GEORGETOWN UNIVERSITY ROUND TABLE ON LANGUAGES AND LINGUISTICS 1993

Strategic Interaction and Language Acquisition: Theory, Practice, and Research

James E. Alatis, *Editor*

Georgetown University Press, Washington, D.C.

Bibliographic notice

Since this series has been variously and confusingly cited as *Georgetown University Monograph Series on Languages and Linguistics, Monograph Series on Languages and Linguistics, Reports of the Annual Round Table Meeting on Linguistics and Language Study,* etc., beginning with the 1973 volume the title of the series was changed.

The new title of the series includes the year of a Round Table and omits both the monograph number and the meeting number, thus: *Georgetown University Round Table on Languages and Linguistics 1993,* with the regular abbreviation *GURT '93.* Full bibliographic references should show the form:

Snow, Catherine E. 1993. Learning from Input in L1 and L2. In: James E. Alatis (ed). Georgetown University Round Table on Languages and Linguistics 1993. Washington, D.C.: Georgetown University Press.

Printed in the United States of America

Library of Congress Catalog Number: 58-31607
ISBN 0-87840-128-8
ISSN 0186-7207

TO THE MEMORY OF ROBERT J. DI PIETRO
WHOSE WORK LINKED THEORY, PRACTICE, AND RESEARCH

A Happy Death

When I die
I will become a more
visible part of what I own.
My world will take me back
and make of me
flowers.
And a little girl's
joy in my beauty
will make her mine.

—Robert Di Pietro
March 6, 1971

Contents

James E. Alatis, *Dean, Georgetown University School of Languages and Linguistics*
Welcoming remarks 1

James E. Alatis, *Dean, Georgetown University School of Languages and Linguistics*
Presentation of Plaque to Mrs. Di Pietro 3

James E. Alatis, *Dean, Georgetown University School of Languages and Linguistics*
Stephen Krashen: An Introduction 5

Stephen Krashen, *University of Southern California*
Some Unexpected Consequences of the Input Hypothesis 6

James E. Alatis, *Dean, Georgetown University School of Languages and Linguistics*
Catherine Snow: An Introduction 22

Catherine Snow, *Harvard Graduate School of Education*
Learning from Input in L1 and L2 23

Anna Uhl Chamot, *Georgetown University*
J. Michael O'Malley, *Prince William County (Virginia) Schools*
Teaching for Strategic Learning: Theory and Practice 36

Cecily O'Neill, *Ohio State University*
From words to worlds: Language learning through process drama 52

Deryn P. Verity, *University of Delaware*
The concept of "rehearsal" in Strategic Interaction 60

Shoko Okazaki, *Georgetown University*
Stating opinions in Japanese: Listener-dependent strategies 69

Catherine Doughty, *Georgetown University*
Fine tuning of feedback by competent speakers to language learners 96

Ruth Jackson, *University of Delaware ELI*
Using strategic interaction in the teaching of writing 109

Joan Morley, *University of Michigan*
Learning strategies, tasks, and activities
in oral communication instruction 116

Karin Ryding, *Georgetown University*
Creating a Learning Community:
Community Language Learning for the nineties 137

Suzanne Flynn, *Massachusetts Institute of Technology*
Marriage for life: Theory, research, and practice 148

Elahé Mir-Djalali, *University of California at Berkeley*
Strategic Interaction: Issues and application to
second language teaching and acquisition 162

Don R. McCreary, *The University of Georgia*
Japanese Dictionaries and *Schadenfreude:*
Editorial Practices and National Prejudices
in Japanese Bilingual Dictionaries 206

James P. Lantolf, *Cornell University*
Sociocultural theory and the second-language classroom:
The lesson of Strategic Interaction 220

Ahmed Mouakket, *Aleppo University*
and the University of Michigan
The concept of kernel sentences as it applies to language acquisition 234

Traute Taeschner, *Università degli Studi di Roma "La Sapienza"*
Foreign language learning in the kindergarten:
A teaching model and some resulting language-acquisition strategies 241

JoAnn Crandall, *University of Maryland, Baltimore County*
Strategic Integration: Preparing language and content teachers
for linguistically and culturally diverse classrooms 255

Ikuo Koike, *Keio University*
A comparative view of English teaching policies
in an international world with a focus on Japanese TEFL policy 275

Louis A. Arena, *University of Delaware*
Strategic Interaction and the teaching of writing:
A comparative study of scenarios vs. traditional prompts
as stimuli for ESL essays 285

Irene Thompson, *George Washington University*
An investigation of the effects of texts and tasks on listening comprehension: Some evidence from Russian 294

Frederick J. Bosco, *Georgetown University*
The place of input in the scenario approach 306

William Frawley, *University of Delaware*
The Computer's Guide to Persons 322

Madeline E. Ehrman, *Foreign Service Institute*
U. S. Department of State
Ego boundaries revisited: Toward a model of personality and learning 330

Virginia Mayer, *Padua Academy/University of Delaware*
Variations on the scenario:
Cooperative and critical thinking in the literature-based classroom 363

Earl W. Stevick, *Lexington, Virginia*
How is strategic memorable? How memorable is "strategic"? 372

Joseph A. Wieczorek, *Loyola College in Maryland*
Students' concepts of Di Pietro's Strategic Interaction: The Scenario 386

Christina Kakavá, *Princeton University*
Conflicting argumentative strategies in the classroom 402

Nadine O'Connor Di Vito, *University of Chicago*
Learner-centered activities: the good, the bad, and the ugly 421

Rajai Khanji, *University of Jordan at Amman*
Interlanguage talk: The relation between task types
and communication strategies among EFL Arab learners 428

Reinhold Freudenstein, *Philipps-Universität, Marburg*
Peace to the world! The contribution of foreign-language teaching
to the goal of world peace 437

Aoi Tsuda, *Osaka University, Japan*
Variability in Foreign Language Education 445

Josep Maria Artigal, *University of Barcelona*
The L2 Kindergarten Teacher as a Territory Marker 452

Phyllis J. Dragonas, *Melrose (Massachusetts) Public Schools*
Making study abroad more effective 469

Marcel Danesi, *University of Toronto*
The Strategic Interaction view of language: Robert J. Di Pietro's Vichian paradigm for theoretical and applied linguistics 480

Frederick H. Jackson, *Foreign Service Institute*
On the implementation of inservice teacher education in an institutional context 492

H. Douglas Brown, *San Francisco State University*
After Method: Toward a Principled Strategic Approach to Language Teaching 509

Dieter Kastovsky, *University of Vienna and Georgetown University*
The structure of the lexicon and language teaching 521

Masaki Oda, *Tamagawa University*
Strategic Interaction: Can it be a relief for foreign-language classrooms? 532

Rebecca Oxford, *University of Alabama*
Gender differences in styles and strategies for language learning: What do they mean? Should we pay attention? 541

Jeanette S. DeCarrico and James R. Nattinger, *Portland State University*
Lexical phrases and Strategic Interaction 559

Anita L. Wenden, *York College, City University of New York*
Strategic Interaction and task knowledge 568

Linda Smith Rutledge, *Central Intelligence Agency*
The Use of Scenarios In The Classroom for the Development of Higher-Level Foreign-Language Skills 587

Jill Robbins, *Georgetown University*
Report on the pilot study of *Learning Strategies for the Japanese Language Classroom* 593

Welcoming Remarks

James E. Alatis
Dean, Georgetown University School of Languages and Linguistics
Chair, Georgetown University Round Table on Languages and Linguistics

Good evening, ladies and gentlemen. My name is James E. Alatis, and I am Dean of the School of Languages and Linguistics and Chair of the Georgetown University Round Table on Languages and Linguistics.

Georgetown is an institution steeped in its traditions. One of those traditions, which has become particularly cherished and regularly recalled since I began chairing the Round Table, is that the Chair should make *very brief* remarks to leave sufficient time for the plenary speakers. So I shall honor that tradition this evening by restricting myself to words of welcome, words of thanks, and a few words of introduction.

First, the welcome. Welcome to Georgetown University, welcome to the Leavey Center, and most of all, welcome to the opening session of the Georgetown University Round Table on Languages and Linguistics 1993. Since that is such a mouthful, feel free to call our gathering GURT '93, for short. This, the forty-fourth annual Round Table, has as its theme Strategic Interaction and Language Acquisition: Theory, Practice, and Research.

Each year, the Round Table brings together college and university professors, program administrators, researchers, government professional staff, elementary and secondary school teachers, authors, and students of languages and linguistics. Here, they have the opportunity to listen, to discuss, and to learn from one another. Some have traveled great distances to be here: from Japan, Korea, and Hong Kong, from Germany, Sweden, Spain, Great Britain, and Poland, from Brazil, Argentina, and Venezuela, from Canada and Mexico. Others have come all the way from the Intercultural Center, a good 100 yards from this room. No matter what the distance, we are delighted to have you join us and we hope you will consider the Round Table *your* conference.

Unlike a few other meetings and conferences that shall remain nameless—but their initials are MLA and TESOL—we have remained small and manageable enough that conversation is still possible. These conversations, through formal presentations, question-and-answer periods, and hallway and coffee break consultations, are a treasured characteristic of the Round Table and one I am committed to maintain. I want to be sure that those who attend the Round Table are participants in the fullest sense of the word. I urge you to take advantage of the proximity of the most important voices in our field to ask questions or begin a scholarly debate. Please don't be shy. You will not ask the dumbest questions at the meeting; that is the prerogative of the Conference Chair.

Before I move on, I would like to take a moment to recognize the organizers, speakers, and participants in the Round Table presessions. I am sure that those of you who had the opportunity to attend any of the presessions on Tuesday and Wednesday will agree that the themes, papers, and discussions were of a caliber that would be the envy of any major national or international scholarly meeting. I congratulate you on your hard work and your wonderful success. I am glad that the Round Table has been able to provide a venue for these presessions, and I hope that there will always be room at the Table for all studies in languages and linguistics.

A moment ago, I mentioned that a strength of the Round Table is its moderate size, and yet we do not wish to emulate the first Round Table, where lore has it that so few attended that everyone could be comfortably seated around a single round table. We need to achieve a certain critical mass, and that, believe me, does not just happen. It's a job that starts in July and keeps on going until it's time to begin planning for the next meeting. Over the course of the year, four fellows were assigned by the Linguistics Department. Their number is joined as the conference approaches by a small army of nearly forty graduate and undergraduate student volunteers. And since I promised to leave at least a few minutes to our plenary speakers, rather than mentioning them all by name, let me suggest instead that we offer them all a round of applause.

I would be remiss, however, were I not to single out the individual who has directed the fellows and volunteers, kept the S.S. *GURT* on course, and generally made Cecil B. De Mille look like a rank amateur. That person is this year's conference coordinator, Ms. Helen E. Karn. To get the word out, via journal listings, printed announcements, electronic bulletin boards, faxes, and telephone calls is a monumental task. This year, the literally thousands of details that make up conference coordination were her responsibility, and her work has been nothing short of superb. Helen, who is working on her Ph.D. in computational linguistics at Georgetown, has brought her considerable technical expertise to the Round Table. I am confident that through her use of the Internet and its countless lists, of which I am blissfully ignorant, we have been able to bring the word of the Round Table to more people than ever before. She has answered the same questions dozens of times and has resisted the temptation to tell us where we could find the answer in the written materials she has been sending us since July. After a twelve-hour day, she has even played it straight when asked "Can you tell me where I should go?" And so, to Helen Karn, with thanks for all you have done and all I know you will be doing, please accept this modest token of our gratitude.

Presentation of Plaque to Mrs. Di Pietro

James E. Alatis
Dean, Georgetown University School of Languages and Linguistics
Chair, Georgetown University Round Table on Languages and Linguistics

This evening and for the next three days, we shall all be participants in a wonderful meeting. This is a promise on which I know I can deliver. My certainty is not just based on GURT's reputation for quality, on its good organization, or even on the superb roster of speakers. For although all these things are very true and critical to our success, it is the conference theme and the wisdom of that theme's framer that prompts me to speak with such complete confidence. You have all seen, I am sure, that the Round Table this year is in honor of the late Robert J. Di Pietro. I felt it fitting to pay tribute to Bob in this way for many reasons: because he was a treasured friend and former Georgetown faculty member, because he was such an important scholar in the field of applied linguistics, but most of all because Bob was the architect of this year's Round Table.

Even while undergoing exhausting and difficult cancer treatments in the last months of his life, Bob remained optimistic and fully engaged in his field. My wife, Penny, and I visited Bob and his wife, Vinnie, frequently during that time. On one occasion, we chatted about possible themes for the upcoming Round Table. A few days later, I received a letter from Bob in which he described the conference theme and its rationale and even proposed speakers. My great regret is that I had hoped that Bob would be one of our plenary speakers. Sadly, Bob succumbed to lung cancer last December 20. He was 59.

Bob, a Cornell Ph.D., had been a member of the faculty at Georgetown for 17 years, where he was a professor of linguistics and Italian. He was Georgetown's first recipient of the Andrew W. Mellon Fund Distinguished Lectureship in Languages and Linguistics. In 1978, he accepted an important appointment as Chair of the Languages and Literature Department at the University of Delaware. While at Delaware, he was a major force in the establishment of their linguistics department, where he became senior professor. A prolific and gifted scholar, Bob contributed more than 300 articles to the field. As an applied linguist, he was proudest of his work that did most to link theory, practice, and research. Throughout his career, he was particularly interested in the teaching and learning of foreign languages. His lifetime of research led to the development of the Strategic Interaction method.

Bob was more than a devoted colleague and respected scholar, he was a beloved husband and father. We are most fortunate this evening to have with us his wife, Vincenza Angela Di Pietro, and his two children, Angela Maria and Mark Andrew. And to them, on behalf of everyone here, I would like to express our sincerest condolences.

A moment ago, I mentioned that Bob was Georgetown's first Mellon Distinguished Lecturer. The plaque that includes the names of those who have been thus recognized hangs near my desk. When I was reflecting on what I would say about a man whose impact cannot be readily summarized in just a few words, I happened to notice that the plaque included a description of the characteristics of the Mellon Lecturer, and I quote, "To recognize distinguished professors who are outstanding in the field of linguistics, who have a broad interest in linguistics, language and culture, and whose approaches are humanistic in character." Little wonder then that Bob was the clear first choice when the lectureship was created, for he never lost sight of the fact that his scholarship was not scholarship for its own sake but in service to others and to learning.

I must add at this point that I do not believe that Bob would have wanted this Round Table to be a sad occasion. Although we all mourn his much-too-early death, I think we can honor his memory best by our full, active, and enthusiastic participation in a conference that includes some of the most important research in applied linguistics today, a subject near and dear to Bob.

I should note that the Round Table is not the only conference in honor of Dr. Di Pietro. The International Conference on Applied Linguistics, which was held at the University of Granada in Spain January 11–13, was dedicated to Bob's memory. Professor Alfred Wedel of the University of Delaware was an organizer and plenary speaker at that conference. During the opening ceremony, the president of the University of Granada presented Professor Wedel with a plaque in honor of Dr. Di Pietro. I think it very fitting that Professor Wedel, who worked closely with Dr. Di Pietro in the Department of Languages and Literature and, later, on the formation of the Linguistics Department, present this plaque to Mrs. Di Pietro.

Thank you very much.

Stephen Krashen: An Introduction

James E. Alatis
Dean, Georgetown University School of Languages and Linguistics
Chair, Georgetown University Round Table on Languages and Linguistics

This evening, we are fortunate to have with us two very distinguished plenary speakers: Stephen Krashen and Catherine Snow. Although both enjoy international recognition as scholars in our field, Professor Krashen is something of a GURT veteran, whereas this is Professor Snow's first time as a GURT plenary speaker.

Professor Steven Krashen received his Ph.D. in 1972 from UCLA and is currently Professor of Linguistics at the University of Southern California. Professor Krashen's areas of research are second-language acquisition and bilingual education. His writings are numerous and widely quoted. His 1982 book *Second Language Acquisition and Second Language Learning* received the MLA's Kenneth W. Mildenberger Medal. His 1973 article, "Lateralization, Language Learning, and the Critical Period," remains, even on its twentieth anniversary, one of the most heavily cited works in our field.

Professor Krashen is a much-sought-after speaker because his writings and addresses have obliged researchers and teachers to rethink their comfortable assumptions and reexamine their theses. His 1985 book, *The Input Hypothesis,* has resulted in a lively and altogether healthy debate in our field.

When we have surveyed GURT participants in the past on their experiences at the conference and their suggestions for the future, one message is repeated again and again: Insist on Krashen—accept no substitute. Not one to mess with success, I am therefore pleased to welcome once again to the podium Professor Stephen Krashen, who will speak on "Some Unexpected Consequences of the Input Hypothesis."

Some unexpected consequences of the Input Hypothesis

Stephen Krashen
University of Southern California

Introduction. My focus here is on unexpected supporting evidence for the Input Hypothesis the hypothesis that we acquire language by understanding messages. The Input Hypothesis is derived from the "comprehension approach" to foreign-language acquisition, from the works of Winitz (e.g. Winitz and Reed 1973), Asher (e.g. Asher 1965), Macnamara (1973), and Nord (1976). In previous publications, I documented supporting evidence, studies showing that more comprehensible input (CI) leads to more language acquisition, both in the informal and formal environment, and I have also documented damaging counterevidence to rival hypotheses (e.g. Krashen 1991).

According to the usual way of doing science, supporting evidence doesn't count for much. Supporting evidence cannot prove a hypothesis, and additional supporting evidence doesn't bring the hypothesis any closer to "truth"; the best you can say about any hypothesis is that it has not yet been falsified. On the other hand, if you find one convincing counterexample, the hypothesis is disproven, and you need to find a better hypothesis.

There is, however, a sense in which supporting evidence helps confirm the validity of a hypothesis. Confirmation of a hypothesis is, in some cases, a test the hypothesis passes, and it seems intuitively obvious that a hypothesis with a great deal of supporting evidence must be more likely to be correct than one with less or no supporting evidence.

What is especially impressive is when unexpected supporting evidence appears, when the hypothesis explains phenomena that it was not originally designed to explain. All the phenomena discussed in this paper are of this kind. In two cases, the phenomena were undiscovered at the time the Input Hypothesis was developed: the Din in the Head, from second-language acquisition, and Facilitated Communication, from work in autism. In another case, the Input Hypothesis was found to be identical to a hypothesis developed in a neighboring field, literacy. And in much of the research presented here, the Input Hypothesis was originally proposed as a post hoc explanation but was subsequently confirmed (the Din, bilingual education).

For those who are unimpressed with supporting evidence, we will also see that rival hypotheses to the Input Hypothesis have a great deal of difficulty explaining the findings discussed here.

The Din in the Head. The Din in the head was first reported by Barber (1980), who noted that when she was using other languages that she was not exceptionally proficient in, she noticed "a rising Din ... in my head; words, sounds, intonations, phrases, all swimming about in the voices of the people I talked with" (30). Barber reported that the Din would occur when she was not actively engaged mentally ("as I walked the streets and museums"), that what she heard was not always comprehensible, and that she had no conscious control over the content of the Din.

In Krashen (1983), I hypothesized that the Din was a manifestation of the LAD in action, and I presented anecdotal evidence showing that the Din was set off by comprehensible input containing "i+1." It appeared to be the case that the Din only occurred after interesting, comprehensible input, not after grammar instruction, and that very advanced acquirers did not experience the Din as much.

Confirmation of the existence of the Din. These speculations were put to the empirical test in three studies (Bradford 1985, Parr and Krashen 1987, de Guerrero 1987). All three studies confirmed that the Din is widespread among beginning language acquirers, ranging from 69.2% to 78.1% (see summary table in Murphey 1990).

More Din after CI than after grammar? Two of the studies investigated whether the Din was more frequent after comprehensible input than after grammar instruction, and results supported the original claim. Table 1, a slightly expanded version of de Guerrero's Table 2, summarizes results from Bedford (1985) and de Guerrero (1987).

It is clear from Table 1 that there are differences between the studies; de Guerrero's students (ESL college students in Puerto Rico) reported more Din overall. But it is also clear that in both groups, students reported more Din in the head after acquisition-type activities than after learning-type activities. There is some noise in the data, but each apparent anomaly has a reasonable explanation.

Bedford's "conversation outside the class" figure is low probably because, as Bedford notes (282–283), a large percentage of his students were foreign-language (not second-language) students and had little chance to converse outside of class. Bedford also found that second-language students reported significantly more Din in the head after conversations outside of class than did foreign-language students.

On the other hand, Bedford's result for "drills in class" is relatively high. Not knowing how students interpreted this category, it is difficult to say what is going on here. Bedford suggests that drills may have provided comprehensible input.

Table 1. Frequency of the Din after acquisition and learning activities

	Bedford	de Guerrero
Acquisition:		
Listening to CI	2.78	3.29
Conversation/class	2.70	3.15
Conversation/outside	2.31	3.06
Reading	2.44	
Learning:		
Grammar in class	2.33	2.83
Drills in class	2.78	2.79
Grammar at home	2.40	2.63

1 = never experienced the din, 5 = very frequently/ always. De Guerrero's questionnaire was on a 0–4 scale, so her scores are adjusted to be comparable to Bedford's.

The low result for reading in Bedford's study is consistent with earlier anecdotal reports, but some people do in fact report the Din after reading. I suspect that the lack of Din reported is due to the fact that second- and foreign-language students rarely read anything that is truly comprehensible and interesting in their target language; they rarely get "lost in a book." As self-selected reading gets more popular in second-language pedagogy, I predict that we will see more "Din in the head" after reading.

De Guerrero included an open-ended question on her survey, asking subjects to list in what other situations they experienced the Din. The most frequent answers were "after hearing songs in English," "after watching movies in English," and "after watching TV programs in English," all sources of comprehensible input.

Level of proficiency. If the Din is a result of language acquisition caused by comprehensible input containing i+1, we would predict less Din among very advanced acquirers, since the comprehensible input they hear and read contains less i+1. Bedford found no relationship between Din frequency and level of proficiency, and de Guerrero actually reported more Din for her more-advanced acquirers. Bedford, however, noted that for his subjects "it is doubtful that any subject in the sample could be described as a very advanced acquirer" (283), and the same was probably true of de Guerrero's subjects.

In Parr and Krashen (1986), we located subjects who were clearly very advanced: graduate students and faculty in foreign-language education who had acquired their second language as adults. Of the subjects interviewed, 25 out of

28 (90%) said they no longer experienced the Din in the head in their second language, clearly confirming that there is less Din among advanced performers.

The Din and grades, aptitude. Bedford found a correlation of only $r=.22$ between the frequency of the Din and grades, and de Guerrero reported no relationship between Din frequency and previous grades in the second language. Bedford also reported a correlation of $r=.056$ between Din frequency and scores on the MLAT (Modern Language Aptitude Test). These results are quite consistent with the hypothesis that the Din is related to acquisition and not learning; grades are typically a measure of how much one has learned, and it has been argued (Krashen 1981) that "aptitude," as measured by the MLAT, can be defined as speed of conscious learning.

The Din in children. Seville (forthcoming) has found that children experience the Din as well. She interviewed children ages 8 to 12 who had been recently reclassified as fluent English proficient. In the interview, she told them a story about a child who acquired English as a second language in the United States and who "started hearing English words and sentences swimming in my head." Saville asked the children if they had had similar experiences. Overall, 57.5% (23 out of 40) said they had experienced the Din. Of the foreign children, 80% had experienced it, many more than the U.S.-born, a reasonable result because the U.S.-born children probably had earlier exposure to English and may have forgotten the Din.

Seville reported that as she read the story, many of the children who had experienced the Din were nodding their heads, and several volunteered their experiences before the story was over. She also noted that those who experienced the Din identified immediately with the story, while those who had not experienced the Din knew right away that they had not.

Other Dins? Several writers have suggested that the Din occurs in other domains as well. Bedford (1985) and Murphey (1990) discuss a musical Din (which Murphey refers to as the song-stuck-in-my-head, or SSIMH, phenomenon). Murphey (1990) suggests that there is a visual Din:

> Artists have told me that when working intensively on a painting they can't get the image out of their heads, that it stays with them when they leave the studio and comes to them at strange moments. (55)

Murphey (1990) also suggests that a kinaesthetic Din exists (56), and Bedford (1985) briefly mentions a possible intellectual Din.

My hypothesis is that what all these Dins have in common is that they occur when we are experiencing something new and attempting to integrate it, that is, when we are learning something ("learning" in the general sense, that is). My "musical Din" seems to occur when I hear a new song or a new kind of music; it doesn't happen with familiar melodies, even ones I like. The kinaesthetic Din also occurs when I am learning some new physical movement, and the intellectual Din occurs when I am attempting to solve a problem, when "incubation" (Wallas 1926) is occurring. Once the tune is familiar, once the movement is mastered or the problem solved, the Din or "infatuation" disappears.

As Stephen Mathews has pointed out to me (personal communication, 1988), the existence of the Din in other domains may point to a commonality between the language module and other aspects of cognition; in all cases, the Din occurs when the brain is dealing with some kind of "i+1." (This is not, in my opinion, a serious counterargument to the hypothesis that the language faculty is a separate module, as argued by Chomsky (1975); one would expect some similarities between the language modules and other "mental organs." The liver and kidneys are different organs, but they still have some points of similarity.)

Literacy. A hypothesis identical to the Input Hypothesis has been presented for literacy development. Working from different sets of evidence, Smith (1988) and Goodman (1982) have hypothesized that "we learn to read by reading," that is, we learn to read by making sense of what we see on the page. Research published in the 1980s extended this "Reading Hypothesis" to other aspects of literacy. It was argued that writing style was also a result of comprehensible input in the form of reading (Smith 1983, Krashen 1984), and that spelling and vocabulary were also acquired by reading (Smith 1983, Krashen 1989).

In Krashen (1991a), I argued that the evidence supporting the Reading Hypothesis was very similar to the evidence supporting the Input Hypothesis for second-language acquisition: More comprehensible input/reading results in more language acquisition/literacy development, both outside of school (exposure studies in second-language acquisition/self-reported reading studies in literacy) and inside school (method comparison studies in second-language acquisition/ sustained silent reading and self-selected reading studies in literacy development). In addition, rival hypotheses in both areas (such as the Skill-Building Hypothesis) fail for similar reasons: The systems are too large and complex to be consciously taught and learned, and there are numerous cases of acquisition without conscious learning.

In addition to the research presented in Krashen (1991a), new research supporting the Reading Hypothesis was presented in Krashen (1992a, 1993). Additional supporting evidence continues to appear regularly, which is, in my view, a good indication that the Input/Reading Hypothesis is correct.

In this section, I review very recent studies (and one recently discovered study) that confirm that more access to print, especially through libraries, and more actual reading result in greater literacy development (Lance, Welborn, and Hamilton-Pennel 1992, Hastings and Hanner 1963, Elley 1992, Foertsch 1992, West, Stanovich, and Mitchell 1993), that direct instruction plays little role in literacy development (Elley 1992, Hastings and Tanner 1963, Foertsch 1992), and that literacy development, in this case vocabulary growth, can occur without formal instruction or language production from reading alone (Dupuy and Krashen in press; Cho and Krashen forthcoming).

Lance, Welborn, and Hamilton-Pennel (1992) reported that the size of school libraries (number of books, videos, serials per pupil; total number of staff hours) was a significant predictor of student performance on standardized tests of reading, even after controlling for socio-economic class.

Hastings and Tanner (1963) is not a new study, but it is one I missed in previous reviews. Four tenth-grade English classes were compared:

- Class 1 spent one period per week in the school library, where students were instructed in the use of "a wide variety of reference materials" to gather information in a number of different areas, "designed to provide some area of interest to all students" (402). This class had no direct instruction on grammar and spelling "except as particular problems arose within the class" (402).
- Class 2 had library work similar to class 1, but in addition "considerable time was given to the teaching of traditional grammar and spelling" (402).
- Class 3 had traditional grammar and spelling and only occasional use of the library.
- As Class 3, Class 4 had traditional grammar and spelling and infrequent use of the library (for browsing only).

Hastings and Tanner reported that Class 1 was the consistent winner on post-testing using standardized Language Skills and Spelling tests done at the end of the year (there were no significant differences at the beginning of the year), while class 2 "was regularly the runner-up" (404). Class 4 consistently finished last. (Differences between 2 and 3 were not significant.) Hastings and Tanner note that "the group that avoided all traditional emphasis on formal grammar and spelling actually yielded results superior in these dimensions ... over the remaining three comparison groups" (404).

Hastings and Tanner do not speculate as to why library use was so effective, but their results are certainly consistent with the hypothesis that these library experiences lead to more reading, which in turn positively affected literacy development.

Elley (1992), the report of the International Association of Educational Achievement, is a study of 9- and 14-year-olds in 32 systems of education, "typically 1,500 to 3,000 pupils per country" (2). In close agreement with other major reports of this kind (e.g. Thorndike 1973), the results strongly support the Reading Hypothesis. First, several findings confirm the importance of access to reading:

- For both the 9- and 14-year-old groups, the size of the school library was "a powerful factor." The effect was especially strong in poorer countries, where, apparently, other sources of reading material are less available.
- Similarly, "in both age groups, the number of books students reported at home showed clear-cut relationships with their achievement levels ... In no country did students achieve well from a background of bookless homes" (66-67).
- More availability of bookstores was associated with reading achievement: "In 22 countries, the highest achievement was shown by 14-year-old students with easy access. By contrast, large numbers of students in the four lowest scoring countries had poor access" (68).

Actual time spent in silent reading in class was investigated as a factor among nine-year-olds. Elley reported that "time spent reading in class is apparently not wasted time" (44); while there was no significant difference between high- and low-scoring countries in a straight comparison, countries that performed better than their socio-economic status would predict engaged students in more in-class reading, while countries that fell below the predicted level did less.

Among nine-year-olds, better reading was associated not only with more books in the library, but also with more borrowing of library books, another confirmation that reported reading relates to literacy development (this variable was not studied among 14-year-olds).

Finally, Elley's report confirmed the inefficacy of direct instruction in reading: More hours of instruction overall and more time devoted to language teaching made some difference among nine-year-olds, but less instruction was actually associated with greater achievement in reading among 14-year-olds. After adjusting for socio-economic differences, the number of textbooks per child was not associated with reading achievement. Also, the amount of reading homework assigned (probed only with 14-year-olds) was not associated with achievement.

Foertsch (1992) is the "Nation's Report Card," the National Association of Educational Progress study of approximately 25,000 fourth-, eighth-, and twelfth-grade students carried out in 1990. The results are very similar to the results of many previous studies of this kind: better reading is associated with the amount of reading students do for school, the amount of reading students do outside of school, and the availability of reading material in the home. Reading achievement was *not* related to the frequency of workbook assignments, journal writing (interestingly, those who wrote a moderate amount had a higher reading achievement than those who wrote daily or who never wrote), or instruction in reading strategies, such as prediction.

An apparent counterexample in Foertsch is the finding that library use was not associated with reading achievement: Students who used the library the most, who took books out daily, performed the worst on reading tests. Only a few students fell into this category, however (3-6%). Also, taking books out of a library daily appears to me to be strange behavior, even for fanatic pleasure readers.

A very clever design by West, Stanovich, and Mitchell (1993) yielded additional confirmation of the reading hypothesis. West et al. observed airport passengers waiting for flights, traveling alone, and classified them as either pleasure readers (read recreational reading for at least ten continuous minutes) or nonreaders. Passengers were asked to fill out a very short form, which took only eight to ten minutes. This form consisted of lists of authors, magazines, newspapers, TV programs, TV newspersons, characters and actors, films, a vocabulary checklist, and a "cultural literacy test." Passengers were also asked to indicate age and educational level.

This amazingly simple procedure yielded very interesting results: Performance on the author-recognition test was highly correlated with airport reading (r=.47), vocabulary recognition (4=.62) and cultural literacy (r=.72). These results also survived multiple regression analyses controlling for age and education. Magazine and newspaper recognition also correlated with vocabulary recognition (r=.48, .47). Knowledge of TV programs did not correlate with vocabulary (r=-.16), but knowledge of newsperson did (r=.34).

Stanovich and colleagues have succeeded in finding relationships between scores on the author-recognition test and other measures of literacy, such as spelling (Stanovich and West 1989). In addition to confirming the Reading Hypothesis, this work promises to simplify research in this area as well.

One in-class and one out-of-class study have confirmed that reading experience and vocabulary gains are clearly related and that vocabulary growth is possible without direct instruction. In Dupuy and Krashen (in press), third-semester French students saw five scenes from the film *Trois hommes et un coffin* (Three Men and a Baby) in French and read the next five scenes in class. Testing revealed significant acquisition of vocabulary contained in those scenes. The out-of-class study (Cho and Krashen, forthcoming), is a case study of a Korean-speaking adult second-language acquirer who had done no book reading in English since coming to the United States, and who was an unconfident speaker of English. She was introduced to the *Sweet Valley Kids* series, books written at the second-grade level, and she became a fanatic reader, reading 15 volumes (about 7,000 words per volume) in about two months' time. An informal assessment of her vocabulary growth revealed that she had been acquiring about 40 new words per book. She has also told us that she feels much more comfortable speaking English informally. At the time of this writing, our subject continues to read this series avidly, and, we hope, will soon progress to *Sweet Valley Twins*, written at the fourth-grade level.

I must emphasize that the research described in this section appeared in the last year (except for Hastings and Tanner and the "forthcoming" and "in press" papers). The research repeatedly confirms the Reading Hypothesis, and it repeatedly makes life difficult, if not impossible, for competing hypotheses. In my view, this year's evidence alone is enough to make the Reading Hypothesis the front runner; combined with the massive amount of evidence that already exists, the case for reading and against direct instruction is overwhelming.

Bilingual Education. In Krashen (1981), I argued that the Input Hypothesis was consistent with research results in bilingual education: One of the reasons properly organized bilingual programs worked was because they provided background information in the primary language that made second-language input more comprehensible. In addition, the Input Hypothesis is consistent with arguments presented concerning the transfer of basic literacy: It will be easier to learn to read in a language we know because it is more comprehensible. And, as many others have said, once you can read, you can read.

The Input Hypothesis also helped explain why models such as concurrent translation were not successful (Legaretta 1979, Fillmore 1986): There is much less comprehensible input in the second language, because students don't have to attend to the message and teachers don't have to make the input comprehensible.

My argument in 1981 was post hoc, but made certain predictions: Successful programs will

- provide comprehensible input in English
- provide subject matter teaching in the primary language without translation
- provide literacy in the primary language.

In our 1988 publication *On Course* (Krashen and Biber 1988), we concluded that more recent programs that were consistent with these principles were successful, converting the post hoc conclusions to hypotheses that were confirmed by research.

Table 2 presents one example, data from the Baldwin Park School District reported by Burnham-Massey and Peña and included in *On Course*. Baldwin Park has a program that comes quite close to the three principles presented above. The children in this table were tested in grade 5; those labelled

Table 2. Performance of former LEP students (graduates of bilingual education) in grade 5 (from Baldwin Park School District)

Measure	Group	N	Mean Score Percentiles
CTBS Reading	bilingual	115	46
	English	492	46
CTBS Language	bilingual	115	50
	English	492	48
CTBS Math	bilingual	115	62
	English	492	58

"bilingual" = former LEP students
"English" = 92% native speakers of English

"bilingual" had participated in the bilingual education program, while 92% of those labelled "English" were native speakers of English (the other 8% were English-dominant). Clearly, the products of bilingual education are doing quite well, achieving around national norms and doing at least as well as and sometimes better than native speakers in their own district. This is certainly contrary to the prevalent view that children in bilingual programs don't acquire English and don't learn subject matter.

Table 3. Longitudinal analysis of LEP children in Baldwin Park

Measure	Gr. 1	Gr. 2	Gr. 3	Gr. 4	Gr. 5
CTBS Reading	19	41	44	52	51
CTBS Language	34	38	45	48	56
CTBS Math	59	55	55	63	67

Table 3 presents a longitudinal view of a subgroup of students that Burnham-Massey and Peña were able to follow through all five grades. Clearly, in grade 1, the bilingual education students don't look very good. The reason for this, as several scholars have pointed out, is that the native speakers are not standing still; the tests get harder every year. It has been estimated, for example, that middle-class schoolchildren who are native speakers of English acquire about 3,000 new words every year (Nagy and Herman 1987).

What is actually going on is that the students in bilingual education are doing better than one year's growth on standardized tests every year, are gaining each year on a rapidly moving target, and are developing their first language at the same time. This data shows that bilingual education is a remarkable success.

Improving bilingual education. As well as bilingual education has done, it can do much better. Bilingual education has been held back, in my view, by the paucity of reading material available in the primary language. My impression is that in most bilingual schools there is little to read in the primary language, and virtually nothing for the child older than ten.

To see how reading can help, let us reconsider the components of successful bilingual education programs:

- Provide comprehensible input in English: As I have argued previously, pleasure reading is one of the best sources of comprehensible input in English.
- Provide subject matter knowledge through the primary language. Research suggests that reading is an excellent source of knowledge. Ravitch and Finn (1987), in their book *What do our Seventeen-Year-Olds Know?*, while essentially an exercise in 17-year-old bashing, reported that those who knew more about literature were those who read more, and those who did best on overall tests of knowledge were those who lived in a more print-rich environment. Similarly, West, Stanovich, and Mitchell (1993) found a significant correlation ($r = .72$) between performance on a test of cultural literacy and a measure of exposure to print, their author-recognition test (described earlier). This relationship held after controlling for age and education.
- Provide literacy in the primary language: The best way of doing this is, of course, through free voluntary reading in the primary language.

School is clearly the place this must happen; children in bilingual programs do not typically come from print-rich environments. Homes of children in all the bilingual programs studied by Ramirez et al. (1991), for example, contained an average of only 22 books.

There is another desirable component of bilingual education programs: continuing development of the first language. It has been argued that continuing first-language development has cognitive advantages (Hakuta 1986) and practical advantages (Simon 1980), and that it helps promote a healthy sense of biculturalism (Cummins 1981). It is a good bet that pleasure reading is an excellent way of promoting high levels of proficiency in the first language.

Facilitated Communication. Recent papers by Biklen, reporting on work by Crossley (Biklen 1990, Biklen and Schubert 1991), describe a fascinating phenomenon: People with autism believed to be incapable of communication were suddenly able to communicate in typing when "facilitated," that is, when a helper would put his or her hand on the writer's hand, sleeve, or arm, or even simply touched the shoulder or sleeve.

The language produced was often amazingly complicated and well-formed, and it often showed great insight into the writer's condition. Within days of beginning to type with facilitation, a kindergarten child wrote: TELL THE KIDS I CAN TALK. I NOT RETARDED (Biklen and Schubert 1991). In his first facilitated session, an autistic 24-year-old typed: I CAN READ. MY MOM FEELS I'M STUPID BECAUSE I CAN'T USE MY VOICE PROPERLY (Biklen 1990: 296).

This kind of complex language can co-exist with echolalia and other forms of autistic behavior. Interestingly, some autistic patients can be successfully facilitated by some people but not by others. One subject (Jonothan, in Biklen 1992) would not be facilitated by his mother, while Edward (also described in Biklen 1990) would only communicate while his mother was facilitating.

This incredible phenomenon has profound implications for the study of autism as well as language acquisition. As Biklen points out, it implies that autism is a problem of expression or praxis (performance, not competence). Facilitated communication also confirms that acquisition is possible without conscious learning ("We can only hypothesize that these children developed literacy and numeracy skills incidentally"; Biklen and Schubert 1992), or output, and with minimal interaction. It also confirms that literacy can be developed without phonemic awareness, phonics, or writing practice, contrary to Adams's conclusions (Adams 1992). The only possible mechanism left to explain such literacy development is comprehensible input. Also, the effect of facilitated communication can be interpreted as a lowering of the output filter, a device designed to explain a lack of performance despite adequate competence (Krashen 1985).

Crossley's discovery has been criticized. One complaint is the insistence that autistic children are simply not capable of doing what Crossley and Biklen said they could do (Cummins and Prior 1992). In addition, there have been claims that the behavior exhibited by Crossley's patients was simply a result of subconscious cuing by the facilitator. One study designed to probe this possibility was done, and it appears to show that some genuine facilitated communication took place (Biklen 1992), but clearer evidence is the fact that facilitated language is often long and complex (Biklen 1992), and Biklen notes that there are "countless instances in which individuals type sophisticated communications where the information is not known to their assistants" (251). In addition, typists reveal "very different personalities despite the fact that they share common facilitators" (253).[1]

---

1. The most recent attack on FC appeared in the *Los Angeles Times Magazine*, February 28, 1993 (Chideya, 1993). The attack focuses on a case history of an autistic child who, through FC, accused her father of abuse which was not substantiated by any evidence. There was suspicion that

Conclusions. The unexpected supporting evidence for the Input Hypothesis included one case in which a similar hypothesis had been proposed in a neighboring field, literacy development, two cases in which the Input Hypothesis accounted for phenomena that were not known at the time the hypothesis was developed (the Din, Facilitated Communication), and two cases in which the Input Hypothesis at first provided a post hoc explanation, but predictions made by the Input Hypothesis were subsequently confirmed (the Din, bilingual education). In three out of the four areas discussed here, the Input Hypothesis was found to be of use outside of second-language acquisition.

As discussed in the introduction, this kind of additional evidence, while it appears to be supportive, does not add to the validity of hypothesis according to the rules of science. We can, however, try to determine whether rival hypotheses can account for these phenomena, and thereby test their validity.

In previous GURT papers (Krashen 1991a, 1992a), I have argued that findings in literacy development are inconsistent with rival hypotheses. Strong versions of all rivals requiring conscious learning (the Skill-Building Hypothesis, the Output plus Correction Hypothesis) are endangered by findings showing literacy development without conscious learning, and Output plus Correction is endangered by findings of the inefficacy of correction as well as its rarity. All rivals dependent on output (Skill-Building, Simple Output, Comprehensible Output, and Output plus Correction) are seriously threatened by studies showing a paucity of output, as well as the lack of a relationship between output frequency and literacy development. The literacy research results discussed here are also inconsistent with rival hypotheses: No relationship was found between literacy development and direct instruction or with writing frequency.

Similarly, the phenomenon of Facilitated Communication shows that literacy development is possible without conscious learning, without output, and with very little interaction, which causes trouble for all rival hypotheses.

The fact that the Din is apparently more likely to be set off by comprehensible input than by grammar study is evidence that it is related to comprehensible input, but it cannot be considered as counter to any rival

---

the source of these messages was the facilitator. Nevertheless, even the mother of the autistic child concluded that FC can work. The following is from the last paragraph (of a lengthy article):

> Although she [the mother] doesn't believe that the method works for all children, she does know of one former student ... who has found new independence. "he started out with full hand support and now he types alone," she says. The boy, who cannot speak, now takes classes with typical students, says [the mother]. "It's wonderful," she says wistfully. "That's what every parent wants." (p. 54)

Chideya's paper also summarizes current research done by D. Wheeler. Wheeler found no evidence for genuine facilitation, but did find some evidence for influence of the facilitator. The study, however, was conducted under what Biklen describes as a high-pressure situation, and was in a very artificial setting with no real communication; apparently, children were only asked to label pictures.

hypothesis, since the Din might be unrelated to language acquisition in general. But the research certainly suggests that it is, because it is less frequently felt by more advanced acquirers. It would be interesting to see whether the Din can be set off by output alone.

Rival hypotheses account for the success of bilingual education only awkwardly. It might be proposed that additional development of the first language simply provides positive transfer, and thus an early boost in production, leading to more comprehensible output, or output plus correction. There is no evidence showing, however, that children produce more language in successful bilingual programs; Ramirez et al. (1991) concluded, in fact, that children in the English-only, early-exit and late-exit programs they studied produced very little language, averaging between 60 and 100 utterances in five hours, less than one utterance per child per class hour, making it unlikely that oral production contributed at all to their language development.

The Skill-Building hypothesis also receives little help from bilingual education research, since successful programs do not contain more skill building. If anything, they contain less (e.g. the El Paso study, described in Krashen 1991b).

This paper presents only a small portion of the research supporting the Input Hypothesis. Despite its massive research support, the full force of comprehensible input has not yet been felt. In fact, rather than probe the effects of massive quantities of comprehensible input, much of today's research appears to be aimed at alternatives, and means of "speeding up" language acquisition artificially, through grammar study. As I have argued elsewhere (Krashen 1992b), this research has thus far failed to show any real success.

My proposal is that we now see what we can accomplish if we fully utilize comprehensible input, if we use comprehensible input-based beginning methods, such as Natural Approach and TPR, sheltered subject matter teaching, provide background knowledge and literacy through the first language, and provide a superrich print environment in the first and second language that includes large libraries with compelling books, magazines, newspapers, and comic books, and classes that promote an interest in reading through literature and story telling. In short, let's put the pedal to the metal and see what the real potential of comprehensible input is. My prediction is that we will see unprecedented success and near-universal reports of a pleasant din in the head of our students.

REFERENCES

Adams, Marilyn. 1992. *Beginning to read.* Cambridge, Mass.: MIT Press.

Asher, James. 1965. "The strategy of total physical response: An application to learning Russian." *International Review of Applied Linguistics 3.* 291–300.

Barber, Elizabeth. 1980. "Language acquisition and applied linguists." *ADFL Bulletin* 12: 26–32.

Bedford, David. 1985. "Spontaneous playback of the second language: A descriptive study". *Foreign Language Annals* 18: 279–287.

Biklen, Douglas. 1990. "Communication unbound: Autism and praxis." *Harvard Educational Review* 60: 291–314.

Biklen, Douglas. 1992. "Autism orthodoxy versus free speech: A reply to Cummins and Prior." *Harvard Educational Review* 62: 242–256.

Biklen, Douglas, and A. Schubert. 1991. "New words: The communication of students with autism." *Remedial and Special Education* 12: 46–57.

Chomsky, Noam. 1975. *Reflections on language*. New York: Pantheon Books.

Chideya, Farai. 1993. "The language of suspicion." *Los Angeles Time Magazine*, February 28, 1993. 34–36, 52, 54.

Cummins, Jim. 1981. "The role of primary language development in promoting success for language minority students." In Office of Bilingual Bicultural Education, State of California. (ed.), *Schooling and language minority students: A theoretical framework*. Los Angeles: Evaluation, Dissemination and Assessment Center, California State University, Los Angeles. 3–49.

Cummins, Robert, and Margot Prior. 1992. "Autism and assisted communication: A response to Biklen." *Harvard Educational Review* 62: 228–241.

de Guerrero, Maria. 1987. "The din phenomenon: Mental rehearsal in the second language." *Foreign Language Annals* 20: 537–548.

Dupuy, Beatrice, and Stephen Krashen. 1993. "Incidental vocabulary acquisition in French as a foreign language." *Applied Language Learning* 4: 19–27.

Elley, Warwick. 1992. *How in the world do students read?* Hamburg: Grindeldruck GMBH.

Fillmore, Lily Wong. 1986. "When does teacher talk work as input?" In Susan M. Gass and Carolyn G. Madden (eds.), *Input in second language acquisition*. Rowley, Mass.: Newbury House. 17–50.

Foertsch, Mary. 1992. *Reading in and out of school*. Washington, D.C.: U.S. Department of Education, Office of Educational Research and Improvement.

Goodman, Kenneth. 1982. *Language and literacy*. London: Routledge and Kegan Paul.

Hakuta, Kenji. 1986. *Mirror of language: The debate on bilingualism*. New York: Basic Books.

Hastings, Dorothy, and Daniel Tanner. 1963. "The influence of library work in improving English language skills at the high school level." *Journal of Experimental Education* 31: 401–405.

Krashen, Stephen. 1981. *Second language acquisition and second language learning*. New York: Prentice-Hall.

Krashen, Stephen. 1983. "The din in the head, input, and the language acquisition device." *Foreign Language Annals* 16: 41–44.

Krashen, Stephen. 1984. *Writing: Research, Application and theory*. Torrance, Calif.: Laredo.

Krashen, Stephen. 1985. *The input hypothesis: Issues and implications*. Torrance, Calif.: Laredo.

Krashen, Stephen. 1989. "We acquire vocabulary and spelling by reading: Additional evidence for the input hypothesis." *Modern Language Journal* 73: 44–64.

Krashen, Stephen. 1991a. "The input hypothesis: An update." In James E. Alatis (ed.) *Georgetown University Round Table on Languages and Linguistics 1991*. Washington, D.C.: Georgetown University Press. 409–431.

Krashen, Stephen. 1991b. "Bilingual education: A focus on current research." *Occasional Papers in Bilingual Education #3*. Washington, D.C.: National Clearinghouse for Bilingual Education.

Krashen, Stephen. 1992a. "Some new evidence for an old hypothesis." In James E. Alatis (ed.), *Georgetown University Round Table on Languages and Linguistics 1992*. Washington, D.C.: Georgetown University Press.

Krashen, Stephen. 1992b. "Under what circumstances, if any, should formal grammar instruction take place?" *TESOL Quarterly* 26: 409–411.

Krashen, Stephen. 1993. *The power of reading*. Englewood, Colo.: Libraries Unlimited.

Krashen, Stephen, and Douglas Biber. 1988. *On course: Bilingual education's success in California*. Sacramento, Calif.: California Association for Bilingual Education.

Lance, Keith, Linda Welborn, and Christine Hamilton-Pennel. 1992. *The impact of school library media centers on academic achievement*. Denver, Colo.: Colorado Department of Education, State Library and Adult Education Office.

Legarreta, Dorothy. 1979. "The effects of program models on language acquisition by Spanish speaking children." *TESOL Quarterly* 8: 521–576.

Macnamara, John. 1973. "Nurseries, streets and classrooms: Some comparisons and deductions." *Modern Language Journal* 57: 250–254.

Murphey, Tim. 1990. "The song stuck in my head phenomenon: A melodic Din in the LAD?" *System* 18: 53–64.

Nagy, William, and Patricia Herman. 1987. "Breadth and depth of vocabulary knowledge: Implications for acquisition and instruction." In Margaret G. McKeown, and Mary E. Curtiss (eds.), *The nature of vocabulary acquisition*. Hillsdale, N.J.: Erlbaum. 19–35.

Nord, James. 1976. "A case for listening comprehension." *Cross Currents Spring*. 5–24.

Parr, Patricia, and Stephen Krashen. 1986. "Involuntary rehearsal of second language in beginning and advanced performers." *System* 14: 275–278.

Ravitch, Diane, and Chester Finn. 1987. *What do our 17-year-olds know?* New York: Harper & Row.

Simon, Paul. 1980. *The tongue-tied American*. New York: Continuum Press.

Smith, Frank. 1983. *Writing and the writer*. New York: Holt Rinehart Winston.

Smith, Frank. 1988. *Understanding reading* (Fourth Edition). Hillsdale, N.J.: Erlbaum.

Stanovich, Keith, and Richard West. 1989. "Exposure to print and orthographic processing." *Reading Research Quarterly* 24: 402–433.

Sternfeld, Steven. 1989. "The University of Utah's immersion/multiliteracy program: An area studies approach to first-year college language instruction." *Foreign Language Annals* 22: 341–354.

Thorndike, Robert. *Reading comprehension education in fifteen countries*. New York: Halsted Press.

Wallas, Graham. 1926. *The art of thought*. New York: Harcourt, Brace.

West, Richard, Keith Stanovich, and Harold Mitchell. 1993. "Reading in the real world and its correlates." *Reading Research Quarterly* 28: 34–50.

Winitz, Harris, and James Reed. 1973. "Rapid acquisition of a foreign language (German) by the avoidance of speaking." *International Review of Applied Linguistics* 11: 295–317.

Catherine Snow: An introduction

James E. Alatis
Dean, Georgetown University School of Languages and Linguistics
Chair, Georgetown University Round Table on Languages and Linguistics

Thank you, Professor Krashen.

Our second speaker this evening is Professor Catherine Snow of Harvard's Graduate School of Education. Professor Snow received her Ph.D. from McGill. Her research centers on first- and second-language acquisition and on socio- and psycholinguistics. Although I have just described several major fields, and most productive scholars could profitably devote their careers to a single aspect of any one of them, I do not exaggerate when I state that Professor Snow has made important contributions to these fields and more. Her list of publications in her curriculum vitae would be an enviable record for an entire linguistics department or research institute; that document lists more than 100 scholarly articles and book chapters. That it is the work of a single individual inspires nothing short of awe.

Professor Snow has been the recipient of education and research grants from, among others, the Spencer and Ford Foundations and the National Institutes of Health. She serves on the editorial boards of nine scholarly journals, and for eight years she has served as editor of *Applied Psycholinguistics*. In her spare time, she is Acting Dean of Harvard's Graduate School of Education. I am beginning to understand why Professor Snow has never spoken at a Round Table before—she hasn't had the time. Ladies and gentlemen, please join with me in welcoming to the podium Professor Catherine Snow.

Learning from input in L1 and L2

Catherine E. Snow[1]
Harvard Graduate School of Education

Input in L1: The standard view. More than 20 years ago, a major effort was initiated to describe the ways adults talk to young children. This research was motivated primarily by skepticism about Chomsky's (1965) description of input as garbled, ungrammatical, degenerate, and complex. Only a little empirical work was sufficient to demonstrate that speech to young children was grammatically correct and quite simple, semantically restricted in topic, and highly redundant (e.g., Snow 1972; reviewed in Snow 1977, in press). More-sophisticated work analyzed the adult speech from a more conversational perspective and identified a further widespread feature of input: It is likely to be formally and semantically contingent, at the utterance level, on the preceding child utterances. In other words, the constraints on semantic and grammatical complexity of input derived to a great extent from the ways adults repeated, recast, expanded, and minimally extended child utterances (see, for example, Cross 1977, 1978). Finally, though the methodological complexities of demonstrating fine-tuning delayed an easy demonstration, research has now made it clear that within individual mother–child pairs, the complexity of the maternal speech increases as the child's speech becomes more elaborated (e.g., Pan, Feldman, and Snow 1993; Sokolov, in press).

The potential value of these features of the input is intuitively obvious. Grammatical and semantic simplicity provides the child with parsable utterances that can be easily mapped onto semantic representations. Redundancy gives the child several chances to analyze and map each utterance and to see relations among utterances that vary minimally in form. Semantically contingent utterances provide adult versions of the semantic intents the child is trying to utter, and they provide utterances that differ minimally but crucially from the child utterances—giving the child rich opportunities to analyze the adult system.

---

1. The work reported on in this paper has been supported by several sources. The Spencer Foundation and the Center for Language Education and Research supported data collection and analysis on bilingual populations. The Home-School Study of Language and Literacy Development, which has been carried out collaboratively with David Dickinson and Patton Tabors, has been funded by the Ford Foundation, the Spencer Foundation, and the Department of Health and Human Services through the Administration for Families and Young Children. My thanks to my several collaborators on both these projects, all of whom have contributed to the ideas presented in this paper.

Oddly, though the value of these modifications seems obvious, it has been rather hard to demonstrate empirically that children with greater access to these features learn language more quickly or easily. I believe this has to do in part with our lack of specific hypotheses about how the various features ought to work and with our lack of differentiated outcome measures for child language. There have been, however, some excellent experimental studies showing positive effects of expansions (Nelson, Carskaddon, and Bonvillian 1973), recasts (see Nelson 1987), and semantically contingent responses (Farrar 1990) on particular features of child-language skill.

Input in L1: The extended view. The standard view of input to first-language learners was derived in a clear way from the standard view in the 1960s and 1970s of what was important about language acquisition. The problem of learning a language was defined primarily as the problem of grammar—figuring out the morphological and syntactic rules of the target language, often from less than perfectly designed data. Major changes in the conception of what language was—what the child had to learn—have occurred during the last 15 years. In the 1960s language was idealized as that which is acquired between the ages of 18 and 36 months—the syntactic core. Language acquisition came to be seen as something that began long before the first two-word utterance, during the many months when the child makes the transition from a few communicative gestures or syllables to a sizable lexicon available for one-word utterances.

Later on, language development was seen to be still drastically incomplete at age three, even in languages where the basic rules of syntax and morphology have mostly been acquired so early. Children at three know very little of the system of discourse rules that governs relations across utterances; they are relatively innocent of the ways genres differ rhetorically; they have not mastered adult levels of pragmatic appropriateness, conversational sensitivity, vocabulary knowledge, metalinguistic skill, or psycholinguistic or phonological fluency. The extended view of what might constitute helpful input to children developed in response to the need to identify contexts in which children master these enormous remaining linguistic challenges (Snow 1989).

With their increased interest in domains of development like lexical knowledge, control over extended discourse, and control over the "decontextualized" language skills that relate to literacy achievement and to school success, researchers formulated new hypotheses about helpful features in the input. The facilitative features proposed included exposure to lots of words and to those words used less frequently in oral language. For example, Beals and Tabors (1993) looked at the words used in low-income families with three- and four-year-old children, in contexts like dinner-table conversations, book reading, and toy play. They analyzed over 500,000 tokens, which comprised about 8,500 types of which only a few more than 2,500 were "rare," that is to say, not on a list of 4,000 words presumed known by third graders. These rare words were most likely to occur during family mealtimes, but familial differences in the use of rare words both at mealtimes and during toy play related to children's vocabulary a year later.

Exposure to extended discourse in the same families studied by Beals and Tabors varied greatly (De Temple and Beals 1991). In some families, as much as 50% of the talk at mealtimes occurred in the context of telling stories or giving explanations. In others, there was no extended discourse at the dinner table. Some mothers, while reading a book with their children, made several comments or questions that extended the conversation beyond the semantically accessible book text, making a link to the real world or asking the child to predict, interpret, or evaluate. Again, some mothers did very little of this "nonimmediate" talk (De Temple and Beals 1991). Exposure to and opportunities to engage in extended discourse and nonimmediate talk, like exposure to rarer vocabulary items, related to children's decontextualized oral-language skills.

These various studies, all carried out in the context of the Harvard Home-School Study on Language and Literacy Development (see Snow 1989 and Snow and Dickinson 1991 for an overview), are examples of the extended view of L1 input put into practice. It should be noted that many others are also engaged in related work, sketching out the ways input in some homes or school settings helps children develop the full array of adult-language skills. Other examples include the collaborative work by McCabe and Peterson (McCabe and Peterson 1991; Peterson and McCabe 1992) on interaction styles that generate narrative skills and Watson's (1989) work on the precursors during parent–child book reading to giving good definitions.

Meanwhile, in L2 research ... While researchers in the field of first-language acquisition were pursuing these lines of thinking, the notion of input had made its entry into thinking about second-language acquisition. Studies of foreigner talk and of the features of classroom discourse in bilingual, immersion, ESL, and foreign-language classrooms have been legion. Krashen has done more than anyone to formalize the hypothesis that the nature and amount of input available to the second-language learner determines speed and ease of acquisition, with his book *The Input Hypothesis* and related papers (see Krashen, this volume).

Though it is clear that input plays a role in L2 acquisition, there are many reasons to think that input will operate somewhat differently in L1 and in L2 contexts. For one thing, we know that L2 learners, who are typically older than L1 learners, are also faster, more efficient, and more capable of intentional learning than younger learners. It may be, then, that they are more resilient, more robust learners in the face of poor input and more able to make use of sparse or badly designed input. As competent speakers of a language, L2 learners have metacognitive and metalinguistic skills that they can apply to the new material of the second language, thus short-circuiting much of the discovery process that optimal input is designed to facilitate. Some of the features of optimal input to L1 learners are responses to their early stage of cognitive development or to their limited attention spans; presumably these features would be absent and perhaps irrelevant to L2 learners. Furthermore, L2 learners typically already know a lot about L1, and their ability to transfer knowledge about how to use language from L1 may effectively supplete much L2 input; this is the presumption underlying the "common underlying proficiency hypothesis" (Cummins 1979, 1981).

In 1983 I started a series of studies of bilingual children, designed to assess exactly how language skills related across languages. I assumed I would find a pattern in which the profile of skills in the earlier-learned language would be replicated in the later-learned language, for precisely the reasons outlined above. The results turned out to be much more complicated. To preview the conclusion: Children developed in L2 the same profile of skills they displayed in L1 only if the contexts for acquiring and using L2 mimicked those of L1. If the two languages were acquired and used in very different contexts (e.g., one at home and one as a curricular language at school, or one as a curricular language at school and the other as a foreign language at school) then the skills from the earlier-learned language did not shape proficiencies in the later-learned language. I will present as examples data from two types of language tasks to illustrate these findings.

The children from whom these data come attended one of two school programs. One group, about 150 children, attended the United Nations International School (UNIS), a large, private, multicultural school in Manhattan. UNIS is an English-curriculum school, but only about half the children attending UNIS are native speakers of English. The rest come from a variety of language backgrounds, often from bilingual households and with a history of schooling in a variety of languages. UNIS children also study French as a foreign language throughout their elementary school years, and the levels of French attained are remarkably good, at least if children have been in the program for several years. UNIS children typically come from middle-class families in which the parents have tertiary education and high educational expectations for their children.

The second group of children attended Spanish–English bilingual programs in the New Haven Public Schools. These children were of Puerto Rican descent and lived in a vibrantly Spanish-speaking community in New Haven. They arrived at school heavily dominant or monolingual in Spanish. Their parents were typically relatively uneducated and either employed in low-wage positions or on welfare. The New Haven bilingual program featured teacher pairing, so that each child spent half the day with a Spanish-speaking teacher learning new material, and the other half with an English-speaking teacher going over recently learned material in English.

The language tasks carried out with these children were designed to tap a wide range of language proficiencies, including those oral-language skills that are highly related to literacy. Thus, for example, we asked children to tell us what a number of simple words meant, in order to see whether they used a "formal" definition or a more conversational, anecdotal way of articulating their word knowledge. We also asked them to describe pictures, both to the experimenter who could see the picture and "so that another child, listening to your description, could draw a picture that looks just like this one." Finally, we asked the children to interview an adult the way a TV talk show host might. This task was designed to reflect conversational skill, but in a more challenging task than simple free conversation in which the adult is likely to do most of the work of keeping the conversation going.

Learning to give definitions in L2. When asked "what does *cat* mean," a child has two general options: to take as a model the Aristotelian or formal definition, which includes a superordinate and some sort of restrictive modifying construction, or to choose a more informal, anecdotal style. Examples of the two styles might be:

> A cat is a domesticated mammal that purrs.

and

> Cats are little and furry, they make good pets, they drink milk, and my grandmother has one.

The informal definition in this case is highly informative but fails to cast the information it contains in the formal structure. While knowledge or use of that formal structure might seem fairly trivial, in fact our studies show that middle-class kindergartners are more likely to give formal definitions than working-class classmates (Dickinson and Snow 1987) and that a tendency to give formal definitions is correlated with age and with literacy skills (Snow 1990).

Looking only at the formal definitions that children give, it is possible to distinguish them in terms of quality. Some use rather vague superordinates (*animal* rather than *mammal, thing* rather than *utensil* or *vehicle*), and choose to provide additional information that is perhaps correct but not sufficiently restrictive (e.g., "a diamond is something that is used in jewelry"). We developed a coding scheme to reflect these quality differences (see Snow 1988, for details). Table 1 presents mean scores on formal definitional quality (FDQ) for some subgroups of children from New Haven and UNIS. All children were

Table 1. Means on quality of formal definitions for various groups (data from Snow 1990, Velasco and Snow 1992).

	English	Spanish/French
Third Graders		
New Haven Good Readers	5.58	6.82
New Haven Poor Readers	3.07	4.02
UNIS tested in French	7.591	7.06
Fifth Graders		
New Haven Good Readers	5.51	6.99
New Haven Poor Readers	3.89	6.05
UNIS tested in French	8.66	7.75

tested in English; the New Haven children were tested in Spanish as well, and the UNIS children in French (a foreign language for most, a home language for some). Many of the larger sample of UNIS children could not perform this task in French, so these data in French and in English come only from the relatively proficient French speakers.

Table 1 shows that older children score higher than younger children, that good readers score higher than poor readers, that UNIS children score higher than New Haven children, that the New Haven children do better in Spanish and the UNIS children in English. None of this is surprising, unless one assumes automatic access in L2 to skills acquired in L1. Table 2 shows, for the UNIS sample, what experiences account for skill in FDQ; in English, grade and experience in English classrooms accounts for almost 25% of the variance in FDQ, with experience using English at home making no contribution to the quality of children's definitions. This suggests, then, that quantity of input in English is not the crucial factor to consider, but it suggests something about the nature of input available in the classroom. Looking at the French FDQ scores confirms that experience using French at home made a minimal contribution to the quality of children's definitions; in other words, children who spoke French at home did not give better definitions than children whose only exposure to French was in a foreign-language classroom!

Table 2. Percent variance explained by regression analyses on English vs French quality of formal definition scores (data from Snow 1990).

	English*	**French**
grade alone	11.6	1.2
home use of language alone	2.6	1.2
school use of language alone	11.8	0.0
grade + home use of language	14.7	4.1
grade + school use of language	24.7	1.4
all three together	24.7	4.2

*the model is significant at $p < .0001$.

Table 3. Length of oral picture descriptions under two conditions by various groups (data from De Temple et al. 1991, Rodino 1992, and Wu et al. in press).

	English		**French/Spanish**	
	ctx	dctx	ctx	dctx
New Hampshire				
5th graders, mainstreamed	90.4	144.2	50.6	79.9
5th graders, bilingual program	--	90.9	--	84.9
3rd graders, bilingual program	--	66.7	--	75.1
UNIS				
students tested in French	83.6	159.1	39.1	66.5
all 3rd graders	82.9	148.2	--	--
all 5th graders	93.2	184.5	--	--

Learning to describe pictures in L2. Assessing the quality of picture descriptions is complex, and in our studies of picture descriptions we include measures of volubility, specificity, complexity, narrativity, and semantic completeness. For the purposes of this paper, I will present only data on length in words, a simple measure but one that correlates well with quality and completeness of the picture descriptions. It can be seen from Table 3 that all groups in all languages differentiate between the two sets of instructions, giving longer descriptions to the distant audience. In addition, fifth graders give longer descriptions than third graders, UNIS children give longer descriptions than New Haven children under decontextualizing instructions, and mainstreamed New Haven children give longer descriptions in English than children still in the bilingual program. However, unlike for definitions, New Haven fifth graders perform better in English, even if still in bilingual classrooms; this (and many other findings about these children's language use) suggests that native-language attrition is occurring even while native-language education is continuing.

L1–L2 relationships. The basic question of interest here is whether L1 skills in tasks like definitions and picture descriptions transfer easily to L2, thus obviating the need for the well-designed and complete input in L2 that was required in L1. One approach to answering this question is to calculate correlations between scores in L1 and L2 on these various tasks. Table 4 presents these correlations for the UNIS children, tested in English and French, and under four conditions: not just contextualizing or decontextualizing instructions, but also written as well as oral production. It is striking in Table 4 that almost no correlations emerge for the oral contextualizing instruction— using language under natural conversational conditions. Under conditions that are more closely related to "school use" of language, either decontextualizing instructions or written mode, the volubility measures show moderate correlations, but other measures show only scattered correlations. It seems that the way one describes a picture in L2 to someone sitting right there is not "borrowed from" or informed by how one does that in L1, though how one writes about a picture is more likely to be.

Analysis of data from the New Haven children showed a pattern of more widespread and robust cross-language relationships (see Table 5). Though not every measure is highly correlated, the cross-language correlation to the same variable was ranked among the five highest correlations (out of 56 within- and cross-language correlations computed) for 15 of 28 variables.

Cross-language correlations for definitions show a similar picture (Table 6). For the UNIS children, these were fairly low, and within-French correlations were much higher than French-to-English correlations. For the New Haven sample, the cross-language correlations for formal definitional scores were high, but those for informal definitions were low. Since we already know that children

Table 4. Cross language correlations: English vs. French picture descriptions (data from De Temple, et al. 1991).

Variable	EOC/FOC	EOD/FOD	EWC/FWC	EWD/FWD
Quantity				
total words	0.25*	0.35**	0.45***	0.57***
t-units	0.19	0.37**	0.44***	0.38***
noun phrases	0.04	0.40***	0.45***	0.53***
lexical noun phrases	0.04	0.35**	0.43***	0.48***
total verbs	0.15	0.20	0.45***	0.45***
adjectives	0.23	0.32**	0.36***	0.51***
Specificity				
revisions	0.05	0.12	0.40***	0.26**
specific locatives	-0.04	0.36**	0.07	-0.11
clarifactory markers	0.04	0.009	0.01	0.44***
lexical nouns/ noun phrases	0.04	0.18	0.003	0.03
Main Theme				
main theme	0.011	-0.09	0.12	0.15
main theme/ total words	0.40**	0.49***	0.11	0.21*
Narrativity				
extra pictorial elements	-0.01	-0.05	0.43***	-0.18
internal states	-0.05	0.13	0.04	0.13
Density				
total words/ t-units	-0.03	0.33**	0.08	0.04
noun phrases/ t-units	0.01	0.32**	-0.01	0.09
verbs/ t-units	-0.05	0.06	-0.03	0.06
adjectives/ t-units	-0.004	0.37**	0.23*	-0.10
revisions/ t-units	-0.15	0.18	0.25**	0.34***
specific locatives/ t-units	-0.10	0.30**	0.05	-0.13
clarifactory markers/ t-units	0.007	-0.04	-0.03	0.01

*P<.05 **P<.001 ***P<.0001

learn how to give formal definitions at school rather than at home, it seems important that the New Haven children are attending a bilingual program, one

Table 5. Cross-language correlations for picture description and definitions variables (data from Velasco and Snow 1992).

	Correlation	Significance	Rank
Quantity			
words	.64	.0001	2
types	.70	.0001	6
utterances	.75	.0001	7
Complexity			
MLU	.01	.90	--
variation	.29	.008	--
NPs	.58	.0001	2
NPs/utterance	.14	.21	--
verbs	.62	.0001	2
verbs/utterance	.01	.87	--
Explicitness			
adj/utterance	.66	.0001	1
conjunctions/utterance	.22	.05	5
revisions/utterance	.26	.02	3
splocs/utterance	.07	.55	--
relatives/utterance	.18	.10	2
clarmark/utterance	.20	.08	4
lexical NPs	.58	.0001	5
lexical NPs/NPs	.03	.80	--
"this picture"	.49	.0001	--
Narrativity			
narrative ratings	.24	.03	4
opening	.42	.0001	1
closing	.12	.27	
dialogue	.02	.87	--
internal state	.02	.88	--
extrapictorials	.26	.02	3
nonpresent verbs	.73	.0001	1
nonpresent verb/verbs	.42	.0001	1
Conversation			
convers features	.59	.0001	1
code-switching	.08	.40	--
prompts	.11	.32	--

in which they have the *same* opportunity to learn how to give formal definitions in Spanish and in English. UNIS children, on the other hand, have very different classroom experiences in English and in French, and those differences in input show up in low cross-language correlations.

Table 6. Cross-language correlations for definitions scores (data from Snow 1990 and Velasco and Snow 1992).

Score	New Haven	UNIS
%FD	.65*	.27**
FDQ	.35*	-.03
IDQ	,14	-.27**
CA	.14	NA

* P<.001 **P<.05

Conclusion. The data presented here suggest, first of all, that assessment of the role of input in language learning must take into account the tasks that the language learner is expected to perform; input that effectively supports the development of skills for one sort of task may not provide a basis for improvement in the skills necessary for a different task. Thus, we found for example that the children who were good at the tasks of giving definitions and decontextualized picture descriptions were not necessarily impressive language users in the TV talk show task (Schley and Snow 1992). Input works in rather specific ways, and in order to support a full range of proficiencies in L1 or L2, it must be relevant to a wide variety of communicative tasks.

A corollary of this way of thinking about input is to recognize that input can be very different in L1 and in L2. The conditions for receiving input can vary as a function of the learner's age, social relationship with native speakers, and context—whether school or home, playground or workplace. Because input can differ so much between L1 and L2, the resultant profiles of skills in L1 and L2 can also be very different. Even proficient bilinguals will confirm that certain topics and types of language interactions that seem easy in one language are difficult in another—common-sense evidence for the conclusion drawn from the studies reported here, that L1 skills transfer to L2 only if the conditions for receiving L2 input and practicing L2 skills mimic those for L1.

REFERENCES

Beals, Diane, and Patton Tabors. 1993, March. "Arboretum, bureaucratic, and carbohydrates: Preschoolers' exposure to rare vocabulary at home." Paper presented at the 60th Anniversary

Meeting of the Society for Research in Child Development, New Orleans.

Chomsky, Noam. 1965. *Aspects of the Theory of Syntax*. Cambridge, Mass.: MIT Press.

Cummins, James. 1979. "Linguistic interdependence and the educational development of bilingual children." *Review of Educational Research* 49: 222–251.

Cummins, James. 1981. "The role of primary language development in promoting success for language minority students." In The Office of Bilingual Bicultural Education, State of California (ed.), *Schooling and language minority students: A theoretical framework*. Los Angeles, CA.: Evaluation, Dissemination and Assessment Center. 3-49.

Cross, Toni. 1978. "Mothers' speech and its association with rate of linguistic development in young children." In Natalie Waterson and Catherine Snow (eds.), *The development of communication*. New York: Wiley.

Cross, Toni. 1977. "Mothers' speech adjustments: the contribution of selected child listener variables." In Catherine Snow and Charles Ferguson (eds.), *Talking to children: Language input and acquisition*. Cambridge: Cambridge University Press. 1–188.

De Temple, Jeanne, and Diane Beals. 1991. "Family talk: Sources of support for the development of decontenxtualized language skills." *Journal of Research in Childhood Education* 6: 11–19.

De Temple, Jeanne, Hsin Frug Wu, and Catherine E. Snow. 1991. "Papa Pig just left for Pigtown: Children's oral and written picture descriptions under varying instructions." *Discourse Processes* 14: 469–495.

Dickinson, David K., and Catherine E. Snow. 1987. "Interrelationships among prereading and oral language skills in kindergartners from two social classes." *Research on Childhood Education Quarterly* 2: 1–25.

Farrar, Jeffrey. 1990."Discourse and the acquisition of grammatical morphemes." *Journal of Child Language* 17: 607–624.

Krashen, Stephen. 1985. *The input hypothesis: Issues and implications*. Torrance, CA: Laredo.

McCabe, Allyssa, and Carole Peterson. 1991. "Getting the story: A longitudinal study of parental styles in eliciting personal narratives and developing narrative skill." In Allyssa McCabe and Carole Peterson (eds.), *Developing narrative structures*. Hillsdale, NJ: Erlbaum. 217–253.

Nelson, Keith E. 1987. "Some observations from the perspective of the rare event cognitive comparison theory of language acquisition." In Keith E. Nelson and A. van Kleek (eds.), *Children's language* 6. Hillsdale, N.J.: Erlbaum.

Nelson, Keith E., Gaye Carskaddon, and John Bonvillian. 1973. "Syntax acquisition: Impact of experimental variation in adult verbal interaction with the child." *Child Development* 44: 497–504.

Peterson, Carole, and Allyssa McCabe. 1992. "Parental styles of narrative elicitation: effect on children's narrative structure and content." *First Language* 12: 299–322.

Rodino, Ana M. 1992. "Y...no puedo decir mas na'." *The maintenance of native language skills by Puerto Rican children in the mainland*. Cambridge, MA: Harvard University Graduate School of Education Qualifying Paper.

Schley, Sara, and Catherine E. Snow. 1992. "The conversational skills of school-aged children." *Social Development* 1: 18–35.

Snow, Catherine E. 1972. "Mothers' speech to children learning language." *Child Development* 43: 49-565.

Snow, Catherine E. 1990. "The development of definitional skill." *Journal of Child Language* 17: 697–710.

Snow, Catherine E. 1989. "Understanding social interaction and language acquisition: sentences are not enough." In Marc Bornstein and Jerome Bruner (eds.), *Interaction in human development*. Hillsdale, N.J.: Erlbaum. 83–103.

Snow, Catherine E. 1991. "Language proficiency: Towards a definition." In Hans W. Dechert and Gabriela Appel (eds.), *A case for psycholinguistic cases*. Amsterdam: John Benjamins.

Snow, Catherine E. 1991. "The theoretical basis for relationships between language and literacy development." *Journal of Research in Childhood Education,* 6(Fall/Winter): 5–10.

Snow, Catherine E., and David K. Dickinson. 1991. "Skills that aren't basic in a new conception of literacy." In Alan C. Purves and Edward M. Jennings (eds.), *Literate systems and individual lives: Perspectives on literacy and schooling.* Albany: SUNY Press.

Snow, Catherine, and Paton Tabors. 1993, March. "Home influences on the development of literacy-related language skills." Paper presented at the 60th Anniversary Meeting of The Society for Research in Child Development, New Orleans.

Sokolov, Jeffrey. In press. "A local contingency analysis of the fine-tuning hypothesis." *Developmental Psychology.*

Velasco, Patricia, and Catherine E. Snow. 1992. "Cross-language relationships in oral language skills of bilingual children." Submitted to *Journal of Educational Psychology.*

Watson, Rita. 1989. "Literate discourse and cognitive organization: Some relations between parents' talk and 3-year-olds' thought." *Applied Psycholinguistics* 10: 221–236.

Wu, Hsin Frug, Jeanne M. De Temple, Jane A. Herman, and Catherine E. Snow. In press. "L'animal qui fait oink! oink!: Bilingual children's oral and written picture descriptions in English and French under varying circumstances." *Discourse Processes.*

Teaching for strategic learning: Theory and practice

Anna Uhl Chamot
Georgetown University

J. Michael O'Malley
Prince William County (Virginia) Schools

Introduction. Our purpose in this paper is to explore the connections between a cognitive theory of learning and instructional applications in the second- and foreign-language classroom. Any body of work such as the one we will describe here has parallels in the field with antecedents that created the context for newer concepts. The more direct antecedents of our work in second-language acquisition are the studies of learning strategies that preceded ours, namely the signal work by Rubin (1975), the subsequent extensive analyses of learning strategies by Naiman, Fröhlich, Stern, and Todesco (1978), and studies by Cohen and his coworkers (e.g., Cohen and Aphek, 1980; Cohen and Hosenfeld, 1981). There were also a number of important ideas in second-language acquisition for which it was difficult to claim any direct antecedent but that represented more pervasive, philosophical positions in second-language acquisition.

Among these were three of Di Pietro's (1987) fundamental views, which served as partial underpinnings for what he referred to as Strategic Interaction, the use of lifelike, dramatic episodes that have personal meaning for students attempting to achieve communication goals in second languages. Di Pietro argued that students participating in Strategic Interaction are *actively processing* information because they generate their own dialogues and cooperate on how to achieve these communication goals. He also noted that through their cooperation, students break from the teacher-dominated classroom and become part of a *speech community*. A third important component of Strategic Interaction is the involvement of students in *self-evaluative processes* so that they reflect on the success of their efforts in attaining communication goals and make adjustments in the substance or style of the message. These components have been part of the contextual dialogue in second-language acquisition of which we have been aware and are compatible with many of the views advanced here. Where we have tried to progress in a different direction from this general context and from others in the field is in assimilating these and other significant views within a cognitive theory and then merging the cognitive theory with second language instruction.

A cognitive–theoretical view of learning. A theoretical model in second-language acquisition is important in explaining what is learned, how learning occurs, and how second-language instruction can proceed most effectively. Moreover, for our purposes, the theory should contain a component that discusses learning strategies and the role they play in learning. We have advocated a cognitive model of learning (e.g., Anderson 1983, 1984, Gagné 1985, Shuell 1986) because the theory is able to accomplish these ends, because the theory has a great deal of generality in explaining learning on a variety of different types of complex tasks, and because the theory seems ideally suited to discussions of second-language acquisition (McLaughlin 1987, O'Malley and Chamot 1990).

In the cognitive model, learning is an active, constructivist process in which learners select information from their environment, organize the information, relate it to what they already know, retain what they consider to be important, use the information in appropriate contexts, and reflect on the success of their learning efforts (Gagné 1985, Shuell 1986). Because learning is a dynamic process, second-language acquisition should occur most effectively with high degrees of learner involvement. Learners in both classroom and nonclassroom settings would analyze what they are learning, think about the learning that occurs, anticipate the kinds of language demands they are likely to encounter, and marshall prior knowledge and skills to apply to new learning opportunities. Furthermore, learners practice, integrate, and refine what they are learning until they are able to execute language functions and skills automatically. It is because of this intricate set of mental processes that second-language acquisition has been construed as a complex cognitive skill (McLaughlin 1987).

Requirements for a theory

What is learned? In cognitive theory, individuals learn at least two types of information that is stored in long-term memory: *declarative knowledge* and *procedural knowledge* (Anderson 1983, 1985). Declarative knowledge consists of "what" we know or can declare, and procedural knowledge consists of the things that we know "how" to do, or processes. Declarative knowledge is stored in memory frameworks, or *schemata,* which are interconnected concepts and ideas. The connections between these concepts are often complex and hierarchical. Depending on prior learning experiences, the concepts are connected with varying strengths of association such that recall of one concept will evoke recall of others, depending on the strength of association.

Language pervades the concepts and other information in schemata through *propositional representations* (Kintsch 1974). These representations maintain the essential meaning of language input by abstracting the complete language used to express the original concepts. Essential meanings may include the ways concepts are related in a sentence, a causal sequence, or a hierarchical relationship, and some of this information can be stored visually in memory. Once learned, these essential concepts and their relationships may be retained even though specific vocabulary terms used to express them are forgotten, as is often found among high school students expected to retain foreign-language vocabulary over a summer.

The second way of storing information in memory, procedural knowledge, concerns what we know "how" to do. This includes both simple and complex physical or cognitive procedures. Procedural knowledge is stored in memory as *production systems,* a series of steps in which there is a "condition" and an "action." The condition and action are connected by an *if–then* sequence, usually with an intermediate "and" clause, which controls whether or not the action follows from the condition. Production systems can be used to explain a variety of language and other complex mental processes, including learning strategies and problem solving.

There are four important features of production systems. First, production systems are goal-oriented. The planning and goal orientation of writing processes illustrate this point. An individual's goals in writing may be to express content knowledge, influence the audience in particular ways, or use words that are particularly appropriate for achieving these goals (Flower and Hayes 1984). Second, production systems are conditional and may proceed in a number of directions depending on the "and" portion of the production. If the condition specified in the "and" portion is not met, the production could go in an entirely different direction. In writing, individuals often plan subsequent portions of text differently depending on the conclusions reached earlier on. Third, production systems are sequential. The last clause of each individual production cues the first clause of the next. Similarly, in writing, individuals often develop a stagewise progression of arguments that are related to earlier reasoning. A fourth feature of production systems is their flexibility. At each step, because of the conditionality, a number of different types of directions can be accommodated. As with production systems, individuals revise their written text in a number of different directions depending on the adequacy with which it meets internal criteria (Hayes, Flower, Schriver, Stratman, and Carey 1987).

Production systems may be the basis for storing the complex linguistic skills underlying communicative competence. Canale and Swain (1980) define communicative competence as the ability to use grammatical, sociolinguistic, discourse, and strategic skills. An individual who is communicatively competent in a second language might engage in exchanges that show exactly the kind of flexibility and adaptability evident in production systems. Communicative competence can be expressed in writing or in oral communication in which the individual adapts to the sociolinguistic features of the communicative context, adapts discourse features and organization to respond to a listener, and deploys communication strategies to maximize the effect of the message.

Production systems can also be used to represent the way that strategic approaches to learning are stored in memory. Imagine a student using a learning strategy such as inferring meaning while reading. The student encounters an unfamiliar word, determines that the word is important for understanding the sentence, pauses to reflect on the meaning of the overall paragraph and sentence in which the word occurs, and determines if the context of the word provides a clue to meaning. The decision to use a particular learning strategy with a second-language task depends on the learner's familiarity with the task, with the strategy, and with prior experiences in using the strategy for similar tasks.

A considerable amount of *metacognitive knowledge* is required in production systems. At each step in the production system, individuals may reflect on the current level of goal attainment, analyze progress toward the goal, and decide to take a different path or even to change the goal. Furthermore, within each step, the learner makes decisions concerning the conditionality expressed in the *and* statement. Learners also recognize the similarity between new and previous language elements or language-learning opportunities. In this regard, metacognitive knowledge entails both matching the pattern of the language elements and context with patterns experienced in the past, and applying strategies that worked in the past to the learning situation at hand. This type of matching requires an interaction between procedural and declarative knowledge, since long-term memory contains experiences with language-learning situations that may have features similar to those of current experiences.

How is new information learned? Apart from identifying the ways information is stored in memory, why is the distinction between declarative and procedural knowledge important? The major reasons are that declarative and procedural knowledge appear to be learned in different ways, and that the information is also retrieved from memory in different ways. This has implications for what teachers do during instruction and what students should do while learning.

Individuals learn declarative information most effectively by establishing links to existing memory structures or schemata and building on previous knowledge. Schemata in long-term memory can be modified by altering an existing concept, adding a new concept to existing schemata, adding new schematic structures, or changing the organizational structure of the schemata. The structure of existing schemata can be restructured by shifting the basis for the organizational framework in memory. For example, one organizational framework for writing is the language in which the text is written, while a second is the purposes the writing accomplishes. Another organizational framework for writing is the genre or topic it represents.

In contrast to declarative knowledge, procedural knowledge is learned most effectively through integrative practice with a complete skill that has meaning and achieves an important goal (Gagné 1985). This approach to learning procedural knowledge can be contrasted with rule-based memorization of linked condition–action sequences. For example, one can learn numerous rules for correct sentence formation and paragraph organization to meet various functional language demands. However, when there are many such rules, as there are in learning a second language, individuals have difficulty in recalling which rule applies in a particular instance, and they find that they need to refer to the rule whenever they are performing a skill. Requiring individuals to remember the rules for executing each step in the sequence is tedious and prolongs learning of the complete action sequence (Gagné 1985).

Instructional implications. This theoretical analysis has direct implications for instruction and learning. To learn new declarative information through a second language, students should identify what they already know about the material, activating concepts learned in their native language. They can expand on this knowledge by checking what they know against new information being presented, by looking for the organization of the new knowledge to determine if it matches their familiar organization, and by looking for new concepts that expand on previous concepts. Clearly the *least* effective way to learn new information would be to construct new schemata out of unfamiliar concepts or language rules. There is no reason to believe that the memory schemata in one language cannot be used to help in solving problems or understanding similar information in a second language, provided that the concepts in each language are similar. That is, the propositional representation can remain the same even though the language used to express it may change.

One preferred method of learning procedural knowledge is to observe and model complete sequences of goal-oriented expert performance. Provided that the language sequence is not too complex to be retained, the novice learner can repeat the sequence and use it to attain the same goal. Interpersonal feedback will indicate whether or not the goal was attained. A second method is to identify manageable but meaningful and integrated components of the complete skill, gain partial mastery over the components by practicing them with feedback, and piece them together to make a complete action sequence that achieves a meaningful goal. The feedback can be either from the teacher or from more-skilled peers. Either of these approaches avoids the tedious learning and compilation of minuscule pieces of knowledge based on rules that are difficult to combine and never seem to achieve a meaningful end. Individuals can improve execution of a skill through practice until it looks like "expert" performance by modeling an ideal performance *or* by referring back to the rules only as needed for refinements in the skill performance. Ultimately, the skill will be performed to resemble the speed, accuracy, and flexibility of expert performance.

An additional piece of information about procedural skills that bears on second-language instruction is that procedural skills are difficult to transfer to new tasks. This may be due to the complexity of the new task, to lack of familiarity between the former task and the new task, or to the fact that learning tends to be situationally embedded. Whatever the reason, the difficulty of transferring procedural skills places extra burdens on instructional design. The second piece of information about procedural skills is that, once learned, they tend to be performed in their original form and are difficult to modify. The reason may be that changing a procedural skill requires a considerable amount of metacognitive effort. One example of the persistence of procedural knowledge is the intransigence of nonstrategic approaches to reading or problem solving. An example in second-language acquisition is the phenomenon of fossilization, in which inaccurate grammatical constructions, incorrect pronunciation, or other errors are retained even after the learner has achieved high levels of proficiency in the target language.

Individuals can have declarative knowledge about complex mental processes such as language-comprehension strategies but be unable to use that knowledge effectively in new situations without conscious effort and deliberation. One way to facilitate the transfer of language processes and strategies is by taking the "high road" to learning. In this approach, individuals are metacognitively aware of parallels between new tasks and more familiar tasks on which the processes have been applied effectively in the past, thereby enabling them to transfer a strategy (Perkins 1989). In using the "low road" to learning, individuals rediscover strategies with each new task because they do not recognize the way the strategies had been used previously. Verbalizing the strategy application often helps learners link potential strategy uses.

Differences in strategy use between good language learners and less-effective learners have been documented in numerous studies (e.g. Abraham and Vann 1987, Chamot and Küpper 1989, O'Malley and Chamot 1990, Vann and Abraham 1990). Rather than attribute these differences in strategic approach to innate learner characteristics such as language aptitude or learning style, we have adopted the approach of researchers who have successfully increased student achievement through explicit learning-strategy instruction (Gagné, Yekovich, and Yekovich 1993, Harris and Graham 1992, Palincsar and Klenk 1992, Pressley and associates 1990). Teaching students how to learn strategies can help ineffective language learners become more successful and good language learners become even more effective and independent.

Effective learning-strategy instruction. The purpose of learning-strategy instruction is to develop autonomous learners by providing students with a repertoire of strategies for approaching various types of learning tasks and guidance in selecting strategies appropriate to the demands of a specific learning task. Second-language learners can profit from a similar approach to learning-strategy instruction as has proved successful with students in first-language contexts (Chamot and O'Malley 1993, O'Malley and Chamot 1990). Key elements are that the strategy instruction is most effective when it is explicit, embedded in the regular curriculum, and maintained over a period of time.

Explicit strategy instruction helps students become consciously aware of their own learning processes, of steps they can take to learn better, and of when to use a strategy or combination of strategies. The awareness that results from explicit strategy instruction develops students' ability to regulate their own learning. Teachers can foster this cognitive development by modeling their own strategic-learning processes, discussing the strategies and their use, having students practice using the strategies, and calling students' attention to examples of strategic learning as they occur in the classroom.

Strategies instruction is most effective when "learning how to learn" is part of the curriculum. Therefore, the instruction should be embedded in the regular curriculum so that students perceive it as part of their regular classwork rather than as an optional activity. Teachers also need to see learning strategies as an integral part of their instruction, otherwise they may perceive it as taking time away from what has to be covered in the curriculum. While initial strategy instruction may seem time-consuming, the potential benefits to students in becoming better learners can justify the initial time commitment. Once students understand a strategy and know when to use it, subsequent strategy practice is performed in connection with regular classroom activities.

Learning strategies are procedural skills and as such require extensive practice before students are able to use them autonomously. Activities with which students practice learning strategies while completing language tasks should therefore be ongoing throughout the year. However, the strategies instruction should be scaffolded so that the teacher gradually reduces the amount of support and frequency of reminders given to students. The intent is for students to begin assuming responsibility for their own choice and use of learning strategies. Once students have developed a rich repertoire of strategies to use with different types of language-learning tasks, they should be able to select strategies independently and apply them successfully.

An instructional model. Our early research on learning strategies with ESL students (O'Malley et al. 1985a, 1985b) led to the formulation of an instructional model for second-language learning based on cognitive learning theory and a focus on explicit learning-strategy instruction (Chamot and O'Malley 1987, 1989, 1993). The Cognitive Academic Language Learning Approach

(CALLA) includes three components in its curriculum design: topics from the major content subjects, the development of academic language skills, and explicit instruction in learning strategies for both content and language acquisition. The CALLA model is based on the belief that instruction should be guided by how students think and learn. Allied with this principle is the idea that language facilitates and illustrates thinking.

The central component of CALLA is instruction in learning strategies. We emphasize that students who are mentally active and who analyze and reflect on their learning activities will learn, retain, and be able to use new information more effectively. Furthermore, students will be able to learn and apply strategies more effectively with new tasks if they have frequent opportunities to discuss and describe their thinking and strategic efforts.

CALLA instruction is organized into five phases: preparation, presentation, practice, evaluation, and expansion. New lessons or units start with the Preparation phase, in which students activate their prior knowledge, including their strategic knowledge, and are made aware of the objectives of the lesson or unit. In the presentation phase, new information is explained and contextualized by the teacher, text, or other medium. The new information may include new language, new content, and new learning strategies. In the Practice phase, students actively use the new information, usually through cooperative group activities. In the evaluation phase, students assess their own level of understanding of the new information. Finally, in the Expansion phase, students reflect on what they have learned and restructure their prior knowledge to include the new information.

The CALLA instructional sequence has proved useful in organizing explicit learning-strategy instruction in both ESL and foreign-language classrooms as follows:

1. *Preparation.* The teacher describes the task and expected student performance and asks students to describe the strategies they could use to complete the task. The teacher writes the names of the strategies on the board, pointing out to students that while individuals often have strategy preferences, it is always useful to increase one's repertoire of strategies.
2. *Presentation.* The teacher models strategic behavior related to the successful completion of the task, usually by thinking aloud while working through the task. The teacher gives the strategy a name, describes the benefits students can gain from using it, and explains when to use it by providing examples of other tasks for which the strategy is appropriate.
3. *Practice.* Students are asked to practice the strategy with the task, often in collaborative groups. Practice is repeated on a regular basis so that

students feel comfortable using the strategy.

4. *Evaluation.* Students assess how effectively they have been able to use the strategy through discussion, learning logs, and thinking aloud as they describe how they worked through the task.
5. *Expansion.* The teacher encourages the application of the strategy to new tasks, identifies students' use of the strategy when it occurs with other classroom tasks, and asks students to describe how they use the strategy at home and in other classes.

Classroom research on language-learning strategies. Research on learning strategy instruction is being conducted by Georgetown University's Language Research Projects as part of the National Foreign Language Resource Center and with additional grant support from the U.S. Department of Education. These studies are investigating learning-strategy instruction and use in secondary school classrooms of Japanese, Russian, and Spanish, and in a university intensive Japanese program (Barnhardt 1992, Chamot 1993, Chamot, O'Malley, and Nishimura 1991, O'Malley 1992, Omori 1992, Robbins 1993). This classroom-based research is designed to (1) identify effective approaches to developing teacher expertise in learning-strategy instruction; (2) describe the relationships between students' use of learning strategies, level of self-efficacy as language learners, and gains in language proficiency and achievement; and (3) determine the degree to which students instructed in learning strategies continue to apply the strategies independently. While data analysis is not complete at this writing, preliminary findings indicate that strategies instruction can be successful under certain conditions.

Professional development. In the current Georgetown University studies, the amount and type of teacher development has emerged as a critical component for successful strategies instruction. Three approaches to professional development of teachers have been taken. First, research staff developed learning-strategy materials based on the foreign-language curriculum of the participating school districts and met individually with teachers to suggest how to teach the strategies lessons. Although teachers indicated that they liked the lessons, classroom observation revealed that both students and teachers perceived the learning-strategy lessons as more of an optional activity than an integral part of their course work. In the second approach, research staff worked intensively with the teacher to develop the lessons jointly, resulting in a smooth integration of the strategies instruction into classroom activities.

The teacher involved in this approach was more experienced in strategies instruction than the other participating teachers and so had less need of support in the form of ready-made lessons. Teacher evaluation indicated that a combination approach would be most helpful for teachers new to strategies instruction. In the third approach, professional development was scaffolded in the same way that we suggested that teachers scaffold their instruction with students. This model of scaffolded instruction is illustrated in Figure 1.

Figure 1. Framework for strategies instruction

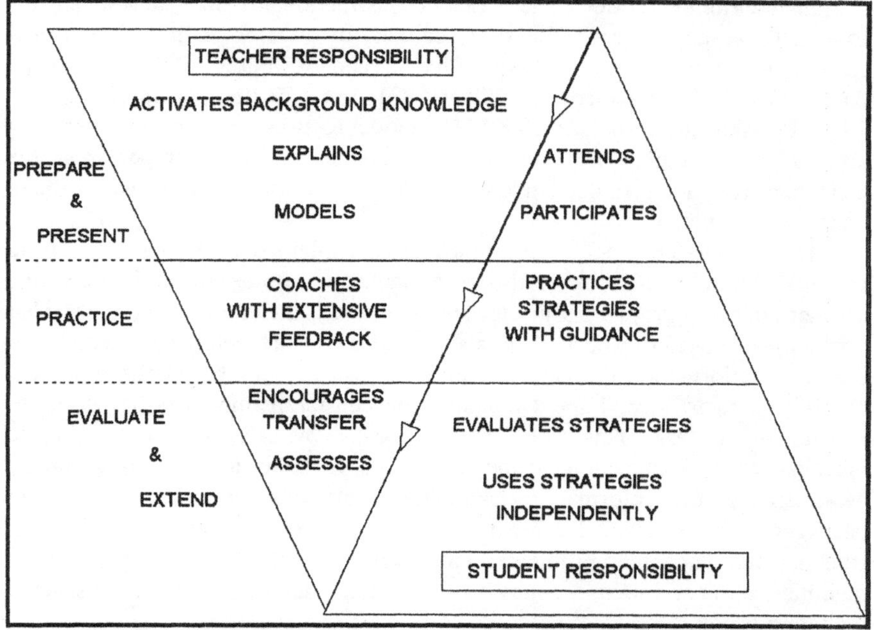

Adapted by El-Dinary and Brown (September 1992) from Bergman (1992), Chamot and O'Malley (1993), and Pearson and Gallagher (1983).

Teachers (or staff developers) begin by providing extensive support in the form of modeling, discussion, and guided practice with the new approach. As students (or teachers learning a new instructional approach) develop expertise, the scaffolding is reduced so that they eventually develop the ability to perform the new approach independently. In the first semester of the current year, scaffolding was provided to teachers through workshops designed to introduce the strategy instruction and through scripted lessons developed in consultation with individual teachers. In the second semester, however, the focus of intervention was changed to one of assisting and supporting teachers in planning their own strategies lessons and providing feedback on the results.

This combination approach has been successful in helping teachers take ownership of the strategies instruction and in helping students realize that the instruction is an integral and important part of their language study. Data collected from teacher interviews at the end of the school year indicated that teachers found the scripted lessons useful as a way of getting into the strategies instruction and that the experience of developing their own strategies lessons in the second semester allowed them to develop confidence in their own competence in developing their students' learning strategies.

Instructional model. The strategic instructional model developed for foreign-language teachers is based on the work of researchers in both first- and second-language learning contexts (Chamot and O'Malley 1993, Hosenfeld, Arnold, Kirchofer, Laciura, and Wilson 1981, Jones, Palincsar, Ogle, and Carr 1987, Pressley and associates 1990). The model focuses on the problem-solving aspects of listening and reading comprehension and emphasizes the metacognitive strategies that students can use to plan for, monitor, and evaluate their own learning.

This illustrated model (see figure 2) is explained to students using an analogy of a mountain climber. First, the mountain climber plans the task. She activates her background knowledge about similar tasks in order to predict what difficulties she can expect. She also decides to pay selective attention to important information that she will encounter in her climb. As the mountain climber starts to ascend the mountain, she constantly monitors her comprehension of the task. This monitoring is assisted by using mental imagery to visualize what is happening in the text one is listening to or reading and by personalizing the information encountered by relating it to one's own background knowledge. During the process of comprehension monitoring, students may encounter problems. These problems are related to problems a mountain climber might encounter in having to devise a way of crossing a mountain brook.

Students are taught how to solve problems encountered in comprehension by using learning strategies. Two recommended strategies are making inferences about unfamiliar language and asking questions for clarification about difficulties that cannot be resolved through inferences. The last part of this comprehension model involves evaluation of comprehension after listening or reading. To evaluate their own comprehension of a text, students summarize the important information orally, in writing, or—eventually—mentally. Another important evaluation strategy is for students to verify the accuracy of the predictions they made during the planning stage. This problem-solving process model of comprehension has been successful in illustrating to both teachers and students the importance of a strategic approach to comprehension of target-language texts.

Impact of strategies instruction. Generally strong correlations between students' reported learning-strategy use and confidence or self-efficacy in their beliefs about their own effectiveness as language learners have been found in the Georgetown University studies. Students who used learning strategies more frequently at the end of the first semester than they had prior to strategies instruction also indicated that they had greater confidence in successfully learning the language. Correlations were also found between gains in language achievement and increases in strategy use from pretest to posttest. Generally, students who made greater gains than their classmates on language-achievement measures also reported more use of learning strategies than their classmates.

Figure 2. Problem-solving process model of comprehension

Plan:
- Set goal for the task
- Activate background knowledge
- Predict/brainstorm
- Selectively attend to elements of language input/output

Monitor:
- Use imagery
- Personalize: Relate information to background knowledge
- Self-talk to reduce anxiety
- Cooperate with peers for practice opportunities

Problem-Solve:
- Question for clarification
- Draw inferences
- Substitute/paraphrase
- Use communication strategies
- Use other cognitive strategies: Elaboration; Contextualization; Resourcing; Grouping

Evaluate:
- Assess whether goal was met
- Verify predictions
- Summarize
- Check performance
- Appraise strategy use

Student attitudes toward learning strategies. A majority of the students instructed in learning strategies reported that the strategies had a positive effect on their achievement and that they applied the strategies independently. Teachers reported that the strategies instruction was most beneficial to students who were encountering difficulties in their language learning and that their most effective language learners were already using most of the strategies and became somewhat impatient with what they perceived as an excessive amount of explicit instruction. Students who had had strategies instruction the previous year or semester remembered the strategies, continued using them when faced with a challenging task, and could share their knowledge of strategies with students new to strategies instruction.

Two important results of the Georgetown University studies were the development of a model that researchers and classroom teachers could use collaboratively for developing and implementing explicit strategies instruction, and the evidence that students perceived the strategies instruction as beneficial to their language-learning endeavors.

Conclusion and research needs. Research on second- and foreign-language learning strategies indicates that more-effective language learners use more task-appropriate strategies than less-effective learners do. Another general conclusion is that high school ESL and foreign-language learners and college foreign-language learners can describe their thought processes as they plan, monitor, and evaluate a language-learning task. Conclusions emerging from current research conducted at Georgetown University indicate that language teachers can, with appropriate support, integrate learning-strategies instruction into their classrooms, that students who report higher levels of learning-strategy use also indicate a higher level of confidence in their ability to successfully complete a language-learning task, and that teachers and most students find strategies instruction beneficial in learning a foreign language.

Research into learning strategies in second- and foreign-language education is a relatively new phenomenon, and many avenues remain to be explored. For example, we need to discover how learning strategies change as students become more proficient in the language they are studying. This type of research will provide insights into differences in skilled learning-strategy use among beginning, intermediate, and advanced students.

Another area of insufficiently researched learning-strategy investigation is the application of learning-strategy instruction to children learning a second language. Important work has been completed in identifying strategies young children use in a bilingual or ESL context (Padron and Waxman 1988), but work remains to be developed on teaching younger students how to use learning strategies with their own language-learning tasks. Another important area of second-language learning-strategy research that needs further investigation is the maintenance of learning strategies over time and the transfer of strategies to new language-learning tasks.

We believe that the important area of future learning-strategy research lies in classroom-centered studies that illuminate the problems and successes of learning-strategy instruction. The analysis of learner characteristics such as learning-strategies applications can be expanded by examining them within a cognitive theoretical perspective. This permits an improved understanding of how learner characteristics influence second-language acquisition in addition to improving our understanding of how information is stored in memory and how language and other knowledge and skills are acquired. Another way to extend the analysis is to focus on characteristics such as learning strategies and motivation that are amenable to instructional influence, rather than focus on those variables that are fixed characteristics of learners (e.g., aptitude, learning style, gender). One by-product of this extended view is a better understanding of additional variables that may influence learning, particularly variables that are related to instruction and to self-directed learning. Because of this focus, different research methodologies may be required than have been used in the past. An extended view of learner characteristics has the potential to reveal how instruction can be adapted to learner characteristics, how learners can gain control over learning opportunities, and how learners can understand and independently pursue second-language learning opportunities.

REFERENCES

Abraham, Roberta G., and Roberta J. Vann. 1987." Strategies of two language learners: A case study." In Anita Wenden and Joan Rubin (eds.), *Learner strategies in language learning*. Englewood Cliffs, N.J.: Prentice-Hall. 85–102.

Anderson, John R. 1983. *The architecture of cognition*. Cambridge, Mass.: Harvard University Press.

Anderson, John R. 1985. *Cognitive psychology and its implications* (Second edition). New York: Freeman.

Barnhardt, Sarah. 1992. *Language learning strategies in a high school Russian classroom*. Unpublished master's thesis, George Washington University, Washington, D. C.

Bergman, Janet. 1992. "SAIL: A way to success and independence for low-achieving readers." *The Reading Teaching* 45: 598–602.

Canale, Michael, and Merrill Swain. 1980. "Theoretical bases of communicative approaches to second language teaching and testing." *Applied Linguistics* 1: 1–47.

Chamot, Anna Uhl. 1993. "Student responses to learning strategy instruction in the foreign language classroom." *Foreign Language Annals*.

Chamot, Anna Uhl, and Lisa Küpper. 1989. "Learning strategies in foreign language instruction." *Foreign Language Annals* 22(1): 13–24.

Chamot, Anna Uhl, and J. Michael O'Malley. 1987. "The cognitive academic language learning approach: A bridge to the mainstream." *TESOL Quarterly* 21(2): 227–249.

Chamot, Anna Uhl, and J. Michael O'Malley. 1989. "The cognitive academic language learning approach." In Pat Rigg and Virginia G. Allen (eds.), *When they don't all speak English: Integrating the ESL students into the regular classroom*. Urbana, IL: National Council of Teachers of English. 108–125.

Chamot, Anna Uhl, and J. Michael O'Malley. 1993. *The CALLA handbook: How to implement the Cognitive Academic Language Learning Approach*. Reading, Mass.: Addison-Wesley.

Chamot, Anna Uhl, J. Michael O'Malley, and Miwa Nishimura. 1991. "Learning strategies in Japanese second language instruction." Paper presented at the annual meeting of the American Council on the Teaching of Foreign Languages, Washington, D.C.

Cohen, Andrew D., and Edna Aphek. 1980." Retention of second language vocabulary over time: Investigating the role of mnemonic associations." *System* 8: 221-35.

Cohen, Andrew D., and Carol Hosenfeld. 1981. "Some uses of mentalistic data in second language research." *Language Learning* 31: 285-314.

Di Pietro, Robert J. 1987. *Strategic Interaction: Learning languages through scenarios*. Cambridge, England: Cambridge University Press.

Flower, Linda S., and John R. Hayes. 1984. "Images, plans, and prose: The representations of meaning in writing". *Written Communication* 1: 120-160.

Gagné, Ellen D. 1985. *The cognitive psychology of school learning*. Boston, MA: Little, Brown.

Gagné, Ellen D., Carol W. Yekovich, and Frank R. Yekovich. 1993. *The cognitive psychology of school learning* (Second edition). New York: Harper Collins.

Harris, Karen, and Steven Graham. 1992. "Self-regulated strategy development: A part of the writing process." In Michael Pressley, Karen R. Harris, and John T. Guthrie (eds.), *Promoting academic competence and literacy in schools*. New York: Academic Press. 277-309.

Hayes, John R., Linda S. Flower, Karen A. Schriver, James Stratman, and Linda Carey. 1987. "Cognitive processes in revision." In Sheldon Rosenberg (ed.), *Advances in psycholinguistics: Reading, writing, and language learning* (Vol. II). Cambridge: Cambridge University Press.

Hosenfeld, Carol, Vicki Arnold, Jeanne Kirchofer, Judith Laciura, and Lucia Wilson. 1981. "Second language reading: A curricular sequence for teaching reading strategies." *Foreign Language Annals* 14(5): 415-422.

Jones, Beau F., Annemarie S. Palincsar, Donna S. Ogle, and Ellen G. Carr. 1987. *Strategic teaching and learning: Cognitive instruction in the content areas*. Alexandria, Va.: ASCD.

Kintsch, Walter. 1974. *The representation of meaning in memory*. Hillsdale, N.J.: Lawrence Erlbaum.

McLaughlin, Barry. 1987. *Theories of second language learning*. London: Edward Arnold.

Naiman, N., M. Fröhlich, H. Stern, and A. Todesco. 1978. *The good language learner*. Toronto: Ontario Institute for Studies in Education.

O'Malley, J. Michael. 1992. "Learning strategies, learner effectiveness, and self-efficacy in foreign language instruction." Paper presented at the American Educational Research Association annual meeting, San Francisco, Calif.

O'Malley, J. Michael, and Anna Uhl Chamot. 1990. *Learning strategies in second language acquisition*. Cambridge: Cambridge University Press.

O'Malley, J. Michael, Anna Uhl Chamot, Gloria Stewner-Manzanares, Lisa Küpper, and Rocco P. Russo. 1985a. "Learning strategies used by beginning and intermediate ESL students." *Language Learning* 35: 21-46.

O'Malley, J. Michael, Anna Uhl Chamot, Gloria Stewner-Manzanares, Rocco P. Russo, and Lisa Küpper. 1985b. "Learning strategy applications with students of English as a second language." *TESOL Quarterly* 19: 285-296.

Omori, Motako. 1992. "Learning strategies in the Japanese classroom." Unpublished master's thesis. Washington, D.C.: Georgetown University.

Padron, Yolanda N., and Hershon C. Waxman. 1988. "The effects of ESL students' perceptions of their cognitive strategies on reading achievement." *TESOL Quarterly*, 22: 146-150.

Palincsar, Annemarie S., and Laura Klenk. 1992. "Examining and influencing contexts for intentional literacy learning." In Cathy Collins and John N. Mangieri (eds.), *Teaching thinking: An agenda for the twenty-first century*. Hillsdale, N.J.: Erlbaum. 297-315.

Pearson, P. David, and Margaret C. Gallagher. 1983. "The instruction of reading comprehension." *Contemporary Educational Psychology* 8: 317-344.

Perkins, David N. 1989. "Teaching meta-cognitive strategies. "Paper presented at the annual meetings of the American Educational Research Association, San Francisco, CA.

Pressley, Michael, and Associates. 1990. *Cognitive strategy instruction that really improves children's academic performance.* Cambridge, Mass.: Brookline Books.

Robbins, Jill. 1993. Report on the pilot study of "Learning strategies for the Japanese language classroom." In James E. Alatis (ed.), *Georgetown University Round Table on Languages and Linguistics 1993.* Washington, D.C.: Georgetown University Press.

Rubin, Joan. 1975. "What the 'good language learner' can teach us." *TESOL Quarterly,* 9, 41–51.

Shuell, Thomas J. 1986. "Cognitive conceptions of learning." *Review of Educational Research* 56: 411–36.

Vann, Roberta J. and Roberta G. Abraham. 1990. "Strategies of unsuccessful language learners." *TESOL Quarterly* 24: 177–198.

From words to worlds: Language learning through process drama

Cecily O'Neill
The Ohio State University

Dialogue and Drama. We have known since the time of Socrates that effective teaching is likely to have the quality of a dialogue. Dialogue is at the heart of drama, which is my field, and also at the heart of every kind of language learning. As Bahktin (1981) points out, in all human creativity with language, dialogue is central. Drama in education rests on the assumption that when students are involved in creating and maintaining a fictional dramatic world, significant learning can occur. The work of Robert Di Pietro rests on the assumption that when students create and sustain meaningful dialogue in fictional situations, significant language learning will occur.

The power of drama arises from the access to and experience of other roles and worlds that it affords. Research has documented (Wagner 1988) the usefulness of drama approaches in the development of oral language, literacy, positive attitudes, and social and cognitive skills. A fairly recent development in the field is what is becoming known as process drama.

Process drama is concerned with the development of a wider context for exploration, a dramatic world, created by the teacher and students working together within the experience, which goes beyond brief "skits" or "improvs" or dramatized stories. In process drama, the group's active identification with and exploration of fictional roles and situations are key characteristics; there is less emphasis on individual expression, theatrical skills, or recreating and enacting an existing story than there is in traditional creative dramatics.

The imagined world of drama involves participants in active role-taking situations in which attitudes and not characters are the chief concern. The goal is the development of students' insight and understanding about themselves and the world they live in through the exploration of significant dramatic contexts (O'Neill and Lambert 1982). The end product of process drama is always the experience itself and the reflection that it can generate. Dorothy Heathcote (Johnson and O'Neill 1984), the British educator who is most closely associated with these developments, believes that drama is never merely stories retold in action but concerns human beings confronted by situations that change them because of what they must face in dealing with those challenges.

Language in Context. Some high school students in a Spanish class were faced with the following challenge: They were asked to imagine that they were adult members of families who had agreed to accept street children from a South American city into their homes. In her role as a welfare worker, the teacher thanked them for their kindness and gave them some background about the conditions under which these children lived. The students asked questions and were given photographs and statistics about the children's lives and the reaction of government agencies to their plight.

Working in groups, the students "created" a particular child whom they would foster. First, they developed names, ages, and circumstances for each child. Next, they began to develop the kind of vocabulary that they felt they would need in welcoming the children into their homes. They wrote letters to the children in Spanish, describing their homes and the life that awaited the children there.

Then they changed perspective. Working in small groups, they created a nonverbal frozen picture, a tableau, of a moment from the children's life on the streets. As the groups watched each others' efforts, they found Spanish words to describe both the situation and what the children within the event were thinking and feeling. Then, in role as the children, they wrote brief letters and journal entries, describing their situation and their hopes for the future.

In the next stage of the drama, they had to work more spontaneously in role in the target language. The teacher became a Spanish-speaking government official hostile to their plans who denies the extent of the children's problems. The students had to convince the official that it would be beneficial to the children to be uprooted from their neighborhoods and taken to a foreign country. Finally, the drama moved on ten years, and each group created a scene that showed the decisions that had been taken and what had happened to their particular child.

As this example demonstrates, in process drama the classroom context is temporarily suspended in favor of new contexts, new roles, and new relationships; as a result, unique possibilities of language use and development are opened up. Drama has the potential to quite significantly change the patterns of communication and interaction in the classroom as well as the teacher's function in setting up these patterns. Because the talk that arises in drama is embedded in context, it is precise, purposeful, and essentially generative. To engage in drama requires an alertness, a quality of listening, verbal resourcefulness, and an immediate and active response. Both listening and talking skills of a high order are demanded and exercised. Students build social skills and become more sensitive listeners and effective conversationalists. They grow in their capacity to send and receive increasingly complex and mature verbal and nonverbal messages.

Dramatic Encounters. Before I encountered Di Pietro's work, I was aware that one of the fields in which dramatic approaches were sometimes used was language teaching. I knew that brief and limited role-plays and simulations were familiar approaches in foreign-language teaching in England, as were language games and other "dramatic" activities. But it was immediately clear that Di Pietro's notion of Strategic Interaction went much further than these short-term, task-oriented, teacher-dominated exercises and was actually more closely aligned to drama in education and theatre. A central difference is Di Pietro's articulation of the essentially structural and dynamic qualities of every dramatic encounter and his recognition that language learning is both a personal and a social endeavor.

For Di Pietro, the essential elements of the dramatic encounter include:

- the ability of language to create and engage students in new roles, situations, and worlds;
- dynamic tension;
- the motivating and challenging power of the unexpected;
- the tactical quality acquired by language under the stress of achieving a goal;
- the linguistic and psychological ambiguity of human interaction;
- the group nature of the enterprise; and
- the significance of context.

All of these aspects of his work are key characteristics of both theatre and drama in education. The single element that immediately marks out his approach from more limited "simulations" and "situations" is his understanding of the significance of tension. Tension is a key quality in all art, and in, particular, dramatic art, although it has not always been recognized as such. Too often in theatre and drama, the much cruder notion of "conflict" is seen as the dynamic force. Viola Spolin, author of the immensely influential *Improvisation for the Theater* (1984: 349), identifies the weakness of this view when she defines conflict as a "device for generating stage energy."

Tension, on the other hand, is an essential structural principle in building imagined worlds. Momentum can only develop if a state of tension is created that will provide a dynamic for the action. Tension is an essential aesthetic element, closely linked with such qualities as time and rhythm. It exists between the situation as it appears at any one moment and the complete action. It can be created in theatre by the ignorance of the characters and the knowledge of the audience, or in strategic interaction by the struggle between the intentions of one role and another. It is never merely suspense, waiting for something to happen, but implies both pressure and resistance. Tension arises as much from what is known as from what is unknown. It is a result not only of what is already apprehended but of what is anticipated. It is this kind of dramatic tension that keeps alive any play, game, or dramatic encounter, including strategic interaction.

Di Pietro understood that traditional classroom role-play offers little real choice to students. He recognized that motivation comes from the opportunity to take on diverse roles in situations that are as authentic and dynamic as possible. In a true dramatic interaction, there is a need to determine, interpret, and respond to the kinds of role being played by others and to cope with any potential interactional ambiguity. This ambiguity is a perfect reinforcer of the need to listen.

In strategic interaction, in spite of role intentions and deliberations during the rehearsal phase, outcomes remain unpredictable. Decision-making is seen as central, as is the need to build bridges between language teaching and the students' own experience. Validating the students' own themes and ideas is fundamental to this way of working, and it gives them a measure of control over the content of the circumstances as well as a sense of empowerment. Strategic Interaction promotes a sense of community and challenges the students to communicate.

Scenarios are always composed of people in a particular relation to each other, achieving goals that are motivating, linguistically challenging, and culturally and personally meaningful. The emphasis is on achieving a communicative goal within the shelter of the group—in other words, through group participation in sense-making. As Tannen (1989) emphasizes, students care more about a situation and the information it contains, and understand it better because they care about it, when they have worked to make its meaning.

For the teacher wishing to operate in this way, a number of implications have to be accepted in the classroom:

- Language is recognized not just as a cognitive activity but as an intensely social and personal endeavor.
- Both students and teachers must be prepared to take risks and entertain alternatives within a functioning speech community.
- The teacher can no longer presume to dominate learning in a traditional way and must be prepared to function in a variety of roles.

Di Pietro proposes roles for the teacher that include those of guide, counselor, consultant and coach, observer, evaluator, commentator, and discussion leader.

Drama in education—and, in particular, process drama—takes the possible functions of the teacher a great deal further. In process drama, the teacher will typically take on a role and enter the developing action, as in the example I gave earlier. This strategy is known as "Teacher in Role." The initial purpose of taking on a role is emphatically not to give a display of acting, but instead to invite students to enter and begin to create the fictional world. When the teacher takes on a role in the interaction, it is an act of conscious self-presentation, and one that invites the students to respond actively, to join in, to extend, oppose, or transform what is happening.

This complex strategy operates to focus the attention of the participants, harness their feelings of ambivalence and vulnerability, unite them in contemplation, and engage them in action. The role presented by the teacher is publicly available to be "read" or interpreted, and participants are immediately entangled in a web of contemplation, speculation, and anticipation. They are drawn together in attending to and building the event as they seek for clues to the nature of the imagined world that is unfolding before them and their place within it. They will be concerned with discovering the nature of the roles they have been endowed with or have adopted, the relationships of these roles to that presented by the teacher, and the powers and functions that the rules of the game may permit them to acquire. Students are challenged to make sense of what they hear and see, to become aware of their responses, and to use these responses as an impetus to action. They are invited not only to enter the dramatic world but also to transform it. Dialogue is at the heart of the encounter with the role, and purposeful response is implicit in the situation.

For the teacher, the advantages of working in role are manifold. The imaginary situation can be established briefly and economically, without lengthy explanations and assigning of parts. Appropriate behavior and language can be modeled, tension can be maintained, and the students can be challenged and supported from within the fictional situation. Criteria of possibility are set up, and appropriate conventions of language and behavior are seen in action. Gavin Bolton (1984: 3) describes the strategy of teacher in role as both a strategy for learning and a significant principle of teaching, which uniquely inverts the assumptions underlying the traditional pedagogical context. As he puts it, "The power relationship between pupils and teacher is tacitly perceived as negotiable."

Drama in the Immersion Classroom. In a two-year research project in immersion schools, drama was used as innovative methodology. Our object was to motivate, enrich, and extend language opportunities for the students by creating dramatic worlds within the immersion classroom. This was a challenging task, as it appeared that the immersion school already presented many of the features of a fictional world. Games, drama, and the notion of the immersion school all depend on the temporary acceptance by everyone involved of an illusion, a closed, conventional, rule-bound and imaginary world within "a space of complicity" (Gouhier 1968: 96).

Bounded by both time and space—the school building and the school day—the signs and signals within the immersion world are selected and manipulated to keep the world of the target language and culture in being. As far as possible, the staff and faculty behave as if the only language available was indeed French or Spanish. Like theatre, the immersion school is real and not real at the same time. In observing the teachers in this setting, it was striking how "dramatized" and expressive their behavior was, how enlarged their gestures, as they used a range of signs and signals in their struggle to draw their students into the world of the target language (Bernhardt 1992).

Teachers in immersion classrooms face a special difficulty. Where the teacher is the only proficient target-language user within the child's world of school, home, and community, it is the teacher's response alone that can really help the child become more proficient in that language. It is her responsibility to create, for example, a French-speaking world and the cultural values that belong to that world. The natural context for language learning within this world shrinks to the input of the teacher and her colleagues.

Classroom discourse, even when conducted in the students' native tongue, rarely offers opportunities for them to explore a range of complex language functions, since these functions arise from personal, sustained, and intensive encounters. The role of adults in sustaining intensive interaction with students is central, and yet in the language classroom it is almost always restricted to narrow teacher/student interactions.

Drama in education, like Di Pietro's scenarios but in a more immediate and flexible format, requires language to be used in meaningful, authentic situations where the focus is on problem-posing and the resolution of a purposeful task. The teacher is cocreator of the dramatic world, and the roles she adopts within this world allow her to diagnose the students' language skills and understanding, support their communicative efforts, model appropriate behaviors within the situation, question their thinking, and extend and challenge their responses.

During our research in the immersion schools, dramatic situations were chosen to fulfill these conditions. Among other roles, students became, for example, young Olympic athletes who had to face the teacher in role as a French immigration officer, astronauts in training for a journey into space, journalists, detectives, zoo keepers, and secret agents. The roles played by students and teachers allowed them to ask and answer questions, interpret responses, pose and solve problems, work in movement and speech, and react appropriately and resourcefully within the fictional situation and the target language.

In one extended session with fifth graders, I took on the role of a substitute teacher who has to accompany a school visit to France. This allowed me to use my fairly limited abilities in French—the students often corrected me—and to challenge the students through my incompetence, not so much in my language as in my role. During the imaginary journey in the bus through France, the students described what they saw out of the windows. After a while, they began to play with their ideas, and one student saw a dead cat!

To be able to play with ideas, words, and concepts immediately implies understanding. Eventually, the bus broke down, and the students were forced to seek help by visiting a lonely house in the woods. Here, two volunteers encountered the teacher (a native French speaker), who took on the role of a strange old lady. With the help of the other students, the volunteers discovered that there was no telephone or car, and the only mode of transport was a horse. There was something sinister about the old lady in the lonely house, and all the students were eager to "read" and interpret her behavior. This encounter had real tension, both for the volunteers and the rest of the class, who were both audience and advisers. The students cocreated the situation, operated within it, encountered obstacles in the shape of both the incompetent substitute teacher and the old lady as well as the difficulties of the journey, and solved the problem and ended the story.

Maxine Greene (1971) suggests that one of the ways working in an art form in the classroom can promote learning experiences is that it allows difficulties to be experienced and overcome. Another example of the teacher as obstacle occurred when I was working with six- and seven-year-olds in London. They were newly arrived from Pakistan and were having additional language instruction in their elementary school. I took on the role of an alien, with no knowledge of English whatsoever. The students welcomed me, and began to try to converse with me in their limited English. First, they gave me instructions—sit down, drink, eat. I was a very slow student and got everything wrong. Finally, one boy, totally frustrated with my poor progress, took me over to an alphabet in Gujurati, and began to teach me that language. My role as a language-impaired alien allowed him to demonstrate his competence.

By adding the strategy of teacher in role to Di Pietro's notion of Strategic Interaction, it is possible to combine and extend many important teacher functions. The rehearsal phase can be built in as part of the action, for example where all the students consulted about the best way to respond to the strange old lady. All of the students can be involved in the situation at once. The situation becomes increasingly "authentic," yet it is still occurring in what Heathcote (1984) calls a ludic, "no-penalty" area.

The kind of pedagogy that Di Pietro proposes is an essentially liberating one. It is above all interactive and challenging, and it promotes student involvement while honoring their genuine aspirations as language learners. Di Pietro's approach and the more extended drama situations I have described possess essential empowering qualities. They closely relate to the characteristics of the kind of liberating education advocated by Friere. These qualities include:

- participation
- cooperation
- the posing of problems
- the validity of student concerns as a basis for classroom content and discourse

- students' control over their own learning of the target language
- the creation of a classroom community of learners, cooperating and pooling its resources
- the importance of the teacher's creativity
- reflection
- self- and peer-evaluation
- the gradual emergence of a sense of coherence.

As Bruner (1986) makes clear in *Actual Minds, Possible Worlds*, education should partake of the spirit of a forum, of negotiation, of the recreation of meaning. He claims that to the extent that the materials of the curriculum are chosen for their openness to imaginative transformation and are presented in a light that invites negotiation and speculation, education becomes part of culture making. Robert Di Pietro clearly both chose and presented the materials of his curriculum in this way, and for that I am grateful for this opportunity to honor him and his work.

REFERENCES

Bahktin, Mikhail M. 1981. *The dialogic imagination*. Austin: University of Texas Press.

Bernhardt, Elizabeth B. (ed.). 1992. *Life in language immersion classrooms*. Clevedon, Avon: Multilingual Matters, Ltd.

Bolton, Gavin. 1984. "Teacher in role and teacher power." In *Drama as education*. London: Longman.

Bruner, Jerome. 1986. *Actual minds, possible worlds*. Cambridge, Mass.: Harvard University Press.

Di Pietro, Robert J. 1987. *Strategic interaction*. New York: Cambridge University Press.

Gouhier, Henri. 1968. "L'essence du theatre." Quoted in Bruce Wilshire (1982), *Role-playing and identity: The limits of theatre as metaphor*." Bloomington, Ind.: University of Indiana Press.

Greene, Maxine. 1971. *The dialectic of freedom*. London: Oliver and Boone.

Johnson, Liz, and Cecily O'Neill (eds.). 1984. *Dorothy Heathcote: Collected writings on education and drama*. Evanston, Ill.: Northwestern University Press.

O'Neill, Cecily, and Alan Lambert. 1982. *Drama structures*. London: Hutchinson.

Shor, Ira, and Paulo Friere. 1987. *A pedagogy for liberation: Dialogues on transforming education*. South Hadley, Mass.: Bergin and Garvey.

Spolin, Viola. 1984. *Improvisation for the theater*. Evanston,Ill.: Northwestern University Press.

Tannen, Deborah. 1989. *Talking voices*. Cambridge: Cambridge University Press.

Wagner, B.J. 1988. "Research currents: Does classroom drama affect the arts of language?" *Language Arts* 65(1).

The concept of "rehearsal" in Strategic Interaction

Deryn P. Verity
University of Delaware

Introduction. Several aspects of its design distinguish Strategic Interaction (SI) as an innovative second-language methodology. One of the most interesting, though least discussed, features of this methodology is the inclusion of a rehearsal phase in the canonical lesson. Understandably, commentators on and practitioners of SI have paid much more attention to the performance phase of the scenario, in which student actors verbally execute their game plans in the target language. By contrast, the rehearsal phase has been the object of much less comment and has been viewed as merely a lead-in to the real core of the lesson. In this paper, I posit the centrality of the rehearsal phase to the success of SI by describing the rehearsal in terms of the Vygotskyan approach.

The rehearsal in Strategic Interaction. Di Pietro (1987) allots something less than a chapter of his book to his notions of rehearsal. However, even these abbreviated comments suggest that he recognizes the rehearsal to be less transparent an activity than it might appear. He begins by reminding the reader that the rehearsal is not a time of learning predetermined parts from a predetermined script, but rather an "opportunity to learn much that is new" (1987: 71). To clarify this statement, he provides five tasks for the learners to accomplish during the rehearsal and four complementary tasks for the teacher.

The tasks set for the teacher are essentially procedural, focusing on the teacher as facilitator and as "knower," in Curran's (1976) sense of the term. Descriptions of tasks are slightly condensed here (1987: 73):

1. Observe and help with group formation if necessary.
2. Offer suggestions if the group seems stuck.
3. Model utterances in the target language.
4. Give explanations, but not lengthy ones (of grammar, culture, etc.).

Only the fourth task allows for the possibility that the teacher might contribute more than management and linguistic expertise to the preparation of the scenario. In addition, all but the briefest and most essential explanations are postponed to the debriefing phase.

The five student tasks, on the other hand, while procedural to some degree, reflect in more radical form Strategic Interaction's stated methodological goal of creating a student-centered, rather than teacher-free, classroom. Tasks are given here in slightly condensed form:

1. Make certain all the members of the group understand the charge given to them.
2. Understand the "ground rules" (use of notes, target and native languages, etc.).
3. Consider all strategic options, and predict alternative outcomes.
4. Participate in choosing a performer.
5. Follow the steps that lead to the group decision of how to play the assigned role.

Unlike those stipulated for the teacher, these tasks are rather interesting. They are, in fact, psychological and psycholinguistic instructions of immense complexity and difficulty. Indeed, it would be challenging even to know whether or not they have been successfully followed. How exactly does one make certain someone else understands; understand something oneself; participate; follow steps that lead to a group decision? Except for the third task—consider the strategic options for the assigned role (the hallmark of SI's psychosocial realism)—there has been little discussion of why these tasks are important and how they can be achieved.

Typically, in fact, Di Pietro's instructions to students have tended to be interpreted on the level of procedure. The classroom set-up for an SI lesson is so different from the traditional one that in many cases it is enough if the students manage to follow such novel operational guidelines as "work in small groups"; "discussion may be in either the target or the first language"; "talk only with the members of your group"; "prepare only one side of the dialogue"; and so forth. Yet anyone familiar with the method realizes that a successful SI lesson cannot be reduced to such descriptive stipulations.

A brief consideration of an unsuccessful SI class will illustrate this anti-reductionistic claim. Most of us who have used SI with a variety of classes have had groups that never seemed to "get it": They work dutifully enough, but they do not explore, extend, or elaborate the roles and situations they have been assigned. Although they appear to be talking to each other during rehearsal, they seem unable to exploit the resources of either the group or the task. In their performances they display incoherent, irrelevant, or fantastical strategies that reflect little linguistic, cognitive, social, or aesthetic effort. My guess is that these groups are not necessarily unwilling to try SI, but that they are unable to engage in rehearsal.

The very processes of rehearsal—interpreting the task, selecting linguistic items, representing that selection to one's groupmates while simultaneously eliminating certain choices in favor of other choices, finally coming to a series of provisional decisions about which strategies to follow first, which alternatives to consider—are so complex as to be impenetrable to a group that struggles even to complete the first task ("be sure that everyone understands the charge given to the group"). Donato's (1988) study of the linguistic structuring of group activity vividly demonstrates how some groups work together and other "groups" merely sit together. My investigation of the rehearsal process from the Vygotskyan psycholinguistic perspective (Verity 1992) suggests that even within a group that is explicitly committed to working (rehearsing) together, the rehearsal must develop along certain lines to fulfill its preparatory functions.

Rehearsal and the Vygotskyan paradigm. Without going into great detail about the Vygotskyan psycholinguistic paradigm, it might be constructive to review here the three basic tenets of this approach.

First, this approach insists upon a genetic, or developmental, perspective, which has several important implications. One implication is that an observer cannot deduce the internal structure of an activity solely from its end results. Development toward a goal is neither unidirectional nor simply cumulative. In the case of SI, what development in the target language has occurred among the participants is not fully recoverable from the public performance of the scenario. Another implication is that the motives and goals of the participants in an activity determine the progress of that activity. As the participants move through the activity, their goals can change; therefore, no predetermined result can be derived from the originating conditions of an activity. In SI, neither the role cards nor the participants' linguistic levels determine what the outcome of the rehearsal will be; ostensibly identical actions may represent very different internal structures.

Thus, the structure of human activity is dynamic, being constantly restructured as it moves through time. Insights into the various phases of an activity and into its meanings (the relationship between motives and goals or between original states and final states, what has been learned, and what changes have occurred in the participants) can be fully revealed only through study of the genesis, or history, of the activity (Kozulin 1986).

Second, the Vygotskyan approach claims that cognition is originally social; knowledge must be "out there" in the world before an individual can appropriate it for personal use. Thus, from this perspective, rehearsal is necessary at the very least to the extent that it requires the group members to externalize their knowledge in order to prepare the selected performer for the performance. As Di Pietro insisted, on the levels of both design and procedure, the apparently solo performer chosen to represent the group's work is in fact a mouthpiece, literally, for the knowledge of many others.

Third, semiotic mediation is seen as the most important tool of human development in the Vygotskyan paradigm. The way that social knowledge becomes individual knowledge is through the semiotic, typically linguistic, mediation of an "other." The primary human semiotic code is clearly language, although other forms of semiotic mediation are, of course, available. Becoming a linguistically mature ("proficient") person in a given code means being able to participate in socially derived and appropriate kinds of symbolic control of the self, of other human subjects, and of the environment (which includes both other human subjects and nonhuman objects). The centrality of linguistic manipulation of and by the environment gives the Vygotskyan approach its psycholinguistic resonance (Wertsch 1985). The relevant question of a Vygotskyan investigation is how the interactions of the individual with the social proceeds through language and time.

To take a Vygotskyan perspective on rehearsal activity, then, is to anticipate that it will serve as more than a preparation for performance—that it should, in fact, represent the collective development of several subjects toward the ultimate goal of autonomous control of the task. It should thus reflect a series of unpredictable states that depend upon language for their instantiation but that may only intermittently resemble anything like a performance. A recent study of the theatrical rehearsal process (Verity 1992) illuminates the fact that a rehearsal is, indeed, not limited to preperformance practice and repetition, but is actually a series of restructurings of knowledge, relationships, and goals. Not a linear procedure progressing cumulatively and unidirectionally from start to finish, the rehearsal is an internally coherent system that "lurches forward," proceeding irregularly and unpredictably, depending upon the nature of the task, the participants, the language, and the kinds of interactions that are involved.

Psycholinguistically, the rehearsal serves two crucial functions for the participants. First, it is *orientational*, in that it requires them to externalize their various definitions of the task at hand. This is a necessary first step in order for these multiple viewpoints to be able to align with each other so they can function as one. Second, it is *proleptic,* in that it represents a zone of development within which the varying levels of expertise among the members serve as scaffolds (Donato 1988). While no single member of the group has all the answers, different members of the group contribute pieces to the various solutions and resolutions that will make up the final performance. The result is that every group member is changed by this interaction to some extent: Some may know more about the target language, others may be more confident in their use of passive knowledge, others may have a cultural or psychological insight. The collaborative, collective effort of rehearsing enriches each student's individual abilities in nondeterministic ways as the group approaches the ultimate goal, autonomy in the face of the task.

Briefly stated, the first function of the rehearsal is to create a shared orientation among group members; the second function is to enable group members to develop control—over the target language, but also over themselves, other people, metalinguistic knowledge, the role, the target culture, and whatever other elements of the scenario are present. As Di Pietro implied when he insisted that the postperformance phase of debriefing be constructed primarily around student requests for information, the preperformance phase is not reducible to roles, linguistic items, or individual strategies: Repeating items x, y, and z a given number of times does not a rehearsal make. Instead, a rehearsal is a time of meaning-making, in which choices and decisions take on meaning only in relation to choices and decisions made in earlier stages.

Orientation. A performance is, by common semiotic definition, an organized concatenation of signs selected from the infinite universe of signs available (Elam 1980). This process of selection cannot take place in any useful way if there is no shared agreement (among the performers, directors, designers, etc.) about the motivation for the choices—in other words, about the background, or semiotic "ground," against which the decisions are made. If the creators of the performance do not share a perspective on the underlying meanings of the play, they will not share motive or goal, and the performance will be incoherent.

The potential interpretations and representations of any play are infinite; our notion of unity and logic demands that choices among potential signs be made with reference to all the other choices made. In addition, there typically are time constraints on the creation of performances. For efficiency, then, as well as for coherence, everyone must share, early in the creative process, a notion of the kinds of possibilities that exist and a notion of the general direction of the work. Where there is a director, much of the orientational obligation falls upon his or her shoulders. Early rehearsals provide the opportunity for the director to help the actors "come around" to seeing the task (i.e. recognizing the fundamental meanings of the play) from his or her viewpoint. The director creates a "parallel definition of situation" with the group of actors (just as the mothers described by Wertsch and Hickmann (1985) try to help their children solve problems by suggesting not just actions for the child to take, but new ways for the child to see the task).

In the SI classroom, there is no director—just as in the experimental theater group, the actors share directorial power and write the script as they rehearse it Paget (1990) describes the possible pitfalls of this exercise). Nevertheless, the beginning of the rehearsal period can be a setting within which parallel definitions of situation arise; initial moves will simply be less clearly motivated without the unifying vision of a director. If this crucial first step is not fully achieved, it is unlikely that a performance will ever be realized. Worse, there might be a "performance," in that certain actors stand before an audience and verbalize, but their words and actions will reflect nothing of the collaborative creative process that preceded the public event. This outcome can be likened to the student actor who never participates fully in rehearsals, but keeps reassuring the drama teacher that he'll get it right "on the night."

To summarize: Without a goal, the operations of the rehearsal are rendered meaningless. The notion of "goal" in SI, of course, has hardly been ignored. It has been well attested that the psycholinguistic strength of the method lies in the goal-directed instantiation of the performance, which arises from partially shared agendas, as in "real life" (Di Pietro 1987; Frawley and Lantolf 1985). However, goals in SI have been invoked primarily in terms of scenario design and performance, the observable playing out of the various entangled strategic moves, and not in terms of the preliminary goal of shaping the game plan itself. It is my belief that the collaborative movement of the actors toward the goal of creating a performance is perhaps even more revelatory of the psycholinguistic validity of SI than the more familiar performances and debriefings.

Prolepsis. The second function of the rehearsal is to create what is called within the Vygotskyan paradigm a "zone of proximal development" (ZPD), a metaphorical space through which each actor or group member develops toward ultimate autonomous control of a task. The ZPD represents the difference between what a learner can do alone and what the same learner can do with the help of expert semiotic mediation. A director, when present, serves as the expert who strategically helps, or scaffolds, the novice to become more expert; when there is no single director, the group members scaffold each other (Donato 1988). Di Pietro does not write explicitly of the phenomenon of prolepsis, but he does enjoin students to "participate" in the group tasks, thus raising an important, if implicit, question.

What does it mean to "participate" in a rehearsal? Follow directions, or strike out independently? Talk a lot, or think a lot? Many factors will influence the answers to these questions. The specific nature of each member's goal will determine the nature of that person's participation in the rehearsal. In addition, the nature of the group's collectivity and the kind of performance being created will help determine the quality of the rehearsal. Di Pietro comments in some detail on the fact that the open-endedness of the scenario leaves more choices in the hands of the student performer/rehearser (1987: 54). As States (1985) says about the written script of a play, the role cards provide a kind of "hypothesis, ... a yearning" toward interpretation that demands to be explored in rehearsal. There are unpredictably many ways to realize what Elam (1980) calls the "spectacular" potential of a given scenario, just as in the theater you can do Shakespeare in modern dress or Mozart operas in the swimming pool. The very recognition that there are many possibilities from which to choose is a qualitatively different kind of knowledge than the belief that there is a single or best solution.

A performance, whether in the theater or in the language classroom, is a kind of text. It is the result of a volitional process of semiotic selection (Strihan 1983). Unlike a printed text, however, many of its meaning-bearing signs are people, not just words and objects. Thus, the selection of signs for the performance text necessarily involves the complexity of human interaction. Rather than merely moving words around on a page, or images around on a canvas, directors (or actors in a collective) must engage and enroll other people to carry out their ideas. The performing actors, who will be the public "signs" reflecting that particular set of semiotic choices, must be committed to those choices.

To achieve such commitment, strategic instruction, explanation, and persuasion will be more useful than fiat. People are, notoriously, difficult to control (indeed, this is one of the essential psychological insights of SI). Ultimately, within the scenario game plan, this means having a strategic back-up plan. First, within the rehearsal, this means using language strategically to create that back-up plan and any others that the performer will bring to the performance. The best ideas in the world will not work if the selected performer cannot, or will not, employ them. This need for attaining a certain level of control within the collaborative environment (over language, over other people, over strategies, over oneself) makes the rehearsal not just an event (a time during which people speak about ideas) but a tool (a way for people to use speaking to create and disseminate ideas).

Rehearsal and the language classroom: Implications for practice. For my study, I recorded an experienced director at work as he guided skilled actors toward the ultimately successful staging of a play. In some obvious ways, this rehearsal process was clearly quite unlike the rehearsal of the SI lesson: The script of the play had been written over 50 years ago and was a standard of the American theater scene. As Di Pietro insists, SI students are not asked to prepare a performance of a prewritten script, but rather to prepare the script and the performance in tandem; indeed, the "script" is rarely written down in any complete form, and then only after one or two viewings and debriefings of the early, performed versions (1987: 84). In addition, the actors I observed were highly trained in the techniques of theatrical performance, while language students are typically not expert performers. In the theater, the director acts as a manager and as chief artist, in that he or she is the final arbiter of most of the many decisions that have to be made about technical details, character interpretation, costumes, and so forth. Conversely, there is no single overseer of the SI rehearsal; neither a student nor the teacher is invested with the kind of wide-ranging authority typically ascribed to a director. In fact, Di Pietro states quite clearly (1987: 68) that SI has been developed to get away from a "teacher-dominated" classroom.

But however dissimilar the two occasions for rehearsal may be, I claim that they share more than a name: A rehearsal, whether in the theater or in the language classroom, is the space within which the very possibility of a performance is collaboratively created. SI is not a methodology that happens to use groups; it is a methodology that depends crucially upon successful group interaction, and this interaction cannot happen without a rehearsal phase.

Insight does not always elucidate praxis. The implications for the language classroom of accepting the complexity of the structure and function of rehearsal are open to exploration. The most obvious implication relates to the use of time in the SI classroom. The rehearsal needs time to get started and then to progress; the time needed may be much longer than the 20 minutes or so originally allotted to it. The impatience of some groups (or teachers) to get to the performance is understandable when the focus of the SI lesson rests upon the performance. When attention shifts to the rehearsal phase as a locus of development, one result may be that students are asked to rehearse the same roles several different times. While I am not advocating allotting a six-week rehearsal period to one scenario, it becomes feasible to devote several class sessions to one set of roles or agendas when the purpose of rehearsal becomes more explicitly exploratory. Such a change of perspective, of course, entails a commitment to do SI in both intensive and extensive ways; not to pluck a scenario out of thin air as a Friday afternoon device, but rather to engage learners in the method so that their own expertise at rehearsing, as well as performing, grows.

Perhaps more interesting are the implications of this perspective for the teacher's role in the language classroom. The key word for the teacher's role in SI is "facilitator," one who makes the lesson, and its associated learning, happen more easily. What can we, as teachers, do to make rehearsal easier for students?

As suggested above, we can simply give them more time to practice rehearsing. In addition, we can become more actively involved in the very activity of rehearsal, serving not only as a source of instant linguistic and cultural reference but also as an expert rehearser. In no way am I advocating that teachers take over rehearsals by dominating group discussions, especially in groups that are able to work together successfully. However, since we see groups in our classes who are *not* able to work well together, and since it appears that performance without sufficient participation in collaborative rehearsal is psycholinguistically less rewarding, why shouldn't we become involved in developing our students' abilities to work collaboratively? While SI may displace the teacher from an outmoded and destructive authoritarian role, it does not remove the need for a skilled and responsive "chain of assistance" (Tharp and Gallimore 1976). Indeed, the Vygotskyan paradigm insists upon the necessity of sensitive and well-targeted strategic instruction for the novice's advancement through the zone of proximal development. Knowing not only *how* a rehearsal works but also *why* can contribute to the teacher's willingness to explore, and to encourage learners to explore, the infinite possibilities of presentation and representation in the second language.

REFERENCES

Curran, Charles A. 1976. *Counseling-learning in second languages.* Apple River, Ill.: Apple River Press.

Di Pietro, Robert J. 1987. *Strategic interaction: Learning languages through scenarios.* New York: Cambridge University Press.

Donato, R. 1988. "Beyond group: Psycholinguistic rationale for collective activity in second language learning." Unpublished Ph.D. dissertation, University of Delaware.

Elam, Keir. 1980. *The semiotics of theatre and drama.* London: Methuen.

Frawley, William J., and James P. Lantolf. 1985. "Second language discourse: A Vygotskyan perspective." *Journal of Applied Linguistics* 6: 19–44.

Kozulin, Alex. 1986. "The concept of activity in Soviet psychology: Vygotsky, his disciples and critics." *American Psychologist* 41: 264–274.

Paget, Derek. 1990. "Oh, what a lovely war: The texts and their context." *New Theatre Quarterly* 6: 244–260.

States, Bert O. 1985. *Great reckonings in little rooms: On the phenomenology of theater.* Berkeley, Calif.: University of California Press.

Strihan, Andrei. 1983. "Semiotics and the art of directing." *Kodikas/Code* 6: 103–108.

Tharp, Roland G., and Ronald Gallimore. 1976. *Rousing minds to life.* New York: Cambridge University Press.

Verity, Deryn P. 1992. *Strategic mediation in the rehearsal process: A psycholinguistic study of directing.* Unpublished Ph.D. dissertation, University of Delaware.

Wertsch, James V. 1985. *Vygotsky and the social formation of mind.* Cambridge, Mass.: Harvard University Press.

Wertsch, James V., and Maya Hickmann. 1987. "Problem solving in social interaction: A microgenetic analysis." In M. Hickmann (ed.), *Social and functional approaches to language and thought.* Orlando, Fla: Academic Press, Inc. 251–266.

Stating opinions in Japanese: Listener-dependent strategies

Shoko Okazaki[1]
Georgetown University

Introduction. In communicating the point of narratives, Labov (1972) suggests, there are two different types of evaluation. In one, external evaluation, the speaker steps aside from a story and explicitly states what the point is. In the other, internal evaluation, the point of the story is communicated by the way the story is presented rather than by an explicit statement made by the speaker. Labov claims that external evaluation is a characteristic feature of middle-class white Americans, whereas internal evaluation is a characteristic feature of black Americans.

When Japanese conversational discourse is examined to see how a specific point is made, we see that the Japanese seem to prefer internal evaluation to external evaluation. In cross-cultural communication, many researchers (for example, Naotsuka and Sakamoto 1981, Hall 1983, Ishii 1984, and Matsumoto 1988, among others) suggest that the point of Japanese speakers' utterances is often difficult for non-Japanese to understand because the Japanese are reluctant to state their opinions directly. Yamada (1989), for example, examined business meetings in Japanese companies and American companies and found that Japanese businessmen have an interactional need for nonconfrontation. They use the exemplification strategy for making their points rather than making their points explicitly and in temporal order.

In this paper, I will examine some of the strategies the Japanese employ when stating opinions and communicating their points in informal settings such as conversations among friends. I will also discuss the possibility of misunderstandings and stereotypes based on different discourse strategies and lack of familiarity with them in cross-cultural settings.

Communication strategies. Different ethnic groups have differing com-

---

1. I would like to thank Dr. Heidi Hamilton of Georgetown University for her encouragement and insightful comments on cross-cultural communication. I also thank Barbara Craig, Riza Meeding, Minako Ishikawa, Patricia O'Connor, and Yuling Pan for reading and commenting on the earlier draft of this paper.

munication strategies. In interactional sociolinguistics, Gumperz (1982, 1992) claims that interlocutors use what he calls contextualization cues to signal what is going on and how the message is to be interpreted. Contextualization cues include paralinguistic cues such as tone of voice, intonation, and voice quality as well as lexical and syntactic cues. These cues are learned through personal contact in a community network rather than from formal teaching in institutions. People who belong to the same speech community are expected to share the governing norms of these cues, and therefore communication is supposed to progress smoothly. In cross-cultural settings, however, participants with different social and cultural backgrounds have different ways of using and interpreting these cues, and therefore, even when the interlocutors speak the same language, miscommunication may occur.

Tannen (1983, 1984) discusses subcultural differences within the United States. She found that speakers from a New York Jewish background use overlap as a show of support for a current speaker, and they regard pauses as malfunctions in a conversation, while British speakers consider overlaps to be annoying interruptions, and they prefer longer pauses for turn-taking. Wieland (1991) also found differences in interpreting overlaps between French speakers and Americans who learned French as a foreign language. The French speakers used frequent overlap as a show of rapport while the Americans who spoke French as a foreign language felt that they were interrupted by the French when conversing in French, and that they were not given a chance to continue to talk.

Hayashi (1988) claims that Japanese speakers use "sync talk," or simultaneous talk, with much greater frequency than their American counterparts in order to achieve a communicative goal such as enjoying conversation in a harmonious atmosphere. In Okazaki (1990), I discussed how Japanese speakers in casual conversations were able to talk simultaneously in a rhythmic way by anticipating sentence boundaries of a floor holder's utterances as well as their propositional content.

Erickson and Schultz (1982) note the importance of rhythmic synchrony in conversations. In a counseling situation, a successful interview is regarded as one in which a counselor and a client (in their case, a college student) participate in an interaction in a rhythmic way, knowing where to come in and where the conversation is headed. In such an interview, the student is likely to obtain more useful information from the counselor. On the other hand, when the interactants do not share the same norms of communication, the result may be a disruption of synchrony in conversation.

These studies suggest that speakers use various discourse strategies that are learned mainly through face-to-face communication in their speech communities, and that these strategies are used not by conscious effort but, in most cases, as automatic responses to certain contextualization cues. Japanese speakers, then, acquire Japanese ways of talking in Japanese society, and they learn how to state opinions and how to interpret others' utterances by the use of different contextualization cues. As long as both a speaker and a hearer share the same norms of communication, the Japanese way of communication functions well between participants, even if it may seem to be inefficient or radically different from other ways of communication of other ethnic groups.

In his discussion of writing strategies, Hinds (1987) suggests a new typology of languages, namely reader responsibility vs. writer responsibility. According to Hinds, written Japanese is a reader-responsibility language in which it is presumably the readers' responsibility to understand the point of the written text. On the other hand, written English is a writer-responsibility language because it is primarily the writers who are expected to make the point explicit and clear for their readers. If the readers cannot understand the exact meaning, then the writer should make every effort to clarify the points rather than expecting the reader to make a special effort to interpret the text appropriately.

Although this distinction is based on the ways people write and read, the typology can be applied to oral communication as well. For example, Tyler and Davies (1990) analyzed an interaction between a Korean teaching assistant and an American student, and they found that the major point of the Korean teaching assistant's argument is initially lost for the American student. Tyler and Davies state that "it is reminiscent of Hinds' (1987) hypothesis concerning a typology of reader/writer responsibility for making the structure of an argument explicitly with Korean convention falling at the reader end of the continuum" (400).

In Japanese conversation, a speaker's point is frequently missing on the surface. Listeners are expected to be sensitive enough to interpret the point and understand where the conversation is headed by the way speakers use contextualization cues. Ishii (1984) calls such a way of communication "*enryo-sasshi* communication," and he points out that it is one of the keys in understanding interpersonal relationships and communication in Japan. *Enryo-sasshi* communication is characterized by the message sender's avoidance of direct expressions of thoughts and feelings (*enryo* "modesty"), and the receiver's sensitivity to the message (*sasshi* "consideration/anticipation"). It is generally believed that the "ethnically homogeneous society of Japan has made it possible for its people to understand each other by means of slight, rather than clear and exaggerated differences" (Ishii 1984: 51).

Hinds (1982: 70) also discusses the Japanese sensitivity to "clues" given in a speaker's utterance:

> Conversational interactants require fewer overt clues in the form of spoken words to carry on successful communication. ... [T]he high incidence of elliptical utterances forces the addressee to be much more receptive to subtle and transitory clues. ... [T]he typical Japanese interactant is sensitive to conversational interaction to a greater degree than the American counterpart.

The observation that the Japanese require fewer overt clues in verbal forms for communication indicates that Japanese culture is what Hall (1976) calls "high-context" communication (Heidi Hamilton, p.c., and Ishii 1984). In high-context communication, most of the information is, as Ishii describes it, internalized into the person or evident from the physical context, and therefore, "little is in the coded, explicit part of the message. High-context interaction is more economical and efficient than low-context interaction" (Ishii 1984: 54). Hall (1983: 62–63) further contrasts Japan with the United States in terms of indirectness in communication:

> The communication strategies of the United States and Japan provide a different perspective in the matter of contexting. Americans lacking extensive experience with the Japanese (particularly older Japanese who have not adapted to European communication patterns) frequently complain of indirection—they have difficulty knowing what the Japanese are "getting at." This is because the Japanese are part of a high context tradition and do not get to the point quickly. They talk around the topic. The Japanese think intelligent human beings should be able to discover the point of a discourse from the context, which they are careful to provide.

Japanese speakers thus do not present much information in verbal forms to communicate the point, and they depend on listeners to use sensitive guesswork or intuition to understand the message.

When successful, such delicate ways of communication bring feelings of satisfaction and involvement among participants. Tannen (1985) describes how filling in unstated information and relationships between propositions requires the listener to share prior communicative experience and background knowledge and to do some of the work of sense making. All of these features contribute to the creation of involvement.

The Japanese speakers seem to be trained from early childhood to understand the message of elliptical and fragmental utterances, and therefore, even though the points are not made explicitly, interlocutors maintain delicate personal interrelationships in communication. A Japanese sociologist, Chie Nakane (1970: 124), emphasizes that "the acquisition of these extremely delicate ways of conducting personal relations requires considerable social training, though most Japanese achieve them through their social life from childhood onwards."

In examination of casual conversations among Japanese speakers, Maynard (1989) suggests "self-contextualization" by speakers through linguistic structures of language and interactional management. She claims that essential characteristics of conversational language in Japanese are found in its fragmented quality and its orientation toward the social packaging of the message. A variety of strategies such as fillers, ellipsis, and postposing makes it possible to design an utterance suited to the occasion of talk. Thus, "it is through these strategies that the mechanism for self-contextualization (encompassing both contextual interpretation and contextual transformation) in Japanese conversation operates" (44).

In her discussion of Chinese discourse, Young (1982) also makes the connection between Chinese linguistic structure and Chinese discourse strategies. Based on the findings of Chao (1968) and Li and Thompson (1976), Young notes that the topic–comment structure is a basic sentence type in Chinese that is significantly different from subject-prominent or topic-prominent languages. In topic–comment structure, the topic bears a loose relationship to its comment, and new or significant information is positioned at the sentence ending. Young claims that this sentence pattern is applied to patterns seen in discourse structures.

> Guided by the insights of these scholars, I will extend their analyses of the functions of the topic–comment utterance to reflect beyond the sentence boundary. I will suggest that in such discourse tasks as explaining, justifying, and persuading, the organization of the discourse mirrors the order presented in the topic–comment utterance. The relationship of the main point to the rest of the discourse is in the order of the semantic relationship of topic to comment. (75)

Thus, Young claims that Chinese speakers prefer to build up information before they arrive at the important message. A similar discourse strategy by South Asians is reported by Gumperz, Kaltman, and O'Connor (1984). South Asian and American speakers of English significantly differ from each other in presenting background information and new information. South Asians first present background information by emphasizing it with stress:

> [South Asians] frequently lead up to a main point by first presenting background information spoken at a high pitch with rhythmic stress, then shift to lower-pitched, less emphatic speech to make their main point. Americans generally do the reverse. That is, they signal their main point with emphatic rhythmic stress and deemphasize the background information, usually by shifting to lower pitch.

Using less stress to make a point is confusing to Americans, who expect speakers to emphasize the point by using more stress and by placing the point in initial position. The different use of strategies employed by speakers thus causes miscommunication. The situation becomes complicated in cross-cultural communication where all the participants may speak the same language but do not share the same norms of communication.

The study. Data for this study are conversations among Japanese speakers and American white middle-class speakers in informal settings. During the conversations, many questions were exchanged among the participants, some of which specifically asked personal opinions on certain topics such as "What do you think about American food?" and "How do you think about the Japanese restaurant, Unkai?" The ways the Japanese speakers and American speakers answered these questions were significantly different. I claim that these differences derive from divergent cultural norms of communication acquired by the speakers in their speech communities.

In the sections to follow, I first describe the methods of data collection, and then I discuss such discourse strategies as use of examples, paralinguistic cues, discourse markers, and sentence-final particles used by Japanese speakers in stating opinions. Finally, I examine different interpretations of these strategies by native speakers of Japanese and native speakers of English. The possibility of miscommunication and the development of stereotypes is also considered.

Data collection. To analyze what strategies the Japanese use to communicate their opinions in informal settings, three conversations were audio-recorded in the United States. One of them was recorded in California, in which the participants were four native speakers of Japanese who speak English as a foreign language and one Japanese American who speaks Japanese as a foreign language. The second conversation was recorded in Washington, D.C., at a lunch table in which the participants were three native speakers of Japanese, one third-generation Japanese who is studying Japanese as a foreign language, and one American who does not know Japanese. The third one was recorded in Washington, D.C., in which four native speakers of Japanese participated. All of the conversations included both male and female Japanese, and the Japanese speakers had been in the United States for less than one year, except for me, who has lived in the United States for five years. I participated in all the conversations.

To supplement the data, I also conducted one open-ended interview with a male Japanese graduate student in Japanese. A conversation among four middle-class American female speakers and me was also recorded for a comparative study. All the American participants in the conversational group are classmates from the same linguistics course. The recording took place in the classroom while we were waiting for a professor.

Both Japanese and American participants seemed a little nervous about tape-recording at first, but as the conversations progressed, the interactions became more natural. The tape-recorded conversations were transcribed and translated into English when the Japanese speakers used Japanese.

Further, two white American students and one Japanese student participated in this study as informants from each culture. I showed the transcripts of the conversations to them and asked them to describe their impressions and interpretations about the participants' utterances and strategies. All the comments were tape-recorded and transcribed. Gumperz (1982) discusses the significance of the information provided by speakers of the same cultural background in understanding interactional assumptions and expectations. In this study, the informants' comments brought deeper insights into my data analysis, and they helped me understand culturally different points of view more clearly.

In the following sections, I will analyze how Japanese state opinions in casual conversations by investigating conversational structures used by the Japanese speakers, conversational structures used by Americans, and the relations of these structures to face concerns.

Conversational structures.

Conversational structures by Japanese speakers. Different languages may have different strategies in constructing discourse. As Young (1982) illustrated, Chinese discourse is structured so that the more important information or the thesis point appears at the end, only after background information is presented. A similar strategy is observed in Japanese conversations. In answering questions such as "What did you think about ______?", the Japanese participants may postpone their statement of opinions until they provide background information from which the listeners can induce a conclusion.

I am not suggesting here that the Japanese never give opinions or answer questions directly. There are many cases in which Japanese speakers state their opinions immediately, depending on topic, interpersonal relationships, settings, and so on. But it seems to be also true that the Japanese speakers are aware of such strategies as providing background information first, and therefore they can patiently wait for the conclusion when the current speaker is using the indirect approach.

The following example illustrates the speaker's avoidance of answering questions immediately. Kazuo, Masao, Shoko, Diane, and Paul are talking about Japanese restaurants in Washington, D.C. Diane and Paul are married, and they are a hospitality family for Kazuo, who has been in the United States for two months. Masao and Shoko are friends of Diane and Paul. Masao is also a good friend of Kazuo, since they are both MBA students at Georgetown University. Diane and Paul invited the Japanese speakers to their house for lunch for the first time. Diane is a third-generation Japanese American who is learning Japanese as a foreign language.

1	Diane:	Have you guys gone to Unkai?
2	Masao:	Well,
3	Kazuo:	I tried once.
4	Masao:	Yes.

→	5	Diane:	How did you think
→	6	Kazuo:	Uh, it's a lunch time.
	7	Diane:	Uh-huh
	8	Kazuo:	Because it's, it's, it costs six dollars,
	9	Masao:	└six dollars
	10	Paul :	└six dollars.
	11	Shoko:	Really::? It's unbelievable.
	12	Diane:	└[laughs]
	13	Kazuo:	Yeah. That's really cheap.
	14		It's uh you know,
	15	Paul:	└Teppan yaki
	16	Kazuo:	└Teppan yaki, yes.
	17		U::m, well, meat? well, I mean uh::
	18	Shoko:	and vegetable and rice and miso soup.
	19	Kazuo:	Yes, chicken? uh::
	20	Diane:	Shrimp? Appetizer?
	21	Kazuo:	Shrimp? and,
	22	Paul:	Scallop?
	23	Kazuo:	Scallop?
	24	Paul:	Beef hot dog.
	25	Kazuo:	Beef [laugh]
	26	All:	[laugh]
	27	Shoko:	Hot dog!?
	28	All:	[laugh]
	29	Diane:	No, really,
→	30	Kazuo:	└and I liked miso soup very much.
	31	Diane:	Uh-huh!
→	32	Kazuo:	Yes, miso soup was very nice.
	33		Six dollars, only six dollars.
	34	Shoko:	└Wo::w!

Diane asks in line 5 what Kazuo thought about a Japanese restaurant, called Unkai. Kazuo's first response is to inform her that he went there for lunch, and the reason for that was because it was less expensive ("because it's it's, it costs six dollars"). He further states what he ate at the restaurant ("Teppan yaki, yes.") in line 16 with some help from Paul, and what was in the food ("well, meat?"). The answer to Diane's question is not given until lines 30, 32, and 33. The listeners' role here is to wait patiently for him to finish providing background information and draw the conclusion. Kazuo's point seems to be that the restaurant was very good and cheap, even though he does not say it directly. This strategy seems to be successful in this conversation; none of the listeners interrupt Kazuo, but they let Kazuo finish his talk and present his conclusion. This might be because this meeting was the first time that Diane and Paul invited the Japanese guests for lunch, and they wanted to be polite to us.

Another example of a similar strategy is observed in a conversation between Bill and Akemi. Bill is a third-generation Japanese American who speaks English as a mother tongue and Japanese as a foreign language. Akemi is studying English as a foreign language, and he has been in the United States for three months. The participants are comparing Japan and the United States. Bill asks Akemi what she thinks about American food.

1 Bill: What do you think about American food?
2 Akemi: American food? Uh ... *nante iuno?*
what can I say?
3 y'know, I'm living with an American family now,
4 so, my, uh host father is a very big man,
5 but in the dinner?
6 Bill: mm hmm
7 Akemi: Um:: he always does not eat so much. Maybe ...
8 I will, I will eat much (laugh) much than
9 him, more than him. So .. but .. uh:: [2.0][2]
10 mm: *tatoeba anmari tabenain-desu-kedo* ..
for example he doesn't eat very much
11 *tatoeba ohiru nanka-ni ranchi-no tokidemo*
for example for lunch, for lunch time, too,
12 *amerika-no hito-tte amari tabenain-desu-yone* ...
the Americans do not eat much, you know, ...
13 *Sonna-koto nai-desu-ka?* [2.0]
Isn't that right?
14 *Eto, watashi-tachi nihonjin-to iunowa,*
Well, we, Japanese,
15 *gohan-o don-to tabete, okazu-o don-to tabete, de*
eat rice a lot, and side dishes a lot, and
16 *honto-ni taberu-tte iu kanji-de taberun-desu-kedo* ...
we eat like we really have meals, but :..
17 [laugh]
18 Bill: mm hmm
19 Akemi: *Wakari-masu-ka? Demo kocchi-no hitotte iunowa*
Do you understand? But people here are
20 *nani-ka .. mm, tatoeba kouiu okashi-o tabetara*
somewhat .. mm, for example, if they eat snacks like these
21 *sore-o yuhan-gawari-ni shite shimattari-toka* ...
they substitute it for supper, or, ...

2. Numbers in square brackets indicate pauses in seconds.

22 *nante iun-desho, shokuji-ni taisuru gainen-ga*
how can I say it, their general idea of a meal is
23 *sukoshi chigau-yona .. kiga surun-desu-kedo...*
a little bit different, I think, but ...
24 Bill: mm hmm

In responding to Bill's question, "what do you think about American food?", Akemi starts by making a statement about her living situation ("I'm living with an American family now.") and talks about her host family's eating habits, that is, her host father does not eat much even though he is big. Then she shifts the topic to talk about eating habits of Americans in general in line 11 ("for lunch, American people do not eat much"). By using *tatoeba* "for example," she provides other instances that made her think that Americans' eating habits are different from the ones in Japan. Only after a long introductory statement and examples, Akemi gives her general thoughts about Americans' eating habits as a response to Bill's question. To Americans, Akemi's concluding statement may not seem to be an answer to the question because she does not say whether she likes American food or not.

One of the tendencies of Japanese conversational structure seems to be to put a long introductory comment about a topic before the thesis statement. Inagaki (1977) points out that it is a characteristic of the Japanese to open their speech, for example, with expressions of humility, apology, excuses, and/or a course of action rather than a main point. In a previous study (Okazaki 1987), I claimed that Japanese speakers provide several opportunities for their listeners to build up a shared background of information by providing preliminary information including socio-cultural knowledge, context-bound presuppositions, and goals of communication that interlocutors must hold in common in order to understand the points of the messages and to proceed smoothly.

In the above example, both Kazuo and Akemi elicited confirmation from the participants and checked their understanding of the information in the course of their talk. Kazuo used *y'know* to examine the participants' meta-knowledge about Japanese food, and Akemi asked *wakari-masu-ka?* "do you understand?" in line 18 before she made a further move toward her conclusion. Her use of examples also provided opportunities to build up shared background information.

What seems to be a significant characteristic of Kazuo's and Akemi's discourse strategy is that instead of giving their opinions directly, they started with general information or background information about a topic, and then, by building up the shared information necessary for the participants to draw the conclusion, they presented their opinions at the end.

What also should be noted is the different use of paralinguistic cues. When uttering his main point about the restaurant ("the miso soup was very nice. Six dollars, only six dollars"), Kazuo's voice became very weak, and it sounded almost like he was whispering this part. To deemphasize the main point with weaker stress is, as Gumperz et al. (1982) suggest, just the opposite of what Americans normally expect. In the Japanese way of communication, however, since all the background information is already presented, there is not much need to emphasize the concluding remarks; listeners are supposed to be able to induce the conclusion by themselves without having the speaker clearly explain the point.

Conversational structures used by Americans. In contrast to the Japanese examples, Americans in my data expressed their opinions more directly. For example, they stated whether they liked a certain kind of food or not, and if they liked it, why they liked it, and if they did not, then why not or what part of the food they didn't like. The following conversation among four middle-class white female Americans and me illustrates this point. The participants are all graduate students. While we were talking casually in a classroom, I asked them for permission to tape-record our conversation. I asked their thoughts about Chinese food first, then later I asked them about Japanese food.

1	Jane:	Well, I love Chinese food, but um, the only
2		problem is when [cough] after, after you eat
3		it and go home and go to bed,
4		I, I always wake up in the middle of the night
5		and I have to get a drink because I get really
6		thirsty.
7	Shoko:	Oh, yeah, yeah.
8	Jane:	I love the hot stuff.
9	Shoko:	mm ... any ... other ... [laugh]
10	Meg:	I like the noodles, I just hate hot
11	Jane:	└Oh I love the noodles
12	Meg:	So, anything that's hot is a problem.
13		I mean, they could do everything but get the hot
14		pepper out, I'd be happy.

In line 1, Jane states her general preference for Chinese food ("I love Chinese food"), then states the part she does not like ("the only problem is ...") in lines 1 through 6, and the reason for that problem ("I love the hot stuff."). Meg also makes her likes and dislikes clear at the initial position of her utterance by saying in line 10, "I like the noodles, I just hate hot." The statements about their opinions of Chinese food appear at the initial position of their utterances, and are followed by reasons. The structure is quite different from Japanese discourse.

When I asked them about Japanese food, the same strategy was used by the participants. Since the Americans had to talk about Japanese food in front of a Japanese classmate (me), there was a greater face threat than there was when they talked about Chinese food. However, the basic strategy of stating one's opinion first and providing reasons second remained the same.

1 Laura: Then, Japanese food,
2 well, I like its organization. [laugh]
3 y'know, the presentation is so nice and I like
4 that.
5 Shoko: Hm
[Ruth walks in.]
6 Ruth: What you guys are talking about?
7 Laura: We're talking about food for recording.
8 Japanese food.
9 Ruth: Oh::
10 Jane: It's much nicer to look at than it is to eat.
11 Shoko: [laugh]
12 Jane: I got so bored with Chines–, with Japanese food
13 when I was in Japan,
14 Shoko: Uh-huh,
15 Jane: that I could eat almost anything instead of it.
16 Meg: Not enough, not enough variety.
17 Jane: But then once I came back, I really, I, I yearn
18 for Japanese food.
19 So, I have certain things I still would like to
20 eat.

Laura states she likes the presentation of food in Japanese dishes. Then, Jane makes a negative comment about Japanese food, saying "it's much nicer to look at than it is to eat." Here, even though Jane's opinion is negative, and therefore it is face-threatening to both Jane and Shoko, Jane expresses her opinion at the first part of her utterance, then she follows up her statement with reasons for that, indicating her possible status as an "expert" about Japan who ate Japanese food so much during her stay in Japan and therefore became bored with it. Using this status as an "expert" on Japan, she may have been more comfortable about stating negative comments in front of a native Japanese.

The next exchange between Meg and Jane also shows that they make their "yes" and "no" clear. Meg asks Jane whether she likes raw fish:

21 Meg: Do you like the raw ... fish?
22 Jane: Yeah.
23 Meg: See, I don't.
24 I can handle the taste but I don't like the

texture. Isn't that weird?
So, it's like I can't get over the feeling
aspect so I can't eat either.
But I love noodle soup.
They have great noodle soup.

Meg's short pause in her question in line 21, "do you like the raw ... fish?" seems to indicate that she thinks that Jane and Shoko may like raw fish even though she does not like it. Jane answers "yeah," but Meg explicitly states that she does not like it. To disagree with the previous speaker can be face threatening. In addition, not only Jane but I could be offended by Meg's negative comment. Therefore, she mitigates her utterance with *see*, then she further provides a reason why she cannot eat raw fish. Thus, even when disagreeing with the previous speaker, Meg states her opinion at the initial position of her utterances and then provides a reason for her opinion.

Americans generally seem to expect their interlocutors to explicitly state their opinions at the beginning of their utterances when they are asked their opinions. Schegloff and Sacks (1973) maintain that the first part of adjacency pairs (such as question–answer, greeting–greeting, and offer–acceptance) presupposes the expectation that the second part will be filled by the next speaker. As Schiffrin (1985) claims, since there is a sequential expectation for a question to be followed by an answer, "answers are often placed in boundary positions of the turn so that their tie to the prior question can be easily established." The answerers then follow with reasoning for their stance because, as Schiffrin (1985: 40) points out, "beliefs, opinions, judgments, and feelings ... are different from assertions and statements of fact because they are representations of internal, cognitive states that are available for neither observation nor verification."

On the other hand, for the Japanese, listeners are expected to be sensitive enough to understand the point based on the background information presented by a speaker. The listeners are responsible as much as, if not more than, the speaker for constructing and continuing the conversation. Even though the adjacency pair assumes that the next speaker will be accountable for supplying the answer, Japanese ways of communication involve listeners in the inductive process of drawing conclusions more greatly than English ways of communication.

Duranti (1986), as well as Goodwin (1986), claims that the audience can be seen as "co-author" of conversations. In other words, listeners' communicative behaviors, including backchannels and eye gaze, influence how speakers talk. In my data of stating opinions, it is not only the speakers who are sensitive to the listeners' response in proceeding in the conversations, but also the listeners who were expected to be sensitive to the direction of the conversations.

Conversational structures and face threat. Indirect ways of communication and face threat have been found to be closely related (Brown and Levinson 1978, 1987). When a speaker makes an utterance that is potentially face threatening to a hearer, then the speaker may use mitigating expressions or indirect expressions and give hints to the hearer about the nature of the speaker's message. In the conversations under study, Akemi was asked what she thought about American food by the third-generation Japanese American. She may have avoided answering the questions directly because she was afraid of damaging the American participant's face by making negative comments about American food.

American students also used hedges such as "well" or "see" when they made statements contradictory to the previous speaker's opinion. The negative nature of the opinion itself may encourage speakers to use more indirect ways of communication. For example, one American student started talking about getting sick from eating Chinese food before she indicated that she did not like Chinese food very much.

This close relationship between indirect ways of speaking and face threat may allow Americans, when they hear Japanese indirect ways of communication, to interpret the Japanese as trying to communicate something negative because they do not state their opinions immediately. On the other hand, the Japanese may be following a different strategy of communication. As an example, Heidi Hamilton (p.c.) suggests that the first impression that Americans would normally have about Kazuo's answer about the Japanese restaurant is that Kazuo did not like the restaurant, and that was why he avoided stating his opinion immediately. Kazuo's positive opinion about the restaurant toward the end of the conversation is, therefore, somewhat surprising, and it may cause confusion for Americans. From the Japanese point of view, however, Kazuo's utterances can be seen as a strategy to avoid confrontation by creating a common ground of information first.

The problem of face is certainly a vital aspect of stating opinions in different ways. Deeper and wider analyses of conversations on different topics with different face threat are needed to gain further insight into this issue.

Discourse strategies for presenting information as to-be-shared. The Japanese speakers try to establish shared information first, before they provide their opinions. By establishing shared background knowledge, and by providing several opportunities for listeners to give affirmative feedback to the current speaker's talk, the speaker moves closer to the conclusion and tries to minimize the possibility of disagreement from listeners. In this section, I will examine some of the strategies Japanese speakers use in my data to present information as to-be-shared by the participants in the conversation. The first to be examined is use of examples. I claim that examples are an effective strategy for presenting background information that needs to be shared by participants when the Japanese speakers use the inductive approach of drawing conclusions.

Then I discuss use of *y'know* as a discourse marker used by Japanese speakers when speaking English and use of *yo-ne* (which roughly means "y'know") when speaking Japanese. I will show that the Japanese participants use *y'know* and *yo-ne* in order to present information as to-be-shared.

Use of examples. Examples are a useful strategy for presenting information as to-be-shared. In her analysis of Japanese and American business meetings, Yamada (1989: 181) finds that the Japanese use an exemplification strategy for point-making, whereas Americans use a temporal sequencing strategy for point-making. In other words, Americans follow three sequential steps: 1. report present situations; 2. supply background as to what has been done to the deal; 3. provide options to be done in the future. In contrast, Japanese "exemplification strategy can be used at any location in the discourse as long as the point made through the example contributes to the topic under discussion." Thus, use of examples is not constrained by linear order in Japanese business meetings. In the informal conversations in my data, examples were used to establish shared background so that all the participants could arrive at the same conclusion as the speaker. Therefore, the speaker may present an example before he or she makes the point.

Akemi uses *tatoeba* "for example" three times in her utterance to make her point. The conversation between Bill and Akemi is repeated below.

	1	Bill:	What do you think about American food?
	2	Akemi:	American food? Uh ... *nante iuno?*
			how can I say?
	3		y'know, I'm living with an American family now,
	4		so, my, uh host father is a very big man,
	5		but in the dinner?
	6	Bill:	mm hmm
	7	Akemi:	Um:: he always does not eat so much. Maybe ...
	8		I will, I will eat much (laugh) much than
	9		him, more than him. So .. but .. uh:: [2.0]
→	10		mm: <u>*tatoeba*</u> *anmari tabenain-desu-kedo* ..
			for example he doesn't eat very much
→	11		<u>*tatoeba*</u> *ohiru nanka-ni ranchi-no tokidemo*
			for example for lunch, for lunch time, too,
	12		*amerika-no hito-tte amari tabenain-desu-yone* ...
			the Americans do not eat much, you know, ...
	13		*Sonna-koto nai-desu-ka?* [2.0]
			Isn't that right?
	14		*Eto, watashi-tachi nihonjin-to iunowa,*

Well, we, Japanese,
15 *gohan-o don-to tabete, okazu-o don-to tabete, de*
eat rice a lot, and side dishes a lot, and
16 *honto-ni taberu-tte iu kanji-de taberun-desu-kedo...*
we eat like we really have meals, but ...
17 [laugh]
18 Bill: mm hmm
19 Akemi: *Wakari-masu-ka? Demo kocchi-no hitotte iunowa*
Do you understand? But people here are
→ 20 *nani-ka .. mm, tatoeba kouiu okashi-o tabetara*
somewhat .. mm, for example, if they eat snacks like these
21 *sore-o yuhan-gawari-ni shite shimattari-toka ...*
they substitute it for supper, or, ...
22 *nante iun-desho, shokuji-ni taisuru gainen-ga*
how can I say, their general idea of a meal is
23 *sukoshi chigau-yona .. kiga surun-desu-kedo...*
a little bit different, I think, but ...

Akemi uses *tatoeba* "for example" in lines 10 and 11 in the place where there is no thesis statement in the preceding text. Therefore, at first, it is hard to understand what these examples are illustrating or supporting. In line 20, *tatoeba* appears after a fragmental utterance of *kocchi-no hito-tte iu-nowa nani-ka ... mm* "people here are somewhat ... mm." *Tatoeba* here introduces her statement about Americans substituting snacks for supper. Use of *tatoeba* indicates the speaker's expectation that listeners will respond affirmatively because it implies "as long as you agree with my example, I can expect that you will understand my point." Further, in the Japanese conversations, what is difficult to express is often illustrated by examples, and the listener's role is to "read between the lines" to find a connection between the examples and the point of the message. In some cases, a speaker may not provide the point in verbal form but will let the listeners induce the point intuitively.

The Japanese informant mentioned that in informal parties, people sometimes start answering questions with *tatoeba* at the beginning of utterances. Thus, the main point of an answer is overtly unstated, and examples are used to let listeners interpret the point and to have them involved in the inductive process of drawing a conclusion. This strategy is illustrated in the following exchange between Kenji and me. Kenji is a graduate student who has been in the United States for about 10 months. Kenji has stated that there are many ethnic groups and geographic areas in the United States and that it is therefore impossible to generalize "what is America." Then I asked him what he thought about American food.

1 Shoko: *Ja, hanashi-wa zenzen kawatte,*
well, changing the subject completely,
2 Kenji: *Hai,*
yes
3 Shoko: *Amerika-no tabemono-wa do-desu-ka?*
how about American food?
4 *Amerika-no tabemono-ni tsuite do omoimasu-ka?*
what do you think about American food?
5 Kenji: *A, tabemono-mo,*
oh, food, too
→ 6 *tatoeba kakohin-ga mise-ni yotte chigau-to omoundesu-yo-ne*
for example, processed food is different depending on stores, I think, right?
7 Shoko: *A::a,*
Yea::h

In this excerpt, Kenji starts his answer to my question with an elliptical utterance, "Uh, food, too," by which he probably meant that "it is difficult to say anything in general about American food just as it is almost impossible to make any generalization about America." But instead of elaborating his opinion explicitly, he uses the exemplification strategy to make his point in line 4. When Kenji said "food, too," it was not very clear in what respect American food is comparable to the United States. The use of examples helped me to fill in the gap between Kenji's utterance of "food, too" and what he really meant by that.

Use of y'know *for shared knowledge.* Schiffrin (1987) claims that one of the functions of *y'know* is to create a situation in which a speaker knows that a hearer shares knowledge about a particular piece of information, and that *y'know* displays the speaker as an information provider who depends upon hearer reception of information. In my data, the Japanese speakers also used *y'know* in building up shared background information when speaking English.

1 Bill: What do you think about American food?
2 Akemi: American food? *Nante iuno?* ["What can I say?"]
→ 3 Y'know, I'm living with an American family now.
4 so, my, uh, host father is a very big man,

Akemi uses *y'know* to bracket the information about her living situation and her host father as necessary background knowledge for the listeners to understand the point. In other words, what follows *y'know* has to be shared by the listeners because her argument builds upon this background information. By using *y'know*, Akemi signals her dependence on the listeners' reception of the information.

The next example also illustrates the use of *y'know* by a Japanese speaker as a signalling mechanism of the speaker's dependence on the listeners' understanding background information.

(Kazuo is talking about how expensive sushi restaurants are in Tokyo.)

1	Kazuo:	Be care, be careful to uh, y'know enter um Ginza
2		restaurants.
3	Shoko:	Oh.
4	Paul:	Ginza.
5	Kazuo:	Yes, Ginza's, Ginza's sushi restaurant.
6	Paul:	uh-huh
7	Kazuo:	It's crazy.
8	Diane:	Why.
9	Kazuo:	Yeah, it's uh if you lose, yes,
10		one night will, y'know, lo–, make you lose money.
11		[laugh]
12	Diane:	Oh, price.
13	Kazuo:	Well, it's exaggeration,
14		but very expensive.

In this conversation, the success of the line of argument Kazuo is presenting depends on the shared knowledge among the participants about Ginza. Ginza is a famous street in Tokyo, probably comparable to Fifth Avenue in New York, where many stores sell a variety of expensive goods. Native speakers of Japanese who were born and raised in Japan generally share this knowledge and have the image of Ginza as an expensive street. Therefore, as soon as I heard *Ginza* in line 3, I responded with "oh," by which I meant agreement with Kazuo about the caution that is required when eating in Ginza. Kazuo's listeners, however, included non-Japanese participants, Diane and Paul. If they do not know what *Ginza* represents, Kazuo's point would not be understood fully. His use of *y'know* before *Ginza* in line 1 therefore can be seen as a signal that Kazuo expects—and depends on—his listeners to understand the implication of *Ginza*.

In line 10, in order to illustrate how expensive Ginza is, Kazuo uses *y'know* again, signalling his expectation of listeners' shared background. His point is that sushi restaurants in Ginza are so expensive that one can lose a lot of money in just one night.

In this conversation, Kazuo also uses an indirect way of answering Diane's question of "why" in line 8.

Kazuo: Yes, Ginza's, Ginza's sushi restaurant.
Paul: uh-huh
Kazuo: It's crazy.
Diane: Why.
Kazuo: Yeah, it's uh if you lose, yes,
one night will, y'know, lo–, make you lose money.
[laugh]
Diane: Oh, price.
Kazuo: Well, it's exaggeration,
but very expensive.

Kazuo states in lines 5 and 7 that sushi restaurants in Ginza are crazy. This statement prompts Diane as in line 8 to ask for the reason why sushi restaurants in Ginza are crazy. Kazuo's answer to this question does not appear until line 14 "very expensive," which is articulated with a weaker stress than the prior part. Here, Kazuo uses the inductive approach to communicate his point: First he gives the illustration of Ginza restaurants ("one night will make you lose money"), and second, he lets Diane induce the point ("Oh, price"). Since Diane understood the point successfully, Kazuo did not have to emphasize his point anymore. Therefore, lines 13 and 14 were articulated with weaker voice than other parts of his utterances.

Sentence-final particles. In Japanese discourse, the sentence-final particle *ne* seems to signal speakers' expectations that listeners share information as necessary background knowledge. According to Maynard (1989: 14), particles are defined as "functional words normally consisting of only a few syllables—which function grammatically and interactionally."

Uyeno (1971) describes *ne* as a particle of a speaker's request for confirmation as well as a listener's show of agreement with the propositional content. Maynard further states that *ne* roughly functions like the tag in English tag questions, and it is often used when soliciting assurance and/or agreement from the listener. Cook (1990: 41) proposes that "*ne* indicates a common ground between the speaker and the addressee by eliciting the addressee's involvement with the speaker."

In the Japanese conversations under study, the participants frequently used *ne* together with *yo* to solicit affirmative backchannels from the listeners when speaking in Japanese. *Yo* is a particle of assertion that adds moderate emphasis. Maynard (1989: 125) suggests that *yo* is "especially useful when the speaker provides a new piece of information." The following example shows use of *yo-ne* by Japanese speakers.

1 Shoko: *Amerika-no tabemono-wa do-desu-ka?*
How about American food?
2 *Amerika-no tabemono-ni tsuite do omoi-masu-ka?*
What do you think about American food?
3 Kenji: *A, tabemono-mo,*
Oh, food, too
4 *tatoeba kakohin-ga mise-ni yotte chigau-to omoun desu-yo-ne*
for example, processed food is different
depending on stores, I think, right?
5 Shoko: *A::a,*
Yea::h

Yo-ne is roughly interpreted as "right?" or "y'know." It is used to present new information as to-be-shared and to-be-accepted by listeners. It signals the speaker's expectation that listeners will agree with the presented piece of information. By putting *yo-ne* at the end in line 5, for example, Kenji tries to elicit an affirmative response from me. One of the implications *yo-ne* conveys is "You agree with me, right? Isn't what I said correct?" By eliciting the affirmative responses through these particles, the speaker continues to build up his argument. He also uses exemplification strategy to make his point.

The next example also shows the use of *yo-ne* as an indication of speakers' dependence on listeners' shared knowledge. The conversation is between Bill and Akemi about American food.

7 Akemi: Um:: he always does not eat so much. Maybe ...
8 I will, I will eat much (laugh) much than
9 him, more than him. So .. but .. uh:: [2.0]
10 mm: *tatoeba anmari tabenain-desu-kedo ..*
for example he doesn't eat very much
11 *tatoeba ohiru nanka-ni ranchi-no tokidemo*
for example for lunch, for lunch time, too,
12 *amerika-no hito-tte amari tabenain-desu-yo-ne ...*
the Americans do not eat much, you know, ...
13 *Sonna-koto nai-desu-ka?* [2.0]
Isn't that right?

After using the exemplification approach, Akemi requests agreement from Bill first by *yo-ne*, and second by asking explicitly "*sonna koto nai-desu-ka?*" "Isn't that right?" Notice that there is a short pause after *yo-ne*. Akemi probably waited for a backchannel from Bill because this is the point where native speakers of Japanese normally give some kind of backchannel. However, no vocalization was made by Bill, and it seems that the lack of backchannels prompted her to ask verbally in line 13 whether Bill thought Akemi's description was correct or not. The idea of the Americans not eating very much was probably difficult for Bill to agree with immediately, which resulted in a two-second pause in line 13 after Akemi's utterance.

The following exchange is an example of a Japanese way of giving backchannels in response to *(yo)-ne*. Kenji explains his thoughts about American food. His point is that it is not possible to make a generalization about American food because it depends on the store, and that if one pays a lot of money or looks for a good store, one can find tasty food. Kenji uses *ne* and *yo-ne* frequently, and I respond to them with backchannels. Further, my backchannels often include *ne* in order to establish rapport. Kenji gives reciprocal backchannels to me after I use *ne*.

	1	Kenji:	*mazu nedan-dewa, nikutoka, ano nanda, yasuitoka*
	2		*-tte iimasu-kedo, iinowa takai-desu-yo-ne*
			First of all, for price, like meat, uh what?
			they say it's cheap or something, but good one
			is expensive, right?
→	3	Shoko:	*Huun, soo-desu-ne.*
			Humm, that's right.
→	4	Kenji:	*Hai.*
			Yes.
	5	Shoko:	*Soo-desu-ne.*
			That's right.
	6	Kenji:	*Katai-nowa mechakucha yasui-desu-kedo::*
			Tough meat is extremely cheap, bu::t,
	7		*iino-wa takai-desu-yo-ne.*
			good one is expensive, y'know
→	8	Shoko:	*Un.*
			Yeah
	9	Kenji:	*Nihon-to anma kawan-nai desu-yo-ne.*
			It's not so different from Japan, y'know.
→	10	Shoko:	*Ee.*
			Uh-huh

Every time Kenji uses *yo-ne* I give backchannels (lines 3, 8, and 9), signalling I am listening. In lines 3 and 5, I also indicate that I agree with him (*soo-desu-ne* "that's right"). In line 4, Kenji also responds to my backchannel with *hai* 'yes' probably because I used *ne* in my utterance. By soliciting affirmative backchannels from me, Kenji continues his argument and presents his conclusion at the end as in line 9 "it's not so different from Japan." As Cook (1990: 42) points out, "*ne* is used to negotiate cooperation" in immediate social interaction.

According to LoCastro (1987), two very important characteristics of Japanese are frequent use of verbal responses that indicate that listeners understand the conversation (Mizutani 1982, Maynard 1989) and presentation of one's interest by using brief comments and/or questions (Kunihiro 1977) According to Kunihiro and LoCastro, the frequency and timing of acknowledgments are different in English and in Japanese. Mizutani (1982) and White (1989) have pointed out that the Japanese have a tendency to use acknowledgements more frequently and quickly than Americans do, not because listeners want to hurry a speaker but because they want to create a supportive atmosphere in a conversation.

I claim that another function of such frequent acknowledgments and backchannels is to establish shared background among participants. Since a Japanese speaker's thesis is often unstated at the initial position of the discourse, in order for the speakers to build up the background information and present their opinions, they need to frequently check listeners' understanding. Use of such sentence-final particles as *ne* and *yo* functions as a mechanism for checking listeners' understanding and attitudes toward the line of argument the speaker is presenting, since they solicit frequent backchannels from the audience.

Implications for cross-cultural communication. The previous sections showed that Japanese speakers may avoid stating their opinions directly at the initial part of their utterances, and they use a variety of strategies to involve listeners in the process of sense making, which Tannen (1985) suggests is an important strategy for creating rapport and involvement. The white middle-class Americans in my data, on the other hand, prefer stating their opinions directly at the beginning of utterances. Reasons for holding that opinion follow their thesis statements.

These differences between Japanese and American interactants may cause misunderstanding in face-to-face communication and may eventually promote negative stereotypes of people from other cultures. In this section, I will discuss comments from my American and Japanese informants about the conversational data. I claim that judgments based on just one system of communication will not only cause misunderstanding but may also contribute to the creation of negative stereotypes against certain ethnic groups as a whole.

I showed the transcripts of my data with English translation to two American informants. They are both students in linguistics at Georgetown University, and are white middle-class Americans. They pointed out that the Japanese speakers did not answer the questions in the way they normally expect, and that it was difficult to understand what the point of their utterances was.

The following excerpts are the American informants' tape-recorded comments on Japanese ways of answering questions:

> [Kenji] is not saying "oh I like tacos," or well, I guess that's Mexican, but "I like hamburgers, I like chicken" you know, whatever else. Um whereas the Americans are definitely focussing on the parts they like and the parts they don't like, and that's how, I think, the Americans normally interpret the question "what do you think about blank food."

> [Akemi] avoided answering the question. She does not talk about like anything she likes or she dislikes. She just has some general thought.

> [Akemi's] point, I guess, is that uh ... in relation to the question, I don't, I don't know how I would say the point.

> I have no idea what [Kenji] is talking about.

When I showed the transcripts to a Japanese informant who is also a graduate student at Georgetown University, he commented that even though the Japanese speakers' utterances sounded as if they were avoiding answering questions directly, it did not strike him as strange or extraordinarily different from what he normally expects from Japanese speakers. He also mentioned that he himself might use the same strategy if he had to make a negative comment. When the Japanese strategy is compared with the American strategy, he said that Americans stated their opinions more directly and clearly, and therefore their utterances were easier to follow.

The Japanese informant's impression was about the same as my reaction to the exchange as a participant observer. The flow of the conversation of the Japanese participants seemed very natural to me. At the time of the conversation, I did not think that the way the Japanese speakers stated their opinions was exceptional or strange. Further, when I asked one of the American informants what the point was in the Japanese speakers' utterances, she said that she had to read between the lines. She was not sure whether what she thought was what the speakers meant. Therefore, she commented "this is how I interpret what the point is. Maybe I'm making this up."

In a writer-responsibility language such as English, it is primarily the author's role to make the point clear, not the reader's. Naotsuka and Sakamoto (1981: 89) claim that Americans presumably think "only things which are clearly communicated in words exist, and only such verbalized communication is trustworthy." In such a culture, speakers are generally expected to state their opinions directly and clearly so that listeners do not have to do the extra work of interpretation and sense-making.

On the other hand, from the *enryo-sasshi* "modesty-anticipation" communicative point of view, listeners are expected to anticipate and interpret the point for speakers who do not state their opinions directly. The listeners' active participation in sense-making is encouraged culturally. A person who is "good at mind-reading and perceiving intuitively another person's thought and feelings is highly appreciated for having what is called '*sasshi* competence' in Japan" (Kobayashi 1980, cited by Ishii 1984: 55).

One of the American informants further suggested that when people talk about Chinese food or Japanese food, it is easier to think of certain dishes. On the other hand, when people talk about American food, it is not so clear what American food really is. As an American informant puts it:

> [American food] doesn't seem to have a clear genre of food? You know, hamburgers and chicken, yeah, but then you start getting all these mixtures and so ... [Kenji] does not have a clear picture again of what constitutes American food maybe? So, he's talking about the whole aspect of American food in general, whether it's cheap or expensive, and you know, whether it's good or bad in general.

Her comment suggests that the Japanese speakers in the present conversations may have been facing a different task of answering the question. That is, when they were asked "what do you think about American food?", the first task for the Japanese speakers is to decide what constitutes American food, or what types of food are thought to be American food, and then to answer the question. The nature of the questions and the complex relationship of face threat involved in the situation need to be taken into consideration in conducting comparative studies.

In face-to-face interaction, however, participants may not be aware of such details of the problem. What should be explained as different tasks of communication can be interpreted as intentional avoidance of answering questions. Further, when mismatches of communicative strategies are repeated over time, lack of familiarity with different communicative systems leads to misconceptions not only about individuals but also about ethnic groups (for example, the Japanese being viewed as too obscure, "beating around the bush," and therefore untrustworthy and insincere). Regarding this point, Young (1982: 84) claims:

> Unfortunately, in cross-cultural interactions, what are generally explained as problems in grammaticality at the sentence level often become interpreted as personality on the level of discourse. It is no exaggeration to say that continuous misperception, misinterpretation and misunderstanding in face to face linguistic encounters can develop into stereotypes that are reinforced over time.

Gumperz et al. (1984: 6) also warn of the danger of making judgments based on just one system of communication; participants who interpret a sequence in terms of one system may fail to see a passage as cohesive and quite normal when the other system is operating.

Conclusion. This study examined the Japanese way of stating opinions, which may be characterized as "listener-dependent" strategies. Thesis statements of Japanese speakers do not appear at the initial position of utterances. The background information is presented first to build up shared information between a speaker and a hearer. Japanese speakers depend on their listeners' ability to make sense out of an inductive approach to conversation building, use of examples, discourse markers, sentence-final particles, and paralinguistic cues. Moreover, such communicative competences as *enryo-sasshi* seem to be at work as cultural norms of communication for Japanese.

Americans in my data, on the other hand, tend to state their opinions first, and then give reasons or evidence in support of their thesis. Americans are more direct in specifying what they like or what they do not like and for what reasons.

For Americans, then, Japanese ways of communication seem very obscure, and it is difficult to understand what the point is. Judgment based on just one system of communication may cause misunderstanding and may also contribute to the development of negative stereotypes. One should not judge other ways of communication simply because one is not familiar with the other systems. The Japanese way of communication functions well among Japanese just as the American way of communication functions well among those Americans who employ the same norms of communication.

What should be noted, however, is that not all Japanese observe the same strategies examined here all the time. There are personal differences; some Japanese may prefer more direct ways of communication. In addition, the same participants may state their likes and dislikes more directly in different settings or on different topics. In the same way, Tyler and Davies (1990) report that an American teacher used an inductive approach, rather than a deductive one, to talk with American students about cheating during examinations.

The present study also indicates that it is essential to provide opportunities for second-language learners to discuss the possible causes of misinterpretation in communicative situations. For example, the position of thesis statements in English discourse and in the students' native language should be pointed out. Direct and indirect ways of expressing one's opinion should also be described, as well as their possible effects on listeners' interpretations. Prosodic conventions and use of examples also need to be examined to bring out the full effect of communicative intentions.

Even though I obtained much more data that indicate tendencies among Japanese speakers similar to the ones examined here, further studies are necessary for more precise understanding of the phenomena. For example, conversations with a wider variety of topics and with differing levels of face threat should be examined. Gender differences, geographical differences, and subcultural differences within the United States and Japan are also issues of great interest. Studies of arguments in colloquial Japanese would be important as well, in order to understand how people disagree with each other and how they make their points in arguments. Comparative studies with American participants need to be conducted with special care in controlling such factors as gender, educational background, interpersonal relationships, settings, and topics, since all of these may significantly influence communicative behaviors of speakers. Cross-cultural communication is a complex and dynamic interaction of various factors.

REFERENCES

Brown, Penelope, and Stephen Levinson. 1978 (revised edition 1987). *Politeness: Some universals in language usage*. Cambridge: Cambridge University Press.

Chao, Yuen Ren. 1968. *A grammar of modern spoken Chinese*. Berkeley and Los Angeles: University of California Press.

Cook, Haruko Minegishi. 1990. "The sentence-final particle *ne* as tool for cooperation in Japanese conversation." In Hajime Hoji (ed.), *Japanese/Korean linguistics*. Stanford: Stanford Linguistics Association.

Duranti, Alessandro. 1986. "The audience as co-author: An introduction." *Text* 6(3): 239–47.

Erickson, Frederick, and Jeffrey Shults. 1982. *The counselor as gatekeeper: Social interaction in interviews*. New York: Academic Press.

Goodwin, Charles. 1986. "Audience diversity, participation, and interpretation." *Text* 6(3): 283–316.

Gumperz, John. 1982. *Discourse strategies*. Cambridge: Cambridge University Press.

Gumperz, John. 1992. "Contextualization and understanding." In Alessandro Duranti and Charles Goodwin (eds.), *Rethinking context*. New York: Cambridge University Press.

Gumperz, John, Hannah Kaltman, and Mary O'Connor. 1984. "Cohesion in spoken and written discourse: Ethnic style and the transition to literacy." In Deborah Tannen (ed.), *Coherence in spoken and written discourse*. Norwood, N.J.: Ablex.

Hall, Edward. 1976. *Beyond culture*. New York: Doubleday.

Hall, Edward. 1983. *The dance of life*. New York: Doubleday.

Hayashi, Reiko. 1988. "Simultaneous talk—from the perspective of floor management of English and Japanese speakers." *World Englishes* 7(3): 269–288.

Hinds, John. 1982. "Japanese conversational structures." *Lingua* 57: 301–326.

Hinds, John. 1987. "Reader versus writer responsibility: A new typology." In Ulla Connor and Robert Kaplan (eds.), *Writing across languages*. Reading, Mass.: Addison-Wesley. 141–152.

Inagaki, Y. 1988. "Madarukoshisa-no shuhen [Around the Japanese sluggishness]." In Tatsuo Iguchi (ed.), *Nihongo Koza* 5. Tokyo: Taishukan Shoten.

Ishii, Satoshi. 1984. "Enryo-sasshi communication: A key to understanding Japanese interpersonal relations." *Cross Currents* XI(1, Spring). 49–58.

Kobayashi, Kaoru. 1980. "Shokuba no ningen kankei [Human relations in organizations]." In Hiroshi Minami (ed.), *Handbook of Japanese human relations*. Tokyo: Kodansha.

Kunihiro, Tetsuya. 1977. "Nihonjin-no gengo kodo-to hi-gengo kodo [Japanese verbal behavior and nonverbal behavior]." In Susumu Ohno and Takeshi Shibata (eds.), *Koza Nihongo* 2. Tokyo: Iwanami Shoten.

Labov, William. 1972. *Language in the inner city: Studies in the black English vernacular.* Philadelphia: University of Pennsylvania Press.

Li, Charles, and Sandra Thompson. 1976. "Subject and topic: A new typology of language." In Charles Li (ed.), *Subject and topic.* New York: Academic Press.

LoCastro, Virginia. 1987. "Aizuchi: A Japanese conversational routine." In Larry E. Smith (ed.), *Discourse across cultures.* Englewood Cliffs, N.J.: Prentice-Hall.

Matsumoto, Michihiro. 1988. "The unspoken way." *Haragei: Silence in Japanese business and society.* Tokyo: Kodansha International Ltd.

Maynard, Senko Kumiya. 1989. *Japanese conversation: Self-contextualization through structure and interactional management.* Norwood, N.J.: Ablex.

Mizutani, Nobuko. 1982. "The listener's response in Japanese conversation." In *Sociolinguistic Newsletter* 13(1): 33-38.

Nakane, Chie. 1970. *Japanese Society.* London: Weidenfield and Nicholson.

Naotsuka, Reiko, and Nancy Sakamoto. 1981. *Mutual understanding of different cultures.* Tokyo: Taishukan Shoten.

Okazaki, Shoko. 1987. "An ethnographic study of English-Japanese bilingual conversation." Unpublished MA thesis. California State University, Northridge.

Okazaki, Shoko. 1990. "Participants' roles and floor management in Japanese-English bilingual conversation." Unpublished paper. Georgetown University.

Schegloff, Emmanuel, and Harvey Sacks. 1973. "Opening up closings." *Semiotica* 7(4): 289- 327.

Schiffrin, Deborah. 1985. "Everyday argument: The organization of diversity in talk." In Teun A. Van Dijk (ed.), *Handbook of discourse analysis* (Volume 3). Discourse and Dialogue. London: Academic Press.

Schiffrin, Deborah. 1987. *Discourse markers.* Cambridge: Cambridge University Press.

Tannen, Deborah. 1983. "When is an overlap not an interruption?: One component of conversational style." In Robert J. Di Pietro, William Frawley, and Alfred Wedel (eds.), *The first Delaware symposium on language studies.* Newark, Del.: University of Delaware Press.

Tannen, Deborah. 1984. *Conversational style: Analyzing talk among friends.* Norwood, N.J.: Ablex.

Tannen, Deborah. 1985. "Relative focus on involvement in oral and written discourse." In David Olson, Nancy Torrance, and Angela Hildyard (eds.), *Literacy, language, and learning: The nature and consequences of reading and writing.* Cambridge: Cambridge University Press.

Tyler, Andrea, and Catherine Davies. 1990. "Cross-linguistic communication missteps." *Text* 10(4): 385-411.

Uyeno, Tazuko. 1971. "A study of Japanese modality: A performative analysis of sentence particles. Ph.D. dissertation." University of Michigan.

Yamada, Haru. 1989. "American and Japanese topic management strategies in business conversations." Ph.D. dissertation. Georgetown University.

Young, Linda Wai Ling. 1982. "Inscrutability revisited." In John Gumperz (ed.), *Language and social identity.* Cambridge: Cambridge University Press.

Wieland, Molly. 1991. "Turn-taking structure as a source of misunderstanding in French-American cross-cultural conversation." In Lawrence Bouton and Yamuna Kachru (eds.), *Pragmatics and language learning.* Monograph Series. Vol. 2. Champaign-Urbana: University of Illinois.

White, Sheida. 1989. "Backchannels across cultures: A study of American and Japanese." *Language in Society* 18(1): 59-76.

Fine-tuning of feedback by competent speakers to language learners

Catherine Doughty
Georgetown University

Abstract. The facilitative potential of feedback by competent speakers to language learners is of vital interest in studies of child language acquisition, second-language acquisition (SLA), and especially classroom second-language acquisition. Interactionist researchers firmly believe that feedback contributes in some important way to learners' developing language. However, although this assumption is intuitively appealing, it has proven difficult to establish empirically that fine-tuning of feedback occurs in any of the above child or adult, first- or second-language acquisition settings, let alone whether finely tuning facilitates language acquisition. It is both difficult to show what portion of a learner's utterance a competent speaker responds to and difficult to know for certain that the language learner correctly interprets the feedback as being directed toward a particular feature of an ill-formed utterance. Recently, however, child language-acquisition researchers have uncovered a number of indicators that adults do finely tune their feedback in child-directed discourse and that children are able to perceive this fine-tuning. The purpose of the study reported was to investigate whether or not second-language teachers similarly finely tune their feedback to learners and, if so, whether learners respond to fine-tuning in ways similar to those discovered in child–adult interaction. Overall, the findings suggest that teachers, as competent speakers of the L2, finely tune their feedback to second-language learners just as parents do when interacting with child language learners. Furthermore, it appears that classroom language learners, like children, notice the finely tuned feedback.

Introduction. For many years now, second-language acquisition researchers have been investigating potential benefits of interaction in the target language. Many of us are convinced both as SLA researchers and as language teachers that interaction makes a vital contribution to second-language acquisition. It is certainly worth noting that this entire meeting of language professionals—GURT '93—is dedicated to the memory of a linguist and language teacher who developed valuable and clever contributions to second-language pedagogy on the basis of this very belief: that interaction contributes to SLA. The fundamental philosophy behind Robert Di Pietro's Strategic Interaction approach to second-language pedagogy is, "that it is as users of the new language that people become learners of it" (Di Pietro 1987: viii).

The research reported here fits squarely in the interactionist view of second-language acquisition. This report is of a preliminary analysis of data from a longitudinal study of the acquisition of French in a foreign-language classroom from two perspectives: that of the interlanguage development of learners over time and that of the nature of classroom interactional sequences that may be facilitating SLA. This report focuses on the latter. My purpose is to present some findings from the analysis of teacher–learner interaction, particularly with respect to teacher feedback to learner utterances. The general belief underlying this work is that teacher feedback on the grammaticality of learner utterances as it occurs during communication is beneficial to learners. However, the questions that I will examine here are much more specific than this. In particular, I will discuss whether teachers, in fact, provide finely tuned feedback to learners, and if they do, what the nature of such feedback is. And, I will discuss the issue of whether language learners notice the teacher feedback and its relevance to their own utterances. Di Pietro might have called this Strategic Interaction, and more recently, language-acquisition researchers have labelled such interaction fine-tuning of feedback to language learners.

Background. The questions of this investigation have been motivated by some fascinating recent work in child language-acquisition research. It is naturally very interesting to draw parallels between child-language studies and instructed interlanguage development because both types of language acquisition involve the interaction of language learners with competent speakers of the target language. Among the variety of special features of child–adult interaction that have been identified and studied, feedback from adults in reaction to child utterances has drawn considerable attention in theory and research. For the moment, feedback may be generally defined as comments by adults (or teachers) pertaining to child (or learner) utterances, though it will become apparent shortly that the operational construct of feedback is indeed much more complex.

The role of feedback in language acquisition is not yet fully understood. Although interactionist researchers hold that feedback is beneficial, it is still relatively controversial whether feedback significantly affects language acquisition. In fact, for a long time, the opposite belief was held by child language-acquisition researchers: It was widely accepted, for example, that adults do not provide linguistic evaluations of their children's utterances. Rather, it was claimed that adults more often react to the truth value of their children's utterances rather than to the well-formedness of the utterances. These claims were based primarily on the findings of Brown and Hanlon (1970), who, in analyzing expressions of parental approval or disapproval of children's utterances, determined that such approval does not depend upon whether or not the child utterances are grammatical. Brown and Hanlon's results were then generalized to a larger claim: In response to children's utterances, adults do not provide corrective, or what is sometimes called negative, feedback regarding what is not possible in the language. It was then assumed that correction or negative feedback is not crucial in child language acquisition.

Recently, however, these claims and this assumption about the role of negative feedback in child language acquisition have been seriously and, I believe, successfully, challenged by several teams of child-language researchers. The challenge has hinged upon criticism of Brown and Hanlon's definition of feedback, which, as noted above, was operationalized as explicit expressions of parental disapproval uttered in response to ill-formed child utterances. For example, Brown and Hanlon searched through transcripts of parent–child interaction looking for instances of metalinguistic comments such as *That's not the correct way to say that* or *No, that's wrong*. Not surprisingly, Brown and Hanlon discovered that such negative feedback rarely occurs.

Brown and Hanlon have been challenged by Hirsch-Pasek, Treiman, and Schneiderman (1984), Bohannon and Stanowicz (1988), and others, who have argued that such *explicit* expressions of parental disapproval or approval are not the right sort of feedback to be looking for in child–adult interaction. Instead, they hypothesize that "parents may show sensitivity to the grammaticality of children's utterances in less explicit ways" (Hirsch-Pasek, Treiman, and Schneiderman, 1984: 81). The less-explicit, alternative indications of adult sensitivity to child-utterance grammaticality that have been suggested by these researchers are responses such as adult recasts of child utterances, adult repetitions of child utterances, and requests by adults for clarification of child utterances.

The difficulty with proposing that feedback of this nature helps children to acquire language is that, because recasting, repetition, and clarification of child utterances are implicit forms of feedback, researchers must find evidence that the child knows that adults are reacting to problems inherent in his or her utterances. Snow (1987) has argued that because children have communicative intent when they produce utterances and because adult feedback interrupts the child's attempt to communicate meaning, the child does indeed notice that something is wrong with how he or she has formulated the intended message.

Snow's claim rests, of course, on whether or not it can be shown empirically that adults react differentially to children's ill-formed versus well-formed utterances. Some recent investigations of child–adult interaction have shown precisely this. There appear to be distributional differences in adult responses to child utterances depending upon whether the child's utterances are well-formed or not. First, mothers tend to interrupt child utterances to seek clarification more frequently after ill-formed utterances than after error-free utterances (Demetras, Post, and Snow 1986). Second, all adults (not just mothers or parents) tend to request clarification of well-formed child utterances less often than they request clarification of child utterances containing one error (c. 7% vs. 38%) (Bohannon and Stanowitz 1988). Moreover, adult exact repetitions almost always (c. 90% of the time) follow errorless child utterances rather than ill-formed utterances, and adult recasts and expansions of child utterances are most often (c. 70% of the time) preceded by ill-formed utterances (Demetras, Post, and Snow 1986). Finally, in their recasts of child utterances, adults often provide "specific contrastive evidence" by giving exemplars of the correct syntactic form or pronunciation immediately after the child error has been uttered. All adults provide such exemplars significantly more often after a one-error child utterance than after a child utterance with multiple errors (c. 29% vs. 18%), and parents provide exemplars significantly more often than do other adults (c. 30% vs.16%) (Bohannon and Stanowitz 1988).

We can summarize these findings by noting that adult, and particularly parental, responses to child utterances provide reliable information to the child about grammatical distinctions in the language they are learning. Furthermore, adults not only provide differential responses depending upon whether the child utterance is well-formed or not, but they also provide language exemplars when the child makes an error. Of course, it should be noted that parents do not appear to spend all of their time teaching their children how to talk in the ways outlined above. In fact, more than 60% of children's language errors are not commented upon by their parents. Nevertheless, when adults *do* provide feedback on child utterances, they provide fairly reliable signals regarding whether the utterance was or was not well-formed, and they concentrate their feedback on utterances that contain only one error.

It is also important to demonstrate whether children respond differentially to their parents' efforts to signal information about their well-formed and ill-formed utterances. Such differential responses would suggest that, at some level, finely tuned parental feedback is noticed by child interlocutors. Two recent studies have shown that children may be sensitive to this finely tuned feedback. Researchers in these studies have discovered that children are more likely to repeat a morpheme when that morpheme is contained in a previous adult recast than when the same morpheme occurs elsewhere in adult utterances (Farrar 1987, reported in Bohannon and Stanowicz 1988). Children also are more likely to imitate adult recasts and expansions than they are likely to imitate adult exact repetitions (c. 26% vs. 4%) (Bohannon and Symons 1988, reported in Bohannon and Stanowicz 1988).

For interactionists, these findings constitute promising evidence that interaction plays an important role in child language acquisition. Thus, the purpose of the present investigation was to discover whether, as competent speakers, teachers provide reliable feedback to language learners regarding the grammaticality of their L2 utterances and, if so, whether learners engaged in working out the rules and conventions of the second language are able to notice the potentially useful information contained in the teacher feedback.

Research Questions and Hypotheses. The specific research questions of this study, all of which were motivated by the above findings in child language-acquisition studies, are:

1. Do teachers finely tune their feedback to second-language learners and, if so, do learners respond to the fine-tuning?
2. When a teacher asks for clarification, does this indicate a well-formed learner utterance or an ill-formed learner utterance? If ill-formed, are there one or many errors?
3. When a teacher repeats, does this indicate a well-formed learner utterance or an ill-formed learner utterance? If ill-formed, are there one or many errors?
4. When a teacher recasts or expands, does this indicate a preceding ill-formed or well-formed learner utterance? If ill-formed, are there one or many errors?
5. When the learner repeats the teacher's utterance, was the teacher's utterance a recast or a repetition?

The overall prediction was that the teacher and the learners would interact in the second language in ways that are very similar to child–adult interaction. Specifically, it was predicted that:

H1: Teachers are more likely to seek clarification of learner utterances with one error than of utterances with many (finely tuned feedback).

H2: Teacher exact repetitions will tend to act as indicators of well-formedness.

H3: Teacher recasts and expansions will function as indicators of problems. These will occur most often after utterances with only one error.

H4: Learners will tend to repeat recasts of their own ill-formed utterances, but not exact repetitions of well-formed utterances.

Subjects. Subjects for this study were the teacher and students in a first-year course in French as a foreign language at a major university in Sydney, Australia. The teacher is a native speaker of Parisian French. This class was chosen on the basis of recommendations by colleagues that the teacher was the most interactionally oriented of the French teachers at the university and that she would likely be willing to participate with her class in research. In fact, she has had quite an impact on the department, and the teaching of French as a foreign language differs substantially from the teaching of other foreign languages in its orientation toward interaction in the classroom. She is herself an applied linguist with a particular interest in gesture and language acquisition. The learners were all members of a class called French 1B—a course only open to those who have not studied French before entering university. Initial class sessions verified that the majority of students in this class were zero beginners in the acquisition of French as a foreign language. There were two false beginners as well.

The French 1B program is mainly organized around interactional activities, but it also teaches about French language structures, functions, and situationally appropriate language use. These two components of the course were separate, with three hours per week devoted to classroom interaction and one hour per week devoted to a lecture on the French language. The noninteractional lecture class was attended by all the French 1B students together, and then they were divided up into small tutorials of fewer than one dozen students for the three hours of target-language interaction. Students also attended a further lab session one hour per week in which they wrote simple compositions, in French, on the computer. The sessions devoted to target language interaction were the focus of the present study.

Procedures. The classroom interactional data was video-recorded. Data were transcribed by two research assistants and the researcher. The transcription of the classroom interaction was accomplished in the first instance using the audio tape, as this was much faster than working from the videotape. Subsequently, the audio transcriptions were checked against the videotapes. This was necessary as the number of speakers involved, even in a small class, makes speaker identification almost impossible from audiotape alone. At that time, corrections were made and contextual notes were made whenever it was felt that these would aid in the interpretation of the interaction. This checking was done by a third research assistant who did not participate in the transcription of the audiotapes.

For the pilot study reported here, three two-hour interaction classes for a total of six hours of classroom interaction were analyzed in order to test the hypotheses of this study. The first class was from the beginning of the year, the second class from about the middle of the year, and the third class from near the end of the year. The transcripts were imported into COALA (Computer Aided Linguistic Analysis) for analysis (Pienemann, Jansen, and Thornton 1992). COALA is a relational data base with a coding interface. It is possible to create user-defined coding categories with COALA, and thus the linguist is not restricted to a structural analysis. The features of teacher–learner interaction that were coded, along with their operational definitions, are given in Tables 1 through 3.

Table 1. Learner utterances

Code	Gloss	Definition
lerr0	no errors	the well-formed learner utterances
lerr1	one error	learner utterances with only one error
lerr+	many errors	learner utterances with more than one error
brief	too brief	learner utterances that were inappropriately brief: example subject without verb
leng	English	learner utterances in English (subjects' L1)
untrans	untranscribable	utterances that were garbled or unclear

Table 2. Teacher feedback

Code	Gloss	Definition
tclar	teacher clarification request	a question or a statement with rising intonation that asks for further clarification of the learner utterance
trep	teacher repetition	exact repetition of the learner utterance
trec	teacher recast	response to an utterance that incorporates content words of the utterance, but also changes the utterance in some way (e.g., phonological, syntactic, lexical) but without adding any information
texp	teacher expansion	response to a learner utterance that provides additional information not contained in the learner utterance
ttrans	teacher translation	immediate translation of learner utterance into French
teng	teacher English	teacher responded in English
untrans	untranscribable	utterances that were garbled or unclear

Clearly some of the categories in Tables 1 and 2 differ from those in earlier child-adult discourse studies. These categories were necessary in order to account for all of the utterances in the teacher–learner interaction. As all subjects shared English as a first or second language, sometimes utterances would be produced partly or completely in English. For example, a learner would produce an utterance in English, and then the teacher would immediately translate the utterance into French. Alternatively, the teacher could simply respond to the English utterance in French, which she often did. Thus we found it necessary to invent the categories "leng," "teng," and "ttrans." Another new category was "brief." Whereas it is quite normal for children to speak in very short utterances, this is not the case for adults. When the learner utterance was too brief, for example, the teacher might ask for clarification or recast the learner utterance into a longer context.

The overall coding strategy involved labeling all teacher and learner utterances, with the exception of one-word *oui-* and *non-*type utterances. Teacher feedback could be readily identified and coded (see Table 2), and then the preceding learner utterance that triggered the feedback could be coded (see Table 1). Finally, if a learner utterance followed the teacher feedback, this too could be coded (see Table 3). Utterances that were not involved in any of the interactional sequences just outlined were coded individually, for example as "lerr0," which might not have gotten any response from the teacher, since it was already well-formed.

Table 3. Learner response to teacher feedback

Code	Gloss	Definition
lrep+	successful learner repetition	learner successfully repeated the teacher feedback—for example, repetition of a recast
lrep-	unsuccessful learner repetition	repetition of the teacher feedback unsuccessfully attempted by learner

Where learner errors were coded, I attempted to assign a label to the interactional sequence that would provide some indication of the nature of the error. COALA allows the coding of tags that can be attached to the entire segment of the discourse that has been analyzed, for example: lerr1 + trec + lrep+ could have the tag "phonological" attached, indicating that the learner's original utterance contained one error in pronunciation. The tags indicated nontargetlike gender, phonology, morphology, lexis, syntax, and pragmatics.

Results and Discussion. The learner utterances and teacher feedback were analyzed across the three classes at once; thus the corpus for this analysis was

Table 4. Total corpus of learner utterances

Learner Utterances	Raw n	%
(a) that received teacher feedback	496	43
(b) that did not receive teacher feedback	582	51
(c) that were responses to teacher feedback	73	6
TOTAL	1,151	100

composed of six hours of classroom interaction. During these six hours, there was a total of 1,151 learner utterances that either were available for teacher feedback or that occurred in response to teacher feedback. This distribution can be seen in Table 4. The teacher provided some type of feedback for 43 percent of learner utterances, and she did not react to 51 percent of learner utterances. Six percent of the learner utterances were in reaction to teacher feedback. It is interesting and perhaps not surprising to note that the teacher in this study provided feedback to learner utterances somewhat more often than adults provide feedback to child utterances (recall that more than 60 percent of child utterances are not reacted to by adults).

Once teacher–learner interaction had been encoded into COALA's relational database, a number of search formulae were applied to the data set in order, informally, to test the hypotheses of this investigation. These formulae enabled systematic searching through the coded transcripts such that teacher–learner utterances could be examined in many combinations. Table 5 is arranged such that the learner utterance types are listed in the first vertical column on the left. Each of the utterances was analyzed with respect to the immediately following teacher feedback. For example, the search formulae "lerr0 followed by tclar" or "lerr0 followed by trep" would reveal well-formed learner utterances followed by teacher clarification requests and teacher repetitions, respectively.

Research questions (RQs) 2 through 4 can be considered with reference to Table 5. In response to RQ2—When a teacher asks for clarification does this indicate a well-formed learner utterance or an ill-formed learner utterance (and, if ill-formed, are there one or many errors)?—it was predicted that teachers are more likely to seek clarification of learner utterances with one error than of utterances with many or no errors. This seems clearly to have been the case: Of the 68 errorful learner utterances, 60 one-error utterances were followed by teacher clarification, whereas only 8 multi-error utterances triggered clarification from the teacher. Furthermore, the teacher never asked for clarification of completely well-formed utterances, though she did sometimes (16 in all) ask for clarification of brief utterances.

RQ3 asked whether, when a teacher repeats, this indicates a well-formed

Table 5. Teacher Feedback to Second-language Learner Utterances.

	tclar	trep	trec	texp	no feedback
lerr0	0	161	24	0	211
lerr1	60	8	174	12	52
lerr+	8	0	9	0	30
untrns	8	0	3	0	11
leng	0	0	7	5	123
brief	16	4	67	0	155
TOTAL	92	173	284	17	582

Read table as follows: 0 tclars follow lerr0; 161 treps follow lerr0; i.e., teachers asked for clarification of well-formed learner utterances 0 times; teachers repeated well-formed learner utterances 161 times.

learner utterance or an ill-formed learner utterance (and, if ill-formed, are there one or many errors)? It was predicted that teacher exact repetitions tend to act as indicators of well-formedness. Again, the findings are strongly in support of the hypothesis. The vast majority (161) of the teacher repetitions followed well-formed utterances. The teacher did not often repeat ill-formed utterances (12 times), but when she did, it was always in response to an utterance with only one error or that was too brief (0 responses to lerr+).

Table 6. Search formulae

recasts	**expansions**
l (err1) precedes trec = 174	l (err1) precedes texp = 12
l (err+) precedes trec = 9	l (err+) precedes texp = 0
l (err0) precedes trec = 24	l (err0) precedes texp = 0

Similarly, RQ4 asked whether, when a teacher recasts or expands, this indicates a preceding ill-formed or well-formed learner utterance (and if ill-formed, are there one or many errors)? And similarly, it was predicted that teacher recasts and expansions tend to function as indicators of problems and that these tend to occur most often after utterances with only one error. This hypothesis is supported by the findings of both recasts and expansions, although recasts are much more frequent in the data than are expansions (recall that the difference between the two is that expansions provide more information whereas recasts contain the same information in a different linguistic formulation). The search formulae in Table 6 reveal these findings, also shown in Table 5.

Finally, RQ5 asked, when the learner repeats the teacher's utterance, was the teacher's utterance a recast or a repetition? The prediction was that learners will tend to repeat recasts of own ill-formed utterances, but not exact repetitions of well-formed utterances.

Table 7 displays the learner utterances that were reactions to teacher feedback. The "no feedback" column is provided for comparison purposes to give an idea of how often learners responded to teacher feedback by repeating the teacher's utterance. Clearly, this was not very often in most categories; however, when learners did repeat the teacher's feedback, it was far more often after a teacher recast (61 times) than after any other kind of feedback. The data were also searched using a formula that could directly address the question of whether learners are likely to repeat the recasts of their ill-formed utterances.

Table 7. Learner Reactions to Teacher Feedback

	lrep+	lrep-	no response to feedback
tclar	5	1	87
trep	4	0	169
trec	61	1	222
texp	0	0	17
TOTAL	70	2	495

Read table as follows: 5 tclars are followed by successful lreps; 61 trecs are followed by unsuccessful lreps = i.e., learners successfully repeated teacher clarification requests 5 times; learners successfully repeated teacher recasts 61 times.

These search formulae, shown below, indicate specifically that learners are more likely to repeat recasts of their own utterances that had only contained one error:

lerr1 precedes trec AND trec precedes lrep	=	72
lerr0 precedes trec AND trec precedes lrep	=	4
lerr+ precedes trec AND trec precedes lrep	=	9

However, these findings must remain tentative, as visual inspection of the data suggested that learners repeat after feedback other than recasts, and neither the search formulae nor the coding categories used in this analysis could uncover these triggers for repetition. Thus, it will be important in future analyses to list out all of the learner repetitions to see what precedes them.

The discovery that the coding for repetition was not refined enough was not the only difficulty in this pilot analysis. Whereas the interactional nature of learner and teacher utterances was generally readily apparent, the coding of the kind of problem underlying nontargetlike learner utterances was much more difficult. Though attempts were made to code for these interlanguage problems, using the sentence tags feature of COALA, it was often difficult to decide exactly what feature of the utterance led to its nontargetlike nature. Demetras et al. (1986) also reported difficulty in attributing error types, even when using a six-judge panel. The problem in both cases is that if the researcher is not sure of the communicative intent of the utterance (which is often the case) and the teacher (or parent) does not respond to the utterance, then it is very difficult to know what the nature of the difficulty with the utterance is. Thus, the refinement of sentence-tag analysis is also a future aim of this ongoing investigation. It will also be important to note whether the teacher provides specific exemplars in her attempts to remedy interlanguage difficulty and whether learners are able to notice and incorporate the exemplars into their own productions.

Conclusion. In light of the findings presented, we can now return to the overall question of this pilot investigation: Do teachers finely tune their feedback to second-language learners, and, if so, do learners respond to the fine-tuning? These findings are the preliminary investigation of a larger corpus and await the confirmation of the further analysis of the entire data set as well as closer scrutiny using more-refined search formulae in the computational analysis. Nevertheless, it appears that this teacher, at least, finely tunes her feedback to learners in ways that are very similar to the feedback that adults provide to child language learners. In other words, the feedback to learners is predictable in the same way that feedback to children is predictable. Interestingly, the reliable, finely tuned feedback is somewhat more frequent in the classroom interaction than in child–adult discourse. It also appears that learners are sensitive to the regularity of the feedback; however, more investigation of the learner responses to feedback is clearly necessary. In sum, the findings of this study may be taken as preliminary evidence that fine-tuning of feedback does occur in the classroom setting, suggesting that, as competent speakers of the L2, teachers provide information to second-language learners about the well-formedness of their utterances. Learners respond to finely tuned feedback in ways that suggest the information the teacher attempts to convey is noticed.

REFERENCES

Bohannon, John, and Laura Stanowicz. 1988. *Developmental Psychology* 24(5): 684–9.

Bohannon, John, and V. Symons. 1988. "Conversational conditions of children's imitation." Paper presented at the biennial Conference on Human Development. Charleston, S.C. April.

Demetras, M.J., Kathryn Post, and Catherine Snow. 1987. "Feedback to first language learners: The role of repetitions and clarification questions." *Journal of Child Language* 13: 275-92.

Di Pietro, Robert J. 1987. *Strategic interaction*. Cambridge: Cambridge University Press.

Farrar, Jeffrey. 1987. "Immediate effects of discourse on grammatical morpheme acquisition." Paper presented at the biennial meeting of the Society for Research in Child Development.

Baltimore, Md., April.

Hirsh-Pasek, Kathryn, Rebecca Treiman, and Maita Schneiderman. 1984. "Brown and Hanlon revisited: Mothers' sensitivity to ungrammatical forms." *Journal of Child Language* 11: 81–8.

Pienemann, M., L. Jansen, and I. Thornton. 1992. "COALA—Computer-aided Linguistic Analysis" (beta test release). Sydney: Language Acquisition Research Centre.

Snow, Catherine. 1987. "Understanding social interaction in language acquisition: Sentences are not enough." In Marc H. Bornstein, and Jerome S. Bruner (eds.), *Interaction in Human Development*. Hillsdale, N.J.: Lawrence Erlbaum.

Using strategic interaction in the teaching of writing

Ruth M. Jackson
University of Delaware ELI

Greeting. In the words of the poet, "On the pulse of this new day," may I say simply, very simply, with hope, Good morning!

Dr. Alatis, Mrs. Di Pietro, family and friends of Dr. Robert J. Di Pietro, and distinguished colleagues: I deem it a very great privilege to be here today at this renowned university to honor the memory and work of Dr. Robert J. Di Pietro, an international scholar and a wonderful colleague. In the months since his passing, I have missed the wit and wisdom in our collaborations and the display of his compassion for his family, friends, and students—a deep caring that came as naturally to him as second-language acquisition seems to come to many five-year-olds. In the brief number of years that I knew Dr. Di Pietro, I came to have a great respect for him—not only for his scholarship but also because of his concern for ESL/EFL students and their opportunities to relax and to enjoy their language studies.

Now, on the promise of a relevant segué in just a short time, allow me to share a personal anecdote about Dr. Di Pietro with you. I first met Robert at a demonstration of Strategic Interaction (SI) that the director of the University of Delaware's ELI had arranged for our faculty. Robert called for some volunteers to be passengers on a bus and I joined in. He told us travelers to react naturally to whatever occurred; then he himself assumed the part of a man with a large bag and boarded the bus. As he started down the aisle, a large snake sprang from the bag. I thought it natural and appropriate to scream—and proceeded to do so. Apparently the act was quite convincing because Robert, who normally would have let the scenario continue to solution, rushed over, great concern furrowing his brow, to ask me if I were all right. Needless to say, the scenario generated a *GREAT* deal of language—on *everyone's* part! Quite a strategic interaction—as far as history is concerned. But there is an example of Robert's compassion for people.

This encounter led eventually to the writing of *American Voices* (1992), our integrated skills reader for highly advanced students. So I feel that I have substantial evidence to support the claim that a solid link can be forged between the use of Strategic Interaction and writing!

Underlying assumptions. On a more serious note, working with Dr. Di Pietro strengthened some of my key assumptions:

- that one of the best goals we as ESL/EFL teachers can have is to lower our students' affective filters to maximize the opportunities for language acquisition to occur;
- that one of the ways to lower our students' affective filters is to provide an atmosphere in which they can relax;
- that one of the ways to provide such a relaxed atmosphere is to create activities in which language learners can work with peers in problem-solving tasks;
- that the use of Di Pietro's approach, Strategic Interaction, and the scenario—the element that "lies at the heart" of the SI approach (1986: 41)—offers students such opportunities; and
- that the use of the scenario can provide opportunities to enhance the development of language learners' writing skills.

When Dr. Di Pietro and I collaborated in the writing of *American Voices*, we followed the principle of structuring all aspects of the book's exercises in such a way that students would be constantly involved and participating in significant interactions. We used SI in order to establish a comfortable student-directed atmosphere, one in which students could control the pace and progress of their language development and, by such mastery, could gain confidence in their language usage.

We titled our book *American Voices* to call our readers' attention to our belief that the writing process begins with *hearing one's own voice*. I mean these words literally *and* metaphorically: The voice heard can be inside or outside the writer's mind, i.e., on the written page. Moving thus from scenario to a clarification of one's values and/or a definition of one's self—to *seeing* the words one believes concretely trawled out on the manuscript page, the language learner becomes author—molding and shaping ideas, sculpting self, defining a personality *and* a personal philosophy.

Clarifying terms. We also experimented with the use of SI in the teaching of writing. Very shortly I will get to some specifics of how SI can be applied in the teaching of writing. Before doing so, however, I believe it necessary to briefly confirm the meaning of the phrase *Strategic Interaction* and the term *scenario*.

Let me explain why I feel it important to do so. My area of expertise lies in what works in the ESL/EFL classroom. In my experience in an intensive English program, where I have been involved in the training of EFL teachers and have given demonstrations for ESL teachers from other universities, I have observed some misconceptions of what Strategic Interaction is and of what a scenario is.

First, *strategic interaction*, as I understand Di Pietro's definition of the phrase in the book of the same name (1986: vii), means an approach to second-language instruction organized around scenarios that are scripts based on real-life happenings that call upon learners to invoke the target language *tactically*, i.e. purposefully and artfully, in dealing with other people. Thus language learners experience language usage in a natural way (see Krashen and Terrell 1983), and they use language to solve real problems. As a result, opportunities for language acquisition to occur are maximized.

Strategic Interaction, as an approach, is not a be-all or end-all unto itself: It is not just a fun time of acting in class once or twice a week. Rather, it can be used as a beginning to initiate language learners' *journey toward self-definition*-not only orally but also with the written word.

Second, a scenario, as Di Pietro defines it, is "a strategic interplay of roles functioning to fulfill personal agendas within a shared context" (1986: 41). Within the scope of this interplay, the scenario is rehearsed, performed, and debriefed. Real-life—and thus strategic—situations are set before the performers who must negotiate their way out of sometimes highly dramatic scenes, e.g., the snake in the bag on the bus.

Now as to what scenarios are not. As we wrote in our *Instructor's Manual to* American Voices (1992: 7), scenarios are not mechanistic role-plays with preprogrammed outcomes. On the contrary, scenarios are open-ended and may be resolved with any number of different endings. The performers do not have to reach any particular conclusion. Instead, they may resolve the situation in any way—save for physical violence—that they choose. Unlike a role play, in which characteristics and personal traits are proscribed for the performers, the directions of a scenario do not predetermine the outcome of the event. The scenario does not proscribe any position, philosophy, or personality trait; a role play, on the other hand, *does*. In a scenario, the student is free within such parameters as age, gender, and occupation—and even age and gender are left open as much as possible in the scenarios of *American Voices*—to develop whatever pathway to a solution he or she chooses.

SI applied to writings. Now to the specifics. Using Strategic Interaction in the teaching of writing can enhance opportunities for students' language acquisition by supporting them in the building of frameworks (schemata) that help them order their ideas and call up vocabulary they can then use in their written assignments. Indeed, having students experience the target vocabulary and the target grammatical structures first orally and then in writing is a procedure that seems to complement Krashen's advice (1982: 21): The instructor is encouraged to focus students' awareness on *meaning* first and move on to structure later.

It is in this moving on to structure—an action that occurs during the *debriefing* stage—that the bridge between SI and writing is most firmly established. The language self-generated in the scenario is "accepted" on the blackboard by the teacher and by the class—and corrected, if necessary—and so the creators of the discourse are validated. The structures thus generated are reinforced in students' minds and *re*-generated, and language acquisition is said to have occurred.

At the upper levels of ESL reading and writing, particularly in English for academic purposes, the use of SI and related activities can be used to familiarize students with the vocabulary of rhetoric. Outlines (schemata), transitions, coherence, parallelism—these are some of the many rhetorical elements that the use of SI can generate and that can then be tried out, practiced more formally in a written assignment, and polished in peer critiquing and revision work. Among the strategic interactive activities that allow students to build such frameworks (schemata) are—in addition to scenarios—reading out loud with a partner, working with a partner to guess the meaning of vocabulary words in context, interactive grammar and usage exercises, peer critiquing of essays, group-written essays, full-circle scenarios, and scenario writing in pairs or small groups.

A few words about Interactive Grammar Exercises: The Interactive Grammar Exercises, which we created for the advanced readers of *American Voices*, are designed to heighten students' awareness of the choices they make when they speak and write in the target language. Students work with their peers to discover the best answers. More than one answer to each problem may be possible, but students, by discussing all the possibilities, must choose the most appropriate ones and be prepared to defend their selections by explaining the rule or the idiomatic usage that prevails in that context.

Results. Di Pietro piloted the use of SI in the teaching of writing with young language learners, while I used it with ESL writers in ESL English for Academic Purposes Reading and Writing Classes Levels 5 and 6 (on the Princeton scale), first piloting the idea at the University of Delaware's English Language Institute in 1988. I had several good results.

First, the SI scenario got my students talking. Then—or hopefully, simultaneously!—it got them thinking. In the talking and thinking, the SI scenario helped them clarify their values. In the talking, thinking, and teamwork, students felt more comfortable and articulated their awareness of this fact.

In addition, I found that the SI scenario helped students develop fluency—both oral and written. And herein lies another of the major connections to writing. In asking students to recall what was said after the performance of the scenario—and often to write it down—the instructor can ask students to check the written accounts against the oral accounts for semantic and syntactic accuracy (or correctness). She or he can then heighten students' awareness of how English grammar works by asking them to observe and to comment on word choice, word order, pronoun reference, embedded clauses, or any specific grammar point that arises during a scenario.

Writing after the performance of a scenario gave my students the chance to employ newly acquired vocabulary and structures in personally meaningful ways, a stated objective of *American Voices* (Jackson and Di Pietro, *Instructor's Manual* 1992: 7). Modeling from the SI dialogue helped students write their own scenarios. In *American Voices*, we often suggest such an assignment as a follow-up activity in which students create their own product after their experience with the target language. We also propose that an essay be written on one issue arising from the scenario as an opportunity for students to respond in writing after reflection and considered word choice.

Actually, the teacher can build a grammatical point into the scenario she or he sets up, as for example using the subjunctive or conditionals in the description of the scenario's situation so that students are guided in their use as the performers negotiate solutions to, say, a potential problem in the neighborhood. And of course, using student-generated materials, as we can observe every day, engages L2 learners more actively in language acquisition—and builds their self-confidence and self-esteem.

I also observed that SI could be used effectively in teaching the development of coherency in writing. This vital attribute of good English prose can be highlighted during the process of heightening students' awareness of the discourse markers used in the scenario. As students recount the events in the performance of the scenario, they can be encouraged to use or to add discourse markers to advance the story line. Thus, discourse markers in spoken English become the transitions in writing that make the written discourse more fluent and more coherent.

Furthermore, by using SI in the teaching of writing, I was able to address the problem of correct pronoun use in number and gender. I found that this problem can first be addressed in oral retelling of a scenario, giving students practice in manipulating the target language—and having fun laughing at the silliness of a reference to a man when a woman is being discussed or vice versa—and then allowing them to be successful in writing them correctly. From confidence gained in the interaction of critiquing scenario performances, my students were able to move with surety into peer critiquing of their own papers. Thus, in a snowball effect, more opportunities were generated for students to learn from peers and from their own increased self-awareness—two of the more effective ways for a person to learn.

Using SI in teaching writing strategies helped my students develop confidence in yet another way: If they "got it right" orally, they knew that they could "get it right" on paper. Of course, it is important to stress that spoken American English is often much more informal than written English, but students get the point.

Both Di Pietro and I found that employing the strategy of using SI in the teaching of writing yielded good results. In oral and written feedback, which I requested at the end of each course, my advanced ESL students told me that they really enjoyed the stimulation that resulted from my use of this approach. I saw student improvement in fluency, coherency, organization, and development, evident in a true rise in the quality of the papers I received, with more than half the class moving from C-level work to B+ or A- work. My students enjoyed the interaction, and I enjoyed reading much clearer papers!

Wider applications of SI. In working on the manuscript that was to become *American Voices*, I saw a wider application of SI to the area of developing writing skills in the target language: Yoking SI and the Experiential Learning Cycle (Concrete Experience, Reflective Observation, Abstract Conceptualization, and Active Experimentation) (Kolb 1984: 40–43) also allows students to expand their vocabulary, to increase the rate of language acquisition, and to generate new language with apparently greater facility. Developing this approach will require further research and work—my homework for next year!

A very important consideration: It seems very logical to me that when students can use the target language to articulate, orally or in writing, their deepest thoughts and convictions—in other words, to define their philosophy and thereby themselves—they have taken major strides in mastering that language and, most likely, have deepened their affinity with that language so that it becomes vital to their personalities. Thus, as the target language becomes *second nature* to the language learner, we may venture to say that language acquisition has truly occurred.

Di Pietro's legacy. I have found Strategic Interaction to be of significant use in teaching my students to write in English more effectively. Using SI in the teaching of writing has enabled me to help my students get at some of their more pervasive problems in writing and to develop their confidence in using written English. I believe that Robert's legacy will continue to have an impact on language teaching and that the influence of his approach will only continue to grow in the coming years.

Dr. Alatis, Mrs. Di Pietro, Di Pietro family and friends, and distinguished colleagues: I believe that the significance of Robert's work and the value of his special approach is finally being fully recognized in this Round Table.

Thank you, Dr. Alatis, for inviting me to share in this very important day.

REFERENCES

Di Pietro, Robert J. 1986. *Strategic interaction: Learning languages through scenarios*. Cambridge:

Oxford Publishing.

Jackson, Ruth M., and Robert J. Di Pietro. 1992. *American Voices: An integrated skills reader.* Boston: Heinle & Heinle.

Jackson, Ruth M., and Robert J. Di Pietro. 1992. *Instructor's manual to American Voices.* Boston: Heinle & Heinle.

Krashen, Stephen. 1982. *Principles and practice in second language acquisition.* New York: Pergamon.

Krashen, Stephen, and Tracy Terrell. 1983. *The natural approach.* Oxford: Pergamon.

Kolb, David. 1984. *Experiential learning.* Englewood Cliffs, N.J.: Prentice-Hall.

Moskowitz, Gertrude. 1978. *Caring and sharing in the foreign language classroom: A sourcebook on humanistic techniques.* Cambridge, Mass.: Newbury House.

Roberts, Jon T. 1982. "Recent developments in ELT: Part II." *Language Teaching* 15: 174–94.

Simon, Sidney B., Leland W. Howe, and Howard Kirschenbaum. 1972, 1978. *Values clarification: A handbook of practical strategies for teachers and students.* New York: Dodd, Mead & Co.

Titone, Renzo. 1982. "Interaction in the language classroom: theories and research models." *Rassegna di Linguistica Applicata* 14: 1–16.

Learning strategies, tasks, and activities in oral communication instruction

Joan Morley
The University of Michigan

Introductory comments. The first part of this paper briefly reviews some benchmark developments in modern second-language theory and practice, ones that have led toward today's strong interest in learner styles, learning strategies, and strategic interaction, in the field of second-language acquisition (SLA) and second-language pedagogy. The second portion of the paper focuses on English for Academic Purposes (EAP) instruction and specifically on EAP oral communication curricula in courses offered by the English Language Institute at the University of Michigan. Developments in learning strategy training in selected oral communication courses are discussed, and a variety of activities, tasks, strategies, and techniques is outlined.

The "power" in the hands of the learner: Tracing the history. The theme for the 1993 Georgetown University Round Table, *Strategic Interaction and Language Acquisition: Theory, Practice, and Research,* is a timely topic and a provocative one. During the 1970s, information appearing in a growing "strategies" literature in second language (SL) learning and teaching focused primarily on *research* and *theory.* In the 1980s, attention to strategies expanded to include a variety of *practice* guidelines and suggestions to SL teachers for direct intervention in facilitating students' development of learning strategies. However, in order to place current strategies work in perspective, it is important to examine some of the fundamental changes in second-language theory and practice that took place from the late 1950s through the early 1970s.

Focus on the learner as active creator in the learning process. The notion of learners as "active creators in their learning process" is perhaps the cornerstone for the single most fundamental change in perspectives on the nature of language and language learning in modern times. And we cannot begin to examine developments in this area without turning at once to the contributions of Noam Chomsky, Roger Brown, and S. Pit Corder. The position that language learning is an active process, which burst upon the academic scene in the late

1950s and early 1960s, appeared near-heretical in the learning-theory climate of the times. It was, indeed, a radical departure from the popular notion of language acquisition—first *or* second—as a behavioral phenomenon, one that attributed language learning to habit formation, to stimulus, to response, to conditioning. Conceptual frameworks of behavioral psychologists such as Skinner (1957) were challenged, and views of earlier cognitive psychologists were re-examined—especially notions of learning as an active process, one enriched by interaction. Some of the writings of Piaget (1926) and Vygotsky (1934/1986) from the 1920s and 1930s were studied with renewed interest (Morley 1991a).

Chomsky (1959) rejected the structuralist approach to language analysis and the behaviorist theory of language learning. He argued that such a learning theory is not a plausible model of the way human beings learn language, since much of human language use is not imitative behavior but novel creation based upon underlying knowledge of abstract rules. This position, along with compelling evidence from the work of Roger Brown (1973) in first-language acquisition from a creative-process perspective (i.e., one in which children work out "rules" from the input available to them) and the work of those who followed began to move the field to a point where it no longer found tenable a concept of the learner role as primarily one of passive repeater of forms and patterns. S. Pit Corder (1967) not only turned our attention to the significance of learners' errors but early on bade us recognize students as prime movers in their own learning process. Corder (1976) observed that:

> Efficient language teaching must work with, rather than against, natural processes, facilitate and expedite, rather than impede learning. Teachers and teaching materials must adapt to the learner, rather than vice versa. (10)

An additional significant page in the history of the second/foreign language field emerged from the Second Congress of the International Association for Applied Linguistics held at Cambridge in 1969. At that conference—hailed by some as a turning point at the end of an "era" in language instruction—a major thrust of the nineteen papers presented was one that focused on insights that might be forthcoming from the field of psychology following a long period of domination by the field by linguistics. In their introduction to the volume of proceedings, Pimsleur and Quinn (1971) noted:

> We would suggest that the focus of our inquiries must move from the language to the learner, from the material to the person who is to absorb it. The more we understand about how students learn, the better we shall teach. (vii)

Prophetically, it seems, the four central themes that emerged from this 1969

AILA congress were ones that pointed toward a "focus on the learner" in a "new era" of second- and foreign-language education. The four themes were:

- a new focus on the individual learner as the central element in the complex process of second-language acquisition
- a desire to bring students into closer contact with "real" language as it is used in the real world by people communicating successfully with each other
- a focus on the so-called receptive skills of reading and listening, long regarded as "passive" skills, as much more complex processes
- an emerging notion that listening comprehension may be the key fundamental skill that has not been adequately understood.

All four "themes" have, indeed, figured prominently in the subsequent development of current directions in second-language theory and pedagogy (Morley 1992a).

Individual learning styles and strategies. With the movement to a view of the centrality of the learner's role as active creator in the language-learning process rather than as passive recipient came the corollary that both similarities and differences will be observed in the way individual learners go about the task of learning. Since the early 1970s, more and more research has focused on the learner and characteristics of the learning process.

Two kinds of learner characteristics are styles of learning and strategies of learning. Brown (1987) presented useful definitions and clear descriptions of these characteristics, which I shall summarize.

Styles of learning are made up of an individual's consistent and rather enduring preferences related to general characteristics of intellectual functioning and personality type. Involved are factors such as greater or lesser tolerance of ambiguity, more or less reflectiveness or impulsiveness, more or less field dependence or independence, orientation more or less toward logical or analytical information, orientation more or less toward imagery and holistic information, and so on.

Strategies of learning are measures taken by language learners to facilitate their own language learning. They are tactics employed by an individual in attacking particular problems in particular contexts. Strategies of learning are of two types: Learning strategies, per se, are learner measures relating to input; communication strategies are learner measures relating to output. Strategies of learning are especially important as they provide some possible ways to account for different degrees of success in language learning. They provide a strong focus for research because (a) successful language learners tend to use "good" strategies more often than unsuccessful language learners and (b) studies show that learning strategies can be improved or modified through training.

Two important articles on "good-learner" characteristics appeared in the mid-1970s, Rubin (1975) and Stern (1975), and since that time there has been an increasing number of studies on these topics. Rubin (1975: 45–48) reported seven characteristics exhibited by good language learners. Good language learners

- are willing to guess and are accurate guessers
- have a strong drive to communicate
- have a lack of inhibition (i.e., they are willing to appear foolish)
- pay attention to form
- seek opportunities for practice
- monitor their own and others' speech
- pay attention to meaning (i.e., they look beyond surface structure).

At the same time, Stern (1975) outlined ten characteristics, many similar to those identified by Rubin, adding that "good" learners also are likely to focus on affective aspects of their language learning and are concerned with "thinking" in the second language. These became part of the Toronto/OISE study on characteristics of good language learners (Naiman et al. 1978). In the 1980s, much new research appeared that refined the earlier research. Work by Faerch and Kasper (1983), Oxford (1985), Wenden (1985), Wenden and Rubin (1987), Chamot and O'Malley (1987), Skehan (1989), and O'Malley et al. (1985) extended and elaborated on theories of learner styles and strategies.

Moving along toward the 1990s, a survey of the "strategies" literature reveals an increasing body of research on learner characteristics, learner styles, and learner strategies. Of special interest to second-language pedagogy is a current focus on classroom-oriented research and practice, which has resulted in articles and teacher reference texts on instructional protocols for learner-strategy training. These works can guide teachers in setting strategies goals and carrying out instructional procedures in their classrooms; they include O'Malley and Chamot (1990), Oxford (1990), Wenden (1991), Scarcella and Oxford (1992), and Oxford (1993).

The importance of strategies training in ESL/EFL. Question: Why is learner-strategies training important today in second-language education? Clearly, as an extension of perspectives on the learner as "active creator" in his or her learning process and the "individuality" of each learner and his or her learning styles and strategies, *learner self-involvement* is a key concept. Personal involvement, self-direction and self-determination, and manipulation of learning states, stages, and environments through conscious as well as unconscious strategies have enormous potential for emerging learner empowerment and, ultimately, increased learner autonomy.

The case for strategies attention has been well drawn for some time by Anita Wenden and Rebecca Oxford. On the basis of research findings, Wenden (1985) has argued that appropriate strategies coursework for developing learner autonomy and empowering learners is of critical importance:

> Learners must learn how to do for themselves what teachers typically do for them in the classroom. Our endeavors to help them improve their language skills must be complemented by an equally systematic approach to helping them develop and refine their learning skills. (7)

Oxford (1993) conveys the importance of strategies and their benefits as follows:

> Strategy training can help students make effective use of multiple strategies. Metacognitive strategies help students keep themselves on track; cognitive, memory and compensation strategies provide the necessary intellectual tools; and affective and social strategies offer continuous emotional and interpersonal support. (22)

At the beginning of the 1990s, as the theme of this Round Table gives testimony, attention to strategies is an important aspect of second-language theory, practice, and research. Today, with the guidance of emerging paradigms and inventories that identify, describe, and categorize learner behaviors into manageable frameworks, it is easier to take strategies training seriously as a learning and teaching goal for ESL and EFL programs across the entire spectrum—kindergarten through grade twelve (K–12), adult education, community college education, four-year college and university education, and business and industry education. The following portions of this paper will look at learning-strategy training in the university ESL milieu.

English for Academic Purposes. English for Academic Purposes (EAP), a subgenre of English for Specific Purposes (ESP), is one of the fastest growing specialty areas within college and university ESL. EAP instruction in institutions of higher education has flourished over the last several years, in both numbers of programs and in linguistic sophistication.

Meeting the EAP language needs of nonnative speaking (NNS) students. According to Institute for International Education figures (1991), there are 407,500 international students in U.S. colleges and universities, the majority of whom are undergraduates. However, in recent years there has been a significant increase in international students enrolling in graduate schools across the country. A recent *NAFSA Newsletter* (1992) reported that during the 1980s, for example, the number of doctorates awarded to non–U.S. citizens more than doubled from 5,221 to 10,666. In 1991, non–U.S. citizens earned 30% of total doctorates; in engineering, a remarkable 59% of the doctorates went to non-U.S. citizens.

To meet the increasingly sophisticated language needs of advanced-level nonnative speaking students, the mission of English-language programs on college and university campuses has been moving toward a focus that is no longer on "general English." Instead, the ESL focus is shifting more and more to one of ESP and especially EAP. The responsibility is one of mounting effective EAP programs that will enable students to succeed, not just survive, and to become fully participating members of the academic and preprofessional communities in their disciplines.

English-language expertise has become a priority academic and professional requirement, whether international higher education graduates choose to return to their home countries or stay in the United States—and more and more students are choosing to stay today, moving into American business and industry and university teaching positions.

University of Michigan EAP program development. Having phased out its intensive course for nonuniversity students in 1987, the primary work of the English Language Institute today is to provide a variety of credit courses in EAP for nonnative speakers enrolled at the University of Michigan and to carry out relevant research (Morley 1991b). Currently over 30 one-credit and two-credit courses are part of the ELI curriculum; ELI courses are taken concurrently with other academic courses. Student enrollments average 450 to 500 in the fall semester and 250 in the winter term. Over 90% of these are graduate students, and most of those are in doctoral degree programs.

Michigan EAP coursework is based on ongoing observation of students' needs in the wide-ranging academic and preprofessional contexts in which they are situated in their various disciplines across the campus. Swales's (1990) three-stage process for ESP course development has been adapted to present ELI curriculum planning. One aspect of this process is an analysis of the target situation and identification of the participants' roles. A second focuses on characterizing the language that expresses these roles, including a linguistic analysis that studies pragmatics and discourse in order to understand the situational texts, both written and oral. The final stage is developing language-learning activities and tasks that allow the specified language to be acquired efficiently and effectively.

Communicative task-based language teaching, with a focus on collaborative work and interactive classroom techniques, is the primary organizing principle of classroom instructional activities. The content of the EAP courses, particularly at the advanced levels, is learner-specific and learner-generated; that is, students in ELI EAP courses write about and talk about material in their own fields and important issues present in the campus milieu, as well as national and international social, economic, and political issues of more general import.

Learning strategies training in EAP oral communication curriculum

The need for oral communication for NNSs in academic and preprofessional career contexts. Traditionally, EAP programming has featured the development of literacy skills, primarily written communication, often to the near exclusion of serious attention to oral communication. Today, in order to meet advanced writing needs, particularly those of graduate students, EAP faculty members have become more and more involved in discourse analysis of written texts in a variety of academic disciplines.

Gradually, however, a new look at EAP coursework in oral communication has emerged as it has become clear that written communication is not the only language skill needed to become a fully participating member of academic and professional communities. Part of being a member of an academic or professional community is learning *both* the written and spoken genre (i.e., the specialized language) of official interaction in that community—specifically, the linguistic forms that mark someone as a member of that community.

In a recent personal communication, a departmental professor–researcher presented a cogent argument vis-à-vis the need for "first-class English-speaking skills" for his NNSs. He reasoned that inasmuch as the execution of hard-science research typically involves hundreds of thousands of dollars per experiment, it is foolish *in the extreme* to skimp on the resources needed to have that research presented by those who execute it. His compelling point was that the NNS graduate student, the department, and the university will all gain if the talks given on the subject at international meetings are given with "first-class English-speaking skills"—perhaps with a dash of elegance, panache, and theatrical flair thrown in.

Clearly, oral communication is as critical to successful academic and professional performance as written communication is. The challenge is to design courses that provide sophisticated EAP and ESP oral communication skills development informed by an examination of academic and professional oral discourse patterns.

Working to meet this challenge, ELI has developed the eleven oral-communication courses listed in Table 1 (Morley, 1993). In addition, a major portion of ELI ITA coursework focuses on features of oral communication in academic contexts. In ELI 993, *College Teaching in the U.S.: Pedagogy, Culture, & Language,* for example, speaking skills and the language of the higher education classroom are key components of the coursework.

Learning strategies, tasks, and activities. Resource materials written by

Wenden (1985, 1991) and Oxford (1985, 1990) have been especially important in presenting the case for strategies training and in providing useful guidelines for strategy-program development.

> Our endeavors to help them improve their language skills must be complemented by an equally systematic approach to helping them develop and refine their learning skills. Learner training should be integrated with language training. (Wenden 1985: 7)

> [L]earning strategies are specific actions taken by the learner to make learning easier, faster, more enjoyable, more self-directed, more effective, and more transferrable to new situations. (Oxford 1990: 8)

Table 1. English Language Institute courses

EAP Oral Communication Courses:	
330	Language & Communication I
331	Language & Communication II
332	Lecture Comprehension
333	Interactive Listening & Communication
334	Academic Speaking
336	Pronunciation I
337	Pronunciation II
338	Voice and Articulation
392	Interviewing
434	(GR/UG) (1) Discussion & Oral Argumentation
601	(GR) (2) Speaking in Research Contexts
International Teaching Assistant (ITA) Courses:	
380	Introduction to ITA Work
381	ITA Presenting Skills
383	ITA Interacting Skills
392	ITA Interactions with Undergraduates
584	(GR) (1) ITA Seminar Practicum
993	(GR) (1) College Teaching in the U.S.: Pedagogy, Culture, & Language

These special academic English courses are designed for and open only to graduate and undergraduate students who are enrolled at the University of Michigan. They carry one or two UG (undergraduate) or GR (graduate) hours of credit.

In reporting on her research, Wenden (1985) describes four groups of learning strategies:

- **Cognitive strategies** are useful in focusing attention on certain aspects of incoming information, in making "input comprehensible," in retaining or storing for future use what they have understood, in developing facility in the use of what they have learned, etc.
- **Communication strategies** are useful when learners experience a gap in their linguistic repertoire or experience miscommunication. They

may include employing their existing knowledge of the L2 by using circumlocutions, explanations, descriptions; using words from their L1; nonlinguistic cues, gestures, drawings, etc.

- **Global practice strategies** focus not on specific aspects of language or communication per se but on utilizing resources in the social environment to create opportunities to practice, to learn, and to develop facility in the use of the second language—through meeting people and talking with people in their living situation, during routine personal activities such as shopping, during leisure activities, from the media, etc.
- **Metacognitive strategies** are used to oversee, regulate, and self-direct their language learning. These include functions of planning, monitoring, and checking outcomes, etc. (Wenden 1985: 4–5)

In suggesting guidelines for strategy training, Oxford (1990: 17) proposes two types:

- **Direct or cognitive strategies,** which learners apply directly to the language-learning itself, include:
  - *memory* strategies (e.g., a focus on remembering more effectively; creating mental linkages; applying images and sounds; reviewing well; employing action)
  - *cognitive* strategies (e.g., using all cognitive processes; practicing; receiving and sending messages; analyzing and reasoning; creating structure for input and output)
  - *compensation* strategies (e.g., compensating for missing knowledge by guessing intelligently; overcoming limitations in speaking and writing)

- **Indirect or metacognitive strategies,** in which learners manage or control their own learning process, include:
  - *metacognitive* strategies (e.g., centering your learning; arranging and planning your learning; evaluating your learning)
  - *affective* strategies (lowering your anxiety; encouraging yourself; taking your emotional temperature)
  - *social* strategies (e.g., asking questions; cooperating with others; empathizing with others).

Learner involvement in ELI pronunciation courses. Three intermediate/advanced pronunciation courses (336, 337, and 338) (see Table 2) are part of the ELI oral communication curriculum. Appendix 1 contains an outline of the rationale and basic instructional features of pronunciation coursework as well as oral communication curriculum in general.

Table 2. Summary Descriptions: Three Intermediate/Advanced ELI Pronunciation Courses

ELI 336 - *Pronunciation I* (the first in a two-course sequence) (1 UG credit)

- an introductory pronunciation course; provides intensive work with English vowels and consonants and their combinations, and basic features of English stress, rhythm, and intonation.
- contextualized practice with two goals: (1) to enable students to modify pronunciation patterns toward more intelligible speech and improved oral communication and (2) to guide students in developing language learning self-monitoring and self-help strategies for present and future use after formal course work ends (especially metacognitive strategies of planning, monitoring, and checking outcomes)
- focuses primarily on micro-level discrete-point pronunciation work; some attention to macro-level global-communicative work

ELI 337 - *Pronunciation II* (the second in a 2-course sequence; may be exempted by 336 teacher) (1 UG)

- focuses on continuation of the work begun in 336; in whole-class sessions, attention focuses on elements of stress, rhythm, and intonation; in small-group and tutorial sessions, attention focuses on extended contextual practice with sounds and sound combinations
- special attention to individual needs through videotaping and critiquing (especially in tutorials) and through individualized self-study programming designed for each student
- special attention to metacognitive strategies of self and peer monitoring and critiqueing

ELI 338 - *Voice and Articulation: Effective Speaking Skills* (1 UG credit)

- an intermediate/advanced pronunciation/speaking class; a focus on stabilizing altered pronunciation and integrating modified speech patterns into extemporaneous speaking
- includes a dual-focus syllabus with more attention to macro level elements of oral communicability and less attention to micro level discrete point pronunciation work
- work includes both pre-planned/rehearsed speaking practice and extemporaneous speaking practice, often with interactive audience participation Question-and-Answer follow up sessions
- initial rapid review of the three pronunciation "systems" (Vs, Cs, SRI), then speaking activities/ tasks that feature a variety of language functions

Explicit attention to learning strategies has long been a part of ELI pronunciation classes; learning strategies have been interwoven into class activities and textbook materials for a number of years (Morley, 1975). In *Improving Spoken English* (Morley 1979), explicit attention is given to speech awareness (a cognitive component of learning), self-monitoring (a metacognitive component of learning), and self-modification of speech patterns (a practice–metacognitive–cognitive component). The *ISE* preface and introduction to students include the following:

> One of the primary concerns of *Improving Spoken English* is to involve students, consciously, in their own learning process as they work to improve their spoken English. Each part of each lesson focuses students' attention on *what* they are doing and *why* they are doing it. Lessons encourage personal involvement by providing students with:
>
> - *ways and means* (a) to take responsibility for their own work and (b) to take a personal pride in their many small accomplishments along the way toward improved spoken English
> - *tools and techniques* with which (a) to monitor others and themselves, (b) to modify their spoken English—in bits and pieces, and (c) to continue to improve their spoken English when they leave the formal classroom and language laboratory. (Morley 1979: vii, viii)

In a more recent text, *Extempore Speaking Practice,* five explicit monitoring checkpoints and learning strategies for rehearsed and extemporaneous speech practice and six explicit learning strategies for imitative speech practice are given (Morley 1992: page xvi).

Strategy focus in selected ELI speaking courses. The kind of specific attention to learner self-involvement developed for the pronunciation courses has been extended to three advanced oral communication courses (434, 601, and the "speaking skills" component of 993) (see Table 3). See Appendix 2 for a summary outline of oral communication self-monitoring guidelines for these three oral communication courses and an oral communication self-assessment sheet.

Strategy focus in ELI listening courses. Two intermediate listening courses are offered in the ELI curriculum (see Table 4). See Appendix 3 for a sample of listening/language-learning goals and purposes as formulated for ELI 333, *Interactive Listening and Communication.*

Concluding Comments. Working with language-learning strategy training as an integral part of coursework in the EAP oral communication context is

Table 3. Summary Descriptions: Three Advanced ELI Speaking Courses

ELI 434 - ***Discussion and Oral Argumentation*** (1 GR credit)

- focuses on advanced seminar-style presentations that feature oral argumentation and interactive challenge-and-defense discussions
- includes two areas of study: (1) organizational patterns of spoken language and (2) effective use of "communicative' pronunciation patterns

ELI 601 - ***Speaking in Research Contexts*** (2 GR credits)

- focuses on tasks in field-specific academic and professional contexts and appropriate language for specific language functions in a variety of genres
- includes dissertation defense, conference paper presentation, panel participation, chairing panels, introducing speakers, job interviews, etc.

ELI 993 - ***College Teaching in the United States: Pedagogy, Culture, and Language*** (1 GR credit)

- ITA intensive workshop designed for foreign-born graduate students who hope to become teaching assistants at the University of Michigan
- a practicum for teaching in a United States setting
- required for all foreign-born LSA graduate students before they can teach
- a special "speaking skills" class focuses on classroom lecture/discussion strategies

challenging and rewarding—both for students and for teachers. The values that accrue are obvious to both students and teachers. Used in an interactive and collaborative-task environment, it is possible to build a strong sense of community within the classroom, one that is supportive, comfortable, and congenial. Common goals of self-involvement, self-challenge, and self-accomplishment help to break down inhibitions and encourage students to take risks (little risks, then bigger risks). It challenges students to try to do difficult—and sometimes frightening—things and to experience the rewards of success (little successes, then bigger successes). For those NNSs who are living isolated and lonely lives (and there are surprising numbers of them), it provides companionship and, for some, even a sense of family: Friendships are begun in class and spill over into private life.

Continued work with more experimental ways to examine and to apply strategies training to regular classroom and laboratory instruction promises to be an exciting new frontier of study and development for learners and teachers alike.

Table 4. Summary Descriptions: Two Intermediate EAP Listening Courses

ELI 332 - ***Lecture Comprehension*** (1 UG credit)

- focuses on lecture listening, note-taking, critical listening, and critical thinking
- includes attention to subject matter comprehension, use of paralinguistic and extralinguistic cues in academic interactions, and cross-cultural differences

ELI 333 - ***Interactive Listening and Communication*** (1 UG credit)

- focuses on various interactive communication situations in the academic context
- includes development of listening strategies in seminar-style class sessions; communication strategies in presenting topics for group discussion; interactive strategies in group collaborative panel presentations; and chairing follow-up audience participation Question-and-Comment sessions

REFERENCES

Brown, H. Douglas. 1987. *Principles of language learning and teaching* (Second edition). Englewood Cliffs, N.J.: Prentice-Hall, Inc.

Brown, Roger. 1973. *A first language: The early stages*. Cambridge, Mass.: Harvard University Press.

Canale, Michael, and Merrill Swain. 1980. "Theoretical bases of communicative approaches to second language teaching and testing." *Applied Linguistics* 1(1).

Chamot, Anna, and Michael O'Malley. 1987. "The cognitive academic language learning approach: A bridge to the mainstream." *TESOL Quarterly* 21(2).

Chomsky, Noam. 1959. "Review of: B. F. Skinner, Verbal behavior." *Language* 35(1).

Corder, S. Pit. 1967. "The significance of learners' errors." *International Review of Applied Linguistics* 5(4).

Corder, S. Pit. 1976. "The study of interlanguage." In G. Nickel (ed.), *Proceedings of the fourth international congress of applied linguistics*. Stuttgart: Hochschul-Verlag.

Faerch, Claus, and Gabrielle Kasper (eds.). 1983. *Strategies in interlanguage communication*. New York: Longman.

Institute of International Education. 1991. *Open doors, 1990–1991*. New York: IIE Publications.

Morley, Joan, Betty Robinett, and Earl Stevick. 1975. "Round robin on pronunciation." *TESOL Quarterly* 9(3).

Morley, Joan. 1979. *Improving spoken English*. Ann Arbor, MI: University of Michigan Press.

Morley, Joan. 1991a. "Current directions in second-language teaching." In W. Grabe and R. Kaplan (eds.), *Introduction to applied linguistics*. New York: Addison-Wesley Publishing Co.

Morley, Joan. 1991b. "Perspectives on English for academic purposes." In James E. Alatis (ed.), *Georgetown University Round Table on Languages and Linguistics 1991*. Washington D.C.: Georgetown University Press.

Morley, Joan. 1992a. "Theory and practice in listening comprehension." In R. J. Courchene et al.

(eds.), *Comprehension-based second language teaching*. Ottawa: University of Ottawa Press.

Morley, Joan. 1992b. *Extempore speaking practice*. Ann Arbor: University of Michigan Press.

Morley, Joan. 1992. "EAP oral communication curriculum: Spoken discourse, meaning, and communicative pronunciation." In James E. Alatis (ed.), *Georgetown University Round Table on Languages and Linguistics 1992*. Washington D.C.: Georgetown University Press.

NAFSA. 1993. "Trends: Noncitizen's share of new doctorates continues to grow." *NAFSA Newsletter*. 44(6)

Naiman, Neil, et al (eds.). 1978. *The good language learner*. Toronto: Ontario Institute for Studies in Education.

O'Malley, Michael, et al. 1985. "Learning strategy applications with students of English as a second language." *TESOL Quarterly* 19(3).

O'Malley, Michael, and Anna Chamot. 1990. *Learning strategies in second language acquisition*. New York: Cambridge University Press.

Oxford, Rebecca. 1985. *A new taxonomy of second language learning strategies*. Washington, D.C.: ERIC Clearinghouse on Languages and Linguistics.

Oxford, Rebecca. 1990. *Language learning strategies: What every teacher should know*. New York: Newbury House.

Oxford, Rebecca. 1993. "Language learning strategies in as nutshell: Update and ESL suggestions." *TESOL Journal*. 2(2).

Piaget, Jean. 1926. *The language and thought of the child*. New York: Harcourt and Brace.

Pimsleur, Paul, and Terence Quinn (eds.). 1971. *The psychology of second language learning*. (Papers from the second international Congress of AILA). Cambridge: Cambridge University Press.

Ries, P., and D. H. Thurgood. 1991. *Doctorate recipients from United States universities*. New York: National Academic Press.

Rubin, Joan. 1975. "What the "good language learner" can teach us." *TESOL Quarterly* 9(1).

Scarcella, Robin, and Rebecca Oxford. 1992. *The tapestry of language learning: The individual in the communicative classroom*. Boston: Heinle and Heinle.

Skinner, B. F. 1957. *Verbal behavior*. New York: Appleton-Century-Crofts.

Skehan, Peter. 1989. *Individual differences in second language learning*. London: Edward Arnold.

Stern, H. H. 1975. "What can we learn from the good language learner?" *Canadian Modern Language Journal* 31(4).

Swales, John. 1989. "Planning an LSP program." Lecture presented at The University of Michigan, Ann Arbor, Mich.

Vygotsky, L. 1934/1986. *Thought and language*. Translated and edited by Alex Kozulin. Cambridge, Mass.: MIT Press.

Wenden, Anita. 1985. "Learner strategies." *TESOL Newsletter* 19(5).

Wenden, Anita, and Joan Rubin. 1987. *Learner strategies in language learning*. Englewood Cliffs, N.J.: Prentice Hall.

Wenden, Anita. 1991. *Learner strategies for learner autonomy*. London: Prentice Hall International.

Appendix 1. Rationale and Basic Instructional Features

I. An Integrated Approach: Dual Focus Program Philosophy
   A. A macro-level focus on general elements of global oral communicability (discourse, socio-
linguistic, strategic competence)
   B. A micro level focus on discrete elements of pronunciation and intelligibility (linguistic/phonetic-phonological competence)

II. Learner Goals: Communicative Competence and Self-help Language Learning Strategies
   A. Learner Goals
      1. Goal one: functional intelligibility.
      2. Goal two: functional communicability.
      3. Goal three: increased self-confidence.
      4. Goal four: speech monitoring abilities and speech modification strategies for use beyond the classroom.
   B. These goals are focused on moving learners along toward development of four communicative competencies (See Canale and Swain, 1980): linguistic/grammatical competence; discourse competence; socio-linguistic competence; and strategic competence.
   C. These goals encompass learners' development of language learning strategies (See Weden, 1985; Oxford, 1990): affective strategies; cognitive strategies; metacognitive strategies; communication strategies; global practice strategies.

III. Learning Dimensions and Learning Objectives: Cognitive, Psychological, Physical
   A. Cognitive/intellectual component of learning: Information objectives
      1. Language information (*cognitive* strategies)
      2. Procedural information (*metacognitive* strategies)
   B. Psychological/affective component of learning: Affective objectives
      1. Learner self-involvement; recognition of self-responsibility; development of self-monitoring skills; development of speech modification skills; recognition of self-accomplishment (*metacognitive* and *affective* strategies)
      2. Comfortable, supportive classroom atmosphere which fosters supportive teacher-student interactions and supportive student-student interactions (*social* strategies)
   C. Physical/performative component of learning: Practice objectives
      1. Speech/pronunciation practice; focus on integration of linguistic, paralinguistic, and extralinguistic components (*communication* strategies)
      2. Pronunciation-oriented listening practice
      3. Spelling-oriented pronunciation practice.

IV. Instructional Planning
   A. Assessment (See Intelligibility Index, Chart 3.)
   B. Instruction: Cycles of three modes of practice.
   [Note: These practice modes move from dependent practice (with model given), to guided practice (with self-initiated rehearsed speech), to independent practice (extemporaneous speech with the content self-selected by the learners to meet their personal, social, educational, and occupational career needs)
      1. Imitative speech practice
      For controlled production of selected speech/pronunciation features (*cognitive, metacognitive* strategies)
      2. Rehearsed practice
      For stabilization of altered pronunciation through the use of relatively "fixed" texts (both oral reading scripts and pre-planned talks), out-of-class self-study rehearsals, and both in-class rehearsals and one-on-one individual work sessions with the "speech coach" (*metacognitive, communication* strategies)
      3. Extemporaneous practice
      For integration of modified speech patterns into naturally-occurring creative speech in both partially planned and unplanned talks (monologues), panel discussions, and audience interaction in a Question-and-Answer or Question-and-Comment audience participation format (dialogues) (discourse, socio-linguistic, strategic competence)

V. Learner Role
   A. Speech "performer"
   B. Learner Awarenesses and Attitudes
      1. Speech awareness.
      2. Self-awareness of features of speech production and speech performance.
      3. Self-observation skills and a positive attitude toward self-monitoring processes.
      4. Speech-modification skills.
      5. Awareness of the learner role as one of a "speech performer" modifying, adjusting or altering a feature of speech/pronunciation, and the teacher role as one of assisting students as a "speech coach."
      6. A sense of personal responsibility for one's own learning, not only for immediate educational and personal needs, but for future career needs.
      7. A feeling of pride in one's own accomplishments.
      8. Building a personal repertoire of speech monitoring and modification skills in order to continue to improve speaking effectiveness in English when the formal instructional program is finished.

VI. Teacher Role
   A. Speech "coach"
   B. Teacher Responsibilities
   1. Conducting speech/pronunciationdiagnostic analyses, and choosing and prioritizing those features that will make the most noticeable impact on modifying the speech of each learner.
   2. Helping students set both long-range and short-term goals.
   3. Designing group program scope and sequence; designing personalized programming for each individual learner in the group.
   4. Developing a variety of instructional formats, modes, and activities (e.g., whole class instruction; small-group work; individual one-to-one tutorial sessions; pre-recorded audio and/or video self-study materials, computer-assisted programs etc. Overall, providing genuine speech task activities for practice situated in real contexts and carefully chosen simulated contexts.
   5. Structuring in-class speaking (and listening) activities with invited NS and NNS guests participating.
   6. Planning field trip assignments in pairs/small groups for real-world speaking practice.
   7. Monitoring learners' speech production and speech performance at all times, and assessing pattern changes, as an on-going part of the program.
   8. Encouraging student speech awareness and realistic self-monitoring.
   9. Always supporting each learner in his/her efforts, be they wildly successful or not so successful.

Appendix 2. Oral Communication Self-Monitoring Guidelines and Self-Help Listening/Speaking Strategies

1. **Monitor your overall clarity of contextualized speech**

   Goal: To increase overall precision and clarity of speech, both sounds (i.e., vowels, consonants) and prosodics (i.e.,stress, rhythm, intonation), by modifying speech in the following ways:
   a. Use open articulation.
   b. Use "fronted" speech.

c. Develop a slower overall pace.
d. Develop the rhythm pattern of English phrases. (See *Rhythmics* summary handout.)
e. Use sufficient volume and project your voice.

2. **Monitor your use of vocal features in oral discourse**

Goal: To increase general vocal effectiveness by focusing on the meaning you wish to communicate. Develop the following features of voice to communicate your exact meaning by marking prominent information in the following ways:

a. Use vocal stress (i.e., longer, louder syllables) and intonation (i.e., rises in tone) to show emphasis.
b. Use variation in speed to show emphasis.
c. Use variations in volume to show emphasis.
d. Keep pitch level normal when you increase volume; don't let pitch rise to high shrill tones; instead, increase energy level for increased loudness.
e. Maintain vocal energy level to the end of the phrase or sentence.
f. Use firm vocal breath support to provide sufficient vocal energy, especially when you speak to a large group.

3. **Strengthen your overall fluency and ongoing planning and structuring of speech**

Goal: To develop overall fluency in the ongoing planning and structuring of speech as it proceeds, in the following ways:

a. TALK! TALK! TALK in this class! Take advantage of every speaking opportunity either as a presenter of "talk" or as a responder who asks questions or adds comments; expand and enrich your English "repertoire."
b. TALK! TALK! TALK outside class! Take advantage of every speaking opportunity in daily contacts. Actively seek speaking "practice" opportunities.
c. LISTEN! LISTEN! LISTEN critically/analytically to a TV evening news show, to a talk show, to an interview show, etc.—every day! Observe and actively analyze "speech delivery" (i.e., speaking skills) as well as content.

4. **Concentrate on raising your general speech intelligibility level**

Goal: to increase overall speech intelligibility level by continued attention to the micro features of pronunciation as well as these macro features. (See the *Speech Intelligibility Index* and the *Dual Focus Chart*.)

5. **Develop your communicative command and control of grammar**

Goal: To increase general communicative command of grammatical constructions, both general academic and field-specific, in the following ways:

a. Identify and modify grammatical problems (i.e., grammatical "gaps").
b. Actively look for ways to develop alternative grammatical structuring to express the meaning you wish to convey.

6. **Broaden your communicative command and control of individual vocabulary words and phrasal units**

Goal: To increase your word and phrasal vocabulary range and communicative command of: field- specific lexicon; general academic lexicon; discourse markers; conversational idioms/slang in the following ways:

a. Actively observe and seek to expand your repertoire of field-specific vocabulary words and phrasal units.
b. Actively observe professors and fellow students in your field and seek to expand your repertoire of general academic words and phrasal units.

c. Actively focus your listening on pronunciation of vocabulary words and phrasal units; focus on both the sounds and the stress/rhythm/intonation patterns of the pronunciation of words/phrasal units.
d. Use your dictionary to look up both meaning and pronunciation of new vocabulary words.
e. Keep a list of idioms and slang expressions; ask friends and fellow students to explain them to you.

7. **Develop your overall use of effective non-verbal features of oral communication**
Goal: Develop overall use of appropriate and expressive nonverbal behaviors in the following ways:
a. Be "listener-oriented"! Establish and maintain rapport with your listeners through eye contact with members of the audience. Develop an "audience-oriented" focus on communication.
b. Use comfortable "in charge" posture and body stance that reflect confidence.
c. Let your facial expressions show your interest and enthusiasm in your subject.
d. Use appropriate head, hand, and arm gestures that grow out of the meaning you wish to convey and complement that meaning. Do not use extraneous distracting gestures (e.g., avoid wringing your hands, picking at your fingers, using wild and inappropriate gestures, "striding "around the room, etc.)

Student Name ________________________________ Date ______________

Oral Communication Self-Assessment: Macro Features

Directions: At the beginning of the term, use the Speech Intelligibility Index to estimate your present intelligibility level. (See *Intelligibility Index* directions.)

Then, as assigned throughout the term, view your video recordings with your partner(s) and evaluate your communicative effectiveness in each of the seven areas. Use the scale of 1–5. Write 2-3 strength/weakness phrases for each category. (See *Oral Communication Self-Monitoring Guidelines*.)

1 = overall, **very good** control; continuing need to use general monitoring strategies
2 = overall, **good** control; continuing need to use both general monitoring strategies and specific monitoring of selected speech/communication features
3 = overall, generally **moderate** control; continuing need to use strategies to develop and/or alter specific features; continuing need to monitor specific features
4 = overall, generally **poor** control; continuing need to follow a prescribed developmental/remedial strategies plan for speech/pronunciation features.
5 = overall, generally **inadequate** control; need to develop and complete a plan to focus on a few selected areas at a time for development and/or remediation.

1. Overall clarity of contextualized speech 1 __ 2 __ 3 __ 4 __ 5 __
   Description: ________________________________
   ____

2. Effective use of vocal features in oral discourse 1 __ 2 __ 3 __ 4 __ 5 __
   Description: ________________________________
   ____

3. Overall fluency and on-going planning and structuring of speech 1 __ 2 __ 3 __ 4 __ 5 __
   Description: ________________________________
   ____

4. Overall speech intelligibility level 1 __ 2 __ 3 __ 4 __ 5 __
   Description: ________________________________
   ____

5. Communicative command and control of grammar 1 __ 2 __ 3 __ 4 __ 5 __
   Description: ________________________________
   ____

6. Communicative command and control of vocabulary words/phrases 1 __ 2 __ 3 __ 4 __ 5 __
   Description: ________________________________
   ____

7. Overall use of effective non-verbal features of communication 1 __ 2 __ 3 __ 4 __ 5 __
   Description: ________________________________
   ____

Appendix 3. ELI 333 - Interactive Listening and Communication (1 credit)

Course Description

1. ELI 333 is an intermediate EAP oral communication course with the overall goal of assisting students in the development of communicative competence in four areas of knowledge and skills. (See Canale and Swain, 1980/1983.)

   - linguistic competence
   - discourse competence
   - socio-linguistic competence
   - strategic competence

2. ELI coursework provides listening/speaking instruction and practice experiences with a variety of interactive communication situations within the academic context. Components of the syllabus include analysis, instruction, and practice in five areas.

   - speech delivery (both micro level and macro level features)(See Morley *Dual Focus Chart*.)
   - grammar in academic contexts (both sentence-level and discourse-level grammar features)
   - vocabulary word/phrasal unit repertoire (field-specific and general academic content lexicon; rhetorical markers; metaphors, similes, analogies, idioms and slang)
   - discourse functions and discourse structures
   - learner strategies (direct, cognitive; indirect, metacognitive) (See Oxford, 1990.)

3. *Interactive Listening and Communication* focuses on the reciprocal listener/speaker role students play in different contexts of English for Academic Purposes on the university campus. It is therefore essential that all class members are fully involved and participate actively in every class session as *both* a listener and a speaker. Critical listening and critical thinking are stressed. Careful listening to the viewpoints of others and respect for the opinions of others is stressed.

   Students study features of speech organization and both macro and micro discourse markers. Videotapes are analyzed for the identification of speaker delivery markers of emphasis, new-versus-given information, attitude, etc. Listening focuses on speaker's use of: pitch rise-and-fall patterns, high-low contrast pattern; intonation contours; use of accelerated/decelerated pacing; use of increases and decreases in volume; use of clear, precisely articulated segments versus "fast speech" reduced segments, etc.

   In class workout sessions and in out-of-class small-group working sessions students view videotape segments and systematically analyze the oral texts, identifying features of effective/ineffective delivery.and patterns of effective/ineffective organization. In preparing and rehearsing collaborative panel reports and individual topic talks students experiment with applying selected effective speech delivery features and speech organization patterns to their own presentations.

Specific Goals

The specific goals of ELI 333 are to enable learners to develop communicative skills in the following areas:

1. Development of Listening Strategies.
   - developing cognitive, metacognitive, communicative, affective and compensatory strategies for enhanced listening comprehension
   - practicing strategy use in both "sheltered" small-group work-out sessions and in "public" seminar-style class discussions

2. Development of Speaking Strategies.
   - planning and presenting small-group collaborative panel reports (i.e., this format includes small group interactive discussions to organize, rehearse, and present collaborative group presentations, chairing panel sessions, responding to questions, and encouraging active constructive audience participation)
   - planning, rehearsing, and presenting individual topic talks on field-specific or social issue topics (i.e., using discourse features of topic development; using description, definition, explanation, cause and effect, comparison and contrast, summary, etc.; using appropriate transitions and topic shifts)

3. Development of Interactive-Speaker Strategies and Interactive-Listener Strategies
   - in responding to follow-up questions and comments
   - in participating in group discussions)

Course Requirements

1. In-class: Attendance at two one-hour sessions per week and bi-weekly individual/small-group tutorial sessions
2. In-class: Daily class participation in both "listener" and "speaker" roles
3. Homework: Small-group work; preparation for collaborative panel reports
4. Homework: Individual or pair work; preparation and rehearsal for class presentations (using video equipment in the ELI Recording Room)
5. Homework: Individual work on audio and video assignments - Language Resource Center (2nd floor, Modern Languages Building)

Creating a learning community: Community Language Learning for the nineties

Karin C. Ryding[1]
Georgetown University

Introduction. I am going to open with a quote from my colleague Heidi Byrnes, from an article published recently in the SLL newsletter, *The SentineLL,* wherein she states that she not only "found it necessary but challenging to reflect more deeply about issues in higher education in general and Georgetown's role within that universe" (1993: 6). In that article she deals with both the social and moral contexts of university education, observing: "As currently practiced, much of education suffers from 'the pain of disconnection' between what people are and what they do" (1993: 7).

The reason I open with this observation is that it calibrates closely with my own experience as a university professor and particularly as a language teacher. That "pain of disconnection" also parallels what Father Charles A. Curran, the originator of Community Language Learning, referred to in 1968 as a "profound core of existential anxiety" (1968: 82), which emerges to confront language teachers in particular because of the nature of the foreign-language learning experience.

Father Curran's Counseling–Learning approach, referred to as Community Language Learning (CLL) in the language-teaching context, has contributed to language-teaching methodology over the past twenty years by dealing with some of "the most profound and elusive issues in the learning/teaching experience, including risk, trust, (in)security, the context and processes of retention, the skillful use of silence, the importance of witnessing and affirming another person's feelings, teacher and learner responsibility and integrity, interpersonal relationships, and stages of psychological growth" (Ryding 1990: 111).

Because of the scope and depth of this approach, and possibly because of the psychotherapeutic/theological viewpoint from which pure CLL theory was originally presented, it has attracted sustained attention but few fully committed practitioners. "Nonetheless, its insights, humanistic values and intellectual integrity have made it a movement to be reckoned with" (Ryding 1990: 111). A small group of CLL practitioners and commentators, including Jennybelle

1. I would like to express my profound appreciation to Jennybelle Rardin for her comments and suggestions on this paper.

Rardin, Pat Tirone, Keiko Samimy, and Dan Tranel[2] have continued to refine and define both theory and practice and to carry out classroom-based experimentation and research. Their focus has been on the central concept of CLL that

> the quality of the relationship between teacher and learners facilitates and enhances learning and is, therefore, prior to and more important than any particular methodology. *Learning is actually made possible by the quality and structure of the personal relationships* (Rardin 1988: viii, emphasis in original).

Innovative "methods." Three innovative language-teaching theories emerged quite contemporaneously in the mid-1970s. Silent Way, Counseling-Learning, and Suggestopedia tended to be treated and discussed together, lumped into one vaguely learner-centered, humanistic category.[3] There is much to be admired in the ingenuity, insight, and creativity shown by each of their founders, but all of these approaches came with a certain amount of impedimenta, such as charts and rods, easy chairs, music, and tape recorders, and all of them were based on new premises about learning, which although they essentially held true, were also somehow peripheral to the experience and training of American foreign-language teachers. Unfortunately, these "innovative" approaches were not only treated as a group, they were dismissed as a group without distinguishing among them what could have long-range, permanent impact on the pedagogy of foreign languages. In this paper I address some of the wider and more enduring implications that Community Language Learning may have for foreign-language teaching, especially in the light of recent educational research and theories of cognition.

This is not to dismiss Suggestopedia, Silent Way, or even the Natural Approach, which came a bit later (Krashen and Terrell 1983). All of these approaches have offered substantial contributions to the field, but here I shall simply focus on Community Language Learning because it is the approach with which I have the most experience and with which I am most familiar.

Community Language Learning. When CLL first developed in the early and mid-1970s, it was indeed innovative in the sense that it took anxiety and feelings of the learners into account, it focused on holistic rather than strictly intellectual learning, it was not grammar-based but proficiency-based, and it reoriented the classroom focus, or "locus of responsibility" (Ames 1992: 265),

---

2. In addition to these practitioners, see Stevick (1973, 1976, 1980, 1990), Ryding (1978, 1979, 1990), and Taylor (1987).

3. See Oller and Richard-Amato (1983), Blair (1982), Richard and Rogers (1986).

from the teacher to the learners. Its philosophy emerged from a background of humanistic psychology and Christian theology, and it reflected a renewed and profound humanistic commitment to the well-being of the learner. CLL theory is expressed and explained in a limited body of writings developed since 1972,[4] but because of the rigorous nature of the approach, which requires training and skill in clinical listening techniques,[5] and perhaps because of the theological flavor of Curran's original presentation of Counseling–Learning theory and practice, it did not attract a large number of adherents.[6]

Although the religious metaphors favored by Curran may have been off-putting to some, nonetheless there is strength and potency inherent in the rich blend of empathy, discipline, knowledge, and conscious risk offered to teachers who undertake CLL training. These issues have become increasingly important and validated in the last decade of this century as a new wave of educational theory has merged with theories of communicative competence in language teaching. The issues I am referring to are those that involve what is termed "situated cognition" (Derry 1992) and education as a moral enterprise,[7] topics not yet widely discussed in language-teaching journals but extremely current in professional publications dealing with broader issues of education, education theory, and educational psychology. It may now be, in our *fin-de-siècle* era, an appropriate juncture for language-teaching theory in particular as well as education theory in general to expand their horizons explicitly to incorporate psychological, humanistic, and ethical concerns.[8]

---

4. See for example, references under Curran, Stevick, Rardin, Samimy, and Ryding.

5. In Young's recent article (1990: 430), which organizes and reviews literature on language anxiety, she laments the fact that "Other than Suggestopedia, ... rarely are instructors given specific examples of how to go about creating a low anxiety atmosphere in the foreign language classroom." She does not mention Curran's work. She refers to "Rardin's" (p. 428) views on existential anxiety, but unfortunately, the Rardin reference is omitted from the bibliography.

6. Stevick (1990: 63) puts his finger on the discomfort that many academics experience with concepts that involve theology: "Many readers in academic circles today have rejected theology, and therefore expect to find theological-type thinking either unintelligible, or worthless, or both. *One possible effect of labeling ideas (government economic policies, language teaching methods, or whatever) as 'theological' is to reduce the likelihood that readers will give these ideas serious attention.*" Emphasis added.

7. In addition to Byrnes (1993), see Long (1992), Shelton (1992), Hellwig (1991), and Burghardt (1992).

8. See especially Lane (1992: 19–56) regarding the critical importance of concepts such as the "identification, maturation and enrichment of self-hood" and "the significance of community for the institution of learning."

Community Language Learning may have a role in the overall development of a coherent theoretical framework for foreign-language teacher education precisely because of its concern with the importance of the teacher/learner relationship and its emphasis on the value of fostering community within the learning situation.[9]

Foreign-language teacher education. As Bernhardt and Hammadou indicate in their 1987 article "A Decade of Research in Foreign Language Teacher Education," one of the salient problems emerging from their analysis is that "general teacher education research has not made an impact on foreign language education" (293). This is only one of their five conclusions, but it is also one of the most important, for it has ramifications for their other conclusions:

1. Foreign-language teacher education is a topic of "very little concern" in the United States;
2. "On the whole, the writings ... indicate *no theoretical framework* [emphasis added] for the statements they contain";
3. "essentially no data exist on effective teacher education programs";
4. "no genuine concern has been exhibited for the preservice education of foreign language teachers." (293)

With respect to the last point, they indicate that the topic of methods course curricula in particular is severely underrepresented, especially with regard to taking "a broad perspective on methods courses" (293).

The lack of a coherent theoretical framework, or paradigm, for foreign-language teacher education has certainly been one factor in its marginalization within applied linguistics today. The methods course is often the only formal exposure that foreign-language teachers receive to language-acquisition theory, learning strategies, a wide range of relatively valid and effective approaches, teaching strategies and techniques, classroom management, and practice teaching. That is, it is necessarily a mix of principle and procedure, of apprenticeship and mastery of theory. But these different aspects of language teaching are sometimes difficult to distinguish, first because each "method" is based on its own principles, whether they be implicit, as in grammar translation, or explicit, as in Community Language Learning; and each method invariably has particular classroom techniques or procedures that suit the principles and calibrate with them. However, this does not mean that either the principles or the techniques are exclusive to one particular approach. Many experienced foreign-language

---

9. "The vision of education and classroom activity associated with culturally situated cognition is that of creating minicommunities and experiences that are simulations and extensions of productive and motivated communities of practice within larger society" (Derry 1992: 417).

teachers are aware of this in the sense that they sift and select what works for them in their classrooms and label their personal approach "eclectic."

Counseling-Learning/Community Language Learning. What Counseling-Learning/Community Language Learning offers to the field is that it incorporates a learning theory into what has been perceived primarily as a "method," and this theory is an especially valid and pertinent one for the particular stage of American educational development in the 1990s. The CLL approach probes the learning situation and the learning experience with a scrupulous concern for the integrity of the learner. It creates an effective matrix for structuring discourse processes and interaction while at the same time constellating the "inner teacher" within the learner and helping students to learn in genuinely individual ways.[10]

Curran and his followers have described and illustrated three disciplinary matrices that are of significance to foreign-language pedagogy in general: the theory of five psychological stages for the learner, the six underlying principles of teaching as reflected in the acronym SAARRD, and the issue of dominance (or eminence) as distinguished from control. All of these have to do with the central theme of Community Language Learning as mentioned earlier: the quality of the relationship between teacher and learners. Moreover, Curran's theory is founded upon the increasingly important theoretical issue of community and its centrality to the learning experience.[11]

In Curran's writings, he focuses on the principles underpinning a counseling approach to teaching and includes discussion of how these principles can be translated into classroom procedure.[12] The importance of these writings resides in their ability to inform and guide teachers with respect to aspects of psychological struggle, transformation, and growth. Many of us experience and witness these events, but we do not completely understand them from a theoretical point of view, and we are not normally equipped with a framework to deal with the various manifestations of these struggles. Most importantly, Curran's

---

10. I see this constellation of the "inner teacher" as parallel to what Woodman refers to as constellation of the "inner healer" (1993: 88) in depth psychotherapy; it is also congruent with what Norman Cousins observed in *Anatomy of an Illness* where he reported the following quotation from Albert Schweitzer: "Each patient carries his own doctor inside him [or her]. They come to us not knowing that truth. We are at our best when we give the doctor who resides within each patient a chance to go to work" (1979:69).

11. "Situated social practice views of cognition suggest that an important first step in educational reform involves addressing the question of how to develop educational communities that are meaningful, engaging, and rich for students" (Derry 1992: 417).

12. See Curran 1968, 1972, 1976, 1978, and 1982.

writings address the elusive concept of classroom community, which is now increasingly recognized as "a crucial prerequisite to truly communicative interaction" (Little and Sanders 1989: 277).

The five stages. The description of the five psychological stages of learner growth offers a sound theory for the development of learners in respect to their relation with the target language.[13] In brief, these psychological stages involve, at first, total dependence of the learner on the teacher, then gradual self-assertion in the language, and at stage three the ability to maintain a "separate existence" in the target language. Stage three is the pivotal stage, wherein future success or stagnation is determined. The learner is functional but still needs help. However, an all-too-common syndrome is for learners, having developed a degree of self-confidence with the language, to reject the teacher and to resist correction; it just doesn't "sink in."

At this point the teacher can become angry or discouraged because her need to offer her knowledge to the learner is frustrated. She may unconsciously want to avoid provoking anger in the learner and subsequently internalize the anger in herself. Having a firm grasp of this developmental theory enables a teacher to comprehend what is actually happening, for example, when a learner seems to resist error correction. Instead of feeling frustrated and perhaps personally rejected, the teacher who possesses a theoretical framework for this development can deal with that resistance in a more mature, healthy, and pragmatic way.

In order for learning to proceed, stage four of Curran's psychological matrix involves what he termed "role-reversal"—that is, the necessity of learners to understand the teacher's need to teach and therefore to put the teacher at ease. If students are to make further progress, this role-reversal is an essential step. A teacher who is attuned to the unconscious dynamics of this situation is much better prepared to take the necessary measures to help her students reach stage four. Stage five is represented by functional independence in the target language.

SAARRD. The six principles signified through the acronym SAARRD can also be of value to any language teacher throughout his or her career.[14] These principles are security, attention, assertion,[15] retention, reflection, and discrimination; they are broad enough to apply whether or not one has been convinced of the efficacy of the entire CLL approach.

---

13. See Curran 1983: 161–176, 1982: 123–130, 1976: 52–59 and Rardin et al. 1988: 81–103.

14. For description and discussion of these principles, see Curran 1982b: 141–45, 1976: 6–8, and Rardin et al., 1988: 110–122.

15. I prefer the term "assertion" to the orthodox CLL "aggression."

Curran believed that learner security was the key component in the language-learning experience and that unless security is attended to by the teacher, insecurity and debilitating forms of anxiety can sabotage even the most genuine conscious attempts to learn. Assertion is a second CLL principle. It refers to student initiation of communication and the resulting self-investment in the learning process. Student attention is a natural result of self-involvement in the learning situation. Reflection, a fourth principle, means that the student is given time to think about the material and digest it; it also means that the teacher systematically undertakes to seek out, and reflect, with "unconditional positive regard," student reactions to the learning experience. The fifth principle deals with retaining the target-language material covered in class: Self-involvement in a meaningful context seems to facilitate ability to retrieve stored material. Discrimination—sorting out, analyzing, and categorizing the details of language structure—is the final principle underlying this approach. In CLL it is initiated by the learners and carried out jointly by the learners and teacher rather than being presented by the teacher alone.

Dominance/control. This is an aspect of CLL that has been widely misunderstood. I would like to clarify it, and I would also like to rectify some misconceptions that have emerged in published descriptions and criticisms of this approach.[16]

In my own training and experience as a practitioner of Community Language Learning, I have been made explicitly aware of the difference between dominance and control, and as a teacher trainer I have found that explanation and illustration of the difference between teacher dominance and teacher control in the classroom has been a significant help to new teachers.[17] In educational psychology, this issue is referred to as the "autonomy orientation" of the teacher: whether she is "autonomy-supporting or controlling" (Ames 1992: 265), that is, whether the teacher encourages learner autonomy and decision-making or discourages it.

Dominance, as I interpret it, refers to the teacher's being the visual and mental cynosure of all classroom activity. In a traditional classroom, students are seated in rows facing the teacher, and she is the central visual point of reference. Furthermore, the teacher is the judge of correctness of all classroom utterances and behaviors. Whereas this is the standard arrangement for lecture-

16. See Richards and Rogers (1986: 113) where the teacher's role in CLL is described as "passive"; Brown (1987: 119) where he expresses concern about the counselor–teacher being *"too* nondirective" and advises that "Supportive but assertive direction from the counselor could strengthen the method."

17. Rardin et al. 1988: 27–28, Curran 1982a: 169–171.

type learning situations, CLL theory focuses on restructuring the teacher/learner relationship so that the teacher *relinquishes her dominance or eminence, while retaining control.* She carefully sets the parameters for the learning experience while providing opportunities at specific levels for students to become actively and meaningfully involved.[18] The teacher structures an atmosphere wherein learner responsibility to herself and to the group is encouraged and deeply engaged.

The concept of control is eloquently explained by Stevick in *A Way and Ways* (1980: 17–23), in which he analyzes the difference between control and initiative. Control is something that the teacher or counselor or knower must possess, understand, and use wisely. Students become anxious if they think that all the aspects of learning are in their hands, and it is utterly essential that the teacher exercise control in establishing and maintaining rules for classroom activity, including efficient structuring of time, setting general tasks for students, guiding, supporting, and focusing activities, and assiduously managing the learning situation. The teacher is also responsible for monitoring correctness and giving diagnostic feedback, showing learners how they are doing in the target language. As Stevick points out, this kind of control creates a powerful learning structure wherein the teacher can then leave the initiative, "the choice of who is going to say what to whom and when" (1980: 19), in the hands of the students.[19] She can thereby structure a learning situation and allow students to maneuver in it under her astute observation and guidance.

Community. A recent article in *Foreign Language Annals* by Greta Little and Sara Sanders entitled "Classroom Community: A Prerequisite for Communication," was the result of an ethnographic investigation of two foreign-language classes. The "unexpected result" of this investigation was the conclusion that "true communicative language learning requires something far more significant than a shift in classroom-management techniques. In fact, communication does not actually take place in the classroom *unless the language learners are a community*" (Little and Sanders 1989: 277, emphasis added).

In this particular article, the authors conclude that "developing this kind of community is first and foremost the responsibility of the students" (Little and Sanders 1989: 279). Based on my own experience, that sense of community

18. "The perception of control appears to be a significant factor affecting [students'] engagement in learning and quality of learning. When teachers are seen as emphasizing independent thinking in addition to content mastery, students are more likely to place value on using effective learning strategies" (Ames 1992: 265).

19. "[M]astery orientations are promoted in classrooms that afford students autonomy and decision making" (Blumenfeld 1992: 274).

does not just happen, but it can be created or fostered with the skillful use of understanding and through structuring of activities based on CLL principles. The Community Language Learning approach is one in which the teacher is explicitly prepared for fostering that community and in which the emergence of community is integral to the effectiveness of the learning experience.[20]

Again referring to recent literature in educational psychology, the construction of community or minicommunities in the classroom has become a central element in what is termed "situated cognition," where learning is increasingly viewed as social in nature. It includes the idea that knowledge is socially "negotiated" within a community and that "any theory of learning or instruction that focuses exclusively on the construction of symbolic knowledge by individuals is regarded as inadequate" (Derry 1992: 416).

It has been suggested that "in cooperative structures *moral* rather than ability concerns underlie motivation; in interdependent situations students focus on helping others, managing resources, and fulfilling responsibility to the group" (Blumenfeld 1992: 277, emphasis added). These new theories stress the social nature of learning and view "peer collaboration as integral to the learning process ... Students construct understanding through actively participating in a community of learners; peers are seen as sources of information rather than as a threat to one's self-esteem" (Blumenfeld 1992: 227). Moreover, "shifting the locus of responsibility from the teacher to the student has also been argued as an effective means of reducing the salience of differential ability levels in the classroom" (Ames 1992: 266).

Community Language Learning, to those who engage in it, creates a powerful learning structure based on an engagement process between the learners and teacher. As Rardin states in her recent book on CLL, "Implicit in most teaching–learning relationships is the notion of the teacher changing the students. What is suggested here is the opposite, namely, that the teacher change himself to accommodate the students" (35). Here is where the "pain of disconnection" mentioned at the beginning of this paper can begin to heal.

Community Language Learning gets learners actively engaged in creating the learning experience, reduces the affective filter, generates large amounts of natural input, provides ample opportunity for acquisition as well as learning, focuses on function as much as form, meets specific student goals, and builds sound group dynamics while attending to affective and intellectual needs on an individual level. Since the approach is neither grammar-based nor teacher-centered, but task-based and learner-centered, it provides a teaching vehicle adaptable to almost any learning situation. It tackles the essence of the language-

---

20. In this regard, see also Long (1990: 50): "Taking a course is not simply fulfilling a private contract; it is a commitment to a process of creating a community for inquiry, receptivity, and discussion."

learning experience not by prescribing a set of teaching procedures but by setting aside the traditional teacher–student relationship and restructuring the learning encounter on bases that take into account the psychological state of the learners and their increasingly well-documented need for structuring and acquiring knowledge within a community. It is a form of conscious humanism that can be used to transform the power behind the desire to learn and the need to teach into an experience that resonates with the deeper notes of the psyche.

REFERENCES

Ames, Carole. 1992. "Classrooms: Goals, structures, and student motivation." *Journal of Educational Psychology* 84(3): 261–271.

Bernhardt, Elizabeth, and Joann Hammadou. 1987. "A decade of research in foreign language teacher education." *Modern Language Journal* 71(3): 289–299.

Blair, Robert W. (ed.). 1982. *Innovative approaches to language teaching*. Rowley, Mass.: Newbury House.

Blumenfeld, Phyllis C. 1992. "Classroom learning and motivation: Clarifying and expanding goal theory." *Journal of Educational Psychology* 84(3): 272–281.

Burghardt, Walter J. 1992. "The Spiritual Exercises as a Foundation for Educational Ministry" in *Review for Religions* (March–April). 166–181.

Byrnes, Heidi. 1993. "Opinions". *The SLL SentineLL* 2(4): 6–12.

Cousins, Norman. 1979. *Anatomy of an Illness*. New York: Bantam.

Curran, Charles A. 1968, 1976. *Counseling and psychotherapy: The pursuit of values*. East Dubuque, Ill.: Counseling–Learning Publications.

Curran, Charles A. 1972. *Counseling–learning: A whole-person model for education*. New York: Grune and Stratton.

Curran, Charles A. 1976. *Counseling–learning in second languages*. East Dubuque, Ill.: Counseling–Learning Publications.

Curran, Charles A. 1978. *Understanding: An essential ingredient in human belonging*. East Dubuque, Ill.: Counseling–learning Publications.

Curran, Charles A. 1982a. "Community language learning." In Robert W. Blair (ed.), *Innovative approaches to language teaching*. Rowley, Mass.: Newbury House.

Curran, Charles A. 1982b. "A Linguistic model for learning and living in the new age of the person." In Robert W. Blair (ed.), *Innovative approaches to language teaching*. Rowley, Mass.: Newbury House.

Curran, Charles A. 1983. "Counseling–Learning." In John W. Oller, Jr., and Patricia A. Richard-Amato (eds.), *Methods that work: A smorgasbord of ideas for language teachers*. Rowley, Mass.: Newbury House.

Derry, Sharon J. 1992. "Beyond symbolic processing: Expanding horizons for educational psychology." *Journal of Educational Psychology* 84(4): 413–418.

Hellwig, Monika. 1991. "Finding God in all things: A spirituality for today." *Sojourners* (December). 11–16.

Horowitz, Elaine K., and Dolly J. Young (eds.). 1991. *Language anxiety: From theory and research to classroom implications*. Englewood Cliffs: Prentice Hall.

Krashen, Steve, and Tracy Terrell. 1983. *The natural approach*. Oxford: Pergamon/Alemany.

Little, Greta D., and Sara L. Sanders. 1989. "Classroom community: A prerequisite for communication." *Foreign Language Annals* 22(3): 277–281.

Long, Edward LeRoy, Jr. 1992. *Higher education as a moral enterprise*. Washington, D.C.: Georgetown University Press.

Oller, John W., and Patricia A. Richard-Amato (eds.). 1983. *Methods that work: A smorgasbord of ideas for language teachers*. Rowley, Mass.: Newbury House.

Richards, Jack C., and Theodore S. Rogers. 1986. *Approaches and methods in language teaching*. Cambridge: Cambridge University Press.

Rardin, Jennybelle P., and Daniel D. Tranel. 1988. *Education in a new dimension: The counseling-learning approach to community language learning*. East Dubuque, Ill.: Counseling-Learning Publications.

Ryding-Lentzner, Karin C. 1978. "The community-language learning approach to Arabic: Theory and application." *Al-Arabiyya* 11: 10–14.

Ryding-Lentzner, Karin C. 1979. "Community language learning." *The Linguistic Reporter* 21(6): 10–11.

Ryding, Karin C. 1990. "Review of Education in a New Dimension." *Language Learning*, 40(1): 111–116.

Samimy, Keiko Komiya. 1989. "A comparative study of teaching Japanese in the audio-lingual method and the counseling learning approach." *Modern Language Journal* 73(2): 167–76.

Shelton, Charles M., S.J. 1992. "Helping college students make moral decisions." *Conversations on Jesuit Education* 2: 6–21.

Stevick, Earl. 1973. "Review article: Counseling-learning: A whole-person model for education." *Language Learning* 23(2): 259–271.

Stevick, Earl. 1976. *Memory, meaning and method*. Rowley, Mass.: Newbury House.

Stevick, Earl. 1980. *A way and ways*. Rowley, Mass.: Newbury House.

Stevick, Earl. 1982. *Teaching and learning languages*. Cambridge: Cambridge University Press.

Stevick, Earl. 1986. *Images and options in the language classroom*. Cambridge: Cambridge University Press.

Stevick, Earl. 1990. *Humanism in language teaching*. Oxford: Oxford University Press.

Taylor, Barry. 1987. "Teaching ESL: Incorporating a communicative, student-centered component." In Michael Long and Jack C. Richards (eds.), *Methodology in TESOL*. New York: Newbury House. 45–60.

Woodman, Marion. 1993. *Conscious femininity*. Toronto: Inner City Books.

Young, Dolly Jesuita. 1991. "Creating a low-anxiety classroom environment: What does language anxiety research suggest?" *Modern Language Journal* 75(4): 426–439.

Marriage for life: Theory, research, and practice

Suzanne Flynn[1]
Massachusetts Institute of Technology

Before I begin, I would like to preface my remarks by saying that it is an honor to be a part of GURT '93. As we all know, Professor Di Pietro's contributions to the fields of language and language learning are vast. His early work in generative transformational grammar and second-language acquisition represents for me one of the earliest and best attempts at an integration of theory, research, and practice within a generative theory of language; in fact, that work served as an important source of inspiration for my own. In *Language Structures in Contrast* (1971), Professor Di Pietro accomplished something that I attempt to achieve in much of my own research and something that I will attempt to articulate here today. The field has suffered a great loss with his death.

Introduction. In the spirit of GURT '93, my paper is concerned with interactions, more precisely strategic interactions, within several familiar domains: theory, research, and practice (the Big Three). In contrast to several recent papers (Flynn 1990, 1991a, 1991b), my principal purpose today is not to argue that these three domains *must* be integrated on some way; rather, my purpose is to illustrate *how* these three domains might be integrated. Demonstrating how this might be achieved demands that we be strategic. We need, for example, to specify which theory, which research, and which practices—even more precisely, we need to specify within each of these domains exactly what might be relevant as well as specifying how any interactions among the domains might hold.

Background. Recognition of the fact that theory, research, and practice are intimately related is not new. For example, Gair (1992) notes that during World War II, the military as well as many civilians needed to be "trained effectively and in the shortest time possible in the use of a wide variety of languages, many of them 'exotic'" (1). To do this, the government sought the help of the American Council of Learned Societies, who in turn contacted the Linguistic Society of America (LSA). As a result, many neo-Bloomfieldian linguists

1. The author wishes to thank Jack Carroll, Jim Gair, and Gita Martohardjono for their comments and suggestions regarding the contents of this paper.

became involved in writing tests and developing teaching materials to teach the various languages that they were commissioned to deal with. Bloomfield himself even worked on a text for spoken Dutch as well as one on Russian.[2]

The approach to language and language learning assumed in this work became more formalized in the articulation of Contrastive Analysis (CA) first by Fries (1945) and later by Lado (1957). Within this context, language learning in general consisted of learning a fixed set of habits over time. Second language (L2) learning, in particular, involved the added component of transfer. It was argued that the L2 learner attempted to transfer the linguistic habits from the first language (L1) to the L2. Where the L1 and the L2 matched, positive transfer took place, and where they did not, negative transfer ensued; with negative transfer, the learner then had to modify the L1 habits to accommodate the L2. While this is an oversimplified account of CA, what is important in both of these examples is that linguistic theory—structuralism—as well as a theory of learning—behaviorism—were productively paired in an attempt to understand L2 learning and to develop pedagogical materials and practices.

The demise of behaviorism as an explanatory account of the language-learning process and the movement away from structuralism within linguistic theory did not immediately sound the death knell for the marriage of theory, research, and practice. The 1960s, with the advent of transformational grammar, also witnessed many attempts to apply the developing theory in language-learning situations. In this context, Robert Di Pietro's book stands out as an important exemplar.

Continued investigation along these lines resulted in the development of Creative Construction (CC) (Dulay and Burt 1974). This work built directly upon proposals made within a generative account of language, and it made one of the first attempts to link L2 acquisition with L1 acquisition in a very direct way. Specifically, CC claimed that L1 and L2 acquisition were essentially the same processes in that they were both guided by the same set of innate principles for language. Development of this work also resulted in an important linkage of theory and language practices in the work of Dulay, Burt, and Krashen (1982). Although I have suggested elsewhere (Flynn 1985) that some of the conclusions drawn were premature in the context of the existing data, this work, nonetheless, represents an important attempt to relate the Big Three.

The disillusionment, skepticism, and disregard of any possible relevant interactions between theory and research, with which I think most of us are familiar, began to emerge when it was discovered that the proposals made within early models of a generative theory of language did not have the psychological reality initially envisioned. For example, working within a transformational

2. However, as noted by Gair (1992), Bloomfield refused to have his name associated with the text on Russian. In its final form, the text appeared under the pseudonym I. M. Lesnin.

model of generative linguistics, many researchers hypothesized that the comprehension and perhaps even acquisition of sentences could be measured by the number of grammatical rules or transformations employed in a sentence's derivation. This was essentially the derivational theory of complexity (DTC); see discussion in Fodor, Bever, and Garrett (1974). After much psycholinguistic testing of the DTC, it was empirically shown that structures that involved fewer transformations were not always easier to acquire or process than those structures that involved more transformations. This finding proved crippling to many.

At the same time that the psycholinguists' hopes for establishing the "reality" of a transformational grammar of language were temporarily undermined, the theory began to evolve and change quite rapidly; in fact, this is still the case. Although the leading ideas of Chomsky's theory have remained constant throughout, the changes in detail have often proved quite frustrating for those attempting to understand the theory and make connections across the relevant domains. What has resulted, as I have discussed at length elsewhere (Flynn 1990, 1991a, 1991b), is that many language pedagogues and L2 researchers believe that linguistic theory has little or no relevance for their respective enterprises. There are also many linguists and researchers who have also traditionally shared this same belief.

Current needs and trends

Linguistic theory. Without going into great detail at this time, we need to pick up and strengthen the traditions initiated in earlier times with respect to the integration of the Big Three. We need to build upon and exploit the fact that linguistic theory aims to represent in a formal manner the structures and processes that underlie a human being's ability to acquire and use language. The grammars that linguists develop are hypotheses about the internal representation of a language in an individual's mind. A generative theory of language, specifically, the theory of Universal Grammar as developed by Chomsky (1986), provides the most promising approach in this regard for several reasons. At present, it is the most well-developed theory of language and language learning currently available.

A theory of UG also provides us with testable hypotheses that can be used to evaluate both the theory itself and the L1 and L2 language-learning processes. "The basic concern of a theory of UG is to determine and characterize the linguistic capacities of particular individuals" (Chomsky and Lasnik 1992: 1). In this context, many of the theory's leading ideas have been supported both theoretically and empirically—this is a major finding in that there is no strong a priori reason that this should be the case. I will develop some of these ideas below.

In addition, the theory allows us to develop unified theories of language acquisition in general. In terms of more specific detail, the theory views language as a function of fundamental principles and parameters.[3] The principles isolated are universally shared by all languages; they interact with a restricted set of parameters that, once set, have deductive consequences for a particular grammar. Parameters within the theory account for the variation observed among natural languages. To exemplify, languages are hierarchically organized; however, languages may differ in terms of the direction of this basic hierarchical configuration. Languages may, for example, branch to the left as in the case of Japanese or branch to the as right as in the case of English. These differences can also be accounted for in terms of a head-initial/head-final distinction.[4]

Minimally, language learning in this framework consists of establishing the parametric values for a particular target language. In the example just described, this would mean a learner would have to establish whether the ambient language branches to the right or to the left. Language learning in this context would also involve the learning of the lexicon as well as mapping the mentally represented grammar onto language-specific structures (see the discussion in Flynn and Martohardjono 1992).

Linguistic theory for L2 research and language pedagogy. Understanding the basic tenets of a theory of UG is essential for language researchers and language pedagogues. For example, the goal of L2 research is an empirical understanding of the language-learning process. This cannot be done without some hypothesis about how the mind is organized and how a grammar might be mentally represented. Current theories of UG provide us with such an initial framework for such investigation as I will develop below in more detail.

Language pedagogues on the other hand seek to develop and foster those structures and processes that enable an individual to acquire a language. In order to develop language competency, language teachers resort to methodologies that reflect some form of a theory of both language and the language-learning process. Without such theories, it would be impossible to teach in any coherent manner as there would be no basis on which to develop curriculum. This means that language teachers already operate with some theory about language and language learning. In this case, then, why not make sure that these theories are the ones that accurately characterize the language to be learned and the language-learning process itself.

In arguing that theory, research, and practice are intimately related, I am

3. What I generally outline in this paper is a *Principles and Parameters* approach to languages. The theory is in flux; a new model, *The Minimalist Program* (Chomsky 1992) is in development. Within this context, as stated elsewhere in the text, the leading ideas of the theory have not changed. The proposed changes do not radically alter the arguments developed in this paper.

4. The exact formulation of this parameter is under much theoretical consideration (see discussion in Lust 1992).

not assuming that the linguistic theory and the empirical research it drives explain all that there is to language learning, nor are all of the concerns of these enterprises necessarily relevant for our language classrooms. In order to participate effectively in a particular linguistic community, one needs more than simply a representation of UG in one's head. I do not say this in an attempt to trivialize either UG or anything else that we need to know in order to develop native proficiency in a target language. What I am suggesting, though, is that in order to determine what in the theory and in the research is relevant, we need to understand both at some level.

Gaining this understanding does not demand knowledge of every new twist and turn that either the theory or the research might take, but it does demand knowledge of some of the leading ideas in both domains as I have stated above.

In this context, I want to make it clear that I am not advocating that we *uncritically* adopt the linguists' formal models of grammars. The relationship between the formal models and the psychology of these models needs to be further verified empirically just as the relationship between formal models of logic and reasoning needs to be empirically established. In other words, I am not proposing that we become disciples who never question the theory; at the same time I am not advocating that we disregard the theory simply because it has not been fully validated. We do not want to become enslaved empiricists either. What I am seeking is a balance and a dialogue between the two enterprises.

I also want to stress that the exchange of ideas among the three domains is not a top-down process; linguists need language researchers and teachers as well. In order to develop explanatory theories of language, which by definition must account for how language learning is made possible, one must utilize the findings that emerge from both formal second-language research and language-education classrooms.

Focus of this paper. Building upon these basic ideas, my goals in this paper are twofold:

(1) Identify and explore specific areas of current linguistic theory and the associated acquisition research that could have consequences for language pedagogy.

(2) Investigate the ways insights and findings in these areas could be translated into, or extended into, practical applications in teaching/learning situations. This would involve positive applications and strategies, but it might also reveal ways current methodologies run counter to the findings of psycholinguistic research and hence might be redirected.

While there are many specific ways findings from language-teaching contexts can be used to inform both theories of language and language learning, I will not develop these in this paper at this time (see Gair 1992 and Flynn and Martohardjono 1992 for some discussion).

L2 research findings: Historical. Let us first begin with a consideration of how linguistic theory and L2 theory have been integrated while at the same time isolating ways this marriage might prove useful in terms of language pedagogy.

From the repeated successes and failures of both CA and CC, we know that:

- The learner's L1 mediates L2 acquisition in some way. This suggests that in contrast to L1 acquisition, L2 learners do not start with "clean slates."
- The errors made by the L2 learners are systematic and are random.
- In addition, many of the errors made by L2 learners replicate those made by L1 learners of the same target language.
- Not all aspects of the L2 are problematic in L2 acquisition. This, in turn, suggests that there might be a finite number of places in the grammar that cause problems, perhaps at those points that grammars allow options.
- Principles independent of the L2 learners' L1s determine the L2 acquisition process at some level. This means that in spite of the differences that might emerge between, for example, Spanish and Japanese speakers learning English as an L2, many similarities also exist between these two groups in terms of the patterns of acquisition and the nature of the errors these learners make.
- L2 learners' hypotheses, like L1 learners', are structure dependent. For example, learners do not form questions like, "Is the man who eating is my father?" on an analogy with such questions as "Is the boy eating?" (see discussion in Zobl 1983, Jenkins 1987, Epstein, Flynn, and Martohardjono 1993). If L2 learners had access only to such things as structure-independent rules, we would expect them to consult only such things as linear orderings in a string of words.

How can we reconcile these seemingly disparate sets of facts within one principled framework? I argue that a theory of UG provides one way we can begin to account for both the contrastive and constructive aspects of the L2 acquisition process outlined above. By capitalizing on the major components of UG, viz., principles and parameters, we can begin to formulate empirical hypotheses about L2 acquisition.

Principles allow us to account for the observed invariance in patterns of acquisition across language groups as well as to account for the close alliance of the L2 acquisition process to the L1 acquisition process. Parameters allow us to account for the variation in patterns among different L1 groups learning a common L2 as well as to account for some of the differences that emerge between L1 and L2 acquisition. L1 acquisition involves parameter setting, and L2 acquisition involves parameter resetting or assignment of new parameter values to existing ones when necessary. These are two related but distinct processes.

To briefly summarize, this UG model for L2 acquisition suggests that at the very least, L2 learners must assign new parameter settings when there is a mismatch between the L1 and the L2, and they must acquire a new lexicon as well as map the internally represented grammar onto language-specific structures.

L2 research findings within a UG framework. In this small but growing field of UG-based L2 research, some very promising and suggestive findings have emerged. While I will not develop these results in great detail, I will highlight some of the most salient findings.

Research from work such as that exemplified in Ritchie (1978), Felix (1988), White (1993), Martohardjono and Gair (1993), and Martohardjono (1993) indicate that L2 learners perform significantly above chance in recognizing violations of UG principles in their target L2s. The principles tested in these studies are abstract and not directly observable in the speech stream, nor is there evidence from the learner's L1 for these principles. For example, Ritchie tested Japanese speakers on their knowledge of the Right Roof Constraint in English, in which extraposition to the right is blocked. The Japanese learners correctly recognized the violations in English even though such constraints were not operable in Japanese, their L1. Similarly, the work of Martohardjono has clearly demonstrated that speakers of L1s that do not instantiate wh-movement at s-structure are able to identify violations of movement in English, their second language (Martohardjono 1993).

Other work has demonstrated that even when a reliance on the L1, viz., transfer, could in fact provide the right solution for an L2 learner, it does not occur. Instead, research indicates that the L2 learner relies on more abstract principles in the construction of the L2 grammar. For example, Flynn (1992) reports that there are certain structures in both English and Japanese that match in terms of their surface-structure manifestations. If L2 learners were relying on strategies that involved transfer from the surface structure of the L1, then those structures that match in both the L1 and the L2 should be very accessible to the learner. However, this is not the case. Japanese speakers do not find those sentence structures in English that instantiate a left-branching structure, for example, easier to acquire than right-branching structures in English. In fact, the left-branching structures are extremely difficult for the learners in that they are in disaccord with the grammar of the new target language.

In another related example, Spanish speakers have available to them both tensed *that* clauses as in "I reminded the man that he had my key" as well as sentences that involve infinitive clauses such as "I reminded the man to go." However, research findings in Flynn, Foley, and Lardiere (1991) indicate that when Spanish speakers are tested in their elicited imitation of both types of structures in English, they find the sentence structures containing infinitive clauses significantly easier to imitate than those containing the tensed *that* clauses. This is true even when the sentence structures are equated in terms of length. This result also matches that for L1 acquisition of English (Cohen 1983) and has been argued to follow from a principle of UG. Taken together, these results are important in that they indicate that L2 learners do not simply transfer surface-structure properties between the L1 and the L2. These findings instead suggest that L2 learners, like L1 learners, have access to abstract linguistic principles such as those that follow from a theory of UG and that they use them in the construction of the new target grammar.

Research has also suggested that one way that we can account for the role of the L1 in L2 acquisition suggested by CA is via parameters. Where parametric values between the L1 and the L2 match, acquisition is enhanced in comparison to the case in which parametric values do not. This has emerged most saliently in studies investigating the acquisition of head-initial languages by head-final L1 speakers (Flynn 1987). Speakers of Spanish, a head-initial language, acquiring English, also a head-initial language, have much less difficulty with complex sentence structures in English that instantiate head-initiality than their head-final Chinese or Japanese counterparts learning English. Moreover, an examination of the nature of the errors made by the Chinese and Japanese speakers indicates that the principal locus of the errors is at points where the structures tested manifest rightwards directionality. This result is interesting in that it isolates the role of parameters in L2 acquisition while at the same time specifying one way we can account for the role of the L1 in a principled manner without resorting to a surface structure contrastive analysis approach.

The results of this program of research have also indicated, as noted by Gair (1992), that the same effects in L2 performance can have very different causes. In an L2 study on restrictive relative clauses with Spanish, Japanese, and Chinese speakers learning English as a second language, results indicated not surprisingly that the Spanish speakers outperformed the Japanese and Chinese speakers due in large part to the shared head-direction parameter setting between Spanish and English. What *was* surprising in the results, however, was the fact that the Japanese speakers and not the Chinese speakers performed very poorly on sentences that involved a gap in object position in the relative clause; for example, they performed significantly worse on sentences such as "The woman that Mary saw" than on sentences such as "The woman that saw Mary."

The explanation proposed for these results relates to the UG claim that relative clauses contain an empty category, namely a variable that must be interpreted in relation to the head noun phrase. In brief, the argument is that there are certain linguistic requirements on the occurrence of null categories of that type. These requirements cannot be met in Japanese for a structural position to the right of a verb, as English requires for the object position. However, this is not the case for Chinese, which does allow such elements in the object position. Thus, what the Japanese speaker must learn is the permissibility of a null element in a specific position in accord with a parameter setting of English, even though elements of that type occur in Japanese relative clauses as well, as the two languages match on the occurrence of such elements in subject position (see Gair, Flynn, and Brown 1992). In another study, Martohardjono and Gair (1993) isolated a related result with Indonesian speakers learning English. The importance of these two examples is the demonstration that similar deficiencies in L2 learning may have different causes, mediated by different UG-related characteristics of the L1; a conclusion that we could not reach if we relied on an analysis of surface structure facts alone derived by simple contrastive analysis.

Relevance for language pedagogy. The outline of a general program of application for some of the relevant results of a UG-based approach to L2 learning is given in Flynn (1990, 1991b). Here I will summarize some of these suggestions as well as build upon them.

Recall that within a theory of UG, language learning consists of establishing the right parameter settings for the target language and the learning of the lexicon. This does not mean that this is all that is involved in becoming a native or native-like speaker of a particular language; it does, however, specify minimally what one must "know" in terms of a basic linguistic competence. Without this base, it would be impossible for a language learner to proceed much beyond a memorized list of common expressions and one-word utterances as a form of communication in a new language.

Above I have outlined a few general ways researchers have been able to document the role of UG in adult L2 learning. To review, the results suggest that L2 learners have knowledge of certain hypothesized abstract principles of UG as well as a knowledge of parameters and the ability to assign new values to these parameters when necessary. Parameters also allow us to account for some of the difficulty encountered by learners in L2 acquisition by appealing to differences in parameter settings between the L1 and the L2. It also allows us to account for the apparent ease of acquisition of certain languages by L1 speakers when there are parametric matches between the L1 and the L2.

Thus, as a minimal program these results are relevant for language teaching in that they tell us *precisely* what kind of linguistic knowledge is available to the adult learner as well as specifying how this core language learning takes place. The results indicate that there are certain kinds of facts and information that we never have to teach our learners, for example, structure dependence, or the abstract constraints that hold on the licensing of certain null elements in sentence structures. The results also tell us that some learners will have to assign new parameter settings where there is a mismatch between the L1 and the L2. And we also know that all learners will have to learn a new lexicon along with the associated properties in these lexical entries.

More specifically, these results are important for language pedagogy in at least three ways: with respect to the nature of (1) the input provided to the language learners, (2) the development of the curriculum, and (3) testing and placement procedures.

With respect to the input, at the most general level, the results indicate that as for L1 acquisition, the learning environment must be rich enough to provide the input necessary for the learner to deduce the right properties of the target language—most importantly parametric settings. While this might seem to be something that we already know, it is not immediately apparent what this actually means. Ideally, we want to simulate in our classrooms as much of a one-to-one learning situation as possible. Students need to hear directed, natural speech, and lots of it. Such a conclusion is especially important in the context of our continued development of computer-aided instructional materials. It seems clear that the UG-based research confirms the fact that learners need natural speech; reliance on, for example, interactive video technology alone to teach a new target language might yield results similar to those achieved with teaching L2s via the television in the early 1960s. This is not to say that the new technologies cannot be useful tools; rather, we need to be strategic about what types of programs we develop with respect to what we know will be most amenable in language acquisition to such methods. The results of the UG-based research program are important in helping us to isolate exactly what can be enhanced in this way.

Another very concrete way that we might reasonably be able to contribute to the language-learning process is to strengthen the process of parameter setting. This should be based on a clear understanding of the parameters concerned and their relation to typological differences between the L1 and the L2. For example, the head-direction parameter provides a tractable property of language that will vary across languages and that will have deductive consequences for grammar construction of a particular target language. One could provide input rich with the ways this parameter is instantiated in the various structures in a target language.

Other examples of parameters that could be subject to such intervention include the fractionalization of the functional category IP (Inflectional Phrase) into Agr (agreement) and/or Tns (tense), or verb raising/lowering and the resultant consequences in terms of such things as adverb placement (Pollock 1989).

With respect to the lexicon, Cook (1991) emphasizes the teaching of vocabulary. In this regard, one wants to specify how particular lexical items can occur in grammatical structures and include a specification of the precise nature of the subcategorization requirements of each item. In this context, it would also be useful to include the features indicated in theta theory such as the semantic-syntactic relations of agent, theme, and experiencer, etc., connected with each lexical item, which in turn partially determines syntactic structure. In this regard, we want to bear in mind the fact that when we are dealing with language groups that are related in some way, e.g. Spanish speakers learning English, we cannot be lulled into thinking that our task is not as great as when we are dealing with language combinations that are not related in this way, e.g. Japanese speakers learning English. Results of empirical study (Flynn 1987) with Japanese and Spanish speakers learning English indicate that the Spanish speakers and not the Japanese speakers make the most errors lexically in their acquisition of English. This finding suggests that a shared family membership does not guarantee ease in acquisition of the target language. In fact, in some ways it might prove to be a hindrance.

With respect to the curriculum, there are a number of ways to design materials so as to deal with the problems directly or indirectly revealed by the UG-based research. These results prove especially relevant in terms of the ordering of the presentation of materials. Traditional orderings of material have followed a sequencing that more closely approximates what a traditional Derivational Theory of Complexity aspired to rather than reflecting what it is in language that must be learned and how it is learned. Most curricula rely on a basic linear model that proceeds from the development of simple utterances (e.g. simple declaratives) to more complex ones. However, such an ordering may in fact reflect the development of performance rather than the development of grammar. I think that I am not stepping too far out of line by suggesting that most language learning that takes place in many classrooms occurs in *spite* of the class. In large part, this is due to the fact that the development of the materials has little or nothing to do with how language learning is in fact occurring. For example, deductive consequences associated with particular parameter settings allow us to consider approaching an exposition of the parameter in some way that would facilitate acquiring the rest of the constellation of features hypothesized to follow from a particular setting.

With respect to testing, the UG-based research incorporates a precise testing of specific features related to the theory that are likely to be overlooked in defining L2 competence when we rely upon available standardized testing instruments. The grammatical aspects that we need to test are in fact just those abstract UG-related features that the theory allows us to identify and that are the objects of investigation in the L2 research described above. Particularly important in this regard is the gap between the results of standardized tests used in grouping the test populations and the results of the research. This is clearly shown by the differences correlated with the L1 *within* groups defined as low, intermediate, and advanced by the standardized tests and the results of these same speakers on the target linguistic structures associated with an empirical test of UG-sanctioned structures. As suggested above, results of currently available standardized tests often place students at the same level. A reasonable assumption to make with such results is that speakers at the same level should perform equivalently on all other dependent linguistic measures. However, the results summarized in Flynn (1987) indicate that this is not the case. Spanish and Japanese speakers at the same level of ESL competence as measured by the Michigan Placement Test perform significantly differently on all other dependent syntactic measures. This result suggests that these standardized tests do not evaluate the critical structures needed to precisely determine the level of competence of each speaker in the target language. The results of the UG-based research provide more precise ways we can accurately measure the L2 competence of our learners.

Conclusions. To conclude, it is clear that our understanding of both the first (L1) and second (L2) acquisition process in terms of an increasingly relevant linguistic theory has implications for L2 pedagogy. This focus is independent of the rapidly changing nature of the fields concerned. At the same time, it is clear that insights derived from language teaching experience have implications for both theories of language and language learning. Given this context, we need to continue to systematically examine how developments in each of these areas interact to inform a comprehensive account of the L2 acquisition process.

Results of the UG-based research can be incorporated into all aspects of the L2 curriculum. What I am proposing is not a discrete point approach to language teaching. Rather, I am advocating that the results of the UG paradigm provide insights that can be incorporated into any language methodology, even in the development of a communicative approach. UG-based research goes a long way in specifying for us *precisely* what must be learned in the course of acquisition and what will be problematic. The examples isolated in this paper would not have emerged without the context of a UG-based research paradigm. Traditional approaches to the language-learning process have simply failed to provide us with the insights needed to develop explanatory theories of language and subsequent language pedagogies.

Continued progress in each of the domains of theory, research, and practice demands an even greater integration of the results from all three.

REFERENCES

Chomsky, Noam. 1992. *A minimalist program for linguistic theory*. MS. Cambridge, Mass.: Massachusetts Institute of Technology.

Chomsky, Noam. 1986. *Barriers*. Cambridge: MIT Press.

Chomsky, Noam, and Howard Lasnik. 1992. "Linguistic theory." MS. Cambridge, Mass.: Massachusetts Institute of Technology.

Cohen-Sherman, J. 1983. "The acquisition of control in complex sentences: The role of structural and lexical factors." Ph.D. dissertation, Cornell University.

Cook, Vivian. 1991. *Second language learning and language teaching*. London: Edward Arnold.

de Bot, Kees, Ralph Ginsberg, and Claire Kramsch. 1991. *Foreign language research in cross-cultural perspective*. Amsterdam: John Benjamins.

Di Pietro, Robert. 1971. *Language structures in contrast*. Rowley, Mass.: Newbury House Publishers.

Dulay, Heidi, and Marina Burt. 1974. "Natural sequences in child second language acquisition." *Language Learning* 24: 37–53.

Dulay, Heidi, Marina Burt, and Stephen Krashen. 1982. *Language 2*. London: Oxford University Press.

Epstein, Samuel, Suzanne Flynn, and Gita Martohardjono. 1993. "The continuous access hypothesis: Some evidence from functional categories in adult L2 acquisition." MS. Cambridge, Mass.: Harvard University and Massachusetts Institute of Technology.

Felix, Sascha. 1988. "UG-generated knowledge in adult second language acquisition." In Suzanne Flynn and Wayne O'Neil (eds.), *Linguistic theory in second language acquisition*. Dordrecht: Reidel Press.

Flynn, Suzanne. 1991a. "Linguistic theory and foreign language learning environments." In Kees de Bot, Ralph Ginsberg, and Claire Kramsch (eds.), *Foreign language research in cross-cultural perspective*. Amsterdam: John Benjamins.

Flynn, Suzanne. 1991b. "The relevance of linguistic theory to language pedagogy: Debunking the myths." In James E. Alatis (ed.), *Georgetown University Round Table on Languages and Linguistics 1991*. Washington, D.C.: Georgetown University Press. 547–554.

Flynn, Suzanne. 1990. "Theory, practice, and research: Strange or blissful bedfellows?" In James E. Alatis (ed.), *Georgetown University Round Table on Languages and Linguistics 1990*. Washington, D.C.: Georgetown University Press. 112–122.

Flynn, Suzanne. 1987. *A parameter-setting model of L2 acquisition: Experimental studies in anaphora*. Dordrecht: Reidel Press.

Flynn, Suzanne. 1985. "Principled theories of L2 acquisition." *Studies in Second Language Acquisition* 7: 99–108.

Flynn, Suzanne, Claire Foley, and Donna Lardiere. 1991. "Who's in control? Adult L2 acquisition of control structures." Paper presented at the Second Language Research Forum, University of Southern California, Los Angeles.

Flynn, Suzanne, and Sharon Manuel. 1991. "Age-dependent effects in language acquisition: An evaluation of "critical period" hypotheses." In Lynn Eubank (ed.), *Point counterpoint universal grammar in the second language*. Amsterdam: John Benjamins. 117–146

Flynn, Suzanne, and Wayne O'Neil. 1988. *Linguistic theory in second language acquisition*. Dordrecht: Reidel Press.

Flynn, Suzanne, and Gita Martohardjono. 1992. "Mapping from the universal to the final state: The separation of universal principles and language specific properties." Paper presented at the symposium on syntactic theory and first language acquisition: Crosslinguistic perspectives, April, Cornell University.

Fodor, Jerry, Thomas Bever, and Merrill Garrett. 1974. *The psychology of language*. New York: McGraw Hill.

Fries, Charles. 1945. *Teaching and learning English as a foreign language.* Ann Arbor, Mich.: University of Michigan Press.

Gair, James. 1992. "Linguistics, L2 acquisition research and pedagogical applications: Restoring the link." Paper presented at SALA XIV, Stanford University, May 23, 1992.

Gair, James, Suzanne Flynn, and Olga Brown. Forthcoming. "Why Japanese object to L2 objects." MS. Cambridge, Mass., and Ithaca, N.Y.: Massachusetts Institute of Technology and Cornell University.

Jenkins, Lyle. 1988. "Second language acquisition: A biolinguistic perspective." In Suzanne Flynn and Wayne O'Neil (eds.), *Linguistic theory in second language acquisition.* Dordrecht, Boston: Kluwer Academic Publishers.

Lust, Barbara. 1992. "Functional projection of CP and phrase structure parameterization: An argument for the "strong continuity hypothesis." Paper presented at the symposium on syntactic theory and first language acquisition: Crosslinguistic perspectives, April, Cornell University.

Martohardjono, Gita. 1993. *Wh-movement in the acquisition of a second language: A cross-linguistic study of three languages with and without overt movement.* Unpublished Ph.D. dissertation, Cornell University.

Martohardjono, Gita, and James Gair. 1993. "Apparent UG inaccessibility in second language acquisition: Misapplied principles or principled misapplications." In Fred R. Eckman (ed.), *Confluence: Linguistics, L2 acquisition, and speech pathology.* Amsterdam: John Benjamins.

Pollock, Jean. 1989. "Verb movement, UG, and the structure of IP." *Linguistic Inquiry* 20: 365–424.

Ritchie, William. 1978. "The right roof constraint in adult-acquired language." In William Ritchie, (ed.), *Second language acquisition research.* New York: Academic Press.

Ritchie, William ed. 1978. *Second language acquisition research.* New York: Academic Press.

White, Lydia. 1989. *Universal grammar and second language acquisition.* Amsterdam: John Benjamins.

White, Lydia. 1993. "UG effects in foreign language learners." Paper presented at workshop on recent advances in generative approaches to second language acquisition. January, MIT.

Zobel, Helmut. 1983. "Markedness and the projection problem." *Language Learning* 33: 293–313.

Strategic Interaction: Issues and application to second-language teaching and acquisition

Elahé Mir-Djalali
University of California at Berkeley

Introduction. Recent studies in the field of language teaching and acquisition suggest the importance of a communicative method and the benefits of meaningful language use for the improvement of learners' performance in the target language and culture. Second-language teachers around the world recognize the need to replace static drills and grammar lessons with spontaneous language use and students' creativity in their classrooms.

In the literature, probably one of the best-known studies of the theory and practice of communicative competence has been provided by Sandra J. Savignon (1972, 1983). Dell Hymes coined the expression "communicative competence" in 1971 to mean the knowledge of sociolinguistic rules combined with grammatical rules to produce appropriate utterances. The phrase has since been widely used, though with a somewhat different definition each time.

A Chomskyan would use "communicative performance" when speaking about the learner's ability to communicate; considering Chomsky's (1965) generally accepted competence/performance distinction, the expression seems more appropriate for referring to students' linguistic performance. Needless to say, the Chomskyan concepts of competence and performance have also been questioned; see in Hymes (1971) the environmental reality of *speech act* redefining competence to include ability for use; and see in Halliday (1970) the concept of functions of language and his argument against the need for this distinction. Savignon points out that both of these were influenced by the theories advanced by Malinowsky (1923, 1935) and Firth (1930, 1937).

The competence/performance issue is one of many in which theory, interpretation, and terminology are disputed. A full discussion about selection and interpretation of different expressions used in our profession is beyond the scope of this paper. What needs to be mentioned is that no matter what terminology is used or what theoretical analysis is made, most second-language teachers are rightly concerned with finding a creative approach to meeting specific requirements of their language instruction.

Objectives are rapidly changing in second-language learning. The goal is no longer a mere fulfillment of school requirements aimed at the intellectual development of individuals, much less the earlier aim of reading old texts and literary works. In these times of rapid global social, political, and economic change, the need for effective communication is very real, and second-language learning remains one of the most important elements of the change.

However, second-language instruction continues to be under the influence of a variety of sociopolitical and economic factors. In addition, the teachers' resistance to abandoning a well-rehearsed teaching practice for an experimental new approach slows down the process of adequately adapted change. Thus, a combination of an audiolingual approach with some role play, and an appearance of interaction with a mixture of instructional tools and materials chosen at random by the teacher, are being used in the most commonly taught languages. As far as the teaching of Persian in the United States is concerned, even less has been accomplished. Some of the programs are considered advanced simply because they no longer use a pure grammar/translation approach.

In most cases, the focus still remains on the formal language instruction as opposed to the students' communicative needs. What we need is a coherently integrated curriculum adaptable to considerations of age, competency level, and cultural awareness of the students, and an approach that is responsive to a variety of learning and teaching styles.

Strategic Interaction. Because language is a social institution used as a tool to communicate with others, its interactive aspect in the dynamics of situations is undeniable. Here, by "communication" I mean "to understand and be understood by native speakers of target languages at a comfortable level that dissipates the inhibiting linguistic barriers." I will not get into the philosophical discussion of what true understanding and communication really means.

At this level, which addresses the more superficial aspect of communication, let us consider the work of Plato as reported by T.J. Saunders (1987: 35, 36): Plato wrote his famous dialogues maintaining that philosophy, as a human activity, is best learned through an exchange of ideas, within the context of rational conversation; "The dialogues always promote Platonic doctrines, but they never *order* one what to think." One step further leads us to the value of a teaching approach that uses the interactional aspect of languages apart from static books and written dialogues.

Language learning as a human activity needs to be interactive, involving the give and take of natural discussions and positioning the learner in a communicative mode that will create the energy and enthusiasm necessary to generate interactive sentences. The focus should be directed toward solving a communication problem, rather than toward conscious classroom performance. The more prescriptive approaches are to be replaced by the dynamic of newly generated material at each interaction. Allwright (1984) argues that the classroom thus generates its own educational materials, and teachers and learners are not only practitioners but also experimenters in the classroom.

Strategic Interaction addresses the language teaching and acquisition process through real-life situations that allow the development of interaction skills. SI is an effective way to achieve and maintain a near-natural linguistic environment in the classroom because it is structured without being dominating, it is open-ended without being haphazard and disorganized, and it addresses all skills at a comfortable level for the learner without being prescriptive. Learning and teaching are both interactive and closely related to the performance level of learners and their linguistic needs, requirements, interests, and goals. I will further expand on these points in the following sections. The outline below of different phases of the SI approach demonstrates the structure of class activities, group management, and learners' participation.

Structure of the SI approach. The SI approach consists of six elements. These are teacher's tasks, the four phases of the interaction itself (rehearsal, performance, debriefing, reinforcement), and students' tasks in the evaluation process.

Teacher's Tasks.

- Review coverage of the subject in textbook and other related materials.
- Review proposed scenarios and prepare others related to the subject.
- Prepare to play several types of interaction roles in the classroom.
- Consider the outline of the grammar that might be used through these interactions.
- Find reading selections that are related to the domain of the key concept under study.
- Prepare some questions derived from the scenarios for writing exercises.
- Prepare to present a model from the students' performance to be used for the evaluation task.
- Prepare to involve students in the evaluation process.

Phase One: Rehearsal. This activity might well take one class session (approximately 45 minutes).

- The students are divided into two or three working groups, according to the task.
- The teacher distributes a scenario role to each group.
- Students are given time to discuss the scenario within each group.
- Students decide on a course of action to accomplish the task or resolve

the problem at hand.

- Students make interaction plans.
- Each group plans several alternative interactions.
- Based on those plans, students ask for additional vocabulary and verify useful grammar points and other cultural issues, according to their needs.

The group work helps dissipate classroom pressures and will encourage most students to participate with others, even if it is by listening only.

Phase Two: Performance. In Phase Two, the class works together in solving the conflict at hand.

- When the students have rehearsed sufficiently, a representative is chosen from each group to enact the scenario role.
- Other students are on stand-by in the group and can make suggestions and come up with helpful expressions as needed by their representative.
- Students are physically grouped together and are involved in listening and participating.
- Depending on availability, the performance may be recorded using audio or video equipment.
- In order to encourage participation from less-forthcoming students, the teacher may ask for suggestions and variations at the final stages of the interaction.

This phase is to be kept as much as possible a group-supported activity.

Phase Three: Debriefing. In Phase Three, the teacher takes a more active role. The discourse used during the interaction will serve as the basis of discussion about important elements of form, grammar, and culture. The students are free to ask any questions they want. An effective way to start the debriefing would be to ask WH-questions about the expressions used, different sounds, different students' ideas, other difficulties, and other ways to convey the same ideas.

- Using schemata to illustrate comments and observations, the teacher will present a model of what was enacted in the interaction.
- Brief grammatical explanations are provided to clarify mistakes of form and structure.
- Phonological corrections are made as necessary by reviewing what was said during the performance.

The audio or video recording could be very helpful in this phase. To facilitate the work of the debriefing, the teacher may want to ask the students to take notes about the major points discussed.

During my work on the research and development project "Learning Persian Language and Culture" (1992), a few adjustments were made to Di Pietro's (1987b) position in *Strategic Interaction: Learning Languages Through Scenarios*. Phase Four: Reinforcement was added to more formally address the reading and writing activities as an extension of class interaction toward reinforcement of those skills. Also, a short list of cultural lexicon, distributed to students with the scenarios, would be helpful to facilitate the *rehearsal* phase and the understanding of basic cultural issues raised in the scenario. Di Pietro's reluctance to prescribe one had been driven by his objection to simply giving students lists to memorize. However, some cultural concepts need to be discussed and described while acting upon them in class. Often there is not a direct entry for those expressions in dictionaries and the students' task-oriented activity is enhanced by simply providing those to them.

Phase Four: Reinforcement

- A relevant reading assignment is provided.
- Related writing activities are done first on an individual basis and then by each group.

From individual creativity the students will move toward collective work of communication with their peers. The classroom experience will provide a common ground for this writing, and the reading should reinforce the experience; the writing is thus a more real-life activity. The style of learning is not dictated, but the task to perform is indicated and the learning style remains up to the ability of the students under the teachers' supervision.

Students' Tasks in the Evaluation Process. Each student is best prepared to answer for him- or herself the following questions. Other students as observers may use good judgment about originality and intelligibility of the interaction.

- Could I have used more of my vocabulary?
- Could I have requested more help from the teacher?
- Was I able to convey what I needed?
- Could other students help more effectively?

The above phases and activities demonstrate the pragmatics of this interactive approach. I have also included here some tentative suggestions about testing, evaluation, linguistic elements, and interaction elements.

Linguistic Elements.

- Pronunciation
- Vocabulary
- Grammar structure
- Comprehension

Interaction elements.

- Skill at turn-taking
- Skill at interrupting for asking questions
- Skill at using the language interactively
- Cultural appropriateness

Evaluation in interactive classroom. The most important principle in testing is that it is done in a coherent situation and within the right context. The student must be aware of the nature of the discourse, the task to be accomplished, and/or the problem to be resolved. Individual records should be kept on each student's performance in all skills.

After the scenario has been performed in the classroom, the teacher looks for points of interaction development and will come up with a dialogue of what was said during the interaction. This will give the students a model to practice with and ask relevant alternative questions. This is also the model on which students can be tested.

The testing of all linguistic elements relating to the use of the language must be done within the student's ability to approach the resolution of the task. The format of the test is primarily oral with reading and writing adjuncts. After the test, the teacher should sit with the students and see if they can evaluate their own work. The test should take only 10 minutes per student to administer, and 5 minutes for the teacher to score.

Issues.

Strategic Interaction is not only an oral approach. This misconception is understandable because of the emphasis placed on situational interaction with scenarios. However, it is easy to dispel that misunderstanding and to see how the SI approach is designed to include and facilitate the development of all other linguistic skills, as well. The pedagogical value of this approach is that it promotes a real-life situation and provides a near-natural context for the introduction of all linguistic skills, which develop out of actual interaction and are addressed through the need for communication within the second language. As we have just seen, the classroom use of interaction involves several phases during which all linguistic skills are addressed based on the requirements of the

Table 1. Tentative score sheet from global skills to detail skills

Global Skill		
Communicative performance, moves made to complete interactive tasks		30
Cultural constraints: gestures and honorifics		20
Discourse coherence		20
Grammatical accuracy		10
Choice of lexicon		10
Pronunciation based on intelligibility in context		10
Detail Skill	Total points:	100

specific phase as well as the learners' ability.

The open-ended feature of scenario interaction and the conversational aspect of different phases are the most innovative steps in this approach; thus, the emphasis has been placed on the oral aspects of interaction, discourse, and real-life roles in Di Pietro's own writing. But, as he noted (1987b: 14, 15), by engaging the students in dialogues, the teacher helps achieve a balance of all three regulatory forces of the Vygotskyan model of learning: *the object* (forms and structure of the target language), *the other* (teacher and others in the class), and *the self* (each learner's own linguistic competence and background).

Di Pietro further notes that while Krashen (1982) advises teachers to strive for meaning first, with structure to be acquired later, he himself suggests that in the context of strategic interactions, one should strive for interaction first, then meaning, and finally structure. Toward this end, Di Pietro enumerates the seven tasks for the teacher: the way to use textbooks and coverage, subject matter, reading selections, writing exercises, grammar logs, and evaluation. Thus, although the available literature on SI puts more emphasis on the oral aspect of communication and the scenario interaction in language learning, the SI does not stop at that. Rather, it provides the ground for the students' tailored needs and interests to be addressed and allows for all styles of learning, contextualized grammar, reading, and writing instruction to take place in a way that completes the process of language teaching and acquisition most effectively. Note that Di Pietro (1987b: 109, 110) also offers suggestions and guidelines for the teaching of literature through Strategic Interaction.

The role of the teacher. The next most important issue is the role of the teacher—classroom management—and the kind of adjustments that need to be made in order to successfully work with SI to the benefit of the students. It is no longer sufficient to choose a good textbook and teach it cover to cover. More is required from the teacher than a certain reassurance that comes with the word *coverage,* when all verb tenses, vocabulary lists, or pronouns in a given language are covered. Using SI requires the teacher to learn how to design interactive curricula, write effective and related scenarios, divide students into groups, and lead the class toward the dynamics of interaction. It also requires the teacher to switch from a role as *know-it-all* instructor with his or her own agenda to fulfill to a role as a guide, a counselor, and a coach who will help learners achieve a goal, a purpose, and the resolution of a question or a communication problem. Di Pietro (1987b: 87) says, "The good teacher is expected to perceive students' difficulties as well as know enough about the cause of these difficulties to give the needed help." Perceiving students' difficulties does not make the teacher a flawless omniscient individual; rather, the issue is the teacher's sensitivity to the needs of the learner more than the teacher's own performance in the target language. Di Pietro further indicates (1987: 92) that "no one, even the so-called native speaker, can know everything about a language," and he suggests that because some questions are harder to answer than others, students can write them down on slips of paper, to be collected at the end of the class session, and be reassured that those questions also will be answered.

Strategic Interaction allows the full range of teacher skills to be used in the classroom. At the same time, the students take the initiative for learning because they must accomplish the tasks before them. The teacher changes, in their eyes, from someone to satisfy to someone who helps them satisfy themselves. Groups have a healthy effect on their individual members because they tend to encourage weaker members through their sharing of the task. The teacher should observe the students as they work in groups; if a student does not cooperate, he or she should be assigned to a new group with other students who did not seem to be cooperating in their original groups. In this way, they will have to motivate each other in order to complete the task the teacher gives them. Working with scenarios, the teacher dictates the task but not the way to achieve it. The SI teacher is involved in an interactive role with the learner, whose communicative needs are generated by the interaction and its requirements, whether those are vocabulary, grammar points, or cultural issues.

Culturally sensitive approach. Culture becomes one of the most effective catalysts for writing successful scenarios since it can be used as the *unshared* or private information part of any scenario. As emphasized by those who have opposed the Chomskyan view of language as a finite set of *formal* or grammatical rules, social and cultural constraints and functions are crucial in language. And, since a successful scenario is one that generates a situation as close as possible to real life, cultural points are the most effective way to address those requirements while writing scenarios. Thus, many cultural issues such as age hierarchy, family relationships, and concepts of time, place, and social practices will become a fact of life for the language learner. Cultural points of historical or religious value can serve most effectively to generate the dynamics of a near real-life situation as they encourage learners to position themselves in an unfamiliar situation and naturally to make the best of it.

Each point of culture within the target language can be referred to as a communication problem on which there is not an automatic consensus; this perspective serves as the unshared part of the scenario and a question to be solved by the learner. A specific issue of cultural difference is first described by the teacher, then addressed by the learners as a task to be completed. The scenario is built around the cultural point, and the class and the teacher explore the possibilities generated in that setting as a way to solve the communication problem.

This brings us to the next point, which is a brief discussion of the scenario and its advantages over other similar classroom activities. Two units presented here from the curriculum prepared for intermediate Persian classes involve cultural issues and will illustrate this use of the scenario.

Scenario. This expression was coined by Di Pietro to label a particular kind of classroom activity that he calls *interlocked tasks.* There are usually two interconnected tasks that form the core of the scenario. Two tasks are interlocked if the function of one depends on the resolution of the other, e.g. a taxi driver and a passenger, a car owner and a tow-truck operator, a tenant's demands for repair and a landlord's prospect of getting higher rent from another party, and so on. The question is how each individual chooses to accomplish the tasks. This entails the genuine involvement of the learner and provides what is called the open-ended character of the scenario.

The main characteristics that separate the scenario from other similar classroom activities such as role-play, simulation, and sociodrama are the following:

- The scenario requires a group of people to interact as themselves, and there are no model utterances prescribed for the task at hand.
- Free thinking by the participants is required in a scenario interaction, as opposed to specific positions to be taken by individuals as indicated on a role card in simulation.
- Students have free choice; unlike role-plays and simulations, the scenario is open-ended, and no definite solutions are set for the participants. Only alternatives and possibilities are discussed, not a specific course of action.

- Uninhibited by bias, the participants are free to feel and express their own opinions and are not limited to a predetermined way to feel about the task or the other participants.

Benefit of group work. Most teachers at some time become frustrated with the dilemma of trying to reach every student in the class while not ignoring the needs of all the others. The traditional solution has been to work one-on-one with each student, hoping to give each equal time to perform or recite. A more recent idea is to allow a silent phase (Krashen and Terrell 1983) in which all the students are allowed to listen without giving any demonstrable feedback to the teacher. In such an approach, the students speak when they feel sufficient confidence to do so. In both cases, the teacher's main contribution of imparting knowledge of the subject matter as well as instructional skills—analytical and applicational—is significantly reduced.

Scenarios, on the other hand, allow the teacher to provide direction and intervention right from the start of instruction without losing the benefits of any silent phase being undergone by individual learners. The teacher can break up the class into small, effective working groups to which she or he may act as a consultant, provider of information, and general guide as needed by each group. Members of the groups also help instruct each other as they acquire different elements of the target language and share their acquired knowledge as needed by others in their groups.

Since the flow of knowledge must eventually be to the individual learner, each group is given a task that represents the group as if it were one individual. Once the group has worked out a number of possible avenues to explore in completing the task, a representative of the group is chosen to interact with a representative of a different group that also has a task to accomplish. As the two representatives interact, they may turn to their groups for help or advice at any time. In this way, the individual receives knowledge that is immediately applicational and functional. This feature of scenario work does away with the traditional methods of instruction that attempt to follow a general regimen of grammar that is supposedly suitable to the entire class.

Description of the phases. The two interlocked roles in scenarios with somewhat opposing agendas generate the dynamics of a purposeful use of the target language as each group tries to achieve its own task or game plan. The goal in the *rehearsal* phase is to understand the task outlined by the scenario, presented in writing; to think and discuss as a group ways to deal with the proposed situation, using the target language with allowances to use the common language as well; and to rehearse in the target language once alternatives are chosen and developed. As learners discuss with each other, they can use dictionaries, take notes, and ask each other and the teacher questions about vocabulary, grammar, cultural points, and protocols in order to prepare for the next phase of the interaction.

The second phase, *performance,* is carried out by individual learners representing their group. The representatives facing each other and backed by the other members of their groups will enact the scenario role based on their choice of the plan of action. The teacher will ensure that each group is actively listening and helping their representatives to achieve the task. The performing students are free to interrupt their interaction for a consultation with their own rehearsal group. During this phase, which could also be recorded, the teacher takes notes and records errors of style, grammar, vocabulary, and pronunciation in preparation for the debriefing phase.

After the performance, the class is brought together as a whole in the third phase, *debriefing.* The teacher's comments and corrections, an outline of the interaction, other proposed alternatives, and grammar points are the highlights of this phase. Each student is allowed to ask questions about the performance and the structural or cultural points used in the interaction. The teacher should lead the discussion and may encourage the students to participate by asking them questions related to the generated responses.

During this phase, the teacher should also address major errors made by the students. It is important for the teacher to discuss the error and not identify the error-maker. The emphasis must always be placed on what the students have managed to achieve, rather than on where they fell short of the mark. The lesson highlights provide fortification and confirmation of what was used during the interaction; then questions are answered, and written assignments and reading passages designed around the scenario are assigned to further *reinforce* the classroom activity and to help develop reading and writing skills.

The *evaluation* is built upon the teacher's schema or outline of the actual interaction: The discourse generated by the scenario is presented and analyzed, questions are asked, and teacher-, peer-, and self-evaluation takes place. By progressing in terms of task completion, involving the students deeply in the target language and its culture, the grammar and cultural points are learned in a functional, interactive way. The solutions achieved in each scenario serve to fix the language in the students' minds.

Strategic Interaction and Persian Curricula. The scenarios in this text are extracted from *Learning Persian Language & Culture,* a set of teaching materials developed in 1991–92 under a grant from the U.S. Department of Education's International Research and Studies Program. The tasks of these scenarios are based on potential points of interaction drawn from Persian culture and society. The attention is focused on learning a cultural point while solving an interaction problem, rather than on learning and reciting scripted material. The teacher's role is to stimulate independent thinking and participation; to provide supportive material including vocabulary as needed, grammar points, and cultural clues; and to give direction so as to guide and not to dictate what to think or say. Several goals are achieved simultaneously: The students first learn about the culture, and then they put their knowledge into practice in a given situation with an open-ended activity. This allows them to review issues in their minds while concentrating on another activity. Thus, students improve their linguistic and socialization skills while their attention is focused on the subject at hand and not on self-conscious performance.

The teaching units from which these samples are drawn (*Noruz* "New Year" and *T^{a}rof* "politeness protocols"; see Appendix) were introduced to an intermediate Persian class at the University of California at Berkeley with very satisfactory results. This was an experimental testing of the pedagogical effect of the product, but it still generated a great deal of interest and enthusiasm among the students. Their evaluations were overwhelmingly positive. Ninety percent reported that the successfully learned cultural point was new to them, or that they had some notion about the events but their ideas were confused until the SI class activity. Pre- and post-testing from the group showed a high degree of content and contextual language acquisition.

This evaluation task was performed in four sessions over three days with a class of ten students officially recognized as intermediate level, but ranging from high-novice to mid-intermediate in most skills. The objective of the testing was to evaluate the effectiveness of the instructional materials and interaction method. A certain degree of English was used in the evaluation sheets and the explanation about the activity; the cultural issues were also introduced to students with the use of some English in order to assure that all learners understood the task at hand.

The task to be performed by the students was more demanding than their usual work in a regular classroom setting, as they were introduced at the same time to new teaching materials as well as a new approach. Thus, the unit on *T^{a}rof* was introduced and used strictly for the purpose of familiarizing the students and explaining what was expected from them. The unit on *Noruz* was used for the actual testing. Both pre- and post-evaluation sheets and written assignments were collected from the students to determine the effect of the class activity. Pre- and post-evaluation was performed by administering the same test twice, first in 15 minutes at the beginning of this process and again in 7 minutes at the end.

The results were extremely encouraging, since the interaction that took place in class and a comparison of the pre- and post-evaluations show that the students who were not previously aware of the cultural issues presented in the lessons were receptive to the teaching material. There were a few students who were already familiar with the specific area of culture treated in the lesson plan; all of them demonstrated confusion about certain activities and relationships in the pre-test, and the lesson helped them put things in perspective as well as providing them with proper Persian expressions and verb phrases to express what they had learned previously in English. Not only did they learn the cultural points, they also improved their functional language skills through interactions.

General acceptance of this new approach was enthusiastic. The practice class prepared students for working with scenarios. By the end, even the most reserved students were involved in the scenario exchange. (The interaction in Persian was recorded on tape.) Eight of the ten students returned the written assignment, and all eight made positive comments about the effect of the teaching methodology, indicating that the cultural presentation had been useful and informative. An analysis of their evaluation tests indicated a clear improvement in their understanding of the issues as well as their ability to speak about them. On the second administration of the test, completed in half the time, 90% of the students showed improvement both in the content of their responses and in their written language performance.

One of the most important results of this testing was that the students responded positively to the new methodology and to the cultural content of the material. It could be concluded that under more favorable conditions (without time constraints, in the course of regular class sessions, and with students' greater familiarity with the interactive approach), the learners' task would be still more performance-oriented and would progress toward much higher proficiency and functional language development.

Conclusion. Most disciplines have been classified either under Arts or Sciences. Language teaching falls under both simultaneously, as educators make use of science to understand and analyze people and their languages while at the same time they engage in the art of detaching the object of learning from its precise mechanics and enhancing classrooms with a live approach to teaching and acquisition. This is a shift of emphasis from the object of the learning to the subject who is learning it. It is encouraging to see that many people agree with this shift and have been working on various approaches and methodologies to fulfill that goal.

Comparing a few of the most recent approaches to second-language teaching with SI further demonstrates some of the obvious advantages of this approach. *Functional/notional* syllabi, for example, need to be related to ordinary experience in order to become more effective than mere communicational devices. One way of ensuring this sort of relevance is to engage students in scenarios that require them to act out roles appropriate to the demands and tensions of those contexts. In the *functional/ notional* approach, functions are itemized and classified in a program, notions in which to express them are taught, references are made to grammar points, and these are practiced in role-play by students hoping to be able to use them one day in the future (Docker

1986: 25, 26). Clearly, the focus is still on language learning, students are given set roles, and they are still provided with the *object* to learn, instead of being in the position of subjects functioning and communicating from their own need for expression.

In using SI, the learner is encouraged into a real situation of speaking the language. As individual learners have their own specific needs and learning styles, they will be naturally asking for what they need to know in order to complete a communication task. Thus, the most important advantage of SI is its practical adaptability to all learners at all levels. Phonology, morphology, and grammatical rules of sentence structure are still taught; what is changed is the way they are presented to the learner as media to provide the most effective communication, which remains the primary goal.

The students are placed in a linguistic environment rather than acting a role. They are being themselves in a system of behavior and communication, experimenting step by step with their own linguistic abilities and needs. Stylistic differences based on age, family relationship, socioeconomic factors, and so on are explored. Students learn to speak, but they also learn how to communicate with people of different sexes, ages, or degrees of familiarity in the target language. The cultural and stylistic dimensions of the language help students through the language learning and retention process as the focus point of interest shifts from the mechanics of the language to the completion of the task.

As pointed out by Krashen (1983b: 261), Richard-Amato (1988: 181), and other linguists in the field, one single method does not provide an adequate language teaching program for all learners. The language teacher needs to know the theory in order to make reliable choices of the teaching material. In addition, beyond theory and methodologies there is a need for pragmatics of an application. Strategic Interaction is an approach through which effective theories of second-language teaching and acquisition are best applied to classroom instruction.[1]

In summary:

- The main advantage of an SI class over the traditional one is that it places students in near-real-life situations, where they learn to think in the language and use it to achieve a communicative goal.
- The learning process takes place *during* interaction, as opposed to the students learning *about* an interaction.

---

1. The SI approach is successfully applied to second language teaching in the following countries: Argentina, Australia, Brazil, Canada, England, Finland, France, Germany, Hungary, Italy, Japan, Jordan, New Zealand, Peru, Poland, Portugal, Singapore, Spain, and Venezuela. The 1987 publication has been translated into Italian, Japanese, Portuguese, and Spanish, and it is being processed into Hungarian.

- In the past, students were taught to memorize different elements of the language; the new approach is to provide an environment where the linguistic skills are naturally developed, used, and reinforced.
- The student is taken from pure memorization of linguistic elements through the experience of developing communicative skills. Thus we work toward the same experience as in natural language learning.
- This approach will allow students to make more errors; but in the interaction, the focus is on communication, not on grammar.
- Practice with the scenarios will help the learner feel situated within a linguistic circumstance, confronted with a problem to solve or a task to accomplish.
- Different points of grammar are practiced as the scenario lessons continue.
- The rehearsal and performance phases are intended to provide practice on pronunciation, lexicon, grammar points, culture points, and useful expressions.
- Grammar points and other elements of the language are explained and taught during the debriefing period, where students still maintain a vivid interest in communication.
- Communicative skills are developed, learned, and internalized as the interaction process evolves.
- Strategic Interaction is not merely a classroom practice tool, as role-play is.
- SI is not only an oral approach to language teaching and acquisition.
- SI is a community-oriented approach, and the open-ended nature of scenarios makes it possible to achieve a natural communicative interaction in the classroom.
- SI is a group activity, yet the individual learners perform, the teacher is fully involved, and language instruction is based on a real-life effort to communicate.
- The psychological factors influencing language learning are under the learners' control.
- All the usual linguistic elements are involved in achieving the communication task: vocabulary, grammar, pronunciation, comprehension, skills at turn taking, cultural appropriateness, etc.
- Scenarios are also excellent feedback on how the student can use the elements of the target language.
- Working through scenarios allows language proficiency to surface and to be reinforced in class and with following activities (writing and reading assignments).

To conclude with a thought from Dr. Di Pietro (1987a: 15, 16):

La vie nous donne des problèmes à résoudre et des difficultés à surmonter. Cette situation ne change pas même si l'on parle une autre langue. J'ai essayé d'introduire cet élément de la vie humaine dans la salle de classe pour donner aux élèves une bonne raison d'apprendre une nouvelle langue.

Translated from French by the author:

In life we encounter problems to resolve and difficulties to overcome. This situation does not change when we switch from one language to another. I have tried to bring this element of human life into the classroom, to provide the necessary inspiration for learning a new language.

REFERENCES

Abbs, Brian. 1980. *Communicating strategies.* London: Longman Press.

Allwright, Richard. 1982 (April). "Communicative curricula in language teaching." Paper presented at the International Conference on Language Sciences and The Teaching of Languages and Literatures, Bari, Italy.

Allwright, Richard. 1984. "The importance of interaction in classroom language learning". *Applied Linguistics* 5: 156–171.

Brown, Joan L. 1986. "¡Diga! Telephone protocols and strategies in the intermediate Spanish conversation course." *Hispania* 69: 413–417.

Carroll, Brendan J. 1966. *The study of language.* Cambridge, Mass.: Harvard University Press.

Carroll, Brendan J. 1980. *Testing communicative performance.* Oxford: Pergamon Press.

Clark, J.L.D. (ed.). 1978. *Direct testing of speaking proficiency: Theory and application.* Princeton, N.J.: Educational Testing Service. (Alexandria, VA: ERIC Document Reproduction Service, N° ED 172 523)

Clark, J.L. D. 1987. *Curriculum renewal in school foreign language learning.* Oxford: Oxford University Press.

DiLaura, Sarajane. 1983. "Teaching without grammar: Title XII experience at the University of Delaware." *FL Annals* 16: 339-342.

Di Pietro, Robert J. 1976a. "Contrasting patterns of language use: A conversational approach." *The Canadian Modern Language Review* 33(1): 49–61.

Di Pietro, Robert J. 1976b. *Language as human creation.* Washington, D.C.: Georgetown University Press.

Di Pietro, Robert J. 1978a. *Language structures in contrast.* Rowley, Mass.: Newbury House.

Di Pietro, Robert J. 1978b. "Verbal strategies, script theory and conversational performances in ESL." In Charles Blatchford and Jacquelyn Schachter (eds.), *On TESOL.* Washington, D.C.: TESOL. 149–56.

Di Pietro, Robert J. 1979a. "The semiotics of role interpretation." In S. Chatman, Umberto Eco, and J.-M. Klinkenberg (eds.), *A semiotic landscape.* The Hague: Mouton. 511–515.

Di Pietro, Robert J. 1979b. "Verbal strategies in the modern language classroom." *The Bulletin of the PSMLA* 57: 3–10.

Di Pietro, Robert J. 1980a. "Role enactment and verbal strategies in the U.S. Virgin Islands." In Edward Blansitt and Richard Teschner (eds.), *Festschrift for Jacob Ornstein.* Rowley, Mass.: Newbury House. 69–81.

Di Pietro, Robert J. 1980b. "The many dimensions of conversational language." In James E. Copeland and Philip Davis (eds.), *Seventh LACUS Forum*. Columbia, S.C.: Hornbeam Press. 467–474.

Di Pietro, Robert J. 1980c. "Verbal strategies: a neglected dimension in language acquisition studies." In Hans W. Dechert and Manfred Raupach (eds.), *Temporal variables in speech*. The Hague: Mouton. 313–21.

Di Pietro, Robert J. 1981. "Discourse and real-life roles in the ESL classroom. *TESOL Quarterly* 15(1): 27–33.

Di Pietro, Robert J. 1982a. "Models for learning and methods for teaching." *JACET Bulletin* 13: 1–7.

Di Pietro, Robert J. 1982b. "Strategic interaction from texts: Converting written discourse into spoken conversation." In William Frawley (ed.), *Linguistics and literacy*. New York: Plenum Publications Company. 387–97.

Di Pietro, Robert J. 1982c. "The open-ended scenario: A new approach to conversation." *TESOL Quarterly* 16(1): 15–20.

Di Pietro, Robert J. 1983a. "Discourse and the creation of a speech community in the foreign language classroom." In M. Heid (ed.), *Kommunikation im klassenzimmer*. New York: Goethe Haus. 90–105.

Di Pietro, Robert J. 1983b. "Form vs. function in discourse studies." *LACUS Forum* 9: 390–397.

Di Pietro, Robert J. 1983c. "From literature to discourse: Interaction with texts in the EFL/ESL classroom." *Canadian Modern Language Review* 40: 44–50.

Di Pietro, Robert J. 1983d. "Real life in the preparation of language teachers." In James E. Alatis, H. H. Stern, and Peter Strevens (eds.), *Georgetown University Round Table on Languages and Linguistics 1983*. Washington, D.C.: Georgetown University Press. 133–142.

Di Pietro, Robert J. 1984a. "Discourse and interaction in the classroom: Bringing Italian to the students." In N. Villa and Marcel Danesi (eds.), *Studies in Italian applied linguistics*. Ottawa: The Canadian Society for Italian Studies. 41–51.

Di Pietro, Robert J. 1984b. "The concept of personal involvement in FL study." *ADFL Bulletin* 15(3): 12–14.

Di Pietro, Robert J. 1984c. "The place of grammar." In R. Hall (ed.), *Eleventh LACUS Forum*. Columbia, S.C.: Hornbeam Press. 498–500.

Di Pietro, Robert J. 1985. "Interaction with literary texts in foreign language instruction." In M. Heid (ed.), *Literarische texte im kommunikativen fremdsprachenunterricht*. Goethe Institut. 431–443.

Di Pietro, Robert J. 1987a. *La dynamique du discours et son application dans l'enseignement des langues vivantes*, tirage à part du *Bulletin AQEFLS*. vol.9, n° 1–2. Montreal: l'Association québécoise des enseignants de français langue seconde.

Di Pietro, Robert J. 1987b. *Strategic interaction: Learning languages through scenarios*. Cambridge: Cambridge University Press.

Di Pietro, Robert J. 1990. *Helping people do things with English*. University of Delaware: English Teaching Forum.

Docker, Julie. 1986. "Strategic interaction: A description and an appraisal." In *Canberra Linguist*.

Firth, James R. (ed.). 1980. *Measuring spoken language proficiency*. Washington, D.C.: Georgetown University Press.

Frawley, William, and James Lantolf. 1984. "Speaking and self-order: A critique of orthodox L2 research." *Studies in Second Language Acquisition* 6: 143–159.

Freed, Barbara. 1984. "Proficiency in context: The Pennsylvania experience." In Sandra J. Savignon and Margie S. Berns (eds.), *Initiatives in communicative language teaching*. Reading, Mass.: Addison-Wesley Publishing Company.

Higgs, Theodore V. (ed.). 1984. *Teaching for proficiency, the organizing principle*. Lincolnwood, Illinois: National Textbook Company.

Higgs, Theodore V., and Ray Clifford. 1982. "The push toward communication." In Theodore V. Higgs (ed.), *Curriculum, competence, and the foreign language teacher* (Vol. 13). The ACTFL Foreign Language Education Series. Lincolnwood, Illinois: National Textbook Co. 57–79.

Hymes, D. 1971. "Competence and performance in linguistic theory." In Renira Huxley and Elizabeth Ingram (eds.), *Language acquisition: Models and methods*. London: Academic Press.

Khanji, Rajai R. 1983. "Two innovative methods in foreign language teaching: Their effects on the acquisition of interactive skills." Ph.D. dissertation, University of Delaware.

Kramsch, Claire. 1981. *Discourse analysis and second language teaching*. Arlington, Va.: Center for Applied Linguistics.

Kramsch, Claire. 1984. "Interactions langagières en travail de groupe." In *Le Français dans le Monde* 183: 52–59.

Kramsch, Claire. 1985. "Classroom interaction and discourse options." *Studies in Second Language Acquisition* 7: 169–183.

Kramsch, Claire. 1986. "From language proficiency to interactional competence." *Modern Language Journal* 70(4): 366–372.

Kramsch, Claire. 1988. "The cultural discourse of foreign language textbooks." In Alan Singerman (ed.), *Towards a new integration of language and culture*. Middlebury, Vermont: Northeast Conference.

Krashen, Stephen. 1982. *Principles and practice in second language acquisition*. Oxford: Pergamon Press.

Krashen, Stephen, and T. Terrell. 1983. *The natural approach*. Oxford: Pergamon Press.

Labarca, Angela, and Rajai R. Khanji. 1985. "On communication strategies: Focus on interaction." *Studies in Second Language Acquisition* 8: 68–80.

Lantolf, J., A. Labarca, and Johanna den Tuinder. 1985. "Strategies for accessing bilingual dictionaries: A question of regulation." *Hispania* 68: 858–864.

Lantolf, James, and Angela Labarca (eds.). 1987. *Research in second language learning: Focus on the classroom*. Norwood, N.J.: Ablex.

McCreary, Don R. 1986. *Japanese-U.S. business negotiations: A cross-cultural study*. New York: Praeger.

Morris, S-J. 1984. "Results of a one-year field test of a new language-teaching methodology." In James Lantolf and Angela Labarca (eds.), *Proceedings of Delaware symposium VI*. Norwood, N.J.: Ablex.

Omaggio, Alice C. 1986. *Teaching language in context: Proficiency-oriented instruction*. Boston, Mass.: Heinle & Heinle.

Puhl, C. 1984. "Synthesizing communicative and rule-based methodologies through the scenarios of strategic interaction." In James Lantolf and Anna Labarca (eds.), *Proceedings of Delaware symposium VI*. Norwood, NJ: Ablex.

Quinn, Terence 1985. "Functional approaches in language pedagogy." *Annual review of applied linguistics* (1984–85), section IV, vol. 5. Rowley, Mass.: Newbury House.

Rivers, Wilga M. (ed.) 1987. *Interactive Language Teaching*. Cambridge: Cambridge University Press.

Roberts, John T. 1982. "Recent developments in ELT (Part II)." *Language teaching* 15: 174–194.

Salah, Ghaida 1983. "The Sequencing of Scenarios according to Complexity in the SI method." Ph.D. dissertation, University of Delaware.

Saunders, Trevor J. (ed). 1987. *Plato: Early Socratic dialogues*. Middlesex, England: Harmondsworth.

Savignon, Sandra J. 1972. *Communicative competence: An experiment in foreign language teaching*. Philadelphia: Center for Curriculum Development.

Savignon, Sandra J. 1983. *Communicative competence: Theory and practice*. Reading, Mass.: Addison-Wesley Publishing Company.

Savignon, Sandra J., and Margie S. Berns. 1984. *Initiatives in communicative language teaching*.

Reading, Mass.: Addison-Wesley Publishing Company.

Savignon, Sandra J. 1987. *Initiatives in communicative language teaching II.* Reading, Mass.: Addison-Wesley Publishing Company.

Tannen, Deborah. 1984. *Conversational style: Analyzing talk among friends.* Norwood, N.J.: Ablex.

Vygotsky, Lev S. 1962. *Thought and language.* Cambridge, Mass.: MIT Press.

Vygotsky, Lev S. 1978. *Mind in society.* Cambridge, Mass.: Harvard University Press.

Wong Fillmore, Lily. 1976. "The second time around: Cognitive and social strategies in second language acquisition." Ph.D. dissertation, Stanford University.

Wong Fillmore, Lily. 1979. "Individual differences in second language acquisition." In Charles J. Fillmore, Daniel Kempler, and William Wang (eds.), *Individual differences in language ability and language behavior.* New York: Academic Press. 203–228.

APPENDIX

UNIT ONE OUTLINE

Underlying concept: **FAMILY** خانواده ، فامیل

Key concept: (New Year) **NORUZ** نوروز

Explanation about Noruz	164
Itemized cultural issues & special events	165
Noruz: vocabulary & expressions	170
SITUATION 1- kh^{a}ne tak^{a}ni خانه تکانی	172
Interaction scenarios	173
Scenarios: vocabulary & expressions	176
Example of classroom interaction	178
New vocabulary used	182
Variation scenarios	183
Scenarios: vocabulary & expressions	185
Teacher's debriefing:	
Written text vs. pronunciation	186
Phonological rules of the spoken language	188
Grammar points	192
Composition topics	200
Vocabulary for composition topics	201
SITUATION 2- hafsin and **tahvile s^{a}l** هفتسین و تحویل سال	202
Interaction scenarios	204
Scenarios: vocabulary & expressions	206
Other related vocabulary	207
Composition topics	208
What we learned	209
SELECTED READINGS	212

NORUZ /noruz/ نوروز IN THE FAMILY*
IRANIAN NEW YEAR

Noruz, one word, combined of two morphemes: **/no/** نو (new), and **/ruz/** روز (day), literally means "new day" and refers to the Iranian New Year. Noruz is Iran's most important national holiday. Officially, only two days are devoted to Noruz, but the schools are out for two to three weeks. The thirteenth day of the new year, **/sizde be dar/** سیزده بدر , is another holiday, which traditionally marks the end of this period of festivities.

The celebration of Noruz dates back several thousand years, to the time of the Achaemenids. Noruz starts at the exact instant of the Vernal Equinox, which occurs each year around the 21st of March, the first day of spring. Although Islam has added additional meaning to this event, it basically remains an old traditional Persian festivity, and this first day of spring marks the beginning of the Iranian calendar year. Like all traditional events, this holiday is marked with a myriad of activities affecting everything from preparations and celebrations to food, clothing, gift giving, charity, and many other social and family activities.

Noruz is a celebration of the first instant of spring and the renewed earth cycle. As such, it symbolizes new life starting along with moderate temperatures, thawing of the ice, fresh water, first blossoms, and flowering of violets, tulips, and hyacinths. These are the themes widely used in thousands of years of Persian poetry and literature, with all their strong symbolism revolving around *Rebirth, Renewal, Nature, Life, Mankind,* and *Spirituality.*

---

* For further reference to "Family" please see chapter 4.in *Iranian and American perceptions and cultural frames of reference* (Szalay and Mir-Djalali 1979).

CULTURAL ISSUES AND SPECIAL EVENTS

The following is a brief explanation of some of the most important activities around Noruz. Prepared in English, it is suitable for all students from novice to advanced levels. Each cultural issue could be used as a *situation* in support of a *scenario* for classroom interaction as demonstrated in this unit.

1 • A complete and thorough house cleaning: **/khªne takªni/ خانه تکانی**. This activity involves an effort to end all unfinished business, return all things borrowed, and end all procrastination in cleaning and organization, in order to feel light and in control of one's own life; it is part of a tradition of good resolutions.

2 • Growing seeds: **/sabze kªshtan/ سبزه کاشتن**, most commonly wheat grains /gandom/ گندم and/or lentils /adas/ عدس. The seeds are grown only in water, for the young to see how a dry closed grain has the potential to grow, develop, and prosper under the right conditions. It has also been reported that historically, many different kind of grains would be grown at this occasion, and the ones showing the strongest growth would be the most prosperous if cultivated that year.

3 • **/hafsin/ هفتسین** (the seven /s/. Notice this word is spelled as /haftsin/ and pronounced as /hafsin/). The /hafsin/ should include at least seven of the following items starting with the /s/ sound, each symbolizing a deeper concept than the object by itself:

/sabze/ سبزه (home grown greens) [symbol of growth, prosperity, and tightly woven roots],

/sombol/ سُنبل (hyacinth) [symbol of the development of the flower from the roots of its bulb],

/sim mªhi/ سیم ماهی (freshwater small carp) [symbol of life],

/samak/ سمک (fish), this expression is rarely used in other contexts,

/sib/ سیب (apple) [the oldest fruit],

/sir/ سیر (garlic) [the oldest bulb],

/somªgh/ سماق (sumac, a condiment) [the oldest condiment derived from a flower],

/serke/ سرکه (vinegar) [symbolic astringent agent],

/senjet/ سنجد (the fruit of the "mountain-ash", a wild tree with olive shaped orange fruit) [symbol of tart and sweet taste],
/samanu/ سمنو (a sweet prepared with the extract of young growth of wheat) [symbol of nature's sweetness],
/sekke/ سکّه (coin) [symbol of permanence and prosperity] and,

/sepand/ سپند (wild rue, a flower seed used as incense) [symbol of good health and good luck this incense is also supposed to protect against evil eyes], this is an older form of the most commonly used expression which is /esfand/ اسفند,

/tokhme morgh/ تخم مرغ (eggs) [symbol of life potential].

/sofreye hafsin/ سفرهٔ هفتسین (the seven /s/set up) is never complete without

/ghor'ªn/ قرآن (the Holy Koran) [spiritual light],

/ªyine/ آئینه/آینه (mirror) [symbol of purity and clarity], and

/sham'o shamdªn/ شمع و شمعدان(candle and candle-holder) [symbol of light and warmth].
As we have seen, the theme of **/hafsin/** mostly turns around spiritual light, purity, clarity, life, respect for the old tradition, warmth, sweetness, prosperity and togetherness. Most people also add:

/noghlo nabªt/ نقل و نبات (/noghl/ نقل is a small white candy made of thin slice of sugar-covered almond, and /nabªt/ نبات is the pure crystallized sugar) [symbol of good fortune and sweetness], with other sweets, and decorated eggs. The symbolic /sim mªhi/ can be substituted with goldfish.

4 • Home-baked pastry: **/shirniye khªnegi/** شیرنی خانگی

/bªghlavª/ باقلوا , /sohªne asal/ سوهان عسل , /nªn nokhodchi/ نان نخودچی ,

/nªn berenji/ نان برنجی , /nªn panjere'i/ نان پنجره ای ,

/reshte be reshte/ رشته برشته , /gushe fil/ گوش فیل , /noghl/ نقل ,

/nabªt/ نبات , etc. These pastries are mostly prepared with /peste/ پسته (pistachio), /bªdªm/ بادام (almond), /asal/ عسل (honey), /kare/ کره (butter), /ªrde berenj/ آرد برنج (rice flour), /khªke ghand/ خاك قند (powder sugar),

/za'far^{a}n/ زعفران (saffron), and /helo gol^{a}b/ هل و گلاب.

5 • Purchase of new clothes, shoes, etc. for everyone in the family. Most often referred to as /rakhte eyd/ رخت عید (New Year's clothing), this expression covers all articles of clothing including shoes, hats, and other accessories, etc. **/leb^{a}se eyd/** لباس عید is also used, but only refers to clothing with the exclusion of articles like shoes. This activity is basically for its /shogune nik/ شگون نیك (good omen). It is commonly believed that your condition at the time of the change of Vernal Equinox will linger with you most of the coming year, and that is the reason for the thorough cleaning, organizing, good thoughts, the sweets, as well as the new clothing, etc.

6 • Preparation for the last Wednesday of the year includes:

/ch^{a}rshambe suri/ چهارشنبه سوری (Wednesday celebration), which reportedly goes back to the time of the Prophet Zoroaster and the celebration of "fire" as the pure and the purifier. The more recent way of celebrating this day involves the arrangement of seven small bushes /botte/ بُتّه , which are set on fire and aligned so that one can jump over them one after the other while singing:

/zardiye man az to/ زردی من از تو

(My yellow complexion be yours)

/sorkhiye to az man/ سرخی تو از من

(Your red complexion be mine)

/^{a}tesh b^{a}zi/ آتشبازی (fireworks) and /gh^{a}shogh zani/ قاشق زنی (making noise with a spoon) are two other activities related to this day, but the latter seems to be fading away.

/h^{a}ji firuz/ حاجی فیروز (a dark complexioned man, wearing red, singing and dancing to amuse children) starts to be seen in the streets around this time. This is a commercialized personality working in the streets to amuse children and get some change. He usually carries a /d^{a}yre zangi/ دایره زنگی (tambourine).

7 • **/eydi/** عیدی (special New Year's gift) is usually given by the eldest to the young, made of a traditional /sekke/ سکّه (coin), or an /esken^{a}se no/ سکناس

نو (new bill), symbolizing the wish "prosperity be with you". Note: the tradition of giving /eydi/, is mostly based on symbolic rather that monetary value.

8 • /hadye/ هدیه (gift), offered by the young to the eldest, is very often either /gol/ گل (flowers), or /shirini/ شیرینی (cakes and pastry). Aside from parents and grandparents vis-à-vis their children, the notion of old and young among acquaintances is most often based on knowledge, wisdom, and seniority, more than actual age.

9 • /dido bªzdid/ دیدوبازدید , refers to visiting, دیدن , and returning visits, بازدیدن. Here again the hierarchy of age, its obligations and its social implications are to be considered. In general, in order to present their best wishes in person, younger people are socially obliged to pay a visit to their seniors, whether members of their family, friends, or acquaintances; the visits are then often reciprocated by the elders, although not required as a rule.

10 • /sizde be dar/ سیزده بدر (the thirteenth day outing). The festivities, greeting cards, flowers and visiting activities generally take place between the first and the 12th day of the New Year. The 13th day, a national holiday, marks the end of the celebration by an outing, generally to fields or green open spaces, in order to make a bond with *nature*. On this occasion the green seeds grown at home are taken to be disposed of in a fresh natural current of water. Once in the fields, unmarried young people, especially girls, are humorously encouraged to make small knots in the grass, along with a wish to be married within the year. This is a symbolic gesture to insure the course of their destiny, /bakht/ بخت (destiny), and the same word is also used in the common expression /bªz shodane bakht/ باز شدن بخت (lit. the opening, starting of the destiny), in conjunction with the knotting of the grass.

SITUATION 1

/kh^{a}ne tak^{a}ni/ خانه تکانی (house cleaning)

Brief explanation by the teacher

To be given before students are divided into groups to work with scenarios and related material:

/kh^{a}ne tak^{a}ni/ خانه تکانی , literally means (house shaking) and is informally pronounced /khune takuni/ خونه تکونی. As implied by its meaning, this activity goes beyond just house cleaning. It encourages an overall review of everything accumulated during the year in order to find, organize and keep all useful things, return all things borrowed and to give to others the things that are not needed by the family. The basis of this tradition is to lighten the burden of extra elements left over from different activities in order to start the new year fresh, unencumbered, and uncluttered, with a thoroughly clean house, mind, and heart. In practice, /kh^{a}ne tak^{a}ni/ of course involves a lot of washing and cleaning of floors, walls, doors, windows, rugs, curtains, and all of the household goods and clothing.

Scenarios

A سناریو

Shirin , your family is getting ready for the Iranian New Year. Everyone is going through his own room and belongings for a final **/kh^{a}ne tak^{a}ni/** (lit. "house shaking", house cleaning). You are helping your older brother **Sohr^{a}b** finish his room. Both of you are disturbed by the fact that your friend **Laura** does not put away her belongings. As she is a guest in your home, you don't know how to make her understand the urgent need for cleaning and tidiness. *How do you do this without offending her?*?

B سناریو

Sohr^{a}b, you want to help your sister **Shirin** inform her friend about the requirements of the yearly **/kh^{a}ne tak^{a}ni/**. While cleaning your own room, deciding which of your books and music will be given away, you offer **Shirin** different strategies, e.g. ask your mother to tell her, have her do it under false pretense, go ahead and do it for her, etc. You finally decide to have a conversation with **Shirin** in front of **Laura**, about the preparations for the Iranian New Year and on the benefits of a thorough house cleaning at this time. *Let's talk with Shirin*

C سناریو

Laura, you are spending your spring vacation with a friend **Shirin**, at her family home. You interpret your friend's zealous effort to clean house not as a sign of respect for her tradition, but as childish immaturity vis-à-vis her family. You think your friend is still very afraid of her parents, and wonder how to help Shirin understand that she is no longer a child. You decide to show her through your actions: all your clothes will stay haphazard, between the suitcase and the closet, until tomorrow--they won't make you do it! *You think.*

Example

Scenario Interaction. The following is an attempt to demonstrate an actual interaction which **might** take place in class. This is not to be memorized and/or enacted by the students. Given the scenarios and the vocabulary, the students should be allowed and encouraged to come up with their own ideas and interactions. They might find a need to speak more about each person's activities, like putting away things, or making decisions about keeping, giving, or throwing away, etc. The teacher is only to help maintain interest and participation, against the backdrop of what has been prepared. The class has been organized into 3 different groups, each with a scenario to work with. The interaction is to take place in Persian.
In this case **Sohr^{a}b (B)** starts the interaction:

1- **B**_ /**Shirin** jun y^{a}det miy^{a}d p^{a}rs^{a}l eydro/ ?
شیرین جون یادت میاد پارسال عید رو ؟
(Do you remember last year's New Year, Shirin dear?)

2- **A**_ /albate ke y^{a}dam miy^{a}d t^{a}rikhi bud/
البته که یادم میاد ، تاریخی بود.
(Of course, I remember it was quite an event.)

3- **B**_ /t^{a} ^{a}kharin daghighe mashghule khune takuni budim/
تا آخرین دقیقه مشغول خونه تکونی بودیم.
(We were busy cleaning house, up to the last minute.)

4- **A**_ /avazesh che ªli bud/ /ba'd az tahvil hame chiz morattabo tamiz bud/
عوضش ، چه عالی بود. بعد از تحویل ، همه چیز مرتّب وتمیز بود.
(It was so nice, to have everything clean and organized, after the New Year.)

5- **B** _ /ba'le vªghe'an ke be zahmatesh miyarzid/
بعله ، واقعاً که بزحمتش میارزید.
(Yes, it was really worth the trouble.)

6- **A** _ /emsªlam dªre dir mishe shªyad behamun gereftªri biyoftim/
امسالم داره دیر میشه ، شاید بهمون گرفتاری بیافتیم.
(It's also getting late this year, we may run into the same problem.)

7- **B** _ /yeki nist be in lorª befahmune ke lªzemeye eyde/
یکی نیست باین "لورا" بفهمونه که لازمهٔ عیده.
(How can we get Laura to understand that this is a New Year's requirement?)

8- **C** _ /chi mige/ ? / in barªdaretam be to dastur mide/ ?
چی میگه ؟ این برادرتم بتو دستور میده ؟
(What is he saying? Your brother also orders you around?)

9- **A** _ /na bªbª/ /dªrim as eydo khune takunihªye gozashte harf mizanim/
نه بابا ، داریم از عید و خونه تکونیهای گذشته حرف میزنیم.
(Not at all, we are talking about **eyd** and other house cleanings in the past.)

10- **B** _ /hameye havªsesh be dastur gereftane kªsh bejªsh harf gush midªd/
همهٔ حواسش بدستورگرفتنه ، کاش بجاش حرف گوش میداد.
(All she can think of is not to take orders, I wish she would listen instead.)

11- **A** _ /hichi nagu badesh miyªd behesh bar mikhore/ !
هیچی نگو بدش میاد ، بهش بر میخوره !
(Don't say anything. She won't like it. She'll get offended.)

12- **B** _ /begzªr balke yªd begire/ /fªrsi khunde ammª hªlª ku tª chiz befahme/

بگذار بلکه یاد بگیره ، فارسی خونده امّا حالا کو تا چیز بفهمه.

(Let it be, she may learn something. She has studied Persian but it'll be a while before she understands anything.)

•*Laura, getting closer to the brother and sister says with a smile:*

13- **C** _ /shirin/ /nemid^{a}nestam be bar^{a}daret^{a}n enghadr nazdik hasti/

شیرین ، نمیدانستم به برادرتان انقدر نزدیک هستی.

(Shirin, I didn't know you were so close to your brother.)

• *Shirin, with laughter, while kissing her brother:*

14- **A** _ /z^{a}heran doshmane khuni hastim/ /amm^{a} eyd fargh mikone/

ظاهراً دشمن خونی هستیم ، امّا عید فرق میکنه.

(We look like fierce enemies, but eyd is different.)

15- **B** _ /etteh^{a}de f^{a}milye ke dar mav^{a}ghe'e mohhem z^{a}her mishe/!

اتحّاد فامیلیه که در مواقع مهّم ظاهر میشه !

(This is family solidarity that appears at critical times!)

16- **A** _ /usulan/ /m^{a} dar f^{a}mil kheyli mottaki behamdigar hastim/

اصولاً ، ما در فامیل خیلی متّکی بهمدیگر هستیم.

(In principle, we are very much relying on each other, in the family.)

17- **B**_ /lor^{a} bahs sare ot^{a}ghe shom^{a} bud k^{a}r be etteh^{a}de famili keshid/!

"لورا" ، بحث سر اطاق شما بود ، کار باتحّاد فامیلی کشید !

(Laura, we were discussing your room, and got into family solidarity!)

18- **C** _ */cher^{a} in/ ? /be ot^{a}ghe man che marbut/ ?

*چرا این؟ به اطاق من چه مربوط ؟

(What is going on? How did my room get into this?)

• *They all look at each other, everybody laughs.*

19- **B** _ /gam^{a}nam shirin behtar tozih bede/

گمانم شیرین بهتر توضیح بده.

(I think Shirin can explain this better.)

• Shirin starts to tell Laura about the way /kh^{a}ne tak^{a}ni/ خانه تکانی should be perceived and accomplished. She explains that traditionally, /kh^{a}ne tak^{a}ni/ is done not only to encourage good cleaning and organizational skills but to discourage procrastination. This practice also helps one to assess things as they are, and to select things based on their utility. In addition, it helps one to think of others and to "put one's house in order". /kh^{a}ne tak^{a}ni/ is an exercise that can be expanded and applied to a wide range of activities. This is why having a cluttered room, with your belongings thrown around, is not what one usually expects to see, at least in this period. Also, in this particular case, it makes the cleaning of other areas more difficult if not impossible.

• *General laughter... Laura finally understands the subtle nature of this situation. She gives in, and starts cleaning up her room.*
• End of class interaction.

Variation Scnarios

A - (Iranian girl): Your American friend is visiting you. You and she were roommates together in college. It is just before Noruz, a time when Iranians must perform certain cleaning tasks (see section on special family activities). Your American friend has just unpacked her suitcase and has her clothing spread around the room. *How will you explain to her that she must put her room in order?*

B - (American girl): You are visiting your friend from college, a member of an Iranian family living in Iran. It is March and almost time for the Iranian new year. You have been shown to your room where you have just unpacked your suitcase and have washed out some soiled laundry in the bathroom. You now need to find a place to dry it. *How will you approach your Iranian friend about this problem?*

UNIT THREE OUTLINE

Underlying concept: **SOCIETY** **/ejtem^a'/ اجتماع**

Key concept: **POLITENESS PROTOCOLS /ta^arof/ تعارف**

ta'^arof: تعارف Politeness protocols 297

I. Explanation and usage 297

II. Cultural examples 299

Invitation to a party 299

Between two friends 301

Cab driver and the passenger 301

III. Key vocabulary & expressions 302

SITUATION 1- mehm^ani مهمانی 304

The expression and its use 305

Interaction scenarios 308

Vocabulary & expressions 310

Composition topics 311

Vocabulary & expressions for composition topics 312

SITUATION 2- t^aksi va mos^afer تاکسی و مسافر 313

Interaction scenarios 314

Vocabulary & expressions 316

Composition topics 317

SELECTED READING 318

T^aROF /ta'^arof/ تعارف

Politeness protocols & Social manners

I. Explanation and Usage

ta'^arof (informal: **t^arof**) refers to a Persian cultural behavior which employs politeness protocols used in a multitude of circumstances. They are not only language- and style-oriented, but have other behavioral consequences; there is not a literal translation in English that covers all the implications of this expression. One of the most commonly used meanings of t^arof refers to formulas used between people involved in saying things for the sake of politeness and not meaning them literally. It should be pointed out that t^arof is generally based on the *modesty* تواضع **/tav^azo'/** of the user, and not on a hypocritical attitude assumed in order to receive favors. It is also understood that some native speakers might choose this approach more frequently than others.

The word **t^arof** is often used by Persian language teachers to refer to a set of expressions used in polite social interactions. It is important to keep in mind that the expressions alone are only a fraction of the larger system of social protocol that is covered by the word t^arof. The formulas represent a deeper concept that has to do with the psychology of people using a given behavior. Once the underlying concept behind t^arof is clarified, it is easier to understand and recognize all its aspects as they translate into native speakers' language and attitude. In short, beyond a set of polite formulas, there is a complete code of conduct connected to t^arof that is based on such characteristics as *modesty* تواضع **/tav^azo'/** and *humility* شکسته نفسی **/shekaste nafsi/**. In accordance with these underlying features, it is quite common in t^arof to observe attitudes and behaviors that imply the following:

- You are better, more important, dearer, and more valuable than I am.
- Your time, life, health, work, and achievements are more important than mine.

Thus, everything else follows the same pattern in **t^arof**, not only in verbal communication, but also in other aspects of social behavior. Note that **t^arof** is used in groups, as well as between just two people without an audience, e.g.:

1 • You receive a call while you are having dinner. You use **tªrof** by not mentioning the interruption even when asked. You would rather have a cold dinner than imply to the caller that they should know better about the time of their call, or that your dinner is more important than they are.

2 • Someone you respect accidentally drops a cup of hot tea on you. You use **tªrof** as you feel it burn. No one else is present; still, in order to avoid implying something negative about the other person, you ignore your condition as if it didn't happen and you did not feel anything.

3 • You are invited to a friend's house. Although the dinner is burnt, you help yourself and use **tªrof** by not acknowledging the smell or the taste of burned food, and by saying how delicious it is (if you are asked), in order to put your host at ease.

4 • Your friend is wearing a new dress to your party, but it is not becoming. You use **tªrof** by saying how beautiful she looks in that new dress, because you know that she will look better with a little more self confidence. You will let her know what you really think later, in **/lafªfe/** لفافه (indirectly).

5 • Someone you respect has made you wait in the rain before showing up for an appointment. He apologizes. You are soaked, but you use **tªrof** and say that you were very comfortable.

SITUATION 2

/shofor tªksi va mosªfer/شوفرتاکسی و مسافر

Brief explanation by the teacher

To be given before students are divided into groups to work with scenarios and related material:

Taxicabs are both available in the streets or, for a higher fee, they may be called to pick you up at your home. A cab driver may choose to pick up other passengers as he drives towards your destination. With some slight differences, taking a taxi in Iran or one that is driven by an Iranian in the U.S. is very similar to a cab ride in any other country, until it gets to the **tªrof**.

The following scenarios are based on true everyday life **t^{a}rof**, in Iran and among Iranians everywhere in the world. This situation has been selected at random, but there are many other cases where similar **t^{a}rof** is used. For example in a store where you have tried to bargain the price of an item down, the shopkeeper may tell you:

/ekhtiy^{a}r d^{a}rid gh^{a}beli nad^{a}re/ اختیاردارید قابلی نداره (please accept if you wish, it is not worth much)

/gh^{a}beli nad^{a}re/ قابل شما را نداره (lit. it does not commensurate with your worth, it is not much to be given to you)

/b^{a}she khedmatetun/ باشه خدمتتون (you are welcome to keep it)

/befarm^{a}yid m^{a}le shom^{a}/ بفرمائید ، مال شما (please, it is yours)

/bebarid pulesham nadid/ببرید، پولشم ندید (you may take it, no need to pay for it)

/ekhtiy^{a}r d^{a}rid moteshakkeram/ اختیار دارید متشکّرم (no, thank you very much)

Scenarios

A سناریو

Cab driver: You have just taken your passenger to his destination. You have learned in talking with him that he is from Washington DC, where you have learned your English and you still have some good friends and family. It has been interesting to meet this passenger, you have had a nice conversation with him, and you want to use **t^{a}rof** with him on the fare he owes you. *How will you politely refuse to accept payment? When do you decide to accept your taxi fare?*

B سناریو

Passenger: You have been taken to your destination by a cab driver in Teheran. You have learned that he has been to the U.S. and has some family in Washington DC, and has visited them recently. So you have had a good conversation with him, but you are in a hurry to attend a meeting and therefore wish to pay the driver without delay. However, there is a cultural matter of **t^{a}rof**, whereby the driver refuses payment until you really insist. *How will you do this and get him to take payment as quickly as possible?*

TEACHER'S DEBRIEFING

During this phase, students are free to ask any questions about the scenario performance, the structure of the sentences, the cultural points, the Key Concept, pronunciation, vocabulary, etc. The teacher encourages this process by asking a few questions. Any of the following might be discussed and students are free to take notes.

FOR THE TEACHER

Written text vs. Spoken word: With the exception of some dialectal and individual differences, standard Persian undergoes phonological transformations to produce the informal speech used in Tehran.These phonological rules will be addressed as we proceed with each lesson. However, at the intermediate level, students should already be familiar with some of these transformations and the teacher will spend more or less time on each point as appropriate. At this time, notice the following general observations as they apply to written vs. spoken Persian language.

There is a clear distinction between the written form and the spoken form in most languages. Based on their communicative needs, individuals with different background, level of education, and socioeconomic status make different uses of the same common native language. Styles may range from the very formal, used in writing, to the informal variety used in everyday interactions with friends and family. The differences in styles may be as small as those found between individuals or as large as those between dialects. Through phonological transformations, Persian offers a wide range of styles in its spoken form.

Among other languages of this group (Indo-European), the general rule is that more formal situations require a speech style closer to written language. However, the sentence structure and the formality of written styles are rarely used in dialogues between people. Generally a set of phonological transformation rules are used to change the same words from formal to informal. Regular spoken languages, no matter how formal, still differ phonologically from the pronunciation used in reading a written text, not only in intonation and sentence structure, but also in vowel and consonant quality. The language used by the media, announcing news over radio and television, is probably the closest spoken language to citations from written material.

The following examples illustrate some of the phonological transformations in Persian. Notice that they are not strictly followed by all users at all times. Some advanced students of Persian with almost perfect pronunciation still sound like reading a written text, because they have not mastered the phonological transformations that occur in the spoken language. Conversely, a new student might sound more advanced as soon as he/she learns to use the spoken form. Practicing the full form of all vocabulary is very important, but just as essential for the students' performance is the early introduction of the spoken form. Let us examine the rules that operate in this class interaction.

Phonological rules: It is important to stress that phonological transformations take place in the spoken language. As such, they belong to the oral performance and students should not be pressured to use the spoken forms in their regular writing assignments. In Persian, as in all Indo-European languages, written words are spelled according to the rules and do not represent these phonological variations. Teaching colloquial writing should be approached with caution if at all. The following is only oral practice

1. In informal speech, the vowel /^{a}/ in medial position followed by /**n**/ and sometimes /**m**/, is pronounced /**u**/:

Rule 1. /^{a}/==> /**u**/~ /^{a}n/ /^{a}m/ ==> /**u**n/ /**u**m/

/sh^{a}ne/ ~ /sh**u**ne/ شانه

/d^{a}ne/ ~ /d**u**ne/ دانه

/j^{a}n/ ~ /j**u**n/ جان

/n^{a}n/ ~ /n**u**n/ نان

/b^{a}m/ ~ /b**u**m/ بام

/b^{a}d^{a}m/ ~ / b^{a}d**u**m/ بادام

/ ^{a}r^{a}m/ ~ /^{a}r**u**m/ آرام

/n^{a}d^{a}n/ ~ /n^{a}d**u**n/ نادان

/ b^{a}r^{a}n/ ~ /b^{a}r**u**n/ باران

From our dialogue:

3-B /kh^{a}ne tak^{a}ni/ ~ /kh**u**ne tak**u**ni/ خانه تکانی

12-B /f^{a}rsi kh**u**nde/ ~

/f^{a}rsi kh**u**nde ast/ ~

/f^{a}rsi kh^{a}nde ast/ فارسی خوانده است ~

13-C /nemid^{a}nestam/ ~ /nemidunestam/ نمیدانستم

7-B /befahm**une**/ ~
/befahm**unad**/ ~
/befahm^{a}**nad**/ بفهماند ~

Notice: In other phonological environments, the vowel /^{a}/ remains unchanged as in many high frequency words: /y^{a}d/ یاد, /d^{a}d/ داد, /^{a}z^{a}d/ آزاد, /^{a}z^{a}r/ آزار, /^{a}v^{a}z/ آواز, /fa'^{a}l/ فعّال, /esteghl^{a}l/ استقلال, /emted^{a}d/ امتداد.

2. In final position, with much less frequency: /^{a}/ ==> /o/.
The main example of this phonological transformation is found in /**r^{a}**/, which is the "postposition" of reference and specificity. Thus we can have the following rules:

Rule 2. /^{a}/==> /**o**/ ~ /**r^{a}**/ ==> /**ro**/ ==> /**o**/
/r^{a}/ را ~ /ro/
/^{a}nr^{a}/ آنرا ~ /^{a}nro/

From our dialogue:
1-B /p^{a}rs^{a}l eydro/ ~ /p^{a}rs^{a}l eydo/

Rule 3. /^{a}/==> /**u**/ ~ /^{a}n/ ==> /**un**/
/^{a}nr^{a}/ آنرا ~ /unr^{a}/ ~ /unro/ ~ /uno/
/inr^{a}/ اینرا ~ /inro/ ~ /ino/

Notice: In these examples /r^{a}/ ~ /ro/ the /r/ is eliminated in the last examples in which the postposition /**r^{a}**/ is simply replaced by the sound /**o**/.

3. In verb forms, the ending sound /-**ad**/ is transformed to the informal ending /-e/ in third person singular, as follows:

Rule 4. /-**ad**/==> /-e/
From our dialogue:

11-A /bar mikhor**ad**/ ~ /bar mikhore/ بر میخورد

12-B /y^{a}d begir**ad**/ ~ /yad begire/ یاد بگیرد

12-B /befahm**ad**/ ~ /befahme/ بفهمد

6-A /d^{a}r**ad**/ ~ /d^{a}re/ دارد

6-A /dir mishav**ad**/ ~ /mishe/ دیر میشود

8-C /dastur midah**ad**/ ~ /mide/ دستور میدهد

14-A /fargh mikon**ad**/ ~ /mikon**e**/ فرق میکند

15-B /z^a^her mishav**ad**/ ~ /mish**e**/ ظاهر میشود

19-B /tozih bedah**ad**/ ~ /tozih bed**e**/ توضیح بدهد

And the third person plural ending in informal speech:
Rule 5. /-and/==> /-an/

/mikhor**and**/ ~ /mikhor**an**/ میخورند

/begir**and**/ ~ /begir**an**/ بگیرند

/befahm**and**/ ~ /befahm**an**/ بفهمند

/d^a^**rand**/ ~ /d^a^**ran**/ دارند

/midah**and**/ ~ /midah**an**/ میدهند

4. /ham/ هم (also), often combines with the preceding word; the **/h/** sound is eliminated and the word is pronounced as **/am/** :
Rule 6. /ham/==> /-am/
From our dialogue:

6-A /ems^a^l **ham**/ ==> /ems^a^l**am**/ امسال هم (also, this year)

/ens^a^n **ham**/ ==> /ens^a^n**am**/ انسان هم (also, mankind)

/^a^nh^a^ **ham**/ ==> /**un^a^am**/ ~ /**un^a^m**/ آنها هم (also, them)

/b^a^z **ham**/ ==> /b^a^z**am**/ باز هم (again) lit.: (other time also)

5. A number of other phonological transformations within this unit and dialogue are:

/**-ts-**/ ==> /**-s-**/ ~ /haftsin/ ==> /hafsin/ هفتسین

11-A /**-u**/ ==> /**-hesh**/ ~ /be'u/ ==> /behesh/ باو

10-B /**-yash**/ ==>/**-^a^sh**/~/bej^a^yash/ ==> /bej^a^sh/ بجایش

11-A /**-chøch-**/==>/**-ch-**/~/hich chiz/==>/hichi/ هیچ چیز

12-B /**-ogz-**/ ==> /**-ez-**/ ~ /bogz^a^r/ ==> /bez^a^r/ بگذار

1-B /**-^a^ya-**/ ==> /**-^a^-**/ ~ /miy^a^yad/ ==> /miy^a^d/ میاید

GRAMMAR

Based on the hypothetical scenario interaction demonstrated in this unit, the following grammar points are likely to be discussed. The teacher will initiate the following points.

1. Polite vs. Familiar (Notice sentences #17-B, 8-C, 13-C in this interaction). As in French and Spanish, Persian uses the plural form of the personal pronoun "**you**" for polite style as opposed to the singular form of the same pronoun, which is used for familiar style.

/shom^{a}/ شما (you) =/= /to/ تو (thou).

/shom^{a}/ شما indicates a sign of respect, based on age difference, family seniority, social status, etc., or it marks distance and a respectful lack of intimacy when used between the sexes. The style of discourse between men and women is another aspect of speech that we will pay special attention to, as we proceed with the lessons. In this interaction we can see:

17-B /lor^{a}/ /bahs sare ot^{a}ghe **shom^{a}** bud/ /k^{a}r be etteh^{a}de famili keshid/ !

"لورا" ، بحث سر اطاق شما بود، کار باتّحاد فامیلی کشید !

(Laura, we were speaking about your room (polite form), and got into family solidarity!)

Notice, **Sohr^{a}b** is speaking to **Laura** on a first name basis, but he addresses her with a **/shom^{a}/**, which indicates a polite and non-intimate relationship between a young man and a young woman.

/to/ تو is generally used among people who are on a first name basis, in the same age group and of the same sex, either family members or close friends and relatives. It is also used by a senior to a junior, without age or sex distinctions, but in those cases a /shom^{a}/ شما is always expected from the junior (whether by age or rank) speaker.

13-C /shirin/ /nemid^{a}nestam be bar^{a}daret^{a}n enghadr nazdik hasti/

* شیرین، نمیدانستم به برادرتلن انقدر نزدیک هستی.

(Shirin, I didn't know you were so close to your brother.)

8-C /chi mige/ ? / in bar^{a}dar**etam** be to dastur mide/ ?

چی میگه ؟ این برادرتَم بتو دستور میده ؟

(What is he saying? Your brother also orders you around?)

In (#13-C), Laura calls Shirin by first name, we know that they are close friends, but she uses the possessive /bar^{a}daret^{a}n/ برادرتان as opposed to /bar^{a}daret/ برادرت She also uses the more formal /nemid^{a}nestam/ نمیدانستم instead of the informal /nemidunestam/. Also in informal speech /hasti/ هستی is usually transformed to /-i/, as in /nazdik **hasti**/ ==> /nazdiki/, نزدیك هستی ==> نزدیکی and she does not use that form either.

A comparison of this sentence with Laura's previous sentence (#8-C) which has a complete informal style, will demonstrate that she has not yet learned how to use the informal speech and needs more practice:

2. <u>Verb omission</u> (Notice sentence #18-C in this interaction). In the following sentence, the verb is omitted at the end of the phrase, as is the practice in less formal speech style:

18-C */cher^a in shod/ ? /be ot^{a}ghe man che marbut/ ?

* چرا این ؟ باطاق من چه مربوط ؟

(What is going on? How does my room get into this?)

/cher^a in/ is an incomplete sentence, she either needs to complete it by a verb and a complement: /cher^a in r^a miguyad/, or she most probably means to use a short interrogation like: /chetor shod/ ? چطور شد ؟

Another point : with an increasing degree of familiarity, the following forms could be used in this construction:

/be ot^{a}ghe man che marbut **ast**/ ~ باطاق من چه مربوط است ؟

/be ot^{a}ghe man che marbut**e**/ ~ باطاق من چه مربوطه ؟

/be ot^{a}ghe man che marbut/ ~ باطاق من چه مربوط ؟

Other examples would be:

/bemanche/ بمن چه (what's it to me?)

/be to che/ بتو چه (what's it to you?)

/be m^a che/ بما چه (what's it to us?)

In all three examples the last part of the sentence, /marbut ast/ مربوط است (it is connected ~ it is related), has been omitted. The full form would be:

/be man che **marbut ast**/ بمن چه مربوط است ؟

/be to che **marbut ast**/ بتو چه مربوط است ؟

/bemª che **marbut ast**/ بما چه مربوط است ؟

3. <u>Yes vs. No - Polite vs. familiar</u> (Notice sentence #5-B in this interaction).

• /ba'le/ بعله can be emphatically pronounced as /ba'::le/, with a long middle vowel, to mean (yes, of course), (certainly, yes). Other variations of this word are /bale/ بله (yes), and the form /bali/ بلی , which is mainly used in writing. The informal /ªre/ آره (yes) used by itself is considered impolite or extremely informal. The form /ªri/ آری is only used in writing and does not carry the same informality as does /ªre/ آره.

• /na/ نه (no), used for negative answers, has the same informal value as /ªre/ آره (yes) if used by itself. The common word for a polite negative answer is /na kheyr/نخیر (no), which is a combination of **informal** /na/ نه (informal no), and **formal** /kheyr/ خیر (formal no).

• Both informal forms, /ªre/ and /na/, are combined with other words to become acceptable in most conversations. The expressions used with آره and نه are of the type /khªnum/ خانم, /ªghª/ آقا , /pedar/ پدر , /mªdar/ مادر , /nane/ ننه , /bªbª/ بابا , and most other kinship words as well as a few terms of endearment: /jªn/ جان , /aziz/ عزیز , /eshgh/ عشق , /ghalb/ قلب , /ruh/ روح Most of the above have a specific connotation in context. The kinship expressions are not exclusively used with the right family figures, but according to what the speaker intends to imply. The following are some of their semantic equivalents in English:

1-/ªre khªnum/ آره خانم (yes) and **not** necessarily (yes ma'am), as خانم loses its formal connotations in making آره less informal.

2-/ªre ªghª/ آره آقا (yes) and **not** necessarily (yes sir)

But:

3-/ba'le khªnum/ بعله خانم (yes) or (yes **ma'am**), emphasis on a formal yes.

4-/ba'le ªghª/ بعله آقا (yes) or (yes **sir**) with formal implications.

5-/na khªnum/ نه خانم (no) or (no **ma'am**) without too much formality.

6-/na ^{a}gh^a/ نه آقا (no) or (no **sir**) without too much formality.

Notice: 3, 4, 5 and 6 are still used among close friends and family. They do not have the same formal connotations as implied in English by most expressions using "ma'am", "madam" and "sir".

7-/kheyr kh^{a}num/ خیر خانم (no) or (no **ma'am**), more formal.

8-/kheyr ^{a}gh^a/ خیر آقا (no) or (no **sir**), more formal.

9-/^{a}re pedar/ آره پدر ~ /^{a}re b^{a}b^a/ آره بابا (yes) and **not** necessarily (yes father)

10-/na pedar/ نه پدر ~ /na b^{a}b^a/ نه بابا (no) and **not** necessarily (no father)

11-/^{a}re nane/ آره ننه (yes) and **not** necessarily mother or nanny.

12-/na nane / نه ننه (no) and **not** necessarily mother or nanny.

Notice: 3, 4, 7 and 8 are to be used in the most formal situations. 9, 10, 11 and 12 could be translated either literally or with a touch of sarcasm. These expressions are used among friends and relatives, with older people or people of the same age group, and they imply closeness. They are also used with the very young.

Notice: /na baba/ نه بابا is often used **to protest** as well as **to deny** (see 9-A in the interaction).

13-/^{a}re j^{a}nam/ آره جانم ~ /^{a}re azizam/ آره عزیزم (yes dear) implies a sense of compassion and caring.

14-/na j^{a}nam/ نه جانم ~ /na azizam/ نه عزیزم (no dear) implies a sense of compassion and caring.

15-/^{a}re amu/ آره عمو ~ /^{a}re d^{a}d^{a}sh/ آره داداش are used by the less educated and the street people, also known as /l^{a}t/ لات and /d^{a}sh mashti/ داش مشدی (notice the phonological transformation of /**d**/ ==> /**t**/ in the last expression).

4. Verb omission and Semantic compounds

(Notice in Scenario A)

(1) /jam'o jur/ جمع و جور . This expression is from:

(2) /jam' kardan va jur kardan/ جمع کردن و جور کردن

and the verb "to do" /kardan/ کردن has been omitted in (1) at both occurrences.

Although (2) literally means (assembling together, matching and organizing), the expression (1) simply means (tidying).

Of the same kind we had among special events in this unit:

/dido b^{a}zdid/ دید و بازدید دیدن و بازدیدن

Some other examples are:

/rafto ^{a}mad/ رفت و آمد رفتن و آمدن

/rikhto p^{a}sh/ ریخت و پاش ریختن و پاشیدن

/d^{a}do setad/ داد و ستد دادن و ستاندن

/zado khord/ زد و خورد زدن و خوردن

/jango jed^{a}l/ جنگ و جدال جنگیدن و جدال کردن

5. <u>Verbs and tenses</u> (Notice in this interaction). Use of past, present, imperative, and subjunctive. Recalling past events and expressing simple wishes:

10-B /dastur gereftan/ دستور گرفتن **inf.** (to take orders)

1-B /y^{a}det miy^{a}d/ یادت میاید **pres.** (do you remember?)

6-A /dir mishe/ دیر میشود pres. (it is getting late)

8-C /mige/ /miguyad/ میگوید pres. (s/he is saying)

8-C /dastur midahad/ دستور میدهد pres. (s/he is giving orders)

9-A /harf mizanim/ حرف میزنیم pres. (we are speaking)

10-B /gush mid^{a}d/ گوش میداد pres. (s/he was listening)

11-A /bar mikhore/ بر میخورد pres. (s/he will be offended)

2-A /t^{a}rikhi bud/ تاریخی بود **past** (it was unforgettable, lit.historical)

3-B /mashgul budim/ مشغول بودیم past (we were busy)

4-A /tamiz bud/ تمیز بود past (it was clean)

11-A /nagu/ نگو **imp.** (don't say)

6-A /biyoftim/ بیافتیم **subj.** (that we fall)

6-A /dar gereft^{a}ri biyoftim/درگرفتاری بیافتیم subj. (that we run into a problem)

7-B /befahmune/ /befahm^{a}nad/ بفهماند subj.(that s/he makes understand)

7-B /ke be'u befahm^{a}nad/که باو بفهماندsubj.(that s/he makes her/him understand)

12-B /y^{a}d begirad/ یاد بگیرد subj. (that s/he learns)

COMPOSITION TOPICS

Choose one of the following topics:

1. Write an essay in which you compare and contrast the New Year in the U.S. and Noruz in Iran. Discuss the different amount and kind of vacation time students get around those festivities.

2. Describe the preparations and the activities around Noruz. Start by enumerating as many of them as you can remember, and then discuss and compare a few activities of your choice.

3. Write to a friend about your new experience at school, learning Persian and getting to know the Iranian culture. Try to catch your friend's attention by telling him/her about some of the totally new and different things you have learned on the subject.

4. What is the underlying cultural meaning of /kh^{a}ne tak^{a}ni/? What are some of the advantages? And why do you think it is important to prepare for a good start?

موضوع انشاء

یکی از موضوعهای زیر رابرای انشاء انتخاب کنید:

۱. عید نوروز را با جشن سال نودرامریکا مقایسه کنید. در مورد طول زمان و نوع تعطیلاتی که دانشجویان دارند توضیح بدهید.

۲. شرحی در مورد تهیّه وتدارکات نوروز بنویسید. اوّل یك یك آنچه بخاطر دارید را نام ببرید و بعد چند عدد از آنها راانتخاب کرده و توضیح بدهید.

۳. در نامه ای بدوستتان در بارهٔ دانشگاه و یاد گرفتن زبان و فرهنگ ایران بنویسید. سعی کنید با صحبت در مورد چند نکتهٔ جدید وتازه توجه او را جلب کنید.

۴. معنیِ اصلی وفرهنگیِ خانه تکانی و فوائد آن چیست ؟ چرادر هر کاری خوب شروع کردن آن مهّم است ؟ بیشتر شرح بدهید.

Japanese dictionaries and *Schadenfreude:* Editorial practices and national prejudices in Japanese bilingual dictionaries

Don R. McCreary[1]
The University of Georgia

Introduction. Japan is a lexicographer's paradise. There are more dictionaries, both monolingual and bilingual, per capita in Japan than in any other country. The buying audience for these monolingual and bilingual English–Japanese dictionaries is over 99 percent Japanese. This is probably due to the Japanese continuing need to borrow, copy, and adapt ideas and technologies coming from the West. I have been fortunate to be involved in this lexicographer's paradise because I have edited two specialized technical dictionaries, the *Japanese–English Science & Engineering Dictionary* 1988, 1,989 pp., and its complement, the *English–Japanese Science & Engineering Dictionary* (in press, c. 1994), with a 6,498-page galley proof. These two dictionaries, with thousands of illustrative sentences, are a definite improvement over previous bilingual English–Japanese technical dictionaries, which have tended to be glossaries, unexemplified word lists. For both dictionaries, virtually all the buyers are Japanese engineers, technicians, scientists, and companies doing technical work, manufacturing, or translation in Japan.

There are some pleasures to be had for the lexicographer in this Japanese "paradise." *Schadenfreude*, a German loanword, means pleasure derived from the misfortunes of others. I first noticed the *Schadenfreude* evident in these dictionaries when I was editing the letter "B" galleys and saw the example sentence for *blast,* "The space shuttle has again shown it can *blast* astronauts into orbit in biblical smoke pillars." This sentence seemed to be heavily infused with a sarcastic anti-Christian connotation, as well as a heavy reference to the *Challenger* tragedy. I then decided to look back at other examples treating the shuttle disaster that I remembered editing, and also to look back at examples mentioning the United States, as well as a few references to women, girls, and females; I had questioned the suitability of many of these for a science and

---

1. I would like to express my thanks to John Algeo for his comments and for the idea of *schadenfreude,* and to Fred Dolezal for his editing and his suggestions. All opinions are my own, of course.

engineering dictionary. National chauvinism and prejudice in lexicography is historically exemplified by Samuel Johnson's (1755) definition: "*Oats,* a grain which in England is generally given to horses, but in Scotland supports the people." To attune the reader to the idea of national chauvinism and prejudice in editorial policy, we will first consider a few of the fifty-two references to women in the new dictionary.

References to Women (fifty-two, all condescending). Allied to lexicographical prejudice and *Schadenfreude* is chauvinism, including the masculine variety. Women in the Japanese engineering world are an outside "other" group, virtually invisible in any engineering office in Japan. Of a total of 226 negative or condescending example sentences, 52 refer to women. References to women seem to be misogynistic, contemptuous, derogatory, condescending, spiteful, and occasionally racist, since non-Japanese women are sometimes the subjects. Unfortunately, the concept of women as poor managers is all too common in scientific and engineering fields in Japan. In fact, women are nearly nonexistent in managerial positions in engineering firms. The editors know the example sentences are intended for a readership that is virtually all male and all Japanese. Their intent has been to write an active learner's dictionary with many example sentences taken from American publications. However, in their selections, they have revealed a good deal of ethnocentrism and chauvinism.

The reader may be wondering about the corresponding delight that is connected with the woes of others in *Schadenfreude*, in this case applied to women. This pleasure may be seen in Japanese comic books and movies for adult men, in which women are objects of all manner of derision and animal-like degradation. The second-class status of Japanese women is slowly changing; however, a more liberated and humane status is not evident in the new 1994 dictionary.

More generally, Sidney Landau (1984) commented on criticisms of sexist bias in dictionaries:

> The author takes the [Thorndike–Barnhart Beginning] dictionary to task for its disproportionate emphasis on Christianity ... from "a" to Yule, we counted fifty-nine references to the word Christmas ... [exemplified by] "Christ came to *save* the world." (Baehr 1964:416) ... The author also shows that the dictionary's illustrative phrases consistently represented girls as good, honest, pure, truth telling, and generally wonderful; whereas boys were represented as violent, cruel, and irremediably wicked. She cites examples: "That cruel boy tortures animals. That cruel boy stoned the dog." And so forth.... The criticism simply illustrates that even an outstanding dictionary conscientiously edited is apt to reflect the cultural

backgrounds and habits of the editors. (Landau 1984:308–309)

Cultural bias, then, should be reported in dictionaries, according to Landau, if they presume to be accurate, but the dictionary need not and should not share bias by reflecting it in definitions and illustrative citations. Regarding biased references to females, here are some example sentences over the past thirty-three years indicating connotations related to women. The first set is from a recent (1988) English–Japanese dictionary, *Shogakukan's Senior Friend Dictionary:*

Woman: an old woman, a married woman, a woman writer.

Female: the female sex, a female child, female flowers.

Girl: shop girl, office girl, a telephone girl.

In the Japanese–English section:

Onna: woman, girlfriend, hostess (in a bar or club), landlady.

Onna no ko: girl, a baby girl.

Josei: woman, female.

We may note the collocations with old, married, and writer, as well as hostess and landlady. Also note that the definitions are not reversible between the English–Japanese and Japanese–English sections in this single-volume dictionary. However, the connotations in these collocations are not as loaded semantically as the following from 1960.

In this older volume, *Kenkyusha's New English–Japanese Dictionary* (1960), we find the following:

Woman: a new woman, an old woman, a woman of pleasure; A whistling woman and a crowing hen are neither liked by God nor men.

Female: a female dress, female education, female charm (weakness), a female sex hormone, the female sex.

Girl: She was married as a mere girl, a shop girl, the leading girl, Jones and his girl. (Kenkyusha, 1960)

In these collocations, which are the complete entries minus the Japanese translations in kanji and kana, some changes are noticeable over nearly thirty years. The "whistling woman" saying does not appear in the modern dictionaries, and most of the glosses are not loaded, with the exception of "hostess," which in Landau's terms is merely accurately reflecting one of the usages in Japan.

As for the glosses for woman, female, and girl in the first dictionary I edited, there were no headwords or glosses at all in the *Japanese–English Science and Engineering Dictionary* (1988); *onna* (woman), *josei* (female), and *onna no ko* (girl) were not included by the editors, and in hindsight, the editors were probably correct in leaving them out. However, in 1993, that editorial decision was reversed for these and many other non-technical words. In the new English–Japanese galleys of the 1994 dictionary, fifty-two derogatory sentences about women were found. A sampling follows:

> *Motivate: Motivating* workers can be a challenge for any manager, but it can be especially difficult for a woman. There's no reason, even in a highly motivated professional crew, that the same kind of sexual tensions that develop here in offices aren't going to develop in space. (This was also used to illustrate *sexual*.)
>
> *Business trip:* What about travelling on *business trips* with colleagues of the opposite sex? (also used for *sex*) There is no reason, however, that a woman should conduct herself any differently on business trips than she does at the office.
>
> *Naive:* Travelling can present certain hazards for women who are *naive* or unsure of appropriate standards.
>
> *Unsure:* ... women who are *unsure* of appropriate standards for personal and professional behavior.
>
> *Sex:* ... ancillary tasks, such as taking notes or making coffee, are still doled out according to *sex*. Males are sometimes called the strong *sex* and females the weaker *sex*.
>
> *Situation:* A woman who finds herself in such a *situation* should never overreact.
>
> *Take notes:* In one case, for example, a woman I know nearly flared up when asked to *take notes* at the first meeting she attended as a manager.
>
> *Female:* The difference between male and *female* pay scales has also been blamed as a reason why women shun engineering.

Fashionably: In the early 1970s, women who dressed *fashionably* in miniskirts and platform shoes were hard pressed to present a business-like appearance.

In favor of: In some cases, men become exceedingly demoralized when they learn that not only have they been passed over for promotion, but that they have been passed over *in favor of* a female.

Favorable: Good manners and politeness can make a very *favorable* impression on a female boss.

Still: Still, she was disappointed at a trade show, when after a lengthy discussion of technical ideas with an exhibitor, he closed the conversation with, "And you're pretty, too." (This was used for *disappointed,* as well.)

Damn: It is inevitable that a woman will eventually encounter some men prone to using foul language, just not [sic] an occasional "*damn*" or "hell."

Discrimination: While several female microwave engineers cite instances of *discrimination* or at least differentiated behavior from both professors and colleagues, they delve into their part for them. [sic]

Wonder: Stereotypes were the rule; if she was married, her male counterparts probably *wondered* aloud what she was doing at the office, instead of staying home taking care of kids. [sic] It may even lead top management to *wonder* whether it was wise to put a woman in charge. Though many women once accepted the wonder woman myth, only a few women are capable of living up with it. [sic]

The connotations of these illustrative sentences, taken out of context from what may have been feminist or otherwise sympathetic American and British texts, are compounded by an editorial tendency to use females as the objects of painful and punishing action verbs. The use of female names along with the frequent use of "she" seems to be a consistent editorial choice. Regarding the pronoun choice of "he," Sidney Landau notes:

> A word about the use ... of "he" as a neuter pronoun. Some linguists and feminist writers have alleged that, in many cases of actual usage, *he* or *him*, used with ostensible neutrality, in fact refers to men only. They are right. (Landau 1984:3)

Similarly, the use of "she" below refers to women only. In these, the sadistic side of *Schadenfreude* is brought out in the open and exposed. A selection follows:

Slice: She *sliced* her finger.

Separate: Mary's blood was run through a machine to *separate* out her white cells.

Sling: The doctor put her arm in a *sling*.

Skin: She had *skin* cancer.

Unconscious: He made her *unconscious* with chloroform.

Look: She *looked* her age.

Verbs with these physically painful or mentally hurtful connotations virtually never occurred with males as their objects.

Schadenfreude and the *Challenger* Space Shuttle. In addition to the above-mentioned "biblical smoke pillars" example that provided the first spark for this paper, there are another 109 references to the *Challenger* space shuttle disaster in the 1994 dictionary. Many of them are in especially poor taste since they refer to the first "Teacher in Space" who was also killed in the explosion.

Obviously, the idea of *Schadenfreude* is shown most clearly here and in the many references to the United States. The Japanese press and media have long taken delight in stories that discredit the U.S. Discrediting both its technology and its innovative endeavors, such as space research, where the U.S. is still visibly ahead of Japan seems to be doubly delightful. That the *Challenger* disaster was a major blow to U.S. technology and proof that American science is inferior to Japanese science is generally accepted among Japanese engineers. This disaster is taken as proof of declining technology in the United States.

The 110 condescending or derogatory references to the *Challenger* space shuttle disaster is so large that one suspects an entire article, extremely critical of NASA, must have been scanned into the database that was used for the example sentences. Then, whenever a potentially negative word came up, this article was searched to see if an appropriately condescending sentence could be found. This was a departure from the earlier neutral stance; i.e., the earlier 1988 Japanese to English dictionary glosses *supesu shatolu* in katakana simply as "space shuttle" with no illustrative sentence, condescending or otherwise. Only five example sentences were found from the 1986 disaster coverage in the entire 1988 dictionary of nearly two thousand pages. This is the entry for space shuttle in the new dictionary:

> *shuttle,* space shuttle, *supesu shatolu,* (in katakana, with two illustrative sentences) Though U.S. astronauts are scheduled to return to space this September in the shuttle *Discovery,* ... The first attempt to put the shuttle into orbit was scrubbed last month only 51 seconds [sic] left in the countdown.

There are some striking examples about NASA and the *Challenger* from the new galley proofs of the 1994 English-Japanese dictionary. One may note that a few of these do not mention the *Challenger* specifically, but given the entire group of 110 examples, the context of every one is obviously related to the shuttle explosion.

> *Vicariously:* Space belonged to everyone finally [sic; NASA was wrongly ellipted] seemed ready to launch both its schoolteacher and the dreams of the children participating *vicariously* from their schools.

> *Astronaut:* Since the shuttle's computer is not programmed to identify which values [sic, valves] have failed, the *astronauts* would not know how to maneuver their craft out of danger.

> *Conclude:* The document *concluded* that because of shifting motion in the boosters at launch, the secondary O rings might not seat properly.

> *Lift-off:* NASA released pictures showing a mysterious puff of black smoke apparently emerging from the booster at *lift-off.*

> *Lend:* The puff of black smoke seen in the NASA photographs *lends* support to theories that an O ring was at fault.

> *Belly:* NASA analysts said that an orange glow had first flickered just past the center of the orbiter, between the shuttle's *belly* and the adjacent external tank. (This was also used for *flickered.*)

> *Blast-off:* When the flame first appeared, a bit more than a minute after *blast-off,* the shuttle had just experienced its maximum aerodynamic stress.

> *Conflagration:* Snaking wildly out of control, the two boosters emerged from the *conflagration,* both clearly intact.

Blast: The space shuttle has again shown it can *blast* astronauts into orbit in biblical smoke pillars.

Blaze: The *blaze* roared up to the heavens.

Whisper: Two days later, he told the press that NASA engineers had "*whispered*" in his ear that because of the O-ring problems they "held their breaths" during every shuttle launch.

Hold one's breath: XYZ engineers has whispered [sic] in his ear that because of the O-ring problems they *held their breaths* during every shuttle launch.

Dinosaur: With NASA and industrial engineers, the NTSB investigators, like paleontologists trying to reconstruct a *dinosaur,* will piece together every available scrap of *Challenger*'s debris.

Assured: But NASA decided that the shuttle could keep flying without an *assured* backup, knowing that the consequences of failure could be "loss of mission, vehicle, and crew."

Vanish: All those laudable projects *vanished,* of course, with *Challenger*'s demise.

In another editorial policy applied to potentially embarrassing example sentences, the editors in Tokyo were fairly vigilant when a Japanese company was named, and replaced the Japanese name with ABC or XYZ. In another editorial change, the switch from NASA engineers to "XYZ engineers" above is an example of an erratically applied editorial policy of masking all company and national names in every example sentence. This editorial practice is generally applied consistently if the example refers to Japan or to the Japanese government. Two examples follow:

Witness: ABC's statements, made as a sworn *witness,* were taken to indicate more bureaucrats made [sic] in the ABC scandal. (Referring to Japan's 1989 Recruit bribery scandal.)

Depression: Mr. E has been hospitalized at Hanzomon Hospital in Chiyoda Ward, Tokyo, for *depression* and other ailments since the case broke July 6th. (Referring to the Recruit scandal.)

This policy is generally very well applied to the JAL jumbo jet crash examples from 1985, so that JAL or Japan Air Lines becomes XYZ, but it is not often applied to the *Challenger* space shuttle examples or to NASA, IBM, the United States, or Americans. Example sentences with negative connotations usually contain a derisive or hurtful reference to NASA, the *Challenger*, to the USA, or to Americans in general. Note the following reference to the JAL crash: "*smash*: The huge U.S.-built Boeing 747 *smashed* into a mountain in a wilderness area in Gumma Prefecture." This editorial practice consequently appears to be discriminatory.

Regarding the national chauvinism and discrimination evident in the new galley proof, I had a conversation with the general editor and the publisher in Tokyo. I asked him why he needed the *Challenger* example sentences. He replied that there was nothing wrong with them. Regarding the examples about the United States, he simply considered them to be factual. He said there was no need to defend their inclusion in the new dictionary. Regarding the derogatory examples about women, he was somewhat mystified and could not see anything wrong with them.

There is one valid point about using the *Challenger* disaster for example sentences. A well-known event as the frame of meaning for the dictionary's example sentence can make an understandable context for more readers, which might help them understand the lexical meaning better. Kromann et al. (1984) also refer to this technique as the "active dictionary" in the active-passive dichotomy of the Sčerba concept. This dichotomy is explained as follows:

> The passive dictionary can take for granted the dictionary user's native-language competence to choose among the equivalents; in the active dictionary a precise and careful glossing of the equivalents is necessary so that the user can be given clear information about the semantic conditions under which he may use each of the possible equivalents in the foreign language. The accumulation of equivalents in an active dictionary, without any meaning-discriminating glosses, is one of the deadly sins of lexicography, but accumulation is possible in a passive dictionary. (Kromann et al., 1984:209–210)

The editors in Tokyo specified to me that the grouping of many equivalents with discriminating glosses in Japanese, followed by useful example sentences, rather than just phrases or single words, was one of their most important goals. This goal has been met for the vast majority of headwords in this new dictionary, and it represents an advancement over other technical English-Japanese dictionaries. Virtually everyone in technical fields in Japan knows about the *Challenger* space shuttle disaster; thus, examples that are complete and illustrative tend to conform to Sčerba's concept, while avoiding the "deadly sin" mentioned above by including numerous discriminating glosses in Japanese, followed by each illustrative sentence and its corresponding Japanese translation.

The *Titanic*. Another topic for *Schadenfreude* in example sentences is the *Titanic* disaster of 1912. In subscribing to the active-dictionary concept above, the *Titanic* disaster presents a context that can make discrimination of meaning more consistent and accurate for the Japanese user, as in the following:

> *iceberg:* Seventy-three years after the "unsinkable" *Titanic* plowed into an iceberg and slowly slipped beneath the waves, the well-known luxury liner has at last been found sitting nearly upright on the frigid Atlantic floor.

However, just as with the *Challenger*, using the *Titanic* and other Western disasters as examples, rather than Japanese ones, is still *Schadenfreude*, despite the passage of time. Examples from World War II, Hiroshima, and numerous domestic tragedies are conspicuously lacking. This seems to illustrate the lack of empathy for non-Japanese. It also brings to mind the victimization complex *(higaisha ishiki)* that Japanese are said to suffer from (van Wolferen, 1990; McCreary and Noll, 1991).

References to the United States. Derogatory references to women, NASA, and the *Challenger*, not to mention the *Titanic,* all suit the expectations of the primary audience for these technical dictionaries, Japanese engineers, scientists, and technicians. Further expectations regarding the United States and Americans were not to be left unfulfilled. There were 31 condescending and derogatory references to the United States and to Americans in the 6,498-page galley proof. Most refer to declining technology or deterioration, or AIDS and other "American" health problems. *Schadenfreude* is evident here since few positive references were to be found, and of course, all Americans are automatically of the other group, the *gaijin* or outside people, and are thus liable to be targets of derision. As in the examples using women as objects, a considerable number place Americans in painful or deadly situations, illustrating the sadistic side of *Schadenfreude*. A selection of illustrative examples follows:

> *One:* As many as *one* in ten American males and *one* in forty women will suffer excruciating pain.

> *Painful:* ... 200,000 Americans hospitalized with costly and *painful* illnesses.

> *Die:* Experts believe that of the more than 140,000 Americans who are killed by traumatic injuries each year, at least 25,000 *die* needlessly because they do not receive the proper care in time.

Shooting: Traumatic injuries, including violent accidents, *shootings,* and stabbings are the leading cause of death among Americans between the ages of one and forty-four.

Wonder: Because an estimated five million Americans use cocaine regularly, it is little *wonder* that infants with symptoms like Aaron's are turning up in epidemic numbers in several cities across the nation. (This sentence is also used for *cocaine.*)

Cost performance: U.S. industry [sic] declining share of foreign markets results in reduced production quantities and a corresponding deterioration in *cost performance* benefits related to economies of scale.

Communicate with each other: Last week it reached an agreement with eighteen Japanese companies to sell technology that would enable different kinds of computers to *communicate with each other,* beating IBM on that front in Japan.

Clout: IBM's aggressive campaign to rescue the ailing machine has raised new fears about its corporate *clout.*

Disturb: They see the U.S. and their employers losing ground and are *disturbed* because they perceive nothing being done about it.

Flaw: The U.S. industry has also been battered by reports of design *flaws,* manufacturing errors, and marketing problems.

Of: The public transportation is very good in Tokyo. And in Los Angeles, there's none to speak *of.*

Difference: There are considerable *differences* in the quality between the Japanese product and American. (This would always be understood in Japan to mean that the Japanese product is always superior to the American.)

Superiority: U.S. technological *superiority* is diminishing with time ... Even if U.S. product superiority were sufficient to offset Airbus financing advantages ...

Look on: The average American too often *looks on* books as furniture.

Put together: Nobody in the United States has ever been able to *put together* a show.

Assertive: Unlike the Japanese, Americans are *assertive* individualists with strong opinions.

Japan as a topic for example sentences. Unlike the thirty-one examples about the United States, there were only twenty-two about Japan and only nine of them were negative, including these two:

Colonial: Relations between the two countries have been cool since 1945, when nearly half a century of harsh Japanese *colonial* rule ended in Korea.

Sour: Discrimination against a large Korean minority in Japan has further *soured* relations.

Others were on the JAL jumbo crash of 1985, although JAL was consistently cut or changed to ABC or XYZ, and the "U.S.-built Boeing 747" cited above was made the subject rather than Japan Air Lines. Ellipsis or the avoidance of naming Japan occurred in, for example,

Death: The death toll made it the worst single plane accident in history.

This definitely refers to the JAL tragedy, although no mention is made of JAL. Instead, positive, prideful examples were chosen when the topic was Japan, as in these:

Proud: Japanese people are justly *proud* of their economic power.

Provide: Japanese robot manufacturers have a reputation for *providing* their customers with complete, efficient systems.

Salable: If the Japanese can get their design into *salable* shape soon, they would enhance their lead in the vital area of semiconductors.

Obsessively: Anxious Europeans have *obsessively* picked over the Japanese experience to find the secrets of economic growth.

The Soviet Union and *Schadenfreude*. America was not the only country skewered by the Japanese editors in the new dictionary. The Soviet Union also came in for criticism. A few negative example sentences about the former Soviet Union exist, largely using the Chernobyl nuclear accident as the topic, which might reflect the so-called nuclear allergy of the Japanese, but also reveals *Schadenfreude*. However, there were only eight in 6,498 galley pages.

> *Diplomat:* Last Tuesday, when a Soviet *diplomat* was trying to elicit West German help with the accident cleanup while providing as little information as possible ...

> *Diplomatic:* Yet the week's gaiety could not conceal that the Soviet's handling of the tragedy had created a severe *diplomatic* setback for Gorbachev.

> *Collide:* The Soviet Union issued an official protest to Washington over an incident in which Soviet and U.S. warships *collided* inside Soviet territorial waters in the Black Sea.

> *Shoot:* If the U.S. does not *shoot* for the moon, the Soviets will get there first.

There were three more on Chernobyl, including these double criticisms aimed at the USSR and the USA:

> *Death:* "Just as we were scared to *death* by Chernobyl," explained a Western diplomat in Moscow, "they were scared to *death* when *Challenger* blew up."

> *Flaw:* The near tragedy exposed operational *flaws* in a Soviet space program that, in manned flight at least, has far outstripped its U.S. counterpart.

Taking into account Japan–Soviet history, the low number of condescending references to the Soviet Union is a number hardly indicative of the sense of danger and wariness that many Japanese have felt toward the Soviets. Could it be that the only truly heartfelt rivalry in Japan that calls for derisive comments about the "enemy" and self-aggrandizing comments about oneself is the Japan–U.S. economic competition?

Conclusion. Obviously, ethnocentrism and a certain amount of xenophobia have long been a part of the Japanese cultural ethos. According to Landau (1984:295), "language expresses bias ... because large numbers of people ... have felt the need to express these biases." The examples quoted above reflect, in a new technical dictionary, the prejudicial, misogynistic, and anti-American biases in the Japanese scientific community. The anti-American bias seen here has parallels in the lexicography of the Cold War era. D.B. Sands (1980–81) examines East German dictionaries and finds national and ideological chauvinism in references to communism, democracy, and capitalism, among other words, in the dictionaries published by that hard-line regime. These definitions were purposeful and were motivated by political correctness, not to mention job security. However, in the Japanese dictionaries examined in this paper, it appears that misogynistic and prejudicial examples were purposely inserted, but not for job security or political reasons, since ideological correctness is certainly not an overt issue in Japan. One wonders if it may be a covert issue, once submerged after defeat in 1945, but now slowly surfacing to once again influence the public consciousness.

Table 1. Editorial topics and number of critical example sentences

Challenger	US	*Titanic*	Women	USSR	Japan*	Total
110	31	21	52	8	9	231
47.6%	13.4%	9.1%	22.5%	3.5%	3.9%	100%

*out of a total of 22 sentences (13 positive)

REFERENCES

Baehr, Ann Ediger. 1964. "An evaluation of the 1952 and 1962 editions of the Thorndike-Barnhart beginning dictionary." *Elementary English* 41(4, April): 413–419.

Kenkyusha's new English–Japanese dictionary. 1960. Edited by Tamihei Iwasaki, and Jujiro Kawamura, gen eds. Tokyo: Kenkyusha Publishing Co.

Kromann, Hans-Peder, Theis Riiber, and Poul Rosbach. 1984. "Active and passive bilingual dictionaries: The Sčerba concept reconsidered." In Reinhard Hartmann (ed.), *Lexeter '83 proceedings*. Tubingen: Max Niemeyer Verlag. 207-215.

Landau, Sidney. 1984. *Dictionaries: The art and craft of lexicography*. New York: Scribner's.

McCreary, Don R. 1986. "Improving bilingual Japanese–English and English–Japanese dictionaries." *Papers in Linguistics* 19(1): 55–66.

McCreary, Don R. (ed.). 1988. *Japanese–English science and engineering dictionary*. Edited by Atsushi Tomii, gen. ed. Tokyo: OHM Publishing Co.

McCreary, Don R. 1989. "Vygotskyan theory applied to Japanese–English lexicography." In *Resources in education*. ERIC Microfiche, File No. ED 304013. 1–14.

McCreary, Don R., and C.J. Noll. 1991. "Cultural, psychological, and structural impediments to free trade with Japan" *Asian Perspective* 15(2, Fall–Winter): 75–97.

McCreary, Don R. (ed.). In press. English–Japanese science and engineering dictionary. Atsushi Tomii, gen. ed. Tokyo: OHM Publishing Co.

Sands, Donald B. 1980–81. "Engaged lexicography: Comment on an East German dictionary." *Dictionaries* 2–3: 39–51.

Shogakukan's senior friend English–Japanese dictionary. 1988. Mutsuo Inamura (General ed.). Tokyo: Shogakukan Publishing Co.

van Wolferen, Karel. 1990. "The Japan problem revisited" *Foreign Affairs* (Fall). 42–55.

Sociocultural theory and the second-language classroom: The lesson of Strategic Interaction

James P. Lantolf
Cornell University

Introduction. In reading through Bob Di Pietro's writings on language teaching and applied linguistics in general, one is struck by his overriding concern with the need to foreground the humanity of second- and foreign-language learners. This concern finds its synthesis in *Strategic Interaction*, the term that characterizes his perspective on language teaching and the title of his 1987 monograph. In his monograph, Di Pietro succinctly presents his position on language learning as follows: "To speak is to be human, and to learn how to speak a new language is to find new ways in which to express that same humanity" (Di Pietro 1987: 12). In what follows I would like to explore, to the extent possible here, the implications of this claim for the language-teaching enterprise. To do this, I will rely on the concept of mind and learning as developed in sociocultural theory, especially as it is reflected in the writings of the two great Russian scholars Mikhail Bakhtin (1981, 1986) and Lev S. Vygotsky (1978, 1986), whose works have been gaining in influence in educational, literary, psychological, and psycholinguistic research.

First of all, Di Pietro insists that the linguistic system, which he often, and fondly, referred to as "the artifact," has to be subordinated to the individual learners/speakers of a language (first or second), with real needs and specific goals, rather than the other way around. In an especially provocative paper (Di Pietro 1983: 390), he makes the following argument:

> We seem to assume that there will always be a grammar which underlies and motivates what people say. This grammar has an existence in and of itself in the minds of many linguists [and, the present author would add, language teachers, materials writers, and test developers]. When utterances do not match the expectations of what grammar should produce, we interpret them as deviant.

Di Pietro's understanding of language as artifact is not restricted to the domain of lexis, phonology, and syntax; it extends to discourse as well. He argues that linguists approach discourse from a corpus-oriented perspective, in which "we collect specimens of conversation which we then analyze according to one of several ethnographic models available." And while this yields important data, "the results are not tied together in a coherent and comprehensive theory of what motivates people to speak to each other" (Di Pietro 1983: 395). Di Pietro's fundamental concern is with how language serves to construct a *self* and with helping learners develop that linguistically configured self in a second language.

Di Pietro, of course, is not the only methodologist/applied linguist to locate the self at the core of his or her pedagogy. Caleb Gattegno and Charles Curran also emphasized the need for language teaching practices to take account of the self (Stevick 1990). As far as I can determine, however, these two psychologists do not conceive of the self in the same way that Di Pietro does. Specifically, they see the self as arising from processes internal to the individual, while for Di Pietro, the self, as linguistically constituted, was derived from the sociocultural milieu in which humans are immersed. To appreciate just what is at issue here, I would like to examine some of the principal features of SI methodology within the framework of sociocultural theory of mediated mind, as represented in the work of Bakhtin and Vygotsky.[1]

Dialogism. Most introductory textbooks in linguistics include a chapter that explores the interaction between language and society, "as if these were two independent entities which just happen to come into contact occasionally" (Fairclough: 23). Sociocultural theory, however, rejects any move to sever the internal link between language and society, insisting on the necessary dialectical interaction of language and society in the formation of the individual self. As Schrag (1987: 125) eloquently puts it, "no 'I' is an island, entire of itself: every subject is a piece of the continent of other subjects, a part of the main of intersubjectivity." For Bakhtin and Vygotsky, the primary means through which humans construct the intersubjectivity out of which a self emerges is dialogue. Both scholars ultimately conceive of the self as always, and everywhere, dialogically mediated. Even when seeming to act alone, human activity is fundamentally social in nature. As Schrag puts it, "one can be alone only because one has already been in communal interaction" (Schrag 1987: 172). Thus, if solitude is not a fiction, it is at least a paradox (Emerson 1986: 32).

To understand the significance of a dialogically constructed identity for language teaching and learning, we need to consider four critical properties affiliated with dialogue in sociocultural theory: Dialogue is *manifold* rather than

1. Although Vygotsky, born in 1896, and Bakhtin, born one year earlier, were contemporaries who produced their most important work following the Russian Revolution, neither man referred to the other's writings, and there is no evidence that they had any mutual contact (Wertsch 1990). Vygotsky suffered an untimely death from tuberculosis in 1934, while Bakhtin continued to write until his death in 1975.

dyadic in nature; it offers humans the potential for realizing *symbolic* freedom; real *meaning* is constructed in, and through, dialogic relationships; and dialogue is the mediational tool through which humans *appropriate* sociocultural patterns in constructing their identity. The first two properties are central to the work of Bakhtin, and although he addresses the final property of dialogue, it forms the cornerstone of much of Vygotskyan research even today. Both scholars were concerned with the question of how meaning is constructed through dialogue.

I will briefly examine these four properties and consider their link to the language-teaching/learning enterprise as I think it was envisioned by Di Pietro. However, the four properties are so tightly intertwined that is it virtually impossible to discuss any one independently of the others. Holquist (1990), in noting this inseparability, coalesces the properties under the heading of *dialogism,* which he sees as a form of *architectonics*—the science of relations that orders parts into wholes (Holquist 1990: 29).

Dialogue is manifold. From Bakhtin's perspective, to conceive of dialogue as consisting of a bipolar relationship between a speaker (*I*) and a listener *(you)* is to fail to appreciate the full power of dialogue to form, liberate, and subjugate the individual. Dialogue, according to Bakhtin, is manifold, consisting of at least three elements: an utterance, a reply, and the relation between the two (Holquist 1990: 38). The thirdness of dialogue, i.e., the relation, is the most important of the three elements because it is here that the self is created and eventually seeks out its contact with the world. To understand this, we need to recognize that a dialogue is not constituted by an *I* and a *you* at all; rather it is composed of at least two *I*'s, each hoping to have its own way but usually not succeeding and therefore finding itself engaged in an interactive struggle to locate the sought-after relation—that is, some other willing to offer an appropriate reply to *I*'s utterances.

Di Pietro captures the dialogic nature of the world through implementation of the *scenario*. At its essence, the scenario brings into contact two *I*'s, each with a unique motive and script that it hopes to actualize through dialogic interaction with a responsive other. Precisely how the dialogue unfolds in a particular time and place, crucially, is unknown. No two dialogic encounters ever result in the same relations between utterances and replies. For Di Pietro, the tension created by the unknown outcome of a dialogic encounter reflects the drama of human interaction. Without dramatic tension, "a scenario is not likely to be successful, no matter how relevant its theme might be to learners' functional needs" (Di Pietro 1987: 3). Similarly, A. A. Leont'ev (1981) distinguishes between stress, an impediment to learning, and tension, an indispensable aid to learning. According to Leont'ev, stress arises when individuals perceive an incompatibility between their goals and capacities, on the one hand, and the demands of a given situation, on the other. Tension, however, allows a person to "settle into" a given activity, and "always leads to the best possible performance" (1981: 70).

Symbolic freedom. The capacity of dialogue to allow the individual to discover linguistically constituted, or symbolic, freedom is perhaps its most intriguing, and at the same time its most controversial, property. From the dialogic perspective, learning a language, first or second, is the struggle to construct one's *voice.* Voice (i.e., a linguistically constituted self) always has a point of view and a motive, and it enacts specific values when speaking or writing in a particular time and place to known or unknown others (Cazden 1992: 193). To fully appreciate what is meant by voice and the potential liberating power attributed to it, we need to first consider Bakhtin's criticism of abstract objectivism, a view of language forcefully put forth by Saussure and, I think it is safe to say, alive and well today in both its linguistic and pedagogical guises.

According to abstract objectivism, language is a "pure system of laws governing all phonetic, grammatical and lexical forms that confront individual speakers as inviolable norms over which they have no control" (Holquist 1990: 42). Meaning, from this perspective, resides entirely in the system—a system so dominant that it obliterates any possibility of subjectivity (1990: 42). While Saussure (via his concept of *parole*) and, in modern times, Chomsky (in his proposals regarding performance) recognize the subjective quality of individual speech, both jettison it from the proper domain of linguistic research, insisting that it is too unsystematic and not worth investigating.

In making the critical, and from the sociocultural stance, equivocal, bifurcation between *langue* and *parole* or competence and performance, and subsequently abandoning the second member of each pair, formal linguistics purges the noise (i.e., subjectivity) from the system and thus achieves the desired homogeneous, albeit abstract, object of study. For Bakhtin and Vygotsky, however, this homogeneity is bought at the expense of the freedom of the individual, because now every individual is imbued with precisely the same set of attributes, and this being the case, real individuality is impossible. As Ilyenkov (1977: 350) cogently states:

> ... unity (or community) is created by the attribute that one individuum possesses and another does not. And the absence of a certain attribute binds one individuum to another much more strongly than its equal existence in both.
>
> Two absolutely equal individuals, each of which has the very same set of knowledge, habits, inclinations, etc., would be absolutely uninteresting to one another, and the one would not need the other. They would simply bore each other to death. It is nothing but a simple doubling of solitariness. The general is anything but continuously repeated similarity in every single

> object taken separately and represented by a common attribute and fixed by a sign. The universal is above all the regular connection of two (or more) particular individuals which converts them into moments of one and the same concrete, real unity. And it is much more reasonable to represent this unity as the aggregate of *different*, separate moments than as an indefinite plurality of units indifferent to one another.

In sociocultural theory, the critical subjective/objective duality is maintained through dialogue. It is through dialogue that individuals simultaneously acquire and surrender their freedom (Bakhtin 1981). This seeming paradox, is, in fact, no paradox at all, once we examine a bit more closely what Bakhtin has to say on this matter.

In order for language to convey meanings for all members of a particular group, e.g. a speech community, it must have an invariant code. But at the same time, there has to be a way to break the code if language is to serve the specific communicative goals of individual members of the group (Holquist 1990: 56). Following the ideas proposed by Jakobson, Bakhtin argues for an ascending scale of freedom beginning with distinctive features and passing through phonemes to lexis and syntax and terminating with utterance. At the lowest level, the code is inviolable, but as we move up the scale we discover enhanced opportunities for freedom (for example, we can exercise greater flexibility with the lexis than with the phonology of our language) until we reach the level of utterance, at which point we break free of the constraints imposed by the grammar of the code and find substantial latitude for creating novel contexts of activity (Holquist 1990: 59). In this way, language binds us into groups while at the same time enabling us to exist as selves.

The mechanism that provides individuals with the opportunity to rise above the grammatical constraints imposed by a language is dialogue. At this level, the fundamental units of language are no longer sounds, words, or sentences, but *utterances*. The utterance is the place where "constancy and systematicity enter into contact and struggle with unique, situated performance" (Wertsch 1991: 50). Parenthetically, it is important to understand that by *dialogue* Bakhtin does not only intend face-to-face verbal interaction but also "verbal communication of any type whatsoever," including books, i.e., verbal performances in printed form (Volosinov 1973: 95).[2] Thus, according to Bakhtin, books, like spoken dialogue, are composed not of sentences but of utterances. Vygotsky, along the same lines, argues that writing is "language without sound ... a conversation with a white piece of paper" (cited in John-Steiner 1985: 348). Utterances,

---

2. Many of Bakhtin's early writings were apparently written under at least two pseudonyms, one of which is Medvedev and the other, Volosinov.

written or spoken, achieve their dialogic status by virtue of the fact that they are, always and everywhere, reactions to previous verbal performances of some other individual, including the self.

Di Pietro (1987) assigns a central role to literary texts as discursive genre in his approach to language teaching. For him, literature is not something students read after they develop their linguistic capacities in the target language. Rather, it is through reading, and interacting with, literary texts that learners, from the earliest stages of their language-learning experience, "can be involved in the act of creation in much the same way that the author was" (Di Pietro 1987: 121).

The study of language conceived of as dialogically embedded utterances is quite different from the way most professional linguists approach their object of study (Holquist 1990: 59). For one thing, the solipsistic posture of at least one version of linguistic theorizing is no longer sustainable because there are no ideal speakers and hearers but only real concrete individuals whose linguistic activity is relative to that of other individuals. At the same time, however, given that utterances are, by their nature, relative phenomena, the freedom achieved through dialogue is not absolute but relative. This is so because utterances are always conditioned by preceding and, importantly, potential future utterances of others; as such, they represent the border between the said and the unsaid (Holquist 1990: 60).[3]

Bakhtin conceives of utterances as comprising a wide array of *speech genres,* or discursive types (Cazden 1992: 194), which he characterizes as "typical situations of speech communication" (Bakhtin 1986: 87). Examples of speech genres include greetings, farewells, congratulations, table talk, intimate conversations among family and friends, and everyday narration (Wertsch 1991: 60). To these, of course, must be added the written genres of literature and scientific discourse. Although discursive genres, in some way, are prepackaged, they are, nevertheless, a resource the individual can draw on in creative and unique ways to achieve specific goals.[4] As Bakhtin (1986: 79) writes: "the generic forms in which we cast our speech, of course, differ essentially from language forms. The latter are stable and compulsory (normative) for the

3. Holquist (1990: 60) points out that in most traditional studies of turn-taking in linguistics, the impact of potential responses is usually overlooked under the assumption that turns are only influenced by the history and not the future of interactions (see, for example, Crookes 1990).

4. Consideration of precisely how goals, communicative or otherwise, are formed and implemented is a major component of Activity Theory, as developed by Vygotskyan psychology. A full discussion of this theory, however, would take us too far afield. The interested reader should consult Wertsch (1985) for a general presentation and Coughlan and Duff (in press) for an L2-based analysis of Activity Theory.

speaker, while generic forms are much more flexible, plastic and free." Once we realize that utterances, as speech genres, offer speakers and writers the opportunity for communicative creativity, we can begin to appreciate Di Pietro's concerns regarding the need to foreground interaction and to background the linguistic system as artifact.

Things are not quite as straightforward as we might like, however. Not all speech genres are equally malleable. For instance, the exchanges that normally occur in such public places as ticket windows, post offices, airplanes, or grocery stores are "maximally codified" (Holquist 1990: 66). Di Pietro recognizes that culturally determined convention dictates the use of specific routinized expressions, or *protocols,* such as "Hi," "Hello"; "Excuse me," "I'm sorry"; "May I help you?" "No thanks, just looking," etc. (1987: 35). He tries to capture the nature of interactionally less-complex exchanges in what he calls *public scenarios,* which he argues can be used from the start of an instructional program (Di Pietro 1987: 24). On the other hand, the discursive types that individuals employ when engaged with close friends or family, or when they find themselves in circumstances that are less commonplace, conventionalized, and normative, are more flexible and diverse. For Di Pietro, such situations require the development and deployment of a plan of communicative action, which he calls "strategy." It is here that the creative dimension of human dialogue is located. However, strategies are still restricted by factors such as speakers' generation, social background, education, topic, and location of the dialogic encounter. Research within Accommodation Theory, for instance, shows that speakers adjust their linguistic output to converge with or diverge from that of their interlocutors in accordance with the speakers' perception of the saliency of sociocultural relationship between them (Zuengler 1982).

All speech genres are, in fact, constrained by one's culture. Even though a speaker/writer develops a plan for accomplishing some communicative goal through saying or writing something in one way and not another, the plan can only be realized through selection of a speech genre imposed by the culture to which the individual belongs, and in this way it is ultimately restricted. Along these lines, Di Pietro (1987: 59) remarks that "it is to be expected that the particular conventions of a society will impose certain constraints on the options for action open to a role player." He nevertheless believes that there is still room for speakers and learners to construct their own voices within the parameters set by a culture. How culture is able to penetrate individuals is a topic I will address shortly.

When we compare native and nonnative users of a language from the dialogic perspective and the struggle for voice, an interesting situation emerges, one not unnoticed by Di Pietro, as evidenced in the following remarks. "Accent and grammatical accuracy play important parts in establishing identities in a foreign language. Yet sounding native can have relatively little to do with successful interaction with the alien society. It is not unusual to find foreigners who are far from accurate in their use of the new language but can, nevertheless, function in society" (1987: 5). Native users of a language appear to be more constrained by their linguistic system than are nonnatives. As Rommetveit (1991: 12) puts it, "mastery of language actually *implies* imprisonment in it." Paradoxically, then, nonnativeness, in some way, bestows greater freedom on the individual.

To illustrate the point, Lantolf and Ahmed (1989) report on a study of an ESL learner who, when interviewed by one of the researchers regarding his various experiences with U.S. culture, exhibited a high level of control over the grammatical features of English he used to talk about such matters. When, quite by chance, the researcher and the learner found their way into a discussion of religious practices in the Christian and Muslim worlds, a topic of intense interest to the learner, a dramatic shift occurred in the interaction—a shift marked by the learner's taking on a different voice, which resulted in his generating more and longer utterances than in the interview, his taking control of topic shifts, and above all, his producing more errors in using the same grammatical structures over which he displayed mastery in the interview. Of course, the second-language literature is full of studies showing systematic variation across tasks. The point here, however, is not just that the learner's performance was variable, but that in order for the learner to construct a voice in his second language, he had to violate the constraints of the abstract grammatical system of the language. To behave otherwise would have meant surrendering to the pull of the system at the expense of his symbolic freedom.

Dialogic meaning. Meaning, according to sociocultural theory, does not reside in the linguistic code or in dictionaries; it results from the relation between voices engaged in dialogue. As Bakhtin writes, "we know our native language—its lexical composition and grammatic structure—not from dictionaries and grammars but from concrete utterances that we hear and that we ourselves reproduce in live speech communication with people around us. We assimilate forms of language only in forms of utterances" (Bakhtin 1986: 95). Under this view, denotation cannot be the unmarked, privileged signification (Cazden 1992: 197) that, according to the "conduit metaphor" (Reddy 1979), is packaged (encoded) by the sender into word containers and transmitted to a receiver, who then opens or fails to open the containers to discover (decode) the message. The meaning, however, is presumed to remain constant; if it does not, we assume there is a defect somewhere in the circuit (Wertsch 1991: 74). When the sender and receiver are native speakers of the language, we attribute the defect to some type of interference such as lack of attention or noise in the system. When, however, nonnative users of the language are at either end of the conduit, we tend to place the problem at their doorstep. In the dialogic understanding of meaning, a difference in the message from the input to the output point is precisely what must occur, because at either end of the circuit is a different voice. Thus, in dialogism meaning is generated as a unique and nonrecurring property of the interaction. It is not transmitted.

Rommetveit (1991: 9) offers an especially persuasive illustration of how meaning is dialogically constructed, which I will slightly recast in the interest of space. It seems that one Saturday morning, Mr. Smith, a firefighter by profession, is mowing his lawn. His wife receives a phone call from a friend, who, at some point in the conversation, says: "That lazy husband of yours, is he still in bed?" Whereupon Mrs. Smith replies "No, Mr. Smith is *working* this morning, he is mowing the lawn." A short time later, Mrs. Smith receives a call from Mr. Jones, Mr. Smith's fishing buddy, who asks: "Is your husband working?" This time, Mrs. Smith answers: "No, Mr. Smith is *not working* this morning, he is mowing the lawn." Rommetveit argues that it is impossible for a representational-computational model of meaning to handle this perfectly acceptable, normal, and yet, seemingly contradictory use of language other than through some post hoc proliferation of entries in the mental lexicon (1991: 10). The point is that Mr. Smith's mowing of the lawn, an event in the world, is made sense of "and brought into language as WORKING by his wife when she is engaged in conversation with a lady accusing him of being lazy. It is equally spontaneously and unequivocally made sense of and brought into language as NOT WORKING when the very same Mrs. Smith is talking about the very same mowing of the lawn to a person who is interested in whether her husband is free to go fishing" (12). The truth of Mrs. Smith's answer in each case cannot be determined by matching a mental representation against a straightforward state of affairs in the world. It is bound by an intersubjectively accepted perspective and a joint concern that implies necessarily perspectival relativity (12).

Clearly, the dialogic construction of meaning, as argued for by Rommetveit, cannot be achieved if the teacher worries about "how many words are being learned and how to teach the future tense or the modal auxiliaries" (Di Pietro 1987: 25) or even a menu of functions, notions, and conversational management formulae. In the SI classroom, the relative difficulty of traditional pedagogical worries like grammatical difficulty and semantic complexity is never at issue. The primary responsibility of the teacher is not to put words in the learners' mouths, as it were, but to provide opportunities for them to engage each other interactionally in the dialogic construction of meaning out of which an identity or voice may emerge. Di Pietro, therefore, insists that the learners must not be constrained by an artifact-based syllabus but must have the freedom to implement their own speech genres. The teacher's task is to offer the learners those aspects of the linguistic system that will allow them to create the utterances they so choose. According to Di Pietro, this is optimally achieved not by means of a "skill-getting/skill-using" framework but on-line when the learners are immersed in the immediacy of a dialogic encounter (1987: 73-74)—that is, when they are struggling to make sense of the concrete world of Mrs. Smith and Mr. Jones.

Appropriation. As a final issue, I would like to consider the implications of the fourth property of dialogism for language teaching: how a self/voice is constructed. In fact, much of the foregoing discussion has already contributed to our understanding of this process. Nevertheless, some important features of the picture remain to be filled in.

Language, as the centerpiece of sociocultural theory, is the most potent tool humans possess for communicating with, and extracting from, the outside world (Emerson 1986: 28). We extract from the outside world by adopting the words embedded in the utterances of those we encounter in dialogue. The words others use with us and about us eventually become words we use with and about ourselves. Thus, for us to have our own voice, we must take on the voices of others that come to us through their utterances. The process of adopting the voices of others is referred to by Bakhtin (1981) as *ventriloquation* and by Vygotsky's adherents, in particular A. N. Leont'ev (1981), as *appropriation* (Leont'ev 1981).[5] This process is one in which "one voice speaks *through* another voice" (Wertsch 1991: 59). No single voice is ever completely unique; it is a hybrid that always carries elements extracted from other voices. Thus, "an utterance that belongs, by its grammatical (syntactic) and compositional markers, to a single speaker, actually contains mixed within it [minimally] two utterances, two speech manners, two styles, two 'languages,' two semantic and axiological belief systems" (Bakhtin 1981: 304–305). Because of the wide variety of alien voices that overpopulate and compete for influence in our mental life, the process of extrapolating an individual voice is not so easily carried out (ibid). It is especially difficult when the voices of others are privileged by the authority of their social endowment.

Bakhtin proposes two means of appropriating the voices of others, both of which have an analogue in the way children learn texts in school: retelling something in the child's own words and reciting by heart the language of others (Emerson 1986: 31). The former is reflexive and responsive (i.e., dialogic) and, above all, is the only opening through which originality and creativity can emerge. The latter is distanced, leaves no room for doubt, questioning, or error (to change a word would be a mistake), and is inherently monologic.

---

5. It should be noted that some researchers of the solipsistic persuasion, such as Fodor, have criticized Vygotsky, in particular, for failing to explain how, in sociocultural theory, the external world can be internalized. The problem, however, as Newman et al. (1989: 69) point out, is that internalization, as a traditional Western concept, is, by definition, an individual constructive process, whereas appropriation is a process that reflects and selects from the events of the external world—a world that is dialogically constituted.

Authoritative discourse

> demands that we acknowledge it, that we make it our own; it binds us, quite independent of any power it might have to persuade us internally; we encounter it with its authority fused to it ... it demands our unconditional allegiance, and allows no play with its borders, no gradual and flexible transitions, no spontaneously creative stylizing variants on it. (Bakhtin 1981: 341).

Authoritative discourse is not permitted to make contact with other voices, because, for one thing, it fails to even recognize the possibility of other voices. It is the kind of univocal voice posited by the conduit metaphor (Wertsch 1990: 79). Originality and creativity are antithetical to monologic discourse, since it seeks to erect a "single collective self" (Holquist 1990: 53).

Examples of authoritative discourse include, but are by no means restricted to, the voices of parents, adults, religious and political figures, governments and other institutions, and teachers. Authoritative discourse is especially insidious in an educational setting designed to maintain the status quo through reproduction of the values of a privileged segment of society (Bourdieu 1990). This reproduction is achieved through implementation of a uniform curriculum, standardized testing (a filtering device), and the lockstep syllabus that compels teachers to "cover material" and, in my view, is reflected in the language teaching endeavor by the slogan "I want them to ________," which may be completed with "know the irregular verbs, be able to tell a story, order a meal in a restaurant, or know how to apologize" in the target language.

Appropriation of a creative, original, and free voice can only come about through dialogue between parent and child, teacher and student, expert and novice. This dialogic process, according to Vygotsky, entails the mutual construction of a *zone of proximal development* (ZPD). Succinctly stated, the ZPD is the negotiated arena that brings to the fore behaviors (cognitive, psychological, emotional, moral) that individuals can perform by themselves and behaviors they can carry out only under the guidance of others (Vygotsky 1978: 68). Through the dialogic interaction of the ZPD, learners extract from experts those utterances that give rise to their unique voices.

Wertsch's (1985) research has shown that the linguistic patterns used by parents and teachers when interacting with children in the ZPD are eventually appropriated by the children when they begin to carry out similar tasks independently. Children select from the repertoire of utterances offered them by other voices during joint distributed mental activity and make these utterances their own by imbuing them with their own interpretations and intentions. In this way, they create their own voice.

Aljaafreh (1992) provides extensive empirical evidence to show how second-language learning is moved forward when teachers and learners interact in a jointed negotiated ZPD. I hasten to mention that not all dialogues in the ZPD necessarily entail only two individuals, one of whom is an expert and the other a novice. Research has shown that individuals interacting in a collaborative format can construct a ZPD, or scaffold, without the intervention of an expert (Newman et al. 1989). Donato (in press), for example, investigates how language learners, working collectively, without intrusion from the teacher, can construct a viable ZPD to help each other and themselves learn the target language.

The ZPD plays a pivotal role at two points in the implementation of scenarios in strategic interaction. During the rehearsal phase, in which learners prepare themselves to participate in the scenario performance, they must be allowed, as far as possible, to construct a collaborative ZPD, with only minimal intrusion from the teacher. At the debriefing stage, in which the learners analyze the performance under the teacher's guidance, the teacher has the responsibility of interacting with the learners in their ZPD. The responsibility here, however, is not just to help learners with the artifactual aspects of the target language but, crucially, to help them develop their second-language voices.

To achieve the necessary interplay between artifact and voice, Di Pietro argued for a negotiated syllabus between students and teachers, which, by definition, cannot be constrained by what the teacher expects to cover. To be sure, in his written texts, he made some concessions to traditional views of the language curriculum and acknowledged that many teachers will not, or cannot, abandon the mandated curriculum, even when their classes are telling them otherwise (Di Pietro 1987: 88)[6]. In personal conversations it was manifestly clear, however, that Di Pietro's beliefs were firmly anchored in the educational philosophy of critical pedagogues like Paulo Freire, Ira Schor, Henry Giroux, and James Gee, who insist that the school curriculum must be dialogically constructed with the students and not imposed on them by education authorities.

Conclusion. Since the early 1970s, language teachers have been counseled to focus on the learner. Some might feel sanguine about the shift of attention from the teacher to the learner. In my opinion, however, what we have brought into focus is a generic, if not statistically idealized, construct, not real concrete individuals. To appreciate this point, we need only look at the experimental literature in our field. In our eagerness to investigate the nature of language learning and the potential impact of teaching on it, we have overlooked the rather obvious fact that in controlled studies, experimental treatments virtually

---

6. Schumann and Schumann (1977) point out that conflicts between the preordained agendas of teachers and the goals of learners, more often than not, give rise to increased negative attitudes among the learners.

never result in unanimous outcomes. There are always learners, as the statistical evidence reported in the studies clearly shows, who appear to be unaffected by the treatment (this number can be as high as 30 to 40 percent of the subject pool). In human terms, it is difficult to imagine that experiments really work when 30 to 40 percent of the subjects fail to succumb to experimental treatments.

I submit that in our eagerness to proclaim support for this or that hypothesis or to make recommendations for future pedagogical practice, not only do we refuse to concern ourselves with statistical minorities, we do not even notice their existence; after all, they are only subjects in an experiment. Here, I think, resides the crux of the problem. *Subject* is an ambiguous term. It can mean one who is passive and under the authority of another, as in the case of a political system or ruler, or indeed, as in the case of an the experimenter and an experimental procedure. It can also mean one who behaves as an agent, an active doer (Fairclough 1989: 39). According to Vygotsky (1979), it is because individuals are subjects in the second, and most important, sense that controlled experiments are problematic; that is, experimental subjects (and learners), as active agents, can, and often do, change the circumstances of an experiment (and the learning situation) while it is in progress (see Coughlan and Duff, in press).

The enduring legacy of Bob Di Pietro is not what Strategic Interaction represents as a set of classroom procedures designed to achieve the elusive goal of *successful* learning. The procedures themselves are secondary to his unswerving commitment to the core principle of the sociocultural stance: Individuals are human subjects with unique histories, goals, and voices, who actively create and recreate their world and themselves. Di Pietro realized, above all else, that we teach real people, not languages.

REFERENCES

Aljaafreh, Ali. 1992. "Negative feedback in second language learning and the zone of proximal development." Unpublished Ph.D. dissertation, University of Delaware.

Bakhtin, Mikhail. 1981. *The dialogic imagination.* Austin: University of Texas Press.

Bakhtin, Mikhail. 1986. *Speech genres and other late essays.* Austin: University of Texas Press.

Bourdieu, Pierre. 1990. *Language and symbolic power.* Cambridge, Mass.: Harvard University Press.

Cazden, Courtney B. 1992. *Whole language plus: Essays on literacy in the United States and New Zealand.* New York: Teachers College Press.

Coughlan, Peter, and Patricia A. Duff. In press. "Same task, different activities: Analysis of an SLA task from an activity theory perspective." In James P. Lantolf and Gabiela Appel (eds.), *Vygotskian approaches to second language research.* Norwood, N.J.: Ablex.

Crookes, Graham. 1990. "The utterance, and other basic units for second language discourse analysis." *Applied Linguistics* 11: 183–199.

Di Pietro, Robert J. 1983. "Form vs. function in discourse studies." In John Morreall (ed.), *The*

Ninth LACUS Forum 1982. Columbia, S.C.: Hornbeam Press. 390–397.

Di Pietro, Robert J. 1987. *Strategic interaction. Learning language through scenarios*. Cambridge: Cambridge University Press.

Di Pietro, Robert J. 1990. "The dialectics of acquisition in an interactive mode." Paper presented at TESOL Convention. San Francisco.

Donato, Richard. In press. "Collective scaffolding in second language learning." In James P. Lantolf and Gabriela Appel (eds.), *Vygotskian perspectives on second language research*. Norwood, N.J.: Ablex Press.

Emerson, Caryl. 1986. "The outer word and inner speech: Bakhtin, Vygotsky, and the internalization of language." In Gary Saul Morson (ed.), *Bakhtin: Essays and dialogues on his work*. Chicago: University of Chicago Press. 21–41.

Fairclough, Norman. 1989. *Language and power*. London: Longman.

John-Steiner, Vera. 1985. "The road to competence in an alien land: A Vygotskian perspective on bilingualism." In James V. Wertsch (ed.), *Culture communication and cognition: Vygotskian perspectives*. Cambridge: Cambridge University Press. 348–372.

Holquist, Michael. *Dialogism: Bakhtin and his world*. London: Routledge.

Ilyenkov, E.V. 1977. *Dialogetical logic: Essays on its history and theory*. Moscow. Progress Press.

Lantolf, James P., and Mohammed Ahmed. 1989. "Psycholinguistic perspectives on interlanguage variation: A Vygotskyan analysis." In Susan Gass, Carolyn Madden, Dennis Preston, and Larry Selinker (eds.), *Variation in second language acquisition*: *Psycholinguistic issues* (Volume II). Clevedon: Multilingual Matters. 93–108.

Leont'ev, A.N. 1981. *Psychology and the language learning process*. Oxford: Pergamon Press.

Leont'ev, A.N. 1981. *Problems of the development of mind*. Moscow: Progress Press.

Newman, Denis, Peg Griffin, and Michael Cole. 1989. *The construction zone: Working for cognitive change in school*. Cambridge: Cambridge University Press.

Reddy, M. J. 1979. "The conduit metaphor: A case of frame conflict in our language about language." In A. Ortony (ed.), *Metaphor and thought*. Cambridge: Cambridge University Press. 284–324.

Rommetveit, Ragnar. 1991. "Psycholinguistics, hermeneutics, and cognitive science." In Gabriela Appel and Hans W. Dechert (eds.), *A case for psycholinguistic cases*. Amsterdam: John Benjamins. 1-17.

Schrag, Calvin. 1987. *Communicative praxis and the space of subjectivity*. Bloomington: Indiana University Press.

Schumann, Francine, and John Schumann. 1977. "Diary of a language learner: An introspective study of second language learning." In H. Brown, C. Yorio and R. Crymes (eds.), *On TESOL '77*. Washington, D. C. : TESOL. 241-249.

Stevick, Earl W. 1990. *Humanism in language teaching. A critical perspective*. Oxford: Oxford University Press.

Volosinov, V. N. 1973. *Marxism and the philosophy of language*. Cambridge: Harvard University Press.

Vygotsky, L. S. 1978. *Mind in society. The development of higher psychological processes*. Cambridge: Harvard University Press.

Vygotsky, L. S. 1979. "Consciousness as a problem in the psychology of behavior." *Soviet Psychology* 17: 3–35.

Vygotsky, L. S. 1986. *Thought and language*. Cambridge: MIT Press.

Wertsch, James V. 1985. *Vygotsky and the social formation of mind*. Cambridge: Harvard University Press.

Wertsch, James V. 1991. *Voices of the mind. A Sociocultural approach to mediated action*. Cambridge: Harvard University Press.

Zuengler, Janet. 1982. "Applying accommodation theory to variable performance data in L2." *Studies in Second Language Acquisition* 4: 181-192.

The concept of kernel sentences as it applies to language acquisition

Ahmed Mouakket
Aleppo University and the University of Michigan

Introduction. I have selected my data based on the analysis of an original Arabic text *Ziqāq l-Midaq* "Midaq Alley" by the Egyptian novelist Najib Mahfouz (1947), together with its English translation by Trevor LeGassick (1966). This text has been analyzed in terms of its formal structures, i.e. kernel sentences and their derivations. Consequently, a set of generalized rules for translating from Arabic into English has been produced in the form of "if such and such in SL, then such and such in TL," with a list of exceptions to the kernels and their derived forms.

The concept of kernel sentences has been discussed and formalized in transformational grammar. According to Chomsky (1957: 80), "the kernel consists of simple declarative active sentences." In terms of their content, kernels are defined as "simple, complete, statement, active, and affirmative" (Cook 1985: 13). A kernel sentence must have all these five features simultaneously; a sentence that lacks any one of these five features is a derived sentence. The contrast between kernel and derived sentences is shown in Table 1.

Table 1. Requisite features of kernel and derived sentences

Kernel	Derived Sentences
1. Simple	1. Compound, complex
2. Complete	2. Incomplete
3. Statement	3. Question, command
4. Active	4. Passive
5. Affirmative	5. Negative

Besides its apparent applications in translation studies, the set of generalized rules that have been generated depending on the concept of kernels can be of use in the field of second-language acquisition. I shall discuss the implications that the concept of kernels has for second-language acquisition in the fourth section of this paper.

Illustrations of the kernels. The kernel sentences will be fully accounted for in my presentation because they are considered basic to our the issue of language acquisition. As for the other structures that are derived from the basic kernels, I shall focus on only two of these structures, the complex and the passive, in addition to one of the exceptional structures, *Munādā* "vocative." A complete list of the rules generated for all the kernels and derived sentences is supplied in the appendix.

Kernel sentences are of three types: transitive, intransitive, and equational.

Transitive Structure. The transitive sentence consists of three basic constituents, which are obligatory in every transitive structure. These constituents are the transitive verb (Vt), the subject noun phrase (NP1), and the object noun phrase(s) (NP2/NP3). To these constituents, one or more adjuncts (Aju) can be added. The subject may be either NP1 or a verb subject-marker affix. The adjuncts to the sentence are adverbs, adverbial phrases, or adverbial clauses of time, place, and manner, as in (1) and (2).

--Vt-- --NP1-- --NP2-- -----------Aju----------
(1) wa ḥadaja š-šāᶜiru l-qādima bi naḏrati-mtinānin (p. 8)
and gazed the poet the newcomer with a look gratefulness

"The ... poet gazed gratefully at the newcomer." (p. 4)

-Vt- -NP2- -------NP1-------
(2) wa qāṭaᶜa-hu sawtun ʻajaššu (p. 9)
and interrupted him voice harsh

"He was interrupted by someone... " (p. 5)

Rules: K1 → [Vt - NP1 - NP2 - (NP3) - (Aju)] Arabic
Condition: This is the unmarked word order.
Ka → [NP1 - Vt - NP2 - (NP3) - (Aju)] English

Intransitive structure. The intransitive sentence consists of two basic constituents, which are obligatory in every intransitive structure. The two constituents are the intransitive verb (Vi) and the subject (NP1). To these two constituents, one or more adjuncts can be added, as in (3) and (4).

---Aju--- --Vi-- -------NP1--------
(3) wa hunā qadima šaxsun jadīdun (p. 11)
and then arrived a person new

"Just then another person arrived." (p. 6)

--------------- NP1--------------- ----Vi---- --Aju--

(4) ḥattā s-sayyid raḍwan l-ḥusaynīy 'ibtasama rāḍiyan (p. 14)
even the Sayyid Radwan Hussayny smiled delighted

"Even Radwan Hussainy smiled delightedly." (p. 9)

Rules: K2 → [Vi - NP1 - (Aju)] Arabic
Condition: This is the unmarked word order
Kb → [NP1 - Vi - (Aju)] English

Equational structure. The universal definition of the equational sentence is that it contains a subject (NP1), an equational predicate (eqp), and a predicate attribute (PA). The predicate attribute may be nominal (NP), adjectival (Adj), or adverbial (Adv). In English all three constituents are required. In Arabic, however, (eqp) is omitted in the present tense but not in other tenses, whereas (PA) is obligatory, as in (5) and (6).

--------Pred-Adv------------ ----------NP1---------

(5) wa bayna l-katifayni wajhun mustadīrun (p. 6)
and between the shoulders a face rounded

"Between his shoulders lies his rounded face." (p. 2)

---NP1--- -Pred-Adj-

(6) 'a^{c}ḍā'u-ka salīmatun (p. 65)
limbs your healthy
"Your limbs are all healthy." (p. 51)

Rules: K3 → [NP1 - (eqp) - { (NP2) - (Adj) - (Adv) }] Arabic
[-pres]
Condition: Eqp is copula, omitted only in the present tense.
Kc → [NP1 - BE - { (NP2) - (Adj) - (Adv) }] English

Derived structures. As mentioned earlier, out of the seven derived forms, only two will be accounted for here, the complex structure and the passive, in addition to the structure *Munādā* 'vocative', which is an exception to kernel structures.

Complex sentence. A complex sentence consists of at least two structures, one main and the other dependent. Complex structures constitute the majority of derived structures that are extensively used in speaking and writing, and they have various types. The examples below reflect some of the many types that the rules, then, will describe.

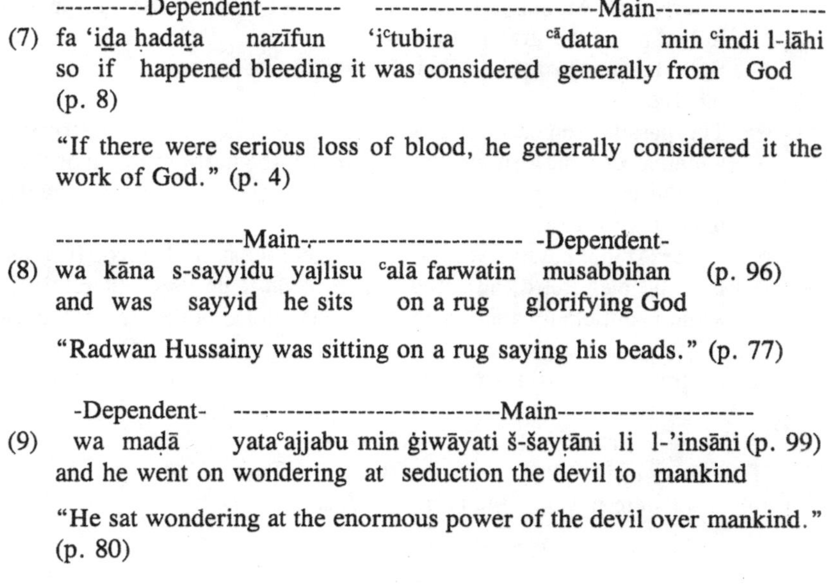

----------Dependent--------- -------------------------Main-------------------

(7) fa ʻiḏa ḥadaṯa nazīfun ʻi^{c}tubira $^{c\bar{a}}$datan min ^{c}indi l-lāhi
so if happened bleeding it was considered generally from God
(p. 8)

"If there were serious loss of blood, he generally considered it the work of God." (p. 4)

---------------------Main-,----------------------- -Dependent-

(8) wa kāna s-sayyidu yajlisu ^{c}alā farwatin musabbiḥan (p. 96)
and was sayyid he sits on a rug glorifying God

"Radwan Hussainy was sitting on a rug saying his beads." (p. 77)

-Dependent- -----------------------------Main----------------------

(9) wa maḍā yata^{c}ajjabu min ġiwāyati š-šayṭāni li l-ʼinsāni (p. 99)
and he went on wondering at seduction the devil to mankind

"He sat wondering at the enormous power of the devil over mankind." (p. 80)

Rules: D-Compx → [Main { K/D } - Dependent] Arabic
D-Compx → [Main { K/D } - Dependent] English
Conditions:
1. Main = Kernel or derived sentence.
2. Dependent may fill one of the following positions:
    a. Subject, object, or object of a preposition
    b. Adverbial position
    c. A clause modifying a noun or an adjective
    d. An aspectual verb
    e. A verb expressing wish or request
3. Conditionals and comparisons are patterned dependencies, with both clauses marked.

Passive Structure. In Arabic, the active sentence is transformed into a passive sentence by using the passive form of the verb, with the object of the active sentence as the grammatical subject and deleting the active subject.

Comparing the passive structures in Arabic with those in English, we may note the following points:

- Both languages use the object of an active sentence as the grammatical subject of the corresponding passive sentence. In English, the role of subject is expressed solely by the word order of the passive sentence, whereas in Arabic it is expressed in addition by the morphological inflection of the grammatical subject.

- Both languages assume that the verb must be transitive and use its passive form.
- The passive sentence in English involves a syntactic construction in which a relevant form of the verb *be* and the past participle of the verb are the constituents, while in Arabic the passive sentence involves a passive verb form.
- In the Arabic passive sentence, the agent must be deleted. If the agent is to be mentioned, an active sentence must be used. In English, the agent is optionally mentioned in a prepositional phrase (a "by" phrase).

To illustrate the passive structure, let us consider examples (10) and (11).

```
        ----V-Pass-----     ---------NP2---------
(10)    fa   nuṣibat           l-'aᶜmidatu            (p. 157)
        so were put up    the (vertical) beams
```

"Vertical struts were put up." (p. 127)

```
        --V-Pass-- -NP2-     ---------------Aju---------------
(11)           xuliq-ta       li-takūna  'aᶜmā  muqᶜadan   (p. 66)
        were created you     to you be  blind   squatted
```

"You were created to be a blind, squatted beggar." (p. 52)

```
Rules: D-Pass → [  V   -   NP1   -   NP2  ]                  Arabic
                [ [+Pass]    Ø      [+Nom] ]
       D-Pass → [ NP2 -  BE  -  Ven - (by-NP1) ]             English
```

Conditions:
1. V = transitive and passive.
2. NP2 = nominative in Arabic.

Munādā 'the person or thing addressed'. Munādā is used for calling to a person or a thing. The munādā structure consists of a noun phrase (NP) preceded by a vocative particle (Voc Part), as in (12).

```
        ----------Command----------  -Voc Part-  --NP--
(12)    ġayyir   mā'a     l-jawzi        yā       sanqaru  (p. 6)
        change   water   the hookah      O        Sankar
```

"Change the water in the hookah, Sankar!" (p. 2)

Rules: Munādā → [(Voc Part) - NP] Arabic
Condition: NP = NP2, takes the necessary inflection.
Vocative → [{ Voc Part } - NP] English
[(You)]
[(Ø)]

Implications for second-language acquisition. The concept of kernel sentences and their derivations has significant implications in the field of second-language acquisition. These can be summarized in the following points:

- The concept of kernels is a universal concept in terms of which almost all natural languages can be analyzed. According to Lyons (1977: 468), "it holds out to the semanticist the prospect of his being able to account for the meaning of all the sentences of a language on the basis of the meaning of a relatively small number of them."
- The universality of the concept of kernels does not necessarily imply that all languages are similar in their basic structures. On the contrary, kernels help to describe the differences as well as the similarities underlying the sentence structures of the languages in question.
- Consequently, one principal effect of depending on the kernels in learning a second language (and perhaps preparing curriculum materials) is to provide the learners with the means and methods of showing the similarities and differences between L1 and L2.
- Mastering the basic structures, or kernels, with their corresponding derived structures of both L1 and L2 enables the learner to operate confidently—formally at first, and later on perhaps more creatively—in transferring any structures between the two languages.

  Field research done so far in this field, however, has not shown lack of interference between L1 and L2 and has not ascertained the extent of interference, whether positive or negative, between L1 and L2 (Klein 1986: 13). But citing certain examples of interference, Klein finds that "speakers of German, for instance, have a strong tendency to use the pronoun 'it' when referring to a child in English, even though they well know that 'it' should be either *he* or *she* (they hasten to correct themselves moreover as soon as they are challenged)."

  Yet the question of "how learners acquire the ability to form basic affirmative sentences" (Littlewood 1984), i.e. kernels, is still an issue that deserves further investigation.
- The concept of kernels seems especially applicable in methods that use translation techniques as a basic strategy for learning a second language—the Community Language Learning method, for example (Brown 1980, Richards and Rodgers 1986).

- Focusing on the kernel level, moreover, will not necessarily distract our attention from the content of the message, i.e. from the functional and communicative potential of language, or what Hymes (1972) refers to as "communicative competence." Once the child begins to capture and internalize the concept of kernels and its applicability, he or she will be able to manipulate the kernel in many ways so as to effect meaningful and communicative linguistic messages.
- The generalized rules for Arabic and English structures show that the agreements between the two languages are far greater than the differences. This might open the way to further investigation in the field of second-language acquisition.
- These generalized rules can also be of use in automatic translation. However, this general system for formal translation is by no means exhaustive; it only gives a general account of the basic and more frequently used structures, based on the analyses made from the data.

REFERENCES

Brown, H. Douglas. 1980. *Principles of language learning and teaching*. New Jersey: Prentice-Hall.

Chomsky, Noam. 1957. *Syntactic structures*. The Hague and Paris: Mouton.

Cook, Walter A. 1985. "Introduction to transformational grammar." Mimeograph. Washington, D.C.: Georgetown University.

Hymes, Dell. 1972. "On communicative competence." In J.B. Pride and J. Holmes (eds.), *Sociolinguistics*. Harmondsworth: Penguin.

Klein, Wolfgang. 1986. *Second language acquisition*. Cambridge: Cambridge University Press.

LeGassick, Trevor. 1966. *Midaq Alley*. Washington, D.C.: Three Continents Press.

Littlewood, William. 1984. *Foreign and second language learning*. Cambridge: Cambridge University Press.

Lyons, John. 1977. *Semantics*. London, New York: Cambridge University Press.

Mahfouz, Najib. 1947. "Ziqaq l-Midaq." *Dar Misr li l-tiba'a*. Cairo.

Nida, Eugen A., and Charles R. Taber. 1969. *The Theory and Practice of Translation*. Leiden: E.J. Brill.

Richards, Jack C., and Theodore S. Rodgers. 1986. *Approaches and methods in language teaching*. Cambridge University Press.

Foreign language learning in the kindergarten: A teaching model and some resulting language-acquisition strategies

Traute Taeschner[1]
Università degli Studi di Roma "La Sapienza"

Introduction. In the following pages, a foreign-language teaching model for children and some empirical results will be presented and discussed. In 1986, the city of Modena started the Modena English Language Project (MELP), introducing English as a foreign language in the last two years of the kindergarten curriculum. The starting age is four years, and the children, divided into groups of at most fifteen pupils, are exposed to three lessons a week. Each lesson lasts from 30 minutes (for the four-year-olds) to 45 minutes (for the five-year-olds). Each year about 600 children enter the project[2]. MELP's main aim is to promote an early contact with English in order to get the children used to its phonological and intonational systems, which are very different from those of Italian and considered difficult for adults to learn.

In the last four years, a Psycholinguistic Research Project (PRP) was added to MELP. The aim of PRP is not simply to evaluate the children's progress in English, but mainly to get further insight into the process young children go through when acquiring a second language in a school setting[3]. The following

---

1. My thanks to Pompea Mocciola and Laura Spadola for their precious help, comments, and suggestions regarding this paper. My thanks also to Anna Lowenstein Corsetti for reviewing the paper so carefully.

2. The project profited from the scientific counseling of Professor Renzo Titone of the University of Rome "La Sapienza" and from Dr. Alfredo Bondi, president of Anils. The project also profited from the work done by a group of Catalan teachers who invented a series of beautiful narrative formats and scripts published in the book *Com fer descobrir una nova llengua* (Eumo Editorial: Barcelona 1984) by Josep Maria Artigal, Fina Anglada, Nuria Aragonès, Maria Dolores Flamerich, Montserrat Ral, Maribel Ruiz, Mariona Ventura, and Mercè Voltas. The first author also participated as scientific adviser and teacher trainer at MELP.

3. Considering the children's young age and the rather natural teaching method used, I don't think that the distinction usually made between *foreign language* and *second language* can be useful in the present context. For this reason the two terms are used interchangeably. The same consideration is made for the terms *acquisition* and *learning* and *L2* and *FL*.

hypotheses were put forward: Considering that the teaching model follows in a certain sense and up to a certain point a natural approach (see the second and third sections below), language strategies similar to those encountered in the process of first-language acquisition can be plausibly expected. For the same reason, phases in L2 progression should resemble phases in L1 acquisition. Underlying these hypotheses is the assumption that the two processes, first-language acquisition and second-language learning in children, are not distinct processes, but that the children, one might say, repeat in another language the path followed in the previous one. First of all, of course, there is the assumption that it is possible to "construct" a natural way of teaching by using appropriate teaching techniques, even in a setting so difficult for L2 language learning as the school setting has been shown to be.

Brief description of the teaching model. A teaching model, called the format model (see principle 1 below), was developed based theoretically on the nature of human communication and on the process of monolingual and bilingual language acquisition (Vygotsky 1962, Austin 1962, Brown 1973, Bruner 1975, Grosjean 1982, Taeschner 1983, McLaughlin 1978, Wells 1985, Slobin 1982, Hakuta 1986). It can be briefly described in ten psycholinguistic principles (Taeschner 1986, 1990, 1992).

Principle 1. In order to learn a language, it is necessary to use it, and the use of a language has as a prerequisite the development of intentions, i.e. the desire to say something to someone. This desire comes into being through the presuppositions speaker A has of the behavior of B. As soon as A has an idea of B or an impression of B or knows how B thinks and behaves, A will want to speak to B. To reach this desire to communicate, shared experiences between A and B are needed. During shared experiences, a certain event takes place, and it is the repetition of the event that causes presuppositions and thus intentions.

For example: A (a teacher) and B (a pupil) decide to go jogging together every day at five o'clock in the afternoon. The first day B arrives at five and A a little later. A also arrives late the second day. After the repetition of the event "coming late," B will now suppose that A usually arrives with delay, and if B is a peaceful person, B will not say anything and will simply arrive late, too. Routines of shared experiences are called "formats" in child-language literature and constitute the primary events (between a prelinguistic child and an adult) for the development of intentions. (For further information see Bruner 1975, Aston 1987, Di Pietro 1987.)

Principle 2. Intentions cannot be commanded by someone else; they are strictly personal. That is to say that a teacher cannot tell a pupil to have the desire to buy a train ticket while comfortably seated in a classroom and without the need for doing so. The desire to buy a train ticket must grow in the pupil. And this natural wish comes into existence in the pupil only when circumstances (either in real life or in imagination) demand it. Current functional approaches (see Halliday 1975, Wilkins 1973, Rivers 1987) make a great deal of use of intentions, but they fail in practice because teachers do not take principles 2 and 3 into account (see next paragraph).

Principle 3. For learning a foreign language, the development of intentions has to occur in the foreign language. It is not enough to have developed the general ability to have intentions in order to use a foreign language, because intentions are attached to the language spoken and understood by the interlocutor. A person has intentions in language Y and uses that language if and only if it is the language of the interlocutor. Thus, for foreign-language use to occur, experiences must be shared with speakers of the target language, either in real life or in the imagination.

Principle 4. Events in narration are interesting; events out of narration are less interesting. We may distinguish two kinds of format: with and without narrative content. The format without narrative content refers to events that are repeated in a similar fashion, as for example, having breakfast. The narrative format is different from the nonnarrative one; it is a sequence of events in which previous events allow us to make predictions about possible future events in the perspective of a concluding final event. It is thus foresight and expectation that creates tension and makes the format interesting.

Principle 5. The process of language acquisition is based on dialogue. As is known from child-language literature, language learning takes place in a dyadic situation: interaction between caretaker and infant. In the dyadic interaction, turn-taking is learned; this means that when A pauses, B begins. In the "multi-dialogue" relationship, which is typical of classroom interactions in which one teacher addresses several children at once, turn-taking gets lost because none of the "group listeners" feels directly compelled to answer.

Principle 6. Language is acquired better and easier in an affective relationship between caretaker and child. This principle has received much attention in developmental psychology and in educational psychology as well. In such studies, the relation between affective problems and learning problems is continually stressed and thus does not need to be further discussed. Positive interactions lead to sympathy and identification, crucial for L2 learning (cf. Schiffler 1980).

Principle 7. For producing foreign language in a classroom situation, children need teachers who do not understand the child's native language. It is not enough to always speak the foreign language while still understanding the children's native language. This behavior ends up with children understanding the foreign language but not speaking it. The foreign language is spoken by the child only if it is the language that makes her talking successful, i.e. understood by the teacher (usually the only L2 interlocutor). If the teacher understands the child's native language, there is no need for the child to use another linguistic code. Second-language production grows, in fact, through the incapacity of understanding the language already known by the learner. (See Taeschner (1983), where the author analyzed at length the phenomenon of children raised in bilingual families without succeeding in becoming bilingual.) Current methodologies may fail because although they stress the need for the teacher to speak only in the target language, they ignore the need to understand only that language.

Principle 8. Language is used in real life and in our imagination, in pretend play or fantasy. If we compare the number of utterances each person produces and the number of unspoken utterances, i.e. the number of real-life events with respect to events that live in imagination, we will see that the latter is much higher.

Principle 9. Meaning is conveyed through words and facial expressions, gestures, body position, previous experience, context, or frame of the event in which communication takes place. Usually adults give too much importance to words, especially at school, forgetting that for children, comprehension is based also and probably primarily on many other cues.

Principle 10. Developmental phases of language acquisition in a natural setting are the best indicators for planning progression levels in foreign-language teaching for children. As several authors have pointed out, target-language progression can best be planned following those phases monolingual children of the target language go through when acquiring the language.

In the Modena Project, three progression levels regarding lexicon and sentence structure were followed. The progression levels were adapted to semesters. A distinction was made between the amount of input given and the expected output. In the first semester, the teaching program begins with single words, gradually progressing to combining two or at most three words in incomplete and complete nuclear sentences[4]. A total of about 100 different words were taught, and about 50% of them were expected to be active production. In the second and third semesters, a slow transition to more complete nuclear sentences, also including amplified sentences with adverbs and noun modifiers, was programmed, and a few of them also were expected. When the story required it, complex and binuclear sentences with connectives were introduced. These structures were expected to be used by the children without connectives. A total lexicon of about 200 different words was taught, and 50%, more or less, were expected in the children's active vocabulary. In the fourth semester, about 100 more words were included in the teaching program, and all types of sentence structures were used, but they were not necessarily expected in the children's production.

Brief description of the model's practical application. Theory and practice are often two separate bodies in foreign-language teaching methodology: theorists not intending (or not able) to create materials, and practitioners failing to work out practical means of interpreting theories. This breach causes many teaching problems and ends up most of the time with children not learning the second language (see Wilkins 1973). In the present approach, a strong effort has been made to overcome this problem by linking psycholinguistic theory to specific classroom activities.

By the term "practice" is meant the activity done in the classroom by teacher and pupils, and in the present context it will be called "teaching technique." It is argued that in a nonnatural setting like the school setting, specific techniques need to be developed in order to promote language learning. The technique developed in the present approach is called "format technique." The term "format" is defined by Bruner as "a routine of shared experiences" (see principle 1).

Two kinds of formats can be distinguished: those with and those without narrative content. For example, having breakfast in the morning is an event that is repeated every day in similar way; it is a format without narrative content. A narrative format can be defined as a sequence of events in which the previous event allows one to make inferences and presuppositions about the next event,

4. Semantic sentence structure analysis based on linguistic analysis by Tesnière (1953), Parisi and Antinucci (1973), and Helbig and Schenkel (1969). As is known, this analysis considers the meaning of the predicate the central part (nucleus) of a sentence, that part that connects the other parts (called arguments) of the utterance. According to this analysis, a sentence is considered a complete nuclear sentence when it is formed by a predicate and its arguments; if an argument is lacking, the nuclear structure is said to be incomplete. If a nuclear sentence also includes words (adjectives or adverbs) not required by the meaning of the verb, it is said to be an amplified sentence. Utterances formed by two nuclear sentences are said to be binuclear. Complex structures are those in which one predicate argument is a sentence or one amplified element is a sentence.

and where the series of events ends with a final important event (cf. Britton and Pellegrini 1990). Both kinds of format are used in the classroom: "asking the teacher for a pencil" is a format without narration, while acting out a story is a format with narration.

The actual narrative format in the classroom (see principle 4) is as follows: A story is invented, taken either from tales or from the children's real-life experiences. A script of the story is made with an accurate description of gestures, mimicry, and body position. Attention is also given to the story structure. These are very clear language indicators, and meaning is conveyed at the beginning by such indicators and then by the foreign word (see principle 9). Thus, during FL lessons the teacher takes advantage of the child's early ability to act out what is in the imagination, which becomes a means of promoting language learning (see principle 8). The "pièce" is executed in the classroom using ancient Greek theatre modalities.[5] A narrator (at the beginning played by the teacher and afterwards also by a child) introduces the story.

Usually a simple story has no more than two to four different roles, and the children all play each role. That is to say, when role A requires the character to be hungry, all children play the role pretending to be hungry. If the complementary role requires a character who cooks for the hungry one, all children play the role pretending to do the cooking. The change of role is signalled by the change of place, body position, facial expression, or any other useful signaling tool. By interpreting all roles all the time, children are always actively engaged in the play, speaking all the time in a dialogue (see principle 5), a dialogue in a world of fantasy in which the child can pretend to be the prince but also the princess, the obedient girl but also the naughty one, and so on (cf. Artigal et al. 1984). While acting out the format, it is not the teacher who is going to tell the pupil what he or she should want or do next, but it is the structure of the story itself, the sequence of plausibly possible events that leads to intentionality. For example, if the children are playing a role in which they pretend eating and eating and eating, their next intention will be the wish to stop eating (see principle 2).

Making theatre in the classroom requires a teacher who is willing to use mimicry and who is also capable of communicating without words. The teacher is supposed to always speak in the foreign language and to pretend to understand only that language (see principles 2, 3, and 7). Furthermore, he or she has to be acquainted with the children's psychology and linguistic processes (see principle 10). The teacher should also be truthfully democratic, capable of

---

5. The present theatre modality is based partly on the work of Artigal et al. (1984). It can of course be easily substituted with any other technique, always in the sense of role play, as for example suggested by Robert Di Pietro's Strategic Interaction. See also Oller and Amato (1983).

interacting with affection (cf. Tausch and Tausch 1973), having as his or her most important educational principle a real, friendly relationship with the children (see principle 6).

The teacher is for the child the most important, if not the only, representative of the foreign language. Only a positive identification with the teacher, on the bases of affection and friendship, will awaken in the child feelings of love and acceptance toward the new language, feelings that are necessary for initiating language learning (cf. Schiffler 1980).

Considering the limited amount of L2 contact a child can get in a classroom, in order to foster L2 memory, a mini-musical was composed for each teaching format (audio memory) and an illustrated book was printed containing the stories for the teaching formats (visual memory). Parents were encouraged to give their children daily contact with the language through the audiocassette and the book.

A typical L2 lesson was divided into activities according to the following scheme:

- Teacher and pupils play the teaching format together.
- They sing and act the mini-musical.
- They make a puppet replay of the story or a story played previously.
- They watch (and read) in their story book. Slides and transparencies of the stories are used as means of eliciting spontaneous conversation.
- A storytelling session closes the lesson. The teacher tells a new and very short story, helped by the children, using already-known words and also many gestures and body and facial expressions.

As homework the children listen to the mini-musical and look at the story book.

Research aims, subjects, and data collection. As already mentioned in the introduction, the aim of the present research is to see if, in a methodological framework like the one described above, kindergarten children will learn a foreign language showing (1) L2 progression similar to progression in first-language development and (2) L2 language-learning strategies similar to L1 language-acquisition strategies. In this context, two linguistic aspects were examined, semantic sentence structure and intonation, comparing the data collected from MELP's FL learners with data collected from monolingual subjects. Considering the important role imitation plays in the process of language acquisition, another aim was to see (3) if FL learners imitated the teacher's intonation patterns and, vice versa, (4) if this imitation was promoted by the teachers by using exaggerated intonation when addressing the children. The latter would mean that teachers naturally employ a common maternal strategy to catch attention and convey meaning: a high pitch in intonational curves and a greater range between maximum and minimum pitch (cf. Fernald et al. 1989).

Fifty-four kindergarten children with a mean age of 6;05 (read: 6 years and 5 months) were tape-recorded in a story-telling task in English, using drawings as visual input. The children were interviewed by a researcher who had first gotten acquainted with them. Interviews were done individually in a quiet room in the kindergarten, and the interviewer showed the drawings one after the other to the children. The drawings referred to formats the children had learned in school, with a few small changes. Two stories (a sequence of nine drawings for each one) were presented to each child. The tape recorder was semi-professional, and wireless microphones were used. The children's productions were transcribed, and two types of analysis were done: semantic sentence structure analysis (structures considered: nuclear sentences, amplified sentences, complex and binuclear sentences) and intonation (parameters considered: maximum fundamental frequency (henceforth F_0 max), minimum frequency (henceforth F_0 min), range, and time. Lastly, analysis was done using a digital sonograph (Visi-Pitch).

Two groups of 25 kindergarten children each were also tape-recorded in a similar story-telling task in Italian. The first group's mean age was 3;6 and the second group's mean age was 5;7. Methods of data transcription and analysis were the same.

FL production of two teachers was collected during classroom interaction, as well as the FL production of five children in the classroom. These data were also transcribed and then analyzed with the Visi-Pitch.

Figure 1. Types of sentence structures produced in story n.1.

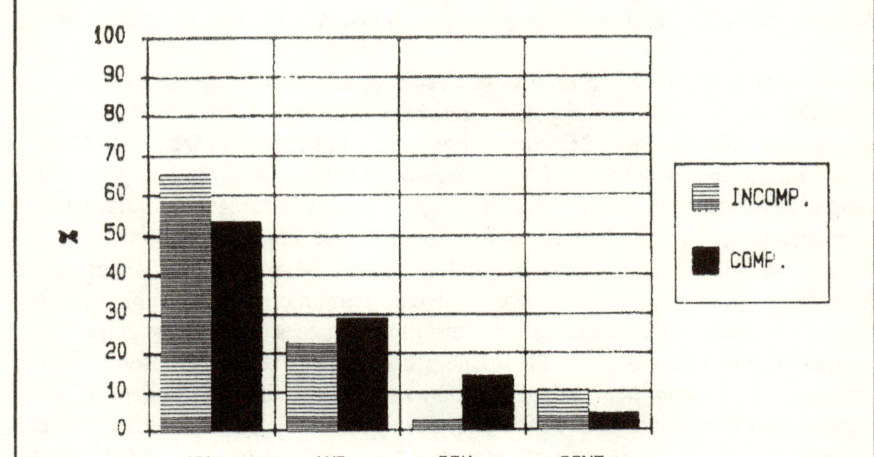

Results. Regarding the first research aim, i.e. to observe if L2 progression is similar to progression in first-language development, results showed that L2 learners' development of sentence structure in FL follows the same pattern monolinguals show when acquiring the first language. As is known from previous research (cf. Taeschner 1983), monolingual children start speaking with single words, vertical utterances, and expressions, followed in the next phase by mainly complete and incomplete nuclear sentences, a smaller number of amplified sentences, and to a much lesser extent binuclear and complex structures. As can be observed in figures 1 and 2, L2 learners, after two years of foreign-language lessons, show the same pattern.

With respect to the second aim, i.e. to observe if L2 language-learning strategies are similar to L1 language-acquisition strategies, it was seen that intonational parameters of children learning a second language in the kindergarten (mean age: 6;05) show the same values and characteristics as smaller children (mean age: 3;6) acquiring the first language and not the values and characteristics of monolinguals of the same age (mean age: 5;7). As is shown in figure 3, the value referring to the distance between minimum frequency and maximum frequency, i.e., the range, is closer to the value displayed by younger monolinguals: Mean range of L2 learners in FL is 313.32 Hz and of young monolinguals 300 Hz while older monolinguals display a lower-frequency range of 200 Hz.

Figure 2. Types of sentence structures produced in story n.2.

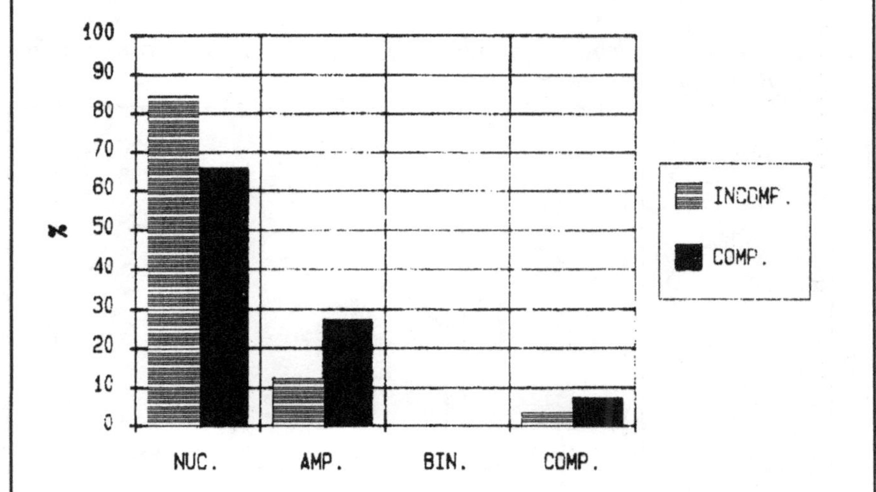

It is known from previous studies that small children's narrations are emphatic and stressed but syntactically and logically poor. In order to give "narrative appearance" to their tellings they use a slower tempo and a rich intonation. Many three-year-olds, in fact, when hearing the request to tell a story, would answer that they were incapable of doing so. Being then persuaded by the teacher to try anyway, they would start with a big initial flourish saying "Once upon a time" and then go on citing one element for each drawing they were shown, producing something like: "... there was a little bird, a little bird, two little birds and here one little bird flies away. Bye bye little bird. The end."

Table 1. Mean range and types of intonational curves shown by L2-speaking children and L1-speaking children

Children	mean age	mean range	Types of intonation curves
speaking a foreign language	6;05	313.32 Hz	• High number of initial peaks • Few falls • High number of final flats
speaking their first language	3;6	300.00 Hz	• High number of initial peaks • Few falls • High number of final flats
speaking their first language	5;7	200.00 Hz	• Many falls • Many bells

Figure 3. Teacher's intonational curve and imitated curves of three children while saying *wolf*.

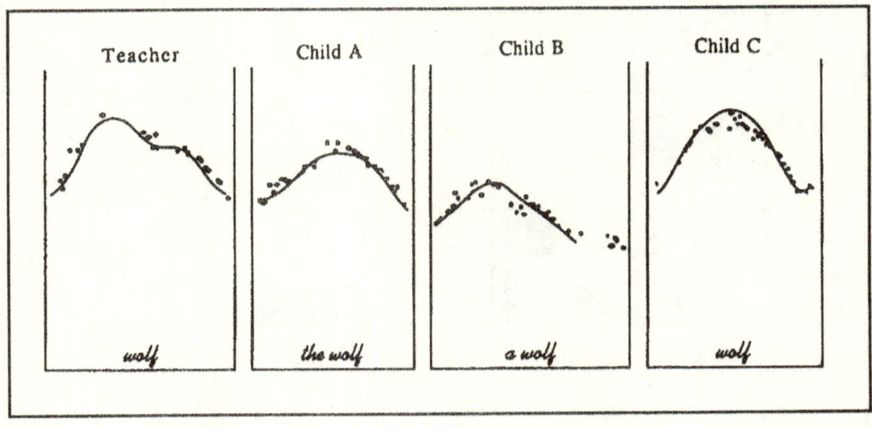

FL narrations were not so purely descriptive, short, and telegraphic, and the

children did believe they were capable of doing the task, thus showing themselves to be cognitively and psychologically more mature, even though they felt the need to insert stress in their story, showing the need to rely on a strategy that will give their narration a stronger story-like appearance. This is probably caused by the lack of trust they have in the meaning conveyed by the utterances they are capable of expressing. Words alone don't seem to be sufficient to express the intentions and other communicative means, even if redundancies such as intonation (and probably also gestures and facial expressions) are used to reinforce it.

Not only exaggerated intonation but also types of curves were similar to those displayed by younger monolinguals: Narratives of three-year-olds and L2 speakers showed a high number of initial peaks, a small number of falls, and a high number of final flats, while older monolinguals displayed many falls and mainly bells.

Regarding the third research aim, i.e. to observe if FL learners imitated the teacher's intonation patterns, it was seen that while learning a second language in the kindergarten, children strongly imitate the teacher's intonation patterns, thus showing a behavior similar to monolingual children's acquiring their first language. Figures 3 and 4 show teacher's curves and the imitated curves of three children.

Regarding the last question, i.e., if imitation was promoted by the teachers using exaggerated intonation when addressing the children, analysis showed, as can be seen in Table 2, the FL teacher using a language with intonation parameters similar to motherese while interacting in the second language with kin-

Figure 4. Teacher's intonational curve and imitated curves of four children saying *mummy*.

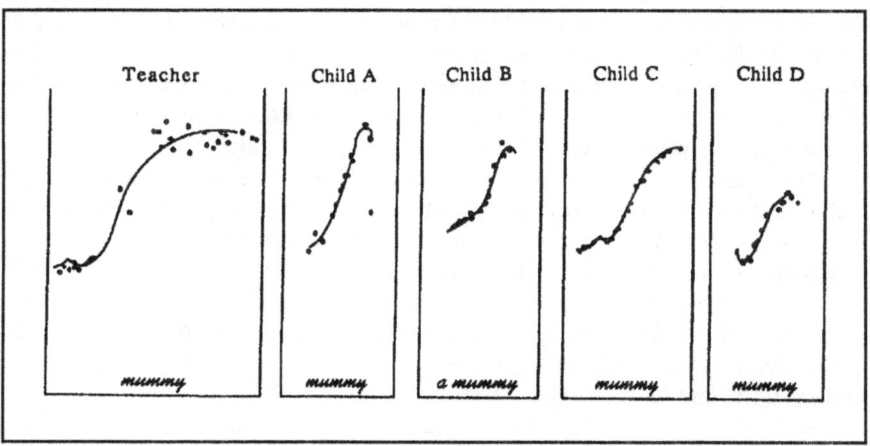

dergarten children. From previous studies on motherese (cf. Fernald et al. 1989), we know that mothers use a different, much higher, and exaggerated intonation when speaking to prelinguistic children when compared with their speech to other adults. Italian mothers, for example, showed a mean range of 130 Hz when speaking to another adult and a mean range of 210 Hz when speaking to prelinguistic children. In the same way, F_0 max mean value was 304 Hz when speaking to adults and F_0 min 174 Hz. Instead, when speaking to prelinguistic children, values were 402 Hz and 192 Hz, respectively (cf. Fernald et al. 1989). FL teachers showed extremely high values, a mean range of 459 Hz, ranging from F_0 max 620 Hz to F_0 min 161 Hz, thus producing an exaggerated motherese. The reason for their exaggerated intonation even when compared to motherese may be due to the fact that teachers interact with several children at the same time and not with just one child or two, as mothers do.

Table 2. F_0 max, F_0 min, and range of Italian mothers speaking to adults and to prelinguistic children and kindergarten teachers speaking to pupils during L2 lessons (frequency values are expressed in Hertz)

	Range	**F_0 max**	**F_0 min**
Mothers speaking to adults	130	304	174
Mothers speaking to children	210	402	210
FL teachers speaking to kindergarten children	459	620	161

According to these results, it is possible to conclude that for the psycholinguistic aspects considered, the process of learning a foreign language in the kindergarten might well resemble the process of acquiring a first language at home. In this sense, the present results are in accordance with most studies reporting on processes of second-language acquisition in older children and in adults. As is known, there is a lively debate at present in the specialized literature as to whether second-language acquisition shows the same learning patterns typical of first-language acquisition or whether it is a process strongly influenced by previous language knowledge. We may say that together with proposals of new teaching methods and new theoretical approaches, it was the hobby-horse of research in second language of the last two decades probably caused partly by crises in the field of contrastive analysis and partly by the emergence of developmental psycholinguistics (cf. Ervin-Tripp 1973, Di Pietro 1987, Felix 1982, Wode 1981, Meisel 1983, Pienemann 1981, Terrell 1980, Dulay, Burt, and Krashen 1982, Swain 1973).

As Hullen (1990: 108) claims, "Learning is dependent on teaching, but teaching is itself also dependent on learning. Teaching methodology must be geared to the mechanism of learning in order to be effective." On the other hand, as Dulay, Burt, and Krashen, 1982: 13–14) state, "The quality of language environment is of paramount importance to success in learning a new language. Teaching a new language means creating for students a part or all of their new language environment." In this sense the present research hopes to contribute to making a little step toward the possibility of giving children a new language environment by basing theory on developmental psycholinguistics and by constructing teaching techniques in harmony with those theoretical principles and that both together be capable of eliciting L1 strategies in a classroom context. L1 strategies should in fact be the simplest, most effective, and functional ones, and as such, desirable to be elicited.

REFERENCES

Artigal, Josep Maria, Fina Anglada, Nuria Aragonès, Maria Dolores Flamerich, Ral Montserrat, Maribel Ruiz, Mariona Ventura, and Mercé Voltas. 1984. *Com fer descobrir una nova llengua.* Barcelona: Eumo Editorial.

Austin, John L. 1962. *How to do things with words.* Oxford: Clarendon Press.

Aston, Guy. 1987. "Casual chat and the teaching of language as co mit." *LEND*, XVI, 1.

Brown, Roger. 1973. *A first language.* Cambridge, Mass.: Harvard University Press.

Bruner, Jerome S. 1975. "From Communication to Language. A Psychological Perspective." *Cognition* 3: 255–257.

Di Pietro, Robert. 1987. *Strategic interaction.* Cambridge: Cambridge University Press.

Dulay, Heidi, Marina Burt, and Stephen Krashen. 1982. *Language two.* New York: Oxford University Press.

Ervin-Tripp, Susan. 1973. "Imitation and structural change in children's language." In Eric H. Lenneberg (ed.), *New directions in the study of language.* Cambridge, Mass.: MIT Press.

Fernals, Anne, Traute Taeschner, Judith Dunn, Mechthild Papousek, Bénédicte De Boisson-Bardies, and Ikuko Fukui. 1989. "A cross language study of prosodic modifications in mothers' and fathers' speech to preverbal infants." *Journal of Child Language* 16: 477–501.

Felix, Sasha W. 1982. *Psycholinguistische Aspekte des Zweitsprachenerwerbs.* Tübingen: Narr.

Grosjean, François. 1982. *Life with two languages: An introduction to bilingualism.* Cambridge, Mass.: Harvard University Press.

Hakuta, Kenji. 1986. *Mirror of language: The debate on bilingualism.* New York: Basic Books.

Halliday, M.A.K. 1975. *Learning how to mean: Explorations in the development of language.* London: Edward Arnold.

Helbig, Gerhard, and Wolfgang Schenkel. 1969. *Wörterbuch zur Valenz und Distribution deutscher Verben.* Leipzig: VEB Bibliographisches Institut.

Hullen, Werner. 1990. "Investigation into classroom discourse." In Hans W. Dechert (ed.), *Current trends in European second language acquisition research.* Clevedon: Multilingual Matters LTD.

McLaughlin, Barry. 1978. *Second language acquisition in childhood.* New Jersey: Lawrence Erlbaum Associates.

Meisel, Jurgen M. 1983. "Transfer as a second-language strategy." *Language & Communication* 3(1): 11–46.

Oller, John Jr., and Patricia A. Richard-Amato. 1983. *Methods that work.* Boston: Heinle and Heinle.

Parisi, Domenico, and Francesco Antinucci. 1973. *Elementi di Grammatica*. Torino: Boringhieri.

Pienemann, Manfred. 1981. *Der Zweitspracherwerb ausländischer Arbeiter kinder*. Bonn: Bouvier.

Slobin, Dan I. 1982. "Universal and particular in the acquisition of language." In Eric Wanner and Lila R. Gleitman (eds.), *Language acquisition: The state of the art 57.*

Schiffler, Ludger. 1980. *Interactiver Fremdsprachenunterricht*. Stuttgart: Ernst Klett Verlag.

Swain, Merrill. 1973. "Child bilingual language learning and linguistic interdependence." Conference on Bilingualism and its Implications for Western Canada, University of Alberta, Edmonton.

Taeschner, Traute. 1983. *The sun is feminine: A study on language acquisition in bilingual children.* Heidelberg: Springer Verlag.

Taeschner, Traute. 1986. *Insegnare la lingua straniera*. Bologna: Il Mulino.

Taeschner, Traute. 1990. *A Developmental psycholinguistic approach to second language teaching*. Norwood, N.J.: Ablex.

Taeschner, Traute. 1992. *Insegnare la lingua straniera con il format*. Rome: Anicia.

Tausch, Reinhard, and Anne Marie Tausch. 1973. *Erziehungspsylogie*. Goettingen: Hogrefe.

Tesniere, Lucien. 1953. *Esquisse d'une syntaxe structurale*. Paris: C. Kliencksieck Librairie.

Vygotsky, Lev S. 1962. *Thought and language*. Cambridge, Mass.: MIT Press.

Wells, Gordon. 1985. *Language development in the pre-school years*. Cambridge: Cambridge University Press.

Wilkins, David A. 1973. "The Linguistic and situational content of the common core in a unit/credit system. In *Systems development in adult language learning*. Strasbourg: Council of Europe.

Wode, Henning. 1981. *Learning a second language*. Tübingen: Narr.

Strategic Integration:
Preparing language and content teachers for linguistically and culturally diverse classrooms

JoAnn Crandall
University of Maryland at Baltimore County

Introduction. It is a pleasure to be a part of this Georgetown University Round Table on Languages and Linguistics, dedicated to the memory of Robert Di Pietro. I had the privilege of studying with Bob Di Pietro at Georgetown, and we remained friends and colleagues after he moved to Delaware and I moved to the Center for Applied Linguistics. Many of you know his early work in contrastive analysis; others of you, especially those who are engaged in language teaching or preparing others to teach second or foreign languages, may be more familiar with what he called *Strategic Interaction* (Di Pietro 1987), an approach to language teaching in which learners are presented with the unexpected and then given the opportunity to resolve the situation through a three-part approach of planning/rehearsal, performance, and debriefing. The goal is to help learners to develop flexibility so that they can function in the range of linguistic situations they are likely to encounter when they leave the classroom.

Now as a teacher educator, codirecting a TESOL/bilingual graduate teacher education program, I see the value of "Strategic Interaction" in another context: teacher education. Strategic Interaction helps our teachers to develop that same flexibility and strategic competence so that they can cope with the incredible challenges that they are likely to face when they leave our teacher-education program. It also helps them to continue their professional development through mentoring, inservice workshops and institutes, and structured opportunities for research and reflection upon their practice. Preservice education represents only the beginning—the rehearsal and initial performances—of a teacher's professional development; inservice education offers the experienced teacher the opportunity to closely examine his or her own practice—a much-needed debriefing in the lifelong learning process required of teachers.

The need for teachers to develop flexibility and strategic competence has never been greater. Because of broad and deep demographic changes in the United States, teachers at all levels of education—elementary, secondary, adult, and college—are being called upon to accommodate and effectively serve an increasingly linguistically and culturally diverse population, a population with different educational experiences and expectations, different English language and literacy proficiency levels, and different types of background knowledge and degrees of familiarity with academic concepts, discourse, and skills. To effectively address this heterogeneity may require some changes in attitudes as well as development of knowledge and skills in cross-cultural communication, language acquisition and development, and effective instructional programs and strategies, and it will require all teachers to rethink the roles they play in educating students.

At a basic level, all teachers will need to consider themselves language and content teachers and will need to learn how to integrate these in their instruction. Content teachers (e.g. regular classroom teachers or teachers of science, mathematics, or social studies) will need to develop strategies to enable all students to learn both content schemata and the oral and written language and discourse conventions required for students to construct and communicate their understandings of those content areas. ESL, bilingual, and other language teachers will need to develop strategies using authentic texts, tasks, and tests from content areas to help students acquire the academic language proficiency and study skills required for successful participation in content-area classes. Students cannot develop academic knowledge and skills without access to the language in which that knowledge is embedded, discussed, constructed, or evaluated. Nor can they acquire academic language skills in a context devoid of content.

To develop this competence, language and content-area teachers need opportunities to interact in teacher-education "scenarios" comparable to those Di Pietro developed for language learners, whereby parties with some shared and some different perspectives on the tasks contribute to the task performance. Language teachers can use these opportunities to develop the strategic flexibility to integrate what they know about language acquisition, learning, and use with knowledge about the demands of the content classroom and the difficulties language-minority students face. Content-area teachers can integrate the knowledge of their own content area with knowledge and skills drawn from language teaching, developing the strategic flexibility to adapt their instruction to make it more comprehensible to students with different levels of English proficiency and degrees of prior experience and knowledge.

How can we best engage teachers in these "scenarios" and prepare them to "strategically integrate" language and content instruction? What can we do to help current teachers to more effectively meet the challenges of a changing student population?

Currently, the Center for Applied Linguistics (Sheppard et al., forthcoming) is conducting a three-year national survey of integrated language and content instruction or "content ESL": "an approach that promotes the integration of English-as-a-second-language (ESL) instruction with subject matter instruction ... taught by the ESL teacher or the classroom teacher (ideally through collaboration) ... in bilingual or monolingual instruction." The survey will provide a good description of the range and extent of content ESL practices and their potential effectiveness, but to date, no one has attempted to conduct a comparable survey of how teachers in these programs acquire and develop the knowledge and skills to function effectively in content ESL situations. Perhaps this is because what they are likely to find is mostly emergency, or stopgap, inservice initiatives. Such initiatives typically provide little or no follow-up and limited opportunity for language and content teachers to work together and learn from each other. Nor do they provide a way for teacher educators from diverse disciplines to share their insights in developing cross-disciplinary teacher-education courses.

Currently, there is limited attention to linguistic and cultural diversity in the preservice preparation of most regular/content-area teachers or to content-area curricula, materials, or discourse in the preservice education of most ESL and bilingual teachers. It is not surprising, then, that the majority of teachers in the survey of content-ESL practices report some inservice education on integrating instruction, often through workshops, but little or no preservice preparation in this area.

A number of promising teacher-education initiatives have been undertaken by schools, colleges, districts, and even states during the past few years that have been directed to helping teachers develop strategies to more effectively cope with changing student populations and to effectively serve both language-minority and majority students by bringing together language and content teachers, especially in inservice education. There have also been some interesting efforts to infuse academic language and integrated language and content instruction into preservice education, though those efforts are recent and limited, primarily directed to ESL and bilingual teachers. The purpose of this paper is to describe some of these initiatives and how we can learn from them. Some initiatives include directions within preservice teacher education that might be expanded to better equip tomorrow's teachers for today's classrooms. Others include directions within inservice education aimed at helping elementary and secondary teachers, as well as adult and college teachers, to more effectively meet the needs of the changing populations in their classrooms.

What may be most effective is a total restructuring of teacher education in a collaborative model that brings together teacher educators, experienced teachers, and teacher candidates from across the curriculum at the school or campus and encourages collaboration with other educational personnel and members of the community in both preservice and inservice education: Such an approach could promote strategic integration of language and content teacher education for all teachers and help alleviate the critical shortage of teachers who are able to effectively teach language-minority students.

The changing demography of U.S. classrooms. For a variety of reasons, including refugee resettlement, immigration, and birthrates, the population of the

United States is changing dramatically. Between the 1980 and 1990 censuses, the number of Asian Americans more than doubled and the Hispanic American population increased by more than half (Bureau of the Census 1991). The effect on the school-age population is profound; during that same period, the Asian school-age population doubled, the number of Hispanic students increased by more than a million, and the total number of limited-English-proficient (LEP) students rose by more than 49% (Chapa 1990). Of the 40 million children in public schools, an estimated 2 to 5 million need some English as a Second Language (ESL) instruction (Council of Chief State School Officers 1990, Boe 1990).

The number of language-minority students is increasing most dramatically in urban school districts: The Los Angeles Unified School District is the first to report a majority of students who come from homes in which languages other than English are spoken, but if forecasts are accurate, by the end of the first decade of the twenty-first century, as many as 50 major metropolitan school districts will have similar populations and will be "educating the new majority" school-age population. Today, it is not unusual to find urban school districts (e.g. Chicago and New York) in which 80 to 100 languages are spoken (National Forum on Personnel Needs for Districts with Changing Demographics 1990), but even districts with declining enrollments report an increase in language-minority students and in the languages spoken by their students. Almost ten years ago, O'Malley and Waggoner (1984) estimated that one out of every two teachers in the United States had an LEP student in his or her class; today, that percentage is surely higher. When both racial and linguistic minorities are counted, 20% of the nation's major school districts are already majority "minority." In Baltimore, where my university is located, and in Washington, D.C., where I live, the population of the schools is already more than 60% ethnically and racially "minority."

The situation in our adult education programs is similar. ESL represents more than one-third of all adult education enrollment, and if one includes the numbers of former ESL students who have moved from ESL to other adult basic education or vocational training programs, language-minority students represent an even greater proportion of the adult education enrollment. The effect on our community colleges, which often serve as both the locus of nonformal, adult education and the transition to more formal college or university education, is especially dramatic. According to a recent survey by The Center for the Study of Community Colleges in Los Angeles, the fastest-growing area of study in our nation's community colleges is ESL (Ignash 1992). That study identified eight community colleges with 70 or more sections of ESL; El Paso Community College reported 429 sections.

Universities also reflect this changing population, not only because of the changing demographics of the United States but also because of the perceived value of American undergraduate and graduate education and the presence of large numbers of foreign students in American colleges and universities. Increasingly, the prestigious teaching and research assistantships are being awarded to these students. The status of English as the primary language for science and technology, international business, international communications, and air and sea travel also attracts international students to English-medium institutions in countries such as the United States. According to the Institute of International Education (1993), there were 420,000 foreign students enrolled in American colleges and universities in 1991–92, a 3% increase over 1990–91.

Not only is the language-minority population growing, it is also constantly changing. Twenty years ago, there were virtually no Cambodian or Vietnamese students in our schools; today, they are part of the fastest-growing population in the United States (Asian and Pacific Americans). At the same time, twenty years ago, there were large numbers of Iranian students in our American universities; today they have been replaced by students from China and Japan. Ten years ago, few educators would have expected to find large numbers of preliterate Hmong or Haitians in adult ESL classes; today, these students are joined by large numbers of Central American students who come to adult ESL and literacy programs with little or no prior education, seeking to combine ESL with first-language literacy, basic education, a high school equivalency program, or some kind of vocational education. In the area of educational demographics, the only constant, it seems, is change.

Developing the attitudes, knowledge, and skills for teachers of language-minority students: Preservice initiatives. Functioning effectively in this continuously changing context of American education requires that teachers develop new sets of attitudes, knowledge, and skills, as well as the strategic flexibility to call upon and adapt these to changing student populations. There is substantial agreement in the field of second-language education on the expected knowledge, skills, and attitudes of ESL and bilingual teachers, whether articulated by Teachers of English to Speakers of Other Languages (TESOL), the Center for Applied Linguistics, or the National Association for Bilingual Education (NABE). While there are some differences, principally related to the role of first-language instruction in bilingual education, there is agreement that both ESL and bilingual teachers need to have opportunities to develop the following kinds of knowledge as well as the related skills to apply that knowledge in educating language-minority students:

- first- and second-language acquisition (psycholinguistics);
- bilingualism, language use, and the relationship between language and culture (sociolinguistics);
- the structure of (American) English (phonology, morphology, syntax);
- methods and techniques of teaching, testing, and evaluating language

learning (pedagogy or andragogy);
- cross-cultural communication; and
- some degree of proficiency in another language.

A group of TESOL professionals invited by the Educational Testing Service to discuss appropriate parameters for the ESL Specialty Exam of the National Teacher Examination, a test mandated in many states as part of K–12 teacher-certification requirements, recommended testing the first five, with the addition of content-based ESL.

There is less consensus on requirements for regular or content-area teachers. However, increased attention to the role of language and literacy in academic achievement and the growing recognition of the importance of parental and community roles in educational achievement have led to (limited) infusion of linguistic and cultural issues into all teacher education and, increasingly, the recommendation of similar knowledge and skills for regular classroom teachers who are likely to have language-minority students in class. Hamayan (1990) suggests four major knowledge areas—second-language learning, bilingualism, sheltering instruction, and grouping practices—as a part of any staff-development program for "mainstream" teachers with "potentially English proficient" (PEP) students in class. Second-language learning would address language acquisition, development, and the role and treatment of errors.Bilingualism would help teachers understand the complex, multifaceted nature of societal and individual bilingualism. Sheltering instruction would help content teachers learn how to use techniques drawn from ESL to make their material more meaningful for language-minority students. And grouping, especially cooperative strategies, would help content-area teachers learn how to make the heterogeneous nature of their classes into an asset. Willig (1990), in her response to Hamayan, suggests a fifth course on cultural awareness, addressing the cultures of the students, the teacher, and the school. Focusing on the community and culture of the students as contexts for teacher education can help "empower minority students," helping students to maintain pride in their culture and language and communicating the value of these for each student's development (Cummins 1986, Clark 1990).

It is interesting to note that these same sets of knowledge and skills are being addressed in the massive state-wide teacher training effort in Florida being undertaken as a result of the META Decree, which mandated inservice education for all teachers with an ESL student in class and set requirements for the training of future teachers. The Florida TOPS program helps teachers understand and develop skills in first- and second-language acquisition and development, cross-cultural communication, and instructional and evaluation strategies for integrating language and content instruction.

As the previous section illustrates, the emphasis in most discussions of teacher education for diverse settings is on making the regular classroom teacher more sensitive to the needs of language-minority students and on the roles that these teachers play in mediating and facilitating both content and language learning. These teachers serve as models of proficient English-language speakers and as cultural guides to the mainstream school community (Hamayan 1990). Far less attention has been paid to helping the ESL or bilingual teacher to become more familiar with the nature of scientific or mathematical knowledge and sensitive to the ways language is used in content-area courses to construct knowledge and evaluate learning, or to the roles that ESL teachers can play in helping students develop content-related thinking and study skills.

Perhaps this is not surprising, since it requires far less expansion to incorporate linguistic insights into one content area than it does to extend linguistic analysis to several content areas, especially at secondary school levels or beyond. Because language-teacher candidates are not provided with substantial structured opportunities to work with their content counterparts in preservice education, they are usually forced, after employment, to learn that content knowledge on the job, attending content-area classes, taking notes, analyzing texts, and interviewing teachers and students in order to develop content-based ESL or adjunct courses focusing on the oral and written language demands of that subject. This can be a terrible burden on secondary school teachers, who have limited planning and preparation time, as well as on college and university teachers, who are usually not compensated for the effort.

At UMBC, where TESOL is a graduate degree, we have unwittingly solved some of the problems of content knowledge by encouraging students from a variety of undergraduate majors—agriculture, biochemistry, business, economics, journalism, nursing, psychology, and sociology, as well as the more traditional backgrounds in foreign languages, English, or international studies—to enroll in our program. Among these students, then, is a range of both language and content instructional knowledge and experiences that can be shared in all courses, especially in those dealing with language acquisition and development, language use, and the practical applications of these in the field experience, the internship, student teaching, and the final project seminar.

Master's programs in TESOL are beginning to address integrated language and content instruction and to provide explicit training in content-based ESL strategies, especially through the basic course in "methods and techniques of teaching ESL," which is likely to discuss instructional approaches such as thematic instruction, sheltered instruction, or adjunct or paired courses and encourage the development of instructional strategies such as cooperative learning, experiential learning, interactive writing, and the use of graphic organizers. This interest in content ESL is evident in recent editions of core "methods" texts such as the second edition of *Teaching English as a Second or Foreign Language* (Celce-Murcia 1992), which includes a chapter on "Teaching Language through Content" by Marguerite Ann Snow, and the second edition of *Methods that*

Work (Oller 1993), which includes chapters on "Content-Based Second Language Instruction" by Donna Brinton, Marguerite Ann Snow, and Marjorie Wesche, and "Sheltered Subject-Matter Teaching" by Stephen Krashen. Another recent text on theory and practice in ESL and bilingual education, *Making It Happen*, edited by Patricia Richard-Amato (1988) deals extensively with integrated language and content instruction. However, only occasionally are entire preservice courses devoted to integrated instruction, and they are likely to be combined with English for Specific Purposes or Vocational ESL, both precursors to content-based ESL, such as the course I taught at American University several years ago on content-based and vocational ESL.

Content-based language instruction is also increasingly likely to be addressed in other core ESL/bilingual-education courses. For example, it is an important focus of two of our required courses in the M.A. program at the University of Maryland at Baltimore County—courses on teaching reading and writing to ESL/bilingual students. These courses discuss academic language development through authentic texts and writing assignments as well as the use of graphic organizers to develop, organize, and communicate ideas.

Similarly, all secondary education teacher candidates are required to take a course called Reading in the Content Areas and Writing Across the Curriculum, which only briefly addresses second-language learners but does focus on some of the same information and teaching strategies as our courses directed to ESL/bilingual teachers. Elementary teacher candidates take courses in reading and language arts, which include thematic teaching, multicultural literature, and interactive writing, all relevant to language-minority students.

If a course on language development or cross-cultural perspectives is required for regular classroom teachers, Patricia Richard-Amato's new collection, *The Multicultural Classroom: Readings for Content-Area Teachers*, should be especially useful. So should the teacher reference texts devoted to integrating language and content instruction (Mohan 1986, Crandall 1987, Brinton, Snow, and Wesche 1989), many of which are also useful as supplementary texts in core courses.

Perhaps the most innovative approach to integrating language and content instruction for ESL and bilingual teachers is a sheltered Spanish content course on "Communications in Bilingual Classrooms," which Robert Milk developed for ESL and bilingual teachers at the University of Texas at San Antonio (Milk 1988, 1990), drawing upon a previous sheltered psychology course taught through French at the University of Ottawa (Brinton, Snow, and Wesche, 1989). While initially designed as a course to further Spanish-language development of bilingual teachers, the presence of ESL teachers provided a model of what language-minority students face when they are being instructed in a second language and an opportunity to test, firsthand, the efficacy of sheltered instruction, or adapting content instruction to make content comprehensible in a second language. Classwork consisted of a series of cognitively demanding tasks, including reading a number of texts (in Spanish) on sheltered instruction and then applying that to the planning and designing of learning activities that integrated Spanish with science, mathematics, and social studies. The results of this experimental course are very promising: Not only did the majority improve their Spanish-language proficiency, but a "clear majority" "felt that they had greatly increased their understanding of the kinds of problems that LEP students encounter in dealing with academic content in a weaker language" (Milk 1988: 57), and all reported increased understanding of how to go about integrating language and content instruction in their own teaching.

A similar course would doubtless be useful to all teacher candidates or even to practicing teachers, given the likelihood that they will have language-minority students in class. If teacher candidates can not experience firsthand what it is like to learn through a second language, at least they can become more familiar with the changing nature of classrooms and schools through their presence in the schools early in their college education (Murray and Fallon 1989; Renaissance Group 1989) and in a fifth year of professional development after their student teaching (Holmes Group 1990).

Increased time in the schools was one focus of the University of Hawaii's Preservice Education for Teachers of Minorities (PETOM) project, which grew out of the work of the very successful Kamehameha Early Education Program (KEEP). The majority of Hawaii's school-age population are linguistic minorities, and many students have their sole experience with Standard American English in the school (Dalton and Moir 1992). The purpose of PETOM was to prepare teachers to provide these students with language and literacy development experiences that they could use not only in classrooms but also later in the community and the workplace.

Besides extensive field experience, PETOM encouraged extensive collaborations among preservice teacher educators in the development and implementation of the program, providing a model of integrated instruction and curriculum integration for teachers to take with them when they leave the program. PETOM also models the principles of "teaching by assistance," drawing upon the work of Vygotsky (1978), whereby teachers and other students assist students through their "zones of proximal development" (where assisted learning occurs and teaching takes place) by means of "scaffolding," including "instructional conversations" (Tharp and Gallimore 1988) or dialogues, writing, or group project work.

The sheltered immersion course at the University of Texas at San Antonio and the PETOM alternative certification program at the University of Hawaii represent only the beginnings of a needed total restructuring of preservice teacher education in line with the current school restructuring and reform movement (Steffens 1992, Collier 1992, Minaya-Rowe 1991). Teacher education must be more integrating from its inception, with greater cooperation among the disciplines and more sustained collaboration among ESL/bilingual and regular teacher-training strands. It is possible to infuse issues of language-minority students into all core education courses (for example, dealing with issues of first- and second-language literacy in the course on reading in the content areas), but I believe it is important to design at least two core courses in which all teacher candidates would participate: language development and cross-cultural communication/multicultural education.

Language development would discuss first- and second-language and literacy development and the cross-transfer of skills, the nature of social and academic language, and the difficulties students face in developing the academic language required for participation in academic instruction. The second would help teachers understand and support the increasing cultural diversity in their schools and communities, identifying ways for teachers and schools to foster cross-cultural understanding and facilitate parental and community involvement in school, helping students retain pride in their own cultures and languages while also developing skills to function in the school culture and beyond. If we can integrate ESL/bilingual and regular teachers in these courses and if we can recruit more members of the students' own communities as teacher candidates, it should not be difficult to create scenarios that invite problem-solving and the sharing of insights across disciplines to more strategically prepare all teachers before they exit from our preservice programs.

These courses would be equally useful to those preparing to teach in adult (and university) education, where issues of linguistic and cultural diversity are equally salient. Adult ESL teacher candidates need opportunities to work collaboratively with other academic (Adult Basic Education, Adult Secondary Education) and vocational teachers, and those preparing to teach at the university level need comparable opportunities with colleagues from across the curriculum. Absent that, participation in an integrated preservice program with peers from other subject areas can provide a useful grounding in the linguistic demands and conceptual objectives of various content areas.

Developing effective teachers of language-minority students: Inservice initiatives. Until preservice education is more comprehensively restructured, much education in integrated instruction will be left to inservice education. Historically, inservice education has consisted of short training sessions or workshops in which teachers learn about new theories or develop a few activities that they can use in their classes. Workshops dealing with integrated language and content instruction, cooperative learning, whole language, or interactive reading and writing, offered during a regular inservice period for elementary or secondary teachers or on Saturday mornings for adult and college teachers, still are the most common form of inservice education for teachers of language-minority students; a number of training manuals, sample agendas, and videos have been developed for this purpose (Short 1990, 1991, Crandall and others 1987).

These workshops may focus on integrating language with only one discipline (mathematics, science, or social studies), or they may deal more broadly with integrating a number of content areas with language through thematic curricula development. At best, these models bring together ESL, bilingual, and regular content teachers and incorporate opportunities for practice, coaching, and reflection. At worst, they are "one-shot experiences with little or no follow-up" (Minaya-Rowe 1991: 267), making it difficult to determine what teachers have learned or how effectively they are applying it in their classrooms.

Gradually, these one-shot training sessions are being augmented or replaced by ongoing programs of professional development that involve opportunities for classroom observations (including the use of videos to observe one's own practice), involvement in a mentoring relationship with an expert teacher or in a peer-coaching relationship with a colleague, research and reflection on one's own practice, and a variety of program improvement efforts such as joint curriculum planning or materials development, identification of appropriate assessment measures, and program evaluation. (See Crandall (1993) for a fuller discussion of inservice education models and practices as they apply to adult ESL.) Actually, professional development occurs naturally in the course of a teacher's work, through participating in textbook-selection committees, curriculum meetings, or conferences; reading professional journals and magazines; and even in informal conversations in the teachers' lounge. Teaching is a lifelong learning process; by identifying their own needs and formulating a professional development plan, teachers can ensure that the focus of that professional development is relevant and appropriate.

Both preservice and inservice programs follow a number of approaches that involve, to some degree, aspects of training, relating theory to practice and practice to theory; mentoring and peer coaching, with some type of "assisted instruction"; and inquiry and reflective practice, with some focus on introspection and classroom-centered or action research, resulting in changes in practice, materials, curriculum, assessment, or an entire program (cf. Wallace 1991, Wrigley and Guth 1992, Crandall 1993). Most inservice education programs involve some of each: New strategies require presentation of theory, demonstrations, and opportunities to plan and practice using that strategy (Di Pietro's planning and rehearsal). They also require some kind of ongoing coaching and mentoring, where helpful feedback is provided (debriefing), and they often lead to new questions about one's own effectiveness as a teacher and the investigation of new strategies for classroom use that require research and reflection.

Training Models. Training models primarily focus on disseminating information and developing teacher knowledge and skills, i.e., competencies frequently established by an education agency or a professional association. To a large extent, much of preservice education is training, since the emphasis is on constructing new knowledge and developing teacher attitudes and skills, although even preservice programs are likely to have many opportunities for collaborative research and reflection, especially in the field experience, student teaching, and other practical courses. Historically, training has also been the principal delivery approach for inservice education, often developed with limited input from teachers. However, a number of training programs, such as intensive summer institutes or year-long programs, are also effective.

One program in which I have been involved for the past four years is a short-term training initiative conducted by the Center for Applied Linguistics in collaboration with schools in the Washington, D.C., metropolitan area, directed by Donna Christian. The Institute uses a school-based model, with each school identifying a team of four or five participants (ESL, content, and resource teachers, and administrators, ideally, the principal). This team works together over a year of activities, beginning with a short summer institute focusing on integrated language and content instruction, whole language, and other instructional strategies appropriate for linguistic minority students. Participants have the opportunity of learning from guest lecturers and other teachers, and they use that knowledge to develop action plans for the school year and outlines of curriculum units and lessons specifying language, content, and thinking or study skills objectives that can be tried out during the school year.

Throughout the year, CAL staff observe classes, provide demonstration classes, serve as substitute teachers to permit teachers to observe their colleagues in other classrooms and other schools, and meet with individual teachers and school teams, discussing problems and successes in implementing the new strategies. Twice a year the participants come back together to share unit and lesson plans they have developed and to demonstrate a portion of a lesson that has been particularly successful. The following summer, a new group of teachers from the same schools engage in a similar program, with some of the previous year's participants serving as master teachers or resources. The result is expanded capacity-building within the schools and a greater likelihood of curricular integration by the teachers.

A number of factors contribute to the success of the institute: interdisciplinary teams of teachers and administrators; the opportunity to relate the training to the classroom, the curriculum, and the school; and the time between sessions to try out new approaches and develop effective instructional units. Similar institutes include the Multi-District Trainer of Trainers Institute (Minaya-Rowe 1991), the Boston University/Boston Public Schools Collaborative (Zanger 1989), and the Language Development Specialist Academy at Hunter College in New York (Romero 1990).

While Romero (1990) is skeptical of the effectiveness of training programs, since they often represent top-down approaches in which the experience and expertise of the teacher is ignored rather than respected and built upon, her Language Development Specialist Academy provides a positive example of a kind of training program. The Academy brings together 20 to 25 expert teachers nine times during a six-month period to share insights, strategies, and materials, to reflect upon their teaching, and to listen to new perspectives. The day begins with reflection upon the past session, then moves to a presentation on research and theory in language development by guest speakers, followed by discussion in small groups and the application of that theory to the development of classroom or training materials. The day ends with demonstrations of successful lessons by the participants, followed by discussion on what principles the lesson exemplified, what theory it supported, and what strategies it used. As a former guest lecturer, I can attest to the high level of discussion, the enthusiastic engagement of the Academy members, and the excellence of this ongoing professional-development program for expert teachers.

Training models, especially when combined with coaching and reflection, have been widely used in adult ESL, perhaps because most adult ESL teachers learn much of their craft on the job and in inservice programs, there being few courses devoted to either adult education or adult ESL in most master's degree TESOL programs. Inservice training permits presentation of effective strategies for teaching, their rationale, and sheltered opportunities to practice the techniques and receive feedback. The Adult ESL Teacher Training Institute (Savage, n.d.) consists of a series of sequenced, skills-based training sessions led by experienced teachers certified as Institute trainers. Prepared video training packages provide the basis for three hours of formal training, including presentation of a technique and its underlying theory, demonstrations, and practice in its implementation. Before the training, program administrators attend a meeting where the training is previewed and Institute staff recommend on-site follow-up and coaching. Strengths of the Institute include the clear presentation of techniques; the development and involvement of experienced teachers, who are nominated locally; the spacing between sessions, which permits application by participants; and follow-up discussion and coaching on site (see Crandall 1993 for more information on the program).

Mentoring or Peer-Coaching Models. The coaching model, as developed by Joyce and Showers (1982), comes close to the three phases of Strategic Interaction, beginning with a presentation of theory, followed by observations and demonstrations of practice, with feedback by an observer and follow-up discussion in a supportive coaching environment. Coaching, whether through mentoring, by a supervisor, or by peer-coaching, provides a way of transferring learning from workshops or university courses to the real contexts of the teacher's classroom (Romero 1990). For that reason, coaching is often incorporated into training programs to make training more personal and manageable and to provide support and feedback during the implementation or practice phase. Teachers as well as students learn best when they are able to engage in instructional conversations and are provided with assistance at their zone of proximal development.

Peer-coaching, because of the confidential nature of the feedback and the removal of the status barriers, encourages development of collaboration and collegiality, which is especially effective when it brings together different teachers who share the same students. An example of a school-based professional-development model using peer-coaching as its centerpiece is one that was developed by the Center for Applied Linguistics for a bilingual middle school program. ESL or bilingual teachers paired with content teachers of the same language-minority students in a series of workshops and activities. These included observing each other's classes, describing the nature of the classwork and the kinds of instructional strategies used, and identifying the potential for transferring these to their own teaching; joint lesson planning; and ongoing peer consultation and collaboration. The success of this type of paired, school-based model requires careful scheduling of classes to ensure that teachers share a planning period and work with the same students over the course of the year.

Mentoring is often a key factor in both the initial success of new teachers and retention of teachers. It is the cornerstone of the University of California at Santa Cruz/Santa Cruz County New Teacher Project (Dalton and Moir 1992), a collaboration between the UCSC Teacher Education Program, the Santa Cruz County Office of Education, and seven school districts in the county. Exemplary bilingual teachers function as teacher advisers to new teachers for their first year of teaching, providing assistance both inside and outside of the classroom, observing and demonstrating lessons, coaching, responding to teachers' dialogue journals, planning lessons, and generally offering encouragement and helping to solve problems. As one principal put it, "The project is supporting new teachers in all the ways that principals would like to but never have the time to do" (Dalton and Moir 1992: 435). During its first three years, the program lost only five of the 155 new teachers served. Moreover, evaluations indicate that it has had a spillover effect, encouraging networking among experienced and new teachers and offering these experienced teachers an opportunity for professional renewal.

Mentoring has also been effectively used at the City University of New York, where experienced or "master" teachers open up some of their ABE/ESL classes to colleagues, who are encouraged to observe as often as possible and are reimbursed for their time. The program permits much-needed cross-disciplinary observations of teachers who provide services to the same students. A similar integration of perspectives is provided in an inservice program developed by the Illinois Resource Center, which brings together ESL, bilingual, and mainstream teachers, focusing on a whole-language approach to literacy and sheltered instruction in the content areas for language-minority students through analysis of literature, demonstration workshops, and peer-coaching.

Reflective Practice/Inquiry-Based Models. As teachers acquire more experience, they are likely to become more interested in specific problems or individual students within their classes, schools, or communities. Through classroom-centered or action research, or group inquiry, teachers can make more-informed decisions about their own practice. Reflective practice or inquiry-based models of professional development place teachers in the center of staff development and encourage them to pause in their teaching to become more active learners and developers of their own theories of teaching and learning (Gebhard 1990). Research questions may emerge from teacher dialogue on common problems and lead to collaborative exploration of possible solutions.

Cochran-Smith and Lytle (1992) describe a preservice and inservice teacher-education program in Philadelphia in which teachers read, research, and reflect upon their own experiences with and attitudes about race, class, and ethnicity and the impact of these upon their classrooms, schools, and communities. In other programs, ESL teachers have joined with content counterparts to systematically investigate the discourse demands of various content areas.

While reflective practice models are more common with experienced teachers, they can also be effective with new teachers as well. Schlumberger and Clymer (1989) discuss a collaborative inservice program for graduate assistants teaching writing to ESL college students. The teachers worked together on placement of students, curriculum design, development of course materials, final course evaluations, and inservice presentations. Through the process, they came to understand not only more about their students and strategies for engaging them in writing, but they also became more aware of how classroom-centered or action research and opportunities for shared discussion could lead to their own development. As Dewey said in 1904, "It is more important to make teachers thoughtful and alert students of education, than it is to help them get immediate proficiency" (quoted in Romero 1990: 489).

Bringing preservice and inservice education together: The professional development school. Perhaps the most promising approach to teacher development is the professional development school. This approach unites preservice and inservice teacher education; includes all educators (aides, counselors, administrators, and teachers) working with language-minority and language-majority students; integrates training, coaching, and research and reflection; brings parents and the community into the teacher-training process; and could serve as a means for increasing the linguistic and cultural diversity of the teaching profession. (Even in ESL, the teachers are overwhelmingly white and Anglo.) The professional development school offers an opportunity to restructure both teacher education and teaching.

Professional development schools are a response to the growing call for professionalization of teaching and are comparable to the clinical experience in medicine (President's Commission on Teacher Education 1992). Teacher education and other departments at the university link up with elementary, middle, or secondary schools and provide a program of teacher education taught at the school, often by teams of experienced teachers and university faculty. Professional development schools offer experienced teachers the opportunity to participate in research with peers and university faculty, something that may be more meaningful than remote doctoral work. New teachers and those preparing to be teachers have the support and assistance of both experienced teachers and teacher educators as they encounter situations that arise in school.

Theory and practice become intimately related in this model, and all teachers are provided opportunities to work on a daily basis with both language-minority and language-majority students and to exchange ideas and to develop strategies to meet the changing scenarios that our diverse schools present. The model can be extended to include adult education and adult ESL, bringing in parental/family literacy courses, citizenship courses, and other programs that will increase parental and community participation and involvement in the schools and will likely also increase students' reading and academic achievement as well.

The professional development school can help solve the critical shortage of bilingual teachers (California Task Force 1991, Boe 1990) by serving as the locus for encouraging bilingual aides and other paraprofessionals to continue their education with classes at the school, moving to the university for completion of their undergraduate degree or developing certification through some kind of alternative certification program. Bilingual aides and paraprofessionals are important resources for preservice and inservice programs, helping to make them more reflective of the linguistic and cultural diversity of the students the school serves. A professional development school is also more likely to facilitate the restructuring of the core curriculum on teacher education, infusing language development and cross-cultural perspectives into all courses and encouraging the transfer of expertise between language and content teachers.

Professional development schools can integrate the three phases of Strategic Interaction—rehearsal, performance, and debriefing—on a regular basis and enable teachers and teacher educators to continue developing the strategic competence needed to effectively integrate all language-minority students into our schools. The implementation of this strategic professional development model could also provide appropriate recognition of the lasting impact of Robert Di Pietro upon language-teacher education.

REFERENCES

Bermudez, A.B. and Y.N. Padron. 1988. "The effects of parent education programs on parent participation." *NABE '88-'89 Annual Conference Journal*. 159–169.

Boe, E.E. 1990. "Demand, supply, and shortage of bilingual and ESL teachers: Models, data, and policy issues." In C. Simich-Dudgeon (ed.), *Proceedings of the first research symposium on limited English proficient students' issues*. Washington, D.C.: U.S. Department of Education, Office of Bilingual Education and Minority Languages Affairs. 23–63.

Brinton, D.M., M.A. Snow, and M.B. Wesche. 1993. "Content-based second language instruction." In John W. Oller, Jr., and Patricia A. Richard-Amato (eds.), *Methods that work* (Second edition). Boston: Heinle and Heinle. 136–142.

Brinton, D.M., M.A. Snow, and M.B. Wesche. 1989. *Content-based second language instruction*. New York: Harper and Row.

California Task Force on Selected LEP Issues. 1991. *Remedying the shortage of teachers for limited-English-proficient students*. Sacramento, Calif.: California Task Force on Selected LEP Issues.

Carter, T.P. and M.L. Chatfield. 1986. "Effective bilingual schools: Implications for policy and practice." *American Journal of Education* 95: 200–234.

Celce-Murcia, M. (ed.). 1991. *Teaching English as a second or foreign language*. 2nd ed. New York: Newbury House.

Center for Applied Linguistics. 1976. "Guidelines for the preparation and certification of teachers of bilingual/bicultural education." In James E. Alatis and K. Twaddell (eds.), *English as a second language in bilingual education*. Washington, D.C.: TESOL. 345–349.

Chapa, J. 1990. "Population estimates of school age language minorities an [sic] limited English proficiency children of the United States, 1979–1988." In C. Simich-Dudgeon (ed.), *Proceedings of the first research symposium on limited English proficient students' issues*. Washington, D.C.: U.S. Department of Education, Office of Bilingual Education and Minority Languages Affairs. 85–112.

City University of New York. 1988. *Research, classroom practice, programs. Improving the odds: Helping ESL students succeed. Selected papers from the CUNY ESL Council Conference*. New York: Instructional Resource Center, City University of New York. [ED 328 069]

Clark, E.R. 1990. "The state of the art in research on teacher training models with special reference to bilingual education teachers." In C. Simich-Dudgeon (ed.), *Proceedings of the first research symposium on limited English proficient students' issues*. Washington, D.C.: U.S. Department of Education, Office of Bilingual Education and Minority Languages Affairs. 361–391.

Cochran-Smith, M., and S.L. Lytle. 1992. "Investigating cultural diversity: Inquiry and action." *Journal of Teacher Education* 43(2): 104–115.

Collier, V.P. 1992. "Response to John Steffens' Presentation." In C. Simich-Dudgeon (ed.), *Proceedings of the second national research symposium on limited English proficient student issues: Focus on evaluation and measurement* (Vol. 2). Washington, D.C.: U.S. Department of Education, Office of Bilingual Education and Minority Languages Affairs. 417–22.

Collier, V.P. 1985. "University models for ESL and bilingual teacher training." In *National Clearinghouse for Bilingual Education: Issues in English language development*. Rosslyn, Va.: InterAmerica Research Associates. 81–90.

Council of Chief State School Officers. 1989. "A concern about . . . educating limited English proficient students: A CCSSO survey of state education agency activities." *Concerns* 26 (March): 1–14.

Crandall, J.A. 1993. "Professionalism and professionalization of adult ESL literacy." *TESOL Quarterly* 27(3): 497–515.

Crandall, J.A. 1993. "Content-centered learning in the United States." *Annual Review of Applied Linguistics* 13: 111–126.

Crandall, J.A. 1987. *ESL through content-area instruction: Mathematics, science, social studies.*

Englewood Cliffs, N.J.: Prentice Hall Regents/Center for Applied Linguistics.

Crandall, J.A., G. Christian Spanos, C. Simich-Dudgeon, and K. Willetts. 1987. *Integrating language and content instruction for language minority students*. Silver Spring, Md.: National Clearinghouse for Bilingual Education.

Crandall, J.A., and G.R. Tucker. 1990. "Content-based instruction in second and foreign languages." In S. Anivan (ed.), *Language teaching methodology in the nineties*. Singapore: SEAMEO Regional Language Centre. 83–96. [ED 312 895]

Cummins, J. 1986. "Empowering minority students: A framework of intervention." *Harvard Educational Review* 56(1): 18–36.

Dalton, S., and E. Moir. 1992. "Evaluating limited English proficient (LEP) teacher training and in-service programs." In *Proceedings of the second national research symposium on limited English proficient student issues: Focus on evaluation and measurement* (Vol. 1). Washington, D.C.: U.S. Department of Education, Office of Bilingual Education and Minority Languages Affairs. 415–456.

Di Pietro, Robert J. 1987. *Strategic interaction: Language learning through scenarios*. New York: Cambridge University Press.

Edmonds, R. 1979. "Some schools work and more can." *Social Policy* 9(5): 28–32.

Feinberg, R.C. 1990. "Response to Hamayan." In C. Simich-Dudgeon (ed.), *Proceedings of the research symposium on limited English proficient students' issues*. Washington, D.C.: U.S. Department of Education, Office of Bilingual Education and Minority Languages Affairs. 398–406.

Galang, R.G. 1992. "Response to John Steffens' Presentation." In C. Simich-Dudgeon (ed.), *Proceedings of the second national research symposium on limited English proficient student issues: Focus on evaluation and measurement* (Vol. 2). Washington, D.C.: U.S. Department of Education, Office of Bilingual Education and Minority Languages Affairs. 423–430.

Garcia, D. 1990. "Response to Ellen Riojas Clark." In C. Simich-Dudgeon (ed.), *Proceedings of the research symposium on limited English proficient students' issues*. Washington, D.C.: U.S. Department of Education, Office of Bilingual Education and Minority Languages Affairs. 498–502.

Glickman, C.D. 1990. *Supervision of instruction: A developmental approach* (Second edition). Boston: Allyn and Bacon.

Goodlad, John (ed.). 1987. *The ecology of school renewal: 86th yearbook of the National Society for the Study of Education*. Chicago: University of Chicago Press.

Hamayan, Else. 1990. "Preparing mainstream classroom teachers to teach potentially English proficient students." In C. Simich-Dudgeon (ed.), *Proceedings of the research symposium on limited English proficient students' issues*. Washington, D.C.: U.S. Department of Education, Office of Bilingual Education and Minority Languages Affairs. 1–22.

Holmes Group. 1990. *Tomorrow's schools*. East Lansing, Mich.: Holmes Group.

Institute of International Education. *Open doors*. New York: Institute of International Education. .

Jew, Victoria. 1992. "Response to Dalton and Noir's presentation." In C. Simich-Dudgeon (ed.), *Proceedings of the second national research symposium on limited English proficient student issues: Focus on evaluation and measurement* (Vol. 1). Washington, D.C.: U.S. Department of Education, Office of Bilingual Education and Minority Languages Affairs. 453–458.

Joyce, B., and Showers, B. 1982. "The coaching of teaching." *Educational Leadership* 40: 4–10.

Krashen, S.D. 1993. "Sheltered subject-matter teaching." In J.W. Oller, Jr.(ed.), *Methods that work* (Second edition). Boston: Heinle and Heinle.

Kreidler, C. 1986. *ESL teacher certification*. Washington, D.C.: ERIC Clearinghouse on Languages and Linguistics, Center for Applied Linguistics.

Kreidler, Charles. 1987. *ESL teacher education*. Washington, D.C.: ERIC Clearinghouse on Languages and Linguistics, Center for Applied Linguistics.

Malarz, Lynn. 1992. "Response to Dalton and Moir." In C. Simich-Dudgeon (ed.), *Proceedings of the second national research symposium on limited English proficient student issues: Focus on evaluation and measurement* (Vol. 1). Washington, D.C.: U.S. Department of Education, Office of Bilingual Education and Minority Languages Affairs. 447–452.

Mercado, C.I. 1985. "Models of inservice teacher training." In National Clearinghouse for Bilingual Education, *Issues in English language development*. Rosslyn, Va.: InterAmerica Research Associate. 107–114.

META Consent Decree. 1990. Tallahassee, Fla.: Department of Education.

Milk, R.D. 1988. "Integrating language and context in the preparation of bilingual teachers." In L.M. Malave (ed.), *NABE '88–'89 Annual Conference Journal*. Washington, D.C.: National Association for Bilingual Education. 57–70.

Milk, R.D. 1990. "Preparing ESL and bilingual teachers for changing roles: Immersion for teachers of LEP children." *TESOL Quarterly* 24(3): 407–26.

Milk, R., C. Mercado, and A. Sapiens. 1992. *Re-thinking the education of teachers of language minority children: Developing reflective teachers for changing schools*. Washington, D.C.: National Clearinghouse for Bilingual Education.

Minaya-Rowe, L. 1991. "Teacher training in bilingual education and English as a second language: Recent research developments." In *Bilingual Education and English as a Second Language: A Research Handbook, 1988-1990*. Hamden, Conn.: Garland Publishing.

Mohan, B.A. *Language and content*. Reading, Mass.: Newbury House.

Murray, F.B. and Fallon, D. 1989. *The reform of teacher education for the 21st century: Project 30 year one report*. Newark, Del.: Project 30.

National Forum on Personnel Needs for Districts with Changing Demographics. 1990. *Staffing the multilingually impacted schools of the 1990s*. Washington, D.C.: U.S. Department of Education, Office of Bilingual Education and Minority Languages Affairs.

O'Malley, J.M. and D. Waggoner. 1984. "Public school teacher preparation and the teaching of ESL." *TESOL Newsletter* 18(3): 1,18–22.

Oller, J.W., Jr. (ed.). 1993. *Methods that work* (Second edition). Boston: Heinle and Heinle.

President's Commission on Teacher Education. 1992. *Teacher education for the 21st century*. Washington, D.C.: American Association of State Colleges and Universities.

Renaissance Group. 1989. *Teachers for the new world: A statement of principles*. Cedar Falls, Iowa: University of Northern Iowa.

Richard-Amato, P.A. 1988. *Making it happen: Interaction in the second language classroom*. New York: Longman.

Richard-Amato, P.A. 1992. *The multicultural classroom: Readings for content-area teachers*. White Plains, N.Y.: Longman.

Richards, J., and D. Nunan. 1990. *Second language teacher education*. New York: Cambridge University Press.

Romero, M. 1990. "Response to Ellen Riojas Clark." In C. Simich-Dudgeon (ed.), *Proceedings of the research symposium on limited English proficient students' issues*. Washington, D.C.: U.S. Department of Education, Office of Bilingual Education and Minority Languages Affairs. 487–498.

Schlumberger, A., and D. Clymer. 1989. "Teacher training through teacher collaboration." In D. Johnson and D. Roen (eds.), *Richness in writing: Empowering ESL students*. New York: Longman. 146–159.

Sheppard, K., et al. forthcoming. "Twenty schools: Content ESL across America." *Final report of OBEMLA contract T291004001*. Washington, D.C.: Center for Applied Linguistics.

Short, D. 1991a. "Content-based English language teaching: A focus on teacher training." *Cross Currents* 18(2): 167–173.

Short, D. 1991b. *How to integrate language and content instruction: A training manual*. Washington, D.C.: Center for Applied Linguistics. [ED 305 824]

Showers, B. 1985. "Teachers coaching teachers." *Educational Leadership* 42(7): 43–48.

Sleeter, C.E. 1992. "Restructuring schools for multicultural education." *Journal of Teacher Education* 43(2): 141–148.

Snow, Marguerite Ann. 1991. "Teaching language through content." In M. Celce-Murcia (ed.), *Teaching English as a second or foreign language* (Second edition). 315–328.

Steffens, J.E. 1992. "Will the LEP train reach its destination? Designing an IHE teacher training program for specific LEP student instructional needs." In C. Simich-Dudgeon (ed.), *Second national research symposium on limited English proficient student issues*. Washington, D.C.: U.S. Department of Education, Office of Bilingual Education and Minority Languages Affairs. 393–416.

Teachers of English to Speakers of Other Languages. 1975. *Guidelines for the certification and preparation of teachers of English to speakers of other languages in the United States*. Washington, D.C.: TESOL.

Tharp, R., and R. Gallimore. 1989. *Rousing minds to life*. New York: Cambridge University Press.

Vygotsky, L.S. 1978. *Mind in society*. Cambridge, Mass.: Harvard University Press.

Willig, A.C. 1990. "Response to Hamayan." In C. Simich-Dudgeon (ed.), *Proceedings of the research symposium on limited English proficient students' issues*. Washington, D.C.: U.S. Department of Education, Office of Bilingual Education and Minority Languages Affairs. 394–398.

Wallace, M.J. 1991. *Training foreign language teachers: A reflective approach*. New York: Cambridge University Press.

Wrigley, H.S. and Guth, G.J.A. 1992. *Bringing literacy to life*. San Mateo, Calif.: Aguirre International.

Zanger, V.V. 1989. "Chats in the teachers' lounge are not enough: Preparing monolingual teachers for bilingual students." In J.J. Foley and L.R. Orlandi (eds.), *Bilingual education: Quality in all languages*. Boston: Massachusetts Association for Bilingual Education.

A comparative view of English-teaching policies in an international world with a focus on Japanese TEFL policy

Ikuo Koike
Keio University

Introduction. It is a great pleasure and honor to present my paper at this 1993 Georgetown University Round Table, particularly because Dr. Alatis has dedicated it to the late Robert J. Di Pietro, who was my teacher, my friend, and mentor of my doctoral dissertation, *The SLA of Grammatical Structures and the Relevant Verbal Strategies*. I also had the great fortune to serve as translator and annotator of the Japanese edition of Dr. Di Pietro's *Language Structures in Contrast* (Newbury House Publishers), which was later published by Taishukan Publishers in Tokyo in 1974.

I would like to turn your attention to the two handouts, "TEFL Profile of Japan" and the outline of today's presentation. You can understand the state of Japanese TEFL in comparison with TEFL/TESL of other countries in the "TEFL Profile of Japan: Its Frame and Problems."

In this paper, I propose a general theoretical framework of factors to establish the foreign-language teaching policies in various countries around the world. Among similar reports on such teaching policies is the work on TEFL in the Polish context reported by Dr. Hanna Komorowska in her article "Second Language Teaching in Poland prior to the Reform of 1990," which appears in the proceedings of the 1991 Georgetown University Round Table edited by Dr. Alatis. When we observe the past and present, static and dynamic features of TEFL/TESL policies in a number of nations, we could assume that there are some factors that help create a framework of policies common to and different from many countries. Since these factors are presumed to exist in TEFL/TESL in Japan, I would like to provide examples of these factors in a concrete form typical of Japanese TEFL.

TEFL/TESL policy and planning are distinctive in each nation. If we could do a detailed analysis of these policies, we could establish some basic criteria that combine to influence foreign-language teaching policy. Here we might recognize that this policy-making is part of human group activities and show the direction of these activities as they relate to sociological, political, economic, educational, and linguistic variables. The common factors and these other variables must then be drawn into a planning unity.

Factors controlling foreign language teaching policy. The first question to ask about making decisions with regard to TEFL/TESL policies is: what are the essential factors controlling foreign-language teaching policy?

From my own experience as a participant and observer in policy-related matters, I would like to propose a set of factors for consideration:

- geography
- history
- race
- politics
- economics
- culture
- language
- education
- communication
- society
- science and technology

Geography or geographic factors. The need to learn foreign languages is based on the density of contact with neighboring countries. Geography is one of the most important factors for establishing a language policy, particularly for foreign/second language teaching. Japan, for example, is surrounded by water and situated hundreds of miles from the Eurasian continent. It is close to the Korean peninsula, China, and Siberia. It was separated and isolated from its neighboring countries except for a limited number of communities whose members were able to communicate directly with the people on the continent. Their land is not linked to the land masses of other countries, thus making it difficult to become integrated. This makes it easy for the Japanese to keep their language from mixing with other languages.

In contrast, European countries share borders with many other European countries, very often creating easy access to these other countries. Japan's remoteness from other major modern countries contributed to its slower positive and active cooperative development with these nations. Japan's segregation policy for more than 200 years had kept it isolated from modern technological culture while Japan prepared itself for a dramatic evolution influenced by western civilization.

History or historical factors. Japan, throughout its history of establishing relations with foreign countries, was limited in its direct experience in international communication. Japan had been culturally and technologically far behind both European and American modernization. The Japanese government practiced a consistent policy of sending abroad small numbers of its best and brightest people for specialized training. The Japanese learned a great deal and eventually became successful in the transfer of technology and in the communication of knowledge—not in the ways and learned words of others, but in very typically Japanese ways.

A large number of Japanese acquired vast amounts of information from translated works. Accuracy, rather than fluency, was the requirement. Such things were seen in the importation of the advanced culture of China and in the importation of European culture and technology in the Meiji Period in the years following 1868. Accordingly, the main focus in foreign-language teaching had been on accurate English translations of Japanese. The grammar–translation method prevailed in every corner of Japanese society.

Now, however, Japan has reached a point of turning away from the period of *grammar-translation* toward the *communicative drill* because of the large scale of requests for mutual understanding and direct communication. Such events have occurred not only in Japan, but in every nation, because of the radical and rapid developments in the communicative approaches to language learning and teaching. The period of the select few who led the majority of cultural illiterates is no more. This has been replaced by the common people's need to communicate directly with foreigners. As a result, teaching methods and materials must develop in such a way as to meet the general needs of communication.

Nowadays, this historical change has necessarily reached a world scale. Communication tools have developed rapidly. All the necessary policies have to be changed in the direction of meeting the needs of methods, speed, and scale. Otherwise, we may be diverted from the mainstream and end up returning to the more conservative approaches of the past.

Race or racial factors. The Japanese people tend to be monoracial, monolingual, and monocultural. Japan may be one of the few countries whose national and racial features are congruent. Many other countries, in contrast, are multiracial and multi-ethnic. The countries of Europe, Africa, the Middle East, South Asia, China, and North and South America have language-planning problems different from those in Japan. There may be frequent conflicts among racial and ethnic groups in assuming leadership and responsibility for their own political, economic, and cultural development. Language, as well as the way of thinking, may be a source of the conflict.

The people in each racial or ethnic group tend to assume a political position toward homogeneity and political independence. They generally speak more than one language, become familiar with different value systems, and become more cooperative with other racial groups.

Language learning, particularly foreign-language learning, is a common everyday problem for Japanese people. Japan, as a generally monolingual and monocultural nation, is different from any other type of monolingual society or country. All the social systems, even including the cultural patterns of feeling and thinking, are unitary in a monolingual and monocultural system.

For example, the Japanese do not have experience with misunderstanding as a result of linguistic diversity. Japan's linguistic and cultural homogeneity provides a setting for communication across districts. We encounter problems when we meet foreigners inside and outside Japan. We are apt to encounter the unfamiliar. We do not know how to adjust to foreigners. We become aware of the gaps in form and function between Japanese and other languages. Some are unnecessarily exaggerated and thus interpreted in ways that portray the Japanese as being either sympathetic or unsympathetic to foreigners. As a result, the Japanese are viewed as unable to communicate with foreigners. TEFL/TESL policies must deal with many problems in raising the level of communication with foreigners and increasing the population of foreign-language learners in Japan, the end result being the achievement of international understanding. This has its dangers in trying to move the majority of people in a single direction toward a single second-language and second-culture awareness.

Economy or economic factors. The revision of TEFL/TESL in Japan has a direct correlation with rapid economic growth. Japan has become one of the leading world economic powers. This status has put Japan in touch with more nations and more people. About 12 million Japanese, or 10 percent of the total population, traveled internationally in 1991. This kind of progress has generated profound interest among the Japanese in acquiring English and other languages for very specific purposes, among them education, business, and tourism. As the Japanese travel about the world and encounter foreign languages, they become self-critical about their ability to communicate in another language. Today, according to a general survey of English teaching in Japan, to which nearly 2,300 business people replied, the following statistics emerge:

(1) how communicative is your English?

not communicative	8.0%
almost not communicative	33.5%
almost communicative	22.8%
communicative	6.7%
half communicative	29.0%

(2) particularly not communicative in

listening comprehension	74.5%
... in speaking	79.4%
... in reading	4.8%
... in writing	14.0%

The responses to the above survey questions suggest that Japanese businessmen suffer from poor communicative ability in English for business purposes. This may be a phenomenon peculiar to the Japanese. However, economic growth is placing greater burdens on the Japanese to learn foreign languages, thus creating a positive environment for the development of a more effective system of second-language instruction in Japan.

At present, the countries of the European Community (EC) have organized themselves to cooperate more and to produce a more powerful political and economic community. The same, I would venture to say, may happen in North and South America. Language policy, such as "Lingua" and other projects in the EC, aims to promote the exchange of teachers and students in the EC, to tighten the bonds among countries, and to create greater economic opportunities throughout Europe.

Politics or political factors. Political factors, when juxtaposed with economic factors, create a new set of defining factors for decision making with regard to foreign-language teaching policy. TEFL/TESL policy can be examined and executed within the framework of a national policy and related to educational and administrative policies. TEFL/TESL policy is normally recognized as important among all schools and college subjects. Generally speaking, the reformation should be consistent with and linked to the former policy; however, drastic changes could be the result.

For example, in 1982 the Japanese government organized the Japanese Ad Hoc Committee for Education Reform. This is the most important policy-making organization created by law. Its objective was to reform the rigid Japanese educational system into a more flexible and dynamic one. In 1984 the Committee concluded that TEFL in Japan does not reflect the efforts expended by many people, and that many people in Japan cannot necessarily respond to the need for international communication. The Committee proposes to reform the TEFL system by establishing clear objectives and by focusing on promoting communicative ability. It also proposed smaller class size, improved teacher training, a communication-centered approach in practical teaching, and other measures. It also strongly suggested that teachers and students follow the revised *course of study*, which is a *national syllabus* for English-language learning and teaching.

The Course of Study was revised in 1987 and is based on the suggestions of the Ad Hoc Committee and the Ministry of Education's Curriculum Design Committee (of which I served as chair in the section of foreign-language teaching at the high school level). This revision included a statement regarding teaching purpose, teaching materials, and teaching methods, and the teaching of pronunciation, grammar, vocabulary, and culture. All are communication centered.

The Government Joint Project, sponsored by the Ministries of Domestic Affairs, Foreign Service, and Education, started the Japan Exchange and Teaching Program (JET) in 1985. The purpose was to enhance international understanding through cooperation with local citizens and by helping to teach English to high school students across the nation. In the summer of 1992, about 3,200 young native-speaker teachers from six English-speaking countries and from France, Germany, and China were invited to Japan. Overall the JET Program has been very successful. Young native speakers who serve as assistant teachers are eager to team-teach with Japanese teachers of English, French, German, and Chinese.

The University Council was established based on the proposal of the Ad Hoc Committee on Educational Reform. Its overall responsibility was to reform the system of strict government control into a system that would give colleges and universities more independence and autonomy in designing and implementing programs of foreign-language learning and teaching. Accordingly, TEFL/TESL in Japanese universities is experiencing some confusion with regard to the value of teaching foreign languages.

Before the changes, policy at the national level read as follows: "Eight credits for one foreign language is obligatory for all university students, according to university law." Now, under the changes, foreign-language learning is no longer obligatory; it is completely optional. Students may take any number of credits and languages and they may take them, if the university allows it, at private language schools. As a result, we can conclude that foreign-language teachers are not necessarily pleased about the turn of events because students are released from the perceived onerous burden of learning languages. Also, under the new regulations, faculty must be evaluated by their students.

In addition, the population of young people is decreasing each year. The Planning Committee on Higher Education at the University Council reported that there were 2.05 million 18-year-olds in 1992; that figure is expected to decrease to about 1.51 million by the year 2000. This decrease may lead to universities and colleges failing economically because of the decreasing population of college-age students. It is not unlike the situation the United States is now experiencing as American universities compete for the same decreasing pool of applicants.

Another problem under discussion with regard to TEFL in Japan relates to the teaching of English at the primary school level. Public elementary schools offer no English lessons, yet the general public is demanding that such programs be offered at this level. The Government Commission on Reforming Foreign Language Teaching Policy and Planning in the Ministry of Education intends to propose an agenda for the twenty-first century that would include a set of responses and directions to this initiative.

The practical conditions under which foreign languages are learned and taught around the world vary widely. However, there are some common themes:

the possibility of teaching English in the elementary schools, the pros and cons of the grammar–translation method, the system of teacher training, and modes of evaluating English-language teaching.

Another political problem is how the Japanese should position foreign-language teaching in a balanced way with other school subjects. Balancing school subject areas and English-language instruction is a delicate matter because of the competition for limited time available during the school day. The political and social question is whether a political decision made by the government can in fact be effective as the Japanese make adjustments to the needs of new generations living in a global society.

Culture or cultural factors. If we accept the immutable fact that everyone has his or her own culture, we can then try to rationalize a relationship between culture and language. We cannot deny the relationship as we consider a TEFL/TESL policy. English became a symbol of modern advanced culture to the Japanese a little over a century ago. English culture was an exotic attraction to progressively minded people, whereas it was less exotic and more exclusive to nationalistically minded people. It is the negative attitude that has produced changes in a system every ten years that excluded the teaching of English in school education. However, over the last 20 years, the situation has changed completely. The English language, and English and American culture, have come to be familiar to the Japanese people. These cultures have influenced the Japanese culture, which has begun to change.

As regards American culture, American people are considered by the Japanese to be simple and open-minded, positive and friendly, and well-mannered; in contrast, one might say that the Japanese people are rather shy in person, and also positive within the Japanese heart and soul, but negative in expressing positive actions, and decentralized in their thinking. Japanese culture is characterized as both superficial and deep, composed of delicate and complex strata.

These characteristics are demonstrated in the way high school English text-books are edited. The majority are written on foreign culture, particularly on the English-speaking culture in English-speaking countries, while the contents of Korean and Chinese texts focus on a similar culture. The nation's culture and ethnicity are reflected in textbook editing.

Language or linguistic factors. Let me begin here by asking a question: Is it possible that language structures or patterns exert some influence on the TEFL/TESL policy of a particular nation? If we consider that many languages in the European context, as Indo-European languages, are similar to English, it is easy to conclude that European learners of English feel more secure learning English than do the Japanese.

If we look at the TOEFL examination, we might generalize that learners from an Indo-European background achieve better scores on the test, while learners from other language families are less successful. According to the 1990–91 TOEFL Test and Score Manual, Japanese test-takers achieved a 491 average, which was ranked third from the bottom among 27 Asian countries, and also 19th from the bottom among all 187 countries. However, in an international Japanese-language test administered in more than 20 countries, the situation was reversed.

Some commentators have said that *language distance* is the major factor in determining the level of language-learning difficulty. Japanese learners of Korean and Korean learners of Japanese are the best and most successful in learning these languages. Another point we must consider is the role of English as an international language. TESL is developing mainly as a field of instruction for immigrants in English-speaking countries such as the United States, Canada, and Australia. TEFL/TESL is commonly provided in multilingual countries in an effort to facilitate communication among a variety of races and ethnic groups in countries such as India and the Philippines. English also works for the international business and culture in monolingual countries such as Japan and Korea.

Generally speaking, a considerable number of countries have at least three languages in use. People use their mother tongue or a vernacular language, another contact language, and an international language such as English, German, or French. This kind of situation has implications for choice of language instruction at the different educational levels, that is, elementary, junior high, and senior high school. As the concept of the global village continues to evolve, the trends to revise and improve foreign-language teaching will become more conspicuous.

Communication or communicative factors. The purpose of TEFL/TESL is closely related to communication and, for secondary schools in Japan, its purposes are (a) to increase communicative ability, (b) to foster active and positive attitudes toward communication, and (c) to develop international understanding. What is the most important purpose? Communication, of course. It is essential for establishing the purpose of TEFL.

Education or educational factors. For the purposes of education, what is the position of TEFL/TESL in the education system in general? The answer is usually very simple: international understanding. For Japan, this has meant, according to the Report of the Ad Hoc Committee for Educational Reform in Japan, that the following objectives were to be established: (a) to balance the development of mind and body; (b) to foster the acquisition of knowledge and promote creativity; (c) to instill an interest in language and culture, thus laying the foundations for international understanding by contrasting domestic affairs in Japan with those of other nations; and (d) to develop each person's freedom, flexibility, individuality, and creativity. TEFL policy promotes international understanding among the above four objectives.

Society or social factors. Generally speaking, policy is established by consensus, first emerging from within the society and later institutionalized by the government through legislation. Once established, it has to apply to the present society and have implications for the future; thus, policy must reflect opinion into the future. TEFL policy making is not exceptional in this regard. In Japan, the government establishes a research agenda by conducting a general survey and creating research advisory committees that consist of specialists and representatives from the public at large. According to the most recent general survey, "TEFL in the Japanese educational system is not effective," that is, 62.6% of junior high school teachers, 58.0% of senior high school teachers of English, 80.24% of returned teachers from overseas Japanese schools, and 74.9% of college students responded in this way.

This survey, *A General Survey of English Teaching in Japan*, was conducted by a research group that I chaired. It has operated for 11 years with financial support from a Ministry of Education grant-in-aid for cooperative research. It is the largest and most comprehensive survey in the history of TEFL in Japan and has had the cooperation of about 20,000 business people, elementary, junior high, and senior high school teachers of English, and university students and university English teachers.

The conclusion I reported above reflects national opinion on the state of English language teaching in Japan and on the internationalization of Japanese society.

Science and technology factors. As the world shrinks, it becomes more of an interdependent global village. Political borders are no longer economic borders, and time is no longer the obstacle it might once have been. Chronologically, while ten years have passed since 1983, more has happened in those ten years than happened in the previous ten, and more people have learned more about more things in less time. Time and distance have been mastered. TEFL/TESL policy must be made to reflect this changing dynamic. That is, responses to change, while they need to be made thoughtfully, also need to be made with some speed to keep up with progress and development.

Conclusion. To conclude, the above factors, when taken together, represent considerations of a comprehensive point of view that calls for important policy changes in the Japanese national setting with regard to the teaching of English and the teaching of other foreign languages. The global economy, global interdependence, and mutual international understanding can be achieved more effectively and efficiently by planning for and establishing human activities, language teaching in this case, that support internationalism.

REFERENCES

Ad Hoc Committee of Educational Reform. 1986. *The second proposal of educational reform: The governmental report of Japan.*

Cheshire, Jenny (ed.). 1991. *English around the world: Sociolinguistic perspectives.* Cambridge: Cambridge University Press.

Coulmas, Florian. 1992. *Language and economy.* Oxford: Blackwell Press.

Council of Europe. 1989. Conference: Language learning in Europe: The challenge of diversity. Strasbourg: Council for Cultural Cooperation.

Educational Testing Service. 1990. *TOEFL test and score manual.* Princeton: Educational Testing Service.

Ek, Jan Ate Van, and John Trim. 1984. *Across the threshold.* Oxford: Pergamon Press.

Honna, Nobuyuki (ed.). 1990. *Varieties of English in Asia.* Tokyo: Kuroshio Publishers.

Koike, Ikuo, et al. 1983. *General survey of English language teaching at colleges and universities in Japan: Teachers' view.* Tokyo: Keio University.

Koike, Ikuo. 1992a. "Foreign language teaching policy in Japan—toward 21st century." *Proceedings of the 10th Anniversary Conference, Educational Linguistics: Retrospect and Prospect'.* National University of Singapore (forthcoming).

Koike, Ikuo. 1992b. "An introductory survey of foreign language teaching policy." *Reports of the Keio Institute of Cultural and Linguistic Studies* (No. 24). Tokyo: Keio University.

Koike, Ikuo. 1986. "Development of English as an international language and the revision of TEFL in Japan." *ELEC Bulletin* 87. Tokyo: English Language Education Council.

Koike, Ikuo, et al. 1985. *General survey of English language teaching at colleges and universities: Students' view.* Tokyo: Keio University.

Koike, Ikuo et al. 1988. *A general survey of English languages teaching: Junior high school and senior high school, primary school, education of Japanese children overseas.* Tokyo: Keio University.

Koike, Ikuo, et al. 1990a. *A general survey of English language teaching: College graduates' view.* Tokyo: Keio University.

Koike, Ikuo, et al. 1990b. *A general survey of English language teaching in Japan.* Tokyo: Keio University.

Komorowska, Hanna. 1992. "Second language teaching in Poland prior to the reform of 1990." In James E. Alatis (ed.), *Georgetown University Round Table on Languages and Linguistics 1991.* Washington, D.C.: Georgetown University Press.

Lambert, Richard, and Sarah Jane Moore (eds.). 1990. "Foreign language in the workplace." *The Annals of the American Academy of Political and Social Science.* California: Sage Publications.

Ministry of Education, Science and Culture of Japan. 1988. *The course of study in foreign language teaching at secondary schools.*

National Curriculum Council. 1991. *National curriculum council consultation report: Modern foreign languages in the national curriculum.* Curriculum Council.

Simon, Paul. 1988. *The tongue-tied American: Confronting the foreign language crisis.* New York: Continuum Publishing.

Strategic Interaction and the teaching of writing: A comparative study of scenarios vs. traditional prompts as stimuli for ESL essays

Louis A. Arena
University of Delaware

This paper is a report of a study that investigated the use of Robert Di Pietro's Strategic Interaction approach in a university-level freshman English composition class at the University of Delaware. While most second-language teachers feel that Strategic Interaction offers a unique approach for the purpose of fostering listening, speaking, and interactive skills using L2, this study concludes that Di Pietro's approach also has much to offer in the acquisition of L2 literacy. Di Pietro's thoughts on the connection between spoken discourse and writing are clear:

> In the strategic interaction of classroom, the skills of reading and writing ideally begin with the performance of scenarios. The belief is that learners develop a strong foundation for literacy in the target language when they can derive the practice of writing from their own active participation in spoken discourse (Di Pietro, 1987: 99).

What this study has done, essentially, is rephrase Di Pietro's belief that writing is easily derived from practiced, interactive spoken discourse into a hypothesis, i.e., qualitatively better writing is derived from practiced, interactive spoken discourse than from the traditional approach of writing from only a prompt or essay question. Traditional approaches assign students an essay-prompt and then ask that they write on the topic and task in the prompt within a time limit, e.g. 30 or 60 minutes. However, by basing essay writing on scenarios, the students are given a unique source from which to draw shared knowledge that is based on rehearsed, interactively performed, and then debriefed spoken discourse.

The shared knowledge that is derived from interactive discourse was the major factor hypothesized that would result in qualitatively better, more coherently written essays. The scenario, after all, is a dialogic text with its own structure, coherence, and negotiated conclusion. The challenge for this study, then, was to find essay prompts that contained some interplay or tension, at least two roles, personal agendas, and some shared context that could be used both traditionally and in scenarios. In Di Pietro's terms, an essay prompt needs to contain at least two roles and an event that involves the unexpected and that requires language to be resolved (Di Pietro, 1987: 41). In addition to these features, the ideal essay prompt is one whose tasks can be assigned as roles and given to two groups of students without informing either group of the other's role. Finally, the ideal scenario essay prompt is one that can be rehearsed, performed, and debriefed in accordance with the Strategic Interaction protocol.

The literature containing the use of scenarios as bases for writing is not replete. Dyer (1982) used scenarios as a basis for writing scripts using computers and word-processing programs. Dalbuono-Glassman and Bosco (1982), in their textbook for teaching Italian, provide a series of descriptions of individuals who usually have opposite tastes or viewpoints. The students are then asked to react to the description by creating a written dialogue between two individuals who shared different views or tastes. Others, such as Danesi (1985), have used scenarios as a prelude to literacy instruction, ranging from dialogic discourse to writing about literature.

However, there has also existed a need for a particular type of prompt that could be used both as a scenario and under the traditional conditions to elicit writing that can be compared empirically. Further, a criterion-referenced, holistic scoring rubric has also been needed for the comparison of essays written from either of the two types of stimuli. And finally, for this study, raters who were experienced in holistic scoring were also necessary for score integrity and reliability. Without such a scoring guide or experienced holistic raters, any comparison of essay scores or the writing contained in essays is of very little value to teachers in the university-level composition classroom.

The essay prompt types selected for this study were designed by the Committee of Examiners for the TOEFL Test of Written English (TWE) under the aegis of the Educational Testing Service at Princeton, New Jersey. The TWE is a 30-minute instrument that directly assesses ESL writing. The TWE was first administered throughout the TOEFL population in 1986. Since then, more than 1,800,000 international students have written a 30-minute essay for the TWE. The TWE prompts are of two types: charts and graphs, and prose prompts. A TWE prompt may contain several types of tasks that require the students to support and develop their essays differently, e.g., compare and contrast; compare and contrast, then take a position; agree or disagree with a given statement, using reasons and/or examples. The TWE prompt-type used for the scenarios in this study is "compare and contrast, then take a position." For example:

> Some people say that the best preparation for life is learning to work with others and to be cooperative. Others take the opposite view and say that learning to be competitive is the best preparation. Discuss these positions and tell which one you agree with and explain why. (ETS, TWE Guide, 1989: 33)

This prompt-type is easily accommodated by Di Pietro's scenario protocol because the two viewpoints can be separated and each can be given to a group of students for development as a scenario. For example, the instructor can rewrite each position contained in such a prompt and give one role to each group, with directions to rehearse a developed position for oral presentation by one member of the group. Two students can then be selected to "perform" the tasks of the prompt as roles. Prior to the performance, the two students are told by the instructor that whatever the topic of discourse is, there must be some accord, negotiated or otherwise, at the conclusion of the performance. After discourse is concluded, the performance is then discussed in the debriefing stage by all members of both groups. Then, approximately two days later, the instructor uses the original TWE prompt containing the two points of view and asks the students to write for 30 minutes.

The TWE prompt type, as such, was conducive to being used both as the basis for a scenario and as the basis for eliciting essays that could be scored by a reliable guide, i.e., the *TWE Scoring Guide* (ETS, *TWE Guide,* 1992: 23). For this study, consequently, four different TWE prompts were used. The protocol and conditions for their use are contained in the Method and Design sections of this paper. The revised TWE Scoring Guide and the six-point TWE scale were used to score all of the essays in this study.

Subjects. A total of 26 international students wrote four essays each, resulting in 104 essays. All of the subjects were matriculated students at the University of Delaware and were enrolled in the three-credit freshman English course that is required for all undergraduates and optional for graduate students. The academic students in this study all had standardized test scores on the Test of English as a Foreign Language (TOEFL) that were high enough (500+) for them to be accepted into regular undergraduate or graduate majors at the University of Delaware with no restrictions as to the number of courses to study. Of these students, 46% scored above 530 on the TOEFL and 30% scored above 550 on the TOEFL.

All of the students were nonnative speakers of English. The native languages of the students were Arabic, Chinese, French, Hindi, Japanese, Korean, Russian, Spanish, Tigrinya, and Turkish. The students participated in this study as a part of the course. In addition to the four essays each student wrote for this study, the students were required to write two additional essays and one full-length research paper. None of the additional writing was considered for this study.

Materials. Four disclosed Test of Written English (TWE) essay topics were used in the study. All were prose topics, that is, they were not chart/graph topics. The topics are contained in the *TOEFL TWE Guide* (1989) and had been used with TOEFL administrations four or five years before; it is not known if these students had seen or written on these essay topics prior to the study, but it is rather unlikely.

The students were asked to write on lined paper, and they were allowed to make notes or an outline within the 30-minute time allowance for completing the essay. All essays were holistically scored using the revised TWE Scoring Guide (1990) by two TWE raters.

Research Design. The participants were divided into two treatment groups, each having a population of 13. Each group was asked to write for 30 minutes on two TWE prose prompts and on two TWE prompts that had first been performed as scenarios. The TWE prose prompts are labeled A and B, and the enacted TWE prompts are labeled C and D. The topic order was counterbalanced such that the groups wrote on Topic A for their first essay and then wrote on Topic C for their second essay; in this manner, the scenario-prompts C and D were counterbalanced between topics A and B, given under traditional conditions. Because the number of students writing on each topic was constant, it is felt that the different orders (counterbalancing of topics) would completely balance each other in examining the performances of the students on topics A and B vs. C and D.

The method for administering topics A and B differed markedly from C and D. Topics A and B were administered according to TWE guidelines, i.e., the students had no idea of the nature of the topic of the tasks required by the prompt. Topics C and D, on the other hand, were administered after specialized, instructional intervention. They were planned (rehearsed) and performed orally with group interaction, and then debriefed according to the guidelines of Di Pietro's scenario protocols prior to being given as topics for writing two days later in class. The constant in the study, however, is that all of the 104 essays were written under the same time limit of 30 minutes.

From an assessment point of view, the rehearsal and performance of topics C and D as scenarios prior to the timed, in-class essay writing of the essays may be viewed as a special condition in the comparison of the performance between topics A and B and topics C and D. However, two factors obviated addressing this view: (1) the population was not large enough to analyze the role that rehearsal had on the actual 30-minute essays and (2) the correlation between the scores for each of the four topics was relatively high, i.e. did not differ significantly. Thus, no formal assessment was attempted as to whether or not the rehearsal and interactive performance of the prompts in scenarios prior to writing constituted a special condition. Moreover, the fact that topics A and B were given as prose prompts under TWE conditions, while topics C and D were performed as scenarios prior to writing, also obviated, for the present, any analysis to assess parallel-form reliability between the two sets of topics.

Procedure. The students were told that they would be asked to write four essays as part of the study and that these essays would be written during the 15-week time period of their class. They were informed that two of the essays would be written on topics A and B, which they had not seen or discussed, and that they would be given 30 minutes to complete their essays. They were then instructed on the scenario protocol of Di Pietro's Strategic Interaction and told that each group would be assigned a portion of a topic as a role to be rehearsed and performed orally before writing. Neither group knew the other's portion (role) of the writing prompt. Each group was then asked to rehearse their part of the topic and to select one person from the group to perform that role before the class.

Thus, two students began discussing, for example, the "best preparation for life." One performer took the view that the best preparation for life was learning to be cooperative while the other expressed the view that the best preparation for life was learning to be competitive. If discourse broke down at any time during the performance, the performer (actor) was free to leave the "stage" and return to his/her group for assistance. After receiving this assistance, the performer returned to the front of the classroom and continued the scenario until a comfortable conclusion was negotiated or reached by both representatives of each group. After the performance, a debriefing session was held in class where both groups discussed questions about certain grammatical points or suggestions for how something might have been expressed differently. On the following day of class, the prompt containing both views was given to all the students, and they wrote on the reconstructed TWE topic for 30 minutes.

Results and Discussion. Scores on topics A and B were derived by administering and evaluating the essays under typical TWE conditions, i.e., no disclosure of the topic in part or whole, 30-minute time limit for writing, and the use of the six-point TWE scale by two TWE raters.

For the essays whose topics were first treated as scenarios (topics C and D), the students experienced a condition of instructional intervention in that the prompts were rehearsed, performed, and debriefed interactively one or two days before writing. In a comparison of the writing performances by the students on the two topics, therefore, the principal effect of interest examined was the difference in the instruction prior to writing. Analyses of variance were conducted on the factor of instruction vs. no instruction and the factor of elapsed time. The one-factor analysis of variance (ANOVA) for the performance on the two sets of topics showed no significant differences between topics A and B and topics C and D essay scores. Actually, one of the most interesting results in the study is the symmetry between the scores on the essays written on the four topics. The two-variable ANOVA of the mean differences of the combined essay scores, however, showed that significantly better scores were generated when the group wrote essays after the prompts had been performed as scenarios.

The mean scores on all of the 104 essays written on the four topics represent the performance effects of the population of students in the study and are presented in Table 1. The average of the mean scores for topics C and D, whose essays were written one or two days after the prompts were rehearsed, performed, and debriefed as scenarios, were actually higher than the mean scores for essays written on Topics A and B, under typical TWE conditions.

Table 1. Performance data: TWE/scenario-TWE topics

Topic A then C			Topic B then D		
N	Mean	SD	N	Mean	SD
26	4.62	.86	26	4.21	.84
26	4.87	.85	26	5.26	.76
TWE Topics A and B mean = 4.41			Scenario-TWE Topics mean = 5.06		

On average, using prompts C and D as the bases for scenarios resulted in essays whose scores were .65 higher on the six-point TWE scale than on the essays written on topics A and B under TWE conditions. This increase is equal to approximately three-fourths of a standard deviation (the mean of the standard deviations). While this increase is certainly significant in an assessment of writing, especially for purposes such as admission to a university or college, such an increase is regarded as only interesting to the writing teacher. In practical terms, a .65 increase does not constitute a "grade-jump," e.g., from a grade of C to a grade of B, or from B to A, in a university-level composition classroom.

What is intriguing in these results is that the average score increase of .65 on a six-point scale in the scenario-prompt essays was *not* due to any extra time given the groups to write essays on *any* of the four topics. While it was tempting to allow more time for writing on the scenario prompts, the variable of 30 minutes was consistently maintained in all of the essay-writing opportunities. However, instructional intervention, i.e. interactively rehearsing, performing, and then debriefing a prompt by the two groups, might have resulted in increased essay scores in any one of several ways. For example, the rehearsal stage may have given the students a much more efficacious preparation for the essay discourse by either suggesting or listening to the trial-run discourse during rehearsal in their respective groups; the performance stage of the prompt by two persons may have afforded visual, kinesthetic, and pragmatic reinforcement for the discourse that was being acted out. Furthermore, the students could observe how the reasoning and support in the discourse contributed to the final, negotiated conclusion of the scenario. The debriefing session afforded the students opportunities to actually revise and/or edit interactive discourse before writing their essays. Finally, the elapsed time (usually one or two days) between the enacted scenario and the actual writing of the essay may have provided the opportunity for the students to further reflect and refine their practiced discourse, such that the 30-minute essay was actually quality writing time. In other words, the students wrote more qualitatively on the scenario topics, within the same 30-minute time span, because they brought successful, interactive, and experiential spoken discourse to the writing table.

The purpose of this study was not to suggest a new method for assessing writing, although it contains some interesting issues for further research in the area of assessment. The purpose of this paper is to illustrate how the Strategic Interaction protocol may be used in the university or college writing classroom. This instructor selected the TWE only because it contains data-derived bases for quantifying any increase in writing scores. The TWE prompts and conditions for writing essays indeed served well as benchmarks for comparing essays written after the scenarios were performed. The *TWE Scoring Guide* for the holistic scoring of all the essays was especially valuable for maintaining interrater reliability and deriving criterion-referenced score reliability.

What Di Pietro's Strategic Interaction approach brings to the pedagogy of university-level writing classes is a method for students to actually experience the entire writing process in interactive, spoken discourse, including all of the benefits of peer-group interaction and support, one or two days *before* the actual act of writing the essay takes place. The application of Di Pietro's Strategic Interaction protocol to TWE prompts, in this study, has resulted in qualitatively better written essays, i.e., the essays were more successfully focused on the writing task, had better organization and clearer development of ideas, reasoning, and illustrations, and experienced more distinctive and negotiated conclusions to the essays than did those written under typical TWE or traditional conditions.

The intent of this study was to investigate the use of Strategic Interaction in college-level ESL composition courses. Because it is difficult at times to distinguish between writing pedagogy and writing assessment in such a study, I hasten to clarify that the intent of the investigation was completely pedagogical; assessment of writing entered into the purpose of the study only as a tool to provide some sort of comparative measure of the writing derived from scenarios vs. traditional prompts.

Di Pietro's method has certain merit in the college ESL composition classroom. And it is only appropriate to Di Pietro and to his students to provide empirical data to support such a conclusion. This study represents some partial data to support continued research using Strategic Interaction in college-level ESL composition classes.

REFERENCES

Arena, Louis (ed.). 1990. *Language proficiency: Defined, teaching, and testing.* New York: Plenum.

Brown, George. 1990. "Cultural values: the interpretation of discourse." *ELT Journal* 44(6): 11–17.

Campbell, C. 1990. "Writing with others' words: Using background reading text in academic composition." In Barbara Kroll (ed.), *Second language writing: Research issues for the classroom.* New York: Cambridge University Press.

Carson Eisterhold, Joan. 1990. "Reading–writing connections: Toward a description for second language learners." In Barbara Kroll (ed.), *Second language writing: Research issues for the classroom.* New York: Cambridge University Press.

Carson, Joan G., and Ilona Leki (eds.). 1993. *Reading in the composition classroom: Second language perspectives.* Boston: Heinle and Heinle.

Caudery, T. 1990. "The validity of timed essay tests in the assessment of writing skills." *ELT Journal* 44: 122–131.

Celce-Murcia, Marianne (ed.). 1991. *Teaching English as a second or foreign language* (2nd edition). New York: Newbury House.

Cumming, A. 1990. "Expertise in evaluating second-language compositions." *Language Testing* 7(1): 31–51.

Curran, Charles A. 1976. *Counseling–learning in second languages.* Apple River, Ill.: Apple River Press.

Dalbuono-Glassman, Eligia, and Fred Bosco. 1982. *Profili: For students of Italian.* Washington, D.C.: Forest House.

Danesi, Marcel. 1985. *Language games in Italian.* Toronto: University of Toronto Press.

de Beaugrande, R. 1984. "Writer, reader, critic: Comparing critical theories as discourse." *College English* 46: 533–59.

Di Pietro, Robert J. 1987. *Strategic interaction: Learning languages through scenarios.* New York: Cambridge University Press.

Dyer, Patricia M. 1982. "Instructional procedures for implementing the strategic interaction method in an intensive E.S.L. program." Unpublished Ph.D. dissertation. University of Delaware.

Educational Testing Service. 1989. *TOEFL test of written English guide* (2nd edition). Princeton, N.J.: Educational Testing Service.

Educational Testing Service. 1992. *TOEFL test of written English guide* (3rd edition). Princeton, N.J.: Educational Testing Service.

Ellis, Rod. 1990. *Instructed second language acquisition.* Oxford: Basil Blackwell.

Flower, Linda, Victoria Stein, John Ackerman, Margaret J. Kantz, Kathleen McCormick, and Wayne Peck. 1990. *Reading-to-write: Exploring a cognitive and social process.* Oxford: Oxford University Press.

Hamp-Lyons, Liz (ed.). 1991. *Assessing second language writing in academic contexts.* Norwood, N.J.: Ablex.

Hubt, B. 1990. "The literature of direct writing assessment: Major concerns and prevailing trends." *Review of Educational Research* 60(2): 237–263.

Kroll, Barbara (ed.). 1990. *Second language writing: Research issues for the classroom.* New York: Cambridge University Press.

Kroll, Barbara. 1990. "Understanding TOEFL's test of written English." *RELC Journal* 22(1): 20–33.

Kroll, Barbara. 1991. "Teaching writing in the ESL context." In Marianne Celce-Murcia (ed.) *Teaching English as a second or foreign language* (2nd edition.) New York: Newbury House/HarperCollins.

Oller, John, and Patricia Richard-Amato (eds.). 1983. *Methods that work.* Rowley, Mass.: Newbury House.

Phelps, L. 1985. "Dialectics of coherence." *College English* 47: 12–29.

Purves, Alan. 1988. *Writing across languages and cultures: Issues in contrastive rhetoric.* Newbury Park, Calif.: Sage.

Redeken, G. 1984. "On differences between spoken and written language." *Discourse Processes* 7: 43–55.

Reid, Joy M. 1993. "Historical perspectives on writing and reading in the ESL classroom." In Joan G. Carson and Ilona Leki (eds.). *Reading in the composition classroom: Second language perspectives.* Boston: Heinle and Heinle.

Ruth, L., and S. Murphy. 1988. *Designing writing tasks for the assessment of writing.* Norwood, N.J.: Ablex.

Scarcella, Robin, and Rebecca Oxford. 1992. *The tapestry of language learning: The individual in the communicative classroom.* Boston: Heinle & Heinle.

Scollon, Ronald, and Suzanne Scollon. 1981. *Narrative, literacy, and face in interethnic communication.* Norwood, N.J.: Ablex.

Swaffar, J. K. 1988. "Readers, texts, and second languages: The interactive process." *Modern Language Journal* 72(2): 123–149.

Tierney, R. J., and T. Shanahan. 1991. "Research on the reading-writing relationship: Interactions, transactions, and outcomes." In R. Barr, M. L. Kamil, P. Mosenthal, and P. D. Pearson (eds.), *Handbook of reading research* 2. New York: Longman. 246–280.

Vaughan, C. 1991. "Holistic assessment: What goes on in the rater's minds?" In L. Hamp-Lyons (ed.), *Assessing second language writing in academic contexts.* 111–126. Norwood, N.J.: Ablex. 111–126.

Zamel, Vivian. 1991. "Acquiring language, literacy, and academic discourse: Entering ever new conversations." *College ESL* 1(1): 10–18.

An investigation of the effects of texts and tasks on listening comprehension: Some evidence from Russian[1]

Irene Thompson
George Washington University

Introduction. Listening comprehension, a neglected skill in comparison with reading, is slowly gaining acceptance among second-language acquisition experts as a researchable area. Its centrality to the acquisition of speaking is now largely accepted, and most modern materials and methodologies give increasing emphasis to activities specifically designed to promote listening comprehension development. Listening comprehension testing, on the other hand, continues to remain somewhat neglected.

While there has been some research concerned with testing reading comprehension in L2, relatively little has been done with the assessment of listening. However, knowledge accumulated from studies of L2 reading assessment may not be fully applicable to measurement of L2 listening skills, since listening differs from reading in a number of significant ways due to differences between the spoken and the written media as well as dissimilarities between oral and written tests (Lund 1991a).

Measuring listening comprehension is difficult because spoken language understanding is an internal, subjective process not open to external observation and can only be. studied indirectly. One way to improve our understanding of this elusive skill is to accumulate data about tests that purport to measure it. By testing specific hypotheses about listening comprehension using data from tests already in existence, researchers can obtain evidence that can be useful in designing future instruments with improved construct validity.

Background. Douglas (1987) called for the development of tests that adequately reflect our understanding of the complexity of the listening skill. He pointed to the need for studying the relationship between empirical stages of L2 listening comprehension development and scales that are supposed to reflect such development, such as, for instance, the ACTFL Proficiency Guidelines (see the Appendix). One such attempt was a validation study of the ACTFL Guidelines for the four skills in English and French (Dandonoli and Henning 1990). A

1. This study was partially supported by Grant PO1700032 from the U.S. Department of Education.

problematic finding of this study was the relatively low validity exhibited by the French and to some extent by the English listening tests. The authors suggested that the low level of construct validity in listening may have been due to factors relating to either the ACTFL Guidelines or the tests that were used in the study. They stressed the need to pay greater attention to characteristics of the listening passages as well as fidelity, memory, speed, and repetitions in order to find ways both the Guidelines and test-development procedures could be modified.

The above-mentioned validation study was originally designed to include Russian, but it was dropped because no Russian tests geared directly to the ACTFL Proficiency Guideline were available at the time. However, a standardized four-skill Comprehensive Russian Proficiency Test (CRPT), intended for students who have completed between two and four years of Russian, was developed by the Educational Testing Service (ETS) in 1990. The listening comprehension portion of the CRPT provides suitable data for examining the effect of passages as well as tasks associated with them.

The listening portion of the CRPT contains 22 multiple-choice questions based on conversations, short lectures, and news reports. The passages are thematically unified by one context that could be described as "a day in the life of an American student in Russia." In the course of the day, the American is involved in a number of informal conversations with Russians, goes on a guided tour, and hears several radio newscasts (weather, sports, and news). The test booklet provides hints as to where and when a conversation or a lecture takes place (e.g., "Later that day, Dan goes on a guided tour of an art gallery"). Test takers listen to each passage once with the questions in front of them. A student's raw score is the number of correct answers. Raw scores can be converted to ACTFL proficiency levels Novice through Advanced.

Each CRPT item was selected to represent one of the following proficiency levels on the ACTFL scale: Novice, Novice High, Intermediate, Intermediate High, and Advanced. A panel of five experts, working as a group, classified the items into the five categories, relying on the descriptions in the ACTFL Listening Guidelines. The classification was based on the stimulus materials and the task demanded of the student. The panel chose 70% as the required probability level for the Rasch analysis, i.e., "An Advanced listener has at least a 70% chance of success on a typical Advanced-level question."

It would have been logical to expect questions classified as "Advanced" to have the highest values of $\theta_{.70}$, those classified as "Intermediate High" to have the next highest value, and so on. However, in many cases the predictions did not correspond to the $\theta_{.70}$ values obtained from the students' responses during the field test. Consequently, the panel was asked to independently reclassify the items so as to bring them closer to the empirical $\theta_{.70}$ values.

The lack of agreement between expected item difficulty (EX) based on the ACTFL Guidelines and empirical data based on test performance (EM) could be attributed to problems with the construct validity of the ACTFL Listening

Guidelines or to the difficulty of translating statements in the ACTFL Guidelines into passage selection and test question development.

Passage variables. There are many factors and interactions of factors that can affect the difficulty of listening passages. "Inside-the-head" factors that affect listening performance include listeners' background knowledge (Samuels 1984, Markham and Latham 1987, Long 1990, Schmidt-Rinehart 1992). "Outside-the-head" factors include characteristics of listening texts and tasks. One feature of oral passages is the extent to which they contain elements of the spoken versus the written language. Tannen (1982, 1985) has suggested that all spoken texts can be arranged along a continuum, with those originating in the spoken language (such as natural conversations) at one end and those originating in the written language (such as newscasts) on the other. Orality and literacy are not directly related to the media in which they are represented because written texts can be read out loud, while conversations can be written down. Tannen (1982: 15) also noted that in the literate mode, the content and the verbal channel are elaborated, while in the oral mode the relative focus is on interaction.

Chafe (1982, 1985) notes that written and spoken language are two different processes because writing is slow, deliberate, and planned, whereas speaking occurs in real time. According to Chafe (1985: 106), spontaneous unplanned speech is produced in a series of spurts that he calls "idea units." These units are spoken with a single intonation contour; they are bound by some form of hesitation, they typically consist of a clause, and they are normally rather short and loosely strung together. Idea units in written language, on the other hand, tend to be both longer and more complex since the writer has more time to use all available linguistic devices to pack information into an idea unit and to place idea units into various relationships with each other. Written transactional language contains densely packed information because readers can process the text at their own pace by previewing, rereading, underlining, and so forth. Speakers, on the other hand, rarely have the time or mental resources to compose such elaborate language. Instead, oral texts typically contain a significant number of formulaic expressions, exophoric pronouns, ellipses, repetitions, false starts, afterthoughts, and so forth.

Rubin and Raforth (1984) argued that "listenability" is a function of the orality of a text. Since orally oriented texts contain more "listenable" features, it is logical to assume that they will be easier for listeners to comprehend. Shohamy and Inbar (1991) reported, for instance, that Hebrew-speaking high school students of English recalled dialogues better than lecturettes, which in turn were recalled better than newscasts. The authors hypothesized that the redundancies, pauses, repetitions, and monitoring of information flow in the dialogue and lecturette gave the listeners more opportunities to process the information they had heard.

Task variables. There is some evidence that listeners' recall of information is affected by tasks they are asked to carry out. Hildyard and Olson (1978) found that listeners did more poorly on memory questions than readers the first time they heard the passages but the differences disappeared in the second presentation. The authors suggested that listeners tend to gloss over details in order to make sense of overall meaning. Shohamy and Inbar (1991) found that tasks requiring inferencing had lower accuracy rates than tasks requiring recall of information explicitly stated in the text. They also found that tasks requiring memory for incidental details presented difficulties for their subjects. Lund (1991b) found some differences in performance depending on whether listeners were asked to recall the gist of an oral passage, were asked to recall details from the passage, or were given no directions at all.

The present study posed three questions:

(1) How did the developmental criteria contained in the ACTFL descriptions for listening correlate with actual listening behavior of students who took the listening portion of the CRPT?
(2) Were orally based texts more "listenable" than those originating in the written language? What features distinguished oral from literate texts?
(3) What task variables were correlated with relative difficulty of test questions?

Subjects and Procedure. Seventy-two students who had studied Russian for two years participated in the study. Data were collected over a period of two years due to small class sizes typical of Russian classes. The test was administered in the beginning of the fall semester of the third year. A small percentage of students who had studied in Russia or who spoke Russian or another Slavic language at home were excluded from analysis because they usually have significantly better listening comprehension than traditional learners who had studied Russian in formal settings, who constituted the majority of the test population.

The test was not very difficult for the students, with an average score of 15 correct (68%), which is higher than the 11 (50%) that could be expected of a 22-item test.

Results

(1) Was there a significant correction between expected (EX) and empirical (EM) values of the items? Figure 1 shows no clear fit between the expected difficulty level and empirical item difficulty. For instance, items classified as Intermediate ranged in difficulty from p = 0.89 to p = 0.52, an item classified as Novice turned out to be the most difficult item of all (p = 0.28), and some Advanced items were no more difficult than items rated Intermediate. If, on the

other hand, questions are arranged in order of decreasing difficulty, as in Figure 2, items judged to belong to one ACTFL level are scattered over different parts of the curve.

Figure 1. Scattergram of item difficulty

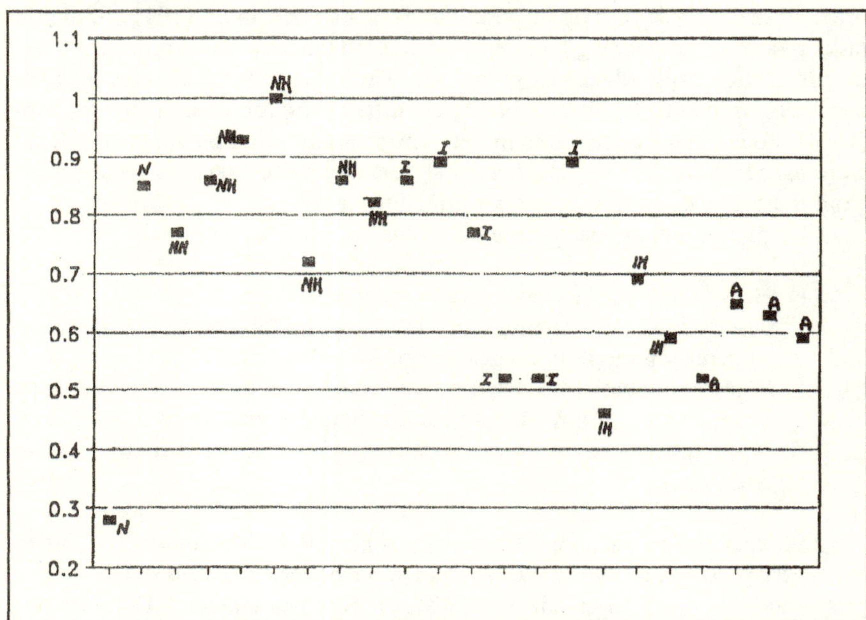

To determine the correlation between expected and empirical item difficulty, ACTFL levels were assigned the following scores: Novice = 0.50; Novice High = 0.75; Intermediate = 1.00; Intermediate High = 1.75; Advanced = 2.00. The Pearson Product-Moment correlation coefficient between empirical and expected difficulty was not significant ($r = 0.41$, df. 20, $p > 0.05$, two-tailed).

Table 1 shows the means for items calibrated according to the ACTFL descriptions. Since there were only two Novice items, they were included in the Novice High group. There was little difference between the means for Novice and Intermediate questions or between the means for the Intermediate High and Advanced groups. For this population, there were only two clearly distinguishable difficulty levels: one at the Novice and Intermediate Low levels and the other at the Intermediate High and Advanced levels.

Within the Novice–Intermediate group, there was a slight reversal in difficulty with the mean for Novice items being slightly higher than the mean for Intermediate questions. Dandonoli and Henning (1990) also found that items associated with Intermediate listening passages in English tended to have lower means than items associated with the Novice level.

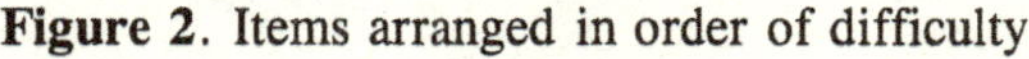

Figure 2. Items arranged in order of difficulty

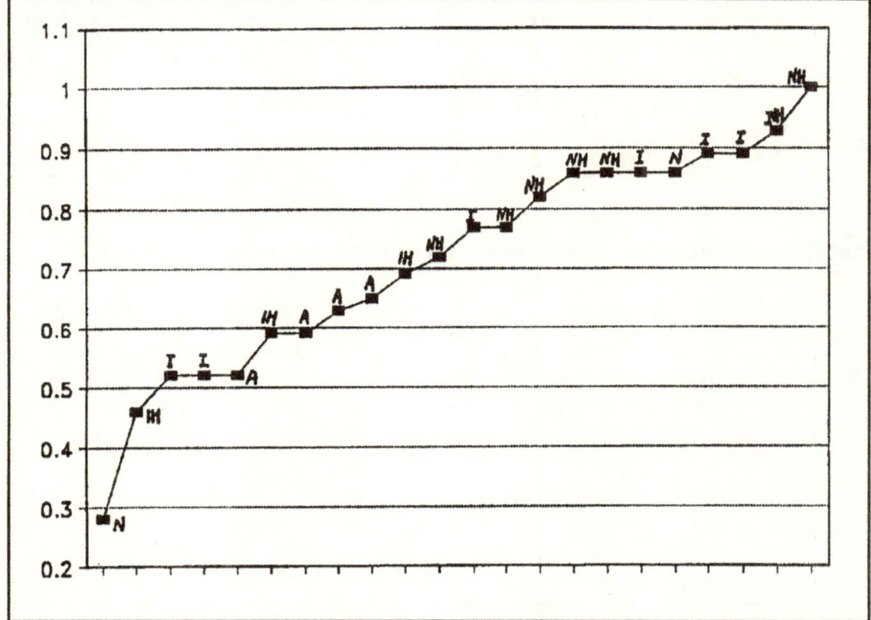

(2) Were orally based texts more listenable than passages that originated in the written language? What features distinguished oral from literate texts? Passages included in the CRPT can be divided into three groups: informal conversations with two or three participants, short lectures by a tourist guide, and radio news. The conversations were modeled on natural speech while the lectures and news reports represented written language that was read aloud. Of the 22 test questions, 12 were based on conversations and 10 were based on lectures and news reports. Table 2 shows that the mean for items associated with oral passages was significantly higher than the mean for questions based on literate texts (0.81 and 0.59 respectively; $t = 3.46$, df 20, $p < 0.01$, two-tailed). It must be noted that all but two (83%) of the questions associated with conversations were rated as Novice, and all but three (70%) of the items based on literate passages were rated as Intermediate High or Advanced.

To establish the relative "listenability" of oral vs. literate passages, they were compared with regard to the following features: number of pausal units; length of pausal units, number of different words used, and the ratio of content words to total number of words in each passage.

Table 1. Means and standard deviations of questions calibrated according to the ACTFL scale

	Novice	Intermediate	Intermediate High	Advanced
Mean	0.79	0.74	0.58	0.60
Standard Deviation	0.20	0.16	0.09	0.05

Table 2. Differences between means for features or oral and literate texts

Text Features	Oral Texts	Literate Texts	t
Empirical difficulty of items	0.59	0.81	3.46*
Number of pausal units	14.80	19.17	1.11
Length of pausal units	2.85	5.07	5.56*
Number of different words	36.17	54.20	5.83*
Percent of content words	0.71	0.93	2.48**

* $p < 0.01$ ** $p < 0.05$

- **Number of pausal units.** On the average, oral texts contained more pausal units than literate passages (mean of 19.17 and 14.80 respectively). However, the difference was not statistically significant ($t = 1.108$, df 20, $p > 0.05$, two-tailed).
- **Length of pausal units.** The mean length of pausal units was 5.07 words in literate texts and 2.85 words in oral passages. The difference was statistically significant ($t = 5.561$, df 20, $p < .001$, two-tailed).
- **Number of different words.** The total number of words in each passage was calculated with repeated words counting as one. The average number of different words in the literate passages was 54.20 as compared with 36.17 in oral texts. The difference was statistically significant ($t = 5.830$, df 20, $p < 0.01$, two-tailed).
- **The ratio of content words to total number of words.** Content words were defined as those not belonging to the following categories: various forms of address, courtesies; formulaic expressions, exophoric pronouns; demonstratives, interrogatives; particles; and various conversation-management devices. Content words accounted for 93%

of the total number of words in literate passages as compared with 71% in oral texts. The difference was statistically significant ($t = 2.48$, df 20, $p < 0.05$).

To find out whether the four text features above were correlated with the empirical difficulty of test questions, Pearson Product-Moment correlation coefficients were computed between them. Table 3 shows the correlations. The empirical difficulty of test items showed significant correlations with length of pausal units and the number of different words in the passages.

Table 3. Pearson Product-Moment correlation coefficients between item difficulty and text features

Text features	Number of pausal units	Length of pausal units	Number of different words	Percent of content words
Empirical difficulty of items	0.10	0.44*	0.47*	0.31

*$p<0.05$

(3) What task variables affected item difficulty? All CRPT questions tested comprehension of factual information of the who/what/when/where type. The questions can be classified into two groups: (1) those requiring recall of structurally important information, i.e., facts related to the main idea(s) of the passage; (2) those requiring recall of incidental information not relevant to the main context. For instance, a question such as "*Where* is X planning to go?" was considered to be structurally important if the conversation dealt with making plans to go somewhere. On the other hand, a questions such as "*Where* did X take place?" was considered to be an incidental memory item if the location of the event had nothing to do with the event itself.

Of the twelve questions based on oral texts, seven required recall of structurally important information and five required recall of incidental information. The average percentage of correct responses for the former was 0.89 as compared with 0.73 for the latter. These numbers were too small for statistical treatment, although they pointed to the apparently greater difficulty of items that required recall of incidental information. Unfortunately, eight of the ten questions associated with literate passages were of the incidental memory type, which made it impossible to compare the two types of questions for texts originating in the written languages, although among questions with the lowest accuracy rates were those requiring recall of numbers (temperatures, various statistics, dates), names of people and places, and incidental details that were mentioned only once or among other details of the same class.

Discussion. The first finding of this limited study points to difficulties in showing a strong relationship between expected difficulty levels based on ACTFL descriptions for the Novice, Intermediate, and Advanced levels and clearly differentiable listening behaviors on the part of this particular group of test takers. Instead of five levels of difficulty used in item calibration (Novice, Novice High, Intermediate, Intermediate High, Advanced), there were only two clearly distinguishable levels: one that included items calibrated as Novice and Intermediate, and the other composed of items rated as Intermediate High and Advanced. This suggests that for learners at this level, there were basically two levels of difficulty: one associated with items based on conversations, and one associated with questions that were based on passages that originated in the literate language. Questions relating to orally based texts were answered more accurately than questions associated with literate passages confirming earlier findings obtained by Shohamy and Inbar (1990). That may be so partly because the oral passages in the CRPT had shorter pausal units, contained fewer different words, and had a lower percentage of content words than literate texts. These features gave listeners more opportunity to process information in the passages. In addition, learners at this level had more experience with listening to situational dialogues than to oral presentation of written texts. Finally, oral texts may have contained more familiar vocabulary than literate passages, although this is difficult to prove empirically since both types of texts consisted for the most part of vocabulary commonly found in first- and second-year Russian textbooks.

With regard to the effects of listening tasks on comprehension, questions requiring recall of incidental details appeared to be somewhat more difficult than questions that were structurally related to the main idea(s) of the passage. This confirmed the results of other studies that found tasks requiring recall of incidental information to be difficult (Hildyard and Olson 1978, Shohamy and Inbar 1990).

The preponderance of memory items associated with literate passages may have been due to the fact that CRPT passages were for the most part descriptive. It may be that descriptive texts lend themselves more readily to detail-type questions. Other types of organization, for instance chronological sequence, might have allowed questions of a different type. Therefore, in selecting oral passages, test developers need to include passages with more than one type or organization.

Summary. Our understanding of processes involved in listening comprehension limits our ability to develop listening tests with high construct validity. As research into the validity of the ACTFL Guidelines (or any other scale) as the basis for construction of listening proficiency tests continues, we need to further investigate those features of texts that contribute to the ease or difficulty with which they can be comprehended and recalled. In particular, we should focus attention on finding ways to objectively measure the orality–literacy dimension of texts as well as their propositional structure. In addition, we need to systematically investigate the effects of task demands on comprehension and recall with particular reference to the role of memory.

REFERENCES

American Council on the Teaching of Foreign Languages. *ACTFL proficiency guidelines.* Yonkers, N.Y.: ACTFL.

Chafe, Wallace. 1982. "Integration and involvement in speaking, writing, and oral literature." In Deborah Tannen (ed.), *Spoken and written language: Exploring orality and literacy.* Norwood, N.J.: Ablex.

Chafe, Wallace. 1985. "Linguistic differences produced by differences between speaking and writing." In David R. Olson, Nancy Torrance, and Angela Hildyard (eds.), *Literary language and learning.* Cambridge: Cambridge University Press.

Dandonoli, Patricia, and Grant Henning. 1991. "An investigation of the construct validity of the ACTFL proficiency guidelines and oral interview procedure." *Foreign Language Annals* 23: 11–22.

Douglas, Dan. 1988. "Testing listening comprehension in the context of the ACTFL Guidelines." *Studies in Second Language Acquisition* 10(2): 245–261.

Educational Testing Service. 1990. *Comprehensive Russian proficiency test.* Princeton, N.J.: Educational Testing Service.

Hildyard, Angela, and David R. Olson. 1978. "On the comprehension and memory of oral versus written discourse." In Deborah Tannen (ed.), *Spoken and written language.* Norwood, N.J.: Ablex.

Long, Donna R. 1990. "What you don't know can't help you: An exploratory study of background knowledge and second language listening comprehension." *Studies in Second Language Acquisition* 12(1): 65–80.

Lund, Randall J. 1991a. "A comparison of second language listening and reading comprehension." *Modern Language Journal* 75(2): 196–211.

Lund, Randall J. 1991b. "The effects of listening tasks on comprehension." Paper presented at Research Perspectives on Adult Language Learning and Acquisition. Columbus, Ohio, October 11–12.

Markham, Paul L., and Michael Latham. 1987. "The influence of religion-specific background knowledge on the listening comprehension of adult second-language learners." *Language Learning* 37(2): 157–170.

Meyer, Bonnie J.F., and George W. McConkie. 1973. "What is recalled after hearing a passage?" *Journal of Educational Psychology* 65: 109–117.

Rubin, Andee. 1980. "A theoretical taxonomy of the difference between oral and written language." In Rand J. Spiro, Bertram C. Bruce, and William F. Brewer (eds.), *Theoretical issues in reading comprehension.* Hillsdale, N.J.: Lawrence Erlbaum.

Rubin, Donald, and Bennett A. Raforth. 1984. "Oral Language: A criterion for selecting listenable materials." MS.

Samuels, S. Jay. 1984. "Factors influencing listening: Inside and outside the head." *Theory into Practice* 23(3): 183–189.

Schmidt-Rinehart, Barbara C. 1992. "The effects of topic familiarity on listening comprehension." Paper presented at the 1992 ACTFL Conference, Chicago.

Shohamy, Elana, and Ofra Inbar. 1991. "Validation of listening comprehension tests: The effect of text and question type." *Language Testing* 8: 23–40.

Tannen, Deborah. 1982. "The oral/literate continuum in discourse." In Deborah Tannen (ed.), *Spoken and written language: Exploring orality and literacy*. Norwood, N.J.: Ablex.

Tannen, Deborah. 1985. "Relative focus of involvement in oral and written discourse." In David R. Olson, Nancy Torrance, and Angela Hildyard (eds.), *Literary language and learning*. Cambridge: Cambridge University Press.

Appendix. ACTFL Proficiency Guidelines for Listening

Novice Low. Understanding is limited to occasional isolated words, such as cognates, borrowed words, and high-frequency social conventions. Essentially no ability to comprehend even yshort utterances.

Novice Mid. Able to understand some short, learned utterances, particularly where context strongly supports understanding and speech is clearly audible. Comprehends some words and phrases from simple questions, statements, high-frequency commands, and courtesy formulae about topics that refer to basic personal information or the immediate physical setting. The listener requires long pauses for assimilation and periodically requests repetition and/or slowed rate of speech.

Novice High. Able to understand short, learned utterances and some sentence-length utterances, particularly where context strongly supports understanding and speech is clearly audible. Comprehends words and phrases from simple questions, statements, high-frequency commands, and courtesy formulae. May require repetition and/or slowed rate of speech.

Intermediate Low. Able to understand sentence-length utterances that consist of recombinations of learned elements in a limited number of content areas, particularly if strongly supported by the situational context. Content refers to basic personal background and needs, social conventions, and routine tasks, such as getting meals and receiving simple instructions and directions. Listening tasks pertain primarily to spontaneous face-to-face conversations. Understanding is often uneven; repetition and rewording may be necessary. Misunderstandings in both main ideas and details arise frequently.

Intermediate Mid. Able to understand sentence-length utterances that consist of recombinations of learned utterances on a variety of topics. Content continues to refer primarily to basic personal background and needs, social conventions, and somewhat more complex tasks, such as lodging, transportation, and shopping. Additional content areas include some personal interests and activities and a greater diversity of instructions and directions. Listening tasks not only pertain to spontaneous face-to-face conversations but also to short, routine telephone conversations and some deliberate speech, such as simple announcements and reports over the media. Understanding continues to be uneven.

Intermediate High. Able to sustain understanding over longer stretches of connected discourse on a number of topics pertaining to different times and places; however, understanding is inconsistent due to failure to grasp main ideas and/or details. Thus, while topics do not differ significantly from those of an Advanced-level listener, comprehension is less in quantity and poorer in quality.

Advanced. Able to understand main ideas and most details of connected discourse on a variety of topics beyond the immediacy of the situation. Comprehension may be uneven due to a variety of linguistic and extralinguistic factors, among which topic familiarity is very prominent. These texts frequently involve description and narration in different time frames or aspect, such as present, nonpast, habitual, or imperfective. Texts may include interviews, short lectures on familiar topics, and news items and reports primarily dealing with factual information. Listener is aware of cohesive devices but nay not be able to use them to follow the sequence of thought in an oral text.

The place of input in the scenario approach

Frederick J. Bosco[1]
Georgetown University

Abstract. Di Pietro's Scenario Approach to L2 instruction incorporates significant features designed to enhance the acquisition process. These include:

(1) an *All-At-Once* contextual framework capable of being held in focal awareness throughout the major phases of instruction (that is, the scenario agendas are presented up front and can easily be held in the mind during the rehearsal, performance, and debriefing phases);
(2) tension-producing situations that require the resolution of uncertainty;
(3) meaningful and sustained student–student interactions through collaborative group work; and
(4) debriefing sessions that focus students' attention on their sociolinguistic needs.

One should not, however, expect the scenario concept to carry the entire burden of second-language development. The underlying pedagogy needs to be carried one step further. I propose extending the Di Pietro model to include an input phase that explicitly brings into focus relevant conversational strategies used by native speakers of the target language in response to the scenarios in question. The framework proposed here involves a four-phase cycle consisting of the rehearsal, performance, and debriefing phases followed by a message-focused input phase directed toward cultural grounding. In this methodology, scenarios serve a threefold function: (1) to promote interactive discourse in the L2 classroom; (2) to generate input from native speakers of the target language; and (3) to establish the basis for instructional materials. I would suggest that message-focused input derived from the scenarios can be embedded in the instructional cycle in a manner consistent with the values of the scenario approach. My purpose is to preserve the strengths of the scenario concept and, at the same time, build on them.

---

1. I am grateful to David P. Harris and Robert G. Walsh for reading the initial draft of this paper and offering valuable comments and suggestions. I should also like to express my appreciation to Carolyn Morse for developing the "Homecoming" scenario and for making available the performance data of her L2 students. Thanks are also due the many friends who provided scenario improvisations and interviews—in particular, Mary Weber and Donald Pilon.

Essential features of Di Pietro's Scenario Approach. The Strategic Interaction (SI) method as described by Di Pietro in *Strategic Interaction* (1987) is a scenario-based strategy developed in response to the need for a holistic approach to second-language instruction. Recognizing the social nature of humans and the universally shared propensity to engage in problem-solving as a group activity, Di Pietro developed SI to promote interactive discourse in the second-language classroom. The method is based on the notion that language learning must take place within the context of discourse generated for the purpose of social interaction. The prime classroom device for this discourse-based approach is the scenario, which is defined as "a strategic interplay of roles functioning to fulfill personal agendas within a shared context" (Di Pietro 1982: 41).

An important ingredient in the scenario is the tension created by giving each role a specific agenda and not sharing all information among the roles. Groups of students work together to rehearse each role and build a game plan for its execution later in the interaction with the other roles of the scenario. Each role allows for the development of a personal agenda. However, changes may be required when the performers meet and try to execute the various roles. The resulting interactive tension may stimulate innovative language use as the performers strive to work out their game plan, come up with alternative plans, or arrive at a compromise position. Rehearsal groups stand ready during the performance to offer advice and guidance to each individual who is playing out a role.

Ideally, execution of a scenario takes place in three phases: rehearsal, performance, and debriefing. It is during the debriefing phase that the teacher leads a discussion of various aspects of the performance. Crucial grammatical points are brought out, as well as matters of conversational organization, vocabulary, pronunciation, and social norms. In terms of teacher-directed classroom activities, debriefing comes closest to the traditional instructional dyad of teacher/student. However, rehearsal as well as debriefing needs to be organized so that students do not lose sight of the intent of the discourse generated by the scenario.

Scope of this study. The basic strength of the scenario approach is that it gives priority to the *strategic* use of language. Teachers utilizing the Di Pietro model are faced with two important questions: What constitute effective interactive strategies with respect to the scenarios in question and where do the performances of the L2 learners break down from a strategic point of view? These questions require us to field test the scenarios in order to determine their appropriateness and to collect a variety of representative *models of language use* from native speakers of the target language. These data can then be used to shape the instructional process. This paper will argue that the Di Pietro model needs to be carried a step forward beyond the rehearsal, performance, and debriefing phases to include scenario-based input gathered from native speakers of the target language and that such input is the basis for schema building. It is suggested that an input phase can be incorporated into the scenario approach without violating the basic tenets of SI. The viability of the scenario that serves both to elicit native-speaker input and to respond to the sociolinguistic needs of the L2 learner will be illustrated by means of a scenario developed for an ESL class. Examples of strategically oriented models elicited from four dyads of native speakers of English will be offered to suggest how such input can be used in the classroom to stay true to the scenario form. Finally, an organization scheme designed to extend the Di Pietro approach to include a formal input phase will be proposed.

Values inherent in Di Pietro's scenario approach. Di Pietro's discourse-based approach to L2 instruction incorporates several significant features designed to enhance the acquisition process. These include

(1) an *All-At-Once* contextual framework capable of being held in focal awareness[2] throughout the major phases of instruction;
(2) tension-producing situations that require the resolution of uncertainty;
(3) meaningful and sustained student–student interactions through collaborative group work;
(4) opportunity for each learner to invest his/her *self* to whatever extent desired;
(5) the activation of individual learning styles by means of small working groups; and
(6) the potential of scenario performances to uncover the sociolinguistic needs of the learners.

One of the most significant features of the scenario approach is an *All-At-Once* situational framework that can be easily held in focal awareness throughout the major phases of the instructional cycle. At the very outset, each group of students is presented with a role assignment that includes a brief description of the situation, together with a communicative goal in the form of an agenda.

---

2. Michael Polanyi (1958) distinguishes between two ways of attending to a thing. *Focal awareness* refers to those things that we consciously attend to in the process of doing something. In reading, for example, the object of our attention is not on the words as graphic configurations or on the texture of the paper, etc., but rather on the conceptions evoked by the text. The text itself, in all its particulars, is in *subsidiary awareness*. Polanyi points out that focal awareness and subsidiary awareness are mutually exclusive. If an experienced pianist shifts his attention from the music he is playing to the observation of what he is doing with his fingers while playing, he may get confused and be forced to interrupt his performance. This happens if our focal attention is shifted to particulars that had previously been in subsidiary awareness.

Each group shares certain basic information with the other group(s), but each is given a different agenda.

Equally significant is that considerable opportunity is provided for social interaction in the classroom. In Di Pietro's approach to second-language instruction, social interaction is promoted in two steps: first, by putting learners together in cooperating groups charged with mapping out procedures to complete a shared task and then by facing off representatives from those groups whose tasks are thematically related (Di Pietro and Bosco 1991). Students are given the opportunity to shape a plan of action, to discuss alternate strategies, to share knowledge, and to assess their own and each other's performance. The classroom itself becomes the *speech community* for sharing and creating knowledge.

Di Pietro's scenario concept has the ancillary value of providing a concrete measure of how well the learner is able to say things in the target language, what competencies have been gained, and what difficulties remain in the areas of language structure and language use. The scenario thus becomes a viable approach to error analysis.

The Scenario

Role A (Female)

Role Identification: You are an outgoing, lively college student. You would like to get to know the new international student in your history class, but he seems quiet and timid.

Shared Information: You invite him to the Homecoming Dance in order to break the ice, and he accepts.

Background and Agenda: A week before the Homecoming Dance, some of your friends invite you and your date to join them for dinner before the dance at an elegant French restaurant.

Possible Conflict: You realize that your date may not be comfortable going to dinner with a large group of your friends.

Your Charge: You meet him on the way to class. How will you convince him to go out to dinner with you and your friends?

Role B (Male)

Role Identification: You are a foreign scholarship student and attend a small college in the Midwest. You are quiet and hold back because of limited experience with English and with American culture.

Shared Information: A woman in your history class invites you to the Homecoming Dance. You accept, happy to have an evening away from your library carrel.

Background and Agenda: Later, friends suggest that the evening may turn out to be expensive if you have to pay for the tickets, go out to dinner, buy flowers, etc. You are living on a tight budget in order to make it through your studies. You need to somehow explain your financial situation. Remember, you are anxious to hold down expenses.

Your Charge: You meet your date before class and have a chance to talk to her about your concerns.

Assessing learner needs by way of scenario performances. Let us consider the "Homecoming" scenario shown above. It was developed for an intermediate-level ESL class. The students in the class, all native speakers of Spanish from Panama, were enrolled at a small community college in Kansas.

Two class periods were devoted to the scenario in question. During the first period, students were divided into two groups and assigned one of the two roles. The instructor took each group aside to explain the role and to help the students develop various approaches to the situation. The students then proceeded to the rehearsal phase. At first, they used Spanish, but gradually shifted to English as they began to come up with the utterances that they planned to use later. At the conclusion of the rehearsal phase, each group selected a representative to enact the scenario in front of the class. Debriefing took place during the second class period. Most of the concerns of the students revolved around grammatical errors. The instructor corrected and explained the troubling grammatical points and suggested alternate approaches to the situation. Following this phase, students were organized into pairs and directed to work through the scenario a second time. Later, the scenario was re-enacted in front of the class by the same two students who were involved in the original performance. The performance was re-enacted to allow students to " ... sharpen their control over the mechanisms of language use" (Di Pietro 1989: 133).

What follows are transcriptions of the performances of two students, Amarilis and Pacifico. The rehearsal and initial performance took an entire class period; the debriefing and second performance took place the following day.

Transcript 1. The first performance of the L2 learners

Opening

She: Hi

He: Hello, hello, Amarilis.

She: How are you?

He: Oh, fine. How are you?

Brings up her agenda

She: I would like to invite you to a dinner ... a pleasure "para" my friends invite you.

He: OK. All right.

She: You go?

He: OK.

Request for information

She: OK. My friends want to know about your culture, about you and also they want ... and also they want to know about some, eh, meals special in your country.

Brings up his agenda

He: Well, I have to ... Maybe I will go, but I don't know if I will have money enough.
She: Oh!
He: Money's a problem.

Resolution

She: This is no problem.
He: Well?
She: This is no problem because my friends and I pay for this.
He: OK. I go.
She: OK. Let's go.
He: I go ... I go to the party. Thank you. Thank you, Amarilis.

Closing

She: See you later.
He: See you later.

Transcript 2. The second performance of the L2 learners.

Opening

She: Hello.
He: Hello, Amarilis.
She: How are you?
He: Oh, fine. How are you?

Brings up her agenda

She: It's a pleasure for my friends and I to invite to a party.
He: OK.
She: Are you going?

Brings up his agenda

He: Well I have to think about it because I don't ... I don't have enough money to go to the party.
She: Oh?
He: Money ... money is a problem.

Resolution

She: It is no problem.
He: Why?
She: Because my friends and I pay for it.
He: OK. I ... I will go to the party.
She: Great.
He: OK. Thank you.

Closing

She: See you later.
He: See you later, Amarilis.

The woman, Amarilis, initiates each of her conversations by advancing directly to the crux of her charge. She makes no reference to shared information, but proceeds immediately to the dinner invitation and does so in a register that appears too formal for the situation. She bypasses the question of where and when the proposed dinner is to take place. Pacifico accepts the invitation initially, notwithstanding his financial condition and his apparent timidity. However, he quickly realizes the implications of the arrangement and blurts out that he has no money. Amarilis assures him that she and her friends would pay for the dinner.

Both performances are marked by relative terseness. In neither performance do the students adequately come to grips with the difficulties inherent in the role assignments. Pacifico, for example, gives no hint as to his reluctance to get in a position in which he might have to sustain a conversation in English with a group of the woman's friends. Amarilis does add an interesting touch to the exchange by suggesting that her friends are anxious to meet Pacifico and to learn about his culture. She uses this validating strategy to encourage Pacifico to accept the dinner arrangement.

There are in both exchanges a number of grammatical errors. Aside from difficulties with word order, the speakers have difficulty with the usage of the forms *it* and *this* and with the modal auxiliaries. For example, when Pacifico says: *I go to the party*, he presumably means *I'll go to the dinner* or *I'll come to the dinner*. There are a number of unmotivated utterances such as *OK, I go* and *Let's go*.

The L2 learners would at this point significantly benefit from native-speaker models in order to gain a better understanding of register, of grammatical usage, and of alternative strategies for dealing with socially complex situations. Such input would be particularly valuable if it were scenario-based and strategically oriented. In order to shape the instructional process, language instructors have the opportunity to use the scenarios to elicit a rich variety of native-speaker responses to the situations. The practice of testing out the scenarios in this way would not only furnish a potentially rich source of data for classroom use, but would serve to highlight potential difficulties inherent in the agendas themselves. In addition, one would gain some indication as to the level of interactive complexity posed by the scenarios. This information is critical to the selection and sequencing of scenarios in a course syllabus.

To illustrate the use of a scenario to elicit strategically oriented native-speaker models, I presented the scenario in question to four dyads of speakers of English and had them improvise in much the same way as did the L2 learners. What follows are the transcriptions of two of the improvisations, followed by a comparison of how the speakers of English developed their agendas as contrasted with the responses of the L2 learners. A full transcription of the improvisations of the third and fourth dyads of speakers of English is included in the appendices.

Transcript 3. Improvisation by native speakers of English (Dyad 1)

Brings up her agenda

She: Some friends have asked us to go out to dinner with them at a French restaurant. Would that be OK with you?

He: Dinner? At a French restaurant? When? What's the occasion?

She: Oh, sorry. They wanted us to join them for dinner before the Homecoming Dance on Saturday.

Brings up his agenda

He: Well … you probably know … I'm on a low budget in order to make it through my graduate studies here in the States. Would it be OK if we shared expenses for the evening?

Resolution

She: This will be my treat. I invited you to the dance and I planned to pick up the entire tab for the evening.

He: That's really nice of you.

She: Then you'll come to dinner?

He: Yes, I'll be glad to.

Transcript 4. Improvisation by native speakers of English (Dyad 2)

Brings up shared information

He: I've been thinking about the Homecoming Dance …

Introduces his agenda

He: Should I pick up the tickets?

She: Oh, no. I already have the tickets.

He: Can I help pay for them?

She: No, no. Remember. I invited you to the dance …

Introduces her agenda

She: Sal, some of my friends have asked us to join them for dinner before the dance. There's a new French restaurant near campus. Everyone is raving about the food.

He: A French restaurant? Won't that be pretty expensive? …

Proposes alternate plan

He: I was thinking of a more private dinner at my place. I wanted to prepare a special dish of mine.

She: Well, I suppose my friends would understand.

He: And you know how tongue-tied I get when I'm in the company of a lot of people.

Resolution

She: I really want you to enjoy the evening. Sure, dinner at your place will be fine.

He: Great. Can I come by your dorm about 5:30 on Saturday?

Closing

She: That'll be fine. I'll be ready. Sal ... it's getting late. We'd better get to class.

Comparing conversational approaches. An examination of the verbal responses of the L2 learners and those of the NSs of English reveals significant differences with respect to the degree of formality/informality, directness/indirectness, and explicitness. Tables 1 through 3 summarize how the speakers dealt with the agendas.

Table 1. Woman's agenda: Extending the dinner invitation

L2 Learners

First Performance

I would like to invite you to a dinner ... a pleasure "para" my friends invite you.

Second Performance

It's a pleasure for my friends and I to invite to a party.

Native Speakers of English

Dyad 1

Some friends have asked us to go out to dinner with them at a French restaurant. Would that be OK with you? They wanted us to join them for dinner before the Homecoming Dance on Saturday.

Dyad 2

Sal, some of my friends have asked us to join them for dinner before the dance. There's a new French restaurant near campus. Everyone is raving about the food.

Dyad 3

Guess what? We got an invitation to join a group of my friends at a swanky French restaurant before the dance.

Dyad 4

Oh, a group of my friends would like to meet before the dance at the Parisienne. It's a very nice restaurant downtown. Is that OK, Amal? ... and the food is great. You'll love it.

The L2 student employs a formal register in her dinner invitation without

Table 2. Man's agenda: Controlling expenses

L2 Learners

First Performance

I don't know if I will have money enough. Money's a problem.

Second Performance

Well, I have to think about it because I don't ... I don't have enough money to go to the party. Money ... money is a problem.

Native Speakers of English

Dyad 1

Well ... you probably know ... I'm on a low budget in order to make it through my graduate studies here in the States. Would it be OK if we shared expenses for the evening?

Dyad 2

A French restaurant? Won't that be pretty expensive?

Dyad 3

Does it mean that much to you to go to the dinner ... or would you rather just the two of us go out for a simple meal? It would be a lot cheaper. But if it means that much to you, I'll go.

Dyad 4

Did you tell your friends we'd definitely be there? Of course, we'll go, if that's what you'd enjoy.

specifying when and where the event is to take place. In the first performance she says: "I would like to invite you to a dinner ... a pleasure 'para' my friends invite you"; in her second performance she does not mention the dinner at all, but instead refers to *a party*: "It's a pleasure for my friends and I to invite to a party." The native speakers of English are more descriptive and matter-of-fact in handling their agenda. One speaker says: "Some friends have asked us to go out to dinner with them at a French restaurant. Would that be OK with you?" Another put it this way: "Guess what? We got an invitation to join a group of my friends at a swanky French restaurant before the dance." Some of the native speakers use hype as part of their game plan. One announces: "There's a new French restaurant near campus. Everyone is raving about the food"; another speaker calls the restaurant *the Parisienne*, and she is equally enthusiastic about the eating establishment. She states: "It's a very nice restaurant downtown and the food is great. You'll love it."

Both the L2 learners and the speakers in Dyads 1 and 2 use a *direct* strategy in talking about expenses, but there are sharp differences. In Dyad 2, the woman

Table 3. The man's concerns about upholding his end of the conversation

L2 Learners

First Performance

(No reference.)

Second Performance

(No reference.)

Native Speakers of English

Dyad 1

I was thinking of a more private dinner at my place ... and you know how tongue-tied I get when I'm in the company of a lot of people.

Dyad 2

(No reference.)

Dyad 3

(No reference.)

Dyad 4

Well, to tell you the truth, I have some trouble meeting new people ... and the conversations go so fast ... and I was thinking ... thinking that we could have a quiet dinner with just one other couple.

has already committed herself to paying the expenses of the dance, and so when she proposes a predance dinner, it is unclear whether she is also paying for the dinner. Thus the man's worry about the expense of the French restaurant could be a negotiating tactic: (1) I don't want you to have heavy dining expenses, too (and let me know who pays for the dinner.); (2) wouldn't a non-French restaurant be more in keeping with your or my budget? Dyad 1 does a lot of negotiating after starting directly. Even this, however, is softened by his "you probably know." He suggests sharing. Thus, even though all speakers in these dyads handle the financial question in a direct fashion, the native speakers' approach is quite different from that of the L2 student.

The preceding discussion is meant to illustrate the importance of collecting and examining scenario-based data for use as possible input in the instructional cycle. The contents and sequencing of the proposed input phase are discussed below.

Proposed instructional framework. Consider the instructional framework outlined below. It consists of Di Pietro's rehearsal, performance, and debriefing phases followed by a proposed instructional (input) phase. The input phase incorporates scenario-based, native-speaker improvisations together with worksheets designed to guide comprehension. The worksheets are meant to provide the learner with a source of language *chunkings*, information schemata and conversational strategies beyond those used in the student–student performances.

- *Phase 1: Rehearsal.* L2 students are divided into groups and assigned roles. Each group is charged with developing an approach to the assigned role.
- *Phase 2: Performance.* A representative from each group is selected to perform the scenario. Participants are encouraged to consult with the appropriate support group as required.
- *Phase 3: Debriefing.* The performance is discussed. Corrections and suggestions are made.
- *Phase 4: Scenario-Based Input.* Comprehension worksheets that provide representative models of language use are made available to the L2 learners. Transcriptions of native-speaker improvisations and interviews together with tapes and/or accompanying videos provide further assistance in schema building.

The comprehension worksheets that form part of the input phase afford the opportunity to cover various aspects of language in a systematic way. Particular attention can be given to how the various scenario roles are portrayed, how information is organized, what transactions are exemplified, what strategies are used, and what choices are made by the speakers in terms of lexicon and grammatical structure. Below is a brief sample of a worksheet designed to incorporate the data discussed earlier.

1. Consider the following responses:

Response A
I would like to invite you to a dinner ... a pleasure "para" my friends invite you.

Response B
Sal, some of my friends have asked us to join them for dinner before the dance. There's a new French restaurant near campus. Everyone is raving about the food.

Which of the following *pieces of information* can you gather from each of the responses?

1. the source of the invitation
2. the nature of the event
3. the type of restaurant
4. the location of the restaurant

5. the amount of time the restaurant has been in business
6. the expected quality of the food

2. Approaches used by the speakers to indicate their lack of enthusiasm for the idea of an expensive evening.

Language used	**Approaches**
Well, I have to ... maybe I will go ... but I don't know if I will have enough money.	Displays hesitancy; is rather direct in bring up his financial situation.
Well, you know, I'm on a low budget in order to get through my graduate studies in the States. Would it be OK if we shared expenses for the evening?	Explanation of state of affairs; introduces alternate proposal.
A French restaurant? Won't that be pretty expensive?	Questions the suggestion; puts the ball in the other court.
Does it mean that much to you to go to the dinner or would you rather just the two of us go out for a simple meal? I'll leave that up to you. If you really want to go, I'll go with you.	A somewhat *hostile* interchange that clearly indicates his attitude towards the suggestion; throws out his own proposal.
It's a French restaurant? Did you tell your friends we would definitely be there? Of course, we'll go, if that's what you want.	Uses a series of questions to indicate his lack of enthusiasm for the idea, but indicates his willingness to sacrifice if that is what is required.

A. Which of the above approaches to the situation do you prefer? Why?
B. Are there other strategies that appeal to you?
C. Which of the approaches listed above would you avoid? Why?

3. Some colloquial expressions found in the improvisations:

To go to a swanky restaurant
Refers to an elegant, fashionable restaurant.

To get tongue-tied
To be unable to speak freely; to have difficulty expressing oneself.

To go *Dutch*
To have each person pay his/her own way.

To split the bill
To divide the costs evenly among the people involved.

To be strapped for cash
To be short of money; to be in financial difficulty.

To be up-front
To be frank, forthright.

To break the ice
To make a beginning; to get through the first difficulties in starting a conversation.

Conclusion. This paper has proposed a strategy for building on the strengths of Di Pietro's scenario approach by extending the model to include a scenario-based input phase designed to introduce native speaker *models* in the instructional design. The framework outlined here entails a four-phase cycle consisting of the rehearsal, performance, and debriefing phases followed by an input phase. I have suggested that field testing the scenarios among a variety of native speakers of the target language provides a valuable source of language data. In addition, such testing furnishes concrete evidence as to the level of complexity of the scenarios in question. This information is critical to the selection and sequencing of scenarios in a course syllabus. In the instructional framework outlined in this paper, scenarios serve a threefold function: (1) to promote interactive discourse in the L2 classroom, (2) to generate interactive models from native speakers of the target language, and (3) to provide the basis for instructional materials.

Appendix A. Improvisation by Native Speakers of English (Dyad 3)

Reference to shared information.

He: I'm happy that you asked me to the Homecoming Dance.

Introduces his agenda.

He: but I hope you understand my situation financially. I am uh ... would I be ... would it be OK with you if we went "Dutch"?

She: That's no problem. I've already purchased the tickets.

Introduces her agenda.

She: Guess what? We got an invitation to join a group of my friends at a swanky French restaurant before the dance.

Proposes an alternate plan.

He: Does it mean that much to you to go to the dinner ... or would you rather just the two of us go out for a simple meal? It would be a lot cheaper ... but if it means that much to you, I'll go.

She: Are you sure this isn't putting you out too much because if it is, we can skip it?

He: I'll leave that up to you. If you really want to go, I'll go with you.

Resolution.

She: Well, we really don't have to go there. I think I'd rather have a simple meal with you, anyway.

Appendix B. Improvisation by Native Speakers of English (Dyad 4)

Reference to shared information.

She: I'm really looking forward to the Homecoming Dance, Amal.

He: So am I.

Brings up his agenda.

He: How do we get tickets for it?

She: (Opens her purse.) I have tickets right here. (Hands them to him.)

He: Oh, that's great. How much are they?

She: This is my treat. I invited you.

Provides cultural note.

She: Have you been to a Homecoming Dance before?

He: I don't think so. Tell me, why is it called "Homecoming"?

She It's during a week when all those who have graduated from the college are invited back for celebrations of all kinds.

He: Ah, I see ... including a dance.

She: Yes, and lots of eating and drinking.

Introduces her agenda.

She: Oh, yes, a group of my friends would like to meet before the dance at the Parisienne. It's a very nice restaurant downtown. Is that OK, Amal?

He: Yes, I guess so. It's a French restaurant?

She: Yes, and the food is great. You'll love it.

He: Did you tell your friends we'd definitely be there?

She: Well, not exactly. We don't have to go ... not if you don't want to.

He: Well, to tell you the truth, I have some trouble meeting many new people ... and the conversations go so fast ... and I was thinking ...

She: Yes, thinking what?

Presents an alternate proposal.

He: Thinking we could have a quiet dinner with just one other couple.

She: One other couple?

He: Do you like Iranian food?

She: Umm. I don't think I've ever had any.

He: A friend of mine and his wife ... they are students here too ... they're from Iran ... and are going to the dance. They mentioned just this morning that they'd like us to come over for dinner ... before the dance.

She: I think I've seen her. Is her name Marva or something like that?

He: Yes, Marveis. And he's Rasheni. (Looks at her.) But if you really want to go to the French restaurant, we could go there.

Resolution

She: And miss a good Iranian meal? I'd love to meet your friends. What time will you come after me?

He: Six o'clock?

She: (nods)

Closing

She: We'd better hurry to class or we'll be late.

He: OK.

Appendix C. An Interview.

The following is an interview of a recent college graduate. The interview is meant to serve as a point of departure for one or more assigned tasks outside the classroom. Each L2 learner, for example, might be asked to interview a college student on campus using the interview questions as a guide. Students would then prepare an oral and/or written report based on the results of their interviews.

Question: Did you ever go to a Homecoming Dance while in college?
Response: Yes.
Question: Just exactly what is a "Homecoming Dance"?
Response: It's a dance held during a week or so or so of celebrations. It's a time for alumni to get back to campus to try to regain their lost youth.
Question: Suppose you had been asked to a Homecoming Dance by a woman in one of your classes and you accepted. Would you pay for any of the expenses involved?
Response: I'd pay for dinner. I would expect her to get the tickets.
Question: What about flowers?
Response: I'd buy her a corsage.
Question: If there were a photographer who was set up to take pictures at the dance, would you pick up the bill for photos of you and your date?
Response: We'd split on the photos.
Question: If you were invited to a dance by a woman in one of your classes and you were having financial difficulties, would you bring up the subject?
Response: I'd say I'm looking forward to a great evening, but I'm strapped for cash.
Question: Suppose a woman in one of your classes had asked you to join her and her friends for dinner at an elegant French restaurant, but you were living on a very tight budget. How would you handle the situation?
Response: Well, of course, it would depend on whether this was a woman I really wanted to get to know. If so, I'd tell her I'd love to go, but I didn't know if I could afford it.
Question: You'd be pretty up-front about it, wouldn't you?
Response: I think that's the best approach in a relationship.

REFERENCES

Di Pietro, Robert J. 1982. Models for learning and models for teaching. JACET Bulletin 13:1–7.

Di Pietro, Robert J. 1987. *Strategic interaction: Learning languages through scenarios*. Cambridge: Cambridge University Press.

Di Pietro, Robert J., and Frederick J. Bosco. 1991. "The scenario: Its use in interactive second language instruction." In Mary E. McGroarty, and Christian J. Faltis (eds.), *Languages in school and society: Policy and pedagogy*. Berlin: Mouton de Gruyter.

Polanyi, Michael. 1958. *Personal knowledge: Towards a post-critical philosophy*. Chicago: University of Chicago Press.

The Computer's Guide to Persons

William Frawley
University of Delaware

Introduction. The chair of a major U.S. university's foreign-language department, one that considers itself cutting edge and teaching for proficiency, once said two very curious things to me:

(1) If a student completes our language sequence and cannot conjugate a verb, then we have failed.

(2) Our instructors should adhere to a target grade distribution so that our classes as a whole consistently produce a certain number of A's, B's, C's, D's, and F's.

This progressive department is cutting a pretty dull edge indeed —not to mention flirting with illegality in predetermining the available grade range! The chair's remarks typify an antiprogressive backlash that has an increasing stranglehold on language instruction. This traditionalist streak, I want to argue, feeds on, reproduces, and supports computationalism. It is the sort of thing that puzzled Di Pietro to near horror and that he always tried to temper through humanism (Di Pietro 1976, 1981, 1987).

Computationalism and its effects. Computationalism is the scientific ideology that thinking is the machine states of the thinker; these states, in turn, are totally characterizable and constituted by formal (or contentless) processes, like configuring and manipulating data structures. In short, a mind is its architecture. Different versions of computationalism bring their respective baggage to this ideology. Connectionism privileges a probabilistically weighted, trained, brain-style network architecture, without representations, categories, rules, or generalizations: A human being is an enormous learning and storage device—behaviorism with a mind. Functionalist, language-of-thought versions split the wetware from the software and focus on the latter's code and on constituent, abstract representations: No computation without representation, so the dictum goes—a mind is a brain's program.

For a significant portion of those working in the human sciences, computationalism is the only way to go—though Searle (1992) persists in objecting. But adherents have very sound motivation: Something of computationalism is undoubtedly correct. Parts of our vision, language, face recognition, spatial orientation, action, and musical cognition are computational in that they operate perfectly well in spite of—in fact, because of—their blindness to how the outside world is put together (Jackendoff 1992). Some of mind is knowledge-as-configuration.

One consequence of computationalism is that intelligence—what thinking can do blindly through its capacity, speed, and organization—is distinct from intentionality—what thinking is about, how it connects to the world (Block 1990). Different schools dissociate intelligence and intentionality in different ways, but computationalism itself requires the distinction. Thus Fodor (1983), Dennett (1991), and Jackendoff (1992) acknowledge the split, but the former two retain intentionality, for quite different reasons, and the latter abandons it.

An appreciation of this epistemological framework lays bare much of the territory in which applied linguistics operates and that Di Pietro's views, in my reading of them, radically confront. Some applied research explicitly follows computationalism. Clear examples are information-processing accounts of second-language learning, where the L2 is a data structure under executive control (McLaughlin 1987), and the work on universal grammar and L2, where the issue is whether innate computational procedures are accessible to nonnative learners. Carroll (1989), for example, not only outlines the influence of computationalism in second-language research, but she also calls for its essential use in the field. Even the schools that seek to displace universal grammar in L2 with functional communicative strategies are baldly computational (though Carroll (1989) would disagree and argue, incorrectly I think, that connectionism is noncomputational; see Fodor and Pylyshyn 1988).

Unsurprisingly, a recent issue of *Applied Linguistics* (Vol. 10, 1989) is devoted to promoting connectionism as the model for applied linguistics built on the primacy of communicative competence! This is a reasonable proposal if only because communicative competence, in the received view, is an architecture—context decontextualized (see Fairclough 1992: 12–36): It is a theory of interactional intelligence and as such is one more computational challenge to its computational competitors.

But there is also much implicitly computational applied work. One example is the influential oral proficiency movement, where a language learner is totally characterized by algorithms. Proficiency is the cumulative machine states—i.e., specifiable configurations—of the assessed. The intentionality of the language learner—what the speaking person is all about—is secondary to the ranked linguistic intelligences that constitute proficiency.

Searle (1980) argues that no machine can have intentionality because that requires understanding, and a machine can perform intelligently without understanding. Computationalists counter that understanding is an effect of the whole computational system—all machine states in their context. Component intelligences in fact support understanding as the essential thinking parts of a thinking system. In the same way, the proficiency movement builds and assesses a non-native understander from the essential components. Understanding is an effect.

The proficiency movement strikes me as a sort of Turing test gone wild. When asked if machines could think, Turing, one of the inventors of computationalism, argued that intelligence is judged only by a system passing a battery of behavioral tests. If the computer passes, it is intelligent: If it fools us, it thinks. Here we are, a nation of High Superiors seeking to upgrade a nation of Novices. When all these persons finally pass the proficiency batteries, they will, at long last, be the machines we hoped they'd be.

When computationalism goes bad. Though computationalism is a scientific ideology, not public policy, it is a natural for policymakers. Not much effort is needed to adopt contentless, determinate, and specifiable knowledge configurations to such things as measurable outcome criteria, program accountability, effective curricula that arm our students with the practical tools to springboard them into the twenty-first century, and, that most recent noble goal, programs that work. (Does anyone hear the chair saying, "If a student completes our language sequence and cannot conjugate a verb, then we have failed" and "Our instructors should adhere to a target grade distribution so that our classes as a whole consistently produce a certain number of A's, B's, C's, D's, and F's."?) Computationalism feeds such empty policy rhetoric by promoting commodification, a managerial agenda, and the technologization of discourse. Di Pietro was against all three.

Commodification. Machine states can be reproduced, packaged, and distributed. The foreign-language and ESL industries are classic examples of how the delinking of intelligence from intentionality supports the commodification of linguistic knowledge: prepackaged curricula, predetermined student and teacher responses, and, worst of all, built-in competency measures (see Apple 1985). Fueled by the computational ideology, commodification lets teachers and students turn over the control of their own defining activities to the publishing houses, or, at least, to people who cannot appreciate teachers' and students' circumstances. How many times must we hear that this language series is not only designed with an eye toward competency, but that it is also teachable?

Commodified educational discourse leans heavily on quantities and skills. Language programs in this vein provide skills training that leads to attainment targets of profiled learners. Thus, Dodds (1992: 503), in outlining the putative successes of a proficiency-centered speaking course in college German, acknowledges that her Advanced and Advanced Plus students could never improve to Superior in one term because "The amount of language needed cannot be provided in such a brief period of time." Dodds is surely right! Since proficiency-oriented curricula require quantities of language skills at the service of target speaker-profiles, one term is just simply is not enough time to fatten an Advanced Plus into a Superior!

For Di Pietro, the commodification of language instruction was a disastrous possibility. Vico taught him the value of the individual and change—language education was connected to emotion and the imagination (Di Pietro 1976)—and these ideas motivated a number of his views of language instruction. For example, he believed that the purpose of language instruction is to facilitate the individual's construction of a self in the second language (Di Pietro 1987: 4–6)—unreifiable consciousness, personal identity, not specifiable knowledge states. No quantity of language skills could ever cumulatively result in a speaking person.

His focus on persons further motivated his view of the proper role of communicative and grammatical competence in language instruction, both of which he saw as commodities. Thus, he remarks that discourse is not cooperative (one of the premises of rational exchange) but manipulative (1987: 10), and that the functional/notional syllabus, built as it is on pragmatics and communicative competence, is really lifeless because it remains outside of the actual execution of a speaker's game plan in an exchange (1987: 38–39).

For Di Pietro, competences grow individually in the language learner. Pedagogical grammar, for instance, is organic, something that develops as the circumstances of the speaking subject transpire, something put down in a logbook after the fact for future reference, not a preranked skill. The commodities of language are important to language instruction as safety valves and reassurances, artifacts the speaking persons make. Thus Di Pietro would have been surprised neither by the studies showing that native and nonnative speakers of the same language have quite different computational states (Coppieters 1987, Carroll 1989; Birdsong 1992, though, objects) nor by those that show no simple relationship between explicit and implicit grammar rules and learner performance (Green and Hecht 1992).

The Managerial Agenda. Commodifying the language curriculum into sets of skills leads to deskilling and managerialism. Students and teachers become parts of the educational delivery system, which means simply that they stop talking to each other. Teachers accept the separation of planning from execution and thus renounce their true skill: an appreciation of the local knowledge of classroom practice. The managerial agenda of technical administrative control and accountability then rushes in to fill the gap between planning and execution. Teachers believe that they have actually chosen their materials because they have cast a vote on a curriculum selection committee (perhaps even one with a student representative), whose report is then forwarded up the line for approval by one of their own who has demonstrated sufficient administrative capabilities by not worrying deans or parents too much and so merits sign-off powers. The skills language teachers "... once had—skills of planning, of understanding and acting on an entire phase of production—are ultimately taken from them by management and housed elsewhere..." (Apple 1985: 71).

Strategic Interaction (Di Pietro 1987) can be seen as a way of recouping local teacher and student power in the language curriculum. The scenarios that drive instruction are schematic and infinite; they are adjusted to local circumstances and require only the tension of self and other, group and individual. Beyond that, they serve only the needs of the person to develop a self through speaking. The learners' collective, not just the group, is at the basis of classroom format, and the collective includes the teacher. Assessment taps everyone involved in the scenario, in all of their roles. Evaluation emerges out of the language activity itself; it is not a profile against which performance is judged.

Di Pietro's method emphasizes the personal agenda (1987: 41ff). One of the great ironies of Strategic Interaction is that as an emergent activity that tries to reinvest teachers and students with educational control, it has to be implemented within the current managerial milieu. Strategic Interaction, I am convinced, can be a success only in an environment that takes administrative risks—one unconcerned about its own authority and thus willing to represent itself to the judging public as unworried about keeping explicit records of comparable outcomes.

Technologization of Discourse. The inherent teachability of determinate information makes it easy for policymakers to link up skills with perceived social needs. Computationalism thus readily serves the technologization of discourse, or the adaptation of language to the demands of social engineering, by condensing discourse into an essential portable toolkit filled with techniques. Discourse then becomes a resource handled by efficiency-and-design specialists whose very occupations are discourse training and gatekeeping (Fairclough 1992: 215–16). In this colonization of the ordinary lifeworld, as Habermas (1984) put it, the activities of interviewing, teaching, and counseling, otherwise tied to the individual's control of his or her public and private self, are increasingly "handled in specific institutional locations by designated social agents" (Fairclough 1992: 215).

Nowhere is this technologization clearer than in a recent purported advance in proficiency testing. Stansfield and Kenyon (1992) report on the development of an oral proficiency interview that can be done validly and reliably without a human interviewer! This is surely a wonderful technological advance since it can be used "... in situations where the administration of a face-to-face test is either impractical or impossible due to the unavailability of a trained interviewer" (Stansfield and Kenyon 1992: 129). It is thus the ultimate in a portable discourse toolkit (with the added benefit of eliminating one of the nasty factors contributing to the inherent variability of the discourse in the testing situation (Ross and Berwick 1992, Young and Milanovic 1992).

Soon the Turing test will take over completely, and the interviewees will be eliminated, too. Imagine a testing room with one tape recorder asking, "What type of sports do you like?" and another tape recorder answering, "None." All this could be videotaped by a camera on automatic pilot, and we could simply get rid of all the humans!

Technologization goes hand in hand with territorialism. Specialists have to protect their specialties. One of the most remarkable and troubling things that Di Pietro and his students have discovered (see Lamb in progress) is that the English-Only Movement has clear support among the foreign-language teaching profession. This is because the exclusion of non-English languages as official speech enhances the foreignness of those languages. With current public rhetoric hammering at us that we live in a global society and must be able to link foreign interests with our own, any movement that can increase the identity and salience of the thing that only foreign-language teachers provide access to is worth their supporting. The otherness of foreign languages protects the foreign-language profession, especially if these very foreign things can be accountably instructed through a portable set of determinate skills.

Strategic Interaction could never serve technologization and concomitant exclusionary interests. Its very purpose is to allow the speaking person to emerge from the unity of the group only to have the comfort of group inclusion to fall back on in times of difficulty. Strategic Interaction seeks to familiarize and personalize the foreign through local, meaningful activity. For Di Pietro, the great failure of technologized foreign-language curricula lay in their reported successes, among which are conjugating speakers falling well within the A range.

Consciousness and postmodern language instruction. I understand Di Pietro's work, generally, as being about the pedagogy of second-language consciousness. Though he never mentioned current views of both consciousness and pedagogy, they mesh nicely with his ideas and offer a broad backdrop.

Dennett (1991) argues against the commonsense (Cartesian) view of consciousness and self as a unified executive overseer or "central meaner," to use his term, in favor of consciousness as the continual, real-time updating of our component subsystems. This Multiple Drafts Model, as he calls it, lends itself to perceived centrality through the way we talk ourselves into unity. The self is the fictional center of gravity of narratives—drafts—that we spin about ourselves and about others to ourselves and to others. Just as there is no need for a central consciousness looking over component subsystems, so there is no need for a unified self. We have as many selves as we have occasions to spin self-accounts.

Though Dennett does not discuss Bakhtin or Vygotsky, this picture of consciousness and the self is a virtual copy of their positions. For Bakhtin

(1981), consciousness is built on the polyphony (many-voicedness) of the speaking subject in heteroglossic (many-languaged) context. For Vygotsky (1978), individual higher thought emerges from the diversity of social thought by the subject's learning to control action through the tension between public and private speaking. Dennett thus appears to be telling us the modern, computational–intentionalist version of Russian dialectical psycholinguistics. A self is a linguistically constructed plurality. He even says, in *Elbow Room* (1984), that a self is the locus of self-control, practically the identical view of the self that Wertsch (1985) attributes to Vygotsky.

Di Pietro hoped that his method would develop L2 consciousness—a second-language self—in the language learner. This is why the personal agenda in the construction of scenarios and classroom practice is so crucial to Strategic Interaction. For Di Pietro, making a proficient native-like speaker is much less important (and probably easier) than promoting a second language as the instrument of a speaking personal identity. Coincidentally, Dennett (1991: 114) notes the connection between his Multiple Drafts Theory and those where the perceived unity of consciousness is the result of scenario spinning.

The epistemological value of multiplicity that Dennett's, Bakhtin's, and Vygotsky's views give to Di Pietro's method is reinforced by its natural connection to postmodernist education. This kind of pedagogy seeks to confront the Modernist (Neo-Enlightenment) view of teaching as the illumination of students through filling them with "the best that has been thought and said." Postmodern education exposes the authoritarian and homogenizing ideology of this kind of pedagogy and seeks to replace it with multiplicity. Marginalized views confront mainstream views to allow a thinking self to emerge from the teaching activity, in contrast to an educated mind that results from being packed with "the best" (i.e., status quo) ideas.

Aronowitz and Giroux (1991) note that this focus on multiplicity and emergence has a number of effects on teacher–student practice. One is that teachers are obligated to have students interrogate the values of their activities in terms of the content of instruction. Strategic Interaction is designed to have students confront and come to terms with the social positionings, or what Bakhtin called *voices,* that a second language allows and inculcates. The teacher and the students are in fact required to discuss the everyday ideological content of the speech that constitutes the Strategic Interaction classroom practice: How else could certain roles and the speech attached to those roles be justified?

In understanding the multiplicity at the basis of speaking and in trying to invest the language classroom with the productive tension of difference, Di Pietro accomplished something he probably never would have anticipated. Such postmodern education removes the teachers from the authoritarian pedestal and lets them be the public intellectuals they thought they were. Likewise, Strategic Interaction obligates the language teacher to be just an ordinary speaker, too.

REFERENCES

Apple, Michael. 1985. *Education and power.* London: Routledge.

Aronowitz, Stanley, and Henry Giroux. 1991. *Postmodern education.* Minneapolis: University of Minnesota Press.

Bakhtin, Mikhail. 1981. *The dialogic imagination.* Austin, Tex.: University of Texas Press.

Birdsong, David. 1992. "Ultimate attainment in second language acquisition." *Language* 68: 706-55.

Block, Ned. 1990. "The computer model of the mind." In D. Osherson and E. Smith (eds.), *Thinking (An Invitation to cognitive science)* (Vol. 3). Cambridge: MIT Press. 247-89.

Carroll, Suzanne. 1989. "Second-language acquisition and the computational paradigm." *Language Learning* 39: 535-94.

Coppieters, Rene. 1987. "Competence differences between native and non-native speakers." *Language* 63: 544-73.

Dennett, Daniel. 1984. *Elbow room: The varieties of free will worth wanting.* Cambridge: MIT Press.

Dennett, Daniel. 1991. *Consciousness explained.* Boston: Little, Brown and Co.

Di Pietro, Robert. 1976. "Humanism in linguistic theory: A lesson from Vico." In Georgio Tagliacozzo and Donald Verene (eds.), *Giambattista Vico's science of humanity.* Baltimore: Johns Hopkins University Press. 341-50.

Di Pietro, Robert. 1981. "Linguistic creativity: A key to contemporary humanism." In Giorgio Tagliacozzo (ed.), *Vico: Past and present.* Atlantic Highlands, N.J.: Humanities Press. 132-43.

Di Pietro, Robert. 1987. *Strategic interaction: Learning languages through scenarios.* Cambridge: Cambridge University Press.

Dodds, Dinah. 1992. "Using proficiency as the organizing principle in an advanced speaking course for majors." *Foreign Language Annals* 25: 497-506.

Fairclough, Norman. 1992. *Discourse and social change.* Cambridge: Polity Press.

Fodor, Jerry. 1983. *The modularity of mind.* Cambridge: MIT Press.

Fodor, Jerry, and Zenon Pylyshyn. 1988. "Connectionism and cognitive architecture: A critical analysis." *Cognition* 28: 3-71.

Green, P., and K. Hecht. 1992. "Implicit and explicit grammar: An empirical study." *Applied Linguistics* 13: 168-84.

Habermas, Jürgen. 1984. *Theory of communicative action* (vol. 1). London: Heinemann.

Jackendoff, Ray. 1992. *Languages of the mind.* Cambridge: MIT Press.

Lamb, Sara. In progress. "The English only movement and the foreign language profession." Ph.D. dissertation, University of Delaware.

McLaughlin, Barry. 1987. *Theories of second-language learning.* London: Edward Arnold.

Ross, S., and R. Berwick. 1992. "The discourse of accommodation in oral proficiency interviews." *Studies in Second Language Acquisition* 14: 159-76.

Searle, John. 1980. "Minds, brains, and programs." *Behavioral and Brain Sciences* 3: 417-58.

Searle, John. 1992. *The Rediscovery of Mind.* Cambridge: MIT Press.

Stansfield, Charles, and D. Kenyon. 1992. "The development and validation of a simulated oral proficiency interview." *The Modern Language Journal* 76: 129-41.

Vygotsky, Lev. 1978. *Mind in society.* Cambridge: Harvard university Press.

Wertsch, James. 1985. *Vygotsky and the social formation of mind.* Cambridge: Harvard University Press.

Young, R., and M. Milanovic. 1992. "Discourse variation in oral proficiency interviews." *Studies in Second Language Acquisition* 14: 403-24.

Ego boundaries revisited: Toward a model of personality and learning

Madeline E. Ehrman
Foreign Service Institute, U. S. Department of State

This conference is devoted to Robert Di Pietro and his concept of Strategic Interaction. Although he was not a specialist in individual differences, he was much aware of the impact of personality factors on learning and the emotional aspects of learning and building a linguistic identity (Di Pietro 1987). I hope that he would have found here material that may enhance understanding of his methodological innovations.

Prologue. Jenny and Keith are successful Foreign Service officers studying a Western European language at the Foreign Service Institute (FSI). They are both about 40. Both of them are having difficulty in their language classes. They score near average for FSI on the Modern Language Aptitude Test (MLAT), though Jenny's MLAT is higher than Keith's.

They have rather different approaches to learning. Keith tells us he wants to know the grammar first, do exercises, and be well prepared before he engages in the many communicative activities in his language class. He wants his tasks clearly defined. He is spending many, many hours on his task and feels guilty when he takes time off, because he feels strongly that he should do perfect work. His difficulty comes especially in the constant communicative class activities, where it is certain that material he hasn't learned will come up. We will see that Keith has what we will call *thick* ego boundaries.

Jenny, on the other hand, really likes to learn through content-based materials. She had some exposure to the language in a previous overseas assignment and enjoyed learning it "by the seat of her pants." She doesn't like it when the flow of content is stopped by structure or vocabulary she does not know. She likes everything she is to learn to be out on the table at once, so that she can integrate it. Her difficulty can be summarized as "things just mush," and she gets overloaded quickly. Jenny has what we will call *thin* ego boundaries.

Introduction.[1] This paper is an exploration of a concept that has variously been called tolerance of ambiguity, language ego, or cognitive flexibility. No matter what the name, many language teachers have found a characteristic of this sort to affect learning, especially in communicative language settings and those in which students are encouraged to cope with authentic input. In general, the more unstructured the learning, the more important this characteristic, both in the classroom and probably even more outside of the classroom in naturalistic settings. At FSI we have observed that almost all of the most successful learners show substantial flexibility and willingness to shift cognitive set, many of them even to the point that they in fact seem to develop a kind of target-language subpersonality when speaking the target language. On the other hand, a student like Jenny, who is very open to input, can get in trouble because of her openness. Conversely, a great many (but not all) of those who have the most difficulty in our classrooms display marked cognitive rigidity. A simple but common example is the student who cannot accept the fact that a word in English doesn't have a one-to-one correspondent in the target language. Keith is this kind of student.

The construct that I address here consists of three parts:

1. the ability to take in new information
2. the ability to hold contradictory or incomplete information without either rejecting one of the contradictory elements or coming to premature closure on an incomplete schema
3. the ability to adapt one's existing cognitive, affective, and social schemata in the light of the new information or experience

This study focuses most on parts 2 and 3. Part 2 is close to what most think of as *tolerance of ambiguity*, that is, acceptance of indistinct lines of separation and messiness of data. This is more a problem for Keith than for Jenny. Part 3 seems very similar to what Piaget (1967) called *accommodation*, in contrast to another process, "assimilation," which is the adaptation of new information to what one already knows. FSI language students appear to be differentiated by their ability to accommodate: to reconstruct their cognitive, affective, and social schemata in the light of new, often unclear information. Both Keith and Jenny have some difficulty at this stage.

---

1. This paper owes a great deal to Dr. Lucinda Hart-Gonzalez of FSI, who provided statistical and methodological support and a great many important suggestions and criticisms from conception of the project to the drafting of this paper. Her work affects this study in far more places than can be specifically acknowledged in this manuscript. Interpretations of the results, however, are mine. Research Assistant Stephanie Lindemann undertook the literature searches that underlie the review of literature; through her comprehension of the concepts and intelligent use of search resources and through her careful critique she made an important contribution to this paper.

I call the overall construct—intake, tolerance of ambiguity, and accommodation—ego boundaries, for two reasons. First, I have operationalized the construct using a questionnaire, the Hartmann Boundary Questionnaire, which was designed to investigate ego boundaries in general, not just for learning. Second, Alexander Guiora has so clearly described the cognitive and affective process involved for the second-language acquisition world using the term *language ego* (1981, 1984). This term *ego boundary* thus indicates that we are dealing with a general phenomenon, but one that has been important to the second-language acquisition field.

This study begins with certain assumptions:

- Constructs like tolerance of ambiguity or ego boundaries are relatively stable aspects of personality.
- They affect a person's behavior across a large number of situations, including, and in particular, learning settings.
- Individuals can be characterized by such constructs in ways that enhance our understanding of learning (and other behaviors). Keith and Jenny have had a history in various settings of experiences that reflect their thick and thin ego boundaries.

In the remainder of this paper, I describe Hartmann's concept of *thin* and *thick* ego boundaries; then I review some relevant literature both from second-language acquisition and from psychology in general. I then describe and discuss findings to date—from the ongoing research study of which the Hartmann Boundary Questionnaire (HBQ) is a part—that are relevant to the ego-boundary concept. I believe that these findings support the idea that the HBQ addresses a stable personality characteristic that is influential in learning. In fact, I believe it to be so influential that I have made it the foundation of a model of learning that I discuss at the end of the paper (Figure 1).

Background

Hartmann's ego-boundary construct. Ernest Hartmann, on whose construct of ego boundaries and questionnaire this substudy is based, made his initial observations from a population of people who suffered from nightmares. He found them to be markedly

> flexible in their identities and social relationships. ... When we tried to describe these people globally, [these] words kept coming up: "unguarded," "undefended," "fluid," "artistic," "vulnerable," "open." The term that seemed best to encompass all this was that they had "thin boundaries" in many different senses. Everything in their minds seemed to flow together. They did not separate things out, nor did they have barriers or walls to

separate themselves from the world. (Hartmann 1991: 16)

Where not extreme, thin boundaries appeared to be characteristic of artists, writers, and therapists. Hartmann speculates that those with thinner boundaries may have an advantage where shifts of focus or novel approaches are required —including philosophy, theoretical mathematics, and learning foreign languages "as native speakers do" (Hartmann 1991: 221). Thin-boundary subjects were found to shift strategies more flexibly and adopt new strategies on a number of tests. Jenny comes out well above the mean in the thin direction. She was formerly a teacher of literature.

In contrast, people with *thick* boundaries had few or no nightmares, said they dreamed rarely, and were quite conventional. In general they were "solid citizens," some of them describable as hard-working and hard-driving and even perfectionistic. In the extreme, they could be concrete-thinking, mechanical, and in need of specific guidelines. Their tendency could be described as excluding stimuli more than including them. "Having thick boundaries feels to them solid, reliable, autonomous, and independent; it is obviously the way to be" (Hartmann 1991: 117). On tests of managing novelty, they were found to be more perseverative even when asked to change strategy or task. Keith is substantially thicker than both Hartmann's and the FSI average. He is a former engineer who specializes now in overseas building maintenance and has not had any exposure to a foreign language since high school.

Relevant research on individual differences. Much of the existing research in second-language acquisition addresses a variety of individual differences among second- or foreign-language learners: The most common of these are age, sex, motivation, anxiety, self-esteem, tolerance of ambiguity, risk-taking, language-learning strategies, and language-learning styles. (See, e.g., Ehrman 1990, Ehrman and Oxford 1990b, Galbraith and Gardner 1988, Oxford 1993, Skehan 1989.) Of these, motivation and anxiety, language-learning strategies, and language-learning styles seem to be most relevant to the ego-boundary concept. Concepts of ego boundary and permeability to new learning are found throughout the literature of learning psychology, clinical psychology, and psychoanalytic theory, as well as for language learning in particular. Representative findings in these areas of interest are addressed below for both language learning and psychology in general.

Second language learning. Language teachers and scholars of language learning are naturally concerned with learner failure to internalize new language data. Discussion of such failures to use input to construct new language and culture schemata pervades the second-language acquisition (SLA) literature. A typical descriptive statement is "... nonnative speakers, when conversing, often transfer the conversational rules of their first language into the second'" (Scarcella 1990: 337). Social distance is adduced as both cause and consequence of such failures, e.g. Schumann (1978a, 1978b). The concept of the *affective filter* that "acts to control entry to further mental processing" (Dulay, Burt, and Krashen 1982: 4) in the well-known Input Hypothesis is another concept that is seen as both cause and effect. Scarcella (1990) describes other research that addresses questions of sociocultural identity retention and maintenance of one's place in a social group that can affect one's ability to internalize a foreign language.

The work of Gardner and his colleagues is widely known for postulating an integrative motive to participate in the target speech community that may enhance the process of internalizing a new language, though this is described as more applicable to informal contexts than to classroom settings (Gardner 1985a). Graham (1984) addresses what he calls *assimilative motivation* or desire to become a full member of a speech community; Trosset (1986) describes the importance of this kind of motivation for an Anglophone in learning Welsh. Motivational factors have a great deal to do with whether a student will even reach the *intake* stage of the ego-boundary concept described above.

Language ego. The second-language theorist who is most associated with a concept of ego-boundary factors in language learning is Alexander Guiora, whose work addresses the inhibitory effects of what he terms *language ego* (Guiora 1981, 1984, Guiora et al. 1972, Guiora et al. 1980), about which he says "What is needed is a 'softening' of the language ego boundaries, to make them more 'permeable'"(Guiora 1984: 10). Guiora appears to be directly addressing all three of the elements of the ego-boundary concept that this study investigates, along with the importance of feelings to one's ability to admit and process new data. This quotation summarizes the cognitive and affective demands on the individual in accommodative processing:

> [T]he task of learning a new language is a profoundly unsettling psychological proposition ... What is required of the learner is not only a cognitive shift in terms of vocabulary, grammar, and syntax, but something much more formidable: the necessity to recategorize information ... that inevitably must lead to a demand to assimilate alternative and new ways to describe and thus conceptualize, and ultimately experience, events in and around us. ... [I]t is here that *individual* differences in the psychological defense systems and flexibilities will be reflected in a capacity (or willingness) to attempt the shifting, to dare the recategorization and the ensuing reconceptualization ... without fear of losing the grip on the psychological integrity for which native language serves as such a powerful anchor [emphasis in original]. (Guiora 1984: 8)

Elsewhere he suggests that "The capacity to tolerate ambiguities and uncertainties is the mark of a certain psychological strength, essential to the understanding of the other. The capacity to entertain an alternate hypothesis about any proposition is the mark of the successful blend of cognitive and affective templates that can lead to new discoveries" (Guiora 1981: 171). Here he directly addresses part 2 of our construct, tolerance of ambiguity.

Tolerance of ambiguity. Tolerance of ambiguity is described as acceptance of confusing situations and lack of clear lines of demarcation (Ely 1989), corresponding to part 2 of the concept described above. A number of researchers have addressed this characteristic. Students who can tolerate moderate levels of ambiguity have been found to be more likely to persist in language learning (Chapelle 1983, Naiman et al. 1978) and to achieve more (Chapelle and Roberts 1986, Reiss 1985) than students who cannot. Ambiguity tolerance, either as a facet of more-general personality characteristics (Naiman et al. 1978, Ehrman and Oxford 1990b) or defined quite narrowly in terms of reactions to specific language-classroom events (Ely 1989), is related to the frequency of use of many kinds of learning strategies. Risk-taking is thought to be related to tolerance of ambiguity. Those who can tolerate ambiguity are more likely to take some risks in language learning; and risk-taking is an essential for progress (Beebe 1983, Brown 1987, Ely 1986, Stevick 1976). Students who avoid risks for fear of criticism from others or self and their language practice becomes stunted.

Managing novelty is a factor of intellectual ability (Sternberg 1989); it involves the ability to keep both the original schema and an alternative hypothesis in mind. A good illustration in the linguistic realm is a study of the ability to provide meaning (through paraphrasing) to linguistically aberrant phrases like "house foot-bird." Subjects showed substantial differences in their ability to manage this novel task (Gleitman and Gleitman 1979). Every second-language learner is faced regularly with this kind of challenge. A study by Horwitz (1982) found that both language aptitude and conceptual level had an impact on communicative competence, but Horwitz attributed the impact of conceptual level to its effect on interpersonal factors rather than cognitive ones.

As the above quotation from Guiora about language learning as a "profoundly unsettling experience" suggests, anxiety plays an important role. Horwitz and Young (1991) clearly show the potentially debilitating effects of language anxiety, a form of performance anxiety that is manifested in the language-learning situation. Horwitz (1990) suggests that in the language-learning environment, there is no such thing as facilitating anxiety; all anxiety in that environment is likely to be debilitating, because language learning is such a complex and emotionally involved process; this seems congruent with Guiora's position. Others (e.g. Bailey 1983, Brown 1987) suggest that some degree of anxiety can indeed be facilitative for language learning, along the lines of the classic Yerkes–Dodson inverted U-curve in which, all other things being equal, different levels of anxiety are differentially facilitative or debilitating (Snow 1989). We can certainly anticipate that internal resources that are drawn off by a necessity to cope with anxiety (or any other demand, such as personal problems, for that matter) will be unavailable for demanding cognitive tasks such as entertaining alternative hypotheses or schemata (see Schwartz 1973).

Learning styles. Galloway and Labarca (1990) suggest that what is perceived as an ambiguous stimulus may well vary among learners; for example, one learner may be disoriented in a naturalistic setting such as the host country, whereas another may have difficulty with the hypothesis generation and testing involved in managing grammar in a structured classroom. One likely dimension along which such variation might be predictable is that of learning style. Language-learning styles are the general approaches students use to learn a new language (Ehrman 1990, Oxford 1990, Oxford, Ehrman, and Lavine 1991, Schmeck 1988). Many learning-styles dimensions from the many available models overlap to varying degrees. Some of them entail an element of ambiguity tolerance; some of these are listed below.

Analytic students tend to concentrate on rules, word analysis, and language comparisons and often avoid free-flowing communicative activities, while global students prefer conversation to rule-learning or analysis (Oxford, Ehrman, and Lavine 1991, Schmeck 1988). The latter are hypothesized to tolerate more ambiguity and have more permeable boundaries. Keith is more analytic; Jenny is very global.

The Myers–Briggs Type Indicator (MBTI) has four general personality scales: Introversion–Extraversion, Sensing–Intuition, Thinking–Feeling, and Judging–Perceiving (Myers and McCaulley 1985). It is one of the most important measures in the present study and closely related to the HBQ; I therefore provide brief descriptions of its dimensions.

Extraverts tend to be energized by external input; introverts receive their energy from the inner world of ideas. We might guess that, in terms of tolerance of ambiguity, extraverts are more comfortable with input from the outside, especially in ambiguous social settings like naturalistic learning, while introverts may manage conflicting ideas relatively comfortably but in a setting where they can work with them alone. On a general measure of tolerance for ambiguity, these two advantages might cancel each other out.

Intuitives think in abstract and large-scale ways, seek to distill principles, and usually like a random (self-generated) approach to learning without excessively clear instructions. Sensing learners, in contrast, prefer facts over abstractions and underlying principles and prefer concrete, sequential learning guided by clear instructions. We can certainly hypothesize a greater tolerance for ambiguity in the former.

Thinking-oriented students prefer logical and impersonal processing, while feeling-oriented learners tend toward problem-solving based on personal considerations, what matters to them and others. The Thinking–Feeling dimension impacts a student's interpersonal relationships and appears to provide information about likely sources of anxiety (Ehrman 1989, 1990). These studies found that thinking students tend to use data analysis strategies much more than their feeling fellows and seem to want a greater degree of control of structures and content. On the basis of this observation, we could guess that feeling students may tolerate certain kinds of ambiguity, e.g., about grammatical structure, more than their thinking classmates.

The last MBTI dimension is Judging (need for closure and structure in life) vs. Perceiving (need to keep options open and keep life flexible). Judgers tend to be deadline-conscious, product-oriented learners; perceivers are often less structured and wish to avoid premature closure, which can sometimes make them more comfortable than judgers with the relatively unstructured aspects of communicative methodology (Ehrman and Oxford 1990a and 1990b). The quickness of judgers to reach closure may mean that they tune out aspects of the language environment prematurely. Perceivers, who prefer to stay open to input longer, can be expected both to manage more input and to tolerate lack of clear boundaries more than judgers. Jenny is an introverted intuitive feeling perceiver (INFP); Keith is an extraverted sensing thinking judger (ESTJ).

Psychology and psychoanalysis. Many of the language-related studies cited above address the affective dimensions that cause learners to exclude input or to be handicapped in their ability to manage the ambiguity new input generates. These are important topics in various fields of psychology other than second-language acquisition. We can divide some of the major contributions in the affective realm into those that have to do with the social impact on identity formation and those that deal with intrapsychic phenomena.

Berger and Luckmann (1966) present a model of learning in the context of social-identity construction. In their model, social interactions of various levels of complexity disrupt established schemata and require various levels of cognitive and affective adaptation in the individual. Face-to-face interaction, especially through the medium of language, requires us to make such mutual adaptations constantly. A very strong challenge to pre-established, "typified" concepts will require corresponding modification in them (or rejection of them). Language is described as a vehicle for transcending boundaries of internal vs. external state, concreteness vs. abstraction, etc., and between various "realities." In this context, Berger and Luckmann describe the process of socialization and acculturation, a process that is open to constant change and readjustment. Tennant (1988) describes the effects of group dynamics on learning, emphasizing the importance of norms, most of which are tacit and often contrary to the explicitly stated norms of a group.

In the individual realm, increased capacity to deal with open systems without clear boundaries and with ambiguous stimuli is seen by some as a characteristic of cognitive maturity beyond adolescent *formal operations*. For example, Rybash et al. (1986) distinguish between the achievement of formal operations (Piaget 1967)—the ability to manage abstractions, but in closed logical systems—versus a more mature capacity to manage an infinite array of interrelated variables and regularly synthesize contradictions. From another point of view, emotional reaction is likely to depend on whether one is in a situation where one knows how to respond. If one is faced with too much new information or incongruity with existing schemata, one must accommodate, and one's feelings will be positive or negative depending on the success of the accommodation (Mandler 1982). Greater maturity is associated with more such coping resources. Greenspan (1989) describes the formal operational period as opening a wider range of resources to cope with ambiguity, contradictions, and much increased variety of experience.

Tennant notes that "[p]sychoanalysis is notably absent from the literature on adult teaching and learning" (1988: 25). This is surprising, in view of the relevance of this approach to cognition and affect in all areas of learning, motivation, and identity formation. Concepts of ego boundary—including Guiora's language ego—are firmly rooted in psychoanalytic thinking.

Psychoanalytic thinking addresses both the intrapsychic and the interpersonal. In the former are concepts of self-cohesion and integrity (Cohler 1989), primitive motivations, e.g., for taking in sustenance, or need for autonomy (Anthony 1989). Piaget, arguably the most influential modern theorist of cognitive development, owed much to psychoanalytic theory and practice and saw his work as a cognitive analogue to Freud's work with affect (Piaget 1973).

Psychoanalysis also addresses the profound riskiness of learning, in which the student faces the danger of discovering his or her lack of capacity or helplessness (Bernstein 1989, Salzberger-Wittenberg et al. 1983) and risk of shame for not knowing (Elson 1989). Stevick (1980), basing his thought on the psychoanalytically oriented work of Ernest Becker (1973), addresses some of these fears in the context of awareness of one's own mortality (1980). Sussman (1989) describes how novelty may arouse defenses against feelings of inadequacy. With this kind of powerful threat carried by new input, it is hardly surprising that we build boundaries.

In psychotherapy, *resistance* is a specialized term referring to a cognitive interference with a patient's ability to take in new data and alter existing self-structures (Rocah 1989). It is also understood as a response to profound personal threats, including a sense of loss of one's origins (Mirsky 1991) that is likely to affect second-language learners more than foreign-language learners. A similar process is implied by such concepts as the *affective filter* in language learning.

Repressed material in the unconscious is similarly "impervious to changes wrought by interaction with the environment" (Klein 1967: 110), thus forcing one to assimilate where accommodation would be more appropriate.

In the interpersonal realm are such powerful concepts as the enduring impact of relations in the family of origin in all one's later relationships, including with teachers. Concern with competition and the envy of classmates, for example, may reflect much earlier competitive relationships with parents and siblings and may cause a learner to limit his or her cognitive capacity or to build insurmountable barriers to input (Cohler 1989). Anthony points out that

> The level of cognition is related to the ability to learn, but the interaction is not a simple one. The overall competence in learning has to do not only with cognitive power, but also the individual's capacity to exchange effectively with the learning environment and thus adapt himself to it with increasing success. (1989: 103)

Learning by identification is also interpersonal. Here one takes in the other and makes him or her part of the learner's own persona. This is a process that begins in infancy and continues throughout life (Piers and Piers 1989). It is the process that makes the kind of social learning described by Berger and Luckmann (1966) possible.

The Hartmann Boundary Questionnaire study. The Hartmann Boundary Questionnaire (HBQ) is part of a study of individual differences being conducted by Rebecca Oxford and me. Data collection and analysis have been underway at the Foreign Service Institute since 1989. The HBQ is one of six instruments; the others are the Modern Language Aptitude Test (MLAT), the Myers–Briggs Type Indicator (MBTI), the National Association of Secondary School Principals Learning Styles Profile (LSP), the Strategy Inventory for Language Learning (SILL), and a composite motivation–affective instrument called the Affective Survey. (Descriptions of these instruments can be found in Appendix A of Ehrman and Oxford, forthcoming.) Students also completed a biographical data questionnaire.

At the end of training, the students were given proficiency assessments resulting in ratings ranging from 0 to 5 for speaking (including interactive listening comprehension) and for reading. For example, R–3 means reading proficiency level 3, S–2 means speaking proficiency level 2. The ratings are equivalent to the ILR/ACTFL/ETS guidelines that originated at FSI and have been developed over the years by government agencies. After training was complete, faculty were asked to rate students. Data were collected by interview in order to get comments as well as quantitative data.

The Hartmann Boundary Questionnaire (Hartmann 1991) was developed for research with sleep disorders and nightmares, using a psychoanalytic theoretical base. It is intended to examine how much individuals keep apart aspects of their mental, interpersonal, and external experience through thick or thin psychological boundaries. It addresses a variety of content dimensions and produces a total score for all of them. The content dimensions are:

- sleep/dreams/wakefulness
- unusual experiences
- boundaries among thoughts/feelings/moods
- impressions of childhood/adolescence/adulthood
- interpersonal distance/openness/closeness
- physical and emotional sensitivity
- preference for neatness
- preference for clear lines
- opinions about children/adolescents/adults
- opinions about lines of authority
- opinions about boundaries among groups/peoples/nations
- opinions about abstract concepts

Hartmann has found that women and younger people score consistently thinner than men and older people. Cronbach's alpha reliability for the HBQ is .93, and theta reliabilities for subscales are .57–.92 (Hartmann 1991). Positive scores indicate thinner boundaries.

In this study, 223 students completed the HBQ and are representative of the much larger sample from which they are drawn. Of the 223, 51% (114) were male and 49% (109) were female; the mean age was nearly 39 (SD = 9); the mean number of languages previously studied was just short of 2; and 43% (97) had master's-level education, while 34% (76) had a bachelor's degree.

For most of the results reported here, the analysis of choice was Spearman's rho on SAS. This is a correlation statistic usually used for rank-order data. When used with interval or ratio data, Spearman's rho provides a more conservative result than the Pearson product-moment correlation. Since some of the measures involved ordered data with uneven intervals, and other measures involved equal-interval data, the choice was for the most conservative correlation coefficient (Spearman's rho) that could be used consistently with all the data.

Analysis of variance (using SPSS for Windows Version 5.0.1) was used for the Hartmann Boundary Questionnaire in combination with end-of-training results. SPSS for Windows principal components analysis with Varimax rotation was applied to the HBQ content categories.

Results and discussion

Descriptive statistics. Table 1 shows the descriptive statistics on the HBQ for the FSI subsample. On every one of the 12 subscales of the HBQ and the total score, the 233 FSI participants proved to have thicker rather than thinner psychological boundaries relative to Hartmann's (1991) broad-ranging samples. Hartmann's normative mean, a total score of 276 (SD 50), contrasts with the FSI mean of 247 (SD 44); lower scores indicate greater boundary thickness. The FSI subsample has thicker boundaries than Hartmann's norm group by one half of a standard deviation, which suggests that they may be less receptive to experiences out of their expected categories, e.g. unexpected information from outside or unconsciously generated material from inside. Jenny's HBQ score is 323, well over Hartmann's mean and dramatically above the FSI mean; Keith's is 197, well below the FSI mean and very greatly below Hartmann's mean.

Table I. Descriptive statistics for the Hartmann Boundary Questionnaire, N-223

Content Categories	Max	Mean	(SD)	Range
People's Experience				
1. Sleep/Dreams/Wakefulness	56	11	(9)	0–40
2. Unusual Experiences (e.g., ESP, "seeing things")	72	17.5	(11)	1–57
3. Thoughts/Feelings/Moods (boundary among states)	68	27	(9)	6–53
4. Impressions of One's Childhood/Adolescence/Adulthood	24	9	(3)	1–17
5. Interpersonal Distance/Openness/Closeness	48	23	(5)	8–34
6. Sensitivity (Physical and Emotional)	20	11	(3.5)	4–18
Orderly Ways of Being				
7. Preference for Neatness and Precision	44	20	(6)	6–38
8. Preferences for Clear Edges and Lines	68	33	(8)	13–55
Boundaries between Elements of Phenomenal Field				
9. Opinions about Children, Adolescents, and Adults	32	19	(5)	6–30
10. Opinions about Lines of Authority	40	25	(5)	12–36
11. Opinions about Boundaries between Groups, Peoples, and Nations	56	34	(5.5)	20–44
12. Opinions about Beauty, Truth, and Other Abstract Concepts	28	18	(4)	8–26
HBQ Total (sum of 1–12): (401 is an outlier)	556	247	(44)	169–312

Higher scores indicate "thinner" mental boundaries; lower scores indicate "thicker" ones.

The FSI mean of 247 (SD 44) for the HBQ Total contrasts with Hartmann's (1991) mean of 276 (SD 50). This suggests that the FSI sample is "thicker" by nearly one half of a standard deviation than the more general sample on which Hartmann's norms are based.

Hartmann's factor analysis (1991) of the data from the HBQ indicates a distinction between categories that represent inner boundaries (between states or modes of cognition and affect) versus outer boundaries (between the individual and the external environment). Factor I relates to sleeping/waking/dreaming, unusual experiences (e.g., ESP), and thoughts/feelings/moods. Factor II relates to preferences in edges, lines, heavy clothing, and opinions about groups, lines of authority, and abstractions. There were no other strong or reliable groupings.

My rotated principal components analysis of the content categories (not of the responses to the items) produced similar findings, except that a preference not to be too neat or exact also appears to fall in Factor II (outer), and access to memories of childhood joins the other inner boundaries in Factor I. Other groupings accounted for far less of the variability and were less stable across two paired subsamples, as was the case in Hartmann's analysis as well.

For purposes of this study, Factor I (Inner Boundaries) is thus composed of the categories Sleep/Wake, Unusual Experiences, Thoughts/Feelings, and Impression of One's Childhood, Adolescence, Adulthood. Factor II (Outer Boundaries) consists of Neat, Edges, Lines of Authority, Openness to Peoples/ Nations, and Comfort with Abstractions. Contrary to the what one might expect from their names, high scores on Neat indicate a tolerance or preference for lack of neatness, and high scores on Edges indicate a preference for demarcations that are not too clear.

Our two students come out as follows on these factors: Keith is well below the FSI mean on Inner Boundaries and somewhat below it on Outer Boundaries; Jenny is well above the FSI mean on both Inner and Outer Boundaries.

Findings. In this discussion of the findings for the HBQ, the main focus is on the two HBQ factors, Inner and Outer Boundaries, and, as appropriate, on the HBQ Total, as a representative of the more unitary construct of ego boundaries that underlies the instrument. The other HBQ scores, Sensitive, Interpersonal, and Opinions (about various life stages) are grouped as *residual HBQ categories*. (Opinions about Life Stages appears to be an almost entirely independent scale. Opinions also intercorrelates with other HBQ scales and with the HBQ Total at by far the lowest level of all the HBQ scales.)

Correlations were considered significant at the $p < .05$ level. Significant correlations from .20 up are considered in data analysis. The low floor is used because this is exploratory work and because there is clear patterning in many of the relatively low correlations. The following material addresses findings with only a few statistics to provide the level of correlation for each measure. All the significant correlations with the HBQ are provided in the appendix. This section addresses correlation findings with the other measures used in the study, then correlations with end of training success (proficiency scores in speaking and reading and faculty ratings). Discussion of each category is included with the general description of the results.

Correlations with Demographic Variables. Female subjects showed a somewhat stronger tendency to thin boundaries than male subjects (HBQ Total .25 $p < .0001$). This finding is consistent with Hartmann's figure: The correlation for gender is comparable to Hartmann's figure of .26 $p < .001$ (Harrison et al. forthcoming). Hartmann's correlation of the HBQ with age is $-.31$ $p < .001$, whereas this sample correlated at less than $-.20$.

The much lower correlation with age of the HBQ for the FSI sample than for Hartmann's may be a result of the relative homogeneity of the FSI sample at middle age (mean age 39 SD 9). The fact that the correlations for sex were similar may have to do with the fact that the sample was balanced with respect to this variable.

Correlations with other measures. The other measures are divided into four categories: demographic variables, cognitive variables (the MLAT and the SILL), affective variables (the Affective Survey), and personality variables (the MBTI and portions of the National Association of Secondary School Principals LSP).

Correlations with cognitive aptitude. The cognitive aptitude measure used in this study was the Modern Language Aptitude Test (Carroll and Sapon 1959), which has been used for many years at FSI. It includes the following subscales, along with a total score and a T-score translation of the total score called the Index: Part I, number learning, Part II decoding phonemic transcription, Part III English vocabulary and decoding odd spellings, Part IV sensitivity to English grammar, and Part V associative vocabulary learning.

The MLAT Index scores for this sample were at about the same level as the current mean for FSI and were thus generally representative of the FSI population. However, if the mean that is indicated by the Index score (Carroll and Sapon 1959) still holds for the population at large, the FSI students fell more than one standard deviation above the general population.

Outer Boundaries correlated with MLAT Parts I, III, and IV, the MLAT total score, and the Index (.27 $p < .003$), whereas neither Inner Boundaries nor the residual HBQ scores correlated with any of the MLAT subscales or the MLAT total. There was a low correlation between Inner Boundaries and the MLAT Index. The HBQ Total correlated with MLAT Part III and the MLAT Index.

The data in this study provide no direct measure of the general intelligence factor *g*. We must therefore infer a level of *g* from indirect indicators. In this study, these are level of education, which tends to correlate with measured intelligence (Anastasi 1988), and MLAT score, of which *g* is a considerable component (Wesche et al. 1982). To the degree that education and the MLAT are valid indicators of intelligence, these correlations may also suggest a *very* slight relationship between general intelligence and thin outer boundaries.

How would this work? First, as mentioned above, one can expect that those who self-select into higher education are both more comfortable with complex input and are more at ease in altering complex cognitive and affective schemata, as is often required by higher education in the kinds of complex and relatively abstract subjects FSI students have usually studied (e.g. political science, economics, anthropology). In addition, FSI students are likely to have acquired learning strategies that enable them to cope with complex new input.[2] It is thus not surprising that FSI student education level correlates with a learning construct that includes ability to take in novel information and accommodate to it.

Despite changes in FSI language-teaching methodology that have made it more communicative and thus require students to cope with increasingly complex input (and output), the data from the project of which this substudy is a part showed that the MLAT continues to correlate with overall learning success at more or less the same levels as it did in the heyday of audio-lingual training (Ehrman and Oxford, forthcoming). This finding suggests that as Carroll (1959) proposed, the MLAT may well be addressing learning abilities that are independent of methodology. Among these is probably a large general intelligence component (see Wesche 1982).

The factor *g* is often described in terms of crystallized and fluid abilities. Crystallized abilities are those skills that have been learned well; they represent the application of good learning abilities and provide a base for further learning. A common example is native-language vocabulary. Fluid abilities are the processing skills involved in solving unfamiliar problems and quick adaptation to new situational variables; they are often tested by logic problems (Groth-Marnat 1984). The MLAT appears to tap both. The MLAT taps crystallized intelligence in the form of sophistication of native language vocabulary and grammar, especially in Parts III and IV. The fluid intelligence aspects probably appear whenever the respondent must change mental sets, particularly in those parts that require quick adaptation to an unfamiliar task. Thus some form of cognitive flexibility may be the underlying fluid ability that is accessed by the MLAT's verbal tasks. An instrument such as the HBQ may directly access at least some of this ability. The fact that it is HBQ Outer Boundaries that correlates most strongly and consistently with cognitive measures is almost certainly a consequence of the accommodative nature of communicative language learning, involving acceptance of novel input, holding apparently inconsistent concepts at the same time, and restructuring complex cognitions such as one's identity structure.

2. This, by the way, is probably the reason that the learning strategy instrument, the SILL, gives much less conclusive information for FSI students than for other populations (Oxford and Ehrman, forthcoming): For the most part, FSI students are already selected from those who have mastered use of many learning strategies.

Correlations with learning strategies. The SILL (Oxford 1989) was the measure of learning strategies that is used in this study. Based on a factor analysis, it divides language-learning strategies into six factors (memory, cognitive, compensation, metacognitive, affective, and social strategies) and calculates a mean to indicate overall reported level of strategy use. (For more discussion of the SILL, see Oxford 1990 and Ehrman and Oxford 1990b.) Both HBQ and SILL were given to 114 participants.

Inner Boundaries and the HBQ Total are similar in correlating with compensation strategies, HBQ residual category Sensitive relates to social strategies and overall strategy use, and Outer Boundaries is distinguished by *negative* correlation with memory (mnemonics) and metacognitive (planning and evaluation) strategies. Level of correlation is illustrated by HBQ Total .23 $p < .0225$ with compensation strategies.

The positive correlation of Inner Boundaries and HBQ Total with SILL compensation strategies suggests that Inner Boundary permeability may affect the element of our construct that involves holding contradictions and incomplete information as one restructures information. The residual category Sensitive is associated with emotional vulnerability (Hartmann 1991); its correlation with social strategies and with overall strategy use may represent efforts to overcome the anxiety raised in the language-learning process. (This conjecture is supported by data from the Affective Survey, discussed below.) Finally, the negative correlation between Outer Boundaries and memory and metacognitive strategies is of interest. It is possible that these two strategy categories represent an application of external structure and discipline on learning that is rejected by students who have thinner outer boundaries. This rejection may be reflected in the learning-style differences that cause some students to have intense difficulty with highly structured programs and prefer self-paced, self-structured programs.

Correlations with Affective Variables. Anxiety was addressed in three places: at the beginning of training by the MBTI–TDI Comfort–Discomfort subscales and their composite Strain scale (see below), at various times during the second half of training by the Affective Survey, and after training in the faculty ratings.

Motivation and anxiety both can be seen as aspects of a general quality of arousal (Snow 1989), but one generally implies approach whereas the other is usually implicated in avoidance. To measure affective arousal and differentiate among its various aspects, Ehrman and Oxford (1991) compiled a composite questionnaire (the Affective Survey) based on questionnaires by Horwitz (1985, 1986), Campbell (1987), and Gardner (1985b) that addressed components of affect. This questionnaire is still in the process of validation at FSI, so as yet there are no norms. The Affective Survey includes sections on different kinds of motivation, beliefs, and anxiety. It also provides a score for negatively phrased items that a respondent endorses. Forty-five participants completed both the HBQ and the Affective Survey.

Inner Boundaries correlated significantly with two anxiety subscales: anxiety about use with native speakers and anxiety about competition, and nearly significantly with a total score representing somewhat pessimistic beliefs about language learning. Outer Boundaries had no correlations at all with any element of the Affective Survey. Students with thin boundaries on the HBQ Total indicated anxiety about competition (.45 $p < .002$) and general discomfort about language learning (.32 $p < .033$). The HBQ residual categories Interpersonal and Sensitive both correlated with a tendency to endorse negatively phrased items about motivation (e.g., I don't really want to learn this language).

Faculty ratings of observed anxiety, rated on a scale of 0 (none) to 3 (severe enough to derail training) correlated only with the HBQ scale Unusual Experiences, one of the Inner Boundaries components. Faculty ratings of extrinsic motivation (vs. intrinsic motivation) correlated with Impressions of One's Childhood, Adolescence, Adulthood, also a component of Inner Boundaries.

The main finding is that Inner Boundaries, the HBQ Total, and HBQ residual score Sensitive correlate variously with anxiety as measured in all three ways. No HBQ element was related to the self-esteem or positive motivation items on the Affective Survey. Outer Boundaries appears to be unrelated to any of the motivation or anxiety measures. There thus appears to be a clear separation between the two factors in the area of affective arousal, suggesting a cognitive vs. affective split between the two factors, as suggested by Greenspan (1989) in his discussion of the concept of ego boundaries in general.

Jenny and Keith report their anxiety on these measures very differently: Jenny scores above average on the anxiety indicators, whereas Keith does not "move the needle" at all. Teacher ratings indicate a low level of performance anxiety for Keith and a very strong level of general anxiety for Jenny.

Correlations with Personality Variables. The HBQ was one of two personality indicators in the study. The other was the MBTI. The MBTI was used in two forms. One was the shorter Form G version with the four scales described above in the literature review (Myers and McCaulley 1985). The other was the factor-analysis-based Type Differentiation Indicator (TDI) version (Saunders 1989), with the same four scales, a fifth Comfort–Discomfort composite scale called *Strain*,[3] two consistency (*polarity*) scores, and 27

3. The individual TDI Comfort–Discomfort (C/D) subscales are a measure of anxiety. Because the MBTI is administered at the beginning of training, these scales and their composite *Strain* thus represent the anxiety level of students early in their training. On the defiant–compliant subscale, defiant (theoretically Discomfort) students have very slightly better and nearly significant speaking ($r=-.12$ $p<.06$ $N=246$) and reading ($r=-.12$ $p<.07$ $N=244$) scores. However, other C/D subscales correlate (but subsignificantly) in the expected direction: Start of training Discomfort

subscales, shown in tables 2 and 3. Subscales 1 through 5 belong to Extraversion–Introversion, 8 through 12 to Sensing–Intuition, 14, 15, 17, 19, and 20 to Thinking–Feeling, and 21 through 25 to Judging–Perceiving. The subscales in the Comfort–Discomfort scale have a dual role. Subscales 6 and 7 also belong to Extraversion–Introversion, subscales 13, 16, and 18 also belong to Thinking–Feeling, and subscales 26 and 27 are also Judging–Perceiving subscales as well as Comfort–Discomfort subscales. Correlations of the four standard MBTI scales with the HBQ are available for 212 respondents, and correlations of the TDI subscales are available for 158 respondents.

The HBQ and the MBTI showed a substantial amount of cross-correlation. Thin boundaries were correlated with the Intuition, Feeling, and Perceiving poles of the four main scales. The correlations were particularly strong for Outer Boundaries. Inner Boundaries and the HBQ Total also correlated in these directions, though more weakly. The correlations of the MBTI–TDI subscales with the HBQ follow this pattern closely (see tables 2 and 3).

Of the HBQ residual scales, Interpersonal Distance/Closeness correlates clearly with Extraversion and Feeling. This scale and Lines of Authority (part of Outer Boundaries) are the only scales to correlate in the direction of Extraversion, though one component of Inner Boundaries (Impressions of Childhood, etc.) correlates with the Introversion pole. Sensitive correlates primarily with Feeling, with the worried pole of subscale 18 Carefree–Worried, and with Strain. It thus reflects the anxiety component of Feeling, which the MBTI–TDI intercorrelations for the FSI population show to be associated with the Discomfort pole of the Comfort–Discomfort scale. Thus Interpersonal is an analogue of Extraversion, and Sensitive is an analogue of anxious Feeling.

The MBTI and the HBQ, though not equivalent by any means, appear to be addressing overlapping domains. In the MBTI world, Inner Boundaries, though it correlates relatively weakly with aspects of Intuition and Perceiving, is most clearly correlated with the anxiety implied by the Discomfort pole of the Comfort–Discomfort scale and its composite Strain. Although there is no direct correlation with Extraversion–Introversion, correlations with the introverted poles (italicized) of subscales 1 (gregarious–*intimate*) and 6 (intrepid–*inhibited*) suggest a possible relationship with Introversion, which elsewhere tends to correlate with higher anxiety and lack of self confidence than Extraversion (Myers and McCaulley 1985, Saunders 1989).

Outer Boundaries, on the other hand, quite strongly correlates with Intuition and Perceiving, and considerably more weakly with Feeling. By MBTI theory, Sensing–Intuition is the scale that directly addresses how people like to take in information, i.e. to learn. It is thus not surprising that the HBQ factor related to input would correlate strongly with this scale. Furthermore, it is also not

---

(anxiety) is debilitating.

Table 2. Myers-Briggs Type Indicator (MBTI) categories and significant HBQ Spearman's correlates. Significance levels are immediately below correlation coefficients.

	HBQ I	HBQ II	Interp	Sens	Opin	HBQ Total
MBTI Main Scales (N = 212)						
Extraversion/Introversion (E/I)	—	—	-.33	—	—	—
			.0001			
Sensing/Intuition (S/N)	.21	.52	—	—	—	.40
	.002	.0001				.0001
Thinking/Feeling (T/F)	.18	.35	.33	.35	.14	.35
	.009	.0001	.0001	.0001	.037	.0001
Judging/Perceiving (J/P)	.20	.54	—	—	—	.39
	.003	.0001				.0001
TDI Subscales (N = 158						
Type Polarity (Consistency)	—	—	—	—	—	—
Comfort Scale Polarity (Consistency on Comfort Scales)	-.25	—	—	—	—	-.17
	.001					.032
Strain (Anxiety/Discomfort Composite)	.38	—	—	.23	—	.26
	.0001			.003		.001
TDI Extraversion-Introversion Subscales						
S1 Gregarious-Intimate	.20	—	-.29	.—	—	—
	.013		.0001	.020		
S2 Enthusiastic-Quiet	—	—	-.24	—	—	—
			.003			
S3 Initiator-Receptor	—	—	-.27	—	—	—
			.001			
S4 Expressive-Contained	—	—	-.39	—	—	—
			.0001			
S5 Auditory-Visual	—	—	-.20	—	—	—
			.013			

(continues)

surprising that thinness is linked with the more flexible pole on this scale: Persons preferring Intuition tend to want considerably less externally imposed structure of any kind (including political) than their Sensing fellows. Similarly, on the behavioral flexibility scale of Judging and Perceiving, thin boundaries are associated with Perceiving, which not only tolerates but often demands delay in closure and seeks to keep options open as long as possible.

The Thinking–Feeling scale correlates at a moderate to low level with Outer Boundaries, with the residual scales Interpersonal, Sensitive, Opinions, and with the HBQ Total, in the Feeling direction. Decision making based on personal meaning and an involved as opposed to a detached stance thus appears to be a pervasive portion of all aspects of the HBQ construct, whereas Inner Boundaries

Table 2 *(cont'd.)*. Myers–Briggs Type Indicator (MBTI) categories and significant HBQ Spearman's correlates. Significance levels are immediately below correlation coefficients.

	HBQ I	HBQ II	Interp	Sens	Opin	HBQ Total
TDI Sensing-Intuition Subscales						
S8 Concrete-Abstract	—	.41	—	—	—	.31
		.0001				.0001
S9 Realistic-Imaginative	.33	.44	—	—	—	.45
	.0001	.0001				.0001
S10 Pragmatic-Intellectual	.23	.31	—	—	—	.32
	.003	.0001				.0001
S11 Experiential-Theoretical	—	.30	—	—	—	.22
		.0001				.007
S12 Traditional-Original	—	.40	—	—	—	.31
		.0001				.0001
TDI Thinking-Feeling Subscales						
S14 Critical-Accepting	—	.25	.23	.21	.22	.22
	.001	.005	.008	.006	.006	
S15 Tough-Tender	—	—	—	.32	—	.21
				.0001		.009
S17 Questioning-Accommodating	—	—	—	—	—	—
S19 Logical-Affective	—	.33	.36	.39	.20	.36
		.0001	.0001	.0001	.014	.0001
S20 Reasonable-Compassionate	—	—	.20		.20	.22
			.011		.012	.005
TDI Judging-Perceiving Subscales						
S21 Stress Avoider-Polyactive	—	.27	—	—	—	.23
	.001	.003				
S22 Systematic-Casual	—	.46	—	—	—	.24
	.0001	.003				
S23 Scheduled-Spontaneous	—	.49	.23	—	—	.31
		.0001	.003			.0001
S24 Planful-Open-ended	—	.37	—	—	—	.18
		.0001				.024
S25 Methodical-Emergent	—	.30	—	—	—	.21
		.0001				.009

HBQ categories: HBQ I = HBQ Factor I (inner); HBQ II = HBQ Factor II (outer); Interp = Interpersonal; Sens = Sensitive; Opin = Opinions about Life Stages. In correlations, Extraversion, Sensing, Thinking, and Judging and their associated subscale poles are negative, and Introversion, Intuition, Feeling, and Perceiving and their associated subscale poles are positive.

is heavily loaded on anxiety, and Outer Boundaries appears reflective of cognitive flexibility (Sensing–Intuition) and behavioral flexibility (Judging–Perceiving).

Table 3. TDI Comfort–Discomfort Subscales of Myers-Briggs Type Indicator (MBTI) categories and significant HBQ Spearman's correlates. Significance levels are immediately below correlation coefficients.

Subscale (Also Belongs To:)	HBQ I	HBQ II	Interp	Sens	Opin	HBQ Total
S13 Guarded-Optimistic (T/F)	-.24	—	.22	—	—	—
	.002		.006			
S16 Defiant-Compliant (T/F)	—	—	—	—	—	—
S18 Carefree-Worried (T/F)	.28	—	—	.28	—	.25
	.0001			.0001		.002
S26 Decisive-Ambivalent (J/P)	.25	—	—	—	—	.22
	.002					.005
S6 Intrepid-Inhibited (E/I)	.22	—	-.22	—	—	—
	.006		.007			
S7 Leader-Follower (E/I)	—	—	—	—	—	—
S27 Proactive-Distractable (J/P)	.34	.24	—	—	—	.36
	.0001	.002				.0001

HBQ categories: HBQ I = HBQ Factor I (inner); HBQ II = HBQ Factor II (outer); Interp = Interpersonal; Sens = Sensitive; Opin = Opinions about Life Stages. In correlations, Extraversion, Sensing, Thinking, and Judging and their associated subscale poles are negative, and Introversion, Intuition, Feeling, and Perceiving and their associated subscale poles are positive. "Also Belongs To": in the factor analysis on which the TDI is based, each of the comfort/discomfort subscales also appeared in one of the major type categories. Thus, for instance, S6 (intrepid-inhibited) is primarily a Comfort/Discomfort scale but is also considered an Extraversion/Introversion scale.

Correlations with Other Variables. The last of the questionnaires used was the National Association of Secondary Schools Principals Learning Styles Profile (LSP) (Keefe et al. 1989). This is a composite learning-styles inventory with seven cognitive function variables that include such traditional scales as field independence and leveling–sharpening. It also includes a scale for sensory input channel (auditory, visual, emotive–kinesthetic), preferred time of day and physical environment for study, and a few other variables, e.g. persistence. Of the students who completed the HBQ, 121 also completed the LSP.

There is only one correlation between the HBQ and a cognitive processing variable on the LSP: HBQ Total correlates $-.20$ $p < .030$ with discrimination ability, which is described as focusing one's attention on important information while ignoring distractions. Students who were thinner on Sensitive and Opinions tended to report a preference for early morning study, whereas those who were thinner on Interpersonal and the HBQ Total rejected afternoon study. *Thin* on Opinions went with a preference for verbal over spatial learning and negatively with consistency of response on the LSP.

The negative correlation between discrimination ability and the HBQ Total suggests that a general openness to stimuli is inconsistent with a developed ability to screen out information. The correlation is low, however, doubtless because no matter how open one is, sooner or later one must set priorities. Jenny's markedly low score on discrimination is illustrative of this point. It is the only score in her LSP profile that was markedly low.

The most consistent information in the LSP was the correlation of the HBQ with learning environment preferences, particularly for an upright posture when studying. Inner Boundaries was also associated with a preference for dim light, possibly a way of minimizing external input that might interfere with the inner world. Outer Boundaries was linked with a preference for background sound while studying, which is consistent with being open to input and an ability to manage more than one externally derived stimulus at a time. The correlation of a preference for background noise with thin boundaries may be interpretable as a form of conceptual polyactivity: a similar measure, TDI polyactive (vs. stress avoider, subscale 21) correlated with learning success at a low level of correlation (Ehrman and Oxford forthcoming). Background sound may thus characterize the kind of person who prefers to do two things at once, e.g. taking notes or doing puzzles during noninteractive lectures. This would seem to be a capacity closely related to the aspect of tolerance for ambiguity that involves holding multiple and often incompatible things in one's head.

Correlations with end-of-training outcomes. End-of-training outcomes were rated in two ways. One was the formal end-of-training interactive proficiency test, which yields scores for speaking and interactive listening and for reading on a scale from 0 (no knowledge) to 5 (native speaker equivalent). The other rating was done by faculty in an interview with a project staff member to fill in a form that addressed overall percentile as a "good" student relative to other FSI students, observed aptitude percentile, estimation of effort in and out of class, motivation, and observed anxiety or emotional upset. The overall percentile rating was also converted into three "faculty ranking" groups comprising the top and bottom 20% and the middle 60%. There were end-of-training scores available in speaking for 119 of those who took the HBQ and in reading for 118 of them.

Overall thin ego boundaries, indicated by the HBQ Total and a preference for low Neatness were associated with end-of-training proficiency test outcomes in both reading and speaking. A preference for fuzzy Edges was correlated with reading proficiency and with faculty ratings of observed aptitude. Neat and Edges are both scales that are included in Outer Boundaries. Outer Boundaries itself correlated .27 $p < .003$ with speaking proficiency, .29 $p < .001$ with reading proficiency, and .22 $p < .056$, $N=78$, with faculty rating of observed learning aptitude. Inner Boundaries did not correlate with any training outcomes.

Results of a one-way analysis of variance (ANOVA) examination suggested that thick boundaries contribute to learning difficulties in FSI's communicatively oriented classrooms. Data for all ANOVAs were restricted to beginners who had at least 17 weeks of training. The HBQ Total differentiated among the lowest 20% based on overall faculty ratings and the other students. The HBQ scale Neat (high scores indicating less preference for order) differentiated between those achieving a score in reading and in speaking of 1 from those who achieved a score of 3 on the end-of-training proficiency test for both speaking and reading. For reading only, Thoughts (permeable boundary between thoughts and feelings) also differentiated between students achieving a tested score of 1 and those achieving the 3 level. Although ANOVAs of the two major factors with any form of end-of-training rating did not prove significant, Neat is an Outer Boundaries component and affects both speaking and reading, while Thoughts, affecting reading only, is an Inner Boundaries component.

In summary, the findings are that Outer Boundaries and HBQ Total correlate, though at a low level, with tested end-of-training proficiency in speaking and reading. Analysis of variance findings for faculty ranking groups suggest that it may be that thick-boundary students are disadvantaged more than thin-boundary students are advantaged. Again, perhaps Keith and Jenny are cases in point: Keith is at risk because of characteristics associated with thick boundaries. Jenny's thin boundaries, on the other hand, are not helpful to her because she does not discriminate among stimuli.

Discussion: Toward a model of learning. Existing research on individual differences such as ego boundaries or tolerance of ambiguity regularly indicates that simple cause-and-effect relationships are hard to find; relationships are for the most part intercorrelated and complex. Figure 1 is an attempt to address some of these relationships, in the form of a tentative model of learning. It is based both on intercorrelations in the data from the project of which the HBQ is a part and on my experience over more than 20 years with language learning and teaching.

Looking at the model vertically, the model suggests that there are a number of tracks that lead concurrently to learning. Individual differences appear in the preferences learners show for one or more of the four tracks. Thus a student may prefer to build learning on close interactions with teachers or native speakers, on cognitive flexibility ("smarts"), on achieving analytical control of material, or on sheer hard work, or on a combination of two or more of these. No student can succeed without some use of strategies from each track, but emphases differ markedly. For classroom learning, at least at FSI, the cognitive flexibility track appears to be indispensable. Students who rely on hard work and control, for example, may achieve short-term success with restricted material but will not master language to the high level they have set as their goal. Indeed, an "effort to play it safe by being obedient, dutiful, and thorough does not usually

Figure 1. A Three-Track Model of Learning

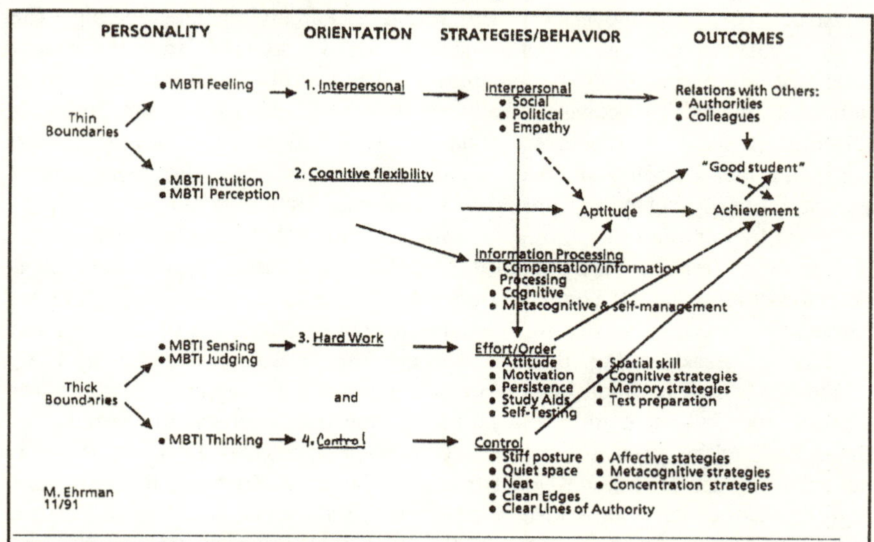

pay off. The student finds herself overwhelmed by quantities of material, undifferentiated detail, boredom, and lost time in an approach to study which has aptly been referred to as 'improvident'" (Entwhistle 1981: 93–103, cited in Henderson and Kegan 1989). Students who rely primarily on their relationships with significant others tend to have a smoother course of learning and enjoy such advantages as accrue to those who engender liking in others. For example, they often are given the benefit of the doubt where their more abrasive colleagues may not be. They may be expert at nonverbal or imprecise verbal forms of communication.

However, interpersonal skills do not compensate for lack of knowledge, ability to tolerate cognitive ambiguity at higher levels of linguistic proficiency, or the capacity to impose a necessary amount of structure on input. On the other hand, FSI faculty can describe a great many students who had very great cognitive ability, including the ability to manage a great deal of complex input, but whose lack of empathy caused considerable question about their success when they left the relatively sheltered world of the language classroom.

Jenny tends to rely heavily on track one, the interpersonal track. We see that she is open to new input, especially that which is associated with her values, which are social and aesthetic. Keith, on the other hand, relies especially on hard work and secondarily on control. Neither is able to reach the point of the accommodative process, which is the key to the cognitive flexibility track, Keith because he does not even complete intake, and Jenny because she tolerates so much ambiguity that she becomes overwhelmed before she can undertake the cognitive and affective operations needed to accommodate.

Looking at the model horizontally, the HBQ Total, representing the whole construct, correlates moderately with Intuition, Perceiving, and Feeling. The level of correlation suggests that the MBTI–TDI and the HBQ are measuring at least part of the same thing, but not entirely. The overlap is less with the shorter version of the MBTI, because it excludes the anxiety measures of the Comfort–Discomfort scale. I hypothesize that the HBQ addresses a set of related constructs that are embedded deep in the psyche, which are in turn expressed by the more overtly behavioral preferences addressed by the MBTI.

This hypothesis leads to the first stage, at the left of the learning model. The primary division is by overall thickness and thinness of ego boundaries as described in this paper. Thin boundaries are then realized either through Outer Boundaries as cognitive flexibility related to input in the form of Intuition and Perceiving, or as Feeling, through aspects of Inner Boundaries and the HBQ residual categories. Thick boundaries are expressed through a preference for Sensing and Judgment for a disciplined, sequential approach to learning, or through Thinking for a structured, controlled approach. Each of these is described by an orientation. Each track has learning strategies that are most regularly associated with it. (More detail on this stage can be found in Ehrman 1989, 1990, Ehrman and Oxford 1990a and b.) All tracks interact to produce outcomes.

We see that Jenny and Keith are prototypic on the horizontal dimension. Jenny is an introverted intuitive feeling perceiver—all the characteristics that are associated with thin boundaries, and she relies heavily on interpersonal and political skills but flounders when she has to deal with material specifically rather than globally. She could be helped by an intervention that enables her to develop discrimination and structuring skills. Keith, on the other hand, is an extraverted sensing thinking judger who works very hard, strives for control, but is quickly overloaded when unmastered material appears and he must access more global processing. He needs help in understanding his perfectionistic tendencies and progressive, confidence-building practice in dealing with ambiguous, slightly over-the-head material. In either case, their teachers must make sure that both feel normal, not defective, as they are helped to learn new skills.

Discussion: In general. It appears that the HBQ Outer Boundaries is related more to the cognitive, relatively (emotional) conflict-free aspects of learning, including cognitive abilities implied in the concept of accommodation. On the other hand, Inner Boundaries appears to relate more to generally negative affective arousal and thus may represent a potential debilitator when very high.

Overall, the expectation appears to be confirmed that the construct of thin ego boundaries as manifested on the HBQ is to be an expression of tolerance for ambiguity. That is, learners who do not require a very orderly and delineated world and who prefer not to draw sharp lines between ideas or images are also those who will welcome the new information and new ways of looking at the world that are entailed by effective language learning to high proficiency levels and who can tolerate the necessary lack of clarity among semantic ranges and grammatical categories as they learn the new language.

The correlation of thin boundaries and learning success might be stronger except that once the new information is in, the student must be able to cope with it. The finding that thick-boundaried learners may be disadvantaged more than thin-boundaried ones are helped seems consistent with my student-counseling experience, in which students have been troubled either by excessive rigidity (thick) or by thin boundaries untempered by an ability to sort, set priorities, and impose a cognitive structure on an overwhelming mass of input. In other words, the latter kind of student can take input and even hold contradictions but seems to fail at the stage where it is necessary to use the input to reorganize concepts. The former (thick) student may not even achieve uninhibited input, possibly because of the threat the ensuing contradictions and knowledge gaps might entail.

The data reported herein show a clear relationship between ego boundaries operationalized by the HBQ and various aspects of learning, not least among them being the outcomes of communicative language training of adults. The HBQ correlates with other variables that also relate to learning success, at about the same level of correlation as do those variables (see Ehrman and Oxford forthcoming for details). These variables include educational level, score on the MLAT, affective elements, and certain personality factors on the MBTI.

Because the FSI sample is relatively homogeneous on the ego boundary variable, nearer the thick end of Hartmann's continuum than the thin end, the amount of variation and hence the strength of the relationships revealed may well be less than they would be in a sample more typical of the range of people who learn foreign languages. This fact suggests that the HBQ may be even more useful than these data suggest.

It appears that personality variables like the HBQ correlate at a high enough level to use for counseling purposes. In fact, the use of the HBQ has proved successful with students very much like Keith and Jenny. However, these variables should not be used directly as predictors for selection purposes, though as part of regression formulas they might contribute to prediction of success. As mentioned above, the correlations may be lower for the FSI sample than for samples from a more general population because of the relative homogeneity of the FSI group on a variety of demographic and personality variables. Further research with other groups of learners might thus demonstrate a greater utility for this kind of variable.

REFERENCES

Anastasi, Anne. 1988. *Psychological testing* (6th edition). New York: Macmillan.

Anthony, E. James. 1989. "The psychoanalytic approach to learning theory." In Kay Field, Bertram J. Cohler, and Glorye Wool (eds.), *Learning and education: Psychoanalytic perspectives*. Madison, Conn.: International Universities Press.

Bailey, Kathleen M. 1983. "Competitiveness and anxiety in adult second language learning: Looking at and through the diary studies." In Herbert W. Seliger and Michael Long (eds.), *Classroom oriented research in second language acquisition*. Rowley, Mass.: Newbury House.

Becker, Ernest. 1973. *The denial of death*. New York: The Free Press.

Beebe, Leslie M. 1983. "Risk-taking and the language learner." In Herbert W. Seliger and Michael H. Long (eds.), *Classroom-oriented research in second language acquisition*. Rowley, Mass.: Newbury House.

Berger, Peter L., and Thomas Luckmann. 1966. *The social construction of reality: A treatise in the sociology of knowledge*. New York: Doubleday.

Bernstein, Helen E. 1989. "The courage to try: Self-esteem and learning." In Kay Field, Bertram J. Cohler, and Glorye Wool (eds.), *Learning and education: Psychoanalytic perspectives*. Madison, Conn.: International Universities Press.

Brown, H. Douglas. 1987. *Principles of language learning and teaching* (2nd edition). Englewood Cliffs, N.J.: Prentice-Hall.

Campbell, Christine. 1987. "Survey of attitudes specific to the foreign language classroom." Unpublished manuscript. Monterey, Calif: Defense Language Institute.

Carroll, John B., and Stanley M. Sapon. 1959. *Modern language aptitude test*. New York: Psychological Corporation.

Chapelle, Carol A. 1983. "The relationship between ambiguity tolerance and success in acquiring English as a second language in adult learners." Unpublished doctoral dissertation. Champaign-Urbana, Ill.: University of Illinois.

Chapelle, Carol A., and Cheryl Roberts. 1986. "Ambiguity tolerance and field independence as predictors of proficiency in English as a second language." *Language Learning* 36: 27–45.

Clark, John. 1986. *A study of the comparability of speaking proficiency across three government language training agencies*. Washington, D.C.: Center for Applied Linguistics.

Cohler, Bertram J. 1989. "Psychoanalysis and education: Motive, meaning, and self." In Kay Field, Bertram J. Cohler, and Glorye Wool (eds.), *Learning and education: Psychoanalytic perspectives*. Madison, Conn.: International Universities Press.

Di Pietro, Robert J. 1987. *Strategic interaction: Learning languages through scenarios*. New York: Cambridge.

Ehrman, Madeline E. 1989. "Ants and grasshoppers, badgers and butterflies: Quantitative and qualitative investigation of adult language learning styles and strategies." Unpublished doctoral dissertation. Cincinnati, Ohio: Union Institute.

Ehrman, Madeline E. 1990. "Owls and doves: Cognition, personality, and learning success." In James E. Alatis (ed.), *Georgetown University Round Table on Languages and Linguistics 1990*. Washington, D.C.: Georgetown University Press.

Ehrman, Madeline E., and Rebecca L. Oxford. 1990a. "Effects of sex differences, career choice, and psychological type on adults' language learning strategies." *Modern Language Journal* 73(1): 1–13.

Ehrman, Madeline E., and Rebecca L. Oxford. 1990b. "Adult language learning styles and strategies in an intensive training setting." *Modern Language Journal* 4(3): 311–327.

Ehrman, Madeline E., and Rebecca L. Oxford. 1991. *Affective survey*. Arlington, Va.: Foreign Service Institute.

Ehrman, Madeline E., and Rebecca L. Oxford. Forthcoming. *Cognition plus: Correlates of language learning success*. Arlington, Va.: Foreign Service Institute.

Elson, Miriam. 1989. "The teacher as learner, the learner as teacher." In Kay Field, Bertram J. Cohler, and Glorye Wool (eds.), *Learning and education: Psychoanalytic perspectives*. Madison, Conn.: International Universities Press.

Ely, Christopher. 1986. "An analysis of discomfort, risk-taking, sociability, and motivation in the L2 classroom." *Language Learning* 36(1): 1–25.

Ely, Christopher. 1989. "Tolerance of ambiguity and use of second language learning strategies." *Foreign Language Annals* 22(5): 437–445.

Entwistle, Noel. 1981. *Styles of learning and teaching*. New York: Wiley.

Galbraith, Vicki, and Robert C. Gardner. 1988. *Individual difference correlates of second-language achievement: An annotated bibliography*. London: University of Western Ontario.

Galloway, Victoria, and Angela Labarca. 1990. "From student to learner: Style, process, and strategy." In Diane W. Birckbichler (ed.), *New perspectives and new directions in foreign language education*. Lincolnwood, Ill.: National Textbook Company.

Gardner, Robert C. 1985a. *Social psychology and second language learning: The role of attitudes and motivation*. London: Edward Arnold.

Gardner, Robert C. 1985b. Motivation Questionnaire. Unpublished manuscript. Prepared for the Defense Language Institute Skill Change Project. Monterey, Calif.: Defense Language Institute.

Gleitman, Henry, and Lila Gleitman. 1979. "Language use and language judgment." In C.J. Fillmore, D. Kempler, and William S.-Y. Wang (eds.), *Individual differences in language ability and language behavior*. New York: Academic Press.

Graham, C.R. 1984. "Beyond integrative motivation: The development and influence of assimilative motivation." Paper presented at the International Convention of Teachers of English to Speakers of Other Languages, Houston, Tex., March.

Greenspan, Stanley I. 1989. "Emotional intelligence." In Kay Field, Bertram J. Cohler, and Glorye Wool (eds.), *Learning and education: Psychoanalytic perspectives*. Madison, Conn.: International Universities Press.

Groth-Marnat, Gary. 1984. *Handbook of psychological assessment*. New York: Van Nostrand Reinhold.

Guiora, Alexander Z. 1981. "Language, personality, and culture, or the Whorfian hypothesis revisited." In Mary Hines, and William Rutherford (eds.), *On TESOL '81*. Detroit, Mich.: Teachers of English to Speakers of Other Languages.

Guiora, Alexander Z. 1984. "The dialectic of language acquisition." *Language Learning* 34(1): 3–12.

Guiora, Alexander Z., W.R. Acton, R. Evarard, and F.W. Strickland. 1980. "The effects of benzodiazepine (valium) on permeability of ego boundaries." *Language Learning* 30: 351–363.

Guiora, Alexander Z., B. Beit-Hallami, R.C. Brannon, C.Y. Dull, and T. Scovel. 1972. "The effects of experimentally induced changes in ego states on pronunciation ability in second language: An exploratory study." *Comprehensive Psychiatry* 13.

Harrison, Robert H., Ernest Hartmann, and Judith Bevis. Forthcoming. "The Hartmann boundary questionnaire: A measure of thin and thick boundaries." Available from Ernest Hartmann, Tufts University School of Medicine.

Hartmann, Ernest. 1991. *Boundaries in the mind: A new psychology of personality*. New York: Basic Books.

Henderson, Ann F., and Robert Kegan. 1989. "Learning, knowing and the self: A constructive developmental view." In Kay Field, Bertram J. Cohler, and Glorye Wool (eds.), *Learning and education: Psychoanalytic perspectives*. Madison, Conn.: International Universities Press.

Horwitz, Elaine K. 1982. "The relationship between conceptual level and communicative competence in French." *Studies in Second Language Acquisition* 5: 65–73.

Horwitz, Elaine K. 1985. "Using student beliefs about language learning and teaching in the foreign language methods course." *Foreign Language Annals* 18. 333–40.

Horwitz, Elaine K., Horwitz, M. B., and Cope, J. 1986. "Foreign language classroom anxiety." *The Modern Language Journal* 70: 125–132.

Horwitz, Elaine K. 1990. "Attending to the affective domain in the foreign language classroom." In S.S. Magnan (ed.), *Shifting the instructional focus to the learner*. Middlebury, Vt.: Northeast Conference on the Teaching of Foreign Languages. 15–33.

Horwitz, Elaine K., and Dolly J. Young. 1991. *Language learning anxiety: From theory and research to classroom implications*. Englewood Cliffs, N.J.: Prentice-Hall.

Keefe, John W. and James S. Monk, Charles A. Letteri, Marlin Languis, and Rita Dunn. 1989. *Learning Style Profile*. Reston, Va.: National Association of Secondary School Principals.

Klein, G. 1967. "Peremptory ideation: Structure and force in motivated ideas." In R. Holt (ed.), *Psychological issues*. (Monograph 18/19, 2 and 3) New York: International Universities Press.

Larsen-Freeman, Diane, and Michael Long. 1991. *An introduction to second language acquisition research*. Oxford: Oxford University Press.

Mandler, George. 1982. "The structure of value: Accounting for taste." In Margaret S. Clark, and Susan T. Fiske (eds.), *Affect and cognition*. Hillsdale, N.J.: Lawrence Erlbaum.

Mirsky, Julia. 1991. "Language in migration: Separation individuation conflicts in relation to the mother tongue and the new language." *Psychotherapy* 28: 618–624.

Myers, Isabel B., and Mary H. McCaulley. 1985. *Manual: A guide to the development and use of the Myers–Briggs type indicator*. Palo Alto, Calif.: Consulting Psychologists Press.

Naiman, N., Frohlich, M., Stern, H.H., and Todesco, A. 1978. "The good second language learner." *Research in education series* (No. 7). Toronto: Ontario Institute for Studies in Education.

Oxford, Rebecca L. 1989. *Strategy inventory for language learning: Version 5.1*. Alexandria, Va.: Oxford Associates.

Oxford, Rebecca L. 1990. *Language learning strategies: What every teacher should know*. New York: Newbury House/Harper and Row.

Oxford, Rebecca L., and Madeline E. Ehrman. Forthcoming. "Language learning strategies: Correlates and outcomes for adult language learners."

Oxford, Rebecca, Madeline E. Ehrman, and Roberta Z. Lavine. 1991. "Style wars: Teacher–student style conflicts in the language classroom." In S.S. Magnan (ed.), *Challenges in the 1990s for college foreign language programs*. Boston, Mass.: Heinle and Heinle.

Piaget, Jean. 1967. *Six psychological studies*. New York: Random House.

Piaget, Jean. 1973. "The affective unconscious and the cognitive unconscious." *Journal of the American Psychoanalytic Association* 21: 249–261.

Piers, Gerhart, and Maria Piers. 1989. "Modes of learning and the analytic process." In Kay Field, Bertram J. Cohler and Glorye Wool (eds.), *Learning and education: Psychoanalytic perspectives*. Madison, Conn.: International Universities Press.

Reiss, Mary Ann. 1985. "The good language learner: Another look." *Canadian Modern language Review* 41: 511–523.

Rybash, John M., William Hoyer, and Paul Roodin. 1986. *Adult cognition and aging*. New York: Pergamon.

Salzberger-Wittenberg, Isca, Gianna Henry, and Elsie Osborne. 1983. *The emotional experience of learning and teaching*. New York: Routledge and Kegan Paul.

Saunders, David. 1989. *Type Differentiation Indicator Manual: A scoring system for Form J of the Myers–Briggs Type Indicator*. Palo Alto, Calif.: Consulting Psychologists Press.

Scarcella, Robin C., and Rebecca L. Oxford. 1992. *The tapestry of language learning: The individual in the communicative classroom*. Boston: Heinle and Heinle.

Scarcella, Robin C. 1990. "Communication difficulties in second language production, development, and instruction." In Robin C. Scarcella, Elaine S. Andersen, and Stephen D. Krashen (eds.), *Developing communicative competence in a second language*. New York: Newbury House.

Schmeck, Ronald R. 1988. *Learning strategies and learning styles*. New York: Plenum.

Schumann, John. 1978a. "The acculturation model for second language acquisition." In R. Gingras (ed.), *Second language acquisition and foreign language teaching*. Arlington, Va.: Center for Applied Linguistics.

Schumann, John. 1978b. *The pidginization process: A model for second language development*. New York: Newbury House.

Schwartz, F. 1973. "Psychoanalytic research in attention and learning." *The annual of psychoanalysis* (Vol. 1). New York: International Universities Press. 199–215.

Skehan, Peter. 1989. *Individual differences in second language learning*. London: Edward Arnold.

Snow, Richard E. 1989. "Aptitude-treatment interaction as a framework for research on individual differences in learning." In P.E. Ackerman, R. J. Sternberg and R. Glaser (eds.), *Learning and individual differences*. New York: W. H. Freeman.

Sternberg, Robert. 1989. *The triarchic mind*. New York: Penguin.

Stevick, Earl W. 1976. *Memory, meaning, and method: Some psychological perspectives on language learning*. Rowley, Mass.: Newbury House.

Stevick, Earl W. 1980. *Teaching languages: A way and ways*. New York: Newbury House.

Sussman, Rita. 1989. "Curiosity and exploration in children: Where affect and cognition meet." In Kay Field, Bertram J. Cohler and Glorye Wool (eds.), *Learning and education: Psychoanalytic perspectives*. Madison, Conn.: International Universities Press.

Tennant, Mark. 1988. *Psychology and adult learning*. New York: Routledge.

Trosset, Carol S. 1986. "The social identity of Welsh learners." *Language in Society* 15: 165–191.

Wesche, Marjorie, Henry Edwards, and Winston Wells. 1982. "Foreign language aptitude and intelligence." *Applied Psycholinguistics* 3: 127–140.

Appendix. Statistical Data

Correlations from .20 up are included in the analysis of the data (lower figures for age are included because of their contrast with Hartmann's findings). This is exploratory research, where it is appropriate to search for patterns in data, in contrast to efforts to build predictive formulas, and thus I investigate the meanings behind the low correlations inherent in personality research.

Correlations were considered significant at the $p < .05$ level. A few subsignificant correlations were included either because the sample number was low (a larger sample might bring the correlation to significance) or because the variable showed patterns in meaningful ways with other, significant correlations. Inner Boundaries is Factor I, and Outer Boundaries is Factor II.

Correlations with Demographic Variables.
Inner Boundaries: Age –.17 ($p < .014$); Sex .18 $p < .011$
Outer Boundaries: Age –.14 ($p < .039$), N = 218; Sex .25 $p < .001$; N=218.
Sensitive .22 $p < .001$, N=214.
HBQ Total: Age –.17 ($p < .014$); .Sex .25 $p < .0001$

Correlations with cognitive aptitude. The cognitive aptitude measure used in this study was the Modern Language Aptitude Test (Carroll and Sapon 1959). It includes the following subscales, along with a total score and a T-score translation of the total score called the Index: Part I, number learning; Part II decoding phonemic transcription, Part III English vocabulary and decoding odd spellings, Part IV sensitivity to English grammar, and Part V associative vocabulary learning. MLAT subscale and total scores were available for 101 students; Index scores were available for 121.

Inner Boundaries: MLAT Index .21 p < .023, N=121.
Outer Boundaries: Part I .20 p < .046; Part III .33 p < .001;
Part IV .24 p < .017; MLAT total score .27 p < .005, N=101;
MLAT Index .27 p < .003, N=121.
HBQ Total: MLAT Part III .22 p < .028, N=101;
MLAT Index .25 p < .006, N=121.

Correlations with learning strategies. The SILL (Oxford 1989) was the measure of learning strategies used in this study. Based on a factor analysis, it divides language-learning strategies into six factors (memory, cognitive, compensation, metacognitive, affective, and social strategies) and calculates a mean to indicate overall reported level of strategy use. Both the HBQ and the SILL were available for 114 participants.

Inner Boundaries: compensation strategies (guessing from context,
filling knowledge gaps, .20 p < .033).
Outer Boundaries: memory strategies (mnemonics) –.23 p < .014; metacognitive strategies
(planning and evaluation) –.21 p < .023.
Sensitive: social strategies (e.g., studying with others) .22 p < .019;
SILL mean .21 p < .027.
HBQ Total: compensation strategies .23 p < .0225.

Correlations with Affective Variables. To measure affective arousal and differentiate among its various aspects, Ehrman and Oxford compiled a composite questionnaire, the Affective Survey (1991), based on questionnaires by Horwitz (1985, 1986), Campbell (1987), and Gardner (1985b) that addressed components of affect. The Affective Survey includes sections on different kinds of motivation, beliefs, and anxiety. It also provides a score for negatively phrased items that a respondent endorses. Forty-five participants completed both the HBQ and the Affective Survey.

HBQ Inner Boundaries: anxiety about use with native speakers
.33 p < .026; anxiety about competition .41 p < .005:
a total score representing pessimistic beliefs about language
learning .29 p < .056.
Outer Boundaries : no correlations at all with any element of the
Affective Survey.
Interpersonal: negatively phrased motivation items .32 p < .032
Sensitive: negatively phrased motivation items .29 p < .051
HBQ Total: anxiety about competition .45 p < .002;
general discomfort about language learning .32 p < .033.

Faculty ratings of observed anxiety, rated on a scale of 0 (none) to 3 (severe enough to derail training) correlated only with the HBQ scale Unusual Experiences (.26 p < .018, N=82), one of the components of Inner Boundaries. Faculty ratings of extrinsic motivation (vs. intrinsic motivation) correlated –.32 p < .02, N=53, with Impressions of One's Childhood, Adolescence, Adulthood, also a component of Inner Boundaries.

Correlations with Personality Variables. The MBTI was used in two forms. One was the shorter Form G version with the four scales described above in the literature review (Myers and McCaulley 1985). The other was the factor-analysis-based Type Differentiation Indicator (TDI) version (Saunders 1989), with the same four scales, a fifth Comfort–Discomfort composite scale called "Strain"[4], two consistency ("polarity") scores, and 27 subscales, shown in Table 2. Correlations of the four standard MBTI scales with the HBQ are available for 212 respondents, and correlations of the TDI subscales are available for 158 respondents.

Inner Boundaries: Intuition .21 $p < .002$; Perceiving .20 $p < .003$;
Strain .38 $p < .0001$.
Outer Boundaries: Intuition .51 $p < .0001$; Feeling .35 $p < .0001$;
Perceiving .54 $p < .0001$.
Interpersonal: Extraversion -.33 $p < .0001$; Feeling .33 $p < .0001$.
Sensitive with Feeling .35 $p < .0001$ and Strain .23 $p < .003$.
HBQ Total: Intuition .40 $p < .0001$; Feeling .35 $p < .0001$;
Perceiving .39 $p < .0001$; Strain .26 $p < .001$.

The patterning of the MBTI-TDI subscales with the HBQ follows the above pattern closely. Specifics are provided in Table 2.

Correlations with LSP Variables. The National Association of Secondary Schools Principals Learning Styles Profile (LSP) (Keefe et al. 1989) is a composite learning styles inventory with seven cognitive function variables that include such traditional scales as field independence and leveling-sharpening. It also includes a scale for sensory input channel (auditory, visual, emotive-kinesthetic), preferred time of day and physical environment for study, and a few other variables, e.g., persistence. Of the students who completed the HBQ, 121 also completed the LSP.

Cognitive processing variable: HBQ Total: discrimination -.20 $p < .030$.
Inner Boundaries: stiff posture -.30 $p < .001$; dim light -.28 $p < .002$.
Outer Boundaries: stiff posture -.27 $p < .004$; background noise .23 $p < .011$.
Interpersonal: afternoon study, -.22 $p < .018$; high mobility .20 $p < .029$;
upright posture -.22 $p < .014$.
Sensitive: early morning study .22 $p < .016$; dim light -.21 $p < .022$.
Opinions: early morning study .20 $p < .029$; verbal over spatial learning -.28 $p < .002$;
consistency -.20 $p < .032$.
HBQ Total: afternoon study; high mobility .23 $p < .011$; stiff posture -.36 $p < .0001$;
dim light -.27 $p < .002$.

Correlations with end-of-training outcomes. End-of-training outcomes were rated in two ways. One was the formal end-of-training interactive proficiency test, which yields scores for speaking and interactive listening and for reading on a scale from 0 (no knowledge) to 5 (native speaker equivalent). The other rating was done by faculty in an interview with a project staff member to fill in a form that addressed overall percentile as a "good" student relative to other FSI students, observed aptitude percentile, estimation of effort in and out of class, motivation, and observed anxiety or emotional upset. The overall percentile rating was also converted into three *faculty ranking* groups comprising the top and bottom 20% and the middle 60%. Of the students

---

4. This individual TDI Comfort-Discomfort (C/D) subscales are a measure of anxiety. Because the MBTI is administered at the beginning of training, these scales and their composite "Strain" thus represent the anxiety level of students early in their training. On the defiant-compliant subscale, defiant (theoretically Discomfort) students have very slightly better and nearly significant speaking ($r=-.12$ $p<.06$ N-246) and reading ($r=-.12$ p.07 N-244) scores. However, other C/D subscales correlate (but subsignificantly in the expected direction: start of training Discomfort (anxiety) is debilitating.

who took the HBQ, 119 had speaking scores on record, and 118 had reading scores on record.

Inner Boundaries: no correlations with any training outcomes.
Outer Boundaries: speaking .27 p < .003; reading .29 p < .001;
faculty rating of observed learning aptitude .22 p < .056, N=78.
Neat: speaking .31, p < .001; reading .33, p < .0001.
Edges: reading .22, p < .017; faculty ratings of observed aptitude .27 p < .018, N=55. (Neat, Edges, and Abstractions are all scales that are included in Outer Boundaries.)
HBQ Total: speaking .25 p < .007; reading .24, p < .008.

ANOVAS for end-of-training data. Data for all ANOVAs were restricted to beginners who had at least 17 weeks of training.

The HBQ Total differentiated among the lowest 20% based on overall faculty ratings and the other students (F (2, 45) = 3.5032, p < .0385).

The HBQ scale Neat (high scores indicating less preference for order, Outer Boundaries) differentiated between those achieving a score in reading and in speaking of 1 from those who achieved a score of 3 on the end-of-training proficiency test (speaking F (2, 62) = 3.7919, p < 0279; reading F (2, 59) = 3.8485, p < .0269).

Thoughts (permeable boundary between thoughts and feelings, Inner Boundaries) also differentiated between students achieving a tested score of 1 and those achieving the 3 level, but for reading only.

ANOVAs of Inner Boundaries and Outer Boundaries with end-of-training ratings of any sort were not significant.

Variations on the scenario: Cooperative and critical thinking in the literature-based classroom

Virginia Mayer
Padua Academy/University of Delaware

Such proverbs as "actions speak louder than words" and "sticks and stones will break my bones, but words can never hurt me" appear to negate the intrinsic value of organized sound for purposes of transfer of information and especially of human feelings. However, although the validity of these sayings may be questionable, the import is acknowledged not because the word is insignificant but rather because the context is most vital and the word operates within this context.

Conventional Scenario. Allowing the literature of any language its active and cultural function in the classroom is a sound base for the development of the corporate and individual thought process in both written and oral form. Language is movement (Schofer 1990: 326), and its literature is a force that is both continuous and contiguous. Yet, literature seeks activation. Frequently the activator is the individual reading alone, creating his or her own images and feelings as he or she decodes the written text. However, in the classroom the activators are indeed plural, and the experience of literature becomes a shared progression.

These activators, students, the "front-line workers," when given responsibility, are able to create judgments and make appropriate decisions resulting in "enhanced productivity" and "improved quality" (Bonstingl 1992: 68). This observation regarding education and the economy has an appropriate corollary to necessary trends in education, emphasizing cooperative learning and critical thinking. The purpose of this paper is to show the "scenario" in concert with literary-based content, and particularly variations that I have termed the simplified scenario, the surprise scenario, and the symphonic scenario, as a significant tool for cooperative learning, critical thinking, and even contextual competition. Particular scenarios will reflect possibilities, both written and oral, for the study of such works as *Antigone* (Anouilh), *Candide* (Voltaire), *Rene* (Chateaubriand), and *Huis Clos* (Sartre 1947).

The scenario is a combination of juxtaposed role playing, undetermined resolution, and significant debriefing (Di Pietro 1983). It is an interesting and active tool for the production of realistic discourse from a literary base. From a portion of the targeted literature, instructors choose an idea or theme to be treated in the scenario. They then write the roles relative to a problem within the theme. If the class is large, the instructor creates several scenarios concerning the same theme. In writing the roles, the instructors provide information exclusive to that role.

For the scenario, the class is divided into as many groups as there are roles; if there are two scenarios, each with two roles, there will be four groups. The students receive their group's role in written form. Together they assess the requirements of the role; they discuss how they will develop this specific role, what vocabulary they will need, and what strategy they will execute.

After a time specified for preparation of the role, one student is selected from each group to play out the role. The role player may be chosen by an instructor or by the group members. If the same group is maintained for several weeks' duration and multiple scenarios are prepared, it is likely that the students, legitimately imposing fairness, will themselves rotate the role player so that all students have an opportunity to perform.

During the performance, the remainder of each group (the nonperforming members) coaches the acting team member concerning the strategy to use as additional information is revealed through the opposite role. The coaches offer the performer suggestions as required. If the performers are truly perplexed, they may signal a *time out* in order to consult privately with fellow group members. The time out is limited to a minute so as not to severely interrupt the problem-solving process now set in motion. In the best interest of the involvement of all students, the number of time outs is also limited.

If the coaching group is small enough and capable of articulate stage whispers, they may vocalize their suggestions (in the target language) directly to the performer without a time out. Often, the coaching group may be more sagacious and linguistically adept than the performer as the spectators observe the trend of the interaction. Therefore, they may call out suggestions for the discourse in a rather excited fashion. Such enthusiasm for the task has a positive effect; this facilitates the performance and assures linguistic processing for the nonperforming students.

The scenario is played out until some type of resolution occurs, e.g. the settlement of the problem evoked by the differences of agenda generated from the roles. Numerous factors may influence the resolution. One factor is that the language skills of the player, and especially of the performer, may be less significant than one might initially expect; likewise the coaching abilities of the entire group may be relatively insignificant. Another factor is that the personality and persistence of the performers perhaps may be indicative of their real-life dealings. A capable student who is not interested in arguing a point may defer to a less linguistically talented student whose persistence will force the confrontation and thus the discourse. In one form or another, resolution will occur as long as time is sufficient to permit its occurrence. The time required to conclude with resolution is not absolutely predictable.

Using François de Chateaubriand's *Rene* as a literary reference point, we shall describe a specific regular scenario. One of the themes of this *mal du siècle* novel is that of suicide. The following could be used to treat this theme in the target language.

Role A: You have just received a telephone call from the hospital where your daughter is a patient. She apparently tried to commit suicide. You speak with her. She insists you say nothing of this situation. You return to your home to think about it.

Role B: You have a friend who seems down— even sad. She does not go out with her friends anymore. She is withdrawn. You telephone her mother to ask her if she had noted these changes.

When the preparation is finished, the two groups come together; the chosen role players are set to commence. The instructor simply introduces the forthcoming drama as a phone conversation. At the direction of the instructor, the friend initiates the call.

The struggle occurs because the friend (Role B) is attempting to discover more information about the daughter; the mother (Role A), respecting her daughter's request, will respond to the friend's inquiries while still preserving her daughter's privacy. However, another dimension will affect the progression of the discourse: that of emotion. The mother is forced to maintain a calm demeanor as the questions and concerns are posed. The mother may have a greater need to share her feelings as well. It is clear that the performers will need to use various tenses and sentence types in order to carry out the scenario. Also significant will be the numerous strategies and coping mechanisms required to reach a resolution.

There is not a tangible goal for the conclusion of this scenario. One is neither buying nor selling. It is information acquisition that is the asset in dealing with the emotional upheaval of the three lives. The mother may or may not release the ultimate information, but it is obvious that emotions will have to be considered.

The preparation and role playing for this scenario will probably require the hour duration of a given class period. Debriefing will require at least two class periods or more (if the scenario has been especially successful in provoking discussion). The syntactic and morphological debriefing will occupy minimal time and is easily integrated at this level into the content discussion. The content discussion regarding the theme of suicide now has a relevant foundation as both role players and team members can make a better association with the involvement in suicide.

The Simplified Scenario. For the simplified scenario, the entire class is divided into two groups; Roles A and B are respectively assigned. The problem to be resolved is uncomplicated. There is no intentional withholding of information, and intrusions are not anticipated. The following is an example of a simplified scenario:

> **Role A:** You must share the car with your sister, who will be returning from college for a three-week period. You will be negotiating with her about the schedule.
>
> **Role B:** You are returning from the university to work during the winter break. You hope to have rather unlimited access to the second family car, but you understand that some "haggling" with your younger sister will probably occur.

Obviously each role will realize the nature of the negotiations, knowing there must be some sense of justice, but desiring personal advantages relative to the individual's requests and schedules. The chosen players do the necessary negotiating. Because all members of each half of the class have focused on a single obvious goal, one player may commence the scenario, and at the discretion of the facilitator (instructor), another student might continue. In fact, several students might perform in succession until resolution is reached.

The scenario cited might serve as an introduction to spark discussion on chapter eight of *Candide*. Comparisons and contrasts may be made from the function and outcome of the scenario to Voltaire's tongue-in-cheek presentation of negotiating "rights" to Cunegonde.

Another simplified scenario that would facilitate discussion via a certain correlation to the moral debate inherent in *Antigone* might resemble the following. This scenario will serve to familiarize students with the feelings of Antigone as she discovers some truths about her own brother, whose reputation she is so intent on protecting.

> **Role A:** You have an older brother whom you adore. You try to persuade your best friend to date him. She has refused him in the past.
>
> **Role B:** Your best friend is trying to persuade you to date her brother, whom she adores. You know he is involved in drugs and a dangerous cult.

The advantages of the simplified scenario are that it is uncomplicated to write and may be structured much like a debate; that the corporate dynamic is heightened as there is a clarified unification to the content; and that the simplified scenario possibly enlists more actual performers who continue an established role. The disadvantages of the simplified scenario are that the nuances of the discourse may be unnoticed, and thus undeveloped, and that the resolution may be attained more quickly than desired for the pragmatic purpose of linguistic practice.

The Surprise Scenario. The surprise scenario will involve three roles. As in the regular and simplified scenarios, Roles A and B will have a certain goal to achieve. Role C will have an interruptive role. However, Role C may not be totally aware of the interruptive nature of the role while preparing for it. Following the allotted time for preparation, Roles A and B will commence their routes to resolution. At a given point, as the facilitator deems appropriate, the instructor (facilitator) will indicate to Role C his or her entrance into the fray. Now Roles A and B must deal with the intrusion of a third party who presents new, more complex, and hopefully more interesting information. The following illustrates a certain example of this genre.

Role A: You are tired of the urban rat race. You have been in contact with a realtor concerning a lovely pastoral property. Having gathered the information needed, you hope to convince your spouse that a move to the country is both feasible and desirable.

Role B: You have just received a wonderful promotion that assures a bright financial future. However, this promotion will necessitate a move from your suburban home because one of the stipulations of the job is that you live within the city limits. You and your spouse are dining out this evening and you are anxious to share the excitement of the new position and subsequent move.

Role C: You are head waiter of a very exclusive restaurant. Tonight you have the rather awesome task of announcing to your clients that there has been a nuclear disaster at a nearby plant, and that the pollution level has reached hazardous dimensions in the local suburban area from which most of your customers come. The radiation levels are very high, and authorities are advising residents not to return to their homes.

With this scenario one has created a backdrop against which one might discuss the yearnings of Rene for the simple life and the reveries that seem to accompany this idealism versus some of the realities contradicting the idyllic life even in that time frame.

Another three-role scenario patterned from the script of *Huis Clos* might evolve like the one on the next page. Subsequent readings of *Huis Clos*, Scene V, will parallel the scenario, provoking questions resulting from the simulated experience.

Among the advantages of the surprise scenario are the expansion of the number of roles and the resultant additional negotiation requiring more sophisticated reasoning and linguistic maneuvering. The three-tiered discourse now pro-

Role A: You desire to impress a young man while attending a cocktail party where there are only a few guests. Your attentions are quite serious, for you are at least infatuated with this man.

Role B: A young attractive woman makes strong advances toward you during a small party at a friend's home. You find yourself quite attracted to her but choose to preserve a somewhat cool demeanor at least for the moment.

Role C: You are attending a small party where an acquaintance of yours appears to be "throwing herself" at a young man. You find the scene quite vulgar, and in your outspoken manner find yourself mocking her actions directly to this acquaintance.

duces a "multidimensional" argument and enhances both the thought process and necessary verbal code as it addresses not only the "proper answer to a question, but often the nature of the question itself" (Paul 1992: 62). As a result of the leveling, new ideas are formed; new possibilities are explored uniting the development of both structure and "content" in simultaneous activity.

One disadvantage to the surprise scenario is that less-capable role players for A and B might not be able to assimilate the additional problem, thus causing a breakdown and/or gap that may actually harm the communicative process to such a degree that serious reparation would be necessary to salvage the event.

The Symphonic Scenario. The symphonic scenario is one in which there will be multiple roles, strong progressive developments, and even change of venue as there is a continuation and sequence to the initial conflict. Like its musical counterpart, there are movements and variations prior to the conclusion and building toward it.

The first two roles will begin the scenario; at the discretion of the facilitator, Role C enters the piece. In this particular scenario the additions of Roles D and E will depend largely on the actions and debate of this third role. Experience has shown that Role C usually arrests the party B. Therefore Roles D and E will usually play their parts. Since it is Role D who will most likely assign the verdict, this is usually the role who secures resolution. Role E usually serves as a summary of the entire situation. However, it is also quite possible that Role E might even serve to reopen the case if certain questions were asked that revealed new information. Also possible might be a confrontation of Roles A and/ or B with Role E. Subroles may also be created to support the primary ones. They would play matching verbal instruments to those of the main roles (e.g. lawyers for the roles A and B, camera operator for the reporter, recorder in the court, and so on). The symphony will play itself out.

Advantages to the symphonic scenario are that a maximum number of students are able to be the front-line role players, that the progression includes vertical as well as linear activity, and that the progression takes students to

Role A: You belong to an animal-rights organization. As an active protest you, with your colleagues, knowing that certain authorities will be watching, stage a "trap the traps" in which you attempt to destroy fifty traps that feed to a well-known furrier.

Role B: You work as a lookout for a large furrier company. Animal-rights activists are known to be in the area, and it is your job to prevent destruction of your company's equipment.

Role C: You are the district sheriff in an area containing miles of woodlands where animals are trapped and subsequently sold to a large furrier in the area. Today you receive a call from the lookouts of this company indicating that a left-wing group attempting to save the animals has been destroying equipment.

Role D: You are a state judge presiding over a case where several animal-rights activists have been accused of destroying equipment belonging to a large furrier.

Role E: You are a reporter for a local newspaper. Today you are assigned to cover the trial involving several animal-rights activists accused of destroying equipment belonging to a furrier in the area.

various "locations" and it layers the action linguistically and socially.

The most significant disadvantage is that if either Role A or B is exceedingly passive, they may terminate the discourse through a weak and early concession. A minor disadvantage to the symphonic scenario is that preparation and presentation usually require more than the hour of a normal class time. Thus, the instructor must impress on the students the importance of not discussing their roles with fellow classmates outside of class so that plot and ending do not become preplanned.

The scenario just cited can be an appropriate introduction and/or review of the study of *Antigone*. Students will find a contemporary corollary on which to base judgments, draw conclusions, and offer possibilities. The examination of the relevance of Antigone has become living literature.

That the thrust of cooperative learning as a method to, among other goals, increase the critical-thinking skills of students is widely accepted, if not practiced. Cooperative learning is not an innovation of current educational calculation. A good portion of our early learning involves cooperative learning. One may witness siblings in action and little friends playing to see how it works—and sometimes how it does not. Learning does not occur in a vacuum, and no subject matter to be learned, mastered, or acquired is as comfortable as foreign language with cooperative learning. Implicit in language is communication within the realm of the cooperative learning domain.

Cooperative Learning for Critical Thinking. If the essence of cooperative learning is to work with a colleague in order to solve a problem, simultaneously increasing the corporate and individual capabilities, then the scenario is a stellar tool for the implementation of this essence. Students work as a team in order to organize strategy for performance; they support and assist a spokesperson and plot new verbal routes.

Syntax becomes pragmatically essential; vocabulary is internalized. Classroom experience has indicated that although students will temporarily retain fewer words than they would from the conventional vocabulary list, they will incorporate more into a durable vocabulary.

From the oral execution of the scenario assignment, both group and individual progress may be further assessed with a written task, which might include a paragraph summary, analysis, or script for a complete theatrical production.

Since it appears that a primary goal of cooperative learning devices is to "teach" critical and even creative thinking skills, it is important to examine the scenario in this realm. Acknowledging that "surrounding any line of thought is a large substructure of background thought" (Paul 1992: 61), the scenario can create the basis for these "background connections" (Paul 1992: 61) in L2 so that a relationship may be linked with the literary text and so that critical thinking about the text will be feasible in L2. A cooperative learning approach fells the "primary barrier to higher order thinking skills programs ... the accepted orientation of teachers to cover or dispense knowledge rather than to work with it" (Young 1992: 49), since any knowledge dispensed by the instructor is for the purpose of immediate incorporation into the problem-solving situation.

The definitions of critical thinking skills are multiple. A singular definition is illusive and perhaps should remain so. Critical thinking, after all, is a rather fluid matter. While it is true that a unique definition is not established, the agreement that "problem solving abilities or cognitive enhancement" (Hunter 1991: 73) can be taught is the positive factor influencing our daily pedagogy. I would like to use five workable categories for our definition of critical thinking. First is the obvious *identification* of the problem, concern, situation, theme, etc. Second is the *reaction* to the problem, whether it be algebraic, social, or philosophical. Third is the *sustenance* of thought and action vis-à-vis the problem. This ingredient will necessitate both discipline and wit. Fourth will be the *projections* and *possibilities* concerning the problem. Fifth will be the *resolution* to the problem based on the choice secured from the integration of the first four considerations. Accepting this structure of a working plan for facilitating critical and even creative thinking within the contained literature-based classroom, the scenario is a crucial tool for delivery.

For too long, literature was either a separate entity from the early language-classroom experience or not dealt with until "advanced" levels. Current trends place more emphasis on language in and from literature in the primary grades in the students' first language (Laughlin and Swisher 1990: ix). Thus the literature is enlivened, critical thinking is produced within its exposure, and the scenario well-coordinates objectives.

Role players identify the problem on numerous levels in the scenario; They react to their discovery; they sustain the verbal struggle by working through a maze of material discovery and language nuances. Within the group, the players discuss possibilities for negotiation. Corporate critical and creative thinking is occasioned. Resolution is secured. It is to be noted that resolution is not synonymous with solution. Other possibilities exist because there are always other scenarios: "Eh bien ... continuons" (Sartre 1947: 76).

When compared to traditional dialogue, enactment of a preplanned situation or nonexperience-based discussion, the simplified, surprise, and symphonic scenarios incorporate the best ideals of the cooperative learning devices while facilitating a schema for enhancing critical-thinking skills. Arthur Costa (1985: xii) parallels thinking to "strenuous movement" and then asserts that instruction does provoke the human thought process to become simultaneously broader and yet more focused, generated more spontaneously and yet "more metaphorically abstract and insightfully divergent." He adds that such "refinement requires practice, concentration and coaching." *Voilà*: The variations on the scenario for the study of literature is a formidable inclusive pedagogy.

REFERENCES

Anouilh, Jean. 1947. *Antigone*. Paris: La Table Ronde.

Bonstingl, John Jay. 1992. "The Total Quality Classroom." *Educational Leadership* 49(6): 68–70.

Chateaubriand, Rene. 1962. *Atala-Rene*. Paris: Garnier Freres.

Costa, Arthur. 1985. *Developing Minds: A Resource Book for Teaching Thinking*. Alexandria, Va.: Association for Supervision and Curriculum Development.

Di Pietro, Robert. 1983. "Unpredictability in Conversational Discourse." Lacus Meeting, August.

Hunter, Eagar. 1991. "Focus on Critical Thinking Skills across the Curriculum." *NASSP Bulletin*. 72–74.

Laughlin, Mildred, and Claudia Swisher. 1990. *Literature based reading*. Phoenix: Oryx Press.

Paul, Richard. 1992. *Critical thinking: Foundation for critical thinking*.

Sartre, Jean-Paul. 1947. *Huis Clos*. Paris: Editions Gallimard.

Schofer, Peter. 1990. "Literature and Communicative Competence: A springboard for the development of critical thinking and aesthetic appreciation or literature in the land of language." *Yonkers: Foreign Language Annals* 23 (September).

Voltaire. 1968. Candide. New York: Oxford University Press.

Young, Lynne. 1992. "Critical Thinking Skills: Definitions Implications for Implementation." *NASSP Bulletin*.

How is strategic memorable? How memorable is "strategic"?

Earl W. Stevick
Lexington, Virginia

Introduction. "Come," says the writer of Ecclesiasticus in his best-known quote, "Come, let us praise those who have become famous. Some of them held sway over kingdoms, some were sage counselors, some composed music or wrote poetry, or were wealthy, and so they won fame in their own generation. There are others," the writer continues, "who are unremembered. But," he assures us, "the unremembered do not include our forebears, for they were people of loyalty and good deeds—people who handed on to us a precious inheritance." Loyalty, good deeds, and a precious inheritance. Remember these.

This year the Georgetown University Round Table on Languages and Linguistics remembers Bob Di Pietro. Bob was the kind of scholar every profession needs more of. He was one who learned from those with the big names, as Ecclesiasticus would have said—but also from those around him, and who responded to them creatively, and then he passed on what he had learned—he made it available to those who otherwise might have had no name, who might otherwise have been forgotten. He made it easier for them to do things worth remembering. Good deeds indeed!

My earliest memories of Bob Di Pietro go back to this same campus, to earlier sessions of GURT or to other professional meetings here, and to the discussion periods that followed the papers. There was one fellow who almost always had a question for the speaker, and that was Bob. Even when others held back, Bob was there to get things started. This was a guy who was eager to learn from everyone—a humble guy who never hesitated to admit he didn't know, if only he thought there was a chance of finding out.

I also remember an opportunity I once had to visit the program at the University of Delaware—a program that had been largely inspired, directed, and generally nursed along under Bob's tutelage. I remember the vitality of that program, and its originality—its combination of freshness and responsibility. To paraphrase one of Bob's dicta about learners (1987: 20), I saw proof that "teachers do not need to lose their creativity in course design through the need to conform to accreditation requirements." But I remember also the very apparent spirit of cooperation and mutual respect among the members of that faculty. Surely Bob had a hand in all this, too. Good deeds again. And on the very first page of his 1987 book, Bob commented on how good it is "to have a friend or two by your side." Beyond all those good deeds, I remember Bob as a kind and loyal friend.

On page 3 of his book, Bob said that "we could go on to conjecture about the psychological forces that are put into play" in any strategic interaction. I'd like to spend the rest of our time today doing just that—talking in some detail about one aspect of the professional inheritance Bob left to us—about the most conspicuous part of that inheritance, which as you know was something he called Strategic Interaction (SI). I'm sure everyone who's here today is well familiar with what SI is about, but just for the record, let me first give my own summary of it as I understand it.

The Strategic Interaction Method. To begin with, Di Pietro recounted the experience of a friend of his who, being in Cairo with very meager control of the Arabic language, had been faced with a plumbing emergency which she handled by somehow piecing together an Arabic sentence that meant "There's water on the bathroom floor!" Not only did she come up with the sentence for the occasion, but she could still remember it 20 years later. "There is no doubt," concludes Di Pietro, "that her success in communicating with the desk clerk helped to fix the utterance forever in her mind" (3). (Page numbers in parentheses in this section are from Di Pietro 1987.)

Taking into account experiences like this one, Di Pietro designed Strategic Interaction as a method that would "value intensity of target-language use over frequency" of use (39). Intensity, in turn, comes from what Di Pietro called "dynamic" (vii) or "dramatic" (3) tension. And tension comes from uncertainty as to how, or even whether, one's own goals will be met (1).

In summary, then, Di Pietro told us that we should reverse the traditional idea that students learn a language in order to use it. "No," he said, "it is as users of the new language that people become *learners* of it" (viii). More shocking than that, he asserted that we can actually help our students to make that reversal!

Di Pietro might have used these ideas as the basis for a neat technique or two, perhaps even for some dazzling demonstrations. But he was convinced that "the dramatic nature of human interactions can be the key to addressing all of the essentials [of language] without having to make each one explicit at all times" (3), and so he had the courage to follow this principle "long and far," as Diller once put it (1978: 70), and to construct a whole method on it, but avoiding the aridity and oversimplification that Diller was criticizing.

Now, anyone who sets out to design a method based on the ideas I've outlined in the last few minutes is going to have to deal with three questions. The most pressing of these three questions is surely "Where is all this dramatic tension to come from?"

Di Pietro's answer to this question about tension begins with careful selection of situations in which learners are likely to want to use the language someday. Let me make four comments about this, though:

- Building lessons around situations is of course as old as the language-teaching profession and has been used in countless existing textbooks.
- This has ordinarily led to the very sequence that Di Pietro was trying to replace: It's led to learning in order to use, rather than to learning through using.
- Asking students to simply memorize and reproduce dialogues for these situations would lead more to tedium rather than to tension; or, as I used to put it (Stevick 1981, chapter 2), too much control by teacher and textbook, and virtually no initiative on the part of the students.
- On the other hand, asking students to simply improvise within generally described situations often requires too much initiative from students compared to the amount of structuring or control on the part of the teacher. The kind of tension this is likely to lead to is academic tension, which draws on a reservoir of equally academic motivation, and which is largely counterproductive.

Di Pietro's answer to this dilemma was to hand out two or more sets of instructions concerning whatever situation he had selected. Some students received briefings from the point of view of the seller, or the landlord, or the hairdresser, or whoever. Others were briefed as buyers or tenants or customers and so forth. And into the two sets of briefings or instructions was built some conflict—some conflict of perception or of interest. Now as we know, the use of conflicting instructions is also not new. I saw Eleanor Jorden doing it in the Japanese program at the Foreign Service Institute in the 1960s, and I heard about something similar from Kent Sutherland in California a few years later.

But where Jorden was using conflicting instructions as a vehicle for applying what had first been learned audiolingually, Di Pietro zoomed in on this device and made it the vehicle for the learning process itself. The name he gave to these sets of instructions was "scenarios." In scenarios, teacher control and student initiative are balanced. Students are now using language in order to reach goals in an uncertain world, and this is apparently what Di Pietro meant by "strategic." As a result, scenarios do not constitute a drain on the students' limited supplies of narrowly academic motivation. Rather, scenarios actually produce a supply of more broadly personal motivation—a kind of motivation that's more akin to what students will be working with in the future outside of class.

Scenarios, then, were Di Pietro's answer to the question about sources of motivation. Around scenarios, Di Pietro designed a three-phase format. The second and central phase of this format consisted of extemporaneous performance of the scenarios.

Another question that faced Di Pietro in turning his insight into a method was "What is to be the relationship between teacher and students?" In most methods, the teacher is presenter, model, director, and evaluator. In SI, by contrast, the teacher is at various times all of these but also functions as coach, consultant, and observer. Students are generally assumed to be receivers, copiers, directed, and evaluated. In SI, they also have additional functions: as role-players, as seekers of advice but also as advice givers, as performers, and as interested observers (21).

The third question that Di Pietro had to deal with was "What other kinds of techniques will fit into this method?" His answer was apparently "Everything!": Everything from free elicitation to existing textbooks, from unconscious absorption of pronunciation and grammar to explicit discussion of them, from monolingual communication to translation when needed—pretty much "the works."

The answers to these second and third questions are embodied in the first and third phases of Di Pietro's format. In the rehearsal phase, groups of students assemble, organize, and rehearse the resources that their representatives are going to be drawing on in the second, the performance phase. In the third phase (the debriefing phase), students and teacher together recall what has just been done in the performance phase, and critique it, and ask questions about it, and generally process the experience so that elements from that experience will be more readily available for use in future scenarios.

The memorability of "strategic." So much for an overview of what to me are the high points of Strategic Interaction. Now to my announced topic: "How is strategic memorable, and how memorable is 'strategic'?"

I'm going to take the two questions of my title in reverse order. The second question is "How memorable is (Di Pietro's use of the word) 'strategic'?" I've often said, sometimes in public (Stevick 1990a), that the word "strategy" is one of the most variously and least precisely used words in our business. Di Pietro provides a welcome exception. Already on the opening page of his preface he tells us that "strategic" interaction is interaction that is carried out "artfully" in pursuit of one's goals. And by "goals" he means very much what we mean by goals in everyday English: He means our constant need to handle the unexpected, in interpersonal situations where the outcome is uncertain.

So in my view, Di Pietro's use of the word "strategic" was definitely memorable. Having said that, I'd like to spend the rest of our time today on the first half of my subtitle: "How is strategic memorable?" This is short for "How is what happens in a Strategic Interaction course memorable to the students?"

Memorability and Strategic Interaction. As a preliminary step to finding out how SI is memorable, we need to be clear in our view of "memory" and how "it" works. This is an aspect of the created order that I've been exploring for quite a few years now. Let me take a few minutes to share with you a view of memory that's somewhat different from the one I held in *Memory, Meaning and Method* (1976). I think it's also different from the views of memory that are implied in much that we still read in publications on language pedagogy today.

Two terminologies. The best-known terminology on the subject of memory is certainly the distinction between so-called short-term memory (STM) and so-called long-term memory (LTM). Instead of STM, many writers these days prefer the term "working memory" (WM), and some writers have divided LTM into two separate parts, which we can call "temporary memory" (TM) and "permanent memory" (PM).

But for our purposes today, I'd like to go one step further, and replace these three terms (WM, TM, PM) with metaphors. My reason for selecting metaphors instead of more standard labels is not that I just want to brighten up my presentation. I'm well aware of the dangers inherent in the use of metaphors or any other figures of speech (Stevick 1990b, chapter 3). But I'm even more concerned about the dangers of such expressions as "short-term memory," "working memory," and the like. Such expressions, it seems to me, can be even more treacherous than metaphors are, mostly because they're less conspicuous. They can very easily become nominalizing reifications, which is my private polysyllabic way of saying that they obscure complexity by giving it a name. If, however, you'd prefer the standard terms, then you're very welcome to substitute them.

The metaphor that I'm going to use instead of WM is "the worktable" (the WT). Now, it's true that the WT (or WM, if you prefer) is a concept closely related to our old friend STM. There are, however, at least three important differences between STM and WM or the WT. One difference is that STM was a stage—a stage through which information passed on its way to LTM. The WT, on the other hand, is really not a stage, but a state—a biologically describable state. A second difference is that with STM, we were mainly interested in what passes through it. With the WT, we are mainly concerned with what happens on it. Third, the very name "short-term" memory focuses on limited duration—on the 20 seconds or so that new material, freshly arrived from the eyes or the ears, can remain freely and directly available for processing. With the WT, we are more interested in its limited capacity—in the fact that only a relatively small amount of information can be in the WT-state at any one time (Klatzky 1984: chapter 2).

Now let's look at the other familiar concept, LTM. By process of elimination, the expression LTM has meant pretty much "whatever remains available in memory after the expiration of the 20 seconds or so that STM supposedly lasts." As we all know, however, some things that are available longer than 20 seconds are in fact available years and even decades later. This is what the term PM refers to. In the metaphor that I'd like to use today, such material is "in the files" (F).

But we also know all too well that other things—things that were still clearly available in memory after 20 seconds or even after 20 minutes—are gone a day or two later. This sort of everyday experience is what the concept called TM is about. Metaphorically, I'll say that such material is "on top of the filing cabinet." It's there at hand; it's ready to be fitted into the files; but it's also subject to being knocked off onto the floor and lost.

Now with regard to the contents of these metaphorical "files," I think it's important to remember that the content of the "files," or LTM, or whatever you want to call it, consists of an almost unimaginable variety of different kinds of information. The kinds we think about first are of course visual and auditory, perhaps with the rest of the so-called five senses thrown in for good measure. In fact, however, there are at least three other kinds of information that simply must be mentioned in this connection. One is information about time, and time of course includes its own diversities: how long ago something happened, how long it lasted, whether it changed while we were watching it or hearing it, and how frequent it's been in our experience. A second additional type of information that's included in the "files" has to do with one's own purposes. And the third type has to do with whatever emotions may have accompanied an experience. In fact, a few writers seem to believe that "memories" are organized around purposes, or emotions, or some combination of both (Schank 1982, Gliner and Gliner 1984). I'm betting today that these writers are correct in this belief.

A further essential point has to do with how all these various kinds of information are stored, and here's where my metaphor of "files" breaks down,because memories are not stored in discrete packets, like a stack of papers in a folder. Rather, they are stored in networks of associations. I'd like to mention six important characteristics of these networks.

1. They are hierarchical. That is to say, they contain items of varying degrees of abstractness and specificity.
2. The items in storage vary continuously. They are not just there or not-there. Each item is at any given time at one or another level of activation, along a continuum.
3. The networks are dynamic. This means that when a message from the senses, or from the WT, activates a particular set of items in the files, activation spreads to other items in the files with which the first items were associated, and from that second set to further sets, and so on. The result is typically a new configuration of items whose level of

activation has been raised high enough to register back on the WT.

4. The spreading of activation through the files is not quite instantaneous, each step does take a certain amount of clock time, but that amount of time is measured in hundredths of a second. This means that there's enough time, while an item is on the WT, for many round trips between the WT and the files, so that a lot can be done from the item, with the item, and to the item. This concept of "spreading activation" among items or units is very widely cited in memory studies these days (Graf, Squire, and Mandler 1984, Klatzky 1985: 18, Nelson and Schmid 1989: 539, Sampson 1987, Johnson 1991).
5. The spreading of activation is an automatic process; it goes on by itself, and it goes on without conscious control. This means that the spreading of activation within the files creates responses, but that the activity of creating those responses does not use up limited capacity the way activity on the WT uses it up. (For a helpful treatment of capacity limits as they affect language learning, see McLaughlin 1987, chapter 6).
6. The strengths of the associations among items are also not a yes-or-no matter. That is, one can't say simply that Items A and B of information either "are" or "are not" connected. These strengths vary along a continuum, and they change as a result of experience.

One of the nice things about viewing long-term storage in terms of the spreading of activation throughout dynamic networks is that we don't have to make an absolute and qualitative distinction between TM and PM. It's my guess—and this guess is central to what I'm saying today—that those items that show the characteristics of being "in PM" are items that participate in rich and complex networks, and particularly in networks that include distinctive items of purpose or emotion or both. Such networks are likely to result from settings and experiences of the kinds that Krashen says "acquisition" is likely to occur in. Similarly, the networks responsible for producing items "from TM" may be relatively simple networks, with not-very-distinctive components of purpose or emotion. These are typical products of the settings in which "learning" (in Krashen's sense) usually takes place.

How information gets to the worktable. In the view I've been developing with you today, the direct source of whatever forms one produces is not LTM, but the WT. And there are three sources from which information about what to say and how to say it can reach the WT.

INFORMATION CAN REACH THE WT FROM THE SENSES. For example, one is producing forms largely in this way when one is doing mimicry-memorization, or the simplest of drills. The advantage of producing from sensory input is that the forms that are being produced are to some extent under conscious management, whether by the learner or by the teacher. The disadvantage in depending on sensory input for the production of forms is of course that you can't depend on it: The content of the WT is constantly being replaced by other content. The Rehearsal and Performance phases of SI allow for lots of sensory input both in the form of props and in the form of long-muscle activities.

INFORMATION CAN REACH THE WT FROM PM (FROM "DOWN IN THE FILES"). Remember that information in PM is information that participates in rich and complex networks of associations, and particularly in associations with important material such as purposes and emotions.

One is producing from PM when one is speaking fluently and with focus on what one is trying to say, rather than on how one needs to say it. This is reminiscent of the products of what Krashen and others have been calling "acquired competence" in contrast to "learned competence."

The advantage of producing primarily from PM is that the content of PM is largely automatic, so that access to it is easy, quick, and usually accurate. Access to what is in PM makes minimal demands on the limited capacity of the WT, which can then be occupied with other concerns. The disadvantage in depending on PM for the production of forms in an SL is that, by the very fact that it is an SL, the content of one's PM in the SL is often inadequate for one's needs.

In planning, rehearsing, and performing an SI scenario, students are required to draw on the full range of the nonverbal information in their PMs—visual, auditory, esthetic, purposive, and all the rest—and they bring these kinds of items to the WT for association with new linguistic forms. Because an SI scenario by its very nature has people working partly in the dark, and with partially conflicting goals, the important purposive category is certain to be well represented.

INFORMATION CAN REACH THE WT FROM TM (FROM "ON TOP OF THE FILING CABINET"). One is producing from the relatively simple and undistinctive networks of TM when one recalls what was on the other side of a vocabulary card, or when one recalls the word or sentence that a certain actor used in a certain scene in the movie one saw last week, for example.

One is also producing from relatively simple networks, which have little that is distinctive either in sensory experience or in purpose or feeling, when one is applying an explicit rule. All these applications of simple, undistinctive networks are reminiscent of what Krashen tells us we are able to do with "learned competence." An advantage of producing from TM is that, to some extent at least, one can control what goes into it. One can exert this control by rote repetition, or by practicing two things side-by-side so that one of them will bring the other to mind, by mnemonics, or in other ways. The disadvantages in depending on TM for the production of forms are that information in TM is subject to crowding and to dissipation (which we don't have time to talk about today); and that getting something out of TM requires more time—more round trips to and fro between TM and the WT—than access to PM does; and that this access depletes the capacity of the WT.

This means that one way of improving one's command of a language is to "stockpile" forms from it by means of conventional academic learning—carefully selecting forms that one expects to encounter soon in settings that will be rich and distinctive. This kind of activity showed up in the practice of some of the gifted language learners I interviewed some years ago (Stevick 1989, especially chapter 6). People apparently differ widely in how much material they can successfully "stockpile" in this way, and for how long (Stevick 1989: chapter 6).

In the Rehearsal phase of SI, students have the opportunity to forge associative networks that are relatively simple, but that they themselves have designed with an eye to making available some of the things they think they'll be needing in the more demanding activities of the Performance phase. Then, in the Performance phase itself, this material is supplied by TM and placed on the WT alongside items of affect and of purpose, and alongside material from the existing complex and rich networks of PM. In this way, the contents—even the structure—of PM is modified. At the same time, however, the results of this interaction become new parts of TM.

Finally, during the Debriefing phase, the new associations that were formed during Performance are available from TM to be connected further with whatever descriptions or summaries or even drills may come out during the Debriefing phase of SI. The results enter TM and will be available for further scenarios (or for other language use) within the hours and perhaps even the days that follow.

Overall, then, the multi-phase Scenario of SI seems to provide plenty of opportunities for the strengths of the WT, TM, and PM to be taken advantage of. But the Scenario also allows the weaknesses of each of these three aspects of memory—the WT, TM, and PM—to be made up for by the other two.

The generation effect and the spacing effect. Now let's look again at "memory," and this time let's consider how new information gets into TM. The best-known way is by repetition while it's still on the WT—what the psychologists call "rehearsal." This was of course the mainstay of the dialogue memorization and of the massive structure drills in audiolingualism. But it was also assumed in the paradigm recital of even more traditional methods.

There is however a second way into TM: a rather interesting one that gets mentioned frequently these days in the experimental literature. This is called the "generation effect." "The generation effect" is not a thing. It's just a noun phrase, but it is a phrase that some writers have been using recently to stand for their observations in a number of rather interesting laboratory experiments. In each of these experiments, the subjects in the control group were given some kind of information. The subjects in the experimental group were required to put together (to "generate") the same kind of information—or at least part of the same information—for themselves in their own heads. Then the subjects were given some sort of task that would measure some aspect of their "memory" for the information.

Just what was generated and how it was generated varied widely from one experiment to another:

- a meaning, expressed as a mental picture, that connects two or more words (Dickel and Slak 1983, Wall and Routowicz 1987);
- a whole word, from the printed word with half of its letters missing (Rabinowitz 1990); or from only one letter plus a hint about meaning (Slamecka and Graf 1978); or from a spoken or written word that is more or less blurred (Hirshmann and Mulligan 1991);
- a native-language "keyword" that will serve in the learner's mind to connect the form of a foreign word with its meaning (Atkinson 1975).

The results turned out to vary with the task. Certain tasks required subjects to know what had happened to go with what, and when. This kind of information is apparently held onto for short periods (TM) fairly easily, but it's less likely to be available permanently. For these tasks, subjects also needed conscious recollection of some part of the study experience. The three most common of these tasks were:

- CUED RECALL OF PAIRED ASSOCIATES: "During the study part of this experiment, you met some pairs of words. Here's one of those words. What was the other word that went with this word?" In FL study, this is like the question "Here's a word that was on one side of a vocabulary card. What was the word on the other side?" Being able to come up with a quick, clear, and accurate answer to these questions can be quite useful to learners by allowing them to benefit from last night's hour with the vocabulary cards.
- FREE RECALL: "During study you met a list of words. Now please give as many of those words as you can." Compare, in our field, "What was in the text that we were supposed to prepare for today?" Prompt and dependable answers here enable one to benefit from what one read or heard last night—or ten minutes ago.
- RECOGNITION: "During study you met a list of words. Here's a word.

> Was this word part of that list?" Our students often have to ask themselves "Am I supposed to know this word?" Recognition or lack of recognition tells one whether it might be worthwhile to continue to try to remember more about that particular word or its meaning.

The results were quite striking. In all three of these tasks—in cued recall, free recall, and recognition—the subjects who had put things together for themselves consistently performed better than the subjects who had had the material given to them (Allen and Jacoby 1991: 270, 272, Gardiner and Parkin 1990: 579, Gardiner and Java 1990: 28, Parkin, Reid, and Russo 1990: 510f., Wall and Routowicz 1987: 1019).

Looking now at SI, SI provides for an extraordinary amount of generating, most conspicuously in its rehearsal phase. Here, with the support—and with the nudging—of the scenario, students have to come up not only with their own lexical meanings but also with their own purposes; not only with their own words and phrases but also with their own discourse structures. Nor should we forget the flexible and supportive role of the SI teacher, which gives rise to more and better generating on the part of the students. Metaphorically speaking, the SI teacher tries to keep the WT steady and to avoid throwing irrelevant or distracting new material onto it. So three cheers for SI and the generation effect!

But don't mortgage the farm and put it all on the generation effect. There are other kinds of tasks—other measures of "memory"—on which the results came out just the opposite from what happened with cued and free-recall tasks and with recognition. On these tasks, the subjects who had "generated" the information did less well with it than the subjects who had merely seen it or heard it. These are tasks that measure what is sometimes called "perceptual fluency" (Allen and Jacoby 1990, Fendrich, Healy, and Bourne 1991, Gardiner and Java 1990, Johnstone, Hawley, and Elliott 1991). I can best explain what this term means by telling you how "perceptual fluency" is measured. One favorite method is through use of a tachistoscope, which flashes words on the screen for very short but variable periods of time. The experimenter notes the shortest exposure that leads to identification of the word. In another method for measuring perceptual fluency, words are shown in partially smudged or obscured form, which gradually clears up. The experimenter notes the degree of clarity that the subject needs in order to identify the word. (Johnstone, Hawley and Elliott 1991: 210).

But what, you may ask, is the relation between tachistoscopes and other specialized viewing equipment used in psychology labs, and what goes on in language study? I would suggest to you that there's a very strong relationship. What really comes in through our senses off a printed page, what really helps us to get the meaning of what we read, for example, doesn't really consist of words or letters. It consists of much smaller dots and lines and angles and curves, and it's from these—actually, it's from only a random sampling of these—that our minds form the letters and the words. "Perceptual fluency" means ease and speed in recognizing the word from relatively few of its components. So the greater a learner's perceptual fluency for a particular word, the less time and capacity that word will require on the WT, and the more time and capacity will be available for dealing with other matters.

Now, what seems to promote perceptual fluency? Not surprisingly, it turns out to be mainly repeated exposure (as I've been finding out in recent months in the process of reviving my college German using *Deutsche Welle* and the monthly audio magazine *Schau ins Land)*. And, what is especially interesting from our point of view as language teachers, the effect of repeated exposure on perceptual fluency was even more marked in experiments that used nonwords (that is, unfamiliar forms) than it was in experiments that used familiar native-language words (Johnstone, Hawley and Elliott 1991: 210).

Here again, SI shows up very well. The same words that students generated (and quite probably even repeated) within the rehearsal phase come up again and again in the performance and the debriefing phases.

There's just one more phenomenon from experimental psychology that I'd like to relate SI to, and that's the familiar distributed-practice effect, also called the spacing effect. This effect has been known for a long time, and it's described in the literature as "robust." A pedagogical application of it was systematically incorporated into the series of readers that we used in freshman German over 50 years ago (Bond 1953). The idea was that all the instances of a new word were not all bunched up together, but that we would learn the word better if there was a certain amount of time and some intervening context between successive occurrences—provided the time between the occurrences was not too long. In the terms I've been using today, we were working with words that had not yet become parts of our PM. In the meantime, a previous occurrence could help in recognizing a new occurrence, but if and only if that previous occurrence was still in TM. And finding the word in successive, related, but slightly different contexts increased the "richness and complexity" of the networks that would be needed for recognizing or producing the word in the future. This moves the word closer to the state where we say it's finally "in PM." Yet again, SI provides for lots of recurrences, at intervals that are irregular, but that are well within the span of TM.

Summary. I've tried to do two things today. I've taken a close look at Bob Di Pietro's Strategic Interaction methodology, and I've shown some of the ways I think it helps learners to hold on to pieces of the new language. But I've also sketched a three-part view of memory (WM, TM, PM)—a view that sees remembering not as action but as interaction—as rapid, recursive, and multidirectional interaction, rather than as a unidirectional flow to and through STM and LTM.

This sketch is clearly preliminary and tentative, but I hope it will be provocative. At least it's more up-to-date than what I wrote 17 years ago! And who knows what will need to be said 17 years from now?

REFERENCES

Allen, Scott W., and Larry L. Jacoby. 1990. "Reinstating study context produces unconscious influences of memory." *Memory and Cognition* 10(3): 270–278.

Atkinson, R. C. 1975. "Mnemotechnics in second language learning." *American Psychologist* 30(8): 821–828.

Bond, Otto F. 1953. *The reading method: An experiment in college French*. Chicago: University of Chicago Press.

Chafe, Wallace L. 1973. "Language and memory." *Language* 49(2): 261–281.

Dickel, M. J., and S. Slak. 1983. "Imagery vividness and memory for verbal material." *Journal of Mental Imagery* 7(1): 121–126.

Diller, Karl. 1978. *The language teaching controversy*. Rowley, Mass.: Newbury House.

Di Pietro, Robert J. 1987. *Strategic interaction*. New York: Cambridge University Press.

Dulay, Heidi, Marina Burt, and Stephen D. Krashen. 1982. *Language two*. New York: Oxford University Press.

Ervin, F. R., and T. Andrews. 1970. "Normal and pathological memory: Data and perceptual scheme." In Francis O. Schmitt (ed.), *The neurosciences*. New York: Rockefeller University Press. 163–173.

Fendrich, David W., Alice F. Healy, and Lyle E. Bourne, Jr. 1991. "Long-term repetition effects for motoric and perceptual procedures." *Journal of Experimental Psychology: Learning, Memory and Cognition* 17(1): 137–151.

Gardiner, John M., and Rosalind I. Java. 1990. "Recollective experience in word and nonword recognition." *Memory and Cognition* 18(1): 23–30.

Gardiner, John M., and Alan J. Parkin. 1990. "Attention and recollective experience in recognition memory." *Memory and Cognition* 18(6): 579–583.

Gliner, J. A., and G. S. Gliner. 1984. "Use of multidimensional scaling of imagery in assessing the organization of environmental stresses in memory." *Journal of Mental Imagery* 8(2): 45–56.

Graf, P., L. R. Squire, and G. Mandler. 1984. "The information that amnesic patients do not forget." *Journal of Experimental Psychology: Learning, Memory and Cognition* 10(1): 164–178.

Hirshman, Elliott, and Neil Mulligan. 1991. "Perceptual interference improves explicit memory but does not enhance data-driven processing." *Journal of Experimental Psychology: Learning, Memory, and Cognition* 17(3): 507–513.

Johnson, George. 1991. *In the palaces of memory*. New York: Knopf.

Johnstone, William A., Kevin J. Hawley, and John M. G. Elliott. 1991. "Contribution of perceptual fluency to recognition judgments." *Journal of Experimental Psychology: Learning, Memory, and Cognition* 17(2): 210–223.

Klatzky, Roberta L. 1984. *Memory and awareness: An information-processing perspective*. New York: W. H. Freeman.

McLaughlin, Barry. 1987. *Theories of second language learning*. London: Edward Arnold.

Nelson, Gayle, and Thomas Schmid. 1989. "ESL reading: Schema theory and standardized texts." *TESOL Quarterly* 23(3): 539–543.

Parkin, Alan J., Thomas K. Reid, and Riccardo Russo. 1990. "On the differential nature of implicit and explicit memory." *Memory and Cognition* 18(5): 507–14.

Rabinowitz, Jan C. 1990. "Effects of repetition of mental operations on memory for occurrence and origin." *Memory and Cognition* 18(1): 72–82.

Sampson, Geoffrey. 1987. "Parallel Distributed Processing." *Language* 63(4): 871–886.

Schank, Roger C. 1982. *Dynamic memory: A theory of reminding and learning in computers and people*. New York: Cambridge University Press.

Slamecka, Norman, and Peter Graf. 1978. "The generation effect: Delineation of a phenomenon." *Journal of Experimental Psychology: Human learning and memory* 4(8): 592–604.

Stevick, Earl W. 1976. *Memory, meaning and method: Some psychological perspectives on language learning*. Rowley, Mass.: Newbury House.

Stevick, E. W. 1981. *Teaching languages: A way and ways*. Rowley, Mass.: Newbury House.

Stevick, E. W. 1989. *Success with foreign languages*. Hemel Hempstead: Prentice Hall International.

Stevick, E. W. 1990a. "Research on what?" *Modern Language Journal* 74(2): 143–152.

Stevick, E. W. 1990b. *Humanism in language teaching*. Oxford: Oxford University Press.

Wall, Harriet M., and Ann Routowicz. 1987. "Use of self-generated and others' cues in immediate and delayed recall." *Perceptual and Motor Skills* 64: 1019–1022.

Students' concepts of Di Pietro's Strategic Interaction: The Scenario[1]

Joseph A. Wieczorek
Loyola College in Maryland
and The University of Maryland at Baltimore County

Introduction. Those of us who teach a foreign or second language (here, both will be designated as the target language, TL) are of at least two distinct orientations: the school whose proponents believe that accuracy first and foremost is critical to the language learning process, also known as the they-*need*-to-know-this syndrome (see Savignon 1992, Valette 1991, 1992); and the group whose members believe in communication first, accuracy notwithstanding. Most proponents of the second inclination would also claim that form follows function, and that function does not eschew form.[2]

Despite the apparent debate between the two camps, there remains one clear focus: Students are involved in the language-learning process. As a result, classroom practitioners and textbook writers have attempted to focus on language process in addition to language product. In this spirit of building a student-centered curriculum, Di Pietro (1987) formalized a humanistic methodology, what he called Strategic Interaction (SI), to provide students with the skills necessary to interact with both native speakers (NS) and nonnative speakers (NNS) of the TL in a realistic framework (see, for example, Schairer 1992).

Use of an SI approach here involves a very practical aspect of language learning. Its focus is entirely on how students envision and have a part in the curriculum. In addition, an SI approach is perhaps the best attempt we can make in an educational setting to validate the TLs we teach as well as speak. As Di Pietro (1987: vii) states:

---

1. I would like to thank Maria Finamore, who helped me to focus the ideas presented here, and Ilona Klein and Margaret Haggstrom, both of whom defined the word *clarity* for me.

2. Recently, I was pleasantly surprised to see how the brochure accompanying my Magnalite Cookware contained the view that "form follows function." While I would not dare make the claim that there is any intrinsic relationship between language and cookware, it is interesting from a classroom perspective that writers in two diverse areas arrive at the same conclusion.

> The classroom can become an ideal location for a[n] ... [SI] approach. There, we can re-create the conditions of social life and provide our students with the help and guidance they need to deal with them.[3]

This article addresses a major component of SI, the *scenario,* which Di Pietro (1987: 2) defines as

> a classroom activity that motivates students to converse purposefully with each other by casting them in roles in episodes based on or taken from real life.

The discussion here will center around students' choice of topic in student-made scenarios. As a result of analyzing such topics, classroom teachers may have to re-evaluate their role in the creation of scenarios to meet the needs of all language learners. Allowing students to create their own scenarios may provide information valuable to classroom teachers, curriculum designers, and textbook authors. Such information includes the range of roles, topics, and ultimately resolutions that may differ significantly from the scenarios designed by instructors.

Even though we realize that an authentic cultural context is necessary for a solid language education, pedagogy has been often slow to respond to making the classroom language a more realistic experience (cf. McPherson, Wieczorek, Haggstrom, and Ward 1992). A promising trend is to make more natural the formerly "unnatural" acts of classroom speech. This symbiosis of both interior conversation (the classroom) and exterior conversation (other social interaction) is the strength of SI and its major component, the scenario.[4]

Again, despite the difference in philosophical perspectives on language learning, there are at least two approaches to the scenario that may interest the pre- and post-baby-boomer generation of language learners and instructors. One, pedagogical in nature, queries the extent to which learners themselves can be involved in the process of creating a learner-centered curriculum, while the other, pragmatic in character, asks how realistic the TL is as used in the classroom, or to what extent the TL serves a specific motivational or engaging purpose. In concrete terms, both approaches consider how what goes on inside the classroom may be applicable to the outside world.

---

3. To paraphrase both VanPatten (1991: 69) and Voltaire, the classroom is not only a place to communicate, it is also the best of all possible places to communicate given the political, linguistic, and educational constraints of languages other than English in the United States.

4. In addition to this kind of interaction, discussed by Doukanari (forthcoming), the NS–NNS interaction is widely discussed (see Shairer 1992, Wieczorek 1991).

Expanding the definition of the scenario. In addition to Di Pietro's concepts of the scenario, *Webster's Twentieth Century Dictionary* offers this definition:

(1) an outline of the plot of a play or an opera, indicating the scenes and the stage directions;
(2) an outline of any proposed or planned series of events, real or imagined.

Although Di Pietro's followers might take issue with the "planned" outcome, the development of the scenario appears to fit the greater part of this description. While it is not an unrehearsed scene, it certainly is not as intricate as the *Ring* cycle. Di Pietro's revisited definition (1987: 41) of a scenario is

> a strategic interplay of roles functioning to fulfill personal agendas within a shared context.

By way of summary, the scenario

- is a source for potential discourse;
- invokes negotiation of meaning and language practice;
- is a social or psychological agenda that suggests shared contexts and interests;
- contains four essential elements: strategic interplay, roles, personal agendas and shared contexts;
- is a source for language practice, since the classroom is the place to communicate.

Instructors and the scenario. An assumption common to the foreign-language (FL) classroom is that most student-centered activities should be generated by the instructor. Part of what we do as instructors is reinterpret grammar for student presentation (cf. Wieczorek 1992), set the curriculum or at least modify it, create a list of methodologies and activities, and either consciously or unconsciously choose a pedagogical philosophy for presentation. While it is also true that instructors frame general parameters of methodology, not all activities need instructor generation. Therefore, it may well be that we can begin to look at student-centeredness and students' roles in how we prepare classroom materials.

Teachers often believe, too, that students' relative success in language experiences is related to their success as teachers. Whether the instructors' perceptions are true or not, a special relationship does exist between the teacher and the learner, just as a special relationship exists between the learner and the material. In one way, then, SI allows for maximum output (and, it is hoped, maximum input) on the part of the students.

Before completely shunning the role of the teacher in making scenarios viable for the classroom, we should first consider both teacher and student in light of strategic interaction. Theoretically, teachers are the curriculum experts. They also plan the syllabus, are often involved in adopting textbooks, and are considered masters of methodology. Ultimately, they establish classroom parameters through language choice and amount of language spoken, the process and procedures of delivering L2 material, and decisions on the division of skills. They equally shape attitudes about the TL and culture and are the presumed authority. If a particular methodology is too new or "foreign" to these language experts, they often find reasons to exclude it from their classroom agendas. We all have heard anecdotal remarks from educators that range from "My students could *never* do that" to "Oh, I always do that in my lessons." We know also that both assertions are probably false.

On the other hand, students are the ones who will eventually speak the language. We seek their motivation, whether sparked by a true interest in learning, by a requirement, or by some other motivation. Some might even go so far as to claim that they regress (or, in the "worst" case scenario, exhibit elements of fossilization) if motivation is not sufficient. Therefore, students set their own agendas. It is doubtful in many cases that they will speak the language beyond the classroom walls (cf. Di Pietro 1987; VanPatten 1991), so they often associate the TL with an academic but not necessarily a social endeavor. At times, due to the nature of the classroom and the correction of "errors" (cf. Wieczorek 1991: 497) and constraints on time due to various academic and personal loads, students may respond either positively or negatively to the tone of the class. In other words, they may be receptive to, be passive about, or react aggressively against the use of scenarios. Lastly, scenarios might work only if the students (or a significantly core group) are risk takers. In all practicality, then, some students may actually enjoy noninteractive grammatical exercises. Such students miss the point that language is a social act and not merely an academic one.

Problems with the scenario. Although it is assumed that instructors using SI will define the parameters and the situations for the scenario, it is equally logical that there are some problems with such an approach. More specifically, personal experience with the scenario in an SI approach yielded some problems:

- Students and the instructor do not always share many of the same life experiences. Factors such as age, life perspectives, political bents, religious affiliation or participation, economic background, work or life responsibilities, independence, travel, etc. may separate students from teachers and from each other.

- Some scenarios may not motivate the students to converse purposefully. As often happens in the FL classroom, the best-laid plans sometimes go awry. Many topics that instructors believe will be stimulating may not inspire students. Furthermore, some instructors may not be comfortable speaking about certain "taboo" matters (for some classrooms, at least) that might actually stimulate conversation among language learners. Such areas include sex, drugs, or other noncurricular activities.
- The episodes chosen may be based on the instructors' lives and not related at all to the lives of the students. If it is true, as Di Pietro suggests, that scenarios should spring from life experience, then there is no compelling reason to assume that students would find motivating what an instructor would. The classroom is the quintessential symbol of multicultural diversity at its best and should be respected as such.
- The social and psychological roles might be too complicated for students or may deal with topics far above students' emotional or linguistic level. Their specific personality types may not even coincide with the topics and roles that they should assume.
- The number of students (perhaps 150+ per year for the average instructor) makes it nearly impossible for teachers alone to create and recreate, as Di Pietro suggests. Imagination has little room to run free when the instructor not only has classroom demands but also holds office hours, attends meetings, answers questions, quiets fears about grades, perhaps conducts research, keeps up on advancements in the field, has a personal life, etc.
- There is something intuitively amiss in instructor generation of most if not all materials in an otherwise student-centered curriculum. It seems logical and noncontroversial to assume that students could be more involved in the language-learning process and that education could become more client-oriented.
- The syllabus allots only a specific amount of time for what some instructors consider the "fluff" of language learning (communicative activities) and not the "stuff" (grammar as conceived by the textbook). The scenario might be one key to the problem of maximizing the time instructors can spend on materials development. In other words, there is a constraint on planning and classroom use of materials.

Perhaps the greatest motivation for looking at student-generated scenarios comes from Di Pietro himself (1987: 63):

> The next task is to pare down restrictions on each personage so that ... students can assume the roles without being forced to take on attitudes and positions in which they might not believe.

So student involvement may be taken to its logical conclusion. Since the students will ultimately use the language taught, Di Pietro's message can be interpreted as this dictum: Let them write their own scenarios. (At least this way, we could envision that the students would be exposed to scenarios at *i* or *i+1*, not *i+20*.) In this light, van Lier's words (1991: 33) become hauntingly prophetic:

> When a person is *receptive* to the language she is exposed to, she will *attend* to it. This attention turns exposure into *input*, language that is received through the senses and made available for mental processing. The learner then needs to *invest* effort (cognitive, emotional, physical) so that the input can be processed. [Emphasis in the original.]

Scenario topics. As previously stated, there has always existed some discrepancy between what instructors envision and what students perceive as interesting topics for discussion, a mélange between intrinsic and extrinsic motivation. Some (both instructors and students) allow texts to dictate what the curriculum is or ought to be. Others manage to change the curriculum as necessary to accommodate particular needs or learning styles. Therefore, instructors, students, and any other interested parties have curricular concerns. In this section, I will address the topics that the instructor found motivational, that the texts found motivational, and that the students found appealing.

Textbook topics for possible scenarios. As a means of curricular sources for scenario topics, instructors might turn to available market materials, represented here by four textbooks (*Connaissances, Contacts, Poco a Poco,* and *Puntos de Partida*), one used at the high school level and three geared for the university level. Selected at random, they represent various pedagogical philosophies and publishers. The books were not chosen because of their strict relevance to scenarios but rather because of their gamut of topics. All areas surveyed are found in Appendix 1. In addition, I wanted to determine whether and in which ways the textbook curriculum differed from my prescribed curriculum. Table 1 shows representative areas where the texts differ from the areas of instructor-generated curriculum.

In brief, the four texts, with minor differences from each other, fit within the general parameters of an established curriculum. Perhaps one significant difference is that the four, including the high school text, appealed to areas associated with later adolescents: a college major, a sister's wedding plans, service station interaction, and car preparation for a trip. In terms of the SI

Table 1. Representative differences among topics of scenarios in four textbooks

Poco a poco	*Puntos de partida*
choice of college major	car preparation (maintenance and repair)
ways of taking leave	nuclear energy
dietary habits/food found in salad bar	
Contacts	*Connaissances*
sister's wedding plans	ecology
interaction with police	service station

scenario, the textbook authors ask us to believe that the areas include shared contexts and fulfill personal agendas. Before deciding whether the textbooks meet the SI criteria, we will look at the instructor-generated scenarios to determine how they set topics for scenarios for use in SI.

Instructor-generated scenarios. Following a subscribed course of study at the high school level, the instructor–researcher selected topics for scenarios that comprised at least 30 different areas. A complete list of the areas is found in Appendix 2. In brief, the topics dealt with daily routine, leisure-time activities, literature and other arts, religion, family matters, the environment, and health issues. Although the instructor-generated topics included areas that were not found in the textbooks (such as an in-depth look at men and women in contemporary society vs. their traditional roles), they did coincide in many areas. Overall, the topics included overriding principles such as communicative function, cultural awareness, and building cognitive skills. The design of the curriculum covered a broad range of skills and potential for SI use, not only for survival skills but also to increase knowledge about the culture through cognitive processes.[5]

Student scenarios. The scenario topics were gathered from high school students in 1991–93. The students were enrolled in the third year of language study in both French and Spanish. They ranged from 14 to 17 years of age and are from an upper-middle socio-economic class. Students were familiar with instructor-generated scenarios, which had been used in approximately 12% of the classroom sessions.

5. Although high school and lower-level university language classes are often presumed to be significantly different, this cursory study found no such difference among the topics.

At the time they were asked to produce scenarios, students were enrolled in honors classes (either by previous recommendation or scheduling needs). The TL was chosen as the language of scenarios and topics specifically because of its appeal to both the instructor and the students as a means of classroom communication.

Students were told to write their own scenarios in the TL. They were further instructed to consider the four essential components of the scenario (strategic interplay, roles, personal agendas, and shared contexts).[6] A total of 247 scenarios were collected from 64 different students over a period of sixteen academic months.

Use of the scenario in the classroom. There are a few caveats for actual use of the scenario in the classroom, not the least of which is the instructor learning the "awful truth": The *koiné* of the foreign-language class might be English, not the TL. Although Di Pietro (1987: 87) suggests post-scenario activities to supplement the language-learning process, it seems logical to assume that pre-scenario activities aiming at sensitizing students to the four skills in a cultural context would be useful. A question of interest is if student-made scenarios can be used in the classroom, and to what extent student-centeredness can aid the instructor in discovering what will intrinsically and extrinsically motivate the students to perform in the L2.

Students' range of topics. A total of 23 different topic choices could be identified for this population. The topics are summed up in Table 2.

Of the 23 topics, the first 4 (school, family, relationships, and violence) accounted for over 54% of topic choice. Of the "school" topics, most could be considered lived experiences, such as explaining why one deserves a better grade, begging for grades, an instructor who hasn't had coffee yelling at students, and plotting the downfall of the instructor by lies and innuendos. Still others deal with some interaction by explaining, for example, how to get out of doing homework or how to tell a friend politely over the phone that you have too much work to be social.

The second largest group of topics, family and relationships, deal with the affective domain of students' lives. Both the constructive side and the negative sides of family life are represented. On the positive side, for instance, a university son returns home for the first time since beginning his college career, or a daughter tries to convince her exhausted father to go to the mall with her. On the negative side, a girl slips out the window while parents sleep but they wait

---

6. Factors such as rating on the ACTFL Proficiency Scale, sex, and general IQ and SAT scores were not filtered out as variables since primary interest was in establishing how students in general would perceive and suggest topics for scenarios.

up for her when she returns at 1:00 a.m., or a father converses with his drunken son about the evils of beer. It is safe to assume that these are probably recently experienced scenarios, a window into what happens when students are away from the classroom.

Perhaps the most unexpected topic was violent crime. The students were more often than not witnesses rather than actual participants in violent crime, but they nonetheless interacted with the perpetrator of the act. Without attributing too much to the sociological aspect of this topic, which probably needs examination by leaders in the psyche of teenagers, it is indeed odd that they would choose to interact with arsonists, rapists, purse snatchers, murderers, and other assorted marginal people.[7]

Table 2. Range of topics for 64 L2 students

Topic	Frequency of topics
school	47
family	30
relationships	30
violence	27
vacation	20
car (driving)	18
social relationships, not romantic	18
party	13
shopping	10
leisure-time activities	8
animals	6
moral dilemma	4
job	3
marriage (wedding day)	2
presidential candidates converse	2
restaurant	2
arts	1
death	1
financial dilemma	1
history: Napoleon and his mother	1
sex	1
social awareness	1
television	1
Total	247

SI and applying students' roles. As far as application of these topics to the SI approach, little work has to be done to assign the roles, explain the dramatic tension, or deal

7. Whenever these topics arose, I allowed the students to interact as they wished. Some consideration was also given to the ethical side of violent crime. I informally asked the subjects why they used such topics. As an automatic reflex, they cited the preponderance of violent acts on TV and in the movies as sources for their topics. At times, discussion ensued concerning the use of various media and their influences so that the "violence" became something of a shared experience. It has been the case that these topics of violence have sparked a great deal of post-scenario topics for writing assignments.

with the resolutions.[8] It also goes without saying that the NNS–NNS interaction, common to the L2 classroom, might be supervised so that the *koiné* remains in the TL, not English.

What is interesting in a cursory study of this type is not only what students did choose as topics, but also what they did not choose. Since this stage in life is often characterized as an egocentric one, it is not surprising that their immediate world was a source of topics for them. As is seen in Table 2, this world included parties, cars, vacation, and shopping. The most glaring absence was one of cultural relevance or sensitivity, what Tom Field (personal communication) calls the "deep culture." Its absence does not necessarily impede a communicative function, but as stated previously, language as taught in the classroom must consist of communication and cognitive skills within a cultural framework. The deep culture here is not of the TL but rather of the American students' experience. A comparison of NNS to NS scenario topics might be fruitful, as well as an analysis of how NSs react to NNS scenarios.

To sum up some of the concepts related to the scenario as discussed here, SI must take into account student-centeredness, the potential complexity of instructor-made scenarios (not to mention a nonshared life experience), increasing discourse proficiency but not necessarily accuracy, cooperative or collaborative learning, incorporation of native-speaker norms (cf. Di Vito 1991), and student involvement both in the evaluation and in the creation of scenarios.

Pedagogical implications. In current pedagogical practices, Galloway (forthcoming) suggests that we constantly drift from method to method, and we even discourage ourselves because we cannot seem to find the "right" method or the ultimate activity to make all L2 learners proficient under all situations in all classrooms. Experienced educators know intuitively that there is no "correct" method, although a particular philosophy may indeed shape the methods used in all ensuing activities and evaluations.

For the scenario and its superstructure the SI approach, and especially for choice of topics under discussion here, several pedagogical implications can be suggested. Their order does not imply relative importance or exclusivity.

- Student-made scenarios should be matched against any existing curriculum, whether instructor-generated or dictated by the text. Convergent and divergent areas of interest will possibly obtain. In the case of the former, motivation is likely to be a factor in extracting and guiding NNS–NNS interaction. Concerning the original question of the

8. Anecdotally, whenever I have used these topics, students seem a bit more free-flowing with their language than they do during discussion of the environment and similar concerns. It goes without saying that the school setting comprises a good deal of the students' lives.

extent to which students may be useful in creating curricular materials, it is obvious that there is some threshold of usefulness to student-generated materials, especially if the instructor is uncomfortable either personally or professionally with the topics and their resolutions.

- The instructor must guide students out of their realm and into others, especially where the "deep culture" should be an issue. Additionally, it is up to the instructor to determine how the students can best be served by using cognition, stimulating both right and left brain hemispheres (cf. Waldspurger forthcoming). If the post-scenario activities are any indication of sharing and exchanging experiences, this bonding may indeed facilitate the mentor role that instructors have in the communicative classroom. I know of no current study that examines the relationship of teacher and student in the second-language acquisition process.
- The use of SI and the scenario, and their application to practice, may respond to van Lier's concerns. In addition, how language theory and research can feed each other is echoed in an SI approach. Certainly, it is the position of this paper that research and pedagogical practice are interdependent and need mutual validation.
- Student-centeredness may indeed play a large role in how language practitioners prepare materials for classroom use. Perhaps the largest implication is that instructors may need to lead students out of common topic choices into other roles that they may adopt as adult speakers of the TL. It is expansion of the linguistic repertoire that best serves the needs of language learners.
- Topic choice by students may need modification by defining roles or changing them so that the SI is facilitated. Di Pietro claims that an important element of the SI is dramatic tension. As a curriculum designer, the instructor may need to transform what students devise to enhance the learning process.
- The topics could be structured so that some spiraling and modifications to increase linguistic and social repertoire is accomplished. Too often the classroom falls victim to compartmentalization of vocabulary and grammar without spiraling previous exposure to the language.
- We must consider the relationship of all the communicative skills beyond what Di Pietro envisioned in the journal and the discussion periods of SI. It is often the case in the L2 classroom that oral practice is solely related to listening, separated from reading and writing within the cultural framework.
- One side question of interest is the validity of the presumed difference between the curriculum in general and textbooks in particular that separate high school from college. However, it seems reasonable to question the practice of separating these areas. Recent phenomena such as

publishers' selling the same book at two different levels with no change at all but the cover, college professors typically writing for high school, and, above all, topics that may not be significantly different between high school and college texts may put this practice into question. In a spirit of continuity or articulation in foreign-language learning, we in the profession have to look at how high school and college students are similar. After all, college students come from high school, and a scholar is not born in September because of a diploma in June.

- The textbook may be a good starting point for sources of curriculum and topics. However, it bears repeating that the textbook is not the only source of curriculum. Teacher training programs might consider emphasizing this factor since it is not uncommon to find instructors chained to the text. Additionally, instructors may have to consider which topics motivate students to use the language purposefully.
- The role of the instructors in such an approach must be re-evaluated to the extent that they feel comfortable with a communicative approach such as SI. Informally, some instructors express that they feel lost in a communicative classroom. It is the job of those supervisors, chairs, or department heads to encourage approaches such as SI.
- There may be some implication for study-abroad programs, since in order for students to write or talk about an experience and NS interaction in that experience, they have to have the experience. Given the nature of the classroom, we can only simulate conversation. Topics that appear in texts, such as changing distributor caps and looking for the gap of a spark plug, may not be as useful as some textbook authors imply, and the socio-political bent of literature as expressed by the Generation of '98 may not be relevant or inspiring.
- We might consider how media materials in an ever-changing technology could reinforce and enhance not only topic choice but the entire communicative classroom. In the ideal classroom there would be enough money to purchase all necessary materials, and students would spend every waking moment using the TL as a means of communication. Since we all know that this is not commonplace, media material may help to keep the students focused on the language.
- As a result of carefully considering SI, the profession has to decide where pedagogy fits in the field of applied linguistics. If we consider how many journals are dedicated to pedagogy as opposed to other academic concerns, we find that there is much work to be done to give practice greater exposure and respect, especially since many of us are language practitioners. Van Lier (1991: 29) perhaps says it the best:

> Current theoretical L2 work does not emphasize pedagogical links, either as sources of data or as targets for application.

Future research. In order to continue along the lines of this article, the following suggestions are made. First, we should look to a variety of groups or populations to determine topic choice, considering variables such as age, sex, socioeconomic class, personality type, language exposure, and L1.

Second, we must determine whether other components of the SI approach are sensitive to motivation through direct student involvement. This might include determining how the instructor and students can interact in curriculum development. Such classroom research in practice will help us to define and redefine the roles of instructor and learner to foster understanding of the TL and the TL culture. We might also consider student interest in responding to the pragmatic needs of many language learners.

Third, we must look at other aspects of the language classroom, especially how culture and cognition can best interact with communication. We could look, for example, at what the role might be of the *koiné* and how the classroom language develops into the L2. Such research might include which strategies (linguistic or otherwise) are used while negotiating the scenario.

Fourth, we could study the influence of the L2 scenario on the way the student perceives that L2. Fifth, we have to sharpen the focus on student-centeredness and how it interacts with other competing philosophies about the classroom. We could then start to determine a general framework that does not rely so much on methodology as it does on real human interaction. The emphasis would therefore fall on use of language, linguistic resources, and developing processes.

Sixth, we could look at how the use of SI can aid in developing proficiency beyond what is commonly done in the classroom. Seventh, such an approach could help determine whether some NS–NNS factors will influence the outcome of the scenario, as opposed to the NNS–NNS interaction in most classroom situations. Eighth, we must look at other areas in which the textbook, the teacher, and the learner can interact and coincide.

Ninth, we might ascertain in what ways high school and college-level language learning is similar by other than tradition or perception. Last, we need to investigate how classroom practice interacts with research in the field of language acquisition and learning.

Conclusions. There is some value to student-centeredness, but not without limits concerning how this student-centeredness can be used in the classroom. Thus, the extent to which students can aid in developing some L2 activities may be finite in the SI approach. However, although there may exist some concerns about not sharing experiences, there are areas that coincide among the text, instructor, and students' concepts of topic choice in the curriculum.

Some topics coincide with professional curricula, some do not. My position is that our task is to continue to discover how students can take an active role in their own learning. We in the profession can learn how the instructor's role can help shape the students' output. In other words, we have to seek to define the relationship between input and output.

This study looked at the practical aspect of language teaching, namely, the use of language and motivation of topic choice. Of the 23 topics gathered from this brief look at scenarios, the topics of school, family, relationships, and violence garnered over 56% of interest among students.

It is no longer sufficient to say that we teach a language if we do not consider not only pedagogy and its importance to the profession but also how we can maximize the time spent on language learning. SI is just one of many ways to help create speakers of the TL. What is hoped is that the instructor, the students, and all curricular materials work together in a partnership in establishing L2 speakers both in and out of the classroom.

Without the necessary combination of teacher and student cooperation, any use or attempted implementation of the scenarios is bound to fail. Teachers need to be open to what the scenario can teach the students and how the transfer of "power" from teacher to student does not mean that instructors do not make a valuable contribution to the learning process. The implications are that students must and will take responsibility for their own learning processes and product. All participants in the classroom are experts in conversational style, methods, and reactions. The key to the foreign- or second-language classroom is to guide and to unlock the door to potential interaction with both native and nonnative speakers of the language. After all, what is behind that door may be a clue to real communication.

REFERENCES

Di Pietro, Robert J. 1987. *Strategic interaction: Learning languages through scenarios.* Cambridge: Cambridge University Press.

Di Vito, Nadine O'Connor. 1991. "Incorporating native speaker norms in second language materials." *Applied Linguistics* 12(4): 383–396.

Doukanari, Elli. [Forthcoming]. "Applying discourse analysis to students' videotaped scenarios: a recent methodology, a new beginning." In Margaret A. Haggstrom, Leslie Z. Morgan, and Joseph A. Wieczorek (eds.), *The foreign language classroom: Bridging theory and practice.* New York: Garland Press.

Galloway, Vicki. [Forthcoming]. "Bridging theory and practice in the foreign-language classroom." In Margaret A. Haggstrom, Leslie Z. Morgan, and Joseph A. Wieczorek (eds.), *The foreign language classroom: Bridging theory and practice.* New York: Garland Press.

Haggstrom, Margaret A., Thomas Ward, Elina A. McPherson, and Joseph A. Wieczorek. 1992 (November). "Four approaches to the oral exam." Paper presented at the ACTFL Convention. Chicago, Illinois.

Hendrickson, James. 1994. *Poco a poco* (Third edition). Boston, Mass.: Heinle and Heinle.

Knorre, Marty, Thalia Dorwick, Bill vanPatten, and Hildebrando Villarreal. 1989. *Puntos de partida* (Third edition). New York: Random House.

Phillips, Elaine M. 1992. "The effect of language anxiety on students' oral test performance and attitudes." *Modern Language Journal* 76(1): 14–26.

Savignon, Sandra. 1992. *The Modern Language Journal Reader's Forum* 76(1): 58.

Schairer, Karen Earline. 1992. "Native speaker reaction to non-native speech." *Modern Language Journal* 76(3): 309–319.

Schmitt, Conrad J., and Jo Helstrom. 1990. *Connaissances oral activity packet*. New York: McGraw-Hill.

Valette, Jean-Paul, and Rebecca Valette. 1993. *Contacts* (Fifth edition). Boston: Houghton-Mifflin.

Valette, Rebecca. 1991. "Proficiency and the prevention of fossilization: An editorial." *Modern Language Journal* 75(3): 325–27.

Valette, Rebecca. 1992. *Modern Language Journal Reader's Forum* 76(1): 58–59.

van Lier, Leo. 1991. "Inside the classroom: Learning processes and teaching procedures." *Applied Learning* 2(1): 29–68.

VanPatten, Bill. 1991. "The foreign language classroom as a place to communicate." In Barbara F. Freed (ed.), *Foreign language acquisition research and the classroom*. Lexington, Mass.: D.C. Heath and Co.

Waldspurger, Theresa. [Forthcoming]. "Stimulating the right brain." In Margaret A. Haggstrom, Leslie Z. Morgan, and Joseph A. Wieczorek (eds.), *The foreign language classroom: Bridging theory and practice*. New York: Garland Press.

Wieczorek, Joseph A. 1991. "Error evaluation, interlanguage analysis, and the preterit in the Spanish L2 classroom." *Canadian Modern Language Review* 47(3): 497–511.

Wieczorek, Joseph A. 1992 (April). "Re-inventing grammar for the classroom." Paper presented at the Kentucky Foreign Language Conference.

Appendix 1. Textbook scenarios and topic choice

	Connaissances	
tourists and tourism	asking and receiving	health
travel in North Africa	directions	driving
travel to tropics	service station	asking for information
housing	interaction	hotel
good manners	friendship	college plans
vacations	ecology	public telephones
expressing preferences	school	
	exchanging money	

	Contacts	
friendship	vacation and other trips	pen pal relationships
meals	French teacher vs.	leisure-time activities
new lodging	principal	grooming habits
expressing personal	driver's test	predicting lifestyles
characteristics	police interactions	plays/movies
plans for college/grad	driver's test	babysitting
school	family	personal qualities
sister's wedding plans	school	shopping

Poco a Poco		
greetings and taking	food	relationships
leave	making reservations	vacations
career plans	problems with	living quarters
social meeting places	accommodations	holidays
family	salad bar choice and	airport/transportation
expressing	description	clothing
suggestions/opinions	social customs	health/medicine
money	shopping college major	dietary habits
household chores	seasonal habits	fine arts
	invitations	

Puntos de partida		
social mores	polling others for	giving advice
expressing (dis)likes	information	school
school	nuclear energy	leisure-time activities
relationships	technology	directions
bargaining (shopping)	economic life in the	defending reasons
personal activities	United States	household chores
pick-ups and social	transportation	service station
interactions	professions	astrology
food	family	careers

Appendix 2. Instructor-generated scenarios

theater	language choice in the	health and health care
cinema–film	United States	school
the bank (money	personal hygiene	relationships
exchange)	bullfights and artistic	community
mail (the post office)	expression	bilingualism
hotel	food	Hispanics in the United
household chores	transportation	States
the arts	regionalism	vacations and travel
religion	family	leisure-time activities
men and women in	environment	celebrations and parties
modern society	expressing (dis)likes	introductions

Conflicting argumentative strategies in the classroom

Christina Kakavá[1]
Princeton University

Introduction. As many studies have shown, engagement in conflict may differ across cultural groups (e.g. Kochman 1981, Schiffrin 1984, Kakavá 1989, Kuo 1991), and different strategies may be used to avoid conflict. For instance, in a cross-cultural study of Japanese and American business meetings, Yamada (1991, 1992) shows that Japanese tend to use silence to avoid confrontational topic shifts, whereas Americans tend to use verbal formulas to close and shift topics.

Engagement in conflict may differ even within a culture. Tannen (1990) claims that many men tend to seek confrontation as a means to negotiate status, whereas many women tend to avoid it because they perceive it as "a threat to connection" and involvement. However, as Tannen points out, men can also use confrontation to create involvement.

In ethnographic studies such as Friedl (1962) and Aschenbrenner (1986), among others, Greeks are reported to be confrontational, but they are also found to enjoy engaging in arguments and even to encourage children to participate in them. This tendency to enjoy arguments has also been documented in studies on auto-stereotypes as reported by Triandis and Vassiliou (1972). The Greeks in these studies were found to "extremely agree" with such statements as "I like arguing with an instructor or supervisor" and "I enjoy a good rousing argument" (323).

Kakavá (1989, 1992, 1993), using an interactional sociolinguistic perspective to discourse analysis, analyzed Greek conversations involving disputes, and she claimed that contentiousness is a form of sociability among Greeks, especially in intimate settings such as with family and friends. This claim is further supported by Tannen and Kakavá (1992), who show that Greeks mark their disagreement with solidarity markers such as first names or figurative kinship terms and personal analogy, evoking what Tannen (1984, 1986, 1990) refers to as the paradoxical relation of power and solidarity. Moreover, Tannen and Kakavá demonstrate that different styles of disagreement emerge from the

---

1. This paper is part of an original study that was directed by Professor Deborah Tannen, whom I sincerely thank. I would also like to thank Paul Fallon for his editorial assistance and his unending support not only for this paper but also for the original study.

qualitative analysis of a casual conversation among Greeks and an American. Whereas the Greek man disagreed directly, the Greek woman agreed briefly and then disagreed. In contrast, the American woman disagreed indirectly.

Most previous and recent studies on Greek have focused on disagreement strategies in casual talk or on disagreement types by gender (Makri-Tsilipakou 1991). Until now, there has been no study that examines argumentative strategies of Greeks or Greek Americans when they speak English in a formal setting such as a university classroom. As part of an investigation of Greek disagreement strategies in different contexts, this paper explores the argumentative strategies that a Greek student used in a classroom setting in an American university. His argumentative strategies are compared to those of a Greek American student and an American student.

I will show that the Greek student tended to be qualitatively more confrontational than the Greek American, and that both the Greek and the Greek American were more confrontational than the American. The Greek strategy involved the expression of strong disagreement followed by accounts. The Greek American strategy was to express disagreement but also to use personal analogies to support a position, a common Greek strategy to create involvement as Kakavá (1989, 1993) and Tannen and Kakavá (1992) have shown. The American strategy was to push "the disagreement rather deep in the turn it occupied," to use Sacks's (1973:58) expression. Disagreement was prefaced with agreement tokens (Pomerantz 1975, 1984) and with deictic shifts to first person plural, which affected the degree of personalization of a claim and mitigated the action of disagreement. I should also point out that these three types of disagreement were issued to people who had different status. Whereas the Greek and the Greek American disagreed with the position of the professor (higher status), the American disagreed with the position of the Greek students (equal status).

These different types of argumentative strategies of negotiating disagreement, I suggest, indicate different argumentative styles that can be indexed to qualitatively different cultural norms assigned to expressing disagreement in a formal setting with people of higher status. In other words, the Greek student (and to a lesser degree the Greek American) transfers Greek sociocultural norms that "allow" these types of confrontational strategies to occur in a rather formal situation such as the classroom and with a higher-status addressee such as the professor. My claim is supported by studies in cross-cultural pragmatics that find that even advanced learners display some form of "pragmatic transfer" when they speak a target language. Further, I address the implications of this sociopragmatic transfer for both native speakers of Greek living abroad and also for people of Greek origin regarding possible cross-cultural misunderstandings and the formation of negative stereotyping.

The study is structured as follows: First I briefly review what researchers have claimed for style and its acquisition. Then I discuss the notions "pragmatic transfer" and "pragmatic failure." Next I describe the classroom discourse that I studied. Then I present a continuum of disagreement types that I identified and I discuss illustrative examples of different types of disagreement from a Greek American, American, and Greek student. Next I discuss implications of the findings for cross-cultural talk and the formation of stereotypes. Finally, I summarize the main points of the study.

Style and its acquisition. Tannen (1984), following Hymes (1974), defines styles as "ways of speaking." These ways of speaking are acquired at a very early stage, as research on developmental pragmatics has shown. It is known that children learn how to talk by socializing with parents and caretakers and later on with peers. As Ochs (1986:2) puts it, children "acquire tacit knowledge of principles of social order and systems of belief through exposure to and participation in language-mediated interactions." Among other researchers, Anderson (1990) shows how children as young as four and five years old show variability of style depending on parameters such as register, task involved, age, and gender of the addressee. Labov (1970), examining the different stages in the acquisition of standard English, claims that by the age of 15, children have a 57% rate of conformity with adult norms. Acquisition progresses steadily to reach 84% conformity levels with adult talk by ages 20–39. This stage is usually attained by middle-class and educated people. However, as Labov notes, not every speaker can acquire a full range of all the different styles available.

Since the participants in this study were educated, middle- to upper-middle class, and between the ages of 20 and 22, one expects that they have acquired the norms of their family and peers and that they would display them in their interaction. Tannen (1981) has found that even when the language spoken is other than native, native interactional habits tend to be retained. In her study of indirectness and ethnicity, she found that Greek Americans had communicative patterns closer to the Greeks' rather than the Americans', even when they had no ability to speak Greek. As Tannen suggests, "conversational style is both a consequence and an indicator of ethnicity" since it "is learned through communicative experience and is therefore influenced by family communicative habits" (1981: 236).

Pragmatic transfer and pragmatic failure. Tannen's views are supported by findings and suggestions from the area of cross-cultural pragmatics. Thomas (1983) has suggested that two types of pragmatic failure exist due to two different types of pragmatic transfer. She refers to the first as "pragmalinguistic failure," which occurs when learners of a target language transfer from the mother tongue "speech act strategies ... which are semantically/syntactically equivalent, but because of different 'interpretive bias,' tend to convey a different pragmatic force in the target language" (101). The other type of failure that she describes, which is relevant to the present study, is "sociopragmatic." She claims that "sociopragmatic failure stems from cross-culturally different perceptions of what constitutes appropriate linguistic behaviour" (99). In other words, a language learner may transfer to an L2 certain L1 cultural norms or principles regarding politeness or considerations of face that may apply differently in L2. The last failure relates to the cross-cultural problems that arise due to different expectations regarding communication and interaction, as Gumperz (1982) has shown between different cultural groups and as Tannen (1984) has demonstrated even within the same cultural group.

This study builds on this research by investigating the argumentative strategies used in the classroom discourse of a Greek, a Greek American, and an American student. The findings will be evaluated in terms of sociopragmatic transfer, which may trigger cross-cultural miscommunication.

Data. The data for this study is a corpus of 40 hours of audiotaped classroom discourse of an undergraduate course on the history of Southern Europe in an American university. I tape-recorded all the sessions for a semester, while doing participant observation and taking field notes. The class consisted of eighteen students representing different ethnic backgrounds including American, German American, Greek, Greek American, Italian, Italian American, and Spanish American. From the 40 recorded hours, I extracted and transcribed two hours that were composed of different excerpts containing opposition. The excerpts include discussion about issues concerning Italy and Greece, since these led to arguments and many students participated in them. I use *argument* as Schiffrin (1987) defines it: "a discourse through which speakers support disputable positions" (18). I believe arguments offer an excellent opportunity to get a sample of candid talk, since participants tend to forget that they are being recorded, as Labov (1972) has claimed, when they discuss topics in which they find themselves engaged.

When Greek political issues were discussed, the professor really had to prompt other students besides the "Greek contingent" to participate. The Greeks seemed to know many facts about the period of Greek history they were discussing (post–World War II), which made many students reluctant to either provide information or present their opinions. In contrast, the Greek students were not shy in expressing their opinions about topics pertaining to Italy or Spain.

There were, however, some qualitative differences among the Greek contingent, which comprised three Greek students and a Greek American. A Greek student, whom I call Pétros, was the only one who did not participate as much in the debates, and his opinions were usually expressed in the form of tentative questions. Some may suggest that this was because his mother was Finnish, he had been living abroad for many years, and he had even attended American high school. Others may argue that the difference can be attributed to his personality. It should be emphasized that even if Pétros were no different from the rest of the Greeks, no claim could be made that all Greek students who study in foreign institutions will behave as the rest of the Greek students did in class.

Table 1. Participants and their disagreement turns

Participants and background (parents' backgrounds in parentheses: father, mother)	Disagree-ment turns	Total turns	% disagree-ment turns
Alberto: Italian (Italian)	0	4	0
Amalía: Greek (Greek)	4	27	15
Andy: American (Greek, Greek-American)	11	55	20
Christina: Greek (Greek)	1	3	33
Ellen: American (Spanish)	1	8	13
Giulia: Italian (Italian, American)	6	9	67
Jeff: American (American)	3	4	75
Lorenzo: Italian (Italian)	4	14	29
Lucy: American (Palestinian, American)	1	4	25
Marta: Italian (Italian, American)	3	14	21
Max: American (German-English, German-Irish)	2	2	100
Minás : Greek (Greek, Greek-American)	19	44	43
Miriam: American (Lebanese, Italian)	2	16	13
Nancy: American (American)	0	0	0
Paul: American (American)	0	0	0
Pétros: Greek (Greek, Finnish)	1	14	7
Philip: American (Hungarian, Irish)	0	4	0
Professor: (American)	31	183	17
Rob: American; (Irish)	0	0	0
Sharon: American (Irish, Canadian-American)	0	0	0
Total turns	89	429*	21

*The grand total in Total Turns is greater than the expected sum of turns in the table (405) because of 19 turns that were assigned to several speakers (e.g. laughter) and because 5 turns were untranscribable.

I now turn to give a quantitative picture of the segments I studied. Table 1 below provides a quantitative picture of the disagreement turns for the whole class and shows the number and percentage of disagreement turns of each class member in about two hours of recorded data. (For more information on the students, please refer to the Appendix.) The first column lists the students' pseudonyms and nationality; their parents' nationality is indicated in parentheses. Where the parents come from different countries, the father's nationality is listed first, followed by the mother's. The second column shows the number of disagreement turns a participant took. The third column gives the total number of turns a participant took in this segment, and the final column gives the percentage of the total turns that contained disagreement. The grand total in Total Turns is greater than the expected sum of turns in the table (405) because 19 turns were assigned to several speakers (e.g. laughter), and because five turns were untranscribable.

In terms of number of disagreement turns, the professor had the highest number, followed by Minás, Andy, and Giulia (19, 11, and 6, respectively), whereas Max (100%), Jeff (75%), and Giulia (67%) had the highest percentage of disagreement in relation to the number of turns. The professor had the greatest number of his disagreement turns (29%, or 10 turns out of 31) with Minás. Next, he disagreed most with Andy and Giulia (for three turns each). He disagreed with other individuals, or with groups of students, one or two times each for the remaining 16 disagreement turns.

As shown in Table 2 below, Minás had the highest percentage of disagreement turns with the professor (89%, or 17 out of 19 occurrences),while Giulia was next (83%, or 5 out of 6 cases). Andy was third with 45% (5 out of 11) of his disagreements with the professor, and last came Miriam (13%, or 2 out of 6 occurrences). Interestingly, the nationalities (Greek, Italian, Greek American, Italian/Lebanese American) of the four students with the highest number of disagreement turns with the professor are associated with very contentious cultural styles.

Table 2. Students who disagreed most with the professor

Student	Disagreement turns with professor	Total turns of disagreement	% disagreement turns with professor
Minás	17	19	89
Giulia	5	6	83
Andy	5	11	45
Miriam	2	16	13

These numbers, however, do not illustrate the qualitatively different types of disagreement employed by the students. For example, even though Max and Jeff had the highest percentage of disagreement turns, their disagreement turns were issued with preagreement sequences and many reluctance markers. Giulia (Italian), Minás (Greek), Amalía (Greek) and Andy (Greek American) were the only ones to issue a range of "strong," "strong yet mitigated," and "mitigated" disagreements (see discussion of the terms below). It is interesting to note that Amalía had most of her disagreement turns with Minás, a fellow Greek but on the other side of the political spectrum. In addition, Giulia and Minás were the only students to engage in what I call "adversative rounds" with the professor, that is, sustained disagreement for a minimum of two consecutive argumentative turns marked by structural repetition, substitution, and competitive overlaps, similar to the ones found in Greek conversations (see Kakavá 1993).

In addition, the total number of turns for each participant was partially affected by the professor, who usually assigned the order of the floor. Some students who may have raised their hands initially but were not called on may have chosen not to contribute to the discussion after a couple of students had already discussed an issue. Other students, due to time constraints, were unable to express their point of view. However, from the information gathered in my field notes, I can report that this did not take place very often, since the students who wanted to make a statement usually managed to do it sooner or later.

Argumentative strategies. By argumentative strategies, I refer to the strategies participants employ to negotiate disagreement. In Kakavá (1993), I define disagreement as "an oppositional stance (verbal or nonverbal) to an antecedent verbal (or nonverbal) action" (Chapter 2.0). The verbal action may be an utterance expressing a speaker's judgment about an object, concept, person, or even course of action. The oppositional stance may also be a nonverbal action in the form of gesture or facial expression. As defined, a disagreement may generate an argument, but it also constitutes argument, since it is part of it. In a study examining disagreement strategies in casual conversations and classroom discourse (Kakavá 1993), I identified three types of disagreement—"strong," "strong yet mitigated," and "mitigated"—which represent different degrees of a force that a disagreement may have along a continuum of possible disagreement responses. The classification was based on structural and interactional criteria and was descriptive in nature. In the original study, I included both the strategies found in Greek casual conversations and English classroom discourse. Here I refer only to the strategies used in the classroom discourse. The category "strong" disagreement includes negative evaluations of a position and contrastive responses with or without repetition. The category "strong yet mitigated" consists of contrastive responses followed by accounts or personal analogies. Finally, the category "mitigated" includes disagreement types in the form of impersonalization, pre-agreement sequences followed by disagreement and accounts, and questions accompanied by hedges and hesitations. Although the Greeks and the Greek American used all types of disagreement, the Americans used only mitigated types of disagreement. The Greeks in the classroom discourse showed a tendency to express disagreement strongly and rather up front, similar to the Greek participants in the Greek casual conversations (Kakavá 1993). Strong forms of disagreement, which tend to be expressed contiguous to a turn and which were abundant in casual Greek conversations, were sparse in the classroom discourse due to the specific participant structure of the classroom (Philips 1972) and the professor's expectations. Students were expected to justify—in other words, offer accounts for—a position whether they agreed or disagreed with it. As a result, accounts were part of their turns, which tended to be rather monologic types of arguments (Schiffrin 1987) since the professor usually orchestrated the turns.

I now turn to analyze a representative example from qualitatively different types of argumentative strategies involving a Greek American, an American, and a Greek student. In order to eliminate factors such as different topic, gender, and time, I have chosen examples from a class discussion by three male students about two authors' books regarding southern Italy. The presentation of the examples follows the chronological order of their turns. I show that the Greek American disagrees directly first with a Greek student's point and then with the professor's position. His disagreement with the professor is accompanied by personalization of his argument. The American prefaces his disagreement with a pre-agreement sequence, he shifts several times between first person singular and first person plural, and finally he expresses his disagreement with a Greek student. The Greek student disagrees directly and strongly with the professor's position and then provides his justification.

The transcription conventions are Tannen's (1984) except for bold, which marks very emphatic stress here. Arrows indicate highlighted parts of the analysis. Underline marks emphatic stress. P stands for talk spoken softly. /?/ indicates that transcription was impossible. The symbol - marks an abrupt cutting off of sound, as in a false start.

The Greek-American student. The following is an example of a turn that displays the use of a "strong yet mitigated" form of disagreement. The shape involves a strong disagreement followed by an account in the form of personal analogy. The excerpt comes from a class discussion on two authors' books about Italy: Carlo Levi's *Christ stopped at Eboli* and Edward Banfield's *The moral basis of a backward society.* The professor had stated his position that both authors presented the same picture of southern Italy but differed in their way of presenting it. For instance, the professor had suggested that Carlo Levi, the Italian author, was more artistic than Edward Banfield, the American author, in his portrayal of southern Italy. Minás, a Greek student, was the first to disagree with the professor's suggestion, and argued that the two authors differed in their perspective. Banfield, according to Minás, "seemed to be more negative" and presented the Italians as "doomed," whereas Levi was more "appreciative" of the Italians and "more objective." Miriam, an American of Lebanese and Italian descent, also disagreed with the professor's position regarding the two authors. She argued that Banfield went to Italy to "prove his theory" about why the southern Italians were acting the way they were, whereas Levi tried to find redeemable qualities in them. The professor disagreed with her point about Banfield, and then Andy, the Greek American, started his turn with what seemed to be disagreement with Minás's position. He claims that Banfield did not present the peasants in southern Italy as "hopeless," which was Minás's prior contention.

(1) (22 March)
156 Prof: Andy and then Jeff.
→ 157 Andy: I think, the- a big thing with the
158 a big difference with Banfield, is that,
159 he- I don't think he stressed the hopelessness.
160 I mean he saw that all these people are hopeless,
161 their- their mindset is hopeless,
162 their, you know, all their concepts are hopeless,
163 but he says that- that could be changed,
164 because, even though it is a harsh landscape,
165 he brings up Saint George Utah,
166 which is a desert,
167 I know, I've been there,
168 but these Mormons have made it bloom,
169 and, you know, he's giving,
170 he's giving an American solution to a problem.
171 Prof: Precisely.
→ 172 Andy: And, I think, that's- that's a big problem,
173 because he [Banfield] doesn't really respect the people,
174 for who they are,
175 and even though Levi is uh from the Piedmont,
176 you know, you know,
177 he does keep a certain amount of respect for these people.
178 And, even if, even if he was harsher
179 than how- u:hm like- like Banfield was,
180 at least he's an Italian,
181 and he can criticize his own country.
→ 182 I mean, sometimes you see an- an American,
183 or some other foreigner coming into Greece,

184 and they would criticize Greece,
185 and I will not appreciate it.
186 But if it's- if it's a Greek that's doing it,
187 it's a different story.-
188 Ss: [laugh]—
189 Andy: You know?

Andy starts his turn disagreeing with Minás's point that Banfield was presenting the Italians as hopeless, since, as he claims, Banfield offered solutions to their problems (lines 159–170). The professor agrees with Andy's point: "Precisely" (line 171). Beginning in line 172 and continuing until 181, Andy shows that he disagrees with the professor and that he aligns with Minás and Miriam. He starts criticizing Banfield for being disrespectful to the Italians, especially since he is not Italian, and Andy questions Banfield's right to criticize a country in which he was not born. This position is supported even further in line 182 when Andy changes footing and creates a parallel between the Italian case and a Greek case:

→ 182 Andy: I mean, sometimes you see an- an American,
183 or some other foreigner coming into Greece,
184 and they would criticize Greece,
→ 185 and I will not appreciate it.
186 But if it's- if it's a Greek that's doing it,
187 it's a different story.

What we see here is a shift in involvement with the topic discussed. The shift is marked with the discourse marker *I mean,* which Schiffrin (1987:309) suggests functions as "an indicator of information which is highly relevant for interpretation of the speaker's overall message." Andy personalizes the argument, and thus he upgrades the degree of involvement with the topic discussed.

Andy did not openly disagree with the professor's position initially. First he disagreed with Minás's point about how Banfield portrayed the Italians, and then he disagreed with the professor's position. However, his disagreement with the professor can be characterized as strong because of the following elements: It displays elements of a strong stance (explicit disagreement on line 172 "I think that's- that's a big problem," personalization of an argument, and expressive intonation (focal stress) on line 185 "I will not appreciate it"). I argue that the shift in the participation framework with the personalization of the argument acts as an interactionally strong form of disagreement, since a participant shows his or her strong commitment to a belief and thus conveys negative affect. However, since the initial disagreement was followed by an account, I characterize it as "strong yet mitigated" to differentiate it from the "strong" forms of disagreement, which were issued without any justification.

The American student. This example illustrates the use of a "mitigated" type of disagreement in the form of pre-agreement followed by mitigated types of disagreement, as indicated by the shifts from first person singular to first person plural. After an Italian and a Greek student take a turn and align with Minás's position by providing further support for his claim that Levi was closer to the Italians and thus understood them better, Jeff, an American student, takes a turn and aligns with the professor's position that both Carlo Levi and Banfield had valuable observations.

279 Prof: And that affection may in parts arise from that.
280 Jeff.
→ 281 Jeff: I agree a lot with what Pétros is saying,
282 and that comes back to the degree of
283 how well Levi might be able to identify for instance a banker,
284 but not to- might be able to-
→ 285 but I think also that-
286 that there- there are a lot of reasons,
→ 287 why we have to be careful,
288 how to interpret how much- I
289 how much we accept both of them.-
→ 290 And furthermore we have to be careful
291 mostly from the standpoint of the studies,
292 and objectively, not to throw Banfield out,
293 due to his- due to just a couple of,
294 either metho- methodological,
295 or other little elements that are distinct,
→ 296 because I think,
297 he did make some valuable observations.
298 Nevertheless, that in some cases,-
→ 299 we have seen /??/ *p*
300 it might be in some cases a little less dramatic,-
301 but nevertheless honest.
302 Prof: Minás prefers to throw the baby out with the bathwater.

First Jeff starts his turn with what I have termed in Kakavá (1993) "enthusiastic agreement" ("I agree a lot with what Pétros is saying"). On line 285 he shows that he disagrees with the position taken by Minás and the others by marking his disagreement with the contrastive marker "but." Note, though, that on line 287, he switches from the first person singular to an inclusive "we"—what Brown and Levinson (1987 [1978]) refer to as impersonalization—

which gives his statements a less personal tone. On line 296 he switches back to the first person singular and attributes "some valuable observations" to Banfield, but then again he switches to a "we" form on line 299. Jeff's position is stated on line 301, where he presents Banfield's observation as "honest."

Thus the American cushions his disagreement with pre-agreement sequences, and then he expresses his disagreement with a mix of impersonal and personal types of assessments followed by accounts. These elements indicate some reluctance on his part to express his disagreement directly, and they make his disagreement seem less confrontational. I now turn to show how Minás, a Greek student, expressed his disagreement with the professor's position (that both writers made similar observations about Italy), which, as noted, was embraced by Jeff, and consequently by another American student.

The Greek student. This example shows another form of "strong yet mitigated" disagreement. The Greek student frames his subsequent talk as disagreement with the professor's position and then moves to the justification of his disagreement. The discussion about the two authors that I referred to in the above examples still continues. In the transcript that follows, the professor restates his opinion concerning the two authors after being challenged by Giulia, a female Italian student, when Minás (a Greek) raises his hand to express his opinion for the second time. (Note that he was the first to disagree with the professor on the issue). I include the whole transcript of Minás's turn to properly contextualize it, even though I focus only on the lines preceded by arrows.

→ 464 Prof: but the- the conclusions about the actual peasants,
465 themselves,
466 that one draws from Levi,
467 are the conclusions
468 that Banfield asks you to draw about these peasants...
469 And I wonder if that's really true.
470 Minás. [calling on Minás]
→ 471 Minás: I disagree.
→ 472 I agree that the- that they both-
473 they both have similarities,
474 and they both have similar ob-
475 actually they both have similar observations.-
→ 476 I disagree in how each one views
477 the effectiveness of or- a solution to the problem.
478 Or that- or something alleviating the problem.
479 It seems that-
480 actually it <u>doesn't</u> seem,

→ Banfield <u>states</u>,
that any sort of action taken by the state,
any sort of economic development,
will be misused,
because these people are inherently and physically,
and physically, uh amoral familists, familists,
these people will **not** know how to develop.
Even if you give them uhm, uhm,
if you- if you make available to them,
the economic resources,
if you.. funnel more investments towards- towards these people,
/they'll handle/ they're amoral familists,
and they will not make good use of them.-
So they are **doomed**.
Whereas, as- as- as Levi, does not-
I don't know if he believes this,
because he really doesn't touch... upon this a lot,
but there's an instance when he claims that,
maybe the fascists are doing the wrong thing.
I mean, here we are preparing for war,
we're going down to Ethiopia,
but we have our, in a way our own Ethiopia in Italy,
and maybe we should uh do something about this.
Now, which means that- that **he** thinks
that the state needs to have a- a greater role for the south,
I don't know if he believes that- that- that this
he does not mention
whether this- this greater role of the state toward the south,
this economic development,
funneled from, you know, central authorities to the south,
might be effective,
it's not stated.
→ But the fact that he does not claim,
specifically, and Banfield does,
that- that any type of solution, any type of investment,
or economic... effort,
to economically develop the south will be doomed,
it might be their difference.

Let us begin with the professor's turn. On line 464, the professor returns to the point that he was making earlier and states that the two authors do not differ in their conclusions:

→ 464 Prof: but the- the conclusions about the actual peasants,
465 themselves,
466 that one draws from Levi,
467 are the conclusions
468 that Banfield asks you to draw about these peasants...

Then the professor opens the floor for more discussion. At that point, Minás is selected again to present his opinion (nobody else had raised his or her hand). Minás frames his upcoming talk as disagreement: "I disagree" (line 471). Notice, however, that he subsequently ratifies the professor's argument, "actually they both have similar observations" (line 475), but then he frames his ensuing talk with another explicit form of disagreement, "I disagree in how each one views the effectiveness of or- a solution to the program" (line 476). Minás raises a new issue that has not been debated before. That issue is about the authors' different perspectives about economic plans that could work in southern Italy. So this is the second time he disagrees with the professor, but on a different issue. Note that Minás indicates his disagreement with the professor even before he justifies his point. Even when he acknowledges that the two authors share observations, again he frames his disagreement as a strong stance: "I disagree..." However, toward the end of his turn (line 518), Minás mitigates his observation with a hedge (the modal *might*), because he bases his point on Banfield's stated position versus Levi's unstated one:

513 Minás: But the fact that he does not claim,
514 specifically, and Banfield does,
515 that- that any type of solution, any type of investment,
516 or economic... effort,
517 to economically develop the south will be doomed,-
→ 518 it might be their difference.

Thus, overall, the Greek student expresses his disagreement explicitly with the professor, then he partially agrees with him, and then he disagrees explicitly with him. His last disagreement is followed by a lengthy account that supports his contesting position. Despite the intermediate partial agreement and the subsequent accounts, Minás's turn is more confrontational because it preposes and highlights a disagreement alignment with "I disagree."

Summary. To sum up, we have seen how three students handled confrontation in a qualitatively different manner. "Strong yet mitigated" forms of disagreement were expressed contiguously by the Greek and the Greek American, whereas "mitigated" forms of disagreement were issued with a delay by the American. Expressing up-front disagreement with a position takes precedence in the Greek case; and in the Greek American case, the personalization of an argument heightens the degree of involvement with the issue discussed. The use of such strategies results in accentuating confrontation. In contrast, in the American case, we have seen an effort to depersonalize an argument and thus minimize the confrontation. Acknowledging a contrasting point or part of a point as right takes precedence over expressing disagreement, which, as shown, is also presented in a mitigated manner.

If I consider that the argumentative strategies are manifestations of two main argumentative styles, then the question is "How do we account for these different styles, considering the fact that both Americans and Greeks belong to a western type of culture that values the expression of individuality within a group?" Yamada (1992) claims this for the Americans in her study, and I also argue the same for the Greeks (Kakavá 1993). The answer is to refer to a continuum of styles that Tannen (1984) advocates. The differences observed between Greek and American speakers can represent relatively different degrees of confrontation on a continuum that ranges from confrontation to nonconfrontation, as evidenced by the argumentative strategies each group uses. The continuum tells us that an American may be perceived to be more confrontational by the Japanese who represent the nonconfrontation pole, as Yamada (1991) claims, but a Greek may be perceived as more confrontational by an American.

I suggest that the Greek and Greek American strategies are indexical to the positive value that Greek culture attaches to expressing an opinion strongly, even when it contests someone else's opinion. Disagreement tends to be a form of sociability in Greek culture, and it is viewed as affiliative rather than as an action threatening solidarity. Stronger types of disagreement demonstrate one's commitment to a belief or position, as the personalization of an argument entails. This kind of cultural norm fosters confrontation in situations that other cultures may inhibit. Rather strong forms of disagreement, I suggest, result from this type of fertile environment for disagreement.

By saying that Greeks tend to express their disagreement rather strongly, I do not claim that Americans never do, or that Americans are not able to disagree strongly in different situations. My observations are based on the evidence from the classroom discourse, a rather formal setting, in which the American students seemed less confrontational than the Greek and Greek American students, who did not shy away from challenging their professor's position with rather strong forms of disagreement. This study's observations about the American students' tendency to mitigate their disagreement and appear less confrontational are supported by Kochman (1981), who found that American white middle-class students tended to avoid confrontations in college classrooms, unlike their fellow black students, who engaged in direct confrontation.

Stereotypes and cross-cultural miscommunication. If we accept that the Greek, and to a lesser degree, the Greek American act according to Greek sociopragmatic norms, which are qualitatively different from American norms, then a "sociopragmatic failure" or cross-cultural miscommunication may arise due to different cultural expectations as to what type of disagreement is expected to be issued not only to a professor but also to other students in a formal setting such as a classroom. Unless professors and students are familiar with Greek argumentative patterns, they may interpret a strong disagreement as a personal attack on them, rather than as a Greek speaker's strong commitment to a position or an idea. Thus they may judge a Greek as "opinionated," "impolite," or "too emotional." Greek students, on the other hand, may interpret the American mitigated disagreement as an effort to be evasive on an issue, or as a sign of being noncommittal, and they may judge an American as "detached" or even "dull." Both types of miscommunication may jeopardize not only personal relations but also a class's smooth operation.

In studies of heterostereotypes, Vassiliou, Triandis, Vassiliou, and McGuire (1972) report that Americans viewed Greeks as "emotionally uncontrolled" and very "argumentative," whereas the Greeks viewed Americans as "emotionally controlled" and "detached." Therefore, differences in argumentative strategies, which represent qualitatively different expectations about "proper" situational argumentative styles, could cause communication problems that may not only hinder the negotiation of agreement and conflict resolution but may also create negative preconceptions among the members of these two ethnic groups.

Conclusion. I have shown two qualitatively different types of argumentative strategies of engaging in confrontation among a Greek, Greek American, and an American student. I argued that the difference in the degree of confrontation represents different styles that can be mapped onto qualitatively different values of expressing disagreement or engaging in confrontation. Even though both Greeks and Americans may view confrontation as a means of individuality within a group, the Greek students tended to be more confrontational than the American, which may lead to negative stereotyping.

In this study I used naturally occurring data from an academic class with fluent speakers of Greek, and I demonstrated that L1 interactional styles of disagreement emerged when speakers used L2, even when they were not born and raised in Greece. This last finding supports Tannen's (1981) claim that cultural communicative habits tend to be retained even if a person is not born and raised in his or her parents' native country.

Although the study is limited in scope since it had a small number of participants, I hope it will act as a springboard for other studies that will explore its findings in other situations, taking into account not only contextual factors but also participants' interactional goals.

REFERENCES

Andersen, Elaine Slosberg. 1990. *Speaking with style: The sociolinguistic skills of children*. London: Routledge.

Aschenbrenner, Stanley. 1986. *Life in a changing Greek village: Karpofora and its reluctant farmers*. Dubuque, Iowa: Kendall/Hunt.

Banfield, Edward C. (ed.). 1958. *The moral basis of a backward society*. Glencoe, Ill.: Free Press.

Brown, Penelope, and Stephen C. Levinson. 1987 (1978). *Politeness: Some universals in language usage*. Cambridge: Cambridge University Press.

Friedl, Ernestine. 1962. *Vasilika: A village in modern Greece*. New York: Holt, Rinehart and Winston.

Hymes, Dell. 1974. "Ways of speaking." In Richard Bauman and Joel Sherzer (eds.), *Explorations in the ethnography of speaking*. Cambridge: Cambridge University Press. 433–51.

Kakavá, Christina. 1989. "Argumentative conversation in a Greek family." Paper presented at the 64th Annual Meeting of the Linguistic Society of America, Washington, D.C.

Kakavá, Christina. 1992. "Re-examining dispreferred second turns." Paper presented at the 37th Annual Meeting of the International Linguistic Association, Washington, D.C.

Kakavá, Christina. 1993. "Negotiation of disagreement by Greeks in conversations and classroom discourse." Georgetown University dissertation. Washington, D.C.

Kochman, Thomas. 1981. *Black and white styles in conflict*. Chicago: University of Chicago Press.

Kuo, Sai-Hua. 1991. "Conflict and its management in Chinese verbal interactions: Casual conversations and parliamentary interpellations." Georgetown University dissertation. Washington, D.C.

Labov, William. 1970. "Stages in the acquisition of standard English." In Harold Hungerford, Jay Robinson, and James Sledd (eds.), *English linguistics*. Glenview, Ill.: Scott Foresman. 275–302.

Labov, William. 1972. *Sociolinguistic patterns*. Philadelphia: University of Pennsylvania Press.

Levi, Carlo. 1947. *Christ stopped at Eboli*. Translated from the Italian by Frances Frenaye. New York: Farrar, Strauss and Co.

Makri-Tsilipakou, Marianthi. 1991. *Agreement/Disagreement: Affiliative vs. disaffiliative display in cross-sex conversations*. Aristotle University of Thessaloníkidissertation. Thessaloníki, Greece.

Ochs, Elinor. "Introduction." In Bambi B. Schieffelin, and Elinor Ochs (eds.), *Language socialization across cultures*. Cambridge: Cambridge University Press. 1–13.

Philips, Susan U. 1972. "Participant structures and communicative competence: Warm Springs children in community and classroom." In Courtney Cazden, Vera John, and Dell Hymes (eds.), *Functions of language in the classroom*. New York: Teachers College Press. 370–94.

Pomerantz, Anita. 1975. *Second assessments: A study of some features of agreements/disagreements*. University of California dissertation. Irvine, Calif.

Pomerantz, Anita. 1984. "Agreeing and disagreeing with assessments: Some features of preferred/dispreferred turn shapes." In J. Maxwell Atkinson, and John Heritage (eds.), *Structures of social action: Studies in conversation analysis*. Cambridge: Cambridge University Press. 57–101.

Sacks, Harvey. 1987. "On the preferences for agreement and contiguity in sequences in conversation." In Graham Button and John R. E. Lee (eds.), *Talk and social organization*. Clevedon, England: Multilingual Matters. 54–69.

Schiffrin, Deborah. 1984. "Jewish argument as sociability." *Language in Society* 13: 311–35.

Schiffrin, Deborah. 1987. *Discourse markers*. Cambridge: Cambridge University Press.

Tannen, Deborah. 1981. "Indirectness in discourse: Ethnicity as conversational style." *Discourse Processes* 4: 221–38.

Tannen, Deborah. 1984. *Conversational style: Analyzing talk among friends*. Norwood, N.J.: Ablex.

Tannen, Deborah. 1990. *You just don't understand: Women and men in conversation*. New York: William Morrow.

Tannen, Deborah, and Christina Kakavá. 1992. "Power and solidarity in Modern Greek conversation: Disagreeing to agree." *Journal of Modern Greek Studies* 10: 11–34.

Thomas, Jenny. 1983. "Cross-cultural pragmatic failure." *Applied Linguistics* 4: 91–112.

Triandis, Harry C., and Vasso Vassiliou. 1972. "A comparative analysis of subjective culture." In Harry C. Triandis, Vasso Vassiliou, George Vassiliou, Yasumaka Tanaka, and A. V. Shanmugam (eds.), *The analysis of subjective culture*. New York: Wiley. 299–335.

Triandis, Harry C., Vasso Vassiliou, George Vassiliou, Yasumaka Tanaka, and A. V. Shanmugam. 1972. *The analysis of subjective culture*. New York: Wiley.

Vassiliou, Vasso, Harry C. Triandis, George Vassiliou, and Howard McGuire. 1972. "Interpersonal contact and stereotyping." In Harry C. Triandis, Vasso Vassiliou, George Vassiliou, Yasumaka Tanaka, and A. V. Shanmugam (eds.), *The analysis of subjective culture*. New York: Wiley. 89–115.

Yamada, Haru. 1991. "Topic shifts in American and Japanese business conversations." *Georgetown Journal of Languages and Linguistics* 1: 249–58.

Yamada, Haru. 1992. *American and Japanese business discourse: A comparison of interactive styles*. Norwood, N.J.: Ablex.

APPENDIX

Alberto, a 21-year-old Italian, born in Milan, Italy. He grew up in Italy and the United States and had been in the United States for ten years. Both parents are Italian. His father is a businessman, and his mother is a housewife.

Amalía, a 22-year-old Greek, born in Athens, Greece. She grew up in Greece and had been in the United States for three years. Both parents are Greek. Her father is a physician, and her mother is a housewife.

Andy, a 20-year-old American, born and raised in Salt Lake City, Utah. His father is a Greek businessman. His mother is first-generation Greek American and she is a housewife.

Ellen, a 19-year-old American, born in Boston, Massachusetts, and raised in Lexington, Mass. Both parents are Spanish. Her father is a professor and her mother is a language instructor for children.

Giulia, a 20-year-old Italian, born in Rome and raised in Rome and Geneva. She had been in the United States for a year and a half. Her father is Italian and a diplomat. Her mother is American and a journalist.

Jeff, a 23-year-old American, born in Ann Arbor, Michigan, and raised in New Hampshire and the Virgin Islands. Both parents are American. His father is a marine industry consultant and his mother is an elementary school teacher.

Lorenzo, a 21-year-old Italian, born in Brescia, Italy, and raised in Italy, the United States, Mexico, and Hong Kong. Both parents are Italian. His father is a businessman and his mother is a housewife.

Lucy, a 21 year old, born in Washington, D.C. She grew up in Bethesda, Maryland. Her father is Palestinian and a professor. Her mother is American and a housewife.

Marta, a 21-year-old Italian, born in Colombo, Sri Lanka. She grew up in different places in Europe and Asia and had been in the United States for four years. Her father is Italian and works as a private consultant, and her mother is American and a housewife.

Max, a 19-year-old American, born and raised in Rhode Island and New York. His father's nationality is German English and he is a politician. His mother is German Irish and a housewife.

Minás, a 22-year-old Greek, born in Athens, Greece, grew up in Greece. He had been in the United States for four years. His father is Greek and a surgeon. His mother was born in the United States but is of Greek nationality, and she's a housewife.

Miriam, a 20-year-old American, born in the Bronx, New York, and raised in Westchester, New York. Her father is Lebanese and he is an accountant. Her mother is Sicilian and she is a teacher.

Nancy, a 20-year-old American, born in Cottage Grove, Oregon, and raised in several states in the United States. Both parents are American. Her father is a manager and her mother is an accountant.

Paul , a 21-year-old American, born in Southfield, Michigan, and raised in Troy, Michigan. His father is a first-generation American (his grandfather was Scotch-Irish) and he is a physical therapist. His mother is first-generation American (grandparents were German and English) and she is a travel agent.

Pétros, a 20-year-old Greek, born and raised in Athens, Greece. He had been in the United States for six years. His father is Greek and he is a civil engineer. His mother is Finnish and she is a housewife.

Philip, a 20-year-old American born and raised in New York. His father is Hungarian and he is a butcher. His mother is Irish and she is a housewife.

Rob, a 21-year-old American, born and raised in Bryn Mawr, Pennsylvania. Both parents are Irish. His father is a businessman and his mother is a housewife.

Sharon, a 21-year-old American, born and raised in New London, Connecticut. Her father is Irish and he is a construction contractor. Her mother is Canadian-American and she is nurse.

Learner-centered activities:
The good, the bad, and the ugly

Nadine O'Connor Di Vito
University of Chicago

Importance of a learner-centered language classroom. "Focus on the learner," "learner-centered," "individual learning styles," "learner motivation and personality," "individual needs and interests": These are the types of terms that we have all become accustomed to hearing in foreign-language acquisition research as well as in the development of pedagogical materials. More and more researchers are now convinced that the personal engagement of language learners in the negotiation of meaningful communication is absolutely essential to the language-acquisition process and, of course, suggestions abound for putting these new research ideas into practice. These include incorporating into our foreign-language classrooms personalized strategy-building exercises, information-gapping tasks, role plays, scenarios, and individualized questions. This increasing focus on the language learner is not just prevalent on the conference circuit; it has become an essential feature of any respectable contemporary foreign-language textbook and of any respectable foreign-language program.

Textbook response to this call. One has only to read the prefaces of a few current editions of widely used textbooks to see the extent to which the language learner has taken center stage. Here are a few examples of statements found in some French-language textbooks that, we might assume, are representative of general tendencies in current textbook development:

> Personalized questions focus on the students and encourage them to tell about themselves, their lives, their opinions, and their activities. (*Pas à Pas*, 1991)

> ... communication exercises encourage students to use what they have learned in an original way by answering personal questions, giving opinions, or exchanging information. (*Contacts*, 1993)

> Each segment of each lesson is intended to furnish the means and provide the opportunity for each student to attempt some personalized communication ... so that no day passes without each student attempting to

> ... express a personal intention. (*Ça marche!*, 1990)

> Students engage in speaking, reading, writing, and listening activities in very much the same way they would in real life, obtaining information, expressing ideas and feelings, observing and describing cultural phenomena, and negotiating meaning with their classmates and instructors. (*Voilà!*, 1992)

Of course, we should applaud these efforts to stress the communicative nature of language and the importance of engaging the language learner in communicative activities. However, as with any popular and good idea, we must avoid the temptation to apply it *willy nilly*. In our mad rush to update and create textbooks with personalized, engaging, communicative activities, we may have forgotten at times to consider whether these activities are merely encouraging our language learners to inappropriately transfer behavioral norms, values, and attitudes, or whether these activities will, in fact, offer language learners opportunities to progress in their development of communicative competence.

Learner-centered activities and the promotion of communicative competence. Over the past two and a half decades, researchers such as Hymes (1971), Bachman and Savignon (1986), Rivers (1986), Tannen (1984), and Kramsch (1986) have contributed to our understanding of communicative competence as the ability to act according to both norms of grammatical acceptability and norms of sociocultural appropriateness. If we are to take seriously this notion of the interrelationship between language and culture and between form and meaning, then we must view language acquisition as the acquisition of more than just different types of grammatical rules or different types of idiomatic expressions or even different customs and practices. If, indeed, communication involves some sort of match between the intent of the speaker and the interpretation of the listener, then it follows that our learner-centered activities should help language learners to

- understand how to express themselves so that their intent will match the way they are interpreted by native speakers and
- interpret native-speaker behavior according to native-speaker norms of interpretation.

In this age of the learner we must recognize, above all, that learner-centeredness alone does not make an activity a good one. *Good* exercises are those that guide the learner to share native-speaker norms of behaving and of interpreting behavior. Learner-centered activities that do not promote such shared norms of communication are, I will claim (somewhat crassly perhaps), *bad* activities. And, finally, *ugly* activities are more than just communicatively inadequate. They are activities that encourage learners to keep or to acquire patterns of behavior that might result in negative evaluation by native speakers or that encourage them to develop or maintain negative stereotypes of native speakers of the target language.

Negative cultural stereotyping or negative misinterpretations of either target-culture behavior or the behavior of nonnative speakers of the target language is a very real and complex problem and one that we in foreign-language teaching cannot afford to ignore. In our classes, evidence of negative evaluation of the target culture can take many forms. It can be the evidence of a feeling of cultural superiority when, for example, students compare the American educational system with other systems and conclude, quite objectively, of course, that the American system is without question better. It may be signalled by a feeling of unease as students view, for example, greeting norms that require much more physical proximity than they are used to. And we have also seen evidence of negative cultural evaluation when students react with disapproving shock to the possibility that some people actually eat horse meat, snails, brains, tongue, or other foods considered exotic or taboo within general American culture.

These signs of incipient cultural stereotyping are, unfortunately, merely the forerunners of more personally informed and, therefore, more dangerous stereotyping that often occurs during extended periods of living abroad. What have our students acquired through our learner-centered activities if they leave our classes, go study in France, and afterwards claim, among other things, that French people are somewhat cold and normally look sad or mean, that they are often frank to the point of being insensitive, or that they tend to be rude and inattentive and interrupt you when you speak? Have we really succeeded in helping our students to acquire communicative competence if French teachers and families in contact with these students claim, among other things, that American students are often spoiled, somewhat self-centered, long-winded, take liberties in the home, are obsessed with money, and are culturally illiterate?

I mention these frightening comments because they are a sad reality, documented in various sociocultural studies (Carroll 1987, O'Connor 1987) and representing fairly commonplace complaints that I have heard while accompanying university groups in French study-abroad programs[1]. I also mention them because they reflect the important issues involved in cross-cultural

---

1. I saw evidence of a good deal of negative cultural stereotyping as director of the University of Pennsylvania study program in La Napoule, France, in 1981 and the Georgetown University summer study program in Tours, France, from 1987 to 1989. From 1984 to 1985, I also collected sociocultural data for my dissertation from 33 Americans studying for the year at the Université de Bordeaux III, Bordeaux, France.

understanding that our language classroom activities, our *learner-centered, personalized activities*, must address if we are to help our students gain true communicative competence. In the February 28, 1993, *Chicago Tribune Magazine*, I was drawn to the tongue-in-cheek statement of Jean Viallet, an American living in Paris: "I've learned to be thicker-skinned and nastier: any American living in Europe shares my position" (p.20).

We cannot wish cultural stereotyping away. Rather, we must acknowledge stereotypes, not as a reality of cultural traits, but as a pointer to areas in which behavior is interpreted differently in two cultures and that, therefore, present obstacles to the acquisition of communicative competence. If people are seen as evidence of a whole culture's tendency to be long-winded and egotistical and other people are seen as evidence of a whole culture's tendency to be rude and inattentive, it seems clear that what is in question here is a cultural difference in behavioral norms and their interpretation. The question is, thus: How do our communicatively oriented activities, our learner-centered activities, deal with such cultural norm conflicts?

Are we personally engaging students to recognize the forms and meanings of their own behavioral norms and to reflect upon the rules of interaction that may be quite different in the target culture? Or are we, in fact, encouraging behavior that invites negative cultural stereotyping, through activities that invite students to talk at length about themselves, their families, their opinions, their likes and dislikes? What preparation for communication in the target language are we giving our students when we have them repeatedly introduce themselves by name to unknown classmates and ask them numerous questions that could easily be considered personal in nature?

Most of us, I would imagine, have used such exercises in our classes and have felt very good about it, and for good reason: They help us to develop an amiable class atmosphere, involve students in interactive communication, and allow them to use and experiment with a variety of lexical items and grammatical structures. But let us stop and think for a moment: How would a student be viewed if she or he actually tried such an activity with a native speaker in any one of a number of countries? In many instances, probably not so well. I was told by one such student in France who would repeatedly try to just go up to French students and introduce herself to them that the normal reaction ranged from suspicious politeness, to incomprehension, to cold stares.

Examples of learner-centered activities that provide questionable preparation for appropriate communicative interaction are numerous. When discussing currency in our foreign-language classes, we often have students practice numbers by indicating real or imagined prices of objects, but how often do we ask students to reflect upon the situations in which money, or prices, or salaries are talked about or are referred to in conversations or in news stories? More importantly, how often do we ask students to reflect upon the social or communicative value of these monetary references?

In discussing professions, a common learner-centered activity is to have students write or discuss their qualifications for a particular job. In such activities, it is not unusual to find American students present themselves as hard-working, enterprising, and aggressive. But although being *aggressive* may be considered a desirable trait in the world of American business, language learners of French should understand that it is wonderful to be *dynamique* or *énergique* (adjectives that might not immediately come to an American's mind), but *agressif* could easily connote undesirable self-centeredness or perhaps an inability to cooperate with others. Do we ever use these learner-centered, personalized activities to help our students discover the many ways words and expressions may encode values and attitudes differently in two cultures?

Bad exercises. Some learner-centered activities, while not encouraging negatively valued behavior or negative cultural stereotyping, nevertheless inadequately prepare language learners for particular communicative situations. Such activities include having students plan imaginary trips by referring to reproduced train schedules whose section of restrictions has been conveniently eliminated. Of course, unless students learn to read the section of the schedule containing all of the travel specifics (e.g. weekend and holiday restrictions, type of train), their classroom practice making individualized plans may merely give them the false impression that they know how to plan a train trip in the target culture. Unfortunately, if one actually attempts to travel by train in France without attending to those schedule restrictions, one is apt to become quickly confused and frustrated.

Good learner-centered activities. We have seen *ugly* and *bad* learner-centered exercises. How can we define a *good* learner-centered activity? First of all, it is clear that the types of activities that we should be developing are those that, at the very least, give students enough information to be able to successfully accomplish their communicative goals, such as knowing that to read a French train schedule, one must consult the section of the schedule containing travel rules and restrictions. They should know that, for example, in order to buy a piece of fruit, many stores require that one first obtain a ticket, pay for the purchase, obtain a receipt, and finally claim the purchase. Therefore, our role-plays at the train station or at the fruit stand should make students aware of these common variables and routines that are important to a successful communicative interaction. *Good* learner-centered activities should help students to confront terms whose meanings may not be so obvious to the culturally uninitiated, so that they may come to discover, for example, that a *salade de concombres* is not a salad of lettuce and cucumbers but a plate of sliced cucumbers in a vinaigrette.

Good learner-centered activities should invite students to think not only about what they do and what they like, but about how their activities and preferences signal their membership to particular social groups and age groups, their level of education, and their socialization as male or female. A *good* learner-centered activity should not just ask students to say what drink they might order in a French restaurant but should encourage them to begin to think about alcohol consumption as part of an intricate system of norms that are used to help people symbolically distinguish between work time and leisure time, to mark particular events, or to build and maintain various types of social relationships. As Douglas (1987:46) has pointed out, "In most societies, drinking is essentially a social act and, as such, it is embedded in a context of values, attitudes, and other norms." What is the significance of happy hours and TGIF outings to local bars? Students should not only know how to order their favorite wine, they should be challenged to examine how, when, why, with whom, and in what quantities alcohol is consumed in their world and in the target culture.

In a *good* learner-centered activity, students are not just asked to describe to fictitious French students the intricacies of the American university system but they are challenged to consider the ways an educational system is a social construct. The rights and responsibilities of teachers and students, the duration of classes, the accessibility of resources, the methods of evaluation, the tuition costs: These are just some of the many particularities of educational systems whose examination can help one understand why people in a specific culture tend to share certain beliefs and attitudes toward education.

Finally, when considering home-life issues in a foreign-language classroom, a *good* learner-centered activity is not just an activity in which students are asked to describe the various rooms in their home; it is, rather, an activity that encourages students to think about the functions of rooms and the ways public and private space are delineated in a home. It is only through such types of personal and engaged reflection that students have any hope of learning how to truly communicate in these target culture settings.

A framework for designing good learner-centered classroom activities. What we need to develop, therefore, are learner-centered activities that, first, encourage students to reflect upon, discover, and understand their own behavior, attitudes, and values and, second, allow students to gain not only interactive skills but real insight into the sociocultural meaning of target-language norms. Given the fact that people tend to perceive and organize new experiences according to their previous experiences, any type of compare-and-contrast activity must go beyond a superficial examination of words and actions to the much more important discussion of their social significance. Depending on the norm in question, our learner-centered activities can challenge language learners to reflect upon behavior in its sociological, emotional, historical, religious, psychological, ecological, geographic, or economic context and to use these different perspectives of their own language norms and of target-language norms as bridges to cross-cultural understanding. The development of cross-cultural understanding should be, of course, at the heart of language acquisition, for such understanding is, undeniably, the soul of true communicative competence.

REFERENCES

Bachman, Lyle F., and Sandra J. Savignon. 1986. "The evaluation of communicative language proficiency: A critique of the ACTFL oral interview." *Modern Language Journal* 70: 380–90.

Brown, Thomas H. 1991. *Pas à pas*. New York: John Wiley & Sons.

Carroll, Raymond. 1987. *Evidences invisibles*. Paris: Seuil.

Douglas, Mary (ed.). 1987. *Constructive drinking: Perspectives on drink from anthropology*. Cambridge: Cambridge University Press.

Heilenman, L. Kathy, Isabelle Kaplan, and Claude Toussaint Tournier. 1992. *Voilà!* Boston: Heinle & Heinle.

Hymes, Dell. 1972. "Excerpts from 'On Communicative Competence.'" In J.B. Pride and Janet Holmes (eds.), *Sociolinguistics: Selected readings*. New York: Penguin Books.

O'Connor, Nadine. 1987. "What non-native narratives can tell us about second language acquisition." Unpublished dissertation. University of Pennsylvania.

Rivers, Wilga M. 1986. "Comprehension and production in interactive language teaching." *Modern Language Journal* 70: 1–7.

Sandberg, Karl C., Georges Zask, Anthony A. Ciccone, and Françoise Defrecheux. 1990. *Ça marche!* New York: Macmillan.

Tannen, Deborah. 1984. "The pragmatics of cross-cultural communication." *Applied Linguistics* 5(3): 189–95.

Valette, Jean-Paul, and Rebecca M. Valette. 1993. *Contacts*. Boston: Houghton Mifflin.

Interlanguage talk: The relation between task types and communication strategies among EFL Arab learners

Rajai Khanji
University of Jordan at Amman

Abstract. The purpose of this study is to compare the effect of two conversation task types, Di Pietro's Strategic Interaction tasks (scenarios) and learner's interview tasks, on the choice of communication strategies used by EFL learners. The study I report analyzes the communication strategies of Jordanian learners of English at the University of Jordan. Tasks have been traditionally assigned to L2 learners in the hope that these interactional activities might result in improving language proficiency. Ellis (1984) has pointed out that the notion of communication strategy might be a useful one for evaluating L2 communicative performance. He recommends that attention should be paid to communication strategies rather than to correctness, intelligibility, or style when evaluating communicative performance. In order to compare the effect of the two task types, I analyze communication strategies from two perspectives: interactional and psycholinguistic. This combination is intended to provide a clearer picture of communication strategies in relation to foreign-language proficiency.

Introduction. Extensive research has been carried out in recent years into learner interaction in the classroom. The central research question in this area is: What classroom tasks provide learners with the greatest amount of opportunities to use the target language in order to promote acquisition? Some types of tasks are often recommended. Examples of such tasks include two-way information gaps (Long 1981), negotiation of meaning (Swain 1985), pair work (Long, Adams, McLean and Castanos 1976), and interactive group work (Bruton and Samuda 1980).

The literature contains many claims regarding the effectiveness of certain tasks in second-language classroom acquisition research. However, there are few studies that substantiate such claims, particularly in the field of teaching English as a foreign language. It is the purpose of this study to compare the effect of conversation task type of nonnative speakers of English on the choice of communication strategies.

The notion of communication strategy, as Ellis (1984) has pointed out, might be a useful one for evaluating L2 communicative performance. Ellis recommends that attention should be paid to communication strategies rather than to correctness, intelligibility, or style when evaluating communicative performance. Ellis (1986) found that one of the learners in his longitudinal study opted for reduction-type behavior in the earlier stages of language proficiency, but he increasingly turned to achievement-type behavior as he progressed. Bialystok (1983) found that advanced learners used significantly more L2-based strategies and significantly fewer L1-based strategies than less-advanced learners.

Method: Participants and Tasks. Forty learners of English who were enrolled in two intensive English classes at the University of Jordan participated in the study. The students were in two conversation courses taught by the same instructor using different pedagogic tasks: Interview (I) tasks and Strategic Interaction (SI) scenario tasks. In one class, the students used the interview task, which required them to practice conversation with each other about topics of their choice. The instructor's job was mainly to guide students and to address their language needs and questions before or during interviews. The other class employed the principles of Di Pietro's Strategic Interaction method. This approach (Di Pietro 1987) is built around the use of "scenarios" that required the students to work through communication problems and enact minidramas on realistic themes (see Appendix).

Procedures. Students from the two conversation classes were assigned to come to the researcher's office in pairs for their oral examination by the end of the fall term of 1991. The oral exam, which later became the interactional data that was audiotaped, transcribed, and then analyzed for communication strategies, represents nearly seven hours of EFL conversations.

Analysis of Communication Strategies. For all 40 students in both groups (the interview task group and the scenario task group), a total of 503 instances of communication strategies were registered. The eight communication strategies most frequently used by students were repetition (24%), message abandonment (16%), language switch (15%), appeal for assistance (14%), circumlocution (12%), retrieval (9%), calque (6%), and overelaboration (4%) (see Table 1). The following is a brief discussion of the communication strategies used by both groups of students.

Repetition. Repetition accounted for 24% of the instances of strategy use. It was registered when learners resorted to repetitions of utterances several times in order to gain more time to think about or plan for a subsequent speech unit. The following utterances taken from the corpus are some examples of this strategy:

Table 1. Frequency of Communication Strategies for All Students

Strategy Type	Observed Frequency		Frequency Rank
	Number	Percent	
Repetition	121	24	1
Message Abandonment	80	16	2
Language Switch	75	15	3
Appeal for Assistance	72	14	4
Circumlocution	61	12	5
Retrieval	46	9	6
Transliteration	30	6	7
Overelaboration	18	4	8
TOTAL	503	100%	

(1) A: The problem is that if I, I, I, if I put a congratulation in the newspaper, then I am cheating.

(2) B: for me it's a problem and I can, I can, I can live without a friend who believe in nonsense.

(3) C: What is good about teaching?
D: to know, to know how, know how the other people thinking, how are the other people thinking.

Message Abandonment. This strategy accounted for 16% of the instances of strategies used. It was registered when learners started talking about a topic but then were unable to complete the utterance due to insufficient knowledge of lexical items. As a result of this conversation breakdown, silence immediately followed. Examples:

(5) E: We must encourage announcement in the newspaper. This will give him a great . . . . (silence)

(6) F: Thank you but this is . . . . [silence]

(7) G: I think it's a kind of . . . . [silence]

(8) H: I said we ought to announce about something . . . . [silence] something that . . . . [silence]

(9) I: You must pay. It's a restaurant not a . . . . a . . . . [silence]

Language Switch. The students used this strategy whenever they could not find the requisite lexical item or structure in the target language and simply rendered it in Arabic. That usually happened following a short period of silence, during which the student groped for a word and then gave up by resorting to his or her first language. This strategy accounted for 15% for all students in both groups.

Appeal for Assistance. This strategy was registered when learners asked for help from either their interlocutors or their teacher. Learners resorted to this strategy by signalling their request for assistance either explicitly or implicitly. This strategy accounted for 14%. Examples:

(10) A: Can you tell me something about family customs in Jordan?
B: <u>Customs? What it means?</u>

(11) A: Did you do your assignment?
B: <u>You mean homework?</u>
A: Yes

(12) B: But sometimes you can work if you have the same ..... <u>I can't find the suitable word.</u>
A: <u>What is the word?</u>
B: I mean [an Arabic word is given].
A: I see, you mean 'qualifications.'

Circumlocution. This strategy accounted for 12%. It was registered when learners tried to describe the features of an object rather than using the intended word or phrase. In this case, learners did their best to achieve the intended meaning by attempting to clarify and explain the message in their mind in various ways. Here are some examples taken from the data.

(13) J: Yes, you can bring to us the <u>list of food</u>. [menu]

(14) A: Do you have any experience in writing?
B: Ya, once I put a paragraph in the magazine. [published]

(15) A: What other qualities in a good teacher?
B: He must not be unfair, he must treat the students as if they are the same. [treat them equally]

(16) K: I know that you dislike this food and you don't understand the things which it consists of. [ingredients]

Retrieval. This strategy accounted for 9%. It was registered when students stopped talking about something for a short while and then continued talking by finding the appropriate target-language item. That is, the learners try to remember a missing utterance that was forgotten, but then remember it. Examples are:

(17) L: My brother works at ..... the Curriculum Department.

(18) M: We had a holiday ..... it is called ..... Labor Day.

(19) N: My mother ..... argued me, ... not argued .... ah ..... urged me to study English.

Calque. This strategy accounted for 6%. It was registered when learners used L2 lexicon and structures to create a literal translation of items that are based on their first language. This is exemplified in the following instances:

(20) I cut him. [interrupt]

(21) Would you like to share me a walk. [join]

(22) My mother is a homewoman. [housewife]

(23) There is two sides for this subject. [point]

(24) I lost seven years in my life. [spent]

Overelaboration. Overelaboration accounted for 4%. It was used when some learners talked about something more than they really needed to. In this case, it seems they wanted to make a good impression on the hearer about their ability to use the target language. Examples are:

(25) A: What TV program did you watch yesterday?

B: I watched after the news a football game about two Jordanian teams. It was interesting, but I slept without see it completely. Did you see it?

Table 2. Total Instances of Strategies For Each Group

Strategy Type	Interview Task Group	Scenario Task Group
Repetition	85	36
Message Abandonment	60	20
Language Switch	49	26
Appeal for Assistance	43	29
Circumlocution	20	41
Retrieval	17	29
Transliteration	16	14
Overelaboration	6	12
TOTAL	296	207

Discussion. In an observational study such as this one, care must be taken not to overinterpret or overgeneralize results. However, some cautious suggestions will be made regarding the use of communication strategies as a means of evaluating communicative performance.

In order to compare the two groups' use of communication strategies, it would seem possible to observe that good language users will resort more frequently to the use of *achievement* strategies and less frequently to *reduction* strategies. According to Ellis (1986: 184), reduction strategies are attempts to do away with a problem when learners give up part of their original goal. In other words, reduction strategies are an indication of low proficiency level. In this study, as in another I have done (Khanji in press), repetition, message abandonment, and code switching are classified as reduction strategies. Table 2 shows that the interview task group (ITG) resorted to the use of reduction strategies more than learners belonging to the scenario task group (STG). In fact, the frequency of use of reduction strategies by the STG learners is almost half the number for the ITG learners.

From a psycholinguistic perspective, the typology of interpreting the use of communicative strategies proposed by Frawley and Lantolf (1985), which is based on the Vygotskyan theory of control, can shed more light on the relation between communication strategies and language proficiency. Using this psycholinguistic interpretation, reduction strategies used by L2 speakers are object-regulated. This means that learners who resort to such strategies exhibit speech that is at a precommunicative stage.

The implication for this study is that the STG learners were less object-regulated than the ITG learners since they used fewer reduction strategies, and consequently their ability to communicate in L2 is comparatively better than that of the ITG learners. In addition, although learners in both groups did resort to using reduction strategies, ITG learners resorted to appeals for assistance more than the STG learners did, which could be seen as further evidence for their lower level of language proficiency.

However, a different picture emerges when we look at the use frequency of the other strategies, i.e. circumlocution, retrieval, calque, and overelaboration. These strategies, which can be described as achievement strategies, are generally used less by the ITG learners than by the STG learners (with the exception of the calque strategy, which is used by both groups about equally). We can classify these strategies from the proposed psycholinguistic model as self-regulation strategies, i.e. strategies that reflect control of the speaking task by their users. Again we notice that the less frequently the learners used self-regulation strategies, the less interactive ability they have, thus losing control of the communication task. We must keep in mind that, according to this model, learners progress in their language proficiency from a state of being *object-regulated* to being *other-regulated,* until finally they attain a state of being *self-regulated.*

Both groups of learners in this study used the same strategies but in varying degrees, reflecting varying abilities in language use. That is, communication strategies were seen as a reflection of a speaker's ability to deal with a task at a particular time. If the variables of the conversation task (interview or scenario) were changed, we might see markedly different results. Therefore, in order to understand the degree to which task type may influence interaction as well as the choice of communication strategies by the students in this study, we have to keep in mind that in the interview task, learners are normally asked to interview each other in a question/answer format without having to argue or to defend a given position, as is the case in the scenario task, where students are deeply involved in a problem-solving situation. The scenario task, therefore, unlike the interview task, creates a dramatic tension in communication due to the dissimilar vested interests of two personalities who happen to encounter each other. In other words, interactants in the interview task simply agree to ask and answer questions, but interactants in the scenario task always argue or disagree in order to win an encounter.

Finally, more recent research studies (Dyer 1983, Miller 1992) show the effectiveness of using scenarios in foreign-language teaching. Dyer found out that the use of occasional scenarios with 206 ESL students of various levels of proficiency and differing language backgrounds increased the acquisition of English and raised student awareness of role analysis, verbal strategies, speech protocols, and interactions in discourse situations. Her study concluded that the use of scenarios contributed to an increase on the test scores (structure and vocabulary) of all students in the study. Moreover, she reported that her students' composition of scenarios on computer terminals indicated the use of more varied structures and more difficult vocabulary. Miller's study of American university students learning Japanese concluded that an interactional approach based on using scenarios and games is both viable and effective in foreign-language instruction.

Conclusion. This study suggests that a scenario task leads to more input, and consequently to more use of *achievement* strategies, than does an interview task. Good interaction in the classroom is difficult to achieve merely by performing an interview task replete with questions and answers on family, job, vacation, or study plans. A scenario task of the type used in this study, which is based on a motivated exchange of language use (i.e. a dramatically charged interaction among speakers who assume psychological roles and experience an emotional depth), leads to good interaction and is thus recommended in a conversation classroom. Problem-solving scenarios, moreover, could provide learners with the opportunity to "push to the limit" their emerging interactive ability. More research in this area is recommended to find out whether or not scenarios will promote a greater quantity of speech or a greater variety of speech acts than will interview tasks or some other type of teacher-led discussion.

REFERENCES

Bialystok, Ellen. 1983. "Some factors in the selection and implementation of communication strategies." In Klaus Faerch and Gabriele Kasper (eds.), *Strategies in Interlanguage Communication*. London: Longman.

Bruton, Anthony, and Virginia Samuda. 1980. "Learner and teacher roles in the treatment of error in group work." *RELC Journal* 11(2): 49–63.

Di Pietro, Robert. 1987. *Strategic Interaction: Learning Languages Through Scenarios*. Cambridge: Cambridge University Press.

Dyer, Patricia. 1983. *Instructional procedures for implementing the strategic interaction method in an intensive English as a second language program.* Unpublished Ph.D. dissertation, University of Delaware.

Ellis, Rod. 1986. *Understanding Second Language Acquisition.* Hong Kong: Oxford University Press.

Ellis, Rod. 1984. "Communication strategies and the evaluation of communicative performance." *ELT Journal* 38: 39–44.

Frawley, William, and James P. Lantolf. 1985. "Second language discourse: A Vygotskyan perspective." *Applied Linguistics* 611: 19–44.

Khanji, Rajai. (in press). "Two perspectives in analyzing communication strategies." To appear in *IRAL* 2.

Long, Michael H. 1981. "Input, interaction, and second language acquisition." In Harris Winitz (ed.), *Native Language and Foreign Language Acquisition.* Annals of the New York Academy of Sciences 379: 259–278.

Long, Michael H., Leslie Adams, Marilyn McLean, and Ferdinando Castanos. 1976. "Doing things with words—Verbal interaction in lockstep and small group classroom situations." In Ruth H. Crymes and John F. Fanselow (eds.). *On TESOL* '76. Washington, D.C.: TESOL.

Miller, Mark. 1992. *Two experimental studies of the effectiveness of interactive game-playing in the acquisition of Japanese by American university students.* Unpublished Ph.D. dissertation, University of Delaware.

Swain, Merrill. 1985. "Communicative competence: Some roles of comprehensible input and comprehensible output in its development." In Susan M. Gass and Carolyn G. Madden (eds.), *Input in Second Language Acquisition.* Rowley, Mass.: Newbury House.

Appendix

1. **Role A:** You've just had a rather serious heart attack and are confined to the hospital. Your doctor seems hesitant to tell you about your condition. Work out a plan to get him or her to tell you exactly what your chances are for a complete recovery.

   Role B: You are a doctor who is treating a patient with a heart condition. This patient has just had a heart attack and is in the hospital. He does not know it yet, but he has just won the national lottery and is a rich man. How will you tell him this news without exciting him so much that he might have another heart attack?

2. An old member of your family needs constant attention because he is sick and needs somebody to look after him; all people at the house are too busy to take care of your old relative. He would like to stay in an old people's home rather than with the family. The members of your family have a divided opinion on this case. How can you reach an agreement regarding this sensitive situation?

3. You are driving your car out of town when it suddenly develops engine problems. You notice that there is a garage just ahead, but the mechanic is getting ready to close for the evening. How will you convince him to fix your car although he seems to be in a hurry to leave?

4. You are enjoying a meal with few friends at a restaurant. Halfway through your meal, the people at the next table complete their lunch and begin to enjoy an after-lunch smoke. You and your friends don't smoke, as it tends to make you cough and makes your eyes tear. Their smoke comes to your table and is ruining the remainder of your lunch. How do you solve this problem?

5. You are a waiter who is not supposed to accept checks from foreign customers. A foreigner, after finishing his meal, wants to pay the bill with a check or a credit card. How will both of you solve this problem, especially when you know that the foreigner has no cash?

Peace to the world! The contribution of foreign-language teaching to the goal of world peace

Reinhold Freudenstein
Philipps-Universität, Marburg

Introduction. The teaching of foreign languages has always been more than just a question of acquiring the linguistic skills necessary for communicative competence. Communication usually takes place in meaningful situations, and the contexts of such situations have been described by curriculum designers in the form of general statements and universal goals. It has been stated, for example, that the teaching of English, French, Spanish, or any other foreign language should promote friendly relations between the people of various countries. Classroom activities should encourage the appreciation of other cultures and contribute to the development of tolerance as a basis for mutual recognition. This list could easily be enlarged. "Peace," however, has so far been excluded from general objectives mentioned explicitly as relevant for foreign-language teaching, at least in Europe.

Why peace education is necessary. It might well be that in the past it simply has been taken for granted that learning a language and living peacefully together with speakers of other languages go hand in hand. It might also be that the idea of peace was implicitly contained in relevant statements on the teaching and learning of other languages. But in a world that has become increasingly aggressive, peace as an educational objective cannot be taken for granted any longer.

Peace education and the teaching of foreign languages should be inseparably combined both in official documents and in classroom activities. There is an important reason for this. Students of today have to learn how to master the challenges of the twenty-first century. The most demanding challenge will probably be to live in a world with a fast-growing population. Living together peacefully is the basis for survival. And one of the prerequisites for peaceful coexistence is the ability to communicate with others in a civilized, friendly—in short, in a peaceful—manner. Thus, *communicative competence*—internationally accepted as the most important objective in the teaching of foreign languages—should be expanded into *communicative peace*, as the Brazilian linguist Gomes de Matos has repeatedly demanded (Gomes de Matos 1991, 1992). It should become the overall concept for everything connected with the teaching and learning of foreign or second languages.

Changes in educational thinking. One of the radical changes that have taken place in foreign-language methodology over the last 15 or 20 years is an increasing awareness of the selection and treatment of content areas that should be covered in the foreign-language classroom. Many aspects of modern life had previously been disregarded or misrepresented in traditional teaching materials. A good example is the role of women in foreign-language textbooks. In the seventies, language educators pointed out in detail what was wrong in this regard (Freudenstein 1978), and since then the discussion about the place of women in society and their representation in schoolbooks has brought about enormous changes. It was not only that learning materials were revised; equally important was the fact that the awareness of the teaching profession had become focused on a problem which was—and still remains—a social challenge.

In the meantime, other deficits have been identified. Why don't we speak about old people and their problems when teaching a foreign language to young people? Why are problems of single-parent families excluded from instructional materials? Why are the handicapped not mentioned in most textbooks? One of the answers is that the teaching of foreign languages in all parts of the world is still more connected with formal aspects of grammar, translation, and vocabulary than with educational concerns. I think the time has come to end this tradition, particularly since many of the common formal aspects of language teaching have been criticized as being superfluous or even useless and are being replaced by elements of alternative methodologies.

In the twentieth century, we have experienced the most dreadful wars in the history of humanity. As the end of this century approaches and a new one is to be mastered by the young generation, it is therefore both justified and necessary to emphasize the notion of peace whenever and wherever possible—including in the foreign-language classroom.

Achievements in peace education so far. Classroom activities aiming at promoting peace are more or less nonexistent. But the idea is gaining ground. The 1990 World Congress of AILA (the International Association of Applied Linguistics) was devoted to the topic "Applied Linguistics, International Understanding, and Peace Education." In the United States, the annual "National Foreign Language Week" in 1991 concentrated on "Peace through Understanding." Particularly in America, peace education in the foreign-language classroom has advanced well beyond the slogan level. In the state of New York, a group of foreign-language educators are trying to integrate materials on nuclear disarmament and international security into everyday teaching.

In Germany, several papers have been published with recommendations for making the foreign-language classroom a place for peace education (Reisener

1990, Raasch 1991). The German UNESCO Commission has supported a project for the promotion of peace education through English-teaching materials for beginning, intermediate, and advanced students (Classen-Bauer 1989). In South America, Francisco Gomes de Matos has demonstrated why the teaching of peace should become the most important assignment for language teachers (1988, 1990). In Japan, the "Global Issues in Language Education Network" is an international body of language teachers who share an interest in peace-related matters like global awareness, social responsibility, and world citizenship. The first LINGUAPAX conference on the content and methods of teaching foreign languages and literatures for peace and understanding was organized by UNESCO in 1987 in the former Soviet Union; meetings in Sitges (Spain, 1989) and Saarbrücken (Germany, 1990) followed (Raasch 1991, 1993).

These are all hopeful signs. But they are still like little islands in a vast ocean of meaningless everyday episodes in the lives of the happy textbook families that dominate the teaching process. I am not just advocating an occasional inclusion of diverse peace items in the foreign-language classroom only. The notion of peace should not be or become just one topic among many others. It should rather be accepted as the overriding idea in the teaching and learning process. Peace deserves to be integrated into the foreign-language curriculum as an all-embracing leitmotif and should be regarded as at least as important as learning to communicate in a foreign language.

Language teaching as a form of peace education. In order to achieve this goal, thinking, research, and action should begin on three levels: (1) curriculum planning, (2) textbook writing, and (3) classroom activities. As these levels indicate, three groups of foreign-language educators are challenged by the new assignment: administrators and people responsible for state, local, or private school planning and development; textbook writers; and the millions of teachers who are actively involved in the teaching of foreign or second languages around the globe.

The curriculum level. Teaching a foreign language means preparing people for communication not only across linguistic borders, but also across cultural and ideological barriers. This can only work if our students are willing to meet and accept others in a truly humanistic way. They should be guided toward talking with fellow human beings rather than merely talking to other people. From there it follows that it should become standard procedure to include peace education as an explicit learning goal in all curricula of foreign- or second-language teaching.

Being able to communicate in everyday situations and being in a position to read and understand literature in another language does not automatically mean tolerance toward different opinions. It is therefore essential that guidelines should prescribe how pupils can be made aware of the fact that each individual has to work personally for a peaceful world. We must equip students with the knowledge, skills, and commitment necessary for becoming *fighters for peace*. Thus peace education should not only be mentioned as a—or even the—leading curriculum item; this could easily be regarded as paying pure lip service to an important educational objective.

Content areas must be identified and described in detail: the relationship between peace and social responsibility, the role of peace in international understanding, the context of peace for justice and human rights, the way the idea of peace can be expressed in class and school projects, and many more. Objectives and activities need to be exemplified in such a way that their relevance can be shown both for people as individuals and for community life. Methods of teaching peace topics should be developed in order to get the message across to the language learners. On the administrative side, every effort should be undertaken to merge peace education and language instruction into a unique concept in which both objectives are regarded as different expressions for the same concern.

In the past, administrators have concentrated too often and too much on only the linguistic elements of language teaching and learning; thus their main interest was focused on formal aspects of language acquisition. In the future they should first and foremost pay attention to what is being communicated, and only then look out for the language forms that need to be learned. It might well be possible that the overall goal of peace education could lead to a new evaluation of the role of linguistic elements once they serve a genuine educational instead of grammatical purpose. On such a basis, *communicative peace* could well be accepted in the same way as *communicative competence* has become the leading objective in the teaching of foreign languages today. If one excludes peace from communication, one is left with a restricted competence. Because of this, "communicative peace" is the challenge for generations of language teachers to come.

Implications for initial and in-service teacher training are obvious. Future teachers will not themselves have experienced, during their school days, how peace education can be put into practice in the foreign-language classroom. They will therefore have to be familiarized with and involved in projects that demonstrate just that. Examples of good ideas, projects, and actions can lead to creative innovations in peace education through language teaching. State officials and administrators responsible for guidelines for the teaching of foreign and second languages must be made aware of this necessity so that the educational needs of the next century can be adequately met on the level of curriculum planning.

The textbook level. I am not aware of any chapter, any lesson, any reading text, or any exercise in traditional foreign-language textbooks or workbooks or on cassettes that deals with the problem or with the challenge of peace. Learning materials devoted to this goal are missing not only in textbooks for beginners but also in readers for intermediate and advanced students. A very popular German textbook for English offers the adjective *peaceful* for the first time in the second year of learning when students have to answer questions while playing the role of Francis Chicester: "'Pacific' means 'peaceful'. Is the Pacific Ocean really so peaceful?" (Hellyer-Jones et al. 1980: 103). In another textbook, *peaceful* is mentioned only in the third year of English, and here in such a way that its meaning is neutralized by the context. In an extract from Edmund Hillary's autobiography, the author writes about adventures that every human being has to master: "Some paths will be more spectacular and others peaceful and quiet—who is to say which is the most important?" (Piepho and Bredella 1979: 111).

There are no differences between textbooks for children and for adults. In connection with looking for a new place to live one can read in a basic course: "I think I'll move to a quiet house in the suburbs some day. You've got peace and quiet, and if you want to go into the city, it's not far away" (Schmitz and Schmitz 1981: 102). There are even textbooks in which *peace* and *peaceful* are not mentioned at all, and the same holds true for textbooks in other foreign languages. *Peace* is treated in a purely formal way; it is a vocabulary item—nothing more. No concepts or appeals are connected with it.

Of course, the presence or absence of peace education cannot be proven by individual words or expressions. And it is also true that the former East European communist countries have misused the word *peace* for ideological purposes in a most horrible way. The Berlin Wall was called "The Wall for Preserving Peace" (Schutzwall für den Frieden). It is therefore necessary to always consider also the context in which these words appear, and it is in this respect that foreign-language textbooks almost systematically exclude peace-related issues.

There is actually no reason for neglecting peace-oriented texts and exercises because of vocabulary or grammar problems, as is often claimed. Texts on peace could be studied and discussed by the learners in just the same way as they have up to now dealt with texts about going shopping, asking the way, or going to a party. Possible topics could be peacemaking during a family quarrel, explaining the causes of violence, demonstrating for peaceful purposes, becoming a peaceful leader of a group—once one has started to think and to talk about subjects like these, students will most certainly provide many more examples that could be integrated into the foreign-language learning process.

Even if one has to use traditional materials, the idea of peace need not be neglected. If peace is regarded as an integral part of language learning, one will easily discover many places in textbook chapters and other teaching materials where the idea of peace can not only be added but can become a central focus of attention. One could design and teach communicative acts of a positive nature. One could devise the task of changing aggressive vocabulary into language that is used in a positive way. I have the feeling that in this way many rather boring texts could be turned into interesting and meaningful learning aids. I was encouraged in this regard by a Japanese language teacher who told me that she had experienced totally different classroom discussions since she had introduced global issues instead of meaningless everyday situations to her students. They were more motivated because they were more interested in the topics.

As the example demonstrates, up till now it has mainly been the teacher's task to include the peace dimension in his or her teaching; it is to be hoped that textbook authors will become aware of the need for *communicative peace* in the foreign-language classroom and write their materials accordingly. In the history of foreign-language teaching it has always been the textbook writers of English who have brought about innovations in the teaching process; this is why they should once again forge ahead and lead the way into a new world of peace-related materials so that other foreign languages can follow.

The classroom level. The classroom is where the real action takes place. Teachers should therefore be guided toward methods of including peace activities into their daily teaching. They must learn that peace is not something for discussion with advanced language students only. It can be put into practice from the very first lesson onwards. Role plays could be set up in which different people have to find peaceful solutions in a difficult or even hostile situation. Dictionary work could be done in order to find words that have to do with peace, e.g. peace-loving, peace-making, peace of mind, peaceful, friendly, good-natured; or when teaching German, friedlich, ruhig, freundlich, störungsfrei, friedvoll, friedfertig, friedsam, and others. One could give pupils the task that whenever a verb with a negative connotation comes up in a textbook story, they should add two new words with a positive attitude. One could explore the vocabulary field in the border area between war and peace.

Specific aspects of *life and institutions* are an integral part of every existing language program; once they are placed in the context of peace education, a new dimension is added to them: What can we do to learn more about a demonstration in Wales? Or the actions of Greenpeace in Australia? Are there possibilities of a letter or fax exchange with students in France? In all activities of this kind, the peace dimension is supposed to open the door of the classroom and to connect the outside world with the teaching process. Students could also be asked to collect peace-related texts and to prepare a reader in the foreign languages they learn with exercises inviting readers to think about the ideas expressed in those texts.

A very promising assignment for advanced students is to identify positive vocabulary in literary texts. One could guide students toward becoming involved in problem-solving activities, e.g. to paraphrase slogans, statements, or proverbs, adding or integrating aspects of peace. Thus, "Drive carefully" could become "Drive peacefully," "Nobody is perfect" could read "Peace is perfect," "Early to bed and early to rise makes a man healthy, wealthy, and wise" could be changed to "Early to bed and early to rise makes people healthy, peaceful, and wise." Likewise in German: "Morgenstund' hat Gold im Mund" could read "Morgenstund' tut Frieden kund," or "Aller Anfang ist schwer" easily changes into "Am Anfang ist auch Frieden schwer." A discussion on environmental conservation could take place in the form of a debate in which opposing parties try to find peaceful solutions to their problems. One could easily think of more examples, and pupils can be very creative in this respect, too, if given the chance to participate actively in the planning of the teaching and learning process.

Peace education is a form of thinking. Peace education in the foreign-language classroom reflects a state of mind; it is something to be permanently pursued. It is in the teacher's mind that language instruction and peace education ought to be regarded as one and the same concern before meaningful activities can be conducted in the everyday teaching situation. Teachers should be convinced that communicative competence has to be combined with peace-oriented thinking, otherwise the challenges of the twenty-first century cannot be met. They must be willing to dedicate time, effort, and professional skill to their work if they wish to contribute to peace in tomorrow's world. Pope John Paul II is supposed to have said: "To reach peace, teach peace."

Teachers must learn to teach peace in such a way that it is not the topic of special exercises that have been particularly selected for that purpose and that are occasionally added to other classroom activities. They must also learn that it is not sufficient merely to talk about peace, but that there are close links to their individual teaching styles. Peace education should be the context for the whole process of teaching foreign or second languages—from the selection of teaching materials and the way of presenting them to the students to a cooperative teacher–student relationship and a relaxed classroom atmosphere.

Benjamin Franklin once said: "Tell me and I forget. Teach me and I remember. Involve me and I learn." I believe that the foreign- and second-language classroom really can involve students in relevant activities that they not only remember but from which they learn how to shape their personal attitudes and actions. Foreign-language instruction by itself and on its own certainly cannot guarantee a peaceful world, but it can—if adequately pursued—help to support efforts of securing peace in all its aspects, from the individual inner calmness to the absence of wars between nations.

REFERENCES

Classen-Bauer, Ingrid (ed.). 1989. *International understanding through foreign-language teaching*. Bonn: German Commission for Unesco.

Freudenstein, Reinhold (ed.). 1978. *The role of women in foreign-language textbooks*. Brussels: AIMAV, Didier.

Gomes de Matos, Francisco. 1988. "Peace and language learning: A checklist." *FIPLV World News* 46: 1–3.

Gomes de Matos, Francisco. 1990. "Integrating peace into the classroom: Guidelines for foreign and second language teachers." *FIPLV World News* 53: 1–2.

Gomes de Matos, Francisco. 1991. "What the world needs now: Communicative peace." *FIPLV World News* 56: 1–2.

Gomes de Matos, Francisco. 1992. "Using foreign languages for communicative peace." *FIPLV World News* 59: 1–2.

Hellyer-Jones, Rosemary, et al. 1980. *Learning English: Compact course 2*. Stuttgart: Klett.

Piepho, Hans-Eberhard, and Lothar Bredella (ed.). 1979. Contacts 7. Topics 1. Enriched Course. Bochum: Kamp.

Raasch, Albert. 1991. "Si vis pacem, pacem para." In Renate Grebing (ed.), *Grenzenloses Sprachenlernen*. Berlin: Cornelsen & Oxford University Press. 275–286.

Raasch, Albert (ed.). 1991. *Peace through language teaching*. Saarbrücken: Universität des Saarlandes.

Raasch, Albert (ed.). 1993. *Language teaching in a world without peace*. Saarbrücken: Universität des Saarlandes.

Reisener, Helmut. 1990. Friedenserziehung durch Fremdsprachenunterricht. *Der fremdsprachliche Unterricht* 2: 30–35.

Schmitz, Albert, and Edith Schmitz. 1981. *Kontakte Englisch*. München: Hueber.

Variability in foreign language education

Aoi Tsuda
Osaka University, Japan

Introduction. The communicative needs of foreign-language learners involve several procedures in teaching: lexical, grammatical, interactional, socio-cultural, and pragmatic knowledge. On the practical level, foreign-language education cannot be separated from the needs, innovations, and development of a society at a particular period. In the light of this viewpoint, Japanese society is one of the typical examples where the whole society is in the process of changing at an accelerated pace. With the growing impact of Japan's economy on the world, increasing numbers of Japanese workers have been stationed abroad with their families. These workers now number more than 500,000, and several thousand of them return to Japan every year. Their children have a problem increasingly recognized as specific to Returnee students, namely, difficulty in re-adapting to Japanese culture and society.

Several years ago, a fact-finding group was organized with the specific purpose of investigating the actual state of Returnee students. The first research project consisted of a preliminary inquiry into the general background of the Returnee students, their linguistic abilities in both English and Japanese, and the psycholinguistic aspects of their cognition and interpretation of reality. I would like to concentrate on the subject I consider most pertinent to the topic of this paper. This research deals with the word associations and social distances of Returnee students, in order to investigate the relationships between language use and the psychological state of mind of the Returnees.

Social and psychological distance measured by word association and evaluation. In the first research project on word association by Yoshida (1985), three different groups were tested. One control group consisted of 32 Japanese students; the second control group consisted of 21 American students; and the third group consisted of 53 Japanese Returnee students. The first two groups were tested in Japanese and in English respectively, and the Returnee group was tested in both languages with an interval of one week between tests. Words that were lexically equivalent in both languages were classified into four different semantic fields: Nature, Daily Life, Society and Thought, and Culture. Two types of analyses were performed on the results: a response item analysis, which compared the actual words that were associated with the stimuli, and a response type analysis, examining the type of associations from a semantic point of view.

Yoshida employed 10 categories to organize the associations: contextual associations, superordinate associations, subordinate associations, coordinate associations, part-to-whole associations, attribute associations, symbolic associations, sound associations, individual associations, and miscellaneous associations, that is, responses that do not fit into the above categories.

Yoshida's results show that the Returnees' responses are distinct, depending on the nature of the stimulus words. Items relating to Society and Thought, and culturally loaded terms such as Kurisumasu/Christmas tend to draw a greater number of different responses of different types in the two languages. Most of the items that related to Nature and to Daily Life, on the other hand, tended to draw similar responses in the two languages. In some cases that were related to Nature and Daily Life, associations of Returnees in English and Japanese were similar to those of the Japanese control group. In other cases, terms related to Society and Thought tended to be similar to those of the control group when tested in Japanese, while in English their responses are distinct from those of the Japanese control group. Yoshida concludes that the Returnees have semantic networks different from the Japanese control group even when they speak Japanese. He cites Taylor (1976: 274), who states that a bilingual must have a complex semantic system, storing some concepts uniquely according to each of the two languages and other concepts in common for both languages, depending on the concepts.

In the section of Yoshida's study that measures Returnees' social distance from the Japanese and American control groups of the first section, he examines how the Returnee students feel about 20 words. As stimuli he uses Acton (1979), including such words as "future," "religion," "United Nations," and "privacy." Yoshida tried to see the evaluation of the Returnee students from two sets of viewpoints such as "optimistic" vs. "pessimistic," "lonely" vs. "merry," "predictable" vs. "unpredictable," "inactive" vs. "active," and so forth. The students were given a scale of six points and asked to mark it after considering the following three factors:

1. How do you feel about the word?
2. How would Japanese feel about it in your opinion?
3. How would Americans feel about it in your opinion?

From his results, Yoshida concludes that the closer the word associations of the Returnees conforms to that of Americans, the further their relative social and psychological distance from the Americans compared with the Japanese. In other words, the more the Returnees acquire the conceptual system of the English language and American culture, the more critical and objective they become toward Americans and their culture, and the more conscious they become of their being Japanese.

Acculturation measured by social and sociolinguistic behaviors. In the second joint research project, the main theme was acculturation in language behavior and patterns of behavior. The research we conducted so far consisted of the following three sections: (1) Japanese proficiency, (2) psychological study of self-disclosure and social adaptation, and (3) sociolinguistic research. Our subjects were 287 university students: 51 American students born and brought up in the United States; 44 Japanese students studying in America; 100 Japanese Returnee students mainly from English-speaking countries such as the United States and the United Kingdom; and finally, as a control group, 92 Japanese students who had never studied abroad. In this brief report, I would like to concentrate on the sociolinguistic research.

In order to investigate the degree of self-assertion comprising the standard of behavior, that is, behavior of oneself and the standard of acceptance, namely, acceptance of the behavior of others, we set out seven situations including school, place of work, and public situations. The approach to our research was as follows: concerning seven situations we asked a total of 32 questions. The subject was supposed to select the one he/she would consider appropriate or write an optional one. Finally, we carried out a quantitative analysis of the answers. By way of example, I will present two situations and questions.

Situation 1: You belong to a certain club at the university. All the club members had a get-together and started to talk about the future activities of the club. Someone proposed an idea. "This coming year let's invite B (a famous singer) for the Freshmen Week Concert in order to encourage freshmen to join our club." Most of your club members eagerly supported the idea. However, you were not very enthusiastic about it. You knew quite well that your club was economically pinched, and even if they succeed in inviting B, there is no telling whether it would do any good in encouraging freshmen to join your club.

Q1. If you are in this situation, what would you say or do in order to express your opinion?

1. If everyone else supports the idea of inviting B, there is not much I can do, so I will keep quiet.
2. I would rather wait for someone else to raise his or her hand and say that he or she is opposed to the idea of inviting B, and then I would say that I am also opposed to the idea.
3. I would raise my hand and say that I am opposed to the idea, giving reasons such as our club is economically pinched or that

even if we succeeded in calling B, it probably would not help too much in getting freshmen to join our club.

The results are shown in the Mean Score as follows: Americans 2.75, Returnees 2.75, Japanese 2.65, and Japanese control group 2.30. As this score decreases, the degree of self-assertion also decreases. The Mean Scores of Americans and Returnees are the same, namely, the majority of them will express their own opinions in front of people, even if their opinions are different from the rest. On the other hand, the Japanese control group's score is close to two points, that is to say, the students tend to wait for someone else to take the initiative in opposing that idea.

Then, in order to find out the degree of acceptance of the behavior of others, we set up the following question and answers.

Q.2. How do you feel when students try to persuade other people, in an attempt to convince them that they themselves are right, and who brave the conflict and confrontation of others?

1. Bad
2. Poor
3. Don't know
4. Fair
5. Good

The Mean Score of each group is as follows: Americans 4.08, Returnees 4.19, Japanese 4.38, and Japanese control group 4.13. Responses from the four groups indicate that there is no statistically significant difference.

Situation 2: Suppose you happen to be in a crowded subway some hot day. Unfortunately, you are standing. The subway for some reason is not air-conditioned. There is an announcement that the air-conditioner is out of order and that the passengers are kindly requested to open the windows.

Q.1. In the above situation what would you do?

1. I don't want to attract the attention of the other people, so I will not open the window.
2. It is too much trouble to open the window, so I will not open it.
3. I would say "Excuse me" and open the window.

The Mean Score of each group is as follows: Americans 2.91, Returnees 2.63,

Japanese 2.48, and Japanese control group 2.43. As the results show, the Mean Score of Americans and Returnees is close to three points, that is, these two groups are liable to respond to the request forthrightly by opening the windows by themselves. On the other hand, almost half of the Japanese answers are that they will not open the windows. With regard to questions measuring attitude toward the behavior of others, we developed the following question.

Q.2 How do you feel about the people who put up with sweltering heat in the crowded subway instead of opening the windows?

1. Good
2. Fair
3. Don't know
4. Poor
5. Bad

The Mean Score of each group is as follows: Americans 3.96, Returnees 3.88, Japanese 3.35, and Japanese control group 3.77. As the number of the score increases, the degree of acceptance of other people's behavior decreases. As revealed by this analysis, we can conclude that the two Japanese groups show a higher degree of acceptance than Americans and Returnees.

In conclusion, in the presentation of this research the following points have been made:

- Linguistic behavior peculiar only to the Returnee students was not observed.
- With regard to the standard of self-assertion, Returnee students show the highest rate, then follow Americans, Japanese studying abroad, and the Japanese control group.
- Concerning the standard of acceptance, Returnee students show the highest rate.
- Among the Japanese control group, a big gap between the standard of behavior and that of acceptance was observed. As regards the standard of behavior, they show the lowest self-assertion, but they have a high acceptance of other peoples' behavior.
- The Americans show a bipolarity with regard to the standard of acceptance. While they point out that their culture is individually oriented, they stress even more strongly the friction caused by their individualism as a negative aspect.

A true understanding of Returnee students will hopefully be achieved through further interdisciplinary endeavors of linguistics, socio- and psycholinguistics, psychology, education, and so on.

Findings and conclusion. The final section of this paper will be devoted to the highlights of these research projects, drawing some conclusions for foreign-language education in Japan. Since the number of Returnee students is constantly increasing, and will continue increasing even more due to the international role Japanese society has to play in greater measure, the educational systems should first of all accept the Returnee students as they are, without forcing them to change. Rather, Japanese educational institutions should recognize the value and contributions of these Returnee students for the ever-growing internationalization of Japanese society. And finally, it is essential to provide suitable curricula to develop the enriching experiences they have already acquired. This could constitute a significant contribution to the development of the students, who could use this Japanese and international experience for the benefit of Japanese society in international, academic, and economic affairs.

More specifically, I would like to propose five points in regard to this perspective.

1. The educational system should be more flexible, in accordance with the interests, needs, and different goals of students with different backgrounds. In foreign-language curricula for example, one pattern is still predominant, that is to say, the grammar and translation method.
2. The education system as a whole should be more internationally oriented, taking into consideration the world in which the students live at present and the world of the future. In foreign-language curricula, for instance, the goal should first of all be toward acquiring greater communicative competence and understanding, and accepting and appreciating value systems of each culture, without any value judgment.
3. The education system should be set up in such a way that students can develop their own way of thinking and expressing opinions. From this viewpoint, the foreign-language curricula should be more student centered than teacher centered.
4. In order to reach this communicative competence and international awareness, the education institutions and the people engaged in foreign-language education should make efforts to create the necessary atmosphere to attain this goal.
5. Finally, it is of the utmost importance to integrate faculty who are native Japanese speakers and faculty who are native English speakers and who share this conception of their ideals.

As a final remark, I would like to quote the great Spanish philosopher Ortega's ideas on the mission of the university, namely, that the mission of the university is to bring the student up to the level of his or her time.

REFERENCES

Acton, William R. 1979. "Perception of lexical connotation: Professed attitude and socio-cultural distance in second language learning." Ph.D. dissertation. University Microfilm.

Acton, William R., and Judith Walker de Felix. 1986. "Acculturation and mind." In Joyce Merrill Valdes (ed.), *Culture bound: Bridging the cultural gap in language teaching*. Cambridge: Cambridge University Press. 20–32.

Beebe, Leslie M. (ed.). 1988. *Issues in second language acquisition: Multiple perspectives*. New York: Newbury House.

Brown, H. Douglas. 1987. *Principles of language learning and teaching*. Englewood Cliffs, N.J.: Prentice-Hall.

Cummins, James. 1979. "Linguistic interdependence and the educational development of bilingual children." *Review of Educational Research* 49: 222–51.

Cummins, James. 1980. "The cross-lingual dimensions of language proficiency: Implications for bilingual education and the optimal age issue." *TESOL* 14: 175–85.

Grabe, William, and Robert B. Kaplan. 1992. *Introduction to applied linguistics*. Reading: Addison-Wesley.

Lobo, Felix, Aoi Tsuda, and Yayoi Sekiguchi. 1989. *A sociolinguistic research of returnee students: Kikokushijo no Bunka Henyoo Hokokusho* [A Research Report on the Acculturation of Returnee Students]. Tokyo: Sophia University Publications. 97–138.

Schuman, John. 1975. "Affective Factors and Problem of Age in Second Language Acquisition." *Language Learning* 25(2): 209–25.

Swain, Merrill. 1984. *Language issues and education policies exploring Canada's multilingual resources*. Oxford: Pergamon Press.

Taylor, Insup. 1976. *Introduction to psycholinguistics*. New York: Holt.

Yoshida, Kensaku. 1985. *Some psycholinguistic characteristics of returnee students: Tango renso to social distance no chosa* [A study of Word Association and Social Distance]. Tokyo: Sophia University Publications. 58–90.

The L2 kindergarten teacher as a territory marker

Josep Maria Artigal
University of Barcelona

"It is as users of the new language that people become learners of it"
—Robert di Pietro

I was a kindergarten L2 teacher for nine years in Catalonia. For the last seven years I have been coordinating and advising on various programs for the introduction of English, German, Swedish, Russian, Occitan, and Catalan as L2 or L3 in kindergartens in Finland, Italy, France, the Basque Country, and Catalonia (Artigal and Camps 1982, Artigal et al. 1984, Artigal 1985, Artigal 1987, Artigal 1990, Artigal 1991b). It was during one of these projects in Italy that, thanks to Traute Taeschner, I was fortunate enough to meet and work with Robert Di Pietro. Knowing him was a great source of enrichment to me, in both theoretical and human terms, and it remains so today.

The topic of my paper is connected with these events. First of all I propose to describe some of the socio- and psycholinguistic variables related to the aforementioned experiments in early multilingual education. Subsequently I will be concentrating on analyzing the one aspect of these experiments that Robert Di Pietro found most interesting and that formed the basis of our discussions: If, as he said, and I agreed, "it is as users of the new language that people become learners of it," then how is it possible for a kindergarten child to become a user of a language that he or she does not yet know?

The necessary requirements for a beneficial early plurilingual program. In the light of many studies carried out in recent years (Genesee, Lambert, and Tucker 1978, Cummins 1979, Swain and Lapkin 1982, Genesse and Lambert 1983, Genesee 1987, Snow 1987, Artigal 1989, Arnau et al. 1992, Vila 1992), it is impossible to state purely and simply, in a generalized way, that school curricula, developed at an early age through languages different from the home language, are in themselves beneficial or harmful to the pupils to whom they are applied. When assessing the viability of this type of education, various sociolinguistic and psycholinguistic variables related to how the languages are acquired must be borne in mind.

In all the programs involving early plurilinguism considered in the present paper, five requirements are fulfilled, and these I will briefly describe.

1. The social status of the languages in question. In all the cases referred to here, the second or third languages introduced in school are socially weaker than the pupils' home language.
2. The attitude and motivation toward the new languages. All the programs of early bi- or trilingualism I will be dealing with are the result of a voluntary choice made by parents and receive their support.
3. The variables related to the teachers' proficiency in the new language and their use of it. Though they interact with their pupils exclusively through the new language, thus respecting the principle of "one language, one person," they are always bilingual and therefore able to understand their pupils when the latter use their home language.
4. The continuing in-service training teachers must receive to ensure that at all times they possess the theoretical and practical knowledge they need in order to guarantee the communicability and efficiency of the interactions conveyed through the new languages. This has been shown by experience to be of vital importance.
5. Finally, the methodological approach used, namely that the new languages are acquired by being used. This implies that, instead of focusing on teaching the L2 or L3, these situations of early plurilingualism emphasize the communication of meaningful tasks through the target languages from the very beginning.

The new language is learned by being used. Though the last of the above considerations may at first sight seem acceptable, it in fact raises several theoretical and methodological questions: First and foremost, how can kindergarten pupils be enabled to make use from the very start of a language they do not yet know?

This, in my view, is the crux of the matter. Once the remaining socio- and psycholinguistic requirements listed above have been met, it is precisely the ability of teacher and pupils to construct meaningful and efficient uses of the new language that becomes the central mechanism of the L2 or L3 learning process between the ages of four and six.

In order to clarify the question of "use as an acquisition mechanism," I will first define three prior assumptions concerning what I mean by a linguistic sign.

First assumption. Linguistic forms operate by means of a set of semiotic functions, that is, linguistic units are a product derived from relational processes with other linguistic units. At the same time, these semiotic functions are, at least partly, independent of the regularities that occur in the world, so it can be said that a "word" is never totally isomorphic with any kind of "world," or, to put it another way, that a "word" is never a "piece of a mirror of the world." Just as Paul Klee states that "art does not reproduce what is visible but makes it visible," we can also maintain that a language is not a set of elements and procedures that make possible the creation of meaning because they are simple "reproducers" of nonlinguistic elements or procedures, but that a language is itself a meaning-making procedure, or, in the words of Klee, a procedure for "making visible." In this sense, according to Vygotsky (1981a), signs are tools of mediation, or to put it another way, making meaning is a process that inevitably introduces a semiotic distancing effect.

Second assumption. As a consequence of the foregoing assumption, linguistic signs are liable to evolve during the acquisition process insofar as their degree of conveyable multifunctionality gradually develops. Therefore, the language-acquisition process—and thus L2/L3 acquisition—is not an accumulation of signs assimilated once and for all but a continuous, semiotic restructuring of signal forms, a progressive functional stratification of signals that has to be constructed. Or, what amounts to the same thing, the initial use of a sign in the new language does not involve the recognition of all the semiotic possibilities that it can have as a sign (Karmiloof-Smith 1979, 1986, 1987, Wertsch 1979, Hickmann 1985, 1987, Silverstein 1987).

Thus, according to this second assumption, one presupposition is established: If during the acquisition process the signs are gradually reorganized, then initially they can be used in such a way that they are dependent on semiotic functions that must for the time being be considered partial or restricted.

Third assumption. As Silverstein (1976, 1985, 1987) has pointed out, indexical functions are among the semiotic functions, that is, indexicality is one form of the semiotic mediation mentioned earlier, one of the ways of creating a distancing effect. In this sense, and returning to an argument proposed by Peirce (1965), a linguistic sign operates as a "vehicle of" both symbolic and indexical functions. Thus, in addition to obvious symbolic functions, any linguistic text—and thus any L2/L3 text—is also built up by means of indexical functions so that the symbolic functions on their own—without indexicality—are no more than an unfulfilled possibility of meaning (Artigal 1990a, 1991, 1992a).

At the same time, indexical functions have an important place in the language-acquisition process. Or to put it another way, in order to solve the "mediation problem"—i.e. finding out how the learner manages to recognize and/or construct semiotic distance—psycholinguistic theories need to use not only a restricted symbolic model but also a semiotic model that includes the indexical functions of the sign as well (Artigal 1992b, De Lemos 1992).

The indexical value of linguistic signs. Following Peirce, I shall define the index as that function of a sign whose existence depends on relations "in presentia" among signal forms and that would become nonoperational, meaningless, as soon as these relations were eliminated.

The index makes meaning through semiotic contiguity as a function of the mutual determination of signal constituents—that is, insofar as it builds a territory of relations in presentia that must be maintained by the interlocutors from the beginning to the end of a given text.

A metaphor may help to clarify this idea of indexical function as a process of establishing a territory of relations in presentia. Let us imagine for a moment a theatrical performance. In such a performance, once a character is brought onto the stage, he or she must be kept in presentia by the spectators—even if he or she leaves the stage—until the curtain falls. In this sense, the way the spectators construe the play depends on a particular set of procedures for maintaining the copresence of a set of characters, for building a territory of contiguities in which these characters may be placed. However, if members of the audience go up to the stage when the performance is over, they will never find the characters from the play. It matters little whether the actors are, or are not, present on the stage; whether they are still wearing their costumes or not; whether they pronounce words from the play or not. When the performance is over, as before it starts, there will be no theatrical characters on the stage who can, and must, be indexically maintained by the audience.

Thus it can be stated that in order to play a meaningful role in the play, the characters need a territory of copresence that is created when the curtain rises and ceases to exist when it falls. Similarly it can be said in some respects that the signs of a text always, and of necessity, operate like theatrical performers. That is, the signs of a text make meaning if they may be placed by the interlocutors in a semiotic territory with boundaries—the curtain that is raised and dropped—where they may be maintained as "copresences." In other words, when the interlocutors use a text they inevitably need to build a shared scenography of contiguities that introduces semiotic mediation, which achieves a distancing effect through territoriality. Otherwise the signal forms they use would be like the characters in a play outside the territory of the performance, ie., they would be devoid of meaning.

It follows then that any meaningful use of a language, including its first uses, will inevitably involve some kind of indexical territory where the signs will have to be placed and maintained.

Joint action as a first indexical territory recognizable by the learners. According to various arguments introduced by psycholinguistics, a child will acquire a new language if it is sufficiently exposed to that language, if its attitude and motivation toward it are positive, but also, and above all, if—when it accedes to the input in question—the input may be processed, that is, "filled" with meaning.

How then is it possible to fill with meaning the forms of a language one does not yet know? The (partial) response I propose is as follows: It is possible to fill with meaning the forms of a language one does not yet know provided the joint action undertaken with others is so organized—ie. as long as the outer boundaries and inner order of what the speakers do are established in such a way—that it can be used cooperatively as a first indexical territory recognized by all the participants, that is, as a topographical mental space that is collectively identifiable.

Obviously this answer rests on the assumption that meaningful and efficient use can be made of the signs of the new language on the basis of semiotic functions that are temporarily being restricted but are capable of being later reorganized. However, as I said before, this semiotically partial but nonetheless efficient use of signs is something that in fact is accepted in my second prior assumption.

In order to explain in what sense joint action operates as a first "shared indexical territory" in the new language, I will begin by referring to the dramatization of one of the stories used to introduce English, German, Swedish, Russian, Occitan, and Catalan as L2 or L3 to pupils aged between four and six years (Artigal and Camps 1982, Artigal et al. 1984, Artigal 1985, Artigal and Taeschner 1990, Artigal 1990b).

Mummy's Cake

A mother and her small daughter make a cake. Once the cake is baked, the little girl wants to eat it, but the mother tells her it is to be eaten later on and puts it away on top of the cupboard. Then the mother goes out shopping and the little girl takes the opportunity to try to reach the forbidden cake. After trying various methods, she finally succeeds by using some magic words, takes the cake, and eats it. Immediately after this the mother comes home and asks who has eaten the cake.

SCRIPT

General Indications	Verbalizations
As soon as all the pupils are in place *, the teacher in place 1a begins to tell the story.	ARE YOU READY FOR A STORY? ONCE UPON A TIME A MOTHER

Figure 1. Classroom map

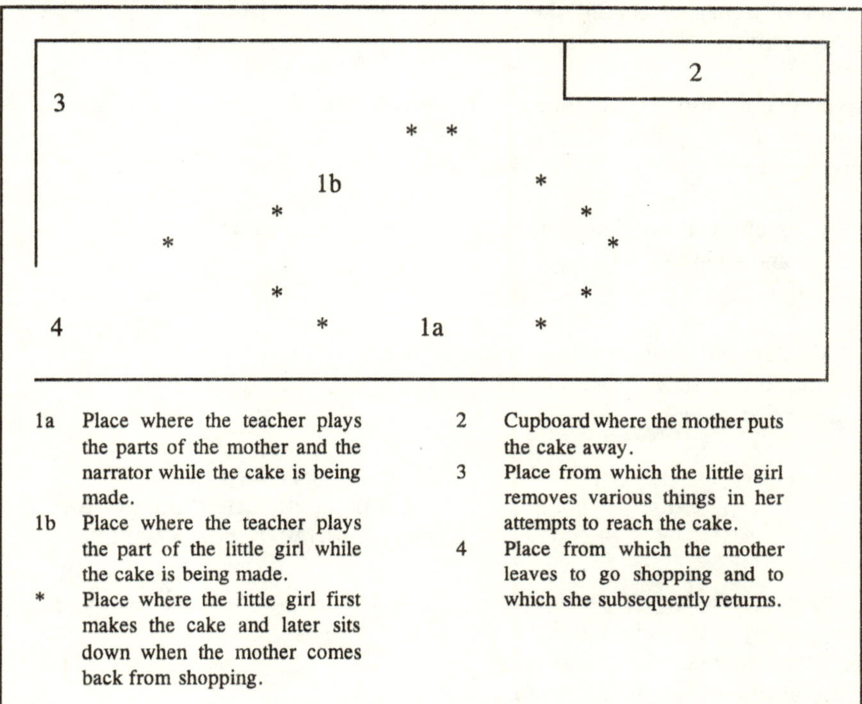

	AND A DAUGHTER WERE MAKING A CAKE
Everyone pretends to tip flour into an imaginary bowl he/she is holding	* flour
Everyone pretends to pour milk into the bowl	* milk
Everyone pretends to put sugar into the bowl	* sugar
Everyone pretends to break an egg and drop the yolk and white into the bowl	* an egg, craack!

Everyone imitates the action and sound of a blender beating the cake mixture	* zzzzzzzzzzzzzzzzz
Everyone puts his or her finger into the mixture, tastes it, looks dissatisfied, and says	* not yet!
Once again everyone imitates the action and sound of a blender beating the cake mixture	* zzzzzzzzzzzzzzzzz
Again they put their fingers into the mixture, taste it, look pleased this time and say	* okay.
	NOW MUMMY AND HER DAUGHTER PUT THE CAKE IN THE OVEN, AND WAIT FOR A WHILE
They open the door of an imaginary oven, put the cake mixture in, close the oven door, and turn the dial to the right temperature. Then they wait a while	* hmmm, it smells good!
They open the oven door, carefully take the cake out, and on seeing it exclaim	* hmmm, what a cake!
Teacher → 1b	AND THE LITTLE GIRL SAID
Playing the role of the little girl they all say	→ Mummy, cake!?
Teacher → 1a	
Playing the part of the mother they all reply	→ mmmh-mmmh, not now, later.
Playing the part of the little girl the pupils say again	→ Mummy, cake!?

Playing the part of the mother the teacher again replies	→ Mmmh-mmmh, not now, later.
Then the teacher alone, playing the part of the mother, picks up the cake and puts it on top of a cupboard	→ Mummy puts the cake high up in the cupboard for later.
Teacher → 1a	AND THEN MUMMY LEFT HOME FOR A WHILE BECAUSE SHE WAS GOING SHOPPING
The teacher alone, playing the part of the mother, moves to 4 saying	→ Mummy is going out. Don't eat the cake. Do you understand me?
The pupils, playing the part of the little girl, answer	→ Yes, Mummy.
The mother repeats	→ Are you going to eat the cake?
The pupils again reply	→ No, Mummy.
The teacher leaves from 4, waits a moment, and then comes in again making gestures to indicate that the mother has gone away	THEN, WHEN MUMMY'S GONE, THE GIRL TRIED TO FIND A WAY TO REACH THE CAKE
Teacher (1a)	* DO YOU WANT TO REACH THE CAKE?
The teacher and all the pupils move to (2) and try to reach the cake	* Ah, ah, ah ...crashhh! I can't!
After a moment's thought they say	* Let's see ... Aha! A chair!
They all move from 2 to 3 repeating	* A chair, a chair, a chair, ...

When they reach 3 they pretend to pick up an imaginary chair and carry it to 2 saying	* A chair, a chair, a chair, ...
When they reach 2 they pretend to put the chair on the ground, climb onto it and try to reach the cake	* Ah, ah, ah ...
However, all they succeed in doing is falling to the ground	* Aaaah ... crashhhh.
	BUT THE CHAIR WAS NO GOOD

This same pattern can be repeated several times with other objects such as "a table," "a ladder," "a box," and so on, each time with the same result. For instance:

Everyone → (2)	* Let's see ... Aha! A table!
Everyone → (3)	* A table. A table, a table, ...
Everyone → (2)	* A table. A table, a table, ...
	* Ah, ah, ah, ...
	* Aaaah .... crashhhh.
	BUT THE TABLE WAS NO GOOD

	SUDDENLY THE CHILD HAD AN IDEA, TO USE SOME MAGIC WORDS
The teacher and all the pupils at 2 thoughtfully look at the cake and finally they say	* Let's see ... Aha! magic words!
They rythmically raise their arms and all say the magic words	* Ho-ho-ho, up we go!
They jump, take hold of the cake and, once they are seated at *, they eat it	* Munch, munch, ... it's delicious!

Teacher → 1a	BUT THEN, SUDDENLY, MUMMY CAME BACK
The teacher leaves from 4. The teacher comes in again making a gesture to imitate the mother and goes to 1a. Then she looks on top of the cupboard, looks surprised, and says	
To everyone	→ Oh dear! What's happened to the cake? Who ate the cake?
One by one	→ Did you eat the cake? Yes or no?
If the pupils answer	→ Yes.
then the mother says	→ Oh! naughty boy/girl.
and smacks their bottoms	→ Smack, smack.
If the pupils say	→ No.
then the mother says	→ That's great! good boy/girl.
and kisses them	→ A kiss.
Teacher → (1a)	AND THAT'S ALL!

The most noteworthy features of the tasks set for the pupils by means of this story can be briefly summarized as follows.

- The tale has a simple plot and deals with a topic akin to the experiences and fantasies of children in the target age group.
- It is narrated, from the very start, by means of a collective dramatization in which the whole class actively plays all the parts that appear in the plot.
- The pupils are absorbed by their own performance, and the actions, gestures, mime, and intonation that teacher and pupils continually develop help to make the plot comprehensible.

Using this type of performance as his or her basic material, the teacher pays special attention to two points that are a crucial and indispensable part of the process of making meaning through the new language referred to above. The first concerns the creation of the classroom map as already described, which, as we will see later on, organizes the joint action in a recognizable way. The second is the arrangement of what we call the boundaries of the story. In the first place there are entry and exit boundaries that—like the curtain that rises and falls—let the children know when they are inside the story and when they are outside of it. In the second place there are a set of internal boundaries that make it possible to delimit "significant units" within the action as it proceeds.

All these external and internal boundaries are achieved by the teacher through the use of "pauses" and "narrative formulae." A pause is a short time during which the teacher stops, drops any body position connected with an action or character in the story, looks at the pupils, and, without actually saying or doing anything, establishes a boundary between the part of the story that has just been acted and the next one to be proposed. A narrative formula is when the teacher, standing in the "place" of the narrator and using the gesture and intonation of the narrator, begins the story with "Once upon a time ...," rounds it off with some other appropriate formula, or gives a brief explanation of what is about to happen in the course of the dramatization.

Experience shows that the pupils do not usually understand these explanations, particularly at the beginning of the new language-acquisition process, but they do immediately recognize their function as the external and internal boundaries of the discourse.

The placing of both pauses and narrative formulae within the classroom map regulates the story internally in a way that is recognizable for all the pupils. In other words, this way of organizing the collective dramatization makes the story—which is told exclusively in the new language—into a semiotic territory that is recognizable, ie. shared and copresent for all the participants. By establishing the inner and outer boundaries of a set of places, moments, and things that are said and done, the teacher is organizing a meaningful semiotic territory that makes it possible for the first uses of the new language to function, that is, he or she regulates a "sharable" mental space that operates as a mechanism for building up the meaning of the uses of the new language.

Let us go back to the dramatization of the story entitled "Mummy's cake" and observe a particular instance of this last argument. If we carefully analyze the script we will notice that the pupils' activity has been structured around three "spaces." When the story begins, all the children are in place 1, sitting on the floor in a semicircle (see the classroom map). In this first "space," which we can classify as (1 + mother + seated pupils), the teacher introduces the main characters—the mother and her little girl—and the "bone of contention"—the cake that the little girl wants to eat and that the mother puts away on top of the cupboard.

Once the plot has been established, the children stand up and, without the "presence" of the mother, move to places 2 and 3. In this second "space," which can be classified as (2 + 3 + no mother + pupils not seated), the pupils try to reach the denouement of the story, that is, get at the cake. Once they have succeeded, they return to place 1 and sit down on the floor again; then the mother "comes back." And it is in this third "space," in this return to the original (1 + mother + pupils seated), that the story finally comes to an end.

This way of organizing the joint activity operates as a shared indexical territory that makes it possible, in the first place, to maintain throughout the tale the signs of the new language, and in the second place to give different meanings to these same signs according to the different spaces in which they are placed. It is precisely this territorialization of the things the class does together that makes it possible to fill with meaning, for instance, the "cake" of the final question:

"Did you eat the cake?"

or that makes it possible to give different meanings to the *cake*s in

"Mummy cake!?"

or

"Oh, dear! What's happened to the cake."

To put it another way, if this indexical territory of shared action were not recognizable, then the form *cake,* which belongs to the new language, could in no case be filled with meaning. This is why the pauses, movements, places, and gestures of the narrator, and positions like being seated or standing, build up a copresent topography, maintained and shared by all the participants, and operate, in short, as the mechanisms whereby the uses of the new language are given meaning.

Just as characters in a play are only characters within the territory of the performance, any element of the new language that cannot be used (understood and/or produced) in a jointly recognizable territory will cease to function as a sign.

From other-regulation to self-regulation. Up to this point I have been arguing that it is possible to use a language one does not yet know because the organization of action undertaken with others can be jointly recognized and used as a first indexical territory.

However this last argument must be completed by another: Though in the first instance the indexical territories of joint action are inevitably regulated by the teacher, later on these meaning-building devices must be self-regulated by the pupils. In order to explain this evolution in the uses of the new language

Figure 1. Stage set of the tale "Mummy's cake": Making the cake

from an initial external regulation to a later internal regulation (Vygotsky 1981b), I will describe some aspects of the way one of the "materials" used from the tale "Mummy's cake" is developed during the school year.

Each tale has its own "stage set" (see Figure 1 and Figure 2). This stage set consists of a large sheet of paper on which the scenery of the action has been drawn together with a set of cut-out characters and objects that can be stuck onto the scenery using "Blue-tack."

Once the tale has been collectively dramatized three or four times, the teacher tells the story again using the stage set as though it were a small "movie screen" on which the characters and objects can gradually be stuck and moved about while the action is being narrated.

The first time the set is used, it is the teacher who tells the story and places the characters and objects in the appropriate places. But as the tale is told again and again, with the help of the set, the teacher lets a pupil "take over" certain characters, in such a way that the pupil occupies an independent place in the discourse. Ultimately the teacher can drop out and leave it up to the pupil to regulate the story-telling alone.

It should be noticed, however, that this self-regulation of the meaning-making mechanisms will now be possible precisely insofar as the pupil has a territory—ie. the stage set—that enables him or her to maintain all the necessary copresences, provides him or her with "spaces" in which to place, indexically, the linguistic forms of the new language, and even enables him or her to signify those parts of the discourse he or she is as yet unable to verbalize.

Figure 2. Stage set of the tale "Mummy's cake": Trying to get the cake

I am referring, for example, to the fact that the set for "Mummy's cake" possesses a cut-out "cake" that can be maintained throughout the tale as an "indexically meaningful character in the play"; to the fact that this type of visual support makes it possible to give different values to the expression "cake" according to the spaces in which it is verbalized; and to the fact that this way of telling the story enables the pupils to overcome the inability to verbalize an expression like

> "But then, suddenly, Mummy came back."

by the simple device of moving the cut-out figure of the mother.

This means that, though at the beginning of the new language-acquisition process, it is the teacher who regulates the indexical meaning procedures, "transfer mechanisms" subsequently appear (Wertsch 1979, 1984, Bruner 1983, Rogoff 1984, Wertsch and Minick 1987, Edwards and Mercer 1988). By means of these "transfers," learners autonomously take over procedures that were initially carried out either by the teacher or under his or her guidance. In this way, by starting from a territory that is recognized and shared from the very outset by all those present, teacher and pupils gradually change the stage set into a territory in which the learners will gradually become more competent to negotiate the regulation of the original script or indeed to gradually modify it.

Final remarks. If as many authors claim (Ausubel 1978, 1985, Coll 1983, 1985), all learning processes necessarily involve the possibility for the learner to establish a link between new things that he or she is in the process of acquiring and some type of pattern of previous knowledge or action, then *those things that the learner (with external support) does with others* operate, at least partially, as a mechanism whereby he or she can accede to *those things that he or she, with internal regulation, will later do without others*. Or, to put it another way, if as Fillmore (1985) suggested, L2/L3 learning cannot be understood simply as the result of exposure to input but must inevitably be viewed as a process dependent on the existing background from which this input is recognized as such, then in the present article I am making three suggestions:

(1) The new language is a "semiotic environment that will be gradually mastered by the child" (Wertsch 1985: 15) and, consequently, the background from which one accedes to it corresponds partly to procedures for recognizing signs.
(2) The process whereby this background is built up includes "social moments," moments at which the development of the ability to recognize is necessarily dependent on interaction with others.
(3) Through this process the teacher necessarily becomes an initial territory maker.

References

Arnau, Joaquim, et al. 1992. *La educación bilingüe*. Barcelona: ICE.UB/Horsosri.

Artigal, Josep Maria, and Remei Camps. 1982. "Didàctica del català, segona llengua, a preescolar." *Actes del 1er Symposium sobre l'ensenyament del català a no-catalanoparlants*. Vic: EUMO. 142–148.

Artigal, Josep Maria, et al. 1984: *Com fer descobrir una nova llengua*. Vic: EUMO.

Artigal, Josep Maria. 1985. *El mètode contextual discursiu per a l'aprenentatge del català abans dels sis anys*. Barcelona: Servei d'Ensenyament del Català. Generalitat de Catalunya.

Artigal, Josep Maria. 1987. "Le programme de 'bain de langue' pour l'enseignement de la langue à des enfants d'immigrés dans les écoles maternelles de Catalogne." *Revue de Phonetique Appliquée*, 82–83–84. 134–142.

Artigal, Josep Maria. 1990a. "Uso/adquisición del lenguaje como construcción de territorio compartido." *Ponencias y comunicaciones del "16 Congreso Nacional de AELFA."* Madrid: Ministerio de Asuntos Sociales, INSERSO. 147-163.

Artigal, Josep Maria. 1990b. "Uso/adquisición de una lengua extranjera en el marco escolar entre los tres y los seis años." *Comunicación, Lenguaje y Educación.* Núm. 7/8. 127-144.

Artigal, Josep Maria, and Traute Taeschner. 1990. *Deutsch für Kinder.* Bolzano: Assessorato all'istruzione e cultura in lingua italiana, Provinzia Autònoma di Bolzano.

Artigal, Josep Maria. 1991. "The Catalan immersion program: The joint creation of shared indexical territory." *Journal of multilingual and multicultural development* 12(1-2): 21-33.

Artigal, Josep Maria. 1992a. "Le storie come 'territorio condiviso'." *Il tedesco-seconda lingua in prima elementare: la sperimentazione in atto.* Bolzano: Assessorato all'istruzione e cultura in lingua italiana, Provincia Autonoma di Bolzano. 33-42.

Artigal, Josep Maria. 1992b. "Some considerations about why a new language is acquired by being used." *International Journal for Applied Linguistics* 2(2): 221-240.

Ausubel, David P. 1978. *Psicologia educativa: Un punto de vista cognoscitivo.* Mexico: Trillas.

Ausubel, David. 1985. "Learning as constructing meanings." In Noel J. Entwistle (ed.), *New directions in educational psychology.* London: The Palmer Press.

Bruner, Jerome. 1983. *Child's talk: Learning to use language.* New York: Norton.

Coll, Cesar. 1983. "La construcción de esquemas de conocimientos en situaciones de enseñanza aprendizaje." In Cesar Coll (ed.), *Psicologia genética y Aprendizajes escolares.* Madrid: Siglo XXI.

Coll, Cesar. 1985. "Acción, interacción, y construcción del conocimiento en situaciones educativas." *Anuario de Psicología* 33(2).

Cummins, Jim. 1979. "Linguistic interdependence and educational development of bilingual children." *Review of Educational Research* 49(2): 222-251.

De Lemos, Claudia. 1992. "Los procesos metafóricos y metonímicos como mecanismo de cambio." *Substractum* 1(1): 121-135.

Edwards, Derek, and Neil Mercer. 1988. *El conocimiento compartido.* Barcelona: Paidós/M.E.C.

Fillmore, L.W. 1985. "When does teachers talk work as input." In Susan M. Gass and Carolyn G. Madden (eds.), *Input in second language acquisition.* Cambridge, Mass.: Newbury House. 17-50.

Genesee, Fred, Wallace E. Lambert, and G. Richard Tucker. 1978. "An experiment in trilingual education." *Language Learning* 28(2): 343-365.

Genesee, Fred, and Wallace E. Lambert. 1983. "Trilingual education for majority children." *Child Development* 54: 105-114.

Genesse, Fred. 1987. *Learning through two languages: Studies of immersion and bilingual education.* Cambridge, Mass.: Newbury House.

Hickmann, Maya. 1985. "The implications of discourse skills in Vygotsky's development theory." In James Wertsch (ed.), *Culture, communication, and cognition: Vygotskian perspectives.* New York: Cambridge University Press. 236-257.

Hickmann, Maya. 1987. "The Pragmatics of reference in child language: Some issues in developmental theory." In Maya Hickmann (ed.), *Social and functional approaches to language and thought.* New York: Academic Press.

Karmiloff-Smith, Annete. 1979. *A functional approach to child language: A study of determiners and reference.* Cambridge: Cambridge University Press.

Karmiloff-Smith, Annete. 1986. "From meta-processes to conscious access: Evidence from children's metalinguistic and repair data." *Cognition* 23: 95-147.

Karmiloff-Smith, Annete. 1987. "Function and process in comparing language and cognition." In Maya Hickmann (ed.), *Social and functional approaches to language and thought.* London: Academic Press. 185-202.

Peirce, Charles S. 1965. *Collected papers.* Cambridge, Mass.: Harvard University Press.

Rogoff, Barbara. 1984. "Adult assistance of children's learning." In T.E. Raphael (ed.), *The contexts of school-based literacy*. New York: Random House. 27–40.

Silverstein, Michael. 1976. "Shifters, linguistics categories, and cultural description." In Keith H. Basso, and Henry A. Selby (eds.), *Meaning in antropology*. Albuquerque: University of New Mexico Press.

Silverstein, Michael. 1985. "The functional stratification of language and ontogenesis." In James V. Wertsch (ed.), *Culture, communication and cognition: Vygotskian perspectives*. New York: Cambridge University Press.

Silverstein, Michael. 1987. "The Three Faces of 'Function': Preliminaries to a psychology of language." In Maya Hickmann (ed.), *Social and functional appoaches to language and thought*. London: Academic Press. 17–38.

Snow, Margerite Ann. 1987. *Innovative second language education: Bilingual immersion programs*. Center for Language Education and Research. Los Angeles: UCLA.

Swain, Merrill, and Sharon Lapkin. 1982. *Evaluating bilingual education: A Canadian case study*. Clevedon: Multilingual Matters Ltd.

Vila, Ilgnasi. 1992. "La immersió lingüística." *Ponències, comunicacions i conclusions*. Segon simposi sobre l'ensenyament del català a no-catalanoparlants. Vic: EUMO. 53–66.

Wertsch, James V. 1979. "From social interaction to higher psychological processes: A clarification and application of Vygotsky's theory." *Human Development* 22: 1–22.

Wertsch, James V. 1984. "The Zone of Proximal Development: Some Conceptual Issues." In Barbara Rogoff and James V. Wertsch (Comp.), *Children's learning in the "zone of proximal development*." San Francisco: Jossey-Bass.

Wertsch, James V. 1985. "Introduction." In James V. Wertsch (ed.), *Culture, communication, and cognition: Vygotskian perspectives*. New York: Cambridge University Press.

Wertsch, James V., and Norris Minick. 1987 (April). "Negotiating Sense in the Zone of Proximal Development." Paper presented at Conference on Thinking and Problem Solving in the Developmental Process: International Perspectives. Rutgers University.

Vygotsky, Lev. 1981a. *Pensamiento y lenguaje*. Buenos Aires: La Pléyade.

Vygotsky, Lev. 1981b. "The genesis of higher mental functions." In James Wertsch (ed.), *The concept of activity in Soviet psychology*. Armonk, New York: Sharpe.

Making study abroad more effective

Phyllis J. Dragonas
Melrose (Massachusetts) Public Schools

For the last ten years, the importance of foreign languages has taken on global dimensions, all of which have had an impact on expanding programs in schools across the country. The impact of the Carnegie Report *A Nation at Risk* and the explicit demands of business, industry, and international trade have had a positive impact on state and local school authorities to provide language learning for students early enough to enable them to acquire acceptable levels of language proficiency. The support for study abroad through the National Security Education Program (1991) and the Neighborhood Schools Improvement Act (1992), which adds foreign languages to the President's America 2000 Program, reinforces the importance of foreign-language learning as a vital connecting link in the interdependent relationships of the modern world.

We have also seen a renewed interest in advancing international exchanges, primarily short-term study abroad at the high school level. Through experience we know that short-term study abroad can provide direct contact with people of other languages and cultures, and that for maximum effectiveness, students must be taken out of the isolated milieu of the classroom and given every opportunity for face-to-face interaction in other cultural linguistic contexts. Such exposure will challenge them intellectually and emotionally, both daily and over an extended period of time. Adolescence is an ideal time for such exchanges to take place, because it is during their formative years that youngsters are most impressionable.

Daily interaction creates a greater awareness of similarities and differences between cultures, which leads to a better understanding of the lifestyles and values that influence everyday behavior. Therefore, as the country prepares for global unity, international exchanges of students are perhaps one of the most direct routes to a major reform in foreign-language education and international studies, a reform that is vital if the ultimate goal of global understanding and better world citizenship is to be achieved.

Lambert claims that an issue that has gained national prominence is the revitalization of study abroad. He believes that it has become clear that the development of truly high levels of language skills is very much enhanced by a period of living abroad in a country where the language is spoken, and that the vehicle for this purpose is study-abroad programs, both those in which acquisition of language skills is the principal purpose and those for which acquisition of language skills is a prerequisite or a by-product (Lambert 1992).

In an attempt to develop a real-life experience that would serve as an added dimension to the study of German, a short-term exchange program was established between the High School of Melrose, Massachusetts, and Gymnasium Oberalster in Sasel, a northern suburb of Hamburg, Germany. Now in its seventeenth year, the program has provided learning experiences conducive to improving communication skills through growing language proficiency and greater cultural awareness. What makes this short-term exchange program unique is that it combines the homestay, which is an implicit learning experience, with an organized immersion institute at each school, which serves as an explicit learning experience that helps students to interpret with greater validity the homestay in each country.

Therefore, the study-abroad exchange program is designed to meet the following objectives:

- to provide a family-life experience by integrating American and German students with German and American host families and partners of the same age
- to provide a balance of structured learning and experiential education through an immersion institute
- to help students sharpen their comprehension skills and gain more facility and confidence in oral communication through daily interaction with native speakers
- to help students acquire a deeper appreciation of the customs, values, beliefs, and viewpoints of Germans and Americans in today's world
- to increase student awareness of each country's position in world affairs, business, and technology
- to provide opportunities for further acquaintance with the civilization of the country through planned excursions and visits to places of historical and cultural interests, and
- to develop more positive attitudes and an understanding of and tolerance for cultural differences (Dragonas 1983).

Predeparture orientation: Adapting to customs, habits, social behavior, and dining. The importance of orientation, or preparation, for an exchange program cannot be overemphasized. The predeparture orientation given to students is essential to the development of an awareness of cultural differences and facilitates adaptation to a new environment. The orientation should focus on the lifestyles, customs, habits, and behavior patterns students will encounter in the home and in social situations, as well as in the school and the community. The importance of having an open mind about other people should definitely be emphasized.

Students are in a foreign country to learn about its culture and to adapt to it, rather than to imitate its ways. To be successful, they must become conscious of the forms of behavior of another culture, which ultimately leads to a better understanding of their own behavior and self-image.

With regard to common courtesies used every day, expressions and vocabulary should be taught that can be used in various situations. Priority should be given to basic and familiar terms that can be mastered and reinforced through repetition in a variety of contexts and in interaction with other people. It may be useful to cite here a few examples of European etiquette. Handshaking, for instance, is always a gesture of courtesy and friendliness. Addressing people by their proper titles, such as Mr., Mrs., and Dr., is observed much more frequently in Germany than in the United States.

Students learn that flowers are the most common expression of friendship and appreciation, and that a hostess customarily expects to receive them from a dinner guest. We emphasize the importance of always being punctual, since in Germany it is discourteous not to be on time for all occasions. In the case of dinner parties, for example, the guests usually arrive within ten minutes of each other, and they all usually leave together.

American students learn that water is not a necessity at the table. They should expect to see wine served with meals, or fruit juice or mineral water for those who prefer it. Students should also expect some differences in eating habits and foods served at various meals. it is also important to be aware that Europeans eat more at a meal than most Americans, and that frequent snacking leaves one with little or no appetite at mealtime, which offends host mothers.

Help in the orientation process can also be provided by students who have participated in past exchanges, since they can answer questions that fall within the scope of their previous experiences. These can be questions regarding relationships with parents and partners, family unity and closeness, expected behavior of young people, food and eating habits, cultural interests and values, and viewpoints and attitudes.

Many of these questions cannot be answered simplistically because there are sociological and economic factors that affect the lifestyles and values of individual families. There are, however, certain generalizations that can be made to prepare students for what to expect and how to respond in various situations.

Homestay: The implicit learning experience. It is the family experience here and abroad that makes the greatest impact on young students. The sense of belonging that develops from the friendship and care of the family helps them to gain the security necessary for successful acclimation to the new cultural environment. The more thoroughly the students allow themselves to be absorbed into the family life, the more at home they will feel in their new surroundings. Rivers claims that having control of the language or being able to communicate orally with some degree of sophistication before arrival in the host country insures more progress during the stay and helps one go beyond superficial impressions of the target culture that often confirm the stereotypes of those less prepared (Rivers 1992: 20). We have also observed that students should have between two and three years of formal study in German prior to going abroad in order to better benefit from the overseas experience. This grounding enables them to interact with their host family and peers at the outset and to follow instruction in school with greater facility and less frustration. Adjusting to their American environment is less difficult for the German students because they can communicate more easily, since English is a required area of study beginning in the fifth grade. American and German participants are usually tenth graders. Every effort is made to arrange partnerships with youngsters of the same age and sex, though exceptions are made where necessary.

Immersion institute: The explicit learning experience. The Melrose–Oberalster Exchange Program operates on a biennial basis and has two phases: The German students spend the month of October in Melrose, and the American partners go to Hamburg in April. Because of the explicit learning experience built into the program, the exchange must take place during the same academic year while both schools are in session. The unique feature of this study-abroad program is the *immersion institute* in each of the partner schools, with separate programs organized to accommodate each group of students. The institute offers a balance of structured learning and experiential education. Since school attendance in the host country is an integral component of the partnership exchange program, a meaningful learning experience has been developed, tailored to the needs of the German students coming to Melrose and later to the American partners going abroad. In design, the *institute* may well be unique; a study of the literature referring to short-term study-abroad exchange programs hosted by individual schools does not show any other models where a major portion of the foreign student's use of time is structured. Because it is conducted in the context of the total school experience, the institute, strategically planned, provides the scene and site for communicative interaction to take place in the language of the host country.

Phase One: The German students in Melrose. The *institute* concept was originally conceived in Melrose in order to provide structured learning experiences for its German exchange students. Its purpose is to give students further insight into, and greater understanding of, American values and society, our political and economic systems, human rights, language, literature, music, the arts, and sports. It further provides opportunities for student participation through discussion and interaction, on a one-to-one basis, with teachers and peers. The institute consists of about fifty sessions given over a four-week period. Most of the sessions are scheduled during the first four periods of a seven-period day. During the last two periods of the day students may either follow their host partners to class or attend classes of their choice. Some of the exchange students select specific courses that are not available in the Gymnasium, such as computer science, computer math, industrial arts, and practical arts.

To facilitate accomplishment of the institute's goals, teachers combine their efforts in an interdisciplinary approach, leading a series of classes or seminars on current issues and topics appropriate to the interests of foreign students. Many of these are also taught by community resource persons. The participating teachers volunteer their free time for as many as two or three hours weekly over a four-week period.

Course content and approach. For the foreign students coming to Melrose, the choice of content must be geared to the level of the group's proficiency in English. This is not difficult to determine, primarily because most of the German students started English earlier and are able to communicate freely. The use of English as the medium of instruction and communication allows them to hear the language constantly in a variety of contexts, which leads to a greater understanding of how language works. For the first time, students hear language functioning in authentic situations, which necessitates their using previously acquired skills. *"It is clear, then, that language skills can be reinforced in the foreign culture where students are integrated with their partners, new friends, and acquaintances and are forced to communicate their thoughts and ideas exclusively in English"* (Dragonas 1983: 69).

In addition to fostering interactive communication and writing, the goal of the institute is to acquaint students with American culture and its institutions, social values, contemporary issues, and economic and international relations. The following course descriptions are examples of the institute's emphasis and approach.

- "City and Municipal Government" is conducted by the mayor, who discusses the structure and operation of the local government. Students are also invited to tour City Hall and visit the various departments of the city to see how they function in comparison with the German system.
- "The Juvenile Courts" seminar offers an overview of the justice system in Massachusetts and the constitutional rights of young people. Taught by a social studies teacher who is also an attorney, it uses a case-study approach. Students are assigned materials to which they are expected to react and respond.
- "Introduction to American Speech and Debate" encourages speaking, group discussion, and debate. Students also learn how to develop a logical argument and to find and use evidence to support their arguments. Each student participates in a debate and attends an after-school

debate with the novice, intermediate, and varsity debate teams. As a special feature of the course, students also attend a reenactment of a debate on the question of women's rights that took place in Melrose in 1872.

- "Changing Roles in American Society" focuses primarily on the role of women in today's society. Students are assigned reading materials on the subject and are shown videos depicting the changing roles of women over varying levels of the work force. Students are encouraged to express their opinions and to compare the changing roles of women in the United States with those in their own country.
- "American Social Structure" gives students a broad insight into and understanding of society and standards of living in the United States. This course does much to dispel the stereotyped notion held by many German students that everyone in the United States is affluent. Indeed, a comparison of the social structures and cost of living in their own home town and in Melrose shows many similarities that the students do not expect.
- "American Values" is designed to bring into perspective some contemporary problems and issues in the foreign policy and economic situations of both countries. The political system is discussed, with concentration on state and national elections. Effective use is made of newspaper articles and magazines; students also participate in the interactive video provided by the school's satellite facility.
- "Poetry and Music" introduces Robert Frost's poems, which are read and analyzed with the help of a teacher of American poetry, who also plays a variety of American folk tunes on the guitar, discusses the origins of the words and music, and involves the group in singing American folk songs.
- "American Sports" introduces students to the rules of football and baseball. They become acquainted with the equipment used to play these games. Classes involve demonstrations, video viewing, and actual practice, as well as attendance at some of the season's games. Students also participate in some intramural sports with their host partners. This encourages more peer interaction and fosters new friendships.

Phase Two: The American students in Hamburg. The second phase of the exchange program takes place in Germany during the spring of the same academic year. This practice maintains continuous momentum and enthusiasm during the whole year, and it permits students in their last year of high school to participate in the exchange. Since the German students came to Melrose first and were hosted by their American partners and families, the Americans going abroad have a distinct advantage over their German counterparts with whom they are already acquainted. They look forward to the reunion.

Essentially, the same format in reverse is used for the institute at Gymnasium Oberalster for the American students from Melrose. Thus, the four-week institute at the Gymnasium offers many sessions on language usage, both oral and written. It provides seminars for discussing current events, politics, and German studies. There is also opportunity for the American students to be integrated with German students in certain classes and to interact with them socially as they become better acquainted and form friendships.

The language courses in German give the American students an opportunity to improve their comprehension and speaking, to expand their vocabulary, and to internalize a number of idiomatic expressions that may be useful in developing scenes for role playing in typical situations. Students write and perform skits, and they develop paragraphs and short compositions, which allows them to use what they have previously acquired or learned in class and corrected with the help of the teachers.

The cultural seminars deal with a variety of topics and are followed by on-site visits where possible. For example, a parent involved with the city government spent four class sessions discussing with students the operation of the Hamburg sanitation department. This series of seminars included a video presentation, many colorful handouts, and an on-site visit to the plant to further illustrate the importance of cleanliness in Germany, a characteristic of German culture.

Another topic of interest shows how Hamburg functions as a city and state, with its two forms of government and separate parliaments. An especially interesting series of discussions deals with the operation of the European Economic Community and the function of Maastricht. In the past year, there were also orientation sessions on what used to be East Germany, which prepared students for their organized excursion to the German Democratic Republic. This excursion included visits to historical and significant places such as Weimar, Leipzig, Dresden, Berlin, and Potsdam.

The organization of education in Germany is of great interest to American students who learn about the various types of secondary high schools and the importance of vocational and technical apprenticeships in these tertiary schools collaborating with business and industry. They also discuss the course of study in the Gymnasium and the importance of high scores on the Abitur, the examination that qualifies students for entrance to the various departments of the university.

An important learning activity of the institute is a seminar devoted to writing a journal in German. Students are shown how to record their impressions, observations, and experiences in the form of a diary. Typical entries include the student's first impressions upon arrival, a description of the host family and their home, weekend and leisure-time activities, reactions to German customs, social and cultural activities, and interactions with people encountered during the course of a day. The diaries are discussed in the German class and shared with fellow American students. In addition to the social and cultural insights the students gain from this experience, the diary provides them with considerable writing practice and affords an excellent opportunity for vocabulary enrichment.

Study tour of East Germany. Integrated into the institute's immersion experience for the American students has been the orientation for the week-long excursions to what used to be East Germany. In the spring of 1988 and 1990 two different groups of Melrose exchange students had the unique opportunity to visit several important cities previously mentioned as well as historic sites including the concentration camp at Buchenwald. The trips were arranged well in advance by Gymnasium Oberalster in cooperation with the Ministry of Education in Bonn, which helped subsidize the cost, and the National Youth Travel Bureau in East Berlin. This organization arranged for student housing and prepared the itinerary, tours, visits, and meetings with youth groups of comparable age on the east side. In addition, the excursion was led by an official guide, who was also well versed in the political, cultural, historical, economic, and social conditions of the country. The students were accompanied by the German teacher in charge of the exchange program and her American counterpart leading the group abroad. Several of the American students were participating in the exchange program for the second time. They had the unique opportunity of visiting East Germany twice: first observing its social and economic problems before the wall came down, and then two years later when the two Germanies became united. Students worked together in small groups writing reports on their observations. This assigned project required the students to become good listeners and keen observers in describing the places visited, the people they met and interviewed, and their impressions of them.

Kramsch believes that in exposing students to experiences where they are totally immersed in face-to-face interactions with people and places, students can develop empathy for other people and other cultures. She further claims that through this reflection and interaction students reach an understanding of and empathy for what they have experienced. *In order to gain empathy one must reflect upon that experience, and that reflection is best achieved through dialogue* (Kramsch: 1993). Rivers also states that a program that attempts to develop systematic progress in cultural understanding, side by side with growing mastery of the language, will ensure that language learners are better able to communicate with speakers of the language in the fullest sense of the word. (Rivers 1981: 341)

Survey on Student Learning Experience. In a short survey of student opinion on the institute, almost all American participants, like their German counterparts, agreed that they had gained more knowledge through their experience in the institute than they would have in an unstructured school environment. They found that keeping a diary in the target language not only helped them increase their vocabulary and express themselves better in writing, it also forced them to learn more about the customs and lifestyles of the people. The students also recognized that their experience abroad made them more tolerant of other people's viewpoints and opinions. In addition, they felt they had developed a feeling of identity with their peers, a desire to know more about them, and a strong willingness to continue to study German. They also believed that through this experience they could understand, speak, read, and write better than they could before going abroad, and that they could communicate their ideas and needs in German with greater facility.

Many students also reported that language and cultural insights were mostly acquired through the family experience and daily contact with German-speaking people. Students became increasingly familiar with current vocabulary, clichés, and expressions, which they used with more confidence and ease.

Assessment. The research in the field quantifying the positive effects of study abroad has been limited. Carroll's research was the only large-scale study concluding that the amount of time spent abroad is a strong predictor of students' listening-comprehension scores (Carroll: 1967). Until a valid instrument becomes available that will measure the success of a learning experience abroad, schools conducting study-abroad programs should set their own criteria and measure these before and after the experience. We should be able to assess noticeable improvement in the use of skills, positive attitudinal changes, and cross-cultural awareness after the students' experience abroad, with the Melrose–Oberalster Exchange Program, the performance of its students as evaluated informally by the American and German teachers involved in the program. Areas considered for this purpose are the following:

- tolerance for cultural differences encountered in the host country
- effort to use the target language and eagerness to participate in and contribute to oral discussion
- noticeable improvement in listening comprehension and written expression
- quality of assigned written projects

Students receive points in the above categories that count toward their final grade in German for the year during which they participated in the exchange program. This serves as an incentive to students to get the most out of the experience, in addition to confirming the seriousness and purpose of the program.

The area that is now being explored is the measurement of the positive effects from study abroad on language proficiency. Fortunately, a remarkable beginning has been made by the National Foreign Language Center in collaboration with the American Council of Teachers of Russian. Brecht, Davidson, and Ginsburg recently completed a major study analyzing the records of American students who studied Russian in eight universities in Moscow and St. Petersburg for a semester. The results of this quantitative data analysis is the first empirical study of language gains made abroad in speaking, reading, and listening. This study also presents evidence that previous language experience, strong grammar, and reading ability are predictors of student success overseas. (Brecht, Davidson, and Ginsburg 1992)

Conclusion. The family homestay, the institute, visits, and excursions are all-encompassing parts of the total cultural and linguistic process that enhances the value of the entire study-abroad experience. A program takes on a special dimension when participants are exposed to or immersed in authentic on-site interactive experiences in the country of the target language.

Foreign-language learning in this country can certainly be strengthened by providing more intercultural exchange programs for high school students. Since long- and short-term study abroad can lead to greater language proficiency and more highly developed cultural understanding, exchange programs should be made available in schools on a much wider basis. Whatever the form of the program, matching funds or other kinds of subsidies should be provided in order to encourage further secondary school participation in international exchange.

If Americans in the twenty-first century are to become linguistically and culturally intelligent, let us begin at the action level in the schools by developing efficient and coordinated systems of language learning and cultural understanding, incorporating study-abroad experiences as integral components of the nation's foreign-language education agenda.

REFERENCES

Boren, David L. 1991. "National security act of 1991." In *The national security education program.* Washington, D.C.: Department of Defense.

Brecht, Richard, Dan Davidson, and Ralph B. Ginsburg. 1991. "The empirical study of proficiency gains in study abroad environments among American students of Russian: Basic research needs and a preliminary analysis of data." In A. Barchenkov, and T. Garza (eds.), *Proceedings of the first soviet American conference on current issues of foreign language instruction.* Moscow: Vyeshaja Shkola.

Carroll, John B. 1967. "Foreign language proficiency levels attained by language majors near graduation from college." *Foreign Language Annals.* 131–51.

DeKeyser, Robert M. 1991. "Foreign language development during a semester abroad." In Barbara F. Freed (ed.), *Foreign language acquisition research in the classroom.* Boston: D.C. Heath and Co.

Dragonas, Phyllis J. 1983. *International homestay exchange programs*. Washington, D.C.: Center for Applied Linguistics.

Dragonas, Phyllis J. 1981. "Foreign language education in the American schools: A response to the national needs and interests." In F.J. Zapp (ed.), *Schule and Forschung: Kommunikation in Europa*. Frankfurt : Verlag Moritz Diesterweg.

Brecht, Richard D., Dan Davidson, and Ralph B. Ginsburg. 1993. *Predictors of foreign language gain during study abroad*. Washington, D.C.: National Foreign Language Center Occasional Papers, June 1992.

Frye, Robert, and Thomas J. Garza 1992. "Authentic contact with native speech and culture at home and abroad." In Wilga M. Rivers (ed.), *Teaching languages in college: Curriculum and content*. Chicago: National Textbook Corporation.

Kramsch, Claire. 1993. *Context and culture in language teaching*. New York: Oxford University Press.

Lambert, Richard L. 1992. "Revitalizing our study abroad programs." *NFLC Perspectives* (Fall): 1–2.

President's Commission on Foreign Languages and International Studies. 1979. *Strength through wisdom: A critique of U.S. capability*. Washington D.C.: Government Printing Office.

Rivers, Wilga M. 1992. "Internationalization of the university: Where are the foreign languages?" In James E. Alatis (ed.), *Georgetown University Round Table on Languages and Linguistics 1992*. Washington, D.C.: Georgetown University Press.

Rivers, Wilga M. 1983. "Talking off the tops of their heads." In Wilga M. Rivers (ed.), *Communicating naturally in a second language*. New York: Cambridge University Press.

Rivers, Wilga M. 1981. *Teaching foreign language skills* (2nd edition). Chicago: University of Chicago Press.

The Strategic Interaction view of language: Robert J. Di Pietro's Vichian paradigm for theoretical and applied linguistics

Marcel Danesi
University of Toronto

Introduction. On October 18, 1708, the start of the school year at the Royal University of Naples, Professor Giambattista Vico, who occupied the Chair of Rhetoric, gave a speech to the student body that was published a year later as his classic treatise on education, *De nostri temporis studiorum ratione* (translated by Gianturco (1965) as *On the Study Methods of Our Time*). With Cardinal Grimani and the Viceroy of Naples in attendance, Vico's speech, an eloquent criticism of Cartesian thought, stunned his audience.

The times had made the intellectual climate of Naples anything but receptive to Vico's captious verbal attack. Scholars throughout the Europe of the times were completely taken with the systematicity and logic of Cartesian method, especially since it seemed to constitute a powerful investigative tool for the study of nature. Cartesianism also dominated the educational scene of the day, causing the older tradition, centered on the study of language and literature, to lose ground to instruction in mathematics, critical philosophy, and the sciences. Vico warned his audience that an emphasis on logic and mathematics was ultimately counterproductive. Natural learning, he emphasized, followed a developmental route that started from concrete modes of thinking, progressing only gradually, and with significant effort, to rational modes. In this developmental scenario, Vico viewed the imagination as the central force in knowledge acquisition. Although it may have seemed that he was advocating a return to classical studies, Vico was attempting to say a lot more to his audience. He was, in fact, arguing for a reconciliation of classical, humanistic education with that of formal, rationalistic education.

Thus it was that at the turn of the eighteenth century—the century of the Enlightenment—an unknown figure climbed upon the intellectual stage of Italy under the spotlight of "radicalness" and "unorthodoxy," an image that would stigmatize him throughout his life. This is perhaps the main reason Vico's magnum opus of 1725, *La scienza nuova* (trans. Bergin and Fisch 1984), which should have guaranteed him a wide readership and a broad range of responses, went virtually unnoticed. Shortly after the book's publication, Vico sent a copy to Sir Isaac Newton, so convinced was he that his *New Science* would do for the study of human nature what Newton's *Principia mathematica* had done for the study of matter. It is not known whether Newton ever received the book. But, as Manuel (1963: 43) suggests, even if he had, Newton "would not have remotely comprehended its meaning." Vico returned with great resolution to his beloved *New Science* a few years later, putting out a revised second edition in 1730. The result was the same—the *New Science* (NS) failed to attract any attention. Depressed but undaunted, Vico returned one last time to the work in 1744. The third edition came out just after his death that same year on January 23.

To this day, Vico remains relatively unknown to the social and educational sciences. The primary reason for the neglect of Vico, as the psychologist Robert Haskell (1987) has recently argued, is the fact that social scientists have only in the last few decades started to become interested in the kinds of things Vico was thinking and writing about over two and a half centuries ago. Vico's ideas on the nature of human rationality, and on how it must have originated in the imagination, are not only highly compatible with current thinking in some of the human sciences, but they are also highly suggestive of future directions for these sciences to pursue. The recent work on the role of metaphor in cognition and communication, for instance, is fundamentally Vichian in nature and scope. The idea that cognition is an extension of bodily experience, a kind of abstracted sensoriality, which is starting to receive serious and widespread attention by some psychologists and linguists, is, as a matter of fact, the unifying principle that Vico used to tie together all the thematic strands that he weaved throughout the NS.

The late Robert J. Di Pietro was one of the first Anglo-American linguists to realize the importance of Vico's thought for linguistics (e.g. Di Pietro 1973, 1976a, 1976b, 1979, 1981). Linguistics aims to study what is perhaps the most fundamental of all the features of human consciousness—the creation and use of language for thinking and communicating. If I had to sum up what Di Pietro has taught a whole generation of linguists in a phrase, I would choose the following one: Robert Di Pietro has shown us that language is not a script-based, disembodied, information-transfer process à la Claude Shannon (1948) or Norbert Wiener (1949), a theoretical model under whose influence many contemporary discourse analysts continue to work. Di Pietro, who read Vico zealously and who often came under his spell, did not see verbal communication as a neutral, abstract information-transfer act. For Di Pietro (1987) it always involved Strategic Interaction (SI), a mode of human interactive behavior that unfolds in terms of the enactment of ego-centered agendas, goals, and affective states. Di Pietro's work on SI has attempted to uproot linguistics from its traditional rational mode of inquiry and to replant it into a terrain that focuses on the imagination. The result is a program for studying human language that, if followed more widely, can lead to a deeper understanding of how humans make sense of the world.

This essay has a specific and a general purpose. The specific purpose is to show how Di Pietro's SI approach is not only inspired by Vico but is Vichian even in its instructional details. The general one is to argue, through Di Pietro's simple yet effective approach to language pedagogy, that a Vichian-inspired perspective of teaching can easily be converted into classroom practices that make education a truly meaningful and rewarding experience.

Di Pietro's Strategic Interaction paradigm. The basis for any Vichian model of language is the imagination. And indeed, the current research in many areas of the behavioral, cognitive, and social sciences informs us that the workings of the imagination, especially as it manifests itself through the medium of the metaphorical capacity, underlie our most fundamental modes of thinking and acting (e.g. Pollio, Barlow, Fine, and Pollio 1977, Lakoff and Johnson 1980, Johnson 1987, Lakoff 1987). The catalogue of findings on metaphor has become an extensive one indeed. Suffice it to say here that when considered cumulatively, the research seems to suggest that discourse is anchored in the capacity to metaphorize. And this is, in fact, the main lesson that linguists invariably learn from the *New Science.* As Vico aptly put it, "metaphor makes up the great body of language among all nations," allowing us to give "names to things from the most particular and the most sensible ideas" (Bergin and Fisch 1984: 147).

In the 1970s, the study of discourse in linguistics was conducted by some within a scientific frame of mind that views human cognitive activity as describable with the notions and models developed by communications engineers and artificial intelligence researchers. In actual fact, that "new" trend was really no more than a modern version of what can be called the "computational fallacy"—the Hobbesian and Cartesian view that the mind's activities operate in mechanical ways. The new impetus and momentum that this fallacy has gained has also rekindled what is perhaps the oldest debate in philosophy: Is "meaning" a derivative of individual experience (the experientialist perspective)? Or, is it "out there," waiting for the innate machinery of the mind to capture and store it independently of bodily processes and individual feelings (the objectivist perspective)?

The emphasis in discourse analysis among those who subscribe to generativist conceptions of language appears to be on cataloguing and explaining speech acts as extended projections of grammatical rules: i.e. generative discourse analysis seemed to be focusing, by and large, on studying the systematic use of the lexical and grammatical devices that allow for economy in cross-reference (e.g. anaphoric and cataphoric reference), ellipsis, discourse-text cohesion, and so on.

Another approach has, of course, been the functional approach of Austin (1962), Joos (1967), Searle (e.g. 1969, 1976), Hymes (e.g. 1972), Halliday (e.g. 1975, 1985), and others that has its roots in the early work of Wittgenstein (1922), Malinowski (1923), Bühler (1934), and Firth (1951). The pivotal research of such scholars has shown that discourse goes well beyond grammatically constrained information transfers. It involves determining *who* says *what* to *whom*; *where* and *when* it is said; and *how* and *why* it is said. It involves, in other words, contextual parameters such as the setting, the message contents, the participants, and the goals of each interlocutor. All these contextual factors are critical in determining the specific form a speech act will assume. A good recent review of the work on speech as a transactional process can be found in Goodwin and Duranti (1992).

What Di Pietro (1987) has added to the study of discourse is a focus on its interactive dimension, i.e. on the use of language to portray roles, speaker identities, and deeply felt life experiences. Few have investigated the intrinsic involvement of the personality dynamics of interlocutors in speech acts as insightfully as has Di Pietro.

At the center of Di Pietro's view of human interaction is the idea that discourse is dependent upon the strategic and tactical value of the words and structures chosen by the speakers. Communication is a goal-oriented activity, and language provides the tools that speakers can use to enact or externalize their "ego-dynamic" states, to use Renzo Titone's (1977) appropriate term. Interlocutors are continually engaged in bringing about the realization of ego-centered agendas and goals through negotiation, manipulation, suasion, and other strategies. Di Pietro (1987: 41) defines *Strategic Interaction*, in fact, as the purposeful and artful use of language when dealing with others. It is an interactive plan deployed by the addresser to relay his or her feelings to the addressee, thus bringing the addressee verbally into the realm of his or her life experiences. SI is quite similar to what Goodwin and Goodwin (1992: 181) have recently designated "assessments": i.e. strategies that "provide participants with resources for displaying evaluations of events and people in ways that are relevant to larger projects that they are engaged in."

In some ways, the study of SI is akin to psychoanalysis. In looking for SI in discourse samples, the linguist, like the analyst, must be trained in the "strategies of the language game," as Peter Farb (1974: 70) has so aptly put it. SI suggests that in verbal exchanges the ego-dynamic level is always a potential factor in shaping discourse. It bears witness to the fact that the individual's motivations and feelings undergird the structuring of speech acts. As Titone (1977) points out, the individual's personality system inheres in a dynamic organization of the psychosocial subsystems within the individual that determine his or her characteristic behavior and thought. It is an open-ended system that allows human beings to relate directly to the outside world. In actual discourse it controls the ability to talk about experience, to adjust to speech patterns according to life situations (including the knowledge of when not to speak), to express attitudes, to retrieve information about oneself verbally, to communicate intentions, and to use language for self-awareness. The ego-dynamic level constitutes, in essence, the "will" to communicate. SI analysis is a direct trace to the workings of this level.

SI seems to reflect a deeply ingrained psychological need to draw attention to our feelings and attitudes. It is a deliberate strategy that implores the addressee to focus momentarily on the addresser's ego-states or feelings. As Goffman (1978: 814) perceptively remarked, our utterances often make "a claim of sorts on the attention of everyone in the social situation." Goffman, incidentally, had previously made us aware in a 1959 study how people used verbal discourse strategically to portray themselves in everyday life. He has come the closest, in my view, to identifying SI as a distinct verbal strategy. Deborah Tannen (1989), too, has recently alluded to the fact that thought and emotions are often intermeshed in discourse. She refers to a passage written by Gregory Bateson in which he remarks that in one of his writings he had attempted "to bring the reader into the room." Tannen (1989: 168) suggests that what Bateson is alluding to is a discourse strategy that constitutes "a way of achieving understanding through involvement."

The study of a phenomenon like SI seems to show that ego-dynamics are at the basis of human cognition. Our affective responses to the world seem to dictate, or, at the very least, guide the choice of the words and structures we continually make in discourse. As in a novel where the author's feelings and perspective shape the form and contents of the storyline, so too SI is one of the means by which the "author" of an utterance reveals his or her feelings and perspectives in an artful manner.

Di Pietro's Strategic Interaction approach and second-language teaching. To make SI the target of second-language teaching (SLT) implies a rather basic rethinking of the goals of language education. If language learners are to become truly proficient in the new language, then they will have to go beyond the literal content of textbooks and exercise manuals.

A typical classroom learner at first only has access to the conceptual system of the native language, not the second language. A Vichian approach in SLT would aim to use this system as a point of departure. The use of the student's innate tendency literally "to imagine" what to do in a given situation implies allowing learners to come up with the crucial concepts involved in typical social scenarios so that they can be reformulated—or reconceptualized—in terms of the target language.

But what would such an approach entail? Above all else, it would imply that the content of a language curriculum should be shaped by the students' imagination rather than by pre-established grammatical or communicative syllabuses. Grammar and communication would be seen as the frameworks that constrain the imagination in humans. SI translates into a classroom approach that provides students with an experiential learning format that allows them to give the content of the curriculum its specific shape while at the same time giving the teacher ample space to provide the formal characteristics that inhere in that content. SI has given us, in other words, a unique opportunity to break away from the traditional notion that the content of a language course must come from pre-established artifacts such as syllabuses or textbooks.

SI constitutes a truly remarkable pedagogical script for teaching language in a Vichian way. At the center of this script is the imagination, which humans continually use to make sense of unexpected circumstances. The human mind is equipped to handle aleatory fluctuations in the environment through the power of its imagination, literally an image-making faculty that generates mental models and plans of how best to accommodate the unexpected situation into a comprehensive life scheme.

The imagination is an epiphenomenal product of brain functioning that confers upon humans the ability to map mental images onto the beings, objects, and events that the senses capture. The units that result from these mappings are what semioticians call *iconic signs*—units of thought that stand for their referents in direct ways. These signs also allow humans to think about their referents away from their contexts of occurrence. The *fantasia*, as Vico called it, can thus "create" new realities totally within the confines of mental space—hence the meaning of *imagination* as a creative faculty. Humans alone have the capacity to "imagine" fictional (context-free) beings, objects, and events. The *fantasia* thus liberates human beings from the constraints imposed on all other organisms by biology. As Verene (1981: 101) puts it, the imagination allows humans "to know from the inside" by extending "what is made to appear from sensation beyond the unit of its appearance and to have it enter into connection with all else that is made by the mind from sensation."

In Vico's model of how humans "imagine," the *ingegno*, "ingenuity, invention," is the crucial faculty of the conscious mind that organizes the iconic signs produced by the *fantasia* into meaningful structures. Whereas the *fantasia* is an epiphenomenal product of brain activity, the *ingegno* is a derivative of the *fantasia*—a kind of "epi-epiphenomenal" activity. It is thus not connected directly to neural processes, operating totally within mental space as it configures iconic signs to form context-free models of world events. "Making sense" is a product of the *ingegno* as it imposes analogical pattern onto the iconic signs that the *fantasia* stores into memory. The brains of all animals have the capacity to form memorable images. This is a survival function. But nonhuman animals lack the ability to transform their images into conceptual structures. Conceptualization inheres in the agreements or resemblances that the human mind alone is capable of making between the images produced by the brain and their corresponding sensory units as registered by the body. As Vico put it: "The human mind is naturally inclined by the senses to see itself externally in the body" (Bergin and Fisch 1993: 78).

The *ingegno* is, therefore, the source of syntax in language and of narrative structure in verbal discourse. It was at the creative nucleus of the earliest myths that humanity literally *invented*. Laws, scientific theories, fictional narrations, and so on are all traceable to the ability of the *ingegno* "to beget"—the word *ingegno* derives etymologically from Latin *in* "in" + *gignere* "to beget."

The *memoria* completes Vico's model of mentality. This is the neurological system that stores iconic thought for future use. While iconic signs are stored in the form of percepts by the *memoria*, the invented structures of the *ingegno* are stored as percept-based categories: i.e. as structures derived from combinations of percepts that underlie our models of space, time, emotions, etc.

In a classroom learning situation, the imagination (consisting of *fantasia*, *ingegno*, and *memoria*) is the students' primary means by which they come to grasp new concepts. The *ingegno* in particular is the faculty that provides the learner with a set of strategies for handling any new situation. While speech acts are predictable to some extent in terms of their overall pragmatic and thematic intent, the verbal pathway entered upon to resolve any communicative act is itself unpredictable because it is dependent upon each interlocutor's *ingegno*: i.e. it is dependent upon the strategic and tactical value of the words, structures, and discourse categories chosen by the speakers. Communication is a goal-oriented activity, and language provides the tools that the speakers can use to reach specific goals. The student's *ingegno* is naturally "programmed" to bring about the realization of goals through negotiation, manipulation, suasion, or a combination of these and other *strategies*, as Di Pietro aptly calls them.

Most approaches to the teaching of communication in the classroom are "finite-state" in orientation. They provide the learner with a checklist of speech acts (making contact, expressing needs, etc.) matched against possible social situations and their linguistic coordinates. The student is thus expected to learn to communicate by selecting the appropriate verbal pathways charted by speech acts and given social situations in an algorithmic, "flow-chart" fashion. Di Pietro's SI, on the other hand gives the students' imagination (or, more specifically, their *ingegno*) full reign to create those very verbal pathways. SI does this by means of "scenarios" that allow the learners to generate their own ways of handling real-life happenings. Di Pietro (1987: vii) defines both *scenario* and *Strategic Interaction* as follows:

> The term "scenario" will be used to give a label to real-life happenings that entail the unexpected and require the use of language to resolve them. The approach organized around scenarios is called "strategic interaction" (SI), to feature the way it calls upon learners to invoke the target language purposefully and artfully in dealing with others.

Let us now look briefly at how Di Pietro's Vichian perspective is converted into a simple and effective classroom routine that any teacher can easily adopt and adapt to the specific language being taught. SI consists of the following phases:

- *Pre-class Preparation:* The teacher selects or creates appropriate scenarios and prepares role cards to describe them.
- *Phase 1 (Rehearsal):* The students form groups and prepare agendas to fulfill the roles assigned to them. The teacher acts as adviser and guide to student groups as needed.
- *Phase 2 (Performance):* The students perform their roles with the support of their respective groups while the teacher and the remainder of the class look on.
- *Phase 3 (Debriefing):* The teacher leads the entire class in a discussion of the student's performance.

The selection or invention of an appropriate scenario will depend, of course, on the stage of linguistic competence reached by the student. Once this has been determined, the teacher can prepare all the necessary role cards deemed appropriate to some learning goal. The basic scenario is one that has two roles that are suitable for performance with one encounter. The following one is a case in point:

Role A: You must return a defective toaster to the department store. Unfortunately, you have lost the purchase receipt and you have your lunch hour to take care of the matter. Prepare yourself for an encounter with the salesclerk.

Role B: You are a salesclerk in a hardware department of a large store. You have been ordered to be careful in accepting returns of merchandise that may not have been purchased at the store. Prepare yourself to deal with someone who is approaching you with a toaster.

In structuring the roles in this way, the teacher has created a situation in which the *ingegno* of the learner is invoked. In order to execute their specific "game plans," each role-player will have to anticipate what the other will say. But it is only in the actual *saying* that the communicative act takes shape and form. Perhaps in no other way is it possible to reproduce the aleatory conditions that characterize normal communication. It is the learners, through their individual *ingegni*, who generate the dialogue within a shared context.

During the rehearsal phase, the students are then asked to explore the ways the scenario can unfold. In Vichian terms, they are asked to reconstruct the workings of the *ingegno*. The role cards tell the students what the particulars of the situation are, but they do not tell them what to do or think. Invariably, students will use their *fantasia* to create the "sense" needed for the situation.

In a certain fundamental sense, the foreign-language learner is like one of Vico's "first poets." Not possessing the formal resources of the target language to successfully carry out a conversation, the student enlists the imagination to generate sense. The student is therefore like a "poet," who must use his or her innate capacity to make sense of a situation by analogy and imagery.

After the performance of the scenario, which stresses fluency before accuracy, the students are asked to analyze the scenario. In other words, the final, debriefing phase brings the learning process back into the domain of traditional pedagogy. It is at this point that the teacher discusses matters of form that have arisen during the performance phase. For Di Pietro, grammar training is a point of arrival, not a point of departure. He describes the role of grammar in SI as follows:

> Grammar is more appropriately viewed as an output than as an input interactive approach. By attending to the ways in which students talk about the structure of the target language and formulate their own explanations, the teacher can gain an insight into their progress. (1987: 98)

SI makes explicit a notion that teachers have always felt intuitively: namely that successful learning of new verbal material depends largely on how the student perceives it. Vico put forward the case that language originated in metaphorical transformations of concrete perception: "the human mind does not understand anything of which it has had no previous impression ... from the senses" (Bergin and Fisch 1984: 110). After this perceptual stage, learning progresses to more abstract modes of knowing. In SI the abstract knowledge of grammar is an "output," or "end-product," of the learning process. The natural process of learning in the human organism goes from a sensorially based form of concrete thought to a more abstract form of cognition. As Vico phrased it: "Men at first feel without perceiving, then they perceive ... finally they reflect with a clear mind" (Bergin and Fisch 1984: 75). This is because the "human mind is naturally inclined by the senses to see itself externally in the body, and only with great difficulty does it come to understand itself by means of reflection" (Bergin and Fisch 1984: 78).

This is why in SI abstract thinking about the target language comes at a later stage than the student's propensities to learn through a more imaginative "poetic style." Di Pietro structures his teaching format according to a "concrete-to-abstract" flow of learning that gives the learner's *ingegno* full reign to explore the new modes of speaking concretely and then to organize them conceptually. It is only after the mind has grasped new concepts in a concrete way that it becomes "ready," so to speak, to make such matters as grammar practice cognitively profitable.

Concluding remarks. In essence, SI is a Vichian-inspired teaching format for imparting true language proficiency in a way that is more reflective of natural language development than any other teaching paradigm of which I am aware. By going from the concrete to the abstract, classroom teaching will follow a natural path of learning that is reflected in the ontogenesis of language. As Vico remarked, children learn by concrete analogy: "the nature of children is such that they name any other men, women, and things by the ideas and names of men, women, and things that bear any resemblance or relation to the first" (Bergin and Fisch 1984: 132). The child develops language by connecting sensory experience to the language samples heard in the environment in a concrete way, and, thus, by building up conceptual abstractions on the basis of concrete modes of thinking and speaking.

Above all else, children attempt, with their *ingegni*, to construct perceptual models of typical events in their environment. SI attempts to follow this natural learning path. In traditional approaches to learning, it is assumed that the learning contents are to be prepared *for* the learner. SI allows the contents to emerge *from* the learner. These are then channeled into the categories of the new language so that the learner can "reflect" upon what has been learned, to use Vico's insightful word.

Vico was concerned with reconciling the orientation of classical, humanistic education with that of formal-rationalistic education. Vico believed that the former tended to make passive listeners out of the learners, and that the latter turned them into abstract, unfeeling automatons. In order to avoid both extremes, Vico advanced an orientation that did not put the two into conflict but rather drew the good qualities from both. So he advocated stimulation of the imagination while at the same time promoting the development of the rational, critical mind.

Drawing from this Vichian conception of language education, Di Pietro has given us an approach to the language classroom that draws out of the learners their imaginative propensities for creating situations. The teacher is charged with imparting the verbal features of the situations, not with providing a priori abstractions about language. For, as Vico once quipped, what is the good of teaching anyone the grammar of a language if that person does not know how to speak it first?

REFERENCES

Austin, J.L. 1962. *How to do things with words.* Cambridge, Mass.: Harvard University Press.

Bergin, Thomas G., and Max Fisch. 1984. *The new science of Giambattista Vico.* Ithaca: Cornell University Press.

Bühler, Karl. 1934. *Sprachtheorie: Die Darstellungsfunktion der Sprache.* Jena: Fischer.

Di Pietro, Robert J. 1973. "Review of Giorgio Tagliacozzo and Hayden V. White." Giambattista Vico: An international symposium. *Foundations of language* 9: 410–421.

Di Pietro, Robert J. 1976a. *Language as human creation.* Washington, D.C.: Georgetown University Press.

Di Pietro, Robert J. 1976b. "Humanism in linguistic theory: A lesson from Vico." In Giorgio Tagliacozzo and Donald P. Verene (eds.), *Giambattista Vico's science of humanity.* 341–350. Baltimore: Johns Hopkins University Press.

Di Pietro, Robert J. 1979. "Language and the imagination." In Paul L. Garvin, and Wolfgang Wölck (eds.), *The fifth LACUS forum.* Columbia, S.C.: Hornbeam. 443–450.

Di Pietro, Robert J. 1981. "Linguistic creativity: A key to contemporary humanism." In Giorgio Tagliacozzo (ed.), *Vico: Past and present.* Atlantic Highlands, N.J.: Humanities Press. 132–143.

Di Pietro, Robert J. 1987. *Strategic interaction.* Cambridge: Cambridge University Press.

Farb, Peter. 1974. *Word play.* New York: Bantam.

Firth, John R. 1951. *Papers in linguistics (1934–1951).* Oxford: Oxford University Press.

Goffman, Erving. 1959. *The presentation of self in everyday life.* Garden City: Doubleday.

Goffman, Erving. 1978. "Response cries." *Language* 54: 787–815.

Goodwin, Charles, and Alessandro Duranti 1992. "Rethinking context: An introduction." In Alessandro Duranti, and Charles Goodwin (eds.), *Rethinking context: Language as an interactive phenomenon.* Cambridge: Cambridge University Press. 1–23.

Goodwin, Charles, and Marjorie Harness Goodwin. 1992. "Assessments and the construction of context." In Alessandro Duranti and Charles Goodwin (eds.), *Rethinking context: Language as an interactive phenomenon.* Cambridge: Cambridge University Press. 65–72.

Halliday, M.A.K. 1975. *Learning how to mean: Explorations in the development of language.* London: Arnold.

Halliday, M.A.K. 1985. *Introduction to functional grammar.* London: Arnold.

Haskell, Robert. E. 1987. "Giambattista Vico and the discovery of metaphoric cognition." In Robert E. Haskell (ed.), *Cognition and symbolic structures: The psychology of metaphoric transformation.* Norwood, N.J.: Ablex. 67–92.

Hymes, Dell. 1972. "Models in the interaction of language and social life." In John Gumperz, and Dell Hymes (eds.), *Directions in sociolinguistics: The ethnography of communication.* 234–272. New York: Holt, Rinehart & Winston.

Johnson, Mark. 1987. *The body in the mind: The bodily basis of meaning, imagination and reason.* Chicago: University of Chicago Press.

Joos, Martin. 1967. *The five clocks.* New York: Harcourt, Brace and World.

Lakoff, George. 1987. *Women, fire, and dangerous things: What categories reveal about the mind.* Chicago: University of Chicago Press.

Lakoff, George, and Mark Johnson. 1980. *Metaphors we live by.* Chicago: Chicago University Press.

Malinowski, Bronislaw. 1923. "The problem of meaning in primitive languages." In Charles K. Ogden and Ivor A. Richards (eds.), *The meaning of meaning.* New York: Harcourt, Brace and World. 234–272.

Manuel, Frank E. 1963. *Isaac Newton historian.* Cambridge, Mass.: Harvard University Press.

Pollio, Howard, Jack Barlow, Harold Fine, and Marilyn Pollio. 1977. *The poetics of growth: Figurative language in psychology, psychotherapy, and education.* Hillsdale, N. J.: Lawrence

Erlbaum Associates.

Searle, John R. 1969. *Speech acts: An essay in the philosophy of language*. Cambridge: Cambridge University Press.

Searle, John R. 1976. "A classification of illocutionary acts." *Language in Society* 5: 1–23.

Shannon, Claude E. 1948. "A mathematical theory of communication." *Bell Systems Technical Journal* 27: 379–423.

Tannen, Deborah. 1989. *Talking voices*. Cambridge: Cambridge University Press.

Titone, Renzo. 1977. "A humanistic approach to language behavior and language learning." *Canadian Modern Language Review* 33: 309–317.

Verene, Donald P. 1981. *Vico's science of the imagination*. Ithaca: Cornell University Press.

Vico, Giambattista. 1965. *On the study methods of our time*. Translated by Elio Gianturco. Ithaca: Cornell University Press.

Wiener, Norbert. 1949. *Cybernetics, or control and communication in the animal and the machine*. Cambridge, Mass.: MIT Press.

Wittgenstein, Ludwig. 1922. *Tractatus logico-philosophicus*. London: Routledge and Kegan Paul.

On the implementation of inservice teacher education in an institutional context[1]

Frederick H. Jackson
Foreign Service Institute

0. Introduction. In a paper she presented at the 1983 Georgetown Round Table, Diane Larsen-Freeman offered a comparison between what she termed *the training process* and *the educating process* of second-language teacher preparation. She described the training process as situation-oriented, with finite objectives and specific criteria for success, and with trainees expected to follow a model presented by the trainer. In contrast, she described the educating process as individual-oriented, with general objectives designed to enable the learner to "adapt to and function in any situation." The educating process was seen as having the goal of enabling the learners to set their own learning agendas; the emphasis was on process rather than results, and success was to be measured by growth, not by attainment of some absolute objective. Both processes were described as necessary, although the educating process was more fundamental. Larsen-Freeman wrote that the training process was "subsumed under the process of educating" (Larsen-Freeman 1983: 265).

In the decade since Larsen-Freeman's paper, several scholars have worked within and expanded upon the contrast she drew. In this paper I propose to examine aspects of the fit between the developing theory of language teacher education and the actual implementation of programs of inservice teacher development in a particular language-teaching institution.

In the first part of the paper I briefly examine some of the insights that have appeared in the recent literature on second-language teacher development. In the second part I look briefly at some factors that have been identified as affecting the implementation of individual and organizational change. With these insights in mind, I turn to a consideration of the specific instance of teacher training and professional development in the School of Language Studies of the Foreign

1. Special thanks are owed to Madeline Ehrman for her interest and advice at a critical point in the development of this paper and to David Argoff and Gary Crawford for their useful comments and suggestions. I have also benefited greatly from discussions—sometimes heated ones—with colleagues at FSI on several of the ideas in this paper. Among the many deserving of thanks in this regard are Madeline Ehrman, Marta Gowland, Lucinda Hart-Gonzalez, Prawet Jantharat, Marsha Kaplan, Jane Malinoff-Kamide, and James Snow. I am, of course, solely responsible for any errors of interpretation or commission.

Service Institute (FSI). The paper concludes with generalizations about implementing developmental change at language-teaching institutions such as FSI.

1. Teacher training and teacher development. In an important 1989 paper, Donald Freeman extended Larsen-Freeman's contrast to propose that the phrase *teacher education* be used as a superordinate term to cover two concepts very similar to Larsen-Freeman's, which he labeled *teacher training* and *teacher development* (Freeman 1989: 37). Training was described as "a strategy for direct intervention to work on specific aspects of the teacher's teaching," while development was "a strategy of influence and indirect intervention that works on complex, integrated aspects of teaching [that are] idiosyncratic and individual" (Freeman 1989: 39–40). Freeman's terminology and definitions have been widely adopted in the field.

1.1 Teacher training. A training model is recognized as an effective way to achieve certain specific behavioral changes in some contexts, such as when novice teachers are being prepared to step into a class for the first time (Freeman 1991: 33), when the teacher educator or supervisor wants teachers to use a specific procedure (e.g. Larsen-Freeman 1992), or when the trainees themselves request training in a particular area (Freeman 1989). However, most writers have emphasized the perceived limitations of the training approach. Richards (1990) and Freeman (1992) assert that typical training models of teacher preparation are based on limited and misguided premises about teaching. Richards describes training strategies as inherently top-down and based upon a reductionist concept of teaching that would define good teaching solely as the implementation of an appropriate behavioral methodology. Richards rejects such a definition as reflecting a view of "teacher as technician," which fails to recognize the actual complexity of the teaching process (1990: 218–219). Other serious limitations that he attributes to the training model are (1) a view of teachers and teaching that treats teaching as atomistic rather than holistic; (2) a failure to address subtle but overriding aspects of teaching such as those involved in teachers' decision-making processes; and (3) the relegation of responsibility for learning success to the teacher trainer rather than to the teachers who undergo training (Richards 1990: 220).

A training procedure can successfully address behaviors, but not complex thinking processes (Richards 1987, 1990, Freeman 1989). However, it is generally recognized that such processes form the core of effective teaching. Freeman writes that "the effects of teacher education lie less in influencing how teachers behave, than in recasting how they think about what they do in classrooms" (Freeman 1992: 1). Richards (1990) urges replacement of the training-focused model of teacher education with a developmental one that would involve teachers in "developing their own theories of teaching, exploring the nature of their own decision making, and developing strategies for critical reflection and change."

1.2 Teacher development. The focus of a developmental model is on expanding and deepening a teacher's existing awareness of the teaching process (e.g. Freeman 1992, Freeman 1991, Larsen-Freeman 1990, Pennington 1992, Richards 1987, Wallace 1991). Freeman (1989) has proposed that teaching be thought of as a series of complex decision-making processes based on the interaction of a teacher's knowledge, skills, awareness, and attitudes. He has also shown (Freeman 1992, 1991) that even novice teachers are not blank slates but bring to any teacher-education program deeply held conceptions of teaching and learning, which have developed over thousands of hours of experience as learners.

Richards (1990: 221) argues that the emphasis in teacher education should be placed on "what teachers know and do and on providing tools with which they can more fully explore their *own* beliefs, attitudes, and practices" (emphasis added). The desirable participation of teachers and teacher trainees in this kind of self-exploration has been referred to as *reflective teaching* (e.g. Bailey 1992, Bartlett 1990, Lange 1990, Pennington 1992, Richards 1990, Wallace 1991).

One of the principal goals of any model of teacher education is to implement change in a teacher's teaching, but Richards (1990) and Freeman (1992) argue that for change to take place, it must be built upon the existing schema about teaching and learning that individuals carry with them. When change does occur, it may not be reflected in observable behavior. Freeman (1989: 38) remarks:

> change does not necessarily mean doing something differently; it can mean a change in awareness ... change is not necessarily immediate or complete ... some changes occur over time, with [the educator] serving only to initiate the process ... some types of change can come to closure and others are open-ended ...

Bailey, in an outstanding recent article about what is involved when language teachers change their teaching behaviors, reports data that indicate that many changes that do occur may take a long time to be implemented in a way that can be observed (Bailey 1992: 276).

1.3 Teacher supervision. The work of Gebhard and his colleagues in exploring models of teacher supervision is also very relevant to a discussion of teacher education (Gebhard 1990, 1991; Gebhard et al. 1990), in that supervisors often carry out the educating and teacher educators often take the roles of teacher supervisors. Gebhard has identified six styles of teacher supervision, which he has termed *directive, alternative, collaborative, nondirective, creative,* and *self-help–explorative*. The first four models are distinct from one another, while the last two are combinations of the other styles. The most common of the styles is the directive model, which has much in common with the training model of teacher education, in that the supervisor uses such techniques as evaluation, direction, modeling, advice, or suggestion to try to effect changes in teachers' behavior. Gebhard argues that this approach to supervision suffers from many of the same kinds of problems that Richards (1990) identified for a training model: (1) the definition of good teaching is relegated to the individual supervisor, (2) the approach may cause feelings of defensiveness and low self-esteem in the teacher, and (3) the supervisor and not the teacher takes responsibility for what happens in the classroom (Gebhard 1990: 156–157). The other three styles of supervision identified by Gebhard are fundamentally developmental in nature, in that each assigns the final choice of what to do to the teacher. Of these styles, alternative supervision involves the most active input from the supervisor, and nondirective supervision involves the least.

Thus far in this paper, our focus has been on the professional growth and development of individual teachers. Now let us look at some of the factors involved in change and development within institutions.

2. Development and change within institutions. Institutions are concerned with the integrity and quality of their programs. To achieve the desired quality, it is often necessary for an institution to implement small or large changes in how it carries out its work, which in turn typically involve changes in how people within the institution do their work. Some such changes are implemented easily, while others may take a long time and a lot of effort to implement successfully. Some changes that have appeared to be well established may evaporate when the attention of the institution is turned elsewhere.

2.1 Factors affecting acceptance of change. Kennedy (1988) summarizes factors that are involved in the implementation and acceptance of change within educational institutions. Kennedy's first point is that "change is systemic, that is to say it takes place in an environment which consists of a number of inter-relating systems." Kennedy lists subsystems in which a language-teaching innovation must operate as follows, in ascending order of power and importance: *classroom, institutional, educational, administrative, political, and cultural*. For example, a classroom innovation that violates systemic values in the training institution in which it takes place will not be implemented successfully, unless the institution is itself willing to change to accept the classroom innovation. Similarly, for the institution to implement a change requires that it fit with the systemic values and procedures of any superordinate educational body, and so on. Although Kennedy does not mention them, it is obvious that there are hierarchical systems within training institutions that will affect the acceptance of innovation in the same way. For example, an innovation tried out by an individual teacher who works as part of a coordinated program of instruction would need to not violate the system of values and procedures of that program.

For innovation to be implemented successfully, there are four clear criteria. The first cited by Kennedy is a dissatisfaction with the existing situation. The greater the dissatisfaction, the more willing the participants are to try out a change. This criterion must be met first; after that, the remaining criteria are feasibility, relevance, and acceptability. Feasibility refers to the resources available to undertake the innovation. Relevance refers to the perceived match between the causes of the dissatisfaction and the suggested innovation. Acceptability refers primarily to the match between the innovation and the existing style and philosophy of teaching of those who will be responsible for implementing the innovation. If these people are directly involved in designing the innovation—that is, if they have some degree of "ownership" in its design— the likelihood of acceptability is significantly increased. Another kind of factor in determining acceptability is the balance of gains and/or losses to those involved in the innovation. If the implementers perceive that the gains to them are less than or only equal to the perceived losses (e.g. in increased work load or responsibility without additional compensation, or with increased professional insecurity or discomfort) then there may be little motivation to change (Kennedy 1988: 336–341).

Kennedy's discussion addresses how innovation may be received within an institution. The model introduced in the next part of the paper deals with how innovation may be brought about through effective leadership and decision making.

2.2 Situational leadership and the implementation of change. The study of management has much that is worth the attention of language teachers and administrators. The work of Hersey and Blanchard (1988) is especially relevant to discussions of models of supervision and of the implementation of change within institutions. They term their theory *situational leadership*. The following is a somewhat simplified summary of it.

Hersey (1985) claims that the selection of a style of supervision should depend on the particular task that the supervisee is to carry out and on the answers to two crucial questions about the supervisee with respect to the task: (1) Is the person able to carry out the task? (2) Is the person willing/motivated/secure enough to carry out the task? There are four possible combinations of answers to the questions. The relationship between the combinations of answers and the respective appropriate supervisory style may be seen in Table 1.

Hersey writes that people grow incrementally in skill and confidence, and that as they grow their need for supervision changes. An individual at Stage I

Table 1. Situational leadership (after Hersey 1985)

Supervisee stage	Indication: leadership or supervision roles
I. Unable and insecure	Leader directed: directing, guiding, telling
II. Unable but willing	Leader directed: explaining, clarifying, persuading, selling
III. Able but insecure	Follower directed: collaborating, encouraging, participating
IV. Able and confident	Follower directed: delegating, observing, fulfilling, monitoring

with respect to a task, such as a worried beginning teacher who is asked to use a new kind of instructional activity with a class for the first time, benefits from clear task-oriented direction from a supervisor, similar to what was mentioned in an earlier section of this paper as *directive supervision* (Gebhard 1990). A training-based style of direction would be appropriate. In complete contrast, an individual at Stage IV with respect to a task, such as an experienced teacher, who is preparing to teach materials that he or she has taught successfully before, needs little if any input from the supervisor for that task.

The other two stages describe individuals who no longer require directive supervision but who do need interaction with the supervisor in order to do the task. At Stage II, the learner has developed confidence in working with the supervisor and is willing to try what the supervisor suggests but has not yet developed skill at the particular task to be undertaken. According to Hersey, this individual needs guidance but not direction from the supervisor in a supportive and encouraging atmosphere. An individual at Stage III in approaching a task has developed the ability to do it successfully but feels insecure about trying it. This individual also needs support from the supervisor, but in a context where it is clear that the learner is the responsible person and the supervisor is in the role of collaborator or consultant (Hersey 1985).

Hersey and Blanchford (1988) use the term *readiness* in describing individuals in the different stages. The readiness of someone at Stage I is said to be *low*; at Stages II and III, it is said to be *moderate*; and at Stage IV it is *high*. At a given time, any person will be at different stages of readiness with respect to the different tasks that he or she has been assigned or has chosen to undertake and will therefore need a different style of supervision for the respective tasks. Also, as the person develops ability and confidence in carrying out a task, the style of supervision should change accordingly.

Hersey and Blanchford (1988: 339–44) use the theory of situational leadership to advance understanding of organizational change as well. They state that there are four levels of change: *knowledge changes, attitudinal changes, individual behavior changes, and group or organizational performance changes*. Of these, knowledge changes are the easiest to make, and attitudinal changes are more difficult because emotion is likely to be involved. Changes in individual behavior are characterized as still harder than the first two, in that people often are unwilling to adopt new behaviors that they recognize as better because they feel comfortable in the old behavior patterns. Changes that affect the performance of an entire organization are the hardest of all to make.

Two ways of implementing organizational performance change are identified by Hersey and Blanchford: *directive change* and *participative change*. Directive change, as the name implies, is top-down and addressed directly at the change that is desired. An example would be an announcement stating "effective Monday all members of the organization will operate in accordance with the procedures in Form 2120." Participative change is in many ways a bottom-up change. It is much more time consuming. It starts by making new knowledge available to the organization in an attempt to effect an attitude that is receptive to the desired direction of change. This may be achieved through group problem-solving. The next steps are to have some individuals pilot the desired new behaviors and then, finally, to have the organization adopt it.

Hersey and Blanchford do not say that one style of implementing change is better than another, although they do note that participative change tends to be more lasting. Instead, they argue, the choice of one style over another should depend upon the situation. Directive change might well be the best alternative for administrative issues that are peripheral to the primary concerns of the staff. Also, if the readiness of the organization for the change is at a level comparable to Stage I in the discussion above—if the staff are neither able nor willing to accept responsibility for effecting a change in a given situation—directive change might be best. However, if organizational readiness is at a higher level and the issue is recognized as important within the organization, participative change would probably be more appropriate. In fact, to attempt to impose major directive change in such a situation could well lead to either open staff hostility and rebellion or to a passive staff that becomes dependent on management for every decision (Hersey and Blanchford 1988: 343–344).

3. Teacher development at the Foreign Service Institute. The Foreign Service Institute (FSI) is the training arm of the State Department. FSI's School of Language Studies currently has approximately 250 native-speaking instructors who teach 63 different languages to adult members of the American diplomatic community.[2] Students are in class at least five hours a day, often for 44 or more weeks. Instructors typically teach four to five hours each day, and they may also participate in other responsibilities, such as proficiency testing. The work of the instructors is overseen by 24 language-training supervisors. In recent years, FSI has focused considerable attention on program development, partly to enable it to open new language programs in, for example, Albanian, Estonian, Mongolian, and Azeri, but also to revise programs that had been based in significant part on textbooks developed in the 1960s and 1970s. An important component of FSI's program development initiatives has been efforts to encourage the continued professional growth of its faculty. To accomplish this, both training-oriented and comparatively development-oriented procedures have been employed at different times. The trend at FSI, as elsewhere, has been to move toward more participative development-oriented activities, but each kind of procedure has met with both successes and relative lack of success. In this part of the paper, we will consider some possible causes for the differing reactions.[3]

3.1 Top-down teacher training at FSI. A largely successful use of top-down training occurred approximately ten years ago when FSI management implemented two major innovations in language programs. The first was the requirement that language programs incorporate interactive activities based around job-related scenarios in ways that resemble Di Pietro's concept of Strategic Interaction (Di Pietro 1983, 1987); the second was the development of a new kind of short situationally based course to provide learners with essential survival skills. In each case, a directive was issued to adopt the innovation, and faculty were directly trained in the new skills and procedures that were required. As follow-up, part of the annual review and evaluation of each language program dealt with how much progress had been made toward implementation. Those programs that had made little progress were encouraged to increase their efforts. The result was that both innovations were adopted by the organization

---

2. Due to the recent increases in the numbers of countries with which the United States has relations, the number of languages taught now is almost 33% more than it was four years ago.

3. It should be remarked that much of the teacher training and development that take place at FSI is conducted by the language training supervisor for the individual language programs. Traditionally, this was carried out through the directive model of supervision (Gebhard 1990). That is, the supervisor directed or guided the teacher's teaching through such means as modeling, suggestion, and evaluation. In practice, even in the past, many experienced instructors were given great autonomy in making teaching and curricular decisions. Recently, while formal evaluation of instructors remains a required part of every supervisor's job, some supervisors have begun to try out other supervisory models. There is no data on how these alternative models are being implemented or received, however, and they will not be discussed further in this paper.

and have for the most part continued in place until the present. Even where the specific innovation has been replaced, most of the principles underlying it have been incorporated into the respective language programs. Thus, these initiatives were largely successful.

Among some senior supervisory and instructional staff, however, there did occur some of the negative effects to morale that Hersey and Blanchford (1988) describe as often resulting from directive change. Some such individuals put off adopting the changes as long as they could. A few developed the required materials but then failed to use them in the language programs. A few developed the new materials to order, but failed to incorporate the desired innovations.

FSI has also successfully used directive change together with training-based implementation to put into effect the adoption of its present test procedure for the evaluation of speaking proficiency. To be allowed to serve as a member of a testing team, every individual is required to satisfactorily complete a rigorous initial training program and to undergo additional training at regular intervals thereafter.[4]

Other attempts to use directive change and a training-based approach have been rather less successful. One of these was the establishment of a clause in teachers' annual written statements of work requiring them to demonstrate professional training and development during the work year. The establishment of such a work requirement serves to establish extrinsic motivation for something that appears to come more effectively from intrinsic motivation (Bailey 1992: 262). One result is that some faculty members "collect" attendance at training sessions in order to obtain higher evaluations, whether or not the sessions are relevant to the individual's needs. Thus, they follow the letter of the directive but not its spirit. Also unsuccessful was the institution of a since-abandoned policy of obligatory attendance at regular teacher-training sessions on such topics as using authentic video materials, teaching the receptive skills, and error-correction techniques. While the quality of many of the sessions was high, and some individual faculty members responded positively to each one, many teachers also reacted defensively, with some interpreting the required attendance policy as an implicit criticism of their work and others rejecting the content as not useful: "too theoretical," "not right for our language," or "the same thing we're doing already." Others signed the attendance sheet and ignored the large part of each presentation. The awareness and knowledge of a few individuals may have been enriched by these sessions, but the majority do not appear to have been affected.

There are several likely reasons why the top-down initiatives in curriculum

4. Testing training also has been shown to serve an important developmental function for FSI faculty who participate in it, in that their increased awareness of testing tasks and of how examinees perform on them often serves to inform and improve their teaching.

development and testing have been by and large successful, while the last two initiatives mentioned have not. The obvious weight of senior management in support of the first initiatives and the existence of clear and persistent follow-up until each project was completed were obvious factors that helped to overcome potential resistance. The fact that the projects could, in fact, be completed suggests another important reason for their success: each of the curriculum development and testing initiatives had finite objectives, was specific in scope, and involved following clearly established models. That is, those projects corresponded to the kinds of activities that Larsen-Freeman (1983) and others have described as being appropriately addressed through a training process. In contrast, *professional growth and development* is a nonfinite objective where progress is relative and the focus is more on process than product. A model of delivery that encouraged individual responsibility for development was needed.

3.2 Movement toward bottom-up developmental approaches. A few years ago, an offering of one of the obligatory training sessions was met with especially obvious expressions of resentment by teachers in one of the instructional departments. This manifestation of disaffection inspired some supervisors and instructors in the department to meet to consider and implement alternatives. The most important of the alternatives chosen were:

- institution of a new policy of voluntary attendance at development sessions
- limitation of the size of activities to no more than 25 participants, with sign-up sheets in advance, but with each session repeated if more than 25 wished to attend
- establishment of no-class blocks of time during each month when development sessions would be held so that no department member would be prevented from attending
- selection of development activities to be offered based on results of a poll of all department members
- involvement of both instructors and supervisors in planning and conducting the sessions.

Among the intended results of these innovations were that polling department members and opening up participation in planning the sessions would increase both the relevance of the training sessions to faculty interests and the acceptability of the content of the sessions through expanded ownership from the department's faculty. In addition, it was thought that limiting the number of people who could participate in any one session might raise interest in attending through a modified law of supply and demand. Each of these intended results was achieved.

It was also hoped that the process of having a team of instructors and supervisors put together a training session would have equal or greater developmental effect on the team than the session had on participants. In the event, the effect of working in the teams on the team members' own knowledge base, self-confidence, and skill in presentation appeared to be far greater, leading to the expanded use of teams like these in other School-wide activities and projects. In retrospect, it is obvious that the problem-solving nature of the planning task was one important reason for this. In addition, inclusion of supervisors on the planning and delivery team as equals with instructors rather than as directors enabled them to relate to the instructors in ways appropriate, in Hersey's (1985) framework, for individuals who are at either the second or third level of readiness. The instructors responded accordingly.

This department's model for inservice development activities was influential three years ago when FSI conducted a review and evaluation of its staff development needs. Indeed, all five of the characteristics of the departmental sessions listed above were also adopted in the FSI-wide plan that was developed then. For example, corresponding to the third point above, in the new FSI plan two afternoon hours every second week are set aside across the School for professional development activity, during which no language classes or tests may be given. During these periods, faculty may read, reflect, meet with colleagues or supervisors, or choose to attend one of the departmental or School-wide professional development sessions that are now offered at those times. The choice is intended to depend upon their individual needs.

The content and format of the new School-wide development sessions were decided during the School-wide review mentioned above. The review was carried out primarily by a team of twelve respected senior faculty members, nine of whom were language instructors and the rest of whom had supervisory rank. Through such means as questionnaires, interviews, meetings, and group discussions, input on staff development needs was obtained from both the management and instructor perspectives. Although there were some differences between the two perspectives—for example, instructors indicated a strong need for ESL training and computer training, while management believed that some other needs were more important—there was also considerable agreement about the content and form of future FSI-wide development activities.

With regard to the form of the activities, the recommendations were that each activity adhere to the five desirable characteristics already listed and also to the following. Each development program was to:

- be delivered over three or more training sessions to allow for follow-up and for ideas to be digested over time;
- include learning activities in which learners would have the opportunity to explore their own understanding of the topic;
- include opportunities for participants to evaluate their own learning.

The recommended content of the activities was of two kinds: (1) specific kinds of procedures that instructors frequently found themselves wanting or needing to perform, such as lesson planning, active listening, teaching conversation skills activities, and using authentic video to teach listening comprehension and (2) longer overviews of some disciplines whose knowledge and theory inform language teaching, including second-language acquisition, descriptive linguistics, reading theory, learning theory, and cross-cultural communication. Programs of each kind of activity have had to be implemented gradually, because of the other heavy responsibilities of the members of each planning team, so that there are now five programs of type (1) available and three of type (2). Other offerings are planned for the future.

Preliminary results of this initiative have been in most ways encouraging. About two-thirds of the faculty have attended one or more of the development activities, and most offerings have had waiting lists of people who wanted to participate but could not get room. Some programs have already been offered three or four times due to demand. End-of-session evaluations have expressed very favorable opinions of the sessions and the presenters, although they have also made suggestions for follow-up and improvement. Anecdotally, several individuals who have participated in sessions have remarked that they now see events in their classes with new insight. Some program supervisors have said that they have observed instructors in staff meetings use concepts and terms that they had been introduced to in a development session. Some supervisors have also stated that when the number of instructors in the language program who are able to use such concepts arrives at some "critical mass," the level of discussion and analysis is significantly heightened.

However, there have also been some more negative comments and reactions among both instructors and supervisors:

A. DELIVERY METHODOLOGY. Several participants in workshops have objected to the use of learning activities designed to make them more aware of their own understanding. Some have indicated that they felt that the activities were a form of test that would "set [them] up" to look bad in front of their peers. Others said that such activities were a "waste of time"—that they had attended the workshop because they wanted to hear from "experts," not from each other. This reaction is similar to one that Richards (1990) has reported of some students in the teacher-development program in Hong Kong; they had expected a knowledge-transmission model of education and were disturbed to find that their expectations were not met. As a result of this feedback, the facilitators of almost every session have reduced the number of these kinds of activities and have increased the use of more traditional methodologies.[5]

B. INSUFFICIENT TIME TO DO RECOMMENDED OUTSIDE WORK. Each development session was asked to suggest work for session participants to do during the two weeks between sessions so as to try to help the participants to reflect about their learning. Such outside activities included reading, group or individual problem-solving, practice of a skill, or observation and analysis of a teaching or learning event. However, almost half of the participants have typically reported that their normal teaching responsibilities are too heavy to permit them to do this work and that their supervisors are unable to provide them any release time because to do so would increase the load on others. Some participants can do some of the assignments at home, but others are unable or unwilling to do this.

C. PRODUCT VERSUS PROCESS, AND THE ISSUE OF EVALUATION. The developmental model of teacher education emphasizes the ideas of process and individual growth. Several supervisors and some senior instructors, however, have raised an important issue that they refer to as "accountability" to urge that workshop developers should explicitly state the behavioral goals and objectives of the session and should then formally evaluate the participants at the end of the session to determine how close they came to the stated objectives. Apparently implicit in this recommendation are a perhaps unrecognized assumption that a training model of faculty development is desired, rather than a developmental one, and the belief that training sessions should be evaluated solely or primarily in terms of their "product." Such a belief would be entirely compatible with some organizational values of the Institute, where the language-training programs are of necessity regularly evaluated on the basis of whether language students achieve their stated training goals. However, the possibility that participants' performance in a development session might end up being evaluated has caused consternation among several instructors who say that they would be much less likely to take risks and explore alternatives.[6]

---

5. Although the feedback from participants was the obvious stimulus for this retreat to more traditional knowledge-transmission methodologies, it also seems clear that most of the workshop facilitators, including the present writer, found such styles more "comfortable." Richards (1990) describes a similar preference among other teacher educators. Hersey and Blanchard's (1988) point, referred to in part 2.2, that behavior is hard to change even when one's knowledge and attitude know what to do would seem almost painfully relevant here.

6. Gebhard et al. (1990: 24) have noted, "When student teachers feel that they or their teaching are being constantly judged, they hold back their ideas." The reaction of these FSI teachers to the idea of being evaluated is comparable.

D. CONCERNS ABOUT RELEVANCE AND ACCEPTABILITY. Some workshop participants have stated that the sessions they attended were "not really relevant" to their teaching situation. Questions about why the sessions were not relevant have elicited statements like the following:

- "We don't have time to do the kinds of lesson plans that the workshop showed us."
- "The Authentic Video workshop showed us a lot of interesting ideas, but we don't have time to go through the video tapes to find good examples for activities."
- "The [Authentic Video] workshop only talked about using authentic video material. We don't have that kind of material in our program yet."

Other comments have addressed concerns about the acceptability within the language program of the ideas that have been gained from the session. One instructor has said that when she wanted to try out an idea from a training session with her class in the language program, she had been discouraged from doing so by a more senior instructor. Another instructor has expressed fear that if she were to try an innovation in her teaching she would probably be less skilled than she is with her familiar procedures and the students, colleagues, and supervisor might be intolerant of her "clumsiness." Although not many of these kinds of comments have been recorded, it is clear that perceived relevance and acceptability may be important for faculty to continue to want to participate in the sessions.

Each of these four important kinds of concerns and objections seems to reflect a mismatch between some systemic expectations of what a development program ought to do or be and what has been attempted in this particular program of development. It will be important to correct this mismatch through improved communication but also probably through accommodation.

4. Conclusions. The new FSI program of faculty development that has been described here is different in many ways from the kind of rich, individually tailored, reflection-driven programs that Richards (1990), Freeman (1992), Gebhard (1990), and others have been recommending for teacher development. In many ways, the activities that make up the program may appear to be closer to a traditional training model. However, its underlying values are fundamentally developmental, very much in the sense that Freeman and others recommend.

Because of organizational constraints, it may not be possible for an institution such as FSI to use a full range of individualized exploratory development activities for an inservice faculty-development program. The requirements of the organization for instructors to coordinate closely together in instructing classes and for as many students as possible to reach the designated learning objectives mean that instructors cannot be permitted to experiment with complete freedom with any and all new procedures or approaches they may wish to try. At an institution like FSI, a language program must, in this sense, be like a machine, with all components working together smoothly to produce the desired product.

However, FSI also needs its instructors and supervisors to have the ability to make the most appropriate instructional decisions for any given learning situation based upon an understanding of as many as possible of the immense number of variables that may relate to that situation. As Gebhard, Freeman, Richards and others have argued, the ability to make those kinds of decisions is not learned through directive supervision or through participation in traditional training in methods and procedures. Such an ability only develops over time through experience in trying something in a class, observing the results, analyzing them in principled ways, and then trying something else. There must be freedom to take risks and learn from the experience, while at the same time, the risks that are taken are not such that they interfere with the abilities of instructors to coordinate together in a program or with students achieving their learning goals.

Development, by definition, involves change. Kennedy's (1988) discussion of change in institutions shows how an intended change needs to respond to and comply with the systemic values, procedures, and attitudes of the organization in which it is to be implemented. On a more individual level, the situational leadership model that was discussed in this paper showed that the style of leadership of the supervisor should depend on the level of readiness of the supervisee (Hersey and Blanchard 1988). An individual who is relatively unready to do a task requires more directive supervision than one who is more ready. By using this model, a supervisor or teacher educator can provide faculty with the opportunity to change and develop while at the same time maintaining those institutional controls that are necessary to ensure that the program functions as it is supposed to.

Simplifying perhaps too much, one may generalize that all three of the quite different models of development and innovation at which we have looked—the developmental model of teacher education, Kennedy's model of implementation of change, and Hersey and Blanchard's situational leadership—have emphasized the importance of beginning with the *existing* situation and building from there. This is true of the people who will be doing the developing, who have their own developed matrix of awareness, knowledge, skills, and attitudes upon which they will build. As Hersey and Blanchard have observed, leadership is ineffective if it assumes that people possess either more or less readiness than they actually have. The generalization is also true of the organizational systems and culture within which the people must operate, which would also appear to have different levels of readiness to tolerate change. To implement development, the levels of both organizational and individual readiness must be addressed.

REFERENCES

Bailey, Kathleen M. 1992. "The processes of innovation in language teacher development: What, why, and how teachers change." In John Flowerdew, Mark Brock, and Sophie Hsia (eds.), *Perspectives on second language teacher education.* Hong Kong: City Polytechnic of Hong Kong. 253-282.

Bartlett, Leo. 1990. "Teacher development through reflective teaching." In Jack C. Richards and David Nunan (eds.), *Second language teacher education.* New York: Cambridge University Press. 202-14.

Di Pietro, Robert J. 1983. "Real life in the preparation of language teachers. In James E. Alatis, H.H. Stern, and Peter Strevens (eds.), *Georgetown University Round Table on Languages and Linguistics 1983.* Washington, D.C.: Georgetown University Press. 133-142.

Di Pietro, Robert J. 1987. *Strategic interaction: Learning languages through scenarios.* New York: Cambridge University Press.

Flowerdew, John, Mark Brock, and Sophie Hsia (eds.). 1992. *Perspectives on second language teacher education.* Hong Kong: City Polytechnic of Hong Kong.

Freeman, Donald. 1989. "Teacher training, development, and decision making: A model of teaching and related strategies for language teacher education." *TESOL Quarterly* 23(1): 27-46.

Freeman, Donald. 1991. "'Mistaken constructs': Re-examining the nature and assumptions of language teacher education." In James E. Alatis (ed.), *Georgetown University Round Table on Languages and Linguistics 1991.* Washington, D.C.: Georgetown University Press. 25-39.

Freeman, Donald. 1992. "Language teacher education, emerging discourse, and change in classroom practice." In John Flowerdew, Mark Brock, and Sophie Hsia (eds.), *Perspectives on second language teacher education.* Hong Kong: City Polytechnic of Hong Kong. 1-21.

Gaies, Stephen, and Roger Bowers. 1990. "Clinical supervision of language teaching: The supervisor as trainer and educator." In Jack C. Richards and David Nunan (eds.), *Second language teacher education.* New York: Cambridge University Press. 167-81.

Gebhard, Jerry G. 1990. "Models of supervision: Choices." In Jack C. Richards and David Nunan (eds.), *Second language teacher education.* New York: Cambridge University Press. 156-66.

Gebhard. Jerry G. 1991. "Language teacher supervision: Process concerns." *TESOL Quarterly* 24(4): 738-43.

Gebhard, Jerry G., Sergio Gaitan, and Robert Oprandy. 1990. "Beyond prescription: The student teacher as investigator." In Jack C. Richards and David Nunan (eds.), *Second language teacher education.* New York: Cambridge University Press. 16-25.

Hersey, Paul. 1985. *The situational leader.* New York: Warner Books.

Hersey, Paul, and Kenneth W. Blanchard. 1988. *Management of organizational behavior: Utilizing human resources* (Fifth edition). Englewood Cliffs, N.J.: Prentice Hall.

Kennedy, Chris. 1988. "Evaluation of the management of chance in ELT projects." *Applied Linguistics* 9(4): 329-42.

Lange, Dale L. 1990. "A blueprint for a teacher development plan." In Jack C. Richards and David Nunan (eds.), *Second language teacher education.* New York: Cambridge University Press. 245-68.

Larsen-Freeman, Diane. 1983. "Training teachers or educating a teacher." In James E. Alatis, H.H. Stern, and Peter Strevens (eds.), *Georgetown University Round Table on Languages and Linguistics 1983.* Washington, D.C.: Georgetown University Press. 264-74.

Larsen-Freeman, Diane. 1990. "On the need for a theory of language teaching." In James E. Alatis (ed.), *Georgetown University Round Table on Languages and Linguistics 1990*. Washington, D.C.: Georgetown University Press. 261–70.

Larsen-Freeman, Diane. 1992. "Punctuation in teacher education." In John Flowerdew, Mark Brock, and Sophie Hsia (eds.), *Perspectives on second language teacher education*. Hong Kong: City Polytechnic of Hong Kong. 309–18.

Pennington, Martha C. 1992. "Reflecting on teaching and learning: A developmental focus for the second language classroom." In John Flowerdew, Mark Brock, and Sophie Hsia (eds.), *Perspectives on second language teacher education*. Hong Kong: City Polytechnic of Hong Kong. 47–65.

Richards, Jack C. 1987. "The dilemma of teacher education in TESOL." *TESOL Quarterly* 21(2): 209–26.

Richards, Jack C. 1990. "Integrating theory and practice in second language teacher education: The role of action research." In James E. Alatis (ed.), *Georgetown University Round Table on Languages and Linguistics 1990*. Washington, D.C.: Georgetown University Press. 218–27.

Richards, Jack C., and David Nunan (eds.), *Second language teacher education*. New York: Cambridge University Press.

Wallace, Michael J. 1991. *Training foreign language teachers: A reflective approach*. New York: Cambridge University Press.

Woodward, Tessa. 1991. *Models and metaphors in language teacher training: Loop input and other strategies*. New York: Cambridge University Press.

Wright, Tony. 1990. "Understanding classroom role relationships." In Jack C. Richards and David Nunan (eds.), *Second language teacher education*. New York: Cambridge University Press. 82–97.

After Method: Toward a Principled Strategic Approach to Language Teaching

H. Douglas Brown
San Francisco State University

In the century spanning the mid-1880s to the mid-1980s, the language-teaching profession was involved in a search. That search was for what has popularly been called "methods," or, ideally, a single method, generalizable across widely varying audiences, that would successfully teach students a foreign language in the classroom. Historical accounts of the profession tend therefore to describe a succession of methods, each of which is more or less discarded in due course of time as a new method takes its place. I will comment on "the changing winds and shifting sands" (Marckwardt 1972: 5) of that history momentarily; but first, we should try to understand what we mean by "method."

What is a method? Three decades ago, Edward Anthony (1963) gave us a definition that has quite admirably withstood the test of time. His concept of method was the second of three hierarchical elements, namely, approach, method, and technique. An *approach*, according to Anthony, was a set of assumptions dealing with the nature of language, learning, and teaching. *Method* was defined as an overall plan for systematic presentation of language based upon a selected approach. It followed that *techniques* were specific classroom activities consistent with a method and therefore in harmony with an approach, as well.

Some disagreement over Anthony's definition can occasionally be found in the literature. For Richards and Rodgers (1986), method was an umbrella term to capture redefined approaches, designs, and procedures. Similarly, Prabhu (1990) thought of method as both classroom activities and the theory that informs them. Despite these and a handful of other attempted redefinitions (see Pennycook 1989), we still commonly refer to methods in terms of Anthony's earlier understanding. For most researchers and practicing teachers, a *method* is a set of theoretically unified classroom techniques thought to be generalizable across a wide variety of contexts and audiences. So, for example, we speak of the Audiolingual Method, the Direct Method, and of the Silent Way or Suggestopedia as methods.

Methods: A century-old obsession. Ironically, the whole concept of separate method*s* is no longer a central issue in language-teaching practice. In fact, almost a decade ago, H.H. Stern (1985: 251) lamented our "century-old obsession," our "prolonged preoccupation [with methods] that has been increasingly unproductive and misguided," as we have vainly searched for the ultimate method that would serve as the final answer.

That search might be said to have begun around 1880 with François Gouin's publication of *The Art of Teaching and Learning Foreign Languages* (1880), in which his Series Method was advocated. This was followed at the turn of the century by the Direct Method of Charles Berlitz. The Audiolingual Method of the late 1940s and the so-called Cognitive-Code Learning Method of the early 1960s followed. Then, in a burst of innovation, the "spirited seventies," as I like to refer to them, brought us what David Nunan (1989) termed the "designer" methods: Community Language Learning, the Silent Way, Suggestopedia, Total Physical Response, and others. This latter flurry was not unlike an earlier period in the field of psychotherapy that burgeoned with a plethora of "methods" of therapy; some of the "designer" terms of that era were T group, encounter group, analytical, Gestalt, marathon group, conjoint family, shock, client-centered, and narcosis therapy, electro-narcosis, biochemotherapy, and analytic psychobiology!

Why are methods no longer the milestones of our language-teaching journey through time? Our requiem for methods might list six possible causes of demise:

(1) Methods are too prescriptive, assuming too much about a context before the context has even been identified.
(2) They are therefore overgeneralized in their potential application to practical situations.
(3) Generally, methods are quite distinctive at the early, beginning stages of a language course, and rather undistinguishable from each other at later stages. In the first few days of a Community Language Learning class, for example, the students witness a unique set of experiences in their small circles of translated language whispered in their ears. But within a matter of weeks, such classrooms can look like any other in a learner-centered curriculum.
(4) Methods are laden with what Pennycook (1989) refers to as "interested knowledge"—the quasi-political or mercenary agendas of their proponents.
(5) It was once thought that methods could be empirically tested by scientific quantification to determine which one is "best." We have now discovered that something as artful and intuitive as language pedagogy cannot ever be so clearly verified by empirical validation.
(6) Finally, there is a curious ethnocentric connotation of methods that smacks of cultural imperialism to many who are not born and bred in Western traditions.

David Nunan (1991: 228) summed it up nicely: "... It has been realised that there never was and probably never will be a method for all, and the focus in recent years has been on the development of classroom tasks and activities that are consonant with what we know about second language acquisition, and that are also in keeping with the dynamics of the classroom itself."

A principled approach. And so, as we lay to rest the methods that have become so familiar to us in recent decades, what assurance do we have today of the viability of our language-teaching profession?

Through the decade of the seventies and into the early eighties, there was a good deal of hoopla about the "designer" methods. Even though they were not widely adopted standards of practice, they were nevertheless symbolic of a profession at least partially caught up in a mad scramble to invent a new method when the very concept of method was eroding under our feet. We didn't need a new method. We needed, instead, to get on with the business of unifying our *approach* to language teaching and of designing effective tasks and techniques that are informed by that approach.

By the end of the 1980s, such an approach was clearly evident in teaching practices worldwide. We had learned some profound lessons from our past wanderings. We had learned to make enlightened choices of teaching practices that were solidly grounded in the best of what we knew about second-language learning and teaching. We had amassed enough research on learning and teaching in a multiplicity of contexts that we were indeed formulating an integrated approach to language pedagogy.

It should be clear from the foregoing that "enlightened" teachers think in terms of a number of possible methodological—or, shall we say, pedagogical—options at their disposal for tailoring classes to particular contexts. An *approach*—or theory of language and language learning—therefore takes on great importance. One's approach to language teaching is the theoretical rationale that underlies everything that teachers do in the classroom.

But one's approach to language pedagogy is not just a set of static principles, "set in stone." It is, in fact, a dynamic composite of energies that changes with one's experiences in learning and teaching. The way one understands the language-learning process—what makes for successful and unsuccessful learning—may be relatively stable across months or years, but it is important not to feel too smug. There is far too much that we do *not* know collectively about this process, and there are far too many new research findings pouring in to be able to assume that one can confidently assert knowing everything about language and language learning.

The interaction between approach and classroom practice is the key to dynamic teaching. The best teachers always take a few calculated risks in the classroom, trying new activities here and there. The inspiration for such innovation comes from the approach level, but the feedback that they gather from actual implementation then informs their overall understanding of what learning and teaching is. Which, in turn, may give rise to a new insight and more innovative possibilities, and the cycle continues.

One's approach may differ on various issues from that of a colleague, or even "experts" in the field (who differ among themselves, of course). There are two reasons for variation at the approach level: (1) an approach is by definition dynamic and therefore subject to some "tinkering" as a result of one's observation and experience; and (2) research in second-language acquisition and pedagogy almost always yields findings that are subject to interpretation rather than giving conclusive evidence.

I would like to suggest that viable current approaches to language teaching are "principled," in that there is perhaps a finite number of general, widely accepted, research-based principles on which classroom practice is grounded. The twelve principles listed in Table 1 compose the sort of fundamental grounding that I am referring to. Those twelve principles, explained in detail in Brown (1994a) and summarized in Brown (1994b), are a part of what most will agree is a relatively undisputed set of "facts" about second-language acquisition. They are briefly summarized here, with references to selected presentations at this year's Georgetown University Round Table.

Table 1. Principles of language learning and teaching

Cognitive Principles
1. Automaticity
2. Meaningful learning
3. Anticipation of Reward
4. Intrinsic Motivation
5. Strategic Investment

Affective principles
6. Language Ego
7. Self-confidence
8. Risk-taking

Linguistic principles
9. The Language-Culture Connection
10. The Native Language Effect
11. Interlanguage
12. Communicative Competence
    - (a) Authenticity
    - (b) Fluency
    - (d) Learner-centered interaction
    - (c) Meaningful, functional, task-based practice
    - (e) Pointed toward language use beyond the classroom

1. Automaticity. Efficient second-language learning involves a timely movement of the control of a few language forms into the automatic processing of a relatively unlimited number of language forms. Overanalyzing language, thinking too much about its forms, and consciously lingering on rules of language all tend to impede this graduation to automaticity. In Earl Stevick's presentation at this conference (pp. 370–384, this volume), the analogy of moving information from one's "worktable" to a "permanent file" is an example of the principle of automaticity.

2. Meaningful learning. Meaningful learning will lead toward better long-term retention than rote learning. One among many examples of meaningful learning is found in content-centered approaches to language teaching, as explained in Crandall's presentation (pp. 254–273, this volume), where students' central focus is on meaningful subject-matter content with language forms acting as a facilitating vehicle to understanding the content.

3. The anticipation of reward. Human beings are universally driven to act, or "behave," by the anticipation of some sort of reward—tangible or intangible, short-term or long-term—that will ensue as a result of the behavior. While long-term success in language learning requires a more intrinsic motive (see principle 4, below), the power of immediate rewards in a language class is undeniable. One of the tasks of the teacher is to create opportunities for those moment-by-moment rewards that can keep classrooms interesting, if not exciting.

4. Intrinsic motivation. The most powerful rewards are those that are intrinsically motivated within the learner. Because the behavior stems from needs, wants, or desires within oneself, the behavior itself is self-rewarding; therefore, no externally administered reward is necessary at all. Robert Di Pietro's (1987) Strategic Interaction technique is firmly grounded in the principle that learners are successful when they generate their own language "material," when the impetus for creative performance comes from within them, and when the teacher is not constantly providing sets of stimuli.

5. Strategic investment. Successful mastery of the second language is due to a large extent to a learner's own personal "investment" of time, effort, and attention to the second language in the form of an individualized battery of strategies for comprehending and producing the language. This principle is cogently illustrated in Chamot and O'Malley's framework for strategies instruction (pp. 37–51, this volume), in which the teacher organizes learner strategy training in such a way that students take more and more responsibility for developing and using successful communication strategies in the language classroom.

6. Language ego. As human beings learn to use a second language, they also develop a new mode of thinking, feeling, and acting—a second identity. The new "language ego," intertwined with the second language, can easily create within the learner a sense of fragility, defensiveness, and a raising of inhibitions. Ehrman's new research on "thick" and "thin" ego boundaries (pp. 327–359, this volume) hints at the possible significance of language ego in the way one goes about achieving language success.

7. Self-confidence. The eventual success that learners attain in a task is at least partially a factor of their belief that they indeed are fully capable of accomplishing the task. This principle is aptly illustrated in virtually all of the papers presented here that examined DiPietro's Strategic Interaction technique. Through group cohesion, planning, and feedback, students were allowed to develop the self-confidence that might in other, more-traditional classroom activities be lacking.

8. Risk-taking. Successful language learners, in their realistic appraisal of themselves as vulnerable beings yet capable of accomplishing tasks, must be willing to become "gamblers" in the game of language, to attempt to produce and to interpret language that is a bit beyond their absolute certainty.

9. The language–culture connection. Whenever one teaches a language, one also teaches a complex system of cultural customs, values, and ways of thinking, feeling, and acting. In Morley's description of the work she is doing with foreign instructors at the University of Michigan (pp. 116–136, this volume), understanding the interaction of language and culture was a key to the instructors' ultimate success in communicating clearly and effectively in an American classroom.

10. The native-language effect. The native language of learners is a highly significant system on which learners rely to predict the target-language system. While that native system will exercise both facilitating and interfering effects on the production and comprehension of the new language, the interfering effects are likely to be the most salient. Suzanne Flynn's plenary presentation on Universal Grammar (UG) (pp. 148–161, this volume) not only recapitulated alternatives to the rather simplistic contrastive-analysis hypothesis but also outlined implications of UG for curriculum development and language testing.

11. Interlanguage. Second-language learners tend to go through a systematic or quasi-systematic developmental process as they progress to full competence in the target language. Successful interlanguage language development is partially a factor of using feedback from others. Teachers in language classrooms can provide such feedback, but more importantly, they can help learners to generate their own feedback outside of the language classroom. Doughty's study (pp. 96–108) of the types of feedback given to language learners gave us some potentially significant pedagogical information.

12. Communicative competence. Given that communicative competence is the goal of a language classroom, then instruction needs to point toward all of its components: organizational, pragmatic, strategic, and psychomotor. Communicative goals are best achieved by giving due attention to language use and not just usage, to fluency and not just accuracy, to authentic language and contexts, and to students' eventual need to apply classroom learning to heretofore unrehearsed contexts in the real world. Lantolf's comments on Vygotsky's insights into language acquisition (pp. 219–232, this volume) reminded us once again of the importance of language as the "negotiation of meaning."

From approach to technique. A principled approach to language teaching encourages the teacher or teacher-trainee to build classroom techniques on the firm foundations of what several decades of research has shown to be applicable. It steers them away from grasping at what may be a very limited "method." It leads them to account for all the contextual variables in a classroom and to create a set of learning experiences that is appropriate for their specific context and purposes. It enables teachers to evaluate what went right and what went wrong in a lesson. It assists them in revising lessons and curricula and in creating new classroom activities and materials. It helps them to devise effective language objectives and to evaluate the accomplishment of those objectives.

Table 2. A Checklist for intrinsically motivating techniques

1. Does the technique appeal to the genuine interests of your students? Is it relevant to their lives?
2. Do you present the technique in a positive, enthusiastic manner?
3. Are students clearly aware of the purpose of the technique?
4. Do students have some choice in:
   (a) choosing some aspect of the technique?
   (b) determining how they go about fulfilling the goals of the technique?
5. Does the technique encourage students to discover for themselves certain principles or rules (rather than simply being "told")?
6. Does it encourage students in some way to develop or use effective strategies of learning and communication?
7. Does it contribute—at least to some extent—to students' ultimate autonomy and independence (from you)?
8. Does it foster cooperative negotiation with other students in the class? Is it a truly interactive technique?
9. Does the technique present a "reasonable challenge?"
10. Do students receive sufficient feedback on their performance (from each other or from you)?

The direct relationship between one's approach and classroom techniques can be illustrated in the way one principle alone generates a number of crucial questions about the effectiveness of a single technique. The principle of *intrinsic motivation*, for example, implies more than a few corollaries that can act as a "test" of a technique's potential for creating or sustaining intrinsic motivation. Consider the checklist in Table 2, each item of which represents a facet of the principle of intrinsic motivation.

We might, for example, consider Di Pietro's (1987) Strategic Interaction technique, and apply the above check list. I think it becomes quite clear that Strategic Interaction does indeed rather dramatically (no pun intended) promote intrinsic motivation!

Another way of looking at the relationship between approach and technique is illustrated in the following list of suggestions for building a sense of *strategic investment* in the classroom. Each of the ten considerations is a principle of language learning/teaching that is reasonably well accepted. They are "good language learner" characteristics that we would all be wise to foster among students in second-language classrooms. For each characteristic, one can name a handful of classroom techniques that foster successful language learning in the classroom.

Building strategic techniques

1. To lower inhibitions: play guessing games and communication games; do role plays and skits; sing songs; use plenty of group work; laugh *with* your students; have them share their fears in small groups.

2. To encourage risk-taking: praise students for making sincere efforts to try out language; use fluency exercises where errors are not corrected at that time; give outside-of-class assignments to speak or write or otherwise try out the language.

3. To build students' self-confidence: tell students explicitly (verbally and nonverbally) that you do indeed believe in them; have them make lists of their strengths, of what they know or have accomplished so far in the course.

4. To help them to develop intrinsic motivation: remind them explicitly about the rewards for learning English; describe (or have students look up) jobs that require English; play down the final examination in favor of helping students to see rewards for themselves beyond the final exam.

5. To promote cooperative learning: direct students to share their knowledge; play down competition among students; get your class to think of themselves as a team; do a considerable amount of small-group work.

6. To encourage them to use right-brain processing: use movies and tapes in class; have them read passages rapidly; do skimming exercises; do rapid "free writes"; do oral fluency exercises where the object is to get students to talk (or write) a lot without being corrected.

7. To promote ambiguity tolerance: encourage students to ask you, and each other, questions when they don't understand something; keep your theoretical explanations very simple and brief; deal with just a few rules at a time; occasionally you can resort to translation into a native language to clarify a word or meaning.

8. To help them use their intuition: praise students for good guesses; do not always give explanations of errors—let a correction suffice; correct only selected errors, preferably just those that interfere with learning.

9. To get students to make their mistakes work for *them:* tape record students' oral production and get them to identify errors; let students catch and correct each other's errors; do not always give them the correct form; encourage students to make lists of their common errors and to work on them on their own.

10. To get students to set their own goals: explicitly encourage or direct students to go beyond the classroom goals; have them make lists of what they will accomplish on their own in a particular week; get students to make specific time commitments at home to study the language; give "extra credit" work.

Here again, we see a practical example of the way a principled approach to language teaching consistently and directly leads to practical classroom techniques. Ten principled maxims or "rules" for good language learning can focus teachers on sound classroom practices.

The ecology of second-language acquisition. Approaches to second-language learning and teaching can become exceedingly complex. Sometimes this complexity is represented in a schematic diagram of some kind. In those flowcharts, the complex interrelationships of various principles discussed above struggle to find themselves graphically represented in what more often resembles those mysterious wiring diagrams pasted on the back of electric stoves than what I like to imagine the human language acquisition process must "look" like—or certainly than the way our *organic* world operates!

One day, in a rebellious moment of simultaneous frustration and inspiration, I was moved in a second-language acquisition class I was teaching to create a different "picture" of language acquisition: one that responded not so much to rules of logic, mathematics, and physics as to botany and ecology. The germination (pun intended) of my picture was the metaphor once used by Derek Bickerton in a lecture at the University of Hawaii about his contention that human beings are "bioprogrammed" for language (see Bickerton 1981), perhaps not unlike the bioprogram of a flower seed, whose genetic makeup predisposes it to deliver, in successive stages, roots, stem, branches, leaves, and flowers. In a burst of wild artistic energy, I went out on a limb to extend the flower-seed metaphor to language acquisition. In Figure 1, I offer my picture of the "ecology" of language acquisition, dedicated to the memory of Robert Di Pietro, who was, not coincidentally, a gardener *par excellence* when he wasn't teaching and training teachers.

At the risk of overstating what may already be obvious to you, I will nevertheless indulge in a few comments on the illustration. The rainclouds of input stimulate seeds of predisposition (innate, genetically transmitted processes). But the potency of that input is dependent on the appropriate styles and strategies that a person puts into action (here represented as soil). Upon the germination of language abilities (notice not all the seeds of predisposition are effectively activated), networks of competence (which, like underground roots, cannot be observed from above the ground) build and grow stronger as the organism actively engages in comprehension and production of language. The resulting root system (inferred competence) is what we commonly call intake. Notice that several factors distinguish input from intake. Through the use of further strategies and affective abilities, coupled with the feedback we receive from others (note the tree trunk), we ultimately develop full-flowering communicative abilities. The fruit of our performance (or output) is of course conditioned by the climate of innumerable contextual variables.

At any point the horticulturist (teacher) can irrigate to create better input, apply fertilizers for richer soil, encourage the use of effective strategies and

Figure 1. The ecology of language acquisition

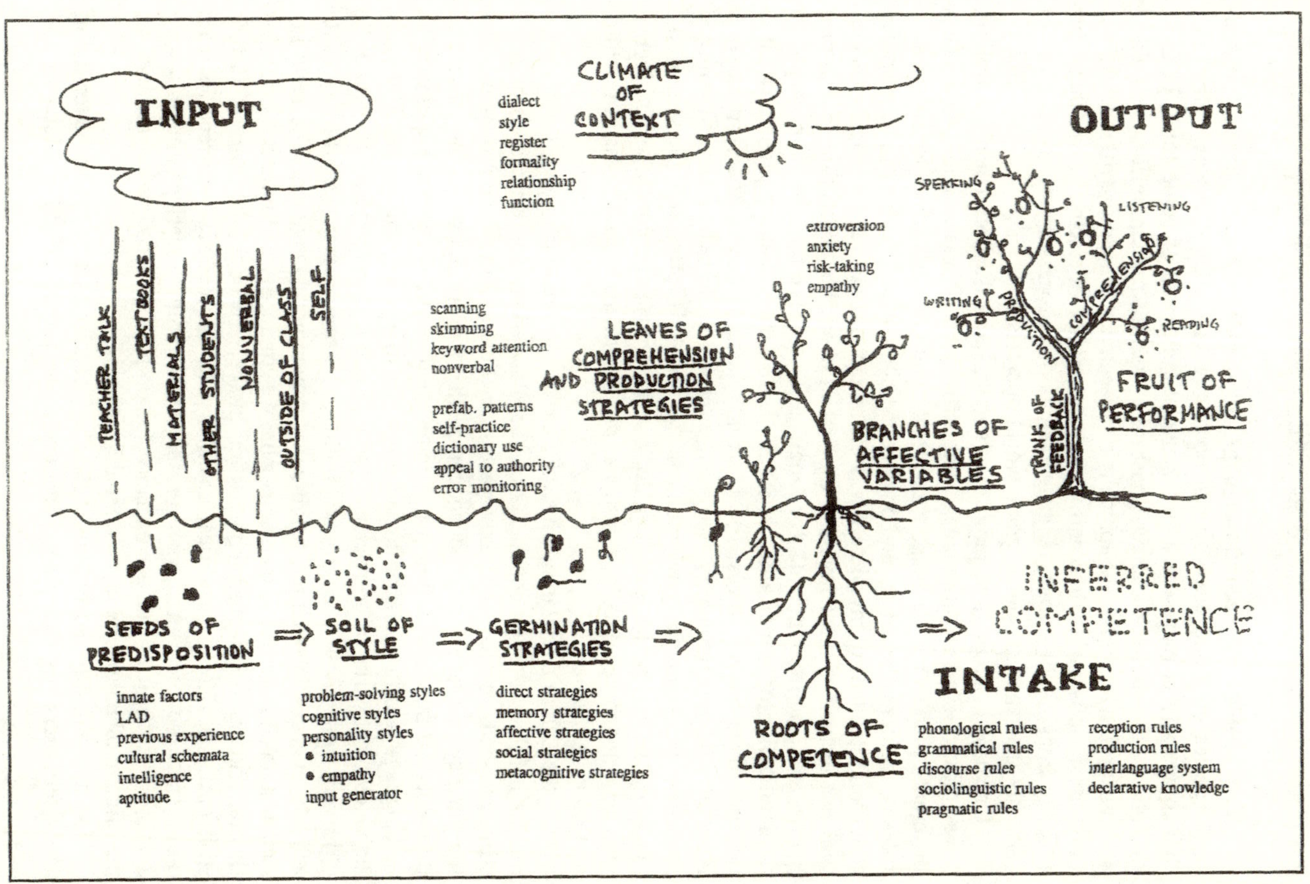

affective enhancers, and, in the greenhouses of our classrooms, control the contextual climate for optimal growth.

No, this is not the kind of extended metaphor that one can "prove" or verify through empirical research. But, lest you scoff at such outlandish depictions, think about how many factors in second-language acquisition theory are conceptualized and described metaphorically: language-acquisition *device*, *pivot* and *open* words, Piaget's *equilibration*, *cognitive pruning,* Ausubel's *subsumption*, *transfer,* social *distance*, *global* and *local* errors, *monitoring*, affective *filter*, *automatic* and *controlled* processing. If a metaphor enables us to describe a phenomenon clearly and to apply it wisely, then we can surely entertain it—as long as we understand that these word-pictures are usually subject to certain breakdowns when logically extended too far.

So, while you might exercise a little caution in drawing a tight analogy between Earth's botanical cycles and language learning, you might just allow yourself to think of second-language learners as budding flowers—as plants needing your nurture and care. When the scientific flowcharts and technical terminology of current second-language research become excruciatingly painful to understand, try creating your own metaphors.

Above all, it is incumbent on us as teachers and researchers to develop a principled, strategic *approach* to second-language acquisition and then to allow that approach to enlighten all aspects of our classroom pedagogy. Sometimes that approach may be best comprehended as an extended metaphor. At other times it may be expressed as a list of established principles. However one's approach is conceptualized, a comprehensive, dynamic, useful set of principles is indispensable to classroom language teaching. Without a principled approach, we flounder, we resort to short-sighted methods, and ultimately we do a disservice to learners. With it, we become empowered to seize every pedagogical moment in the classroom by creating optimal learning experiences for our students.

REFERENCES

Anthony, Edward. 1963. "Approach, method, technique." *English Language Teaching* 17: 63–67.

Bickerton, Derek. 1981. *Roots of language*. Ann Arbor, Mich.: Karoma Publishers.

Brown, H. Douglas. 1994a. *Principles of language learning and teaching* (Third edition). Englewood Cliffs, N.J.: Prentice Hall Regents.

Brown, H. Douglas. 1994b. *Teaching by principles: An interactive approach to language pedagogy*. Englewood Cliffs, N.J.: Prentice Hall Regents.

Chamot, Anna Uhl, and J. Michael O'Malley. 1993. "Teaching for strategic learning: Theory and practice." In James E. Alatis (ed.) *Georgetown University Round Table on Languages and Linguistics 1993*. Washington, D.C.: Georgetown University Press.

Crandall, JoAnn. 1993. "Strategic integration: Content-based language programs and teacher development." In James E. Alatis (ed.) *Georgetown University Round Table on Languages and Linguistics 1993*. Washington, D.C.: Georgetown University Press.

DiPietro, Robert. 1987. *Strategic interaction: Learning languages through scenarios*. New York: Cambridge University Press.

Doughty, Catherine. 1993. "Fine tuning of feedback by competent speakers to language learners." In James E. Alatis (ed.) *Georgetown University Round Table on Languages and Linguistics 1993*. Washington, D.C.: Georgetown University Press.

Ehrman, Madeline E. 1993. "Ego boundaries revisited: Toward a model of personality and learning." In James E. Alatis (ed.) *Georgetown University Round Table on Languages and Linguistics 1993*. Washington, D.C.: Georgetown University Press.

Flynn, Suzanne. 1993. "Marriage for life: Theory, practice, and research." In James E. Alatis (ed.) *Georgetown University Round Table on Languages and Linguistics 1993*. Washington, D.C.: Georgetown University Press.

Gouin, François. 1880. *L'art d'enseigner et d'étudier les langues*. Paris: Librairie Fischbacher.

Lantolf, James P. 1993. "Vygotsky and Bakhtin in the second language classroom: A case for strategic interaction." In James E. Alatis (ed.) *Georgetown University Round Table on Languages and Linguistics 1993*. Washington, D.C.: Georgetown University Press.

Marckwardt, Albert D. 1972. "Changing winds and shifting sands." *MST English Quarterly* 21: 3–11.

Morley, Joan. 1993. "Interactive listening and communication: Activities, tasks, strategies." In James E. Alatis (ed.) *Georgetown University Round Table on Languages and Linguistics 1993*. Washington, D.C.: Georgetown University Press.

Nunan, David. 1989. *Understanding language classrooms: A guide for teacher-initiated action*. New York: Prentice Hall.

Nunan, David. 1991. *Language teaching methodology: A textbook for teachers*. New York: Prentice Hall.

Pennycook, Alastair. 1989. "The concept of method, interested knowledge, and the politics of language teaching." *TESOL Quarterly* 23: 589–618.

Prabhu, N.S. 1990. "There is no best method—why?" *TESOL Quarterly* 24: 161–176.

Richards, Jack C., and Rodgers, Theodore S. 1986. *Approaches and methods in language teaching*. New York: Cambridge University Press.

Stern, H.H. 1985. "Review of Oller and Richard-Amato (1983), Methods that work: A smorgasbord of ideas for language teachers." *Studies in Second Language Acquisition* 7: 249–251.

Stevick, Earl. 1993. "How strategic is memorable? How memorable is strategic?" In James E. Alatis (ed.) *Georgetown University Round Table on Languages and Linguistics 1993*. Washington, D.C.: Georgetown University Press.

The structure of the lexicon and language teaching

Dieter Kastovsky
University of Vienna and Georgetown University

Lexical–Semantic Structures. As has repeatedly been pointed out during this conference, language-acquisition and language-teaching theories have always reflected—and interacted with—contemporary linguistic theories. Thus, part-of-speech-based traditional grammar acted and still acts as the framework for the grammar-translation method of language teaching. Behaviorist neo-Bloomfieldian structuralism produced the audiolingual method with pattern practice and the language laboratory; and generativism, which regards language as rule-governed activity, was the source of notions such as interlanguage and the interpretation of language acquisition as hypothesis formation. This interaction is most obvious in the domains of phonology, morphology, and syntax, but it also concerns the lexicon and thus has consequences for vocabulary teaching.

Here, however, the interaction between linguistic theory and language-teaching methodology has had some problematic side effects, which were due to certain theoretical assumptions characterizing the dominating linguistic theories, especially in the United States, but not only there. First of all there was the semantic bias of (neo-)Bloomfieldianism, still to a certain extent detectable in generative linguistics (cf. Kastovsky 1986: 93ff., 1992: 287ff.), which necessarily led to a disregard of the semantic aspects of vocabulary teaching. And, second, there was the conception of the lexicon as an unstructured "appendix of the grammar, a list of basic irregularities" (cf. Sweet 1913: 31, Bloomfield 1933: 274, Chomsky 1965: 142), which seemed to make systematic vocabulary teaching a futile enterprise.

Thus, the teaching of vocabulary has always been somewhat of a Cinderella —at least in Europe, but probably also in the United States, and it has never been influenced by linguistic theorizing to the same extent as other domains. It might therefore not be inappropriate to again draw attention to some aspects of European lexicology and lexical semantics, which, despite the present popularity of prototype theory, should be re-examined as to their usefulness for language teaching, especially in combination with another aspect of the lexicon, viz.. word-formation (derivational morphology), which also has not figured too prominently in language-teaching methodology. Both taken together will, I think, provide a powerful tool for a more systematic and principled approach to vocabulary teaching.

I will start out from the assumption that the lexicon of a language is by no means unstructured but is organized into larger units called lexical fields, as was postulated by structural semanticists such as Trier in the thirties and Coseriu, Lyons, Lehrer, and many others in the sixties and seventies (cf. Kastovsky 1982: ch. 4). According to this view, lexical items sharing a common semantic denominator are related to each other on the basis of paradigmatic oppositions, at the same time dividing a semantic continuum among them in a language-specific manner. These oppositions constitute semantic dimensions and semantic features specifying these dimensions, which in turn characterize not only the sense relations between the lexical items in question but also their internal semantic structures.

Thus, both aspects are interdependent: A lexical field is constituted by lexical items standing in opposition to each other, and these oppositions at the same time establish one or several semantic dimensions and corresponding feature specifications, which characterize the sense relations obtaining in the lexical field between the lexical items and their internal, micro-semantic structure. To take a classical textbook example: The opposition between *stallion* and *mare* constitutes a dimension *SEX* within the lexical field *HORSE,* which is further specified as [male] and [not male] by complementary semantic features. Similarly, the opposition among *walk, swim, fly* establishes the dimension *MEDIUM* with the equipollent feature specification [solid surface], [liquid], and [air].

The relationship among such oppositions, their underlying dimensions, and the respective semantic features leads to the establishment of various sense relations such as antonymy, complementarity, hyponymy, etc. (cf. Lyons 1977: 270 for a comprehensive list), whose properties depend on the nature of the dimension, the number and type of features characterizing it, and their function. In this respect one may distinguish between inherent features such as [male] or [air] in the above examples and contextual features ("lexical solidarities," cf. Coseriu 1967), which are related to the selection restrictions of early generative grammar and constitute syntagmatic relations, for example:

(1) a. bark $\supset$ $\text{dog}_{\text{Subj/Ag}}$, see, look $\supset$ $\text{eye}_{\text{Instr}}$, kiss $\supset$ $\text{lip}_{\text{Instr}}$, fell $\supset$ $\text{tree}_{\text{Obj/Pat}}$
b. confess $\supset$ $[+\text{ HUMAN}]_{\text{Subj}}$, elapse $\supset$ $[\text{TIME}]_{\text{Subj}}$

Thus, the meaning of *dog* is included in *bark* as Subject and Agent, the meaning of *eye* is included in *see, look* as Instrument, the meaning of *tree* is included in *fell* as Object/Patient; *confess* implies a Subject with the feature [HUMAN] and *elapse* includes the notion of [TIME] as Subject.

This so-called Aristotelian or checklist theory of semantics has recently been criticized by the adherents of prototype theory, who regard linguistic meaning from a basically referential point of view and define the meaning of a lexical item in terms of an ideal referent or prototype (a Platonic idea?). But as Lipka (1987) and I (Kastovsky 1988) have tried to show, these two approaches are not genuine alternatives but correlative organizational principles of the lexicon, a view corroborated by psycholinguistic studies, e.g., Aitchison (1987: 5). It would therefore be premature to totally abandon this structuralist approach to semantics, especially since it receives strong support from the domain of word-formation, with which it systematically interacts (cf. Kastovsky 1988). And it is this interaction which will be discussed and exemplified in the next part of this paper, while the final part will focus on some implications for vocabulary teaching.

Word-formation and semantics. In this section I will first outline some general properties of word-formation, then I will discuss the relationship between paradigmatic lexical structures (sense relations) as well as syntagmatic relations (lexical solidarities) and word-formation. Finally, I shall turn to the functional aspects of word-formation.

Word-formation and sense relations. It may safely be assumed that every human language will have word-formation patterns in order to systematically extend the vocabulary and adapt it to the changing communicative needs of the speech community. The principal characteristics of word-formation syntagmas is their motivated status; i.e., unless they have become lexicalized and/or idiomatized, their overall meaning can be derived from the meanings of their parts and some underlying constructional meaning according to the compositionality principle underlying human language in general.

Word-formation syntagmas are based on a determinant/determinatum (modifier/head) relationship, the order of the two constituents being language-specific. In English it is usually modifier/head. As Marchand (1969: 11) has argued, this binary structure results from a general tendency "to see a thing identical with another already existing and at the same time different from it." Put differently, a certain extralinguistic phenomenon (concept) is identified with something known and already categorized linguistically, but at the same time it is differentiated from it, because the identified object/concept differs from the general category by an additional property. Thus a space-going vessel is identified as a *ship,* but since it is distinct from normal ships by the fact that it doesn't travel on water but into outer space it is called a *spaceship.* This specification may assume quite different forms, but the crucial point in our connection is that it largely seems to follow the sense relations postulated by structural semanticists for the simplex lexicon.

Thus the example already quoted, viz. *ship* and *spaceship,* illustrates the sense relation of hyponymy; for example, the more comprehensive field *SHIP:*

(2) *SHIP:* barque, frigate, schooner – steamship, sailing ship, spaceship – freighter, tanker, etc.

Thus, the simple lexical items *barque, frigate, schooner* function as hyponyms of the superordinate term (archilexeme) SHIP in the same way as the compounds *steamship, sailing ship, spaceship,* i.e., compounding basically serves to produce hyponyms in those instances where there is no simplex hyponym in the lexicon: A compound always is a hyponym of its head. The same is true of certain prefixes, for example:

(3) write : rewrite; tell : foretell; author : co-author; husband : ex-husband

And, as the examples *freighter, tanker* in (2) demonstrate, suffixation also produces hyponyms in certain instances.

Another sense relation that characterizes certain word-formations is complementarity, i.e. the relationship between the base and the prefix, as in:

(4) edible : inedible; transformable : untransformable; white : nonwhite; steward : stewardess; widow : widower; bearded : beardless

This sense relation is the same as between *dead : alive; man : woman; true : false.* Antonyms, exemplified by *long : short; high : low; good : bad* in the simplex vocabulary, are also frequently created by word-formations, for example:

(5) kind : unkind; wise : unwise; natural : unnatural; loyal : disloyal; hairy : hairless.

Directional oppositions of the type *to open : to close* have their parallel in prefixal reversative verbs such as

(6) tie : untie; lock : unlock; militarize : demilitarize; join : disjoin; arm : disarm, etc.

Obviously, word-formations typically occur in those instances where there is no primary, i.e. simple, lexical item to represent a term in the respective sense relation created by a potential opposition within a given lexical field. And it is the semantic dimensions, which determine the internal structure of lexical fields, that are of the utmost importance for this parallelism and also for the overall organization of the vocabulary. Elsewhere (Kastovsky 1981: 441) I have illustrated this with a brief analysis of the lexical field *HIT,* for example:

(7) a. HIT / kick : punch : slap : (beat) ⇒ <INSTRUMENT> → hit with the knee, elbow, hammer, club, cudgel, etc. → to hammer, club, cudgel, cosh, etc.
b. HIT / bash : smack : pound : knock : beat ⇒ <MANNER>

(8) scrape : peel : bark : skin : debark : dehusk, etc.

HIT, the superordinate term, is unspecified with regard to the instrument or manner involved in the action. The opposition among *kick, punch,* and *slap* constitutes a dimension of <INSTRUMENT> by implying the meanings of *foot, fist,* and *flat instrument;* in other words, it establishes a lexical solidarity at the same time. *Beat* involves an optional, i.e. inferential, feature [with a stick]; this feature is often present by implicature but may be cancelled by the context. Another dimension, <MANNER>, is constituted by the series *bash, smack, pound, knock, beat,* etc. But the dimension <INSTRUMENT> is of course not exhausted by these examples; other possibilities can be realized by syntactic paraphrases such as *hit with the knee, elbow, hammer, cudgel, club,* etc. And if a fixed expression is needed, word-formation intervenes and produces verbs like *hammer, club, cudgel, cosh,* etc.

Another example is *scrape,* defined as "to remove (unwanted material) from a surface by pulling or pushing an edge firmly across it repeatedly" (LDCE) as compared to verbs like *peel, bark, skin, debark,* etc. *Scrape* does not imply a specific object, but it contains a specification of the <MANNER> in which the removal is done. The other verbs are based on the dimension <REMOVED OBJECT> but are neutral with regard to <MANNER>.

Word-formation and lexical solidarities. As already mentioned, examples like *kick, punch, scrape* represent lexical implications, called "lexical solidarities" by Coseriu: The meaning of another lexical item or even a whole class of lexical items, e.g. HUMAN BEING, is included in the meaning of the item in question. Lyons speaks of encapsulation in such instances. These examples illustrate purely semantic implications. In the case of word-formation, on the other hand, the semantic implication is accompanied by a formal one: A specific lexical item has not only semantically, but also formally and morphologically become part of another lexical item, which is motivated by this fact in the sense of Saussure's notion of "relative motivation." It is this formal–semantic motivation, the analyzability and/or transparency of a complex lexical item, that is the most essential property and very *raison d'être* of word-formation.

We thus again observe a remarkable parallelism between semantic structures characterizing simple lexical items and word-formation. Moreover, since word-formation must be regarded as rule-governed, this parallelism suggests that the lexicon is indeed not an unordered conglomerate of lexical items but has internal structure. Or as Aitchison put it from a psycholinguistic perspective: "words are not just stacked higgledy-piggledy into our minds ... they are organised into an intricate, interlocking system" (Aitchison 1987: 5).

Another important aspect of this interaction and parallelism is the fact that purely semantic implications (lexical solidarities) and semantic implication accompanied by formal inclusion (motivated complex lexical items, i.e. word-formation syntagmas) are only opposite end points on a scale of motivation, not an all-or-none phenomenon, due to the phenomenon of lexicalization/idiomatization and other factors. This is illustrated by the following examples:

(9) thief/theft : steal; bite : tooth; big/small : size; kill : die : dead/not alive

(10) father : patern/al; mother : matern/al; mouth : or/al; sun : sol/ar

(11) consume : consump/tion; deceive : decep/tion

(12) science : scient/ist; pirate : pira/cy

(13) fly : fligh/t; give : gif/t; high : heigh/t; wide : wid/th; sing : song

(14) rob : robb/er; shoot : shoot/ing; look vb : look sb; thick : thick/ness; erase : eras/er, hammer sb : hammer vb; father : father/ly; legal : legal/ize; break itr. : break tr.

The examples in (10) are lexical solidarities or other types of purely semantic implications. Type (15), on the other hand, exemplifies the other end point of the scale, viz. fully motivated word-formation syntagmas produced by productive word-formation rules.

The remaining groups fall in between these extremes. (11) contains items that are in principle analyzable, and there is a limited possibility of new formations, but it differs from (15) in that the formations are neo-Latin; i.e., analyzability is only possible on a foreign basis, since the bases of the derivatives do not exist in English as independent lexical items. Type (12) is also basically foreign, but in terms of analyzability it is closer to (15); it is completely unproductive, however, even on a foreign basis and involves a great deal of mainly idiosyncratic morphophonemic alternations. The pairs are usually independent loans from French and Latin, where they were/are derivationally connected. Type (14) is the native parallel. Type (13) resembles (12) in that it is foreign, and the derivative can be analyzed as containing an allomorph of the basis, which occurs as an independent word in English. But it differs from (12) in that the suffixes are productive, and therefore morphophonemic alternations between bases and derivatives could be handled by appropriate morphophonemic rules, though these will have to be lexically governed. The crucial factor again is the fact that the meaning relations exemplified by all these types are the same, which points to a homogeneous organizational principle of the lexicon.

The function of word-formation. Let me now turn to the functional aspect of word-formation, which, incidentally, can also be envisaged as a scale. Word-formation patterns exist in order to create new lexical items, and these will of course serve the typical function of lexical items (words), viz. to act as designations, as labels, as names for nameworthy segments of extralinguistic reality, i.e. for categories that are salient enough to require a name instead of merely being described by a syntactic construction. This function is typically served by many N + N compounds of the type *polar bear, teaspoon, tablespoon, eggplant, space shuttle,* etc., but not only by these, of course; for example, *cheeseburger, beefburger, nannygate, Irangate,* etc. There is, however, another function, called syntactic recategorization, by means of which a certain amount of syntactic material is converted into nouns, adjectives, or verbs, cf. the following examples from detective and science-fiction stories:

(15) a. ... do we assume that the *stone-chucker, wire-stretcher, composite letter-writer, dumper of green lady and telephonist* are one and the same person and that this person is also the *murderer* of Miss Cost? ... Miss Pride ... is convinced that the *ringer-up* was Miss Cost.

b. ... and whether our own conversation doesn't sound a little *potty*. It's the *pottiness,* you know, that's so awful.

c. Solarians did not bud, they *birthed;* and the female was always the *birther*. She remained female for life, no matter how many times she *birthed*.

d. "Don't you know a single person who *ought to be murdered*?" He wondered why his host should appear to set so much store by his acquaintance with *potential murderees,* but hardly liked to ask.

e. At the end of it, either they would *split up* or decide to make it permanent, and up to now Rodger had been silently determined that it was going to be a *split*.

f. It's *blood* on his hands. His hands get *covered with blood,* not visible to anybody else, and he goes and washes them. ... He wouldn't give his name and didn't mention *bloody* hands.

g. He made *fists* ... He *defisted* to gesture.

h. If that's not *civil, civilise* it and tell me.

This function might be regarded as a subcategory of textual pronominalization and enhances textual cohesion.

Such formations overtly incorporating syntactic relations are of course also integrated into the vocabulary and can become labels as well, so that one and the same lexical item, depending on the context, may either function as recategorization, as in (16 a) or as label, as in (16 b), i.e. the function is context-dependent, for example:

(16) a. And he knew no one was going to take him offstage and *beat* him; the *beating* of prisoners was not authorised.

b. ... a larger male not only stole his peanut but gave him a *beating*.

One essential consequence of this observation is that syntactic functions/thematic roles/deep-structure cases are required in a description of the word-formation patterns of a language (cf. the "transformational hypothesis" of the sixties), and it would seem that on the basis of the interaction between simple and complex lexical items, such functions also play a role in the semantic description of simple lexical items such as *author, doctor, architect* (primary agent nouns), *curtsy, curse* (primary action nouns), *knife, fork, shovel, comb* (primary instrument nouns), as had already been suggested by Weinreich (1966) in his seminal paper, which sparked off generative semantics and lexical decomposition.

Consequences for language teaching. So far I have talked about properties of the lexicon as postulated by a linguistic description that assumes that the meanings of lexical items are, at least to a certain extent, describable on the basis of oppositions, dimensions, and semantic features specifying these dimensions. Moreover, I have tried to show that there is a close relationship between such semantic structures and the semantic make up of word-formation syntagmas, where these semantic structures are made explicit, at least to a certain extent. Let me now turn to the practical relevance of these observations for language teaching.

Of course, new lexical items will have to be introduced through an appropriate contextualization, both in terms of linguistic and extralinguistic context. Scenarios or frames provide the requisite setting for this. But, as has already been pointed out by structural semanticists such as Coseriu, this leads to a vocabulary structure that is organized on the basis of extralinguistic associations—a so-called *Sachfeld.*

While this extralinguistically based organization of the vocabulary is certainly relevant and even necessary, it is not sufficient. As we have seen, the vocabulary of a language is not merely a nomenclature for the labeling of segments of extralinguistic reality, it is structured. And it is this complex structure that the language learner has to acquire, too, although under incomparably more difficult conditions than the child acquiring its mother tongue. Therefore, it would seem that a more systematic attention to the various types of relationship between simple and complex lexical items is called for in vocabulary teaching.

Thus, if new lexical items are introduced, they should not only be suitably contextualized, but they should be introduced together with their antonyms, complementaries, hyponyms, etc., both simple and complex. Thus, a speaker of German should not only be exposed to the lexical items *bus, monkey,* or *snail,* but at the same time also to their field neighbors *coach, ape,* and *slug,* in view of the fact that English has a categorial distinction between these on the level of the primary vocabulary, which German lacks (cf. *Bus, Affe, Schnecke*). Inversely, a speaker of English should be made aware of the fact that this distinction, obligatory in English, is neutralized in German, but can be actualized by making use of compounding, cf. *Menschenaffe* ("ape"), *Nackt-schnecke/Hausschnecke* ("slug"/"snail"). Put differently, vocabulary teaching should explicitly relate semantic and morphological/derivational structures on a contrastive basis to a much greater extent than has been done so far.

Similarly, syntagmatic relations should also be made more explicit. Thus, a student of German has to be made aware of the fact that *eat* and *drink* are matched by two lexical items in German, viz. *essen/fressen* and *trinken/saufen,* depending on whether the Subject/Agent is a human being or an animal (with the appropriate remarks on metaphorical usage). It cannot be denied, of course, that such observations have always been included in textbooks and language courses to a certain extent. What I would like to suggest, however, is that vocabulary teaching should be based to a much greater extent and much more systematically on these relationships.

Moreover, in view of the fact that every language has its own lexical–semantic organization, which hardly ever matches that of another language, the learner should be made aware of this fact—but should also be shown that there are escape hatches when s/he wants to express something for which either just s/he or the target language itself does not have a straightforward equivalent, escape hatches in the form of paraphrases or word-formations. This of course implies that vocabulary teaching might also have recourse to making linguistic structures explicit, not only grammar. And it may even turn out that in the former area, cognitive–explanatory teaching produces much better results than in syntax or morphology.

Another domain that should be included more systematically, especially at the more advanced level, is the role of word-formation as a means of creating textual cohesion exemplified in (15) above. This will of course be more relevant for written rather than spoken language, but it seems that languages differ markedly as to the use of these devices. A study done by a student of mine (Indra 1991) has shown, e.g., that English uses such lexical-coreference means much more frequently than German, regardless of the text type involved.

Finally, one might want to ask whether one should encourage students to actively apply word-formation rules in creating new lexical items. If second-language learning is indeed very similar to first-language acquisition, then the answer is "yes," since children are always much more creative in this area than adults who have a larger simplex vocabulary, while the child has to find stopgaps. And just as the child in first-language acquisition gradually unlearns abortive formations, so the second-language learner will gradually find that not anything goes, and that there are restrictions, if they are pointed out to him or her. Thus, active use of word-formation rules should not be discouraged, although the major emphasis should nevertheless be on their passive application in recognition tasks and in relating word-formation structures to the overall makeup of lexical fields.

Thus, it would seem that a certain amount of cognitive teaching and learning in the domain of vocabulary is not only useful but necessary in view of the fact that the vocabulary of a language has its own complex structure and grammar, if one believes that second-language learning requires a cognitive approach—a belief that the author of this paper shares.

References

Aitchison, Jean. 1987. *Words in the mind. An introduction to the mental lexicon.* Oxford: Blackwell.

Coseriu, Eugenio. 1967. "Lexikalische Solidaritäten." *Poetica* 1: 239–253.

Coseriu, Eugenio. 1973. *Probleme der strukturellen Semantik.* Tübingen: Narr.

Indra, J. 1991. "Word-formation and text cohesion." Unpublished M.A. thesis. University of Vienna.

Kastovsky, Dieter 1981. "Lexical fields and word-formation." In H. Geckeler et al. (eds.), *Logos Semantikos: Studia lingustica in honorem Eugenio Coseriu 1921–1981* (Volume 3). 429–445.

Kastovsky, Dieter. 1982. *Wortbildung und Semantik.* Tübingen: Francke.

Kastovsky, Dieter. 1986. "Problems in the morphological analysis of complex lexical items." *Acta Linguistica Academiae Scientiarum Hungaricae* 36: 93–107.

Kastovsky, Dieter. 1988. "Structural semantics or prototype semantics?: The evidence of word-formation." In Werner Hüllen and Rainer Schulze (eds.), *Understanding the lexicon: Meaning, sense and world knowledge in lexical semantics.* Tübingen: Niemeyer. 190–203.

Kastovsky, Dieter. 1992. "The formats change—the problems remain: Word-formation theory between 1960 and 1990." In Martin Pütz (ed.), *Thirty years of linguistic evolution.* Amsterdam: John Benjamins. 285–310.

Lehrer, Adrienne. 1974. *Semantic fields and lexical structures.* Amsterdam: John Benjamins.

Lipka, Leonhard. 1987. "Prototype semantics or feature semantics: An alternative? Perspectives on language in performance." In Wolfgang Lörscher and Rainer Schulze (eds.), *Studies in linguistics, literary criticism and language teaching and learning*. Tübingen: Narr. 282–298.

Lyons, John. 1963. *Structural semantics: An analysis of part of the vocabulary of Plato*. (Publications of the Philological Society 20.) Oxford.

Lyons, John. 1977. *Semantics* (Vol. 1 and 2). Cambridge: Cambridge University Press.

Marchand, Hans, 1969. *The categories and types of present-day English word-formation* (Second revised edition). Munich.

Sweet, Henry. 1913. *Collected papers*. Oxford: Oxford University Press.

Trier, Jost. 1931. "Der deutsche Wortschatz im Sinnbezirk des Verstandes." *Die Geschichte eines sprachlichen Feldes*. (Vol. 1) Von den Anfängen bis zum Beginn des 13. Jahrhunderts. Heidelberg: Winter.

Weinreich, Uriel. 1966. "Explorations in semantic theory." In Thomas Sebeok (ed.), *Current trends in linguistics* (Vol. 3). 395–477.

Strategic Interaction: Can it be a relief for foreign-language classrooms?

Masaki Oda
Tamagawa University

Introduction. In our daily life, everyone has to face a series of problem-solving activities. Some problems are fairly easy to solve, while others require a tremendous amount of effort to deal with. Figure 1 below illustrates an example of the latter type of problem-solving activities I had to face recently, in a form of a role-card.[1]

Figure 1. Being invited to a conference

> You are invited to present a paper at a conference. Though the conference organizer has agreed to waive your registration fee, you are responsible for transportation and accommodations. In addition, you have found out that the commencement of your university is scheduled on the first day of the conference. Decide what to do, and inform the conference organizer of your plan as soon as possible.

Like a famous phrase from Hamlet, you have to decide whether or not to accept the invitation to the conference, taking various factors into consideration. You must consider when and where the conference is held, what the theme is, and what you are expected to do in your presentation including topic and length. With these pieces of information, you then have to deal with the two big problems described in your role card: expenses and schedule, both of which require extensive interactions with other people. In my case, I had to talk with our chairman, the dean, and several office personnel in the university to secure my travel expenses. At this point, my role card was supposed to have been as Figure 2.

---

1. My special thanks to Yuko Taniguchi-Oda for her insightful comments and suggestions regarding the content of this paper, and to the participants of JALT Omiya Chapter meeting in April 1992 for their input to the scenario presented in this paper.

Figure 2. Getting your travel expenses

> You decided to accept an invitation to present a paper at Georgetown University during the second week of March. However, you need to get some help for your travel expenses from your university. Talk to the people concerned, and secure your travel expenses.

The goal I had to achieve was to get money, and the first part of Figure 2 had already been solved at this point, as far as I was concerned.

When you deal with other people, you cannot read their minds. You can only guess what is likely to be in their "role-cards" based on your experience and your interactions with them. Once you have secured your travel expenses, you have to work out your schedule. In my case, I had to make a judgment about whether or not to attend the commencement of my university, based on how important it would be for me. I decided to attend the commencement since it would be the one for those students who were my first group of advisees.

The next step you must take is to get back to the conference organizers and tell them you accept the invitation but that you cannot present your paper on the first or second day of the conference. You have to interact with them (and they have their own "role-cards") and come up with the best possible solution. My solution was to schedule my presentation on the last day.

What did the process of solving a series of problems illustrated above tell you? Obviously, it showed us how complex human interactions are. At the same time, it implied that we are dealing with such a series of problem-solving activities every day, even at this moment. It is supposed to be a very important aspect of language teaching, yet most of you would agree that it had been talked about very little among language-teaching professionals until Di Pietro (1987) put together the elements of human interaction illustrated above and proposed Strategic Interaction (SI). I believe that it is a good option for foreign-language classes, particularly those emphasizing communication.

In this paper I will discuss if SI can be one of the options for foreign-language classrooms in college, with special attention to EFL in Japan. In the following section, I will discuss the prevailing problems of teaching EFL in Japan, from both teachers' and learners' standpoints. Next, I will point out some specific problems that are unique to Japan. I will then discuss how much SI can help EFL teachers overcome these problems with some examples from my own classes. Finally, I will give a conclusion and prospects for future foreign-language courses using SI.

Background. Many foreign-language teachers never seem to be completely satisfied with their teaching conditions. There are too many students in one class, there are too many items to cover in a short period, the students have very little exposure to the target language, the students are not motivated, and so on. While most of these problems are beyond each individual teacher's control, the general public usually blames the teacher for not helping his or her students master the target language after they have completed the language course.

The situation in Japan is not an exception. As Osanai (1992: 39) points out, the criticism of English (foreign) language teaching that appears in Japanese newspapers usually includes one of the following arguments:

- After having taken EFL courses for six years at secondary schools and four years at college, most students still *cannot speak* English;
- English that is useful for communication is not taught at school because EFL teachers themselves *cannot speak* English;
- People *cannot speak* English because of the current education system, which focuses heavily on college entrance examinations.

EFL teachers would respond to such criticisms by arguing that their teaching conditions need to be improved first: They want more class hours to cover the items to teach, smaller classes, more time and financial support for their own professional development in English-speaking countries, and so on.

In the past decade, such a debate between EFL teachers and the general public has been a favorite pastime in various newspapers, on TV programs, and at conferences on language teaching. However, nobody has ever been successful in making both sides happy at the same time, no matter how many ideas for improving English-language teaching have been proposed.

In June 1991, the Japanese Ministry of Education announced the revised standards for colleges and universities, which abolished foreign-language requirements at higher education institutions (cf. Reinelt 1993: 2). Foreign-language classes, including those of EFL at the college level, therefore, are facing a major turning point. We cannot afford to spend time criticizing each other. Instead, we need at least some "relief" for our foreign-language classrooms. Teachers must seriously consider what their learners need, while the general public must be aware of the various constraints on teachers.

It is said that there are more than 8,000 tenured or tenure-track faculty teaching English at colleges and universities in Japan. This number constitutes approximately 65% of the entire population of those teaching foreign languages at that level (cf. Abe 1992: 82). At present, it is very unlikely that the number of EFL classes would radically decrease in the next few years, as most college freshmen have had to study English, the only foreign-language subject for entrance examinations, for many years before entering a college or a university. Nevertheless, the fact that the status of EFL classes is not guaranteed by the revised standards will force colleges or universities to offer programs that attract their students.

What then attracts students? According to a survey conducted of 10,315 college students in Japan by Koike et al. (1991), 60.1% responded that they desire to get *communication-based* training in EFL at the college level (27). As I have stated elsewhere, however, language teachers have never been consistent about defining *communication,* although many of them, in fact, have positive attitudes about communication as an objective of language teaching and thus attempt some sort of communicative language teaching (Oda 1992a). Dubin and Olshtain (1986) also point out that the term *communicative* has been defined so differently by different people, "as with the tale about five blind men who touched separate parts of an elephant and so each described something different" (69). It is not the purpose of this paper to give a black-or-white definition of *communication*: I would only like to say that the students want something different from what they have at present. Perhaps they, as well as the general public, expect more training in spoken English that they can use outside their college classrooms. In the next section, I will examine the conditions of teaching EFL at Japanese universities and will look into the possibilities of developing communication-oriented spoken English courses using SI.

Adopting new methods or techniques for EFL classes at Japanese Universities: Conditions to be considered. Traditionally, the most common way for language-teaching professionals to improve their teaching conditions is to adopt new methods or techniques in their classes. In the past two decades, various "innovative" methods or techniques, such as Total Physical Response, the Silent Way, and Community Language Learning (cf. Richards and Rodgers 1986) have been brought to Japan mostly from English-speaking countries. In addition, presentations on Computer Assisted Language Learning (CALL) and video are usually the most popular ones at professional conferences on language teaching such as TESOL, ACTFL, or JALT (The Japan Association of Language Teachers).

Many of these methods and techniques, however, require "good" teaching conditions such as small class size, well-motivated students, a teacher with native-like proficiency in the target language, and a sufficient amount of exposure to the target language. In addition, special equipment and/or training for teachers are often regarded as prerequisites for adopting some of those methods or techniques. Nonetheless, very little has been said about the possible modifications teachers can make in case their teaching conditions do not meet the level required by the proponents of the particular method or technique they are trying to adopt. As a result, teachers often overlook the fact that a method that requires a small class size does not necessarily work in larger classes.

In the case of English classes at Japanese universities, there are four major areas to consider before adopting any new methods and/or techniques. First of all, they are not ESL classes but EFL classes. Moreover, in most Japanese universities, each class usually meets once a week for 90 minutes. Therefore, the amount of the students' exposure to English is very limited.

Second, the class size is quite large. According to Koike et al. (1990), 592 out of 981 teachers (60.3%) responded that the maximum number of students in one class acceptable to them was 60. In fact, that is the typical size of a "general" English class at a Japanese college. Besides, many students are taking English only because they have to: I once taught an English class for engineering majors that had more than 70 students, all of whom had failed English in the previous year. Since foreign-language classes had been required before the revised standards were proposed by the Ministry of Education, and English was the only foreign language offered to them that year, the students had to take and pass English courses. Needless to say, the degree of the students' motivation was not always high enough.

Third, the teachers' backgrounds must be taken into account. Those teaching English at colleges or universities do not necessarily specialize in TEFL. In fact, Koike et al. (1990: 130) report that only 210 out of 1,008 teachers (20.8%) they surveyed were specialists in foreign-language teaching, including TEFL. Other specialties include literature, linguistics, and comparative cultures. From this figure, it is natural for us to assume that the options of methods or techniques they can use in their classes are somewhat more limited in comparison with those available to TEFL specialists.

Lastly, we have to consider the fact that most teachers who are teaching English in college are Japanese-speaking teachers. Although there are more native English speakers who are teaching in college nowadays, they are usually reserved for courses for English or international relations majors. In fact, there are considerably few native English speakers who hold full-time positions teaching college.

The Japanese-speaking teachers also have some problems. A major one is that, besides the lack of constant exposure to English in Japan, about 31% of these teachers have never had a chance to visit an English-speaking country (Koike et al. 1990: 18). As I stated earlier, students want to learn how to "communicate" with someone in English. It is not my intention to say that being a native speaker of English is a qualification to teach the language. It is, however, certainly a disadvantage for many English teachers who have never had a chance to communicate in English if they are to teach communication-oriented classes.

Does Strategic Interaction work in Japanese universities? Taking what I have discussed in the previous section into consideration, while meeting students' needs, I believe that SI can be an option for EFL classes at Japanese colleges and universities for at least the next decade.

A typical classroom procedure for Strategic Interaction (SI) can be classified as a type of role playing (cf. Di Pietro 1987). Each student is instructed, usually through a role card, what s/he is expected to do. In the case of SI, such an instruction is called a "scenario." Like what is commonly called a "simulation" in which each participant "is asked to work out his [sic] own attitude to the problem, and his [sic] own strategy for dealing with it [in a given situation]" (Livingstone 1983: 1), SI expects each participant to deal with the given problem in his or her own way.

The major difference between SI and the other role-playing techniques is that in SI, there is always a conflict between the roles; i.e, the instruction given to each participant is carefully designed so that the situation in which all the roles have achieved their goals completely satisfactorily at the same time could never happen. This creates *dramatic tension,* since each participant must impose his or her ideas on the others in order to achieve his or her goal. Di Pietro (1987: 3) emphasizes the importance of dramatic tension as follows: "Without the element of dramatic tension, a scenario is not likely to be successful, no matter how relevant its theme might be to learners' functional needs."

As I mentioned earlier, one of the problems of teaching English in Japan is the lack of students' exposure to English. I do not simply mean the amount each student hears or reads English: The important thing is how frequently the student is put into a situation in which s/he is under the pressure of using English to get something done. As SI is an approach that attempts to recreate dramatic tension of human interaction in classrooms, it is supposed to be helpful for EFL classes at Japanese colleges or universities. Let us look at an example and see how such dramatic tension is created through scenarios. Figure 3 below is the one I have actually used in my freshman English class.

Figure 3. Next door neighbors. (From Oda 1992b)

Role A: You meet your next-door neighbor in the elevator. Though no pets are allowed in this apartment complex, you often hear a cat meowing from next door. Your little baby is allergic to cats. Tell your neighbor that you do not want them to have a cat.

Role B: You meet your next-door neighbor in the elevator. Your daughter is going to a high school entrance exam next week, but she has been suffering from the sound of music coming from next door. Tell your neighbor that you want them to turn the volume down.

When students are asked to work on the above scenario, the very first thing both roles A and B have to consider is how to tell their neighbors something that they do not want to tell them. I believe that this is quite a common question we ask ourselves in our daily lives, for example, a child has to tell his or her parents that s/he failed an exam, or a boss has to tell his or her worker that s/he is fired. In the case of this scenario, neither role A nor role B has concrete evidence that a cat is certainly in B's apartment or that A is certainly playing the music too loud. They are just making their best guess based on the information available to them in addition to their experience. Both **A** and **B** are afraid of offending the others by saying what they are not supposed to say. Therefore, both of them are required to plan carefully *how* to express their ideas in addition to *what* ideas to express in order to avoid possible disasters such as breaking up the relationship with their neighbors.

Notice that this whole process is very similar to the series of problem-solving activities presented in the first section of this paper. In other words, this type of activity can, in fact, bring a real-life situation with dramatic tension into the EFL classroom. If so, then, it is a response to the Japanese general public who want EFL classes in which students can learn English that helps them get something done in real life.

SI would also solve another problem I listed in the previous section. While some students taking EFL at college have a considerably low level of proficiency in English, SI can still be beneficial for those students. Di Pietro (1987) states the difference between SI and real life as follows:

> Unlike real life, however, [the students] are given the opportunity to discuss their options and plan their strategies in groups (the rehearsal phase) before having to face the other party in the scenario (the performance phase). They are even permitted to interrupt their conversation and return to their supporting groups if they feel the need for on-the-spot help. (1)

This means that the students feel much secure when they perform a scenario, while they can still experience dramatic tension.

SI also seems suitable for large classes. The most common problem of teaching in a large class is that it is very difficult for the teacher to make his or her students actively participate. In SI, however, the teacher can easily divide the class into small groups to work on a scenario. The teacher can also assign four or five students to work on the same role. In the actual performance, one will represent the group and act out the scene, while others are expected to help the person if necessary. In this way, those students who are not acting can also actively participate. The debriefing phase (87–98) can also encourage everyone's active participation. From the foregoing, I can say that SI is an option for both large classes and low-level students.

It is not clear at this moment if SI could solve the other two problems I pointed out in the previous section: those related to the qualifications of the teachers and those related to the lack of opportunities for professional development. However, SI can be used for training teachers themselves who have sufficient linguistic knowledge but little experience in actually interacting with someone in English.

Conclusion and Prospects. In this paper, I have addressed the question if SI can be a relief for foreign-language classrooms in college, with a special emphasis on EFL in Japan. Considering the impact of the revised standards proposed by the Japanese Ministry of Education from which foreign-language requirements were eliminated, I stated that the priority for future EFL courses would be the content that attracts students. Both teachers and students have been suffering from the fact that, in Japan, they had very little exposure to English. In addition, big classes, low motivation, and low level of proficiency were among other negative factors that have prevented teachers from having more communicatively oriented EFL courses. It was found that SI would help the teachers, providing their students with the exposure to the target language and encouraging the students to participate actively in their classes. However, we still have to solve the problems described in the role card in Figure 4 below:

Figure 4. Strategic Interaction and the future of TEFL

> You are an EFL teacher. You have just finished a presentation on Strategic Interaction at GURT '93. Your audience has asked you several questions including (1) How to sequence the scenarios in your semester-long EFL course, (2) How to evaluate the students' performance, and (3) How to deal with varieties of English. Discuss with people and come up with good answers.

This is a role card assigned to everyone in the field. Each of us needs to interact actively with other colleagues in order to complete the tasks assigned to the role, because I believe this was the role that our enthusiastic leader Robert Di Pietro had wished to play but was unable to.

REFERENCES

Abe, Yoshiya (ed.). 1992. *Kokusai bunkagaku to eigo kyoiku* [Intercultural studies and English language education]. Tokyo: Tamagawa University Press.

Di Pietro, Robert. 1987. *Strategic Interaction: Learning languages through scenarios.* Cambridge: Cambridge University Press.

Dubin, Fraida, and Elite Olshtain. 1986. *Course design: Developing programs and materials for language learning*. Cambridge: Cambridge University Press.

Koike, Ikuo, et al. 1990. *Wagakuni no eigo kyouiku ni kansuru jittai to shouraizo no sogoteki kenkyu* [A general survey of English language teaching in Japan]. Tokyo: JACET.

Livingstone, Carol. 1983. *Role play in language learning*. Essex: Longman.

Oda, Masaki. 1992a. "Communication in college EFL curriculum: An identity crisis?" Paper presented at the 31st JACET conference, Tokyo.

Oda, Masaki. 1992b. "Strategic interaction for foreign language classrooms." Paper presented at JALT Omiya Chapter Meeting, Omiya.

Osanai, Takeshi. 1992. "Gakko eigo kyoiku masukomi taisakuron" [How to deal with criticism of English language teaching in mass-media]. *Gendai eigo kyoiku* [Modern English Teaching] 29(6): 38–40.

Reinelt, Rudolf. 1993. "Introduction." *The Language Teacher* 15(2): 2.

Richards Jack C., and Theodore S. Rodgers. 1986. *Approaches and methods in language teaching*. Cambridge: Cambridge University Press.

Gender differences in styles and strategies for language learning: What do they mean? Should we pay attention?

Rebecca L. Oxford[1]
University of Alabama

In the movie *My Fair Lady,* hero Rex Harrison cries in frustration, "Why can't a woman be more like a man?" This rather misogynistic question must be radically changed in light of research on second-language (L2) learning styles and strategies. Much better queries might now be: What are the unique gifts of women and men in language learning, and how much variation is there both within and between the sexes? What does all this mean, and is it important to pay attention to it? The greatest concern here is gender differences in L2 learning styles and strategies. However, before discussing our central theme we need to take a quick look in the first part at social and cognitive development and language use. The second part discusses the main research on L2 learning styles and strategies, the third part analyzes possible responses in future research, the fourth part examines implications for instruction, and the fifth part is the conclusion.

This paper offers many generalizations about women and men, but readers should be aware that the research cited here does not, of course, apply to every individual woman and man. I am presenting trends that, while meaningful, nevertheless might not capture the essence of each person. I don't intend to stereotype human beings, no matter what the gender, but I do propose to synthesize the research in the clearest and most accessible way possible.

Social and cognitive development and language use. Here are some of the key points from decades of research, both quantitative and qualitative. In the domain of social development, girls and women show greater interest than men and boys in social activities and are more cooperative and less competitive (Maccoby and Jacklin 1974). Women prefer *gentle* social interaction more than

---

1. The author presents some of the concepts in a different form in a paper entitled *Evidence and Instructional Implications of Gender Differences in Second/Foreign Language Learning Styles and Strategies*, to be published in *Applied Language Learning*. The author offers a far shorter discussion of several of these topics in a chapter in editor Jane Sunderland's forthcoming Prentice-Hall book, *Exploring Gender*.

aggressive social interaction (with aggression defined as the intent to harm others), and the opposite is true of men (Maccoby and Jacklin 1974, Gilligan 1982, Hyde and Linn 1986).

Girls are more likely than boys to show continuing need for social approval and desire to please others through good grades and social behavior (Mansnerus 1989, Nyikos 1990). Women smile and laugh significantly more than men in a social setting (Hyde and Linn 1986).

In cognition, boys and men generally outperform girls and women on tests of mental object rotation, depth and vertical–horizontal perception, map reading, mechanical reasoning, and some kinds of mathematics (Hyde and Linn 1986, Maccoby and Jacklin 1974, Weiner and Robinson 1986). Boys and men are consistently more variable than girls and women in quantitative reasoning, spatial visualization, spelling, and general knowledge (Feingold 1992). Cognitive gender differences among adolescents have slightly decreased over the past generation but are certainly not gone (Feingold 1992).

In terms of native language (L1) development and use, girls surpass boys at verbal tasks at most ages, starting with saying first words and sentences earlier, then speaking in more complex sentences and scoring higher on tests of verbal ability and reading (Cahn 1988, Gage and Berliner 1975, Larsen-Freeman and Long 1991, Halpern 1986, Owen et al. 1981, Maccoby and Jacklin 1974, Slavin 1988). Women's L1 speech shows more empathy, concern, deference, encouragement of other speakers, negotiation, detail-remembering, uncertainty, submersion of personal identity, and grammaticality than men's speech (Fishman 1978, Lakoff 1975, Tannen 1986, 1990, Kramarae 1981). Women use L1 monosyllabic responses to show interest, while men use the same to discourage interaction (Fishman 1978). Women using their L1 ask three times as many questions as men (Fishman 1978). In the L1, men use more verbal expressions of power and aggression, adversarial-argumentative style, interruption, ridicule, and analytical critique (Belenky et al. 1986, Tannen 1986, 1990).

L1 differences become transferred to the L2. For instance, men dominate L2 conversations, but women initiate more negotiations of meaning, trying to understand and communicate clearly (Gass and Varonis 1986). In the L2, females are more sensitive than males to differences in dialects, especially the social meaning (differential social prestige) of each dialect (Eisenstein 1982).

One possible cause of gender differences in social and cognitive development and in language use is generalized socialization, including but not limited to the subordinate role of women in our society (Jacklin 1983, Kramarae 1981, Nyikos 1990, Eccles 1989, Slavin 1988, Orlofsky and Stake 1981, Crawford and Gentry 1989, Thorne et al. 1983). Another cause might be physiology (Moir and Jessel 1991, Springer and Deutsch 1989), which is avidly discussed nowadays in terms of *brain sex*. Personal motivation is yet another factor (Davies 1993). Strong motivation toward development of certain social, cognitive, or language-use skills can overcome some of the influences of generalized socialization and physiology.

Gender differences in L2 learning styles and strategies. *Learning styles* are the general, broad approaches used to learn a new language or any other subject. Styles have cognitive, affective, physiological, and social aspects; they are not limited to the narrower concept of *cognitive style* (Keefe 1979, Cornett 1983).

> Learning style [is] a consistent pattern of behavior but with a certain range of individual variability ... Styles then are overall patterns that give general direction to learning behavior. (Cornett 1983: 9)

Styles are not immutable throughout the lifespan. In fact, some psychologists assert that integrating of contrasting styles is a sign of developmental maturity. It is likely that generalized socialization, physiology, and personal motivation have differentially strong effects on the nature of a person's learning style at given times of life.

Some individuals who discover their styles, particularly people who are closure-oriented, might fixate on a particular set of style characteristics as their unchanging identity—"This is who I am" (Davies 1993). They might go further and expect or want all instruction to be presented to them in terms of their "permanent" style preferences. Such people should be made aware that some fluctuation of style is entirely normal and that they, like all other learners, might benefit from stretching their style through learning new behaviors that are not part of their stylistic comfort zone.

Let us discuss gender differences (and what they might mean in the L2 instructional environment) in each relevant style dimension in turn, although some researchers (e.g. Schmeck 1983, Willing 1988) suggest all these dimensions might be ultimately related to a single contrast—analytic vs. global. Style dimensions included here are sensory preferences, objective/subjective ways of knowing (thinking vs. feeling), reflection and impulsivity, brain hemisphericity, and field independence/sensitivity. Then I describe learning strategies as a manifestation of learning style and explain gender differences observed in L2 learning strategies.

Gender differences in sensory preferences. One of the most obvious aspects of learning style concerns sensory preferences. These are the perceptual modes or learning channels through which students take in information. They include visual, auditory, tactile, and kinesthetic preferences.

Visual students prefer to learn via the visual channel; therefore they like to read, need the visual stimulation of bulletin boards and movies, must have written directions, and often prefer working alone. Auditory students enjoy the oral–aural learning channel; thus, they want to engage in discussions, conversations, and group work and typically require only oral directions. Tactile students need to touch and manipulate objects. Kinesthetic students require movement and frequent breaks in activity.

A learning style preference characterized by tactile and kinesthetic channels might be related to the spatial ability prominent in the masculine gender role, as is the case in one study (Hansen 1982). In L2 classrooms we might expect that tactile and kinesthetic students might more often be boys or men than girls or women. We might also predict that nontraditional women (those who have chosen to follow gender-role patterns different from the traditional norm) would show these preferences more frequently than traditional women. L2 activities—for both child and adult learners—should involve some movement for kinesthetic people and manipulation of objects for tactile people.

Linkages between gender and auditory preferences are not clear, although listening studies (Eisenstein 1982) suggest that L2 auditory ability might be greater in women than in men. The relationship between gender and visual preference in the L2 setting is not yet determined. Because L2 learning requires an integration of the senses, especially visual and auditory, L2 teachers must help this integration occur through activities that require both modes simultaneously or in sequence.

Clearly, much more research needs to be done in the area of gender differences in sensory preferences. This area of learning style deserves far more attention, especially in the L2 instructional setting.

Gender differences in objective/subjective ways of knowing (thinking vs. feeling). Belenky and colleagues (1986) conducted extensive interviews with college men and women. These researchers argue that in general the two sexes have different ways of knowing, men more often through "objectivity and thinking" (abstract analysis) and women more often through "subjectivity and feeling" (personalized experience). This finding supports research with the Myers–Briggs Type Indicator (MBTI) showing that a majority of women in our culture have more of a feeling approach (emotional, personal, subjective, empathic, merciful) than a thinking approach (analytic, impersonal, objective, factual, just) (Lawrence 1984, Myers and McCaulley 1990).

This research might suggest that men and women, in general, employ different routes in L2 learning. More men than women might take the thinking approach, thus focusing on rules, facts, and logic and avoiding the more personal interactions. More women than men might like the feeling approach, in which there is a great deal of social interaction and cooperative learning and a high degree of empathy.

Gender differences in reflection and impulsivity. The women in the Belenky et al. (1986) study wanted to reflect before judging, thus displaying tendencies toward the learning style of reflection and toward language modes of deference and increased empathy. The men in the study rapidly jumped to conclusions and interrupted, showing a slant toward the learning style of impulsivity and toward the language mode of lack of deference and decreased empathy.

In psychological research, reflection is defined as the tendency to stop and consider options before responding to a question or problem, often resulting in greater accuracy, while impulsivity is the tendency to respond immediately and often inaccurately. (Unfortunately, fast-accurate and slow-inaccurate are not part of the typical research paradigm of reflection and impulsivity.) When gender differences in reflection and impulsivity are found in children and adolescents, girls are usually more reflective (Shipman and Shipman 1985).

Yet this line of research is confounded by some other investigations. If girls and women are more reflective than boys and men, what are we to make of the frequent assumption that reflection is associated with analytic, field independent individuals—more often men than women? And how does this fit in with the finding that girls and women are often more accurate in spelling and grammar than boys and men?

Perhaps there are at least two kinds of reflection that apply to language learning and use. One type might be analytic reflection that allows the person to apply grammar and spelling rules logically, carefully analyze sociolinguistic factors in order to produce the appropriate response, and conduct detailed self-evaluation. Another type might be global reflection that enables the learner to recognize and use holistic patterns of grammar and spelling, instinctively comprehend social interactions and situations without analysis, and conduct global self-evaluations. Both kinds of reflection are potentially important. It is entirely possible that these different types of reflection, if well researched, would show gender differences that might help answer many remaining questions about reflection and impulsivity.

In the L2 area, the *perceivers* on the MBTI (those learners who could refrain from leaping to conclusions too rapidly and who might therefore be called reflective learners) were better at learning languages than the *judgers* (those who needed quick closure) (Ehrman and Oxford 1988, 1989, 1990). The perceivers/reflectives stayed open to gather new clues, which would help them to understand the meaning. Likewise, in other L2 research, impulsive learners had problems because of their premature, inaccurate responses; an imposed *wait time* was helpful (Parry 1984, Galloway and Labarca 1991). However, too much concern for accuracy can lead to destructive anxiety, diminishing L2 performance, as Ehrman and Oxford (1990) found empirically. If carried too far, reflection in an L2 situation can be immobilizing, especially in a fast-moving, intensive program (Leaver 1991). A balance between reflection and impulsivity appears desirable for L2 learning, especially when conversational fluency—not just accuracy—is an important focus.

Gender differences in brain hemisphericity. Brain hemisphericity or lateralization (right, left, and integrated) is a feature of many learning-style surveys and books. Right-hemisphere dominant individuals—those whose right side of the brain typically dominates their thinking processes—tend to be more field dependent (less able to separate the details from a confusing background), global, and emotion-oriented, according to Willing (1988). Left-hemisphere dominant people—those whose dominant brain hemisphere is the left—are more field independent, analytic, and logic-oriented (Willing 1988). Both hemispheres deal with language differently. The left hemisphere interprets the meaning of words, while the right hemisphere interprets verbal tones, patterns, and musical qualities of the language.

What about gender differences in brain dominance? We see from several sources (Springer and Deutsch 1989, Elias 1992, Associated Press 1992) that:

- In men, the left hemisphere might be more lateralized (specialized) for verbal activity and the right hemisphere may be more lateralized for abstract or spatial processing.
- Women might use both the left and the right hemispheres for both verbal and spatial activity, thus showing more integrated brain functioning and less hemispheric differentiation.
- In women as compared to men, part of the corpus callosum (the bundle of brain fibers linking the left and right hemispheres) is bigger in relation to overall brain weight, allowing more information to be exchanged between the two hemispheres.

Other research contradicts the idea that brain hemispheres are more integrated in women than in men. For example, some research implies that females are usually more right-hemisphere dominant than males because of their often-observed field sensitivity, discussed below (Good and Brophy 1986, Shipman and Shipman 1985).

Based on the research just noted, men might usually process the L2 more readily through the left-hemispheric, analytic mode, but women might more often process the L2 through the right-hemispheric, global mode or through an integration of left- and right-hemispheric modes. Mixed-gender L2 instruction should use aspects of both modes, thus including a variety of analytic activities and global-fluency tasks.

Gender differences in field independence/sensitivity. Linked with brain hemisphericity is field independence/sensitivity. Gender differences have often been found for field independence/sensitivity through many different measures: tests of perception in tilted rooms, embedded figures tests, and rod-and-frame tests. As adolescents and adults—and sometimes even as children—men are usually more field independent and women are more field sensitive (Good and Brophy 1986, Shipman and Shipman 1985, but see Lusk and Wright 1981 for a different view).

Field independence refers to the ability to easily separate the key details from an ambiguous context through the use of analysis; it is often linked with left-hemisphere dominance. Research with all ages suggests that field-independent people are less sensitive to the social context, are more detached and more logical than field-dependent people, and prefer more structured, analytical learning (Oxford 1990a). In contrast, field sensitivity or dependence is the lesser ability to separate details from the background easily and the greater tendency toward global impressions; it is often related to right-hemisphere dominance. Field-dependent people tend to be more sensitive to the social context, are perceived as more outgoing and more considerate than their field-independent peers, and do well with less structure in their learning (Oxford 1990a).

Field-independent learners, often boys and men, have advantages in L2 achievement (Hansen and Stansfield 1981), but this might be related to the analytic nature of most written L2 achievement tests and many grammar-based L2 activities. Field-sensitive individuals, often girls and women, with their more interpersonal and global orientation, might do better in less analytic aspects of overall L2 communicative competence, such as sociolinguistic competence, discourse competence, and strategic competence, but more evidence is needed on this point. L2 teachers should probably offer a combination of both more-structured, analytical activities and less-structured, globally communicative activities. In this way, all students receive what they need.

Strategies—a manifestation of learning styles. Learning strategies are more specific than learning styles and are often a manifestation of learning styles. Strategies are the particular behaviors that learners employ, usually intentionally, to enhance their understanding, storage, retrieval, and ultimate use of information (Rigney 1978, Oxford 1989). In the L2 area, examples include note-taking, seeking conversation partners, developing empathy with the target culture, skimming, previewing, and guessing to understand what is read or heard. Almost two decades ago, researchers made lists of strategies presumed to be essential for the "good language learner." Rubin (1975) suggested that good language learners guess willingly and accurately, want to communicate, are uninhibited about mistakes, focus on both structure and meaning, take advantage of all practice opportunities, and monitor their own speech and that of others. Another early list (Naiman, Frohlich, and Todesco 1975) added that successful L2 learners think in the language and use affective (emotional) strategies to cope with the strains of language learning. Unfortunately, none of these researchers mentioned that the concept of the good language learner is highly related to learning style, which is in turn strongly associated with cultural background (Oxford, Hollaway, and Horton-Murillo 1992, Davies 1993).

Later L2 researchers found that appropriate strategy use is often related to better learning performance (Ehrman and Oxford 1988, Wenden and Rubin 1987, Wenden 1991, O'Malley and Chamot 1990, Cohen 1990, Brown 1989, 1991). Mere frequency of use of learning strategies is not as important as orchestrating the use of strategies to fit the requirements of the task and the goals of the learner. Unsuccessful L2 learners often use just as many strategies as effective L2 learners, but the former use them randomly (Vann and Abraham 1989) instead of in an orchestrated, knowledgeable fashion. Strategy training studies have shown that L2 performance can frequently be improved through teaching students to use new strategies or improve their application of already-known strategies (O'Malley and Chamot 1990, Oxford and Crookall 1989).

Gender differences in learning strategies. Only recently have researchers noted that the choice of L2 learning strategies is often gender-related and depends crucially on L2 learning style, which is also frequently linked to gender (Ehrman and Oxford 1988, 1989, Oxford and Ehrman 1988, Oxford 1990a, 1990b, 1990c, Nyikos 1990, Willing 1988). If learners are not pressed by the situation or the teacher, they tend to employ L2 learning strategies that are directly congruent with their favored learning style.

For instance, the analytic, field-independent learner (probably a man or boy) ordinarily selects strategies involving logic, such as deductive reasoning, whereas the global, field-dependent learner (often a woman or girl) chooses non-analytic strategies that involve searching for the main idea and intuitively guessing from multiple contextual clues—frequently social ones—when some pieces of information are missing. The visual learner (who could be either sex) seeks extensive visual input through reading, the auditory learner (frequently a woman or girl) engages in lots of social interaction and uses auditory memory devices like rhyming, and the tactile/kinesthetic learner (typically a man or boy) likes total physical response and manipulating objects. The reflective learner (often a woman or girl) considers different angles and the social context before responding and is devoted to answering correctly, while the impulsive learner (often a man or boy) jumps in with a quick response and may want to dominate, regardless of correctness of the response. These descriptions do not imply that all women or all men prefer to use certain strategies; these illustrations do, however, show that the favored style dimensions, which are frequently gender-related, can have a direct effect on the specific L2 learning behaviors chosen.

Oxford, Nyikos, and Ehrman (1988) were the first to publish a review of studies involving gender differences in L2 learning strategies. At that time, out of a selection of over 80 investigations of L2 learning strategies, only four mentioned gender differences at all (Politzer 1983, Ehrman and Oxford 1988, Oxford and Nyikos 1989, Nyikos 1987).

Politzer reported that women college students used social strategies for L2 learning significantly more often than their male peers—a difference that Politzer did not explain but that might be related to gender differences in social orientation (see the section above on development). Ehrman and Oxford found that women in an intensive adult learning setting, compared with men, reported significantly greater use of L2 learning strategies in four categories: general study strategies, strategies for negotiating meaning, self-management strategies, and functional practice strategies. Oxford and Nyikos discovered that female college students, contrasted with males, used L2 learning strategies significantly more often in three of five factor-analytically derived categories: formal rule-based strategies, general study strategies, and conversational input-elicitation strategies. The gender differences found in the second and third studies might be associated with women's greater social skills, stronger verbal skills (including pattern usage), and greater conformity to academic and linguistic norms. Nyikos observed significant gender differences among university students in using memory strategies for German vocabulary learning. After training in the use of these strategies, men outperformed women in the color-plus-picture combination, which was explained as potentially related to men's putatively greater visual-spatial acuity. However, women surpassed men in the color-only condition, which was explained by women's greater interest in color (often as a social attractor).

Other studies also found gender differences in strategy use. For example, Oxford, Park-Oh, Ito, and Sumrall (1993) discovered gender-difference trends among high school students studying Japanese by satellite. Although all students used strategies of various kinds, women tended to use many cognitive strategies, social strategies, and affective strategies more often than boys; gender differences were not as strong in metacognitive, compensation, and memory strategies. Boys did not surpass girls in strategy use in any of the main strategy categories. Girls also outperformed boys in terms of motivation and Japanese language achievement. In a different study, Green and Oxford (1992) found that Puerto Rican university students learning ESL had gender differences in strategy use, with women consciously employing strategies significantly more often than men in metacognitive and social categories and nearly significantly in affective and cognitive areas. In a study of ESL learners in Australia, Willing (1988) discovered interesting gender differences in L2 learning strategies. More of the significant differences in strategy choice, when they occurred, favored women, but these differences did not clearly separate women from men on the basis of any underlying sensory preferences.

When L2 strategy research has considered gender, it has usually—though not always (see Tran 1988)—demonstrated gender differences in strategy frequency, with women consciously choosing to use particular sets of strategies more often than men. Women especially tended to use general study strategies, social strategies, affective strategies, and certain conversational or functional practice strategies more frequently than men across a number of studies, thus usually showing a greater range of frequently used strategy categories. Men and women tended to use somewhat different memory strategies in a study of vocabulary learning. Differences in frequency and patterns of strategy choice might explain why women often show better L2 classroom performance than men (although of course informal, nonclassroom-based language development in the target country might reveal something different if research were conducted).

Research summary. So far this paper has explained potentially important differences in learning styles and strategies. Some auditory style preferences have been shown more by women than by men. In many investigations women have been more reflective than men. Research on learning styles suggests that males might have more strongly specialized brain hemispheres than women, with the left hemisphere in men being dominant for language. Some research suggests that, compared with men, women more readily use the right hemisphere or else use both hemispheres in an integrated way for language processing. Research tends to show that, compared with women, men are somewhat more field independent, analytic, objective, and logically minded in processing language and in other areas of life, while women have been found to tend toward more field sensitive, globally patterned, subjective, and emotional capabilities.

L2 learning strategy research shows that women reported consciously using more strategy types more frequently than men. In the available studies, women more often than men reported greater tendencies toward using general study strategies, social and emotional strategies, and conversational or functional strategies. Across most though not all studies, men typically failed to report greater conscious strategy use in any of the major strategy categories.

Possible research responses in the future. What are some possible responses to such gender differences? How can researchers react in the future? Possible reactions are: the ostrich response, the depth response, the epistemological response, and the truth-in-reporting response.

The ostrich response. The ostrich response ignores or downplays the observed gender differences. For instance, Baumeister (1988) suggests that gender differences should not be reported at all, because such reporting might perpetuate and legitimize the gender distinction, which then might justify continuing unequal treatment of women and men by society. Chipman (1988) calls for de-emphasis on gender differences in general on the grounds that many of those differences, though statistically significant, are small. (Yet even Chipman does not fully subscribe to the ostrich response, though she seems at first to champion it. Chipman herself cites several gender differences that are relatively large, as in spatial-rotation ability and aggression.) We in the L2 field should not bury, obfuscate, or tone down results related to gender differences in styles and strategies. If we do so, we will lose some possibly explanatory information that could help students and teachers alike.

The depth response. The depth response looks at gender differences from other angles and with greater depth. For example, Feingold (1992) wants researchers to look not just at differences in means for men and women but also at gender differences in the degree of variability within each group; men tend to be much more variable than women on many cognitively based traits. Hyde (1981) enjoins researchers to look at the actual size of a statistically significant difference, not just at the existence of that difference. Rothblum (1988) suggests that nonsignificant and small sex differences should be published to emphasize any similarities—not just differences—between women and men. In the L2 field, we should not overemphasize gender differences artificially by publishing just the contrasts and not mentioning areas of similarity. Looking at variability and at size of statistical difference rather than just at L2 style and strategy means makes a great deal of sense.

The epistemological response. The epistemological response demands a new philosophy of knowledge. Riger (1992) wants to see a new so-called feminist epistemology in which the scientific tradition enlarges to honor ("feminine") personalized, naturalistic, socially contextualized, qualitative research on an equal footing with ("masculine") objectified, experimental or quasi-experimental, socially decontextualized, quantitative research. Actually, Cronbach presented the idea of such a balance two decades ago (1975). See Lincoln and Guba (1985) for a detailed description of naturalistic inquiry, which provides information unavailable purely through traditional, quantitative means. In the L2 area, and particularly in the realm of L2 learning styles and strategies, a blend of qualitative and quantitative research would be very valuable. This research balance might be viewed as a *feminist epistemology*, but even more than that it is a well-grounded, intelligent *human epistemology*, because it offers better and more comprehensive data that fit and benefit all people.

The truth-in-reporting response. The truth-in-reporting response requires good, complete research reporting. The American Psychological Association argues that even in the traditional quantitative model, all researchers should specify the number of women and men in every study (Gannon et al. 1992; see also Denmark et al. 1988). This seems like a reasonable *sine qua non* for the L2 area, as for any other research field in psychology and education. Such reporting does not require much extra work and could be of great advantage. Without this information, we will never understand how women and men learn languages and how to help them do it more easily.

Implications for L2 instruction. Four classroom implications of the research in this paper concern assessing styles and strategies, accepting gender-related differences, using style and strategy information for tailoring instruction, and using the information to prepare the learning environment.

Assessing styles and strategies. It is very important to assess the learning styles and strategies of L2 students and even to assess the styles and strategies of L2 teachers. This can be done using one or more learning-style instruments (Schmeck 1983) and learning-strategy measures (see Cohen 1990). Helping students understand their observed L2 styles and strategies can become part of general *learner training*, which has been shown to be of significant benefit to L2 learners (Wenden 1991, Ellis and Sinclair 1989, Brown 1989, 1991, Cohen 1990, O'Malley and Chamot 1990, Oxford 1990b).

Accepting gender-related differences. Teachers and students should not be surprised if gender-related differences appear in the style and strategy assessments. All participants should feel free to discuss these differences openly, bringing up any sociocultural (and perhaps biological) influences that might have helped create any contrasts between women and men, girls and boys. It is useful to emphasize what useful skills people of different styles and strategies can learn from each other, both across and within gender boundaries. In addition, cross-gender likenesses should also be highlighted in the discussion.

Using style and strategy data for tailoring instruction. By using the data, teachers are better able to spot any style conflicts and strategy difficulties in the classroom. Teachers can also vary their instructional techniques to meet the needs of students with contrasting styles and strategies of learning. Suggestions include: providing a wide range of activities (analytic and global; visual, auditory, tactile, and kinesthetic; reflective and impulsive); using an imposed wait time to require or encourage impulsive or conversation-dominating students, often men and boys, to reflect before responding; offering speeded games and skits that make good use of these students' rapid answering; giving reflective students, often women and girls, lots of opportunity to think and ask questions before responding; consciously encouraging some students to be more spontaneous through multiple activities in small groups; teaching students to use strategies that go beyond their preferred styles. (For instance, global students can learn to do grammatical analysis, while analytical students can learn to make global predictions.)

Using style and strategy data for preparing the learning environment. Style and strategy data can also help the teacher prepare a learning environment that welcomes and accommodates women and men alike. The learning environment can establish the class as either exclusive, limiting which styles are accepted, or inclusive, welcoming everyone. Lively bulletin boards, attractive exhibits of cultural artifacts (especially touchable or manipulable items), eye-catching wall decorations, videos, tapes, creative use of space with areas for movement activities, comfortable seating (a small sofa or cushion along with regular desks), and flexible seating for individual reading or group activities can send positive messages to all students.

Conclusion. This chapter is not the final word on gender differences in L2 learning styles and strategies. In fact, it is one of the earliest comprehensive presentations of the theme. It is somewhat unusual in offering gender differences in social and cognitive development and language use as a prelude to discussing L2 learning styles and strategies. Even though much more research is necessary to flesh out the constructs I have begun to sketch here, readers can nonetheless start garnering useful instructional implications from the research offered in this chapter. Later L2 investigations will substantiate or somewhat alter these implications, but in the meantime, sufficient information exists to support applying these ideas in the classroom, at least on a tentative basis. We must continue to discover what gender differences in L2 styles and strategies mean, and we must pay attention to these findings in order to provide optimal instruction to learners.

REFERENCES

Associated Press. 1992, Aug. 1. "Study shows brains differ in gay, heterosexual men: Anterior commissure area larger in homosexuals." *The Washington Post A2.*

Baumeister, Roy F. 1988. "Should we stop studying sex differences altogether?" *American Psychologist* 43: 1092–1095.

Belenky, Mary F., Blythe M. Clinchy, Nancy R. Goldberger, and Jill M. Tarule. 1986. *Women's ways of knowing: The development of self, voice, and mind.* New York: Basic Books.

Brown, H. Douglas. 1989. *A practical guide to language learning: A fifteen-week program of strategies for success.* N.Y.: McGraw-Hill.

Brown, H. Douglas. 1991. *Breaking the language barrier: Creating your own pathway to success.* Yarmouth, Maine: Intercultural Press.

Cahn, Lorynne D. 1988. "Sex and grade differences and learning rate in an intensive summer reading clinic." *Psychology in the schools* 25(1): 84–91.

Chipman, Susan. 1988. "Far too sexy a topic: Review of *The psychology of gender: Advances through meta-analysis*." In Janet S. Hyde, and Marcia C. Linn (eds.), *Educational researcher,* 17(3): 46–49.

Cohen, Andrew D. 1990. *Language learning: Insights for learners, teachers, and researchers.* New York: Newbury House/HarperCollins.

Cornett, Claudia E. 1983. "What you should know about teaching and learning styles." Bloomington, Ind.: *Phi Delta Kappa Educational Foundation.*

Crawford, Mary, and Margaret Gentry (eds.). 1989. *Gender and thought: Psychological perspectives.* New York: Springer-Verlag.

Cronbach, Lee. 1975. "Beyond the two disciplines of scientific psychology." *American Psychologist* 30: 116–127.

Davies, Catherine. 1993, Mar. 8. Personal communication.

Denmark, Florence, Nancy F. Russo, Irene H. Frieze, and Jeri A. Sechzer. 1988. "Guidelines for avoiding sexism in psychological research." *American Psychologist* 43: 582–585.

Eccles, Jacqueline S. 1989. "Bringing young women to math and science." In Mary Crawford and Margaret Gentry (eds.), *Gender and thought: Psychological perspectives.* New York: Springer-Verlag. 36–58.

Ehrman, Madeline E., and Rebecca L. Oxford. 1988. "Ants and grasshoppers, badgers and butterflies: Qualitative and quantitative exploration of adult language learning styles and strategies." Paper presented at the Symposium on Research Perspectives on Adult Language Learning and Acquisition, Ohio State University, Columbus, Ohio.

Ehrman, Madeline E., and Rebecca L. Oxford. 1989. "Effects of sex differences, career choice, and psychological type on adults' language learning strategies." *Modern Language Journal* 73: 1–13.

Ehrman, Madeline E., and Rebecca L. Oxford. 1990. "Adult language learning styles and strategies in an intensive training setting." *Modern Language Journal* 74: 311–327.

Eisenstein, Miriam. 1982. "A study of social variation in adult second language acquisition." *Language learning* 32: 367–391.

Ellis, Gail, and Barbara Sinclair. 1989. *Learning to learn English: A course in learner training.* Cambridge: Cambridge University Press.

Elias, Marilyn. 1992, Aug. 3. "Difference seen in brains of gay men." *USA Today.* 8D.

Feingold, Alan. 1992. "Sex differences in variability in intellectual abilities: A new look at an old controversy." *Review of Educational Research* 62(1): 61–84.

Fishman, Phylla M. 1978. "Interaction: The work women do." *Social Problems* 25: 397–406.

Gage, Nathan L., and David C. Berliner. 1975. *Educational psychology.* Chicago: Rand-McNally.

Galloway, Vicki, and Angela Labarca. 1991. "From student to learner: Style, process, and strategy." In Diane W. Birckbichler (ed.), *New perspectives and new directions in foreign language education.* Lincolnwood, Ill.: National Textbook Co. and ACTFL. 111–158.

Gannon, Linda, Tracy Luchetta, Kelly Rhodes, Lynn Pardie, and Dan Segrist. 1992. "Sex bias in psychological research: Progress or complacency?" *American Psychologist* 47(3): 389–396.

Gass, Susan, and Evangeline M. Varonis. 1986. "Sex differences in NNS/NNS interactions. In Richard Day (ed.)," *Talking to learn: Conversation in second language acquisition.* Rowley, Mass.: Newbury House. 327-351.

Gilligan, Carol. 1982. *In a different voice: Psychological theory and women's development.* Cambridge: Harvard University Press.

Good, Thomas L., and Jere E. Brophy. 1986. *Educational psychology* (Third edition). New York: Longman.

Halpern, Diane F. 1986. *Sex differences in cognitive abilities.* Hillsdale, N.J.: Erlbaum.

Hansen, Jacqueline, Charles W. Stansfield. 1981. "The relationship of field dependent–independent cognitive styles to foreign language achievement." *Language Learning* 31: 349–367.

Hansen, Martha J. 1982. "Spatial performance, activity preferences, and masculinity-femininity." Paper presented at the annual convention of the American Psychological Association,

Washington, D.C.

Hauck, LaVerne S. 1985. "Differences in information-mapping strategies in left- and right-brain learners." Paper presented at the annual meeting of the American Vocational Association, Atlanta, Ga.

Hyde, Janet. 1981. "How large are cognitive gender differences?" *American Psychologist* 36: 292–301.

Hyde, Janet, and Marcia C. Linn (eds.). 1986. *The psychology of gender: Advances through meta-analysis*. Baltimore: Johns Hopkins Press.

Jacklin, Carol N. 1983. "Boys and girls entering school. In Michael Marland (ed.), *Sex differentiation and schooling*. London: Heinemann.

Keefe, James W., ed. 1979. *Student learning styles: Diagnosing and prescribing programs*. Reston, Va.: National Association of Secondary School Principals.

Kramarae, Cheris. 1981. *Women and men speaking*. Rowley, Mass.: Newbury House.

Lakoff, R. 1975. *Language and women's place*. New York: Harper and Row.

Larsen-Freeman, Diane, and Michael Long. 1991. *An introduction to second language acquisition research*. London: Longman.

Lawrence, Gerald. 1984. "A synthesis of learning style research involving the MBTI." *Journal of Psychological Type* 8: 2–15.

Leaver, Betty L. 1991, Nov. 24. Personal communication.

Leaver, Betty L. 1986. "Hemisphericity of the brain and foreign language teaching." *Folia Slavica* 8: 76–90.

Lincoln, Yvonne S., and Egon G. Guba. 1985. *Naturalistic inquiry*. Newbury Park, Calif.: Sage.

Lusk, Edward J., and Haviland Wright. 1981. "Differences in sex and curricula on learning the Group Embedded Figures Test." *Perceptual and Motor Skills* 53(1): 8–10.

Maccoby, Eleanor E., and Carol N. Jacklin. 1974. *The psychology of sex differences*. Stanford: Stanford University Press.

Mansnerus, Laura. 1989, Aug. 6. *SAT separates girls from boys*. New York Times. Sec. 4A. 27-28.

Moir, Anne, and David Jessel. 1991. *Brain sex: The real difference between men and women*. New York: Stuart/Carol.

Myers, Isabel B., and Mary H. McCaulley. 1990. *Manual: A guide to the development and use of the Myers-Briggs Type Indicator*. Palo Alto: Consulting Psychologists Press.

Naiman, Neil, Maria Frohlich, and Angie Todesco. 1975. "The good second language learner." *TESL Talk* 6(1): 58–75.

Nyikos, Martha. 1987. *The effect of color and imagery as mnemonic strategies on learning and retention of lexical items in German*. Dissertation, Purdue University, West Lafayette, Ind.

Nyikos, Martha. 1990. "Sex-related differences in adult language learning: Socialization and memory factors." *Modern Language Journal* 74(3): 273–287.

O'Malley, J. Michael, and Anna Uhl Chamot. 1990. *Learning strategies in second language acquisition*. Cambridge: Cambridge University Press.

Orlofsky, Jacob L., and Jayne E. Stake. 1981. "Psychological masculinity and femininity: Relationship to striving and self-concept in the achievement and interpersonal domains." *Psychology of Women Quarterly* 6(2): 218–233.

Oxford, Rebecca L. 1989. "Use of language learning strategies: A synthesis of studies with implications for strategy training." *System* 17: 235–247.

Oxford, Rebecca L. 1990a. "Language learning strategies and beyond: A look at strategies in the context of styles." In S.S. Magnan (ed.), *Shifting the instructional focus to the learner*. Middlebury, Vt.: Northeast Conference on the Teaching of Foreign Languages. 35–55.

Oxford, Rebecca L. 1990b. *Language learning strategies: What every teacher should know*. New York: Newbury House/HarperCollins. Now Boston: Heinle & Heinle.

Oxford, Rebecca L. 1990c. "Styles, strategies, and aptitude: Connections for language learning." In T. Parry and C.W. Stansfield (eds.), *Language aptitude reconsidered*. Englewood Cliffs,

N.J.: Prentice-Hall. 67–125

Oxford, Rebecca L., and David Crookall. 1989. "Language learning strategies: Methods, findings, and instructional implications." *Modern Language Journal* 73: 404–419.

Oxford, Rebecca L., and Madeline E. Ehrman. 1988. "Psychological type and adult language learning strategies: A pilot study." *Journal of Psychological Type* 16: 22–32.

Oxford, Rebecca L., Mary E. Hollaway, and Diana Horton-Murillo. 1992. "Language learning styles and strategies in the multicultural, tertiary L2 classroom." *System* 20(3).

Oxford, Rebecca L., and Roberta Z. Lavine. 1991. "Teacher-student "style wars" in the language classroom: Research insights and suggestions." *Bulletin of the Association of Departments of Foreign Languages* 23 (2): 38–45.

Oxford, Rebecca L., and Martha Nyikos. 1989. "Variables affecting choice of language learning strategies by university students." *Modern Language Journal* 73: 219–300.

Oxford, Rebecca L., Martha Nyikos, and Madeline Ehrman. 1988. "Vive la différence? Reflections on sex differences in use of language learning strategies." *Foreign Language Annals* 21(4): 321–329.

Oxford, Rebecca L., Young Park-Oh, Sukero Ito, and Malenna Sumrall. 1993. "Learning Japanese by satellite: What influences student achievement?" *System* 21(1).

Parry, Thomas S. 1984. *The relationship of selected dimensions of learner cognitive style, aptitude, and general intelligence factors to selected foreign language proficiency tasks of second-year students of Spanish at the secondary level.* Dissertation, Ohio State University, Columbus, Ohio.

Politzer, Robert L. 1983. "An exploratory study of self-reported language learning behaviors and their relation to achievement." *Studies in second language acquisition* 6: 54–68.

Riger, Stephanie. 1992. "Epistemological debates, feminist voices: Science, social values, and the study of women." *American psychologist* 47(6): 730–740.

Rigney, Joseph W. 1978. "Learning strategies: A theoretical perspective." In Harold F. O'Neil (ed.), *Learning strategies*. New York: Academic Press. 265–285.

Rothblum, Esther D. 1988. "More on reporting sex differences." *American psychologist* 43: 1095.

Rubin, Joan. 1975. "What the "good language learner" can teach us." *TESOL Quarterly* 9(1): 41–51.

Schmeck, Ronald R. 1983. "Learning styles of college students." In Ronna F. Dillon, and Ronald R. Schmeckl (ed.), *Individual differences in cognition* (Vol. 1). New York: Academic Press. 233–279.

Shipman, Stephanie, and Virginia C. Shipman. 1985. "Cognitive styles: Some conceptual, methodological, and applied issues." In Edmund W. Gordon (ed.), *Review of research in education* (Vol 12). Washington, D.C.: American Educational Research Association. 229–291.

Slavin, Robert E. 1988. *Educational psychology: Theory into practice* (Second edition). Englewood Cliffs, N.J.: Prentice-Hall.

Springer, Sally, and George Deutsch. 1989. *Left brain, right brain.* New York: Freeman.

Tannen, Deborah. 1986. *That's not what I meant!* New York: Morrow.

Tannen, Deborah. 1990. *You just don't understand: Women and men in conversation.* New York: Ballentine.

Thorne, Barrie, Cheris Kramarae, and Nancy Henley. 1983. *Language, gender, and society.* Rowley, Mass.: Newbury House.

Tran, Thanh V. 1988. "Sex differences in English language acculturation and learning strategies among Vietnamese adults age 40 and over in the United States." *Sex Roles* 19(11–12): 747–758.

Vann, Robert, and Roberta Abraham. 1989. "Strategies of unsuccessful language learners." Paper presented at the annual meeting of Teachers of English to Speakers of Other Languages, San Francisco, Calif.

Weiner, Neil C., and Sharon E. Robinson. 1986. "Cognitive abilities, personality, and gender

differences in math achievement of gifted adolescents." *Gifted Child Quarterly* 30(2): 83–87.
Wenden, Anita. 1991. *Learner strategies for learner autonomy: Planning and implementing learner training for language learners.* Englewood Cliffs, N.J.: Prentice-Hall.
Wenden, Anita, and Joan Rubin (eds.). 1987. *Learner strategies for language learning.* Englewood Cliffs, N.J.: Prentice-Hall.
Willing, Ken. 1988. *Learning styles in adult migrant education.* Adelaide, S. Australia: National Curriculum Research Council.

Lexical phrases and Strategic Interaction

Jeanette S. DeCarrico and James R. Nattinger
Portland State University

Introduction. In his book *Strategic Interaction*, DiPietro provides detailed arguments for the use of scenarios in the language-learning classroom, scenarios in which students consciously plan strategies for interacting with others and in which they "are led to create discourse in the target language that embodies the drama of real life" (DiPietro 1987: 41). He emphasizes the crucial role of strategies, noting that "all scenarios require strategies" (31).

We find DiPietro's arguments for Strategic Interaction compelling ones, and we agree that strategies are crucial in effective communication. Indeed, in our own research, we have found that strategies and other functional units in conversation are considerably more pervasive and more varied than is revealed by the work of DiPietro and others. In this paper we suggest a framework that allows for more comprehensive categories of strategies and related functional units. At the same time this framework limits the categories to those deemed most pedagogically useful by redefining the functional units themselves.

We begin by outlining DiPietro's three categories for strategies. The expression "strategies" is used for the first of these categories; the others are "learning and communicating strategies" and "protocols." We then redefine all such categories as form/function units of prefabricated language, the "lexical phrase," and show how this unit allows for a more comprehensive framework of pedagogically useful categories.

Strategies include disclaimers, used for blunting possible criticism (I don't know how to tell you this but ...); postscripts, used to play down the significance of a request (While we're on the subject ...); and apologies (I really don't deserve it, but I hope you will ...). They also include the oneup, for verbalizing one's advantage (I told you so), refusals (Thanks, but ...), and defensive strategies such as changing the topic (By the way ...).

Learning and communicating strategies seem mainly to refer to requests for clarification or to ploys nonnative speakers use to make themselves understood (Please repeat; How do you say that in X?).

Protocols are different from strategies in that their use is dictated more by cultural convention than by intentions of speakers. They include such functions as salutations (Hi, how are you?), moving in traffic (Excuse me), rites of passage (Best wishes), holidays (Happy New Year), daily functions (Glad you could come; Must you go so soon?), and conversational management (Hello there; I'll talk to you later).

Lexical Phrases and Classifications. As described in Nattinger and DeCarrico (1992), lexical phrases are *chunks* of language of varying length, "conventionalized structures that occur more frequently and have more idiomatically determined meaning than language that is put together each time" (Nattinger and DeCarrico, 1992), and several researchers, such as Hakuta (1974), Wong-Fillmore (1976), Peters (1983), now put lexical phrases and other prefabricated language at the center of work in language acquisition. An important aspect of lexical phrases is that, unlike ordinary collocations or idioms, lexical phrases are associated with particular discourse functions.

Collocations are sets of words that tend to occur together; we say "rancid butter" and "sour cream," for instance, but we don't say "sour butter" or "rancid cream."

Idioms are language chunks that have idiomatic meanings, such as "kick the bucket" or "hell bent for leather."

Lexical Phrases are conventionalized language chunks that have more or less idiomatic meanings, but they also have associated discourse functions: "I'm sorry to hear that X" is used to express sympathy; "by the way" is used to shift a topic in discourse; and the indirect speech act, "could/would you X," is used to make requests.

Another important aspect of lexical phrases is that while some of them, such as "by the way," are set phrases allowing no variability, others are more like skeletal frames that have slots for various fillers, such as "could/would you X," where either "could" or "would" can be chosen, and X is a slot that is filled with a VP, such as "Could you pass the salt?" These phrases include short, relatively fixed ones, such as "a __ago," or longer phrases or clauses such as "I'm (very) sorry to hear that X," "the __er X, the __er Y", each with slots for various fillers. Examples of these variations are shown in (1).

(1) a. a __ago: a year ago, a month ago, a long time ago
    b. I'm (very) sorry to hear that X: I'm very sorry to hear that your father is ill; I'm sorry to hear that you lost the race.
    c. the __er X, the __er Y: the higher the climb, the thinner the air; the longer you wait, the sleepier you get.

Lexical Phrase Categories. The categories we have devised reflect an attempt to group lexical phrases according to function in a way that will reflect the requirements of spoken and written language and, at the same time, be pedagogically useful. These groups are not traditional grammar categories by gories of meaning and pragmatic characteristics of discourse and conversational structure that exist in many different types of situations. They are somewhat similar to Wilkins's notional–functional categories, where emphasis is on the lexicon needed to perform specific speech functions for common situations (Wilkins 1976). We emphasize that ours are intended to be pedagogical as well as theoretical categories, devised to use as practical instruments for the classroom, but also, we feel, adhering closely to current work in discourse analysis and speech act theory.

We refer to these groups as *social interactions*, *necessary topics*, and *discourse devices*. Under social interactions we list lexical phrases that are markers describing social relations. Necessary topics are those topics about which learners will be asked, or ones they will need to talk about frequently. The third group, discourse devices, are types of lexical phrases that connect the meaning and structure of the discourse. In what follows, we give examples of each type, together with illustrations of typical lexical phrases used to perform these specific functions.

1. *Social Interactions*: Social interactional markers, those that describe social relations, consist of (a) categories of conversational maintenance, and (b) categories of functional meaning relating to conversational purpose.

   a. *Conversational Maintenance* (regularities of conversational interaction that describe how conversations begin, continue, and end).

Summoning:	Excuse/pardon me (sustained intonation); Hey/hi/hello, (Name); How are you (doing)? Lookit; I didn't catch/get your name; Do you live around here? Hello, I'm + NAME; Good morning/afternoon/evening, (how are you?) What's up?
Responding to summons:	Uh-huh? Hi/hello, (Name); How are you (doing)? What's going on/ happening? Hello, I'm + NAME; (I'm) fine, thanks, (and you)?
Nominating a topic:	What's X? (By the way) Do you know/ remember X? Have you heard about X?
Clarifying:	(1) audience: (I) beg your pardon? Excuse/pardon me? What did you mean by X/when you said X? (2) speaker: What I mean/I'm trying to say is X;

	(2) speaker: What I mean/I'm trying to say is X; How shall I put it ? Let me repeat;
Checking comprehension:	All right? (Do you) understand (me)?
Shifting a topic:	Say, by the way; This is (a bit) off the subject/track, but X; Where were we/was I? Oh that reminds me of X.
Shifting turns:	(Well), so O.K., (Look/listen), excuse/pardon me; Could I say something here?
Closing:	Well, that's about it; I must be going; (It's been) nice talking to you/meeting you; I've got to run/go/do X; I mustn't keep you any longer;
Parting:	Goodbye; See you later; (Well) so long (for now);

b. *Conversational Purpose* (types of Speech Acts, i.e. functions that describe the purposes for which conversations take place).

Expressing politeness:	Thanks (very much); If you don't mind;
Questioning:	Do you X? Is/are there/it/they X? (rising intonation)
Answering:	Yes, (there/it/they is/are) (X); No, (there/it they is/are not) (X).
Requesting:	Modal Verb + Pro + VP (i.e., Would you (mind) X?); May I X?
Offering:	Modal Verb + Pro + VP (i.e., May/Can I help (you)?) Would you like X?
Complying:	Of course; Sure thing; I'd be happy/glad to.
Refusing:	Of course not; No way; I'd rather you X; I'm sorry but (I'm afraid/I think that) X;

Complimenting:	NP + be/look + (intensifier) + ADJ; I + (intensifier) + like/love + NP.
Asserting:	It is (a fact/the case that) X; I think/believe that X; It's said that X; Word has it that X; It seems X; I read (somewhere) that X; There is/are/was/were X;
Responding:	1. acknowledging (simple reinforcers): (Yeah) uh huh; mmhm; (And then) what happened (next/then/after that)? 2. accepting: Yeah, I know; (OK), right; Oh, I see; No kidding; 3. endorsing: Yes, that's so/correct/right; I absolutely/ certainly/completely agree; (That's) a (very) good/excellent point; There you go; That's great; 4. disagreeing: Yes, but (I think that) X; Well, (sustained intonation), no; I don't (really) agree (with you/X);
Expressing gratitude:	Thanks very much/a lot (for X); I (really) appreciate your thoughtfulness/kindness/doing X;
Expressing sympathy:	I'm (very) sorry about/to hear (about) X; (Wow,) that's/how terrible/awful; What a shame/pity/terrible thing;

2. *Necessary Topics*: These lexical phrases mark topics about which learners are often asked, or ones that are necessary in daily conversations.

Autobiography:	My name is ____, I'm from ____, I'm (a) ____ (years old);
Language:	Do you speak ____? How do you say/spell ____? I don't speak ____ very well; I speak ____ (a little);
Quantity:	How much/big is ____? (Not) a great deal; Lots of ____.

Time:	When is X? What time X? For a long time/ ____ years; (a) ____ ago; Since X; At/it's ____ o'clock; On ____day; The ____ before/ after ____;
Location:	Where is ____? What part of the ____? Across from ____; Next to ____; To the right/left (of ____); How far is ____? ____ blocks (from ____).
Weather:	Is it going to X? It's (very) ____ (today)! I'm ____;
Likes:	I like/enjoy ____ (a lot); I don't like/enjoy ____ (at all); I'd like to X; ____ is lots of fun; (What) do you like to X?
Food:	I'd like (to have) ____/to make a reservation (for ____); The check; A table for ____; Serve breakfast/lunch/dinner;
Shopping:	How much is ____? I want to buy/see ____; It (doesn't) fit(s); (Not) too expensive; A (really) good/bad buy/bargain; ____ cost(s) (me/you/them) ___dollars;

3. *Discourse Devices* (lexical phrases that connect the meaning and structure of the discourse).

Logical Connectors:	Therefore; As a result (of X); Nevertheless; Because (of) X; In spite of X;
Temporal Connectors:	The day/week/month/year before/after ____; And then; After X then/the next is Y;
Spatial Connectors:	Around here; Over there; At/on the corner;
Fluency Devices:	You know; It seems (to me) that X; I think that X; By and large; At any rate; If you see what I mean; And so on; So to speak; As a matter of fact;

Exemplifiers:	In other words; It's like X; For example; To give you an example;
Relators:	The (other) thing X is Y; X has (a lot)/doesn't have (much) to do with Y; Not only X but also Y;
Qualifiers:	It depends on X; The catch is; It's only in X that Y;
Evaluators:	As far as I know/can tell; Frankly (speaking); There's no doubt that X; (I'm (not) absolutely/pretty sure/positive/certain but) I think that X; I guess; At least;
Summarizers:	To make a long story short; My point (here) is that X; OK, so (level intonation);

Conversational Discourse. In conversational discourse, social interactions and discourse devices are the basic pragmatic organizers and provide patterns for the framework of the discourse; necessary topics, introduced basically for their pedagogical usefulness, provide patterns for the subject of discussion. A diagrammatic representation of this relationship might be:

Necessary Topics
↓
Social Interactions————————————————Discourse Devices

Most conversational encounters, if they are not of the briefest, phatic sort, are composed of a patchwork of patterns from all three of these categories. For example, one of the most basic interactions at the beginning of a conversation is to get the attention of the person one is talking to. When that person responds to the summons, the next step is to get the partner to attend to the topic of discourse; one then begins to offer information about the selected topic. In this way the participants cooperate to build a conversation. After the purpose of the conversation has been satisfied, the participants close the dialogue, and they part.

The following is a relatively simple, reconstructed dialogue that illustrates some typical lexical phrase functions in conversation (with labeled lexical phrases), including their interconnected functions:

(2) Bill: Hey, Sally. What's up? (summons: SI)
Sally: Hi, Bill. How are you doing? (response: SI)

Bill:	Pretty well, thanks. (response: SI) By the way (topic shift: SI), did you hear about my new car? (topic nomination: SI)
Sally:	No kidding (response: SI), a new car? (clarification: SI)
Bill:	Uh-huh (response: SI). I bought an old Volvo (shopping: NT) the day before yesterday. (time: NT)
Sally:	Hey, that's great (response: SI). How much did it cost you? (shopping: NT)
Bill:	It seems to me that it was a really good buy (assertion: SI) (evaluator: DD) (fluency device: DD) (shopping: NT), and what's more, (conjunction: DD) there isn't anything wrong with it (assertion: SI)—as far as I can tell (evaluator: DD), at any rate (fluency device: DD)
Sally:	Yeah, it's a beauty (response: SI); you were lucky to find it (assertion: SI). Oh, guess what (topic shift: SI)? Word has it that Jack just got a big promotion (assertion: SI). Did you hear about it (question: SI)?
Bill:	Yes, I heard (answer: SI). The other thing I heard is that he gets to move into a fancy big office (relation: DD) on the top floor (location: NT).
Sally:	No kidding, that's great (response: SI). Well, I've got to run now (closing: SI). See you later (parting: SI).
Bill:	Well, then (closing: SI), so long for now (parting: SI).

Person A (in this case, Bill) initiates the conversation by summoning the attention of B (in this case, Sally) with the lexical phrases "Hey, NAME" and "What's up?" B responds to the summons, and after A responds to B, A then shifts the topic ("By the way") and nominates a new topic ("Did you hear about X?"), and so on.

Bill's remark beginning with "It seems to me that" is typical of the complex utterances that often occur after a topic has been established and information is being presented about it. Evaluators, fluency devices, and other discourse devices begin to play a part in the evolving conversation. Moreover, the lexical phrases themselves begin to serve several purposes simultaneously.[1] For example, the beginning of Bill's utterance "It seems to me that," bears a multiple function: It marks a social interaction, for it is a routinized way of making an assertion, and at the same time it serves as a couple of discourse devices—as an "evaluator," because it marks the assertion as personal opinion, and as a "fluency device," because it is a bigger piece stitched into the discourse

---

1. It is not unusual that a single lexical phrase should have multiple functions. Speech Act theory has also had to allow for the fact that many categories cannot be defined as nonarbitrary and discrete types.

than the similar phrase "it was X." Being a bigger chunk, it gives the speaker more time to plan for the next routine and thus promotes fluency.

In form, it is an expansion of the lexical phrase "I'm (not) (absolutely/pretty) sure/positive/certain (but I think) (that) X," and it certainly allows A more time to gather thoughts than would a minimal form of the same lexical phrase, such as "I think X," or simply the bald assertion, "it is X."

It would be unreasonable for a teacher to condemn such fluency devices as linguistic crutches or as verbose, empty filler, for they serve an extremely important function, especially at the beginning and intermediate stages of language learning, of promoting fluency and of thus motivating learning.

Conclusion. In this paper we have suggested categories of lexical phrases that we feel are theoretically sound yet pedagogically useful for the second-language classroom. We also feel that they are especially well suited for teaching within DiPietro's framework of Strategic Interaction within scenarios. That is, with respect to classroom practice, these categories can serve as a more comprehensive framework from which particular form/function units can be selected for teaching within a given scenario; further, they can serve as a guide for selecting various scenarios themselves for a particular classroom, depending on the specific goals and needs of the students.

Finally, we emphasize that the overall goal should not be just teaching the functions of appropriate lexical phrases within given scenarios. Rather, formal aspects must also be considered. Students should also be taught to recognize and analyze more and more on their own these lexical phrase frames as they encounter them outside the classroom; and as they gain familiarity with various expansions of these frames, they should be guided toward finding their own way to the formal rules of syntax as well.

REFERENCES

DiPietro, Robert J. 1987. *Strategic interaction: Learning languages through scenarios.* New York: Cambridge University Press.

Ervin-Tripp, Susan. 1976. "Is Sybil there? The structure of some American English directives." *Language in Society* 5: 25–66.

Hakuta, Kenji. 1986. *Mirror of language: The debate on bilingualism.* New York: Basic Books.

Manes, Joan, and Nessa Wolfson. 1981. "The compliment formula." In Florian Coulmas (ed.), *Conversational routine.* The Hague: Mouton.

Nattinger, James, and Jeanette DeCarrico. 1992. *Lexical phrases and language teaching.* Oxford: Oxford University Press.

Peters, Ann. 1983. *The units of language acquisition.* Cambridge: Cambridge University Press.

Richards, Jack C. 1980. "Conversation." *TESOL Quarterly* 14: 413–432.

Tannen, Deborah. 1986. *That's not what I meant!* New York: William Morrow and Company.

Wardhaugh, Ronald. 1985. *How conversation works.* Oxford: Basil Blackwell.

Wilkins, D. 1976. *Notional syllabuses*. London: Oxford University Press.
Wong-Fillmore, Lily. 1976. "The second time around: Cognitive and social strategies in second language acquisition." Unpublished doctoral dissertation. Palo Alto, Calif.: Stanford University.

Strategic Interaction and task knowledge

Anita L. Wenden
York College, City University of New York

Introduction. Strategic Interaction is a communicative approach to language learning that calls upon learners to use the target language purposefully and skillfully in communicating with others in the context of a scenario, which replicates real-life situations. Students are assigned roles that oblige them to work out and implement personal game plans to seek a resolution to the problem that is the focus of the scenario. The dramatic tension that results as personal agendas clash and conflict in role enactment makes Strategic Interaction realistic and involving (Di Pietro 1987).

According to Di Pietro, Strategic Interaction is a learner-centered approach to language teaching that recognizes that "the students' learning is under their own control ..." (10); that students (should be allowed to) control much of their own learning (11); that the teacher may orchestrate activities, but it is the students who fulfill them in their own ways (11–22). For Di Pietro, this means that the teacher must not always "dominate instruction" and should, therefore, "loosen the reins" on the students, allowing them to "direct their own learning" as they work through the normal course of events leading to scenario execution on their own (68). Furthermore, it is the basic assumption of the approach that a well-constructed scenario will motivate students to participate autonomously (or take control) and, therefore, learn. However, simply giving students the freedom to direct their own learning is not enough for them to be truly self-directed or autonomous learners. Students will also need to learn the "technology" of learning to successfully navigate their way through the procedures "required for them to prepare for, enact, and evaluate the enactment of a scenario." Di Pietro recognizes this to some degree, stating that "all scenarios require strategies" (31). Included in the kinds of strategies he describes are learning strategies, though he does not refer to any of these strategies by name.

The purpose of this paper is to introduce another, relatively ignored, component of the learning technology needed by learners to participate autonomously in communicative language-learning tasks in general and in Strategic Interaction in particular, i.e. task knowledge. Figure 1 outlines the components of task knowledge as these apply to language learning. Implicit in each of the main categories is a key question learners need to ask and answer about a learning task teachers set for them or that they set for themselves, however general (e.g. improve my writing) or specific (learn to edit for incorrect tenses), in order for learning to be under their control as they complete the task, i.e., What is the purpose of this task? Why am I doing it? What kind of task is it? What do I have to do to complete it? What resources do I need to do so? Will it be hard or easy?

Figure 1. Task knowledge

Task purpose
Relevant to my personal goals
achievement
instrumental
Opportunity for learning vs. demonstration of competence

Task classification
Kind of task

Task demands
Resources required and available to do the task
Knowledge
Skills
Dividing the task (subgoals)
Order
Strategies
Hard/easy

In fact, teachers will either consciously or unconsciously seek answers to some if not all of these questions when they prepare a course or a lesson or select a specific set of tasks that make up the lesson. In other words, task knowledge is specialized knowledge about language and language learning/teaching (i.e. about methodology) that teachers acquire through professional training and experience. Thus, it may be assumed that a book in teacher education, such as *Strategic Interaction,* provides answers to these questions for those teachers who wish to use scenarios in their classrooms and, in so doing, outlines the task knowledge necessary to teachers who intend to use the methodology. What is contended here is that some of that same information intended only for the teacher is task knowledge that could be provided to the student.

To determine what kind of task knowledge students would need in order to participate in Strategic Interaction scenarios successfully, *Strategic Interaction: Learning Language through Scenarios,* Di Pietro's methodology book describing why and how teachers should use scenarios in the language classroom, was analyzed according to the categories outlined in Figure 1. In the first part of the paper, I will report on the analysis. Then, I will refer to research that points to the role of task knowledge in learning. My concluding comments will outline the implications of insights derived from both the research and the analysis for classroom practice.

Task knowledge and Strategic Interaction. The categories in figure 1 point to the kinds of task knowledge that students need about Strategic Interaction to take control of their learning. They should understand:

- why Strategic Interaction will help them improve their second/foreign language
- what kind of a task it is
- what they must do to complete the task and what resources will be necessary to do it[1]

Task purpose. Knowledge of task purpose refers to an understanding on the part of learners of whether a particular language-learning activity is learning oriented or performance oriented. That is, will it provide an opportunity to develop and acquire the basic linguistic skills they lack (e.g. more vocabulary, fluency) or those they need for survival or professional purposes (e.g. how to interview for a job)? The former refers to achievement needs and the latter to instrumental needs (Breen 1987). On the other hand (Boekhaert 1992), is the task perceived primarily as a test of their existing competence? Or is it a situation that requires that they show how well (or how poorly) they can use the language?

Task purpose and Strategic Interaction. Di Pietro provides information about the purpose of Strategic Interaction in the introductory chapter of his book. He advises that students be made to understand that the achievement of a nativelike accent and grammatical accuracy are two unrealistic goals that cannot be achieved in the classroom. As regards Strategic Interaction, interactive proficiency for participation in discourse is what it aims to help learners achieve. Students can expect to develop proficiency in responding to the demands and challenges of human interaction—to learn to express personal desires and views and to negotiate these views and desires with their classmates. At the same time, they can also expect to learn the grammar and vocabulary they need to perform these language functions.

Learners should be made to reflect on the learning purposes of a class using Strategic Interaction. Teachers who intend to use scenarios as the main methodology in their classrooms should, first of all, help students become aware of their own goals and expectations. Students should, then, be helped to contrast these with what can be realistically achieved in the classroom and with the interactive goals that are particular to Strategic Interaction.

Kind of Task. Classifying a learning task is a prerequisite to determining task demands. Learners need to determine what *kind* of task it is in order to understand how to complete it. Basic to classifying a language-learning task is an understanding of the nature of language and of how language learning is different from subject-matter learning. They also need to realize, for example,

---

1. See Breen 1987: 25 for similar questions.

that a writing task is different from a listening task or a listening–speaking task, i.e. the differences between the spoken language and the written language, and how social context can further distinguish two apparently similar communication tasks one from the other.

Strategic Interaction's assumptions about language. What general notions about spoken language are important for students to understand in order to participate in scenarios with understanding? In chapter 1, Di Pietro refers to four.

Multidimensional nature of language. In the section entitled "The Three Dimensions of Language" (6–8), Di Pietro refers to three functions or levels of language used in scenarios: information exchange (with its grammatical orientation), transaction (with its focus on negotiation and the expression of speaker intentions), and interaction (with an emphasis on how language works to portray roles and speaker identities).

How is this translated into task knowledge for students? Students who are expected to participate in scenarios should be made aware of the fact that

- language is the means of doing things with other people;
- it has many functions, depending upon what we want to do;
- three of these functions will be used in scenarios, i.e information exchange, transaction, and interaction.

Moreover, to help them learn to use language on these three levels, students will need to know about and learn to attend to

- the differences in grammatical structures that frame different information (information exchange)
- the nonverbal aspects of language that suggest intent (transaction) and
- the expressions that demarcate different social roles (interaction).

Ambiguity of language. Di Pietro also sets aside a section of chapter 1 to discuss the ambiguity of language and the relevance of ambiguity to discourse. He notes that other than structural ambiguity, a concept that was popular around 1960, ambiguities in the dimensions of transaction (a speaker's intent) and interaction (a speaker's role) are probably of even greater significance for speakers of a language (8). In other words, a speaker's intent is not always clear, nor are the psychological roles being played by others.

Students should also be made aware of the ambiguity of language as they prepare their scenarios. They should be helped to understand that language is not always to be interpreted literally and that the information exchanged, the intent of a speaker, and even the role the speaker plays are not always clear.

The humanist dimension of language. Di Pietro argues for a holistic and humanistic view of language teaching. He considers it a behavioral science and the basis of human intervention with language as not only cognitive but social and personal as well. He notes, "To speak is to be human and to learn to speak is to find new ways in which to express that same humanity" (12). Oftentimes language learners approach language learning instrumentally. Learning the language is related to an academic or work need. Students need to be helped to understand that learning a language is a broadening experience that expands one's human potential. Moreover, by pointing out to students that language is multidimensional, they can be made to see not only the cognitive but also the social and personal dimensions of human interaction that are facilitated by language.

Task demands. Knowledge of task demands means knowing what knowledge and skills are necessary to complete the task and whether these are available. That is, learners need to ask themselves if they will need world knowledge and if so, about what topics and situations. They need to determine what kind of specific knowledge about language and language use as well as what skills they will need. Then, they must determine whether this knowledge is part of their existing store of background knowledge or whether they must seek resources external to themselves. Learners will also need to know how to break up the overall task into learning objectives, each one dealing with a subcomponent of the task and, if relevant, in which order to complete each. That is, what comes first and what follows? Finally, knowledge of task demands requires that learners realize that they may need to use strategies to complete the task and which ones they should use. It is the answers to these questions that will determine whether or not the task is conceived of as hard or easy. Learners who have been able to accurately assess these various aspects of the task and who have the resources and skills required will find the task easy.

Task Demands and Strategic Interaction. In chapter 4, "Rehearsing and performing the scenario," Di Pietro acknowledges that "Teachers and students working through an interactive methodology for the first time may need some direction in what they are supposed to do during the rehearsal phase" (71). In other words, he points to the need not only to inform teachers but also to inform students about the task's demands, and his ensuing discussion provides the following outline of the knowledge and skills required.

World and culture knowledge. World and culture knowledge is especially important during the rehearsal phase of a Strategic Interaction. Di Pietro acknowledges that students may want to "know more about the cultural matrix of the utterance" (74). Certainly, learners will need to have some knowledge of the cultural background that provides the context for the scenario. When necessary, they will also need world knowledge that may relate to a particular issue that arises in the scenario in order to be able to consider realistic and authentic options.

Let us consider, for example, what prior knowledge would be needed for a language learner to participate in the following scenario role (from Di Pietro 1987: 74):

> You are a young executive in a large firm. You have invited a client to dinner in an expensive restaurant. If you can impress this client, you might win a large account and also be given a raise and a promotion by your boss. As the dinner progresses, you discover that you have left your wallet with all your money and credit cards at home. What do you do?

First, the learner/student would need to have an understanding of the *business culture,* which provides the context for the meeting. For example, what does it mean to be a young executive? How does a large firm differ from a small firm? The student needs to understand what it means to win a client's business and how one goes about doing so. Moreover, the student needs to have some knowledge of expensive restaurants and what is appropriate behavior in these restaurants. He or she must also know about credit cards. If experience has not provided students with this background knowledge, it needs to be provided for them so they can participate in the scenario authentically.

World knowledge about different approaches to dealing with the problem is also necessary. Di Pietro lists five that would be appropriate for the above role: analytic, idealistic (attempting to gain the guest's sympathy), pragmatic (accepting the situation and joking about it), realistic (perhaps the client will lend the money, the problem is not really that bad), synthesist (this must have happened before—talk to the manager). Moreover, he bids the teacher provide direction if students are having difficulty. That is, students with little or no experience with that type of role will need this aspect of task knowledge provided.

Linguistic/socioliogustic knowledge. Linguistic and sociolinguistic knowledge is necessary for students to be able to enact the scenario in a realistic manner. This requires the following categories of knowledge regarding the use of language in social contexts.

KNOWLEDGE OF DISCOURSE STRUCTURE. Interactive discourse (i.e. the scenario) is the basic activity of Strategic Interaction, and in his discussion of the performance phase of the scenario, Di Pietro describes two aspects of discourse structure that are important. First of all, performance prototypes that guide the enactment of various scenarios differ in variability. In some cases a discourse may be quite open ended, as when the intended goals of the participants are not mutually known. Di Pietro gives the example of a husband and wife trying to determine who is to take care of their child on a day when both have pressing commitments. In other cases roles and preferred outcomes are mutually known and so the discourse structure is more fixed as when, for example, a scenario deals with a dissatisfied customer and the complaint personnel of a department store. In other cases, yet, discourse structure is quite routinized as when one orders dinner in a restaurant or calls a particular office for specific information. Learners need to know that these differences exist. They need to know how the discourse that forms the context of a particular scenario proceeds.

Second, in his discussion of conversational management, Di Pietro refers to the conversation format of a discourse that dictates when participants should take their turns at speech, how they should open and close a discourse, and under what circumstances they are free to change the topic under discussion. Learners should also be made aware of this aspect of discourse structure.

KNOWLEDGE OF CULTURAL INTERACTION STYLES refers to culturally appropriate choice of topic and language forms. Di Pietro notes that "cultural differences influence the style of interaction in ways that we are just beginning to understand" (1987: 75). Successful participation in a scenario will require students to know that cultural interaction styles differ and to have at least a rudimentary knowledge of the cultural interaction style appropriate to participating in a particular scenario.

Certainly work in cross-cultural communication has shown that approaches to business negotiations vary from culture to culture. Directness, establishing trust, dealing with feelings, and clearly specifying options are all factors that are treated quite differently from culture to culture.[2] A student participating in the above scenario would need to know about these factors.

They will further require knowledge of how language within cultures varies depending upon whom one is talking to, i.e. of how language is tailored to fit role relationships (79). For example, students participating in the above scenario would need to know that interaction with the client and with the waiter would differ. Di Pietro refers to the use of familiar forms of address (in languages such as French and Spanish), word choice, idioms, intonation, style, and other variables affecting language use, concluding, however, that it is not possible or

2. For illustrations of these differences, see "Communicating across Cultures" from the video series *Valuing Diversity* available from Intercultural Press (Yarmouth, Maine).

even desirable to make students aware of all these variables. However, he does advocate that students be assisted in fitting the language to how they perceive themselves in the role they are playing and that students be made aware of the pragmatic function of socially variable language.

GROUP SKILLS. Students are divided into groups in order to complete the tasks that constitute the rehearsal phase. They continue to function as a group during the performance phase, advising their selected "actor" whenever he or she consults with them. Therefore, while Di Pietro does not refer to group skills explicitly, this implies that learners should also have a rudimentary knowledge of group process. They need to know how to participate in a group (ask questions, agree, disagree, contribute ideas, and so on).

Dividing the task/order. Besides knowing what knowledge and skills are necessary to complete the task, learners must also know how to divide it up in such a way that the objectives that constitute the overall task goal can be achieved in the proper order.

Three phases of Strategic Interaction. Strategic Interaction consists of three phases, each with its specific action and learning objective: rehearsal, performance, and debriefing. The objective of the rehearsal phase is to develop a game plan to be executed in the target language during the coming performance phase (70). That is, learners are expected to create a script for a personal role to realize a given agenda. For this reason, Di Pietro emphasizes the fact that rehearsals are an opportunity to learn much that is new.

As for the performance phase, he notes, it is not to be construed as entertainment but as the working out of two or more game plans—a real-life negotiation. Therefore, in this second phase of Strategic Interaction, students should conceive of themselves as fitting into one of three roles, each with its own specific objective, i.e. scenario performer (negotiating), group member (consulting), or onlookers (witnessing). Finally, with its focus on building competence in the target language, the debriefing phase is the phase of Strategic Interaction that most closely resembles the traditional activities of the classroom. During this phase, the teacher first provides feedback on the transactional and interactive aspect of the scenario. She then moves on to comment on the language used during the enactment, and in response to the questions asked by students she may provide a mini grammar lesson. Students need to understand what the objectives of these three phases are and how they contribute to improving their interactive proficiency.

Steps to be followed during phase 1 and 2. Once the objective of each phase is clear, students need to know what to do to proceed through each phase.

REHEARSAL PHASE. During the rehearsal phase, individual participants and the group as a whole need to follow the specific steps that lead to a group decision of how to play the assigned role. These steps are:

(i) understanding the role they are to discuss and what they have to do
(ii) thinking about the problem and weighing diverse ways to resolve it
(iii) proposing their ideas to the group and discussing ideas of others
(iv) deciding on a plan of action and picking someone to execute it during the performance.

Learners need to know what these steps are.

PERFORMANCE PHASE. The student who is selected to participate in the performance of the scenario needs to know how to proceed through the enactment. Di Pietro lists the following steps:

(i) appraise situation
(ii) consider the options for resolving it
(iii) anticipate the responses of others in the chosen options
(iv) apply the options by interacting with others in conversation
(v) review the results and integrate the forthcoming information within a personal conceptual framework

Of course, the first three steps will already have been followed during the rehearsal phase when options are considered and selected. However, once faced with a real opponent or counterpart, these steps take on a new meaning. Learners should be made aware of how all five of these steps can be used to guide them through the negotiation that is the focus of the scenario—whether they are actors, consultants, or onlookers.

Strategic knowledge. While the steps described above outline how the action and learning objective of each phase is to be achieved, strategies are necessary for students to navigate their way through each step successfully.

According to Di Pietro, during the rehearsal phase, students are permitted to "enlist each other's aid or ask the teacher ... about matters relevant to the charge" (72). That is, they are encouraged to use clarification strategies to facilitate their learning. The steps students must follow to complete the task suggest the need for other learning strategies not explicitly named by Di Pietro. For example, to be certain they have understood their charge and to know when to ask questions, students need to monitor their comprehension. They need to elicit background knowledge to determine what they know about the context of the role they are discussing and to predict outcomes in order to choose and evaluate options as they devise their game plan. Moreover, as they plan the utterances necessary to implement their game plan, they must be able to self-assess, i.e. to know what language they know and do not know so as to elicit the help of the teacher. Learners need to be made aware of the kinds of strategies they should use during the rehearsal phase.

In his discussion of the performance phase of Strategic Interaction, Di Pietro refers to the need for communication strategies, although he does not refer to them explicitly in that way. "It is especially important," he says, "for second language learners to have access to those conversational management devices that are applicable when limited knowledge of the target language leads to a breakdown in communication" (84), and he suggests ways for teachers to provide them. Of course, they will also be needed for learners to participate in the group discussion that takes place during the rehearsal phase and during the debriefing phase. Students will also need to know how to selectively attend to the relevant features of language that will enable them to determine what information is being communicated as well as the intentions and social roles of the participants.

At the outset of the debriefing phase, teachers are asked to engage students in an evaluation of the transaction and interactive aspects of the performance—another learning strategy, one that requires knowledge of appropriate criteria for assessment. In his discussion, Di Pietro suggests questions that a teacher can ask, i.e. What was the outcome? Were the intentions of the participants met? Could there have been other solutions? Learners need to learn to use these questions as evaluation criteria. The importance of asking questions for clarification of particular grammar points is another strategy that Di Pietro explicitly advocates using during the debriefing stage. At this time, he also suggests, students can also be encouraged to keep a grammar log, yet another learning strategy, to record lesson highlights and make them available for future use. Lesson highlights include vocabulary, structures, and conversational strategies.

In sum, Di Pietro describes six different learning strategies that should be used to participate in one or other of the three phases of Strategic Interaction: clarification, eliciting background knowledge, predicting, evaluating, monitoring, and selective attending. He also refers to the need for communication strategies ("conversational management devices"). Learners need to be made aware of the need to use these strategies, and they need to know which strategies are appropriate for which task during which phase in order to be able to participate effectively in a scenario.

Figure 2 summarizes the task knowledge specific to Strategic Interaction described above. This is knowledge that learners need in order to self-direct their participation in scenarios with benefit. The schema highlights the fact that the background knowledge requisite for providing learners with task knowledge is derived from domain-specific knowledge, strategic knowledge, and person knowledge.

Figure 2. Schema of Task Knowledge for Strategic Interaction

Task Purpose
Interactive proficiency

Kind of Task
Oral/aural; multidimensionality, ambiguity, and humanist function of the language

Task Demands

Culture and world knowledge of the setting and problem that provide the context for the scenario; approaches to solving the problem

Linguistic knowledge of different performance prototypes; techniques for conversational management; differences in cultural interaction styles

Group skills

ACTION OBJECTIVES

(1) devise a script
(2) perform the script
(3) discuss language use associated with the performance

STEPS DURING THE REHEARSAL PHASE

(1) understand the role
(2) weigh diverse ways to resolve the problem
(3) propose one's ideas to the group
(4) decide on a plan of action
(5) pick someone to execute it

STEPS DURING THE PERFORMANCE PHASE

(1) appraise the situation
(2) consider the options for resolving it
(3) anticipate the responses of others
(4) apply the options by interacting with others
(5) review the results
(6) integrate the forthcoming information within a personal conceptual framework

STRATEGIC KNOWLEDGE

(1) need to use strategies
(2) which strategies to use (e.g. predict, self-assess, selective attending, evaluate, clarification)

As outlined in figure 2, to assess task demands, learners will need specific knowledge about language and how language works, they will need culture and world knowledge specific to the setting of the scenario, and they will need knowledge of group skills. Such specialized knowledge is referred to as *domain-specific knowledge*. Domain-specific knowledge will also be necessary for learners to be able to classify a task accurately and to determine what linguistic need it best meets (i.e. task purpose). Learners will need to draw upon their *strategic knowledge* to determine that need to use strategies and to select those most appropriate to the task. Finally, in order to know whether they will have the knowledge and skills required for the task and, therefore, to decide whether it will be hard or easy, they need to have knowledge of their own acquired competence. This last kind of knowledge is referred to as *person knowledge*. Figure 3 summarizes these relationships among the various components of task knowledge and the knowledge sources it builds upon.

Figure 3. Source of Task Knowledge

task purpose	domain-specific knowledge
task classification	domain-specific knowledge
task demands	
what resources	domain-specific knowledge
how (subgoats/order)	domain-specific knowledge
strategies	strategic knowledge
hard/easy	person knowledge (competence)

Utility of task knowledge. *Concept of task knowledge.* The notion of task, person, and strategic knowledge, as three categories of metacognitive knowledge or beliefs learners can hold about a cognitive enterprise, was the outcome of Flavell's memory research (1977, 1979). In these writings, Flavell described two subcategories of task knowledge. First, there is knowledge about the kind of information available during a cognitive enterprise, an understanding of what such information implies for how the cognitive enterprise should best be managed, and how successful one was likely to be in achieving the goal. The second subcategory includes metacognitive knowledge about task demands or goals—the realization of how demanding or difficult a particular task can be.[3]

A very similar notion was included as one of the components of Newell and Simon's (1972) general problem-solving model. In their model, "problem space" refers to the knowledge and information known or potentially available to the problem solver that may be useful in solving the problem. It includes problem goal and subgoals and the possible states of the problem that may occur as the

3. See Wenden 1987; 1991 for applications of these categories to second language learning.

solver moves toward the solution. Operators or mental procedures, which enable the individual to move from state to state, as well as knowledge of the constraints under which a problem is to be solved, are also included in the problem space.

More recently, in noting the role of reflection and reconstruction in a cognitive constructive view of learning, Paris and Byrnes (1989) refer to research that has shown that in approaching a task, school-age children ask "What is the purpose of this task? What can I do to solve the problem? Should I try hard? What do I already know about this task?" These are all questions that refer to the need aspect of task knowledge.

Research. During the last two decades, research and theory from a variety of disciplines have indicated the importance of task knowledge by demonstrating the influence of one or another of its components on learning. The following summary of some of the insights drawn from a selected review of the literature lists four of the ways task knowledge, derived from a learner's domain-specific knowledge, strategic knowledge, and/or person knowledge, influences and enhances the learning process.

Perception of task demands and task purpose indirectly influences the quality of learning. Boekhaerts's (1992) model of adaptable learning, which integrates research on motivation, anxiety, and self-efficacy, provides insight on how perception of task demands and task purpose influences a learner's decision to invest personal resources in acquiring new skills, i.e. to engage him- or herself in the learning opportunity provided by a task. According to the model, three factors influence this decision. The first factor is a learner's perception of task demands—the task and the physical, social, and didactic context in which it is embedded and—though not explicitly stated in Boekhaerts' model, but referred to elsewhere (1992: 2)—the task goals or purpose. A second factor, activated domain-specific knowledge and skills relevant to the task, provides information on the learners' competence. A third factor consists of learners' self-concept, anxiety, and goal structure.

As noted in Figure 4, a learner's decision to engage in a task is the outcome of a cost–benefit appraisal that weighs task knowledge (i.e. perception of task demands and task purpose) against three aspects of person knowledge: level of competence, self-concept, and goal structure. Level of competence refers to the domain-specific knowledge and skills relevant to the task available to the learner to do the task. Self-concept refers to learners' sense of self-efficacy. That is, do they have confidence in their ability to learn in general and as it applies to this specific task? Self-concept will determine learners' belief in their ability to learn in that situation. Finally, goal structure refers to learners' personal strivings—their long- and short-term goals. Is the task relevant to them?

Figure 4. Task knowledge and learning intention

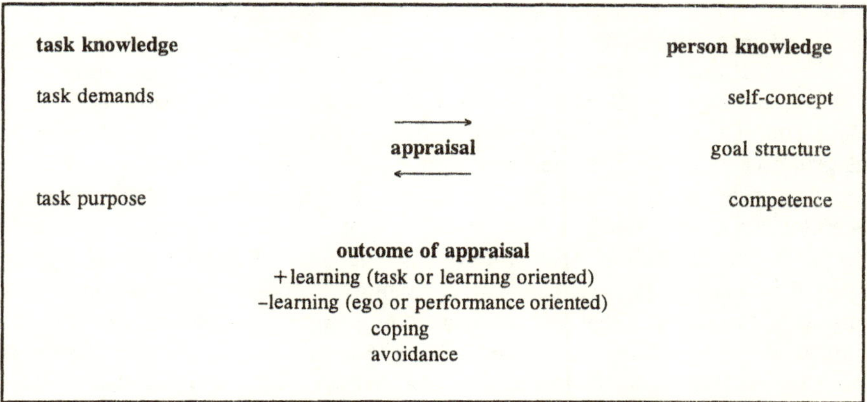

Boekhaerts's research has shown that students do conduct these appraisals. Moreover, if, as a result of learners' awareness of their competence vis-à-vis the task's demands and its perceived attractiveness, the appraisal is positive, they'll activate learning processes and there will be a gain in resources. If, on the other hand, they perceive that they do not have the competence and question the utility of the task, the appraisal is negative and they'll choose coping strategies to prevent loss of resources or discomfort or avoid the task altogether (cf. Volet 1992 and Schunk 1990 for similar conclusions).

It is this final determination of learning intention, influenced by a learner's perception of task demand and task purpose, that bears directly on the quality of the learning process. It determines whether students choose challenging tasks that they may have difficulty doing or tasks that will make them look competent or "smart" (Elliot and Dweck 1981, Bandura and Dweck 1981, Dweck 1989). That, in turn, determines how much effort they'll be willing to expend. Further, it influences their criteria for evaluating success (will it be based on a learning gain? or on approval from an outside source?), how much control they feel over a task/their learning, and their attribution of causes of task outcome (ability vs. effort). (See Volet 1992 for similar conclusions.)

Perception of task demands and task purpose indirectly influences the transfer of learned strategies. In her schema of three key factors affecting transfer, Wong (1991) includes a learner's decision to use the task as an opportunity to learn. This decision, as has just been noted, is based on the learner's perception of the task's purpose. Wong reports on research that has shown that this perception and the subsequent decision to learn is a prerequisite for the use of conditional knowledge (i.e. the determination of whether it is appropriate to use a strategy to do a particular task) and, therefore, predicts the use or transfer of effective, learned strategies (Nolen 1988).

"Nature of instruction" is the second factor in Wong's schema. According to Wong, if one wishes to enhance the likelihood of transfer, it is important to teach students to apply effort and metacognition, i.e. to be "mindful," while acquiring a new skill or strategy and in the decision process for selecting an appropriate strategy. This means helping learners learn to seek relationships between previous tasks and the current task and to determine whether the abstracted principle related to a previously learned skill or strategy is applicable to this new task. Both of these processes will need to build upon task knowledge gained by classifying each task, i.e. determining what kind of a task it is. She also refers to research that has documented how mindfulness enhanced the learning of normally achieving college students (Salomon and Gloverson 1987b) as well as learning-disabled students (Wong, Wong, Perry, and Sawatsky 1986).

Task knowledge indirectly influences the use of strategies. According to Boekhaerts's model (referred to above), learners' perception of task demands activates relevant domain-specific knowledge, i.e. acquired prior knowledge and skills related to the subject matter of the task. Research has shown that the existence of such a knowledge base, also referred to as expert knowledge, can influence the use of strategies.

Insights from research on the relationship between domain-specific knowledge and memory performance in children has shown that there are at least three ways that the knowledge base relates to strategy use (cf. Pressley, Borkowski, and Schneider 1987, 1990). For example, research that looked at the relationship between the meaningfulness of words and the use of organizational strategies in memory tasks showed that domain-specific knowledge facilitates the use of particular strategies (cf., for example, Frankel and Rollins 1985, Schneider 1986, Bjorklund 1988, Hasselhorn 1990). Research has also shown that rich domain-specific knowledge can diminish the need for strategy activation (Chi 1985, Rabinowitz and Chi 1987), and that insights gained from the automatic activation of well-established semantic memory relations (i.e. well-organized domain-specific knowledge) can lead to spontaneous strategy use on the part of learners. That is, in reviewing learned material, for example, learners may note how it is organized, and as a result, they may initiate the use of this organization strategy in the learning of other materials. That is, domain-specific knowledge generalizes strategy use to related domains (Ornstein 1986, Bjorklund and Jacobs 1985).

Research contrasting approaches to categories of learners further supports the influence of domain-specific knowledge or task familiarity. Stein (1986) notes that the main difference between studies that find young children capable of strategic processing and those that do not lies in the type and familiarity of materials and tasks used. When children are familiar with the content of a task, they perform like adults. As regards novice and expert learners, not only do experts in an area learn more when studying new information in their domain of expertise than do novices, they also represent (or organize) their knowledge differently and have different recall strategies. (Schneider 1992).

Domain-specific knowledge has also been seen as a necessary complement to the efficient use of writing-process skills. This is the thesis proposed by Stein (1986), who maintains that good composing requires certain types of knowledge and that without it the efficient use of process skills is limited. Her review of the literature on knowledge and process in writing outlines the following distinct types of domain-specific knowledge that must complement writing-process skills, i.e. knowledge about the functional goals of composing, different discourse forms, and domain-specific or topic knowledge and how it relates to discourse forms.

As noted by Boekhaert (1992) the activation of domain-specific knowledge is dependent upon the learners' perception of task demands. It is the perception of task demands that either activates the knowledge automatically or that makes the learner aware of the need to retrieve it. Then, once available, the domain-specific knowledge facilitates the use of appropriate strategies. Thus, task knowledge indirectly influences the efficient use of strategies and the outcome of learning.[4]

Perception of task demands guides and controls the execution of a task. Insights from theory on the writing process, specifically Flower and Hayes's (1981) theoretical model of the subprocesses specific to writing, describe how learners' perception of task demands also determines the specification of goals and subgoals both at the outset of a writing task and throughout the process of completing it. The model assumes that the writer's knowledge store and the writer's interpretation of task demands continually guide and control three major subprocesses particular to writing: planning, translating, and reviewing. During the planning process, writers must first attempt an interpretation or representation of task demands in order to set goals of how the writing should proceed. Then, as they proceed with the task, translating ideas into linguistic form and reviewing/revising what has been written, it is the perception of the changing task demands that further guide actions and decisions (i.e. the use of strategies, retrieval of appropriate knowledge, change of goals). In fact, research has shown that writers maintain awareness of these goals, using them as a guide as

4. For research conclusions in learner strategy research in second language learning that suggest a similar relationship between task knowledge and strategy use, see Vann and Abraham 1990 and O'Malley and Chamot 1990.

they proceed through the task. Young children, for example, can stop and identify some of the goals motivating their composition behavior and their problem-solving behavior (Stein and Jewett 1986, Stein and Levine 1986) while they are performing a task and after it is over (Stein 1986). In other words, it is knowledge of task demands that influences the use of metacognitive strategy in writing (cf. Wenden 1991 for a similar conclusion).

Implications. Basing his rationale for Strategic Interaction on Showstack (1982), Di Pietro claims that there are only two things that are clearly provided by the teacher: exposure to the target language and motivation to continue studying the language. This paper's intent has been to demonstrate that this is not so. To facilitate learning, it is important, though not sufficient, for teachers to create conditions necessary for learners to learn. They need in a formal and explicit way to share with them their own expertise as teachers—to help them learn how to learn. It has already been acknowledged that learning strategies are the key to effective learning (cf. for example, Robin 1989, O'Malley and Chamot 1990, Cohen 1990). This paper has argued for another aspect of learning that is even more basic, i.e. task knowledge.

REFERENCES

Bandura, M., and Carol S. Dweck. 1981. "Children's theories of intelligence as predictors of achievement goals." Unpublished manuscript, Harvard University, Cambridge, Mass.

Best, Deborah L., and Peter A. Ornstein. 1986. "Children's generation and communication of mnemonic organizational strategies." *Developmental Psychological Strategies* 22: 845–853.

Bjorklund, David F., and J.W. Jacobs. 1985. "Associative and categorical processes in children's memory: the role of automaticity in the development of organization in free recall." *Journal of Experimental Child Psychology* 39: 599–617.

Bjorklund, David F. 1988. "Acquiring a mnemonic: Age and category knowledge effects." *Journal of Experimental Child Psychology* 45: 71–87.

Boekaerts, M. 1992. "The adaptable learning process: initiating and maintaining behavioral change." In *Applied Psychology: An International Review.*

Chi, Michelene T.H. 1985. "Interactive roles of knowledge and strategies the development of organized sorting and recall." In S.F. Chipmain, J.W. Segal, and R. Glaser (Eds.) *Thinking and learning skills: Research and open questions* Vol. 2: 457-483. Hillsdale, N.J.: Erlbaum.

Cohen, A. 1990. *Language learning: Insights for learners, teachers, and researchers.* New York: Newbury House.

Di Pietro, Robert J. 1987. *Strategic Interaction: learning languages through scenarios.* New York: Cambridge University Press.

Dweck, Carol S. 1989. "Motivation." In A. Leagold and R. Glaser (eds.) *Foundations for a psychology of education.* 87–136. Hillsdale, N.J.: Erlbaum.

Elliot, E.S. and Carol S. Dweck. 1981. *Children's achievement goals as determinants of learned helplessness and mastery-oriented achievement patterns: An experimental analysis.* Unpublished manuscript, Harvard University, Cambridge, Mass.

Flavell, John H., and Henry M. Wellman. 1977. "Metamory." In R. V. Kail, Jr., and J.W. Hagen (eds.) *Perspectives on the development of memory and cognition.* Hillsdale: NJ: Erlbaum Associates.

Flavell, John H. 1979. "Metacognition and cognitive monitoring: A new area of cognitive-developmental inquiry." *American Psychologist* 34: 906–911.

Flower Linda, and J. Hayes. 1981. "A cognitive process theory of writing." *College Composition and Communication* 365-387.

Frankel, M.T., and H.A. Rollins. 1985. "Associative and categorical hypotheses of organization in the free recall of adults and children." *Journal of Experimental Child Psychology* 40.304-318.

Hasselhorn, M. 1990. "The emergence of strategic knowledge activation in categorical clustering during retrieval." *Journal of Experimental Child Psychology* 50.53-80.

Newell, Allen, and Herbert Simon. 1972. *Human Problem Solving.* New York: Prentice-Hall.

Nolen, S.B. 1988. "Reasons for studying: Motivational orientations and study strategies." *Cognition and Instruction.* 1,2: 117–125.

O'Malley, J. Michael, and Anna Uhl Chamot. 1990. *Learning strategies in second language acquisition.* New York: Cambridge University Press.

Paris, Scott G., and James P. Byrnes. 1989. "The constructivist approach to self-regulation of learning in the classroom." In Michael Pressley, John G. Borkowski, and Wolfgang Schneider. 1987. *Cognitive strategies: Good strategy users coordinate metacognition and knowledge.* In R. Vasta, and G. Whiteburst (eds.) Annals of Child Development Vol. 1. 5:89–129. New York, N.Y.: JAI Press.

Pressley, Michael, John G. Borkowski, and Wolfgang Schneider. 1990. "Good information processing: What it is and how education can promote it." *International Journal of Educational Research* 13: 857–867.

Rabinowitz, M., and Michelene T.H. Chi. 1987. "An interactive model of strategic processing." In S.J. Ceci (ed.) *Handbook of the cognitive, social and physiological characteristics of learning disabilities.* Vol 2 83–102. Hillsdale, N.J.: Erlbaum.

Rubin, Joan. 1989. "How learner strategies can inform language teaching." In V. Bickley (ed.) *Proceedings of LULTAC,* Institute of Language in Education, Department of Education, Hong Kong.

Salomon, Gavriel, and Tamar Globerson. 1987. *Rocky roads to transfer.* Second Annual Report to the Spencer Foundation. Tel Aviv: Tel Aviv University.

Schunk, D.H. 1990. "Introduction to the special section on motivation and efficacy." *Journal of Educational Psychology,* 82, 1: 3-6.

Schneider, Wolfgang. 1992. "Domain specific knowledge and memory performance in children." *Educational Psychology Review.*

Showstack, R. 1982. "Language teaching vs Language learning systems." *Systems* 10: 179-89.

Stein, Nancy, and J. Jewett. 1986. "A conceptual analysis of the meaning of basic negative emotions: Implications for a theory of development." *Measurement of Emotion in Infants and Children,* Vol. 2, ed. by C.E. Izard and P. Read. New York: Cambridge University Press.

Stein, Nancy, and M. Levine. 1986. "Thinking about feelings: The development and use of emotional knowledge." In R.E. In B.E. Snow and E. M. Farr (eds.) "Aptitude learning and instruction" Vol 3: *Cognition, Cooation, and Affect.* Hillsdale, N.J.: Lawrence Erlbaum.

Stein, Nancy. 1986. "Knowledge and process in the acquisition of writing skills." E.Z. Rothkopf (ed.) *Review of Research in Education* 13: 225-258.

Vann, Roberta J., and Roberta G. Abraham. 1990. "Strategies of unsucessful language learners." *TESOL Quarterly* 24: 177-98.

Volet, S.E. 1992. "Modelling and Coaching of Relevant Metacognitive Strategies for Enhancing University Students' Learning." *Learning and Instruction.*

Wenden, Anita. 1987. "Metacognition: An Expanded view on the cognitive abilities of L2 Learners." *Language Learning* 37,4.573–596.

Wenden, Anita. 1991. "Metacognitive Strategies in L2 Writing: A Case for Task Knowledge."

Georgetown University Round Table on Languages and Linguistics 1991, ed. by James E. Alatis. Washington, D.C.: Georgetown University Press.

Wong, B.Y.L. 1991. "On the thorny issue of transfer in learning disabilities interventions: Towards a three-prong solution." Invited address, Fourth European Conference for Research in Learning and Instruction, Turku, Finland. [B.Y.L. Wong, Simon Fraser University, Faculty of Education, BurBaby, B.C. Canada V5A 1S6.]

Wong, B.Y.L., R. Wong, N. Perry, and D. Sawatsky. 1986. "The efficacy of a self-questioning summarization strategy for use by underachievers and learning disabled adolescents." *Learning Disability Focus*, 2: 20-35.

The use of scenarios in the classroom for the development of higher-level foreign-language skills

Linda Smith Rutledge
Central Intelligence Agency

Introduction. Use of scenarios, designed for use in foreign-language classrooms by Dr. Robert J. Di Pietro, is a methodology designed to elicit free-flowing, unscripted conversation. They have been used at the Language Training Division of the Central Intelligence Agency (CIA) to assist students in developing higher-level language skills.

As defined informally in Dr. Di Pietro's *Strategic Interaction: Learning Languages through Scenarios,* scenarios are real-life happenings that involve the unexpected and require the use of language to resolve a dilemma. The dialogue in a scenario is not scripted, the ending is variable, and the student plays himself or herself when enacting a scenario.

Because the dialogue is not scripted and because the student is being himself or herself in the situation, the resolution of a scenario cannot be predicted, and no two enactments of a scenario will ever be the same. The words the student uses in acting out the scenario become more than conveyors of information. They contribute to the student's reaching a goal, and therefore they assume a tactical worth. Also, because there is no way to know in advance how the situation will play out, the interacting students must pay attention to what is being said. The students must additionally be ready to make adjustments in their game plans as the conversation unfolds. In achieving the proper interactions, students must also take into consideration the setting and nonverbal elements, such as their intonation, facial expressions, and gestures.

Comparison of scenarios and role plays. In a role play, the student is given a part. He or she portrays someone else and does what he or she is told to do, says what he or she is supposed to say. The target language is used to practice previously learned material. The actors *and* audience know what will be said and done. In a scenario, the student plays herself or himself within a framework. She or he is given a situation but is not told what to say or do. Aspects of the target language are taken from the enactment of the scenario and used as the basis of discussion and exploration of language use. Neither the actors nor the audience know just what will be said or done; the interaction contains an element of uncertainty and dramatic tension.

Rationale for the use of scenarios. Scenarios allow instructors and students to recreate or simulate the conditions of life and provide students with the help and guidance they need to deal with them. The instructor can isolate potentially stressful situations, bring them into the classroom, and control them. Unlike real life, students have the opportunity to discuss their options and plan strategies in groups. They can even interrupt a conversation and return to the supporting group for on-the-spot help. Also, scenarios make allowances for differences in students. Shy students can be excellent learners of a language without wishing to perform before the entire class. The shelter of the group enables them to participate without undue stress.

Subject matter for scenarios. The best themes for scenarios come from real life. This is one reason students can be such valuable authors of scenarios. It does not take long to learn the technique for writing a scenario, and in scenarios that they write, students can capture situations that interest them or bother them or with which they feel a need to grapple. Some other sources of intriguing ideas or situations for scenarios are letters seeking advice, such as letters to Dear Abby or Miss Manners, newspaper articles on human interest stories, and literature.

Creation of scenarios. In creating a scenario, the instructor (or student) sets the scene for the participants. The scenario usually consists of two "roles." In writing a scenario, the author (language instructor or student) must:

- *Interlock the assigned tasks.* The tasks given to the participants should be interrelated. The students need a reason to interact.
- *Share some information with all participants.* The students must know enough about the situation to be able to begin. The shared information helps orient them and give them a context.
- *Retain some private information.* Unshared information helps motivate each participant to continue the interaction until the ambiguity is resolved.

In grouping students, Di Pietro recommends that no more than eight participants make up the groups assigned to each role. Large classes can work around this restriction by working on two or more scenarios at the same time. Students should be allowed to form their own groups as often as possible. They will form groups whose members feel comfortable with each other. This sets a positive, relaxed atmosphere for participation, for communication, and for mutual support. Members of each group will normally form a circle. Each group should be separated by enough distance to prevent eavesdropping during the rehearsal phase.

Phases of classroom implementation. The three phases of classroom implementation of the methodology as outlined by Di Pietro should be preceded by *preclass preparation*. This involves creating or selecting scenarios and preparing role cards. It might also include reviewing with the class grammatical structures that could be effectively used or introducing specialized terminology to facilitate the upcoming interactions.

Phase 1: Rehearsal. During rehearsal, the students break into groups and prepare to fulfill their roles (one role per group). The members of the group are given a piece of paper that contains their part of the scenario—the shared information and their private information. At the same time, the second group gets a piece of paper with the shared information and *their* private information.

The group maps out possible game plans to put into action in the target language during the performance phase. The rehearsal allows students to discuss with peers in a nonthreatening setting what they are going to do; it reduces the tension level for all of them. Di Pietro also found that in working in this fashion, the group has greater knowledge than its individual members. Working together produces a synergy that allows the group to generate conversation of a higher level than any of them would be able to create or utter individually. Discussion among the students may be in their native language or in the target language or in a combination of both, but the game plan is prepared to be delivered in the target language.

During the rehearsal, the members of the group may consult each other, the instructor, dictionaries, texts, or anything else they need. The students, especially the one chosen to act during the performance, may make and use notes. The teacher acts as an adviser and offers guidance when it is requested. Students should be allowed to take as much time as necessary to make their preparations. The instructor observes the behavior of the students and leads them into the next phase when they are ready.

Phase 2: Performance. A chosen person from each group performs his or her role. This is done with the support of the group. At any time the player can call for a break and go back to the support group for guidance on what to say or do next; the group may also choose to call their representative back to the group for advice or assistance. These strategies are particularly effective when the performer encounters a part of the other performer's game plan that she or he had not anticipated.

During the performance, the teacher and the rest of the class are spectators. This phase is usually shortest. It can be a few minutes long, or it can go 15 minutes or more. This will depend on the students' level and their involvement in the situation. Di Pietro found that the average length of scenario performances is about five minutes.

Phase 3: Debriefing. The teacher leads the whole class in a discussion of the performance. Students are invited to think of alternative solutions to the situation and how those alternatives might have played out. After discussion of the performance as a speech event, the instructor and class will want to move on to the speech used and look at it in terms of grammar, vocabulary, pronunciation, and cultural conventions. This is the time, particularly if a transcript of the performance has been made, to look at recasting it in a more fluent style, to lead the class in expanding on what was said, to give explanations of points the students question, and to do exercises of various types.

In discussing the speech used during the performance, the instructor must take special pains not to identify a particular person as having made an error. To embarrass a student would be to discourage all the students from being willing to participate in further scenarios. Rather, if errors are remarked upon, it is done for the edification of all. As students participate in the discussion and ask questions, instructors are cautioned to keep explanations simple and direct. Launching into a long discussion of a particular grammar point may not answer the question asked and may well lose the interest and attention of all the students.

Again, the time necessary for this phase will vary. It is up to the instructor to monitor the behavior of the students and decide when it is time to move on.

The debriefing may be followed by complementary reading and/or writing activities. Students may read newspaper articles related to the situation they enacted or write letters as follow-ups to one of the characters in a scenario. Perhaps the scenario involved an accident. The students might need to write up a report about what happened. Alternatively, the group can collaborate to produce a written version of what was said or a written version of what might happen as a result of the interactions in the original scenario.

Language proficiency. Employees of the United States government whose work assignments require language ability are tested. Their abilities in speaking, reading, and understanding are assigned proficiency scores ranging from 0 to 5. A rating of 0 means no language ability, 1 is elementary proficiency, 2 is limited working proficiency, 3 is general professional proficiency, 4 is advanced professional proficiency, and 5 is native ability. The goal of language students at the Central Intelligence Agency is level 3 for field assignments. (For difficult languages, the goal is level 2.)

The student who attains a level 3 in speaking ability is able to speak with enough structural accuracy and vocabulary to effectively take part in most formal and informal conversations on practical, social, and professional topics. The student may make some errors when using the language, but the errors do not interfere with understanding and seldom disturb the native speaker. Examples of ways the level 3 student can use language in a work setting include answering objections, clarifying points, justifying decisions, understanding the essence of challenges, stating and defending policy, conducting meetings, and delivering briefings.

Scenarios and the CIA. Di Pietro presented a series of workshops to the instructors of the Language Training Division (LTD) of the Central Intelligence Agency in 1990. He talked about his methodology and taught the instructors how to write scenarios. Di Pietro was invited to the CIA because instructors were concerned that language students frequently plateau at the 2 or 2+ levels (limited working proficiency). The instructors were interested in learning a technique that might assist them in helping students make the jump to level 3. Also, most of the language instructors at the CIA are native speakers of the languages they teach. They have no experience at the sorts of activities their students will perform in the course of their jobs. They view scenarios as an opportunity to make the language the students learn more job relevant and useful.

The instructors wrote 75 unclassified scenarios during the time that Di Pietro worked with them. These scenarios reside in a central computer system for the use of any language instructor. Typical of the scenarios they created is the following:

"The meeting's the thing. . ."
Realia for the scenario: A detailed city plan

Role A: You have to arrange a meeting with the president of Total Security. The meeting needs to be held as soon as possible and in a private place so as not to compromise what you will talk about. Call and make the arrangements. Be sure to get accurate directions.

Role B: You are the Director of Development of Total Security. You've been told to take any calls from Role A and make arrangements for a meeting between Role A and your president. The president is involved in meetings from 9:00 a.m. to 8:00 p.m. for the next week and can't make the arrangements herself. Also, she has said she wants you to be present at any meeting so she has a witness to anything said. Try to set up a meeting for next week for the three of you. Agree on the time and place.

In this scenario, the tasks are interlocked in that Role A and Role B must talk to each other to accomplish their goals. The *shared* information is that there should be a meeting between Role A and the president of Total Security and that it should take place soon. Also shared is the city map that will be used for making the meeting arrangements. The *unshared* information for Role A is that he or she wants the meeting to be in private; for Role B the unshared information is that he or she has been directed to set up the meeting and be present when it takes place.

The instructors who went back to the classroom and used the scenarios developed during the workshops with Di Pietro (or scenarios they or their students wrote) report that the students enact scenarios with great enthusiasm. The students' comments indicate that they appreciate the opportunity to tailor their language training more specifically to the jobs they will be holding and to practice practical situations in the safety of the classroom.

There has not been formal testing of control and test groups to evaluate the effectiveness of scenarios in helping students reach level 3. However, the instructors and students who use them are very pleased with their incorporation into the curriculum. They are a welcome addition to an instructor's bag of tricks to help students learn and to keep them motivated and involved.

Summary. Scenarios have been in use in foreign-language classrooms of the Central Intelligence Agency since 1990 to assist students in the development of higher-level language skills. Although there has not been controlled testing of the effectiveness of the method, the instructors who use scenarios in their classes say that the students take part in them with great enthusiasm. Learning to write scenarios is not a complicated process, and students are able to quickly learn to write them. This allows the students to set up situations typical of what they might encounter in future work assignments and tailor their language training to better prepare them for those assignments.

REFERENCE

Di Pietro, Robert J. 1987. *Strategic interaction: Learning languages through Scenarios*. New York: Cambridge University Press.

Report on the pilot study of *Learning Strategies for the Japanese Language Classroom*

Jill Robbins
Georgetown University

Research on learning strategies and language learning. This project is based on the work of J. Michael O'Malley and Anna Uhl Chamot, who have directed research toward the description of learning strategies used by second- and foreign-language learners.

Definitions and classification of learning strategies. As with any new field of study, there are several working definitions of learning strategies that have been used as guidelines for research. The definition used in this study is "*Learning strategies* are the thoughts or behaviors that individuals use to help them comprehend, learn, or retain new information" (O'Malley and Chamot 1990: 1). Wenden (1987) identified the specific characteristics of *language-learner strategies* as language-learning behaviors that (1) refer to specific actions, not learner characteristics; (2) can be observable or non-observable; (3) are problem oriented; (4) contribute to learning directly or indirectly; (5) may be consciously employed; and 6) are amenable to change.

McGroarty (1988) studied learners of Spanish and Japanese and identified behaviors that predicted achievement in the foreign language. Learning strategies that were associated with success in learning Japanese were divided into two categories: *seeking input* and *practicing output*. In the first category, the effective strategies were guessing meaning from gestures, asking teacher about exceptions, listening to L2 (target language) radio, and watching L2 TV. In the *practicing output* category, the effective strategies were thinking first in L2, not being afraid to volunteer in class, and thinking of alternative expressions. Although the students in McGroarty's study did not receive direct instruction in learning strategies, she suggests that their successful techniques can be taught in order to improve the performance of other learners of the foreign language.

O'Malley and Chamot's strategy classification scheme was developed based on the distinction in cognitive psychology between metacognitive and cognitive strategies, adding a third category for social–affective strategies.

- *Metacognitive strategies* involve executive processes in planning for learning, monitoring one's comprehension and production, and evaluating how well one has achieved a learning objective.

- *Cognitive strategies* are those in which the learner interacts with the material to be learned. This can be achieved by manipulating it mentally, as in making mental images or elaborating on previously acquired concepts or skills, or physically, as in grouping items to be learned in meaningful categories or taking notes on important information to be remembered.
- *Socio-affective strategies* are those in which the learner either interacts with another person in order to assist learning, as in cooperation or asking questions for clarification, or uses some kind of affective control to assist a learning task.

Originally developed for ESL students, this tripartite scheme has been validated for students of other foreign languages (O'Malley and Chamot 1990).

Previous training programs in learning-strategy instruction for foreign language learners. A study conducted by Chamot and Küpper (1989) with learners of Russian and Spanish provided information on the different ways that effective and ineffective learners applied metacognitive, cognitive, and social-affective strategies to learning tasks. Both groups were found to use learning strategies, but the more-effective students had a greater range of strategies and used them more appropriately than the less-effective students. One component of the study was *course development*, in which instructors selected and taught strategies for listening, reading, and speaking. It was found that learning-strategy instruction could be implemented by the foreign language instructor rather than a researcher. The success of the teacher-implemented strategies instruction depended on the teachers' interest in learning strategies, their development of techniques for instructing students in the effective use of learning strategies (e.g. modeling, providing practice opportunities), and their ability to motivate students by proving the value of learning strategies. These findings influenced decisions made on how to integrate learning-strategy instruction with a Japanese curriculum in the current study.

A number of other studies have been carried out to describe learning strategies used by foreign-language learners and experiments with strategy training. Oxford et al. (1990) reviewed strategy training programs and concluded that training that is integrated into regular classroom tasks is most effective and that the training should be overt and explicit, thereby allowing learners to transfer, monitor, and evaluate their strategy use. Learners with these abilities are more self-directed, confident, and efficient.

Proposal for the project. Japanese has become an important language for Americans to learn, and it is taught at increasing numbers of schools throughout the country. Yet, because of the language's unique characteristics, one cannot assume that research on learning strategies for other languages, especially Indo-European languages, can be applied to the teaching of Japanese. In 1990, a proposal was made to the Department of Education, International Research and Studies Program, for a three-year study titled "Learning Strategies in Japanese Foreign Language Instruction." The study was carried out by Language Research Projects of Georgetown University.[1]

This study addressed four research questions:

(1) Which learning strategies are selected by Japanese instructors as most beneficial to their students?
(2) How can learning strategies be taught to high school and college students of Japanese?
(3) Do students instructed in learning strategies apply the strategies independently and do they continue to apply them in subsequent levels of language study?
(4) Do students who use learning strategies more frequently show greater language proficiency and perceive themselves as more effective learners than students who use strategies less frequently?

The first two years of the study were designed as a pilot study, with the third year an experimental study, comparing classes receiving strategies instruction with classes not receiving the instruction.

Procedures of the study.

Development Study. The first student-centered activity of the project was to determine, through interviews with students at beginning and advanced levels, what they were already doing to learn Japanese. The information gained from these interviews was used to develop a *Learning Strategies Questionnaire* (LSQ), which asked students to indicate the frequency of their application of learning strategies to particular tasks. Other instruments developed and pilot tested during the first year of the project were a *Self-Efficacy Questionnaire* (SEQ), which asked students to indicate on a Likert-type scale the degree to which they feel able to perform specific language-learning tasks, and a *Proficiency/Achievement Test* (PRF), which included reading and listening tasks. The SEQ and the PRF

1. The principal investigator during the first year of the study was J. Michael O'Malley; from October 1991 the principal investigator was Richard T. Thompson. The project director is Anna Uhl Chamot. The research associate in the first year was Lisa Küpper, and from October 1991 was Jill Robbins. Data analysis was done by research associates Pamela El-Dinary and Jill Robbins. Consultants were Miwa Nishimura, Motoko Omori, Sachiko Shudo, Kazue Watlington, and Fumiko Yuasa.

tests were geared to the instructional level; for example, the high school students were not taught romaji (Japanese written in the Latin alphabet), so they were not asked any questions dealing with learning it or requiring them to use it.

Strategies chosen for instruction. The first research question was answered in the course of developing and pilot testing a resource guide for learning-strategy instruction for Japanese. This resource guide was based on a guide developed by Chamot and Küpper (1989) and was reviewed by the Japanese instructors and consultants during the first year of the study. This resource guide was closely matched to the specific curriculum of each level of Japanese and to the goals of the Japanese programs at the schools involved in the study. Since the college beginning-Japanese program emphasized speaking and listening skills, strategies that help with listening comprehension and oral communication were chosen for instruction. At the high school level, reading and writing in hiragana were emphasized along with the development of basic vocabulary and knowledge of grammatical structures. Therefore, the strategies chosen for the high school class were intended to help with memorizing new material through elaboration, imagery, and focusing attention.

Japanese names were given to some of the strategies; teachers involved in the project wanted to be able to refer to the strategies without switching into English. At the high school level, the students did not accept the use of Japanese names, so the teacher decided to use only English names for the strategies. In the college class, teachers continued to use Japanese names for the strategies, when possible. This allowed them to use only Japanese as the language of instruction. The learning strategies selected for use at both levels, and the definitions given to students, are listed below.

(1) Metacognitive Strategies.
- Directed Attention *(Syuutyuu)* – Deciding in advance to pay attention to a learning activity and to ignore distractions
- Selective Attention *(Pointosyuutyuu)* – Deciding to pay attention to specific aspects of a language listening or reading activity.

(2) Cognitive Strategies.
- Contextualization *(Bamen Zukuri)* – Using real objects to associate meanings with words or phrases, acting out words or phrases; putting language into its real-life context.
- Creative Repetition – Varying the ways you repeat, making up stories, new dialogues, etc.
- Grouping *(Nakamawake)* – Classifying and sorting vocabulary words in a way that is personally meaningful to you, remembering words or other information based on previous groupings.

- Imagery *(Imeezi)* – Using actual pictures or forming a specific mental image to help remember new material.
- Personalization *(Genzituka)* – Making meaningful personal associations with new material.
- Prediction *(Yoki)* – Using what you know to predict what will be said in an exchange or to anticipate what might be said in discussion of a topic.
- Silent Repetition *(Ansyoo)* – Letting the most recent sound to enter your ears echo, or play back, for a few seconds after hearing it, in order to gain more time in which to process the information and understand it fully.

(3) Social–Affective Strategies.

- Questioning *(Chekku)* – Asking for confirmation that you have correctly understood another's speech; showing your understanding of what has been said to you without committing yourself to a response immediately.
- Cooperation – Working with classmates in a noncompetitive manner to help each other practice and improve language skills.

Learning-strategy instruction. The second year of the study, involving the implementation of learning-strategy instruction, was aimed at translating the resource guide into actual classroom practice. The high school group was the Level 1 Japanese class at a suburban high school. The college group was the Intensive Japanese Level 1 class at a private university, with 20 students. Following the administration of the pretests, the learning-strategy instruction began with several worksheets that asked students to reflect on how language learning is different from learning other subjects and to report on the learning techniques they had developed in their first month of studying Japanese.

The second research question, "How can learning strategies be taught?", was answered over the course of the second year of the study, as a process evolved for presenting learning strategies. After the teacher had made the students aware of the singular requirements of language learning, she told them about the value of learning strategies for improving their language-learning ability. The teacher introduced individual strategies one at a time and suggested specific activities for practice in the classroom or outside of school. The teacher first described each strategy, then modeled it. The teacher then led the students through a specific activity in which the strategy could be used and asked them to respond to questions on worksheets about the value of the strategy for their own study of Japanese.

As the year went on, the teachers involved with the study continued to provide their lesson plans to the researcher, who wrote strategy lessons that were closely blended with their daily classwork. Certain elements of the curriculum for elementary Japanese seemed to lend themselves to the use of particular strategies. For example, when numbers were first taught, the Silent Repetition strategy was introduced: Students were told to let the sound of the number echo in their minds, or play it back silently to themselves, until they could process it and figure out what number was being said. Then, when the numeral quantifier *-tu* was taught, the Selective Attention strategy was suggested: Students were asked to listen to a series of sentences. In each sentence, they were to listen for the number by paying attention to what word was attached to the suffix *-tu*. The use of other numeral quantifiers was practiced through Contextualization: Students were asked to hold props such as newspapers, apples, books, sheets of paper, and so on, while they said the number of items and used the correct numeral quantifier, which changes with the type of object being referred to.

Later in the year, when phone numbers occurred in the college-level dialogues, the strategy of Silent Repetition was practiced again in an information-gap activity (Student Worksheets 21A and 21B, in Appendix A) that required students to ask each other for phone numbers of local businesses. The students were instructed to wait for a moment before writing down the number, to let it "echo" in their mind. They were given a reason for the practice of this strategy: There may be times when you can't ask the speaker for a repetition, such as when you hear a number on the radio or get a recording on the telephone.

Another strategy that was found especially useful for the college-level curriculum is Prediction *(Yoki)*, used to improve listening comprehension when working with the tapes that accompany the textbook. Student Worksheet 21C shows how this strategy was applied: First, students were told the situation in the tape: A woman was calling a university to speak to a professor. Then, students were asked to think of the type of language they might hear; in this case it would be polite, using ritual phrases typical of telephone conversations. Some specific questions were asked about the conversation, and students were asked to predict what words might be used in answer to those questions. The teacher then played the tape, and the students listened for the answers to the questions. Students wrote the answers on the worksheet, comparing their original predictions with what they heard.

Each class was observed in the process of receiving the instruction and practicing the strategies. Worksheets often asked for student feedback in the form of comments on how useful certain strategies were to them, and on the areas of difficulty they encountered in their study of Japanese. A midyear review and survey of their strategy use was conducted. The results of this survey helped to clarify how well the students understood each strategy and asked whether students were using the strategies on their own, outside of class.

One of the problems that arises when providing learning-strategy instruction at the beginning level of any foreign language is the need for teachers to explain the strategies in English. Teachers who are using a communicative style of teaching try to use the target language in class as much as possible. The teachers involved in this study felt somewhat awkward when the time came to explain strategies in English; switching out of Japanese seemed to disturb the flow of their instruction. Giving the strategies Japanese names was one way that this problem was addressed. Teachers felt that if they could remind students to use strategies while still speaking Japanese, it would help them to fit the strategy instruction and practice more closely with their curriculum. The students at the high school level didn't relate to the Japanese names for the strategies, and halfway through the year the teacher decided to refer to strategy names in English. At the college level, the students were more willing to learn the strategy names in Japanese, but they seemed to prefer using the English names to discuss them. A possible reason for the students' reluctance to use Japanese strategy names is that they are not *thinking in Japanese* about their learning processes. If they were, using the Japanese strategy names would make sense. But since they are thinking in English, they naturally use strategy names in English to describe their thought processes.

The problem of having to use English to describe strategies and lead students through practice in strategies is more serious with a language like Japanese than it is with languages that are more closely related to English. In a parallel study (conducted by Language Research Projects) with learners of Spanish, teachers were able to use more of the target language to conduct the strategies instruction, and they used only Spanish names for the strategies. Still, even the Spanish teachers were concerned that they had to use some English for the initial explanation and modeling of strategies. Future research at more advanced levels of Japanese will address the question of the extent to which the target language can be used for strategies instruction.

Results. At the end of the school year, each class was given the *Proficiency Posttest* to measure students' achievement in Japanese. The *Learning Strategies Questionnaire* was given to determine how their strategy use had changed over the year, and the *Language Learning Self-Efficacy Rating* was given to find out if their confidence level had changed as a result of their experience in class, along with the experience of receiving strategy instruction.

Independent use of learning strategies. The third research question of this study, regarding students' use of learning strategies, has two parts: (1) Do students instructed in learning strategies apply the strategies independently? and (2) Do they continue to apply them in subsequent levels of language study? The first part of this question can be answered with qualitative data; during the first year of the study, students were asked on worksheets and on the midyear questionnaire to describe how they studied the various elements of their Japanese curriculum (vocabulary, speaking, listening, reading). The students' descriptions of their techniques for studying Japanese were coded for strategies.[2] Based on their descriptions, it appears that students did apply strategies independently and that they had many more strategies at their disposal than the set that was taught to them. Their strategies were creative and individual; while some students relied on brute memorization, others made up stories with their new words. One student didn't believe in using phonetic spelling of Japanese words, another relied on the phonetic spellings to remember how the words sound. One student imagined a Japanese family and visualized them acting out scenes to connect new words with. Appendix B contains a list of representative student comments, showing the strategies they used.

Table 1 compares the self-reported strategies of high school and college students. It is apparent from the important position of Kinesthetic and Auditory Practice and of Repetition that rote memorization is a very high priority to their study of Japanese. This is probably because vocabulary building is the major focus at the beginning level of language learning. In contrast, Repetition was much lower on the college student's list of strategies; it was replaced by strategies that assist in listening (*selective attention*) and speaking (*contextualization*) tasks. Comparing the high school and college classes overall, the college students self-reported significantly more metacognitive strategies ($t=3.40$, $df=28$, $p=.002$) than the high school students.

Most of the self-reported techniques fell into the category of cognitive strategies. These strategies reflect, on the whole, an approach that is more focused on accomplishing specific learning tasks, like memorizing and immediate understanding. The goals of the third year of this study are to provide more instruction and practice in metacognitive and social-affective strategies, which guide overall learning and understanding.

The qualitative information collected from the student responses throughout the second year was found to be very useful in making adjustments to the study for its third year. Changes were made in the initial presentation of learning strategies, presenting them within a model of how they could be applied. This model included the steps Planning, Monitoring, Problem-Solving, and Evaluation. Through the use of this model, the researchers intend to familiarize students with the metacognitive processes involved in learning.

---

2. At the high school level, the total number of self-reported strategies and the categories of strategies they represented were significantly correlated with the corresponding LSQ data. For metacognitive strategies: $r=.425$, $p=.050$; cognitive strategies: $r=.626$, $p=.005$; social-affective strategies: $r=.466$, $p=.034$. At the college level, correlations were found between total self-reported strategies and total LSQ average: $r=.672$, $p=.002$, and also between the self-reported social-affective strategies and social-affective strategies on the LSQ: $r=.489$, $p=.038$.

Table 1. Self-reported strategy use at high school and college levels

High School		College	
Strategy	Freq.[1]	Strategy	Freq.[1]
Kinesthetic/Auditory Practice	0.88	Selective Attention	0.93
Selective Attention	0.81	Contextualization	0.86
Repetition	0.81	Grouping	0.86
Associations	0.75	Directed Attention	0.79
Directed Attention	0.69	Prediction	0.71
Imagery	0.63	Imagery	0.71
Grouping	0.50	Personalization	0.57
Questioning	0.50	Repetition	0.43
Cooperation	0.38	Silent Repetition	0.43
Resourcing	0.31	Self Management	0.36
Translation	0.31	Kinesthetic/Auditory Practice	0.36
Practice with others outside class	0.31	Questioning	0.36
Using nonverbal cues	0.19	Resourcing	0.30
Self management	0.13	Associations	0.21
Inferencing	0.13	Cooperation	0.21
Note-taking	0.13	Practice with others outside class	0.21
Prediction	0.06	Inferencing	0.14
Transfer	0.06	Deduction/Induction	0.07

1. Percentage of students reporting this strategy.
Strategies above the dashed line were reported by 50% or more of the students.

Continuation of independent strategy use. Most of the students who were in the first-year classes are now studying Japanese at the second-year level. These students have been given the LSQ and SEQ and have been rated by their teachers. Preliminary results indicate that the level of strategy use remains constant in individual students over the first year following learning-strategy instruction.

Examination of strategy use, self-efficacy, and proficiency. The quantitative results obtained from the study should be interpreted with caution because of the small size of the student sample. Analysis of the LSQ showed no significant differences across instruction groups or from pretest to posttest. Some strategies increased in use slightly from pre- to posttests, but at the college level none were statistically significant. At the high school level, the strategy that increased significantly in frequency of use was production monitoring (checking one's oral or written production as it's taking place), at $t=2.71$, $df=9$, $p=.024$. This was not among the strategies selected to be taught, but it was apparently learned through the students' experience over seven months of language study.

Do high school students who use strategies more often have greater language proficiency? In the following discussion, all results are from the posttests unless specified otherwise. A correlation analysis was performed with Proficiency (PRF) and Learning Strategies Questionnaire (LSQ) scores. The relationship between the total score on the PRF and the total score on the LSQ was not significant at $p \leq .05$. However, the reading section of the PRF did correlate with the total LSQ ($r=.598$, $p=.026$). The listening section of the PRF correlated with the reported use of vocabulary strategies on the LSQ ($r=.697$, $p=.009$). This led to the question, "Was the listening section really more of a test of vocabulary?" On examination, the "listening" test was found to contain items that depended upon the students' knowledge of vocabulary in order to answer correctly. By reading the question (in English) before hearing the conversation given for each test item, a student could (using the strategy Selective Attention) simply listen for the Japanese word that would answer the question.

Teacher ranking was based on the students' abilities across all language skills. This ranking was one of our measures of proficiency. A correlation was also done on teacher ranking of the high school students and overall LSQ scores; it showed no significant results at $p \leq .05$. When strategies were classified into categories, however, teacher ranking correlated with use of cognitive ($r=.471$, $p=.033$) and social-affective ($r=.435$, $p=.046$) strategies. Although the differences found when comparing proficiency groups were not statistically significant with the small sample, some patterns emerged. At the high school level, the high-proficiency group reported more frequent use (frequency of 3.29 on a scale of 1 = never to 5 = always) of strategies overall than the low-proficiency group (frequency of 2.61).

Do college students who use strategies more often have greater language proficiency? A correlation analysis was performed on the mean averages of the LSQ with the PRF for the college class. A moderate correlation was found between the reported use of vocabulary strategies on the LSQ and the overall score for the PRF ($r=.549$, $p=.026$). A moderate correlation was also found between the reading proficiency section of the PRF and reported use of vocabulary strategies on the LSQ ($r=.585$, $p=.018$).

Another correlation analysis was done on the teacher's ranking of students with their LSQ scores. A moderate correlation was found between teacher ranking and overall LSQ (r=.502, p=.028). Teacher ranking also correlated with reported use of metacognitive strategies on the LSQ (r=.688, p=.003). A t-test showed that the high-proficiency group used metacognitive strategies more frequently than the low-proficiency group (t=3.27, df=8, p=.011).

Do students who use strategies more frequently perceive themselves as more effective learners than students who use the strategies less frequently? The findings of this study indicate that there aren't *any* students who don't use learning strategies. From the results above, we know that while all students use some learning strategies, the higher-proficiency students tend to use learning strategies more often than lower-proficiency students. To find out if students who use strategies more often see themselves as more effective learners, their scores on the Self-Efficacy Questionnaire (SEQ) were compared to their LSQ scores. The SEQ asked students to rate their abilities to perform specific language-learning tasks, such as memorizing a list of kanji, reading and pronouncing a dialogue, and so on. Tables 2 and 3 show the correlations between the SEQ and the LSQ. At the high school level, there was an overall relationship between strategy use and self-efficacy (r=.691, p=.013). This relationship was not significant at the college level.

Table 2. High School SEQ and LSQ posttest correlations

Students: 10	SEQ AVG	Hir. & Kat. Voc.	Kan. Voc.	Hir. & Kat. Dia.	Hir. & Kat. Rdg.	Soc. Sit.
LSQ AVG	**r=.691** **p=.013**	**.691** **.013**	.009 .490	**.736** **.008**	**.773** **.004**	**.651** **.021**
Task 1: Vocabulary	**.591** **.036**	**.757** **.006**	-.245 .247	**.733** **.008**	**.775** **.004**	**.545** **.051**
Task 2: Listening	.475 .083	.361 .152	.298 .201	.366 .149	.366 .149	.435 .104
Task 3: Speaking in Class	**.642** **.023**	**.536** **.055**	.106 .385	**.653** **.020**	**.692** **.013**	**.624** **.027**

Bold type indicates significant correlations.
Key: Voc. = vocabulary; Dia. = dialogue; Rdg. = reading; Rom. = romaji; Hir. = hiragana; Kat. = katakana; Kan = kanji; Soc. Sit. = social situation.

Some interesting patterns emerged at both high school and college levels. At the high school level, the use of strategies for listening didn't seem to have anything to do with self-efficacy. Perhaps this was because listening to tapes was not required at the high school level, and there was not as much emphasis on oral skills as at the college level. A similar situation existed with the high school students' self-efficacy rating on kanji vocabulary, which was unrelated to all aspects of learning-strategy use; at the high school level kanji was not taught until late in the year, so the students had no experience in learning kanji when they took the posttest LSQ.

Table 3. College SEQ and LSQ Posttest Correlations

		Vocabulary			Dialogue		Rdg.	
Students: 15	SEQ AVG	Rom.	Hir & Kat	Kan.	Rom.	Hir., Kat., Kan.	Hir. & Kat.	Soc. Sit.
LSQ AVG	r= .436	.428	.226	**.500**	.408	**.536**	.223	.239
	P= .052	.056	.208	**.029**	.065	**.020**	.212	.195
Task 1: Vocab.	-.110	.158	-.426	.0009	.057	.078	-.268	.007
Learning	.348	.286	.056	.499	.420	.390	.167	.489
Task 2:	**.460**	.132	**.461**	**.443**	.388	**.442**	.421	.235
Listening	**.042**	.319	**.042**	**.049**	.076	**.049**	.059	.199
Task 3: Speaking in	**.473**	.397	.312	**.495**	.380	**.639**	.290	.199
Class	**.037**	.071	.129	**.030**	.081	**.005**	.147	.237

Bold type indicates significant correlations.
Key: Rdg.= reading; Rom.= romaji; Hir. = hiragana; Kat.= katakana; Kan.= kanji; Soc. Sit.= social situation

At the college level, the individual SEQ tasks on Table 2 that were *not* significantly correlated with LSQ were relatively easy; they probably didn't require the college students to frequently employ learning strategies. Those SEQ tasks that *were* significantly correlated with LSQ were more challenging ones: reading and memorizing kanji vocabulary and reading dialogues written in kana. These tasks would be easier for those students with a strong repertoire of learning strategies. Overall correlations between listening and speaking LSQ scores and the average of SEQ scores reflects the emphasis of the college Japanese curriculum: Speaking and listening are of fundamental importance. Those college students who have developed a set of effective strategies for listening and speaking would have the most self-confidence in language learning in this situation.

There seems to have been a definite change along these lines over the seven months since the pretests were given. Only two correlations showed up between the pretest LSQ and SEQ; those were on romaji vocabulary learning and kanji vocabulary. This is evidence for the value of learning-strategy training that is integrated with a particular curriculum: If learners are given the strategies they need to meet the specific demands of their program, they will feel more confident about their language-learning ability.

Conclusions. Although the number of students participating in this study was small, some patterns appeared that tend to confirm earlier research on learning strategies and point to directions for future research. For example, students do use learning strategies independently, and they have a wide range of cognitive strategies that they apply to their study of Japanese. As in Vandergrift's (1992) study of novice learners of French, these Japanese novice learners used predominantly cognitive strategies. As Vandergrift suggested, these cognitive strategies can be augmented by the governing influence of metacognitive strategies and the motivational benefits of social–affective strategies. Future strategies instruction should emphasize the value of metacognitive and social–affective strategies in guiding language learning.

At both high school and college levels, proficiency seemed to be related to the use of vocabulary-learning strategies. The teacher's ranking of students' proficiency was also related to strategy use. Additionally, college students at the high-proficiency level used a greater number of strategies at a higher frequency than did lower-proficiency college students. Among the important questions that arise in relation to strategies training, we must ask: Why don't the lower-proficiency students use learning strategies as much as their peers? Is it because they don't know what the strategies are (perhaps the instruction in this study wasn't getting through to them), or is it that they don't know how to apply the strategies to language-learning tasks? At what age or instructional level is it appropriate to teach the metacognitive strategies needed for task evaluation?

Finally, questions arise that deal with the level of difficulty faced by most Americans who are learning Japanese and with the teaching methods that are used in U.S. schools. In the interest of having more students continue their study of Japanese beyond the elementary level, it would be beneficial to use a method that helps students to feel more confident about their ability to learn the language, which is what learning-strategy use seems to do. If learning strategies are integrated with the curriculum, would there be a lower attrition rate in Japanese classes? And would the students who remain in the class be able to reach a higher level of proficiency, thanks to their use of learning strategies?

As the economic and cultural ties between the United States and Japan become stronger, it will be increasingly important for Americans to achieve more than an elementary understanding of the Japanese language. Since so little is known about how Americans are learning Japanese, further research into the questions raised by this study is imperative. Producing a generation of American students with ample opportunities to gain fluency in Japanese will require that we carefully examine our methods of teaching it and look for ways to improve the learner's prospects for success in learning Japanese. Learning-strategies instruction merits further research as a way of promoting successful Japanese language learning.

REFERENCES

Chamot, Anna Uhl, and Lisa Küpper. 1989. "Learning strategies in foreign language instruction." *Foreign Language Annals* 22(1): 13–24.

McGroarty, Mary. 1988. *University foreign language learning: Spanish and Japanese*. Los Angeles: Center for Language Education and Research, University of California.

O'Malley, J. Michael, and Anna Uhl Chamot. 1990. *Learning strategies in second language acquisition*. Cambridge: Cambridge University Press.

Oxford, Rebecca, David Crookall, Andrew Cohen, Roberta Lavine, Martha Nyikos, and Will Sutter. 1990. "Strategy training for language learners: Six situational case studies and a training model." *Foreign Language Annals* 23(3): 197–215.

Vandergrift, Laurens. 1992. *The comprehension strategies of second language (French) listeners*. Unpublished doctoral dissertation, University of Alberta (Canada).

Wenden, Anita. 1987. "Incorporating learner training in the classroom." In Anita Wenden and Joan Rubin (eds.), *Learner strategies in language learning*. Englewood Cliffs, N.J.: Prentice-Hall.

Appendix A. Samples of Learning-strategy Instruction

The following lessons are related to the textbook *Japanese, The Spoken Language,* by Eleaner Harz Jorden with Mari Noda

Material: Lesson 12 A Application and Utilization
Worksheets: Student Worksheet 21 (A and B versions) - Denwa Bangoo - Ansyoo
Objectives: To practice **Ansyoo** (Silent Repetition) with telephone numbers.

Description of Activities

1. For application A, p.329, hand out the worksheet, being careful to give alternating students the A and B versions. Have students sit back to back, and ask their partners for the telephone numbers they lack on their own sheets. Tell them,

> "When you are given the phone number, don't write it down as you hear it. After listening to the phone number, use **Ansyoo**—play back the number in your mind, immediately after you hear it. Then write it down. In a real-life situation, you will be able to use this skill, **Ansyoo**, for the times when someone says a number too quickly for you to write it down—or when you hear a number on the radio, for example, and can't ask for a repetition."

Name:_______________________________ Date:_____________________

****

Student Worksheet 21 A - Denwa Bangoo no Ansyoo

****

Instructions:

- Sit with your back to your partner.
- In Japanese, ask your partner for these telephone numbers.
- When your partner says the number, *don't write it down as s/he says it.* Wait a few seconds and **try to hear it echo in your mind.** As you may remember, this is the strategy called **Ansyoo**, or Silent Repetition; playing back a sound immediately after hearing it.
- After you have heard the number *a second time,* as it echoes in your mind, **write it down**.

This technique may seem like an extra step for you now, but in the future there will be times when you won't be able to ask for a repetition—hearing a number on the radio, or getting a recording on the telephone. If you practice this now you'll develop a skill that will help you in such situations.

Ask the number of:	(Use Ansyoo!)	Tell the number of:	
Riggs Bank		Vital Vittles	944-2296
G.U. Bookstore		Parking Office	688-4355
Tower Records		Domino's Pizza	342-0100
Financial Aid		Japanese Dept.	688-5918

Name:______________________________Date:____________________

****

Student Worksheet 21 B - Denwa Bangoo no Ansyoo

****

Instructions:

- Sit with your back to your partner.
- In Japanese, ask your partner for these telephone numbers.
- When your partner says the number, *don't write it down as s/he says it.* Wait a few seconds and **try to hear it echo in your mind**. As you may remember, this is the strategy called **Ansyoo**, or Silent Repetition; playing back a sound immediately after hearing it.
- After you have heard the number *a second time,* as it echoes in your mind, **write it down**.

This technique may seem like an extra step for you now, but in the future there will be times when you won't be able to ask for a repetition—hearing a number on the radio, or getting a recording on the telephone. If you practice this now you'll develop a skill that will help you in such situations.

Ask the number of:	(Use Ansyoo!)	Tell the number of:	
Vital Vittles		Riggs Bank	835-7378
Parking Office		G.U. Bookstore	688-7482
Domino's Pizza		Tower Records	331-2400
Japanese Dept.		Financial Aid	688-4547

Material: Lesson 12 B CC 1, Drills A, G, H

Worksheets: Student Worksheet 21C - Yoki (Prediction) and Pointosyuutyuu (Selective Attention

Objectives: To get more practice using **Yoki** (Prediction) and **Pointosyuutyuu** (Selective Attention) with the Core Conversations.

Description of Activities

---

1. Before viewing Core Conversation 1 on the tape, have students think about the conversations and make predictions on the worksheet. First ask what style they expect that the caller will use: polite or casual style. Then ask them to think about what usually takes place during phone conversations. For example, the person who answers the phone usually identifies the location called, the person called is either there or not there, and if that person is not there, the caller either calls back or asks for a return call. Based on this background knowledge, students can assume the three questions on the worksheet might be answered by the conversation. Have them predict what words they will hear that will answer those questions: For the first question, the name will have 'daigaku' ('university' attached to it. For the second question, the professor will have the title 'sensei' after his name. Tell students,

"Now that you have made predictions about the words you might hear in answer to these questions, listen selectively for those words when I play the tape. When you hear one of those words, you know the answer will be adjacent to it."

Name:_______________________________Date:____________________

****

Student Worksheet 21 C - Yoki and Pointosyuutyuu

****

Instructions: Before listening to the tape of CC 2 and 3, think about the conversation you are going to hear. In #2, a woman is calling a professor at a university. What type of speech do you expect to hear? ____

I. Jot down any words you think you might hear in answer to these questions:

1.	What university did she call?	
2.	Whom does she want to talk to?	
3.	Is the person called in?	

II. Now listen to the tape. Answer the questions if you can. If not, listen again.

1.	What university did she call?	
2.	Whom does she want to talk to?	
3.	Is the person called in?	

III. Have you used this technique, **Yoki** (predicting) at home when you listen to the audio tapes? Does it help you? If you haven't used it on your own yet, give it a try, and see if it works for you.

Appendix B. Student Comments on Strategy Use

Metacognitive Strategies

Directed Attention

- Listen carefully
- Divorce myself from distractions
- Give your undivided attention when listening to a foreign language

Selective Attention

- Look for key words or phrases
- Remember the key aspects of characters (strokes)
- Ignore unknown words—listen to what I know
- Look at the sentence structure
- Listen for the main idea
- Read for comprehension of detail and imagery
- Listen for the correct way of pronouncing the new vocabulary
- Pick out the words I do understand and try to make an educated guess about what was said

Prediction

- Think of the topic/phrases in book
- Review and look ahead in the book so you have an idea of what will be said
- Think up many vocabulary words that might fit the situation of the core conversation

Self-Management

- Say only what I know and get help on what I don't know
- Speak on tape and listen to myself
- Speak slowly
- Work on pronunciation
- (I use Prediction) so I can be calm when the question is asked
- Say them in my head and see if I say it right

Cognitive Strategies

Silent Repetition

- Let what is said echo in my mind

Kinesthetic or Auditory Repetition

- Air-brush characters (draw in the air with a finger)
- Write it down to get a better feel of it
- Write it again and again
- Read aloud while thinking about inflection of how the words is said
- Say while writing

Associations

- Remember sight and sound associations
- Use flashcards with pictures on them
- Look for any similarities between the Hiragana and Kanji spellings
- Think of an English word that sounds like the Japanese word
- Relate to what I already know about Japanese

Personalization

- Associate with things in my life
- Associated the characters with something familiar

Creative Elaboration

- Teach to others
- Create stories or dialogues with new vocabulary

Contextualization

- Use the context of the sentences in the core conversations to help me remember new vocabulary
- Connect the new vocabulary to real objects / picture the object in my mind as I look at the word
- Act it out using my hands as puppets
- Try to imagine a situation where you use the word or phrase
- Use in everyday conversation
- Listen and create a response to what I'm hearing

Imagery

- Relate the calligraphy to a picture of something
- Imagine myself as a participant
- Visualize social situation or objects
- Draw a picture to represent the meaning
- I listen very carefully and get all these pictures of what's being said
- Remember and visualize the video
- Visualize myself speaking to a Japanese speaker

Resourcing

- Use the class tapes and books
- Look for Japanese books in the library

Grouping

- Break down the vocabulary to certain situations
- Remember an opposite or similar word
- Group words together based on form (i.e. V,ADJ,N)
- Group vocabulary for certain ideas (family names, travel words, colors, etc.)
- Separate flashcards

Note-taking

- Write down words I have difficulty pronouncing

Deduction/Induction

- Read the grammar so that I understand how and why I use the new vocabulary the way that I do

Transfer

- I think of what English words it reminds me of
- Japanese characters are almost the same as Chinese
- I'm Chinese so it helps to understand a little bit about a foreign language
- Use phonetic spelling
- Don't use phonetic spelling

Inferencing
- Watch the other speaker's body language and facial expressions
- When I don't know what everything means I listen to certain things and reason it out
- Recall what the teacher said just before and see what little clues I can find

Social and Affective Strategies

Questioning
- Ask the teacher
- Ask peers—they speak slowly and have the same amount of vocabulary as you

Cooperation
- Practice through in-class group work
- Study with a classmate
- Practice with others
- Play games in Japanese
- Create opportunities for practice by motivating friends to use Japanese
- Have friends quiz me
- Since tapes are too fast, I work with my Japanese partner and have her repeat *slowly* every sentence
- Use words I've already learned with friends and family members

www.ingramcontent.com/pod-product-compliance
Lightning Source LLC
LaVergne TN
LVHW090756070826
844660LV00022B/1002

9780878401284